# DEPRESSION

New Directions in Theory,
Research, and Practice

# DEPRESSION

## NEW DIRECTIONS IN THEORY, RESEARCH, AND PRACTICE

*Edited and with Commentary by*

## C. Douglas McCann and Norman S. Endler
*York University*

## WALL EDITIONS
WALL & EMERSON, INC.
*Toronto*

Requests for permission to make copies of any part of the work should be mailed to:
Wall & Emerson, Inc., Six O'Connor Drive, Toronto, Ontario, Canada M4K 2Kl.


Canadian Cataloguing in Publication Data

Main entry under title:

Depression : new directions in theory, research, and practice

ISBN 0–921332–28–9

1. Depression, Mental.
2. Depression, Mental - Treatment.
I. McCann, Douglas, 1951-      .
II. Endler, Norman S., 1931-      .
RC537.D46  1989          616.85'27          C89-095202-7

ISBN 0–921332–28–9
Printed in Canada by T. H. Best Printing Company.
1 2 3 4 5    94 93 92 91 90

# Table of Contents

## PART III: PSYCHOBIOLOGICAL FACTORS

## PART IV: BIOLOGICAL FACTORS

# Preface

During the last fifteen years (since the mid 1970s) there has been a proliferation of research with respect to both psychological and biological factors in depression. Concomitant with the empirical work, many new theories regarding both biological and psychological antecedents of depression have been developed. These theories have been developed in tandem, with first one theory and then another being in the forefront. While biological and psychological theories and research programmes have developed in parallel, there have been few attempts at syntheses and integration.

The present book focuses on new directions in theory, research, and practice in depression. By focusing on both biological and psychological factors, the aims of this book include attempts to highlight and draw some attention to the parallel developments in various areas of depression research, practice and theory. By making active researchers aware of what others are doing in their vineyards, it is hoped that a synthesis of biological and psychological factors will produce a more definitive understanding of depression. By making readers aware of the work of some of the leading researchers in the field, it is hoped that further research and understanding of the area will ensue. This book provides a comprehensive and current survey of biological and psychological factors in depression.

The book is organized into four parts. Each part has an introduction, written by the editors, which provides the theme of the section, followed by a number of chapters written by leading experts in the field. All chapters are current and are original to this book. The four parts are relevant to the following themes:

Part I:     Psychosocial factors
Part II:    Psychological factors
Part III:   Psychobiological factors
Part IV:    Biological Factors

Parts II and IV focus on psychological and biological factors, whereas Part I attempts to integrate psychological and social factors and Part III attempts to integrate psychological and biological factors. The introduction to each part provides specific information about the various chapters.

The section at the end of the book, following the indexes and entitled "About the Editors and Contributors," provides a brief biographical sketch and information about the current research interests of the contributors. In addition to providing a more human touch about the scientists involved, the information about the contributors' current research interests should encourage additional reading in and study about various aspects of depression.

The book is aimed at both professionals and students in the fields of psychiatry, psychology, social work, and psychiatric nursing. The book should prove useful as a text for upper-level undergraduate and graduate courses in depression and other affective disorders. Such courses are found in psychology and psychiatry programs in universities and medical schools across the United States and Canada. In addition, scholars working in the field, clinical psychologists, psychiatrists and social workers, and persons working in mental health institutions, hospitals and associations will benefit from a reading of the material in this book.

We would like to thank the various contributors who agreed to write original chapters for this book. We would also like to thank the CIBA-Geigy Canada Limited, Pharmaceuticals Division, and especially its Medical Director, Evert C. Vos, M.D., Ph.D., for providing us with a small research grant, which assisted us in completing this book, especially the indexes. Work on this book was completed while the first editor (McCann) held research grants from Natural Sciences and Engineering Research Council (NSERC) and Social Sciences and Humanities Research Council (SSHRC), and while the second editor (Endler) held a Killam Research Fellowship, Canada Council, and a research grant from the National Health Research and Development Program (NHRDP) Health & Welfare Canada. We would also like to thank Sandra R. Locke and Barbara Devlin for their secretarial assistance, and Charlene Mahon for preparing the indexes. Finally we wish to thank our spouses for their tolerance and patience while we were preparing this book.

C. Douglas McCann
Norman S. Endler
*York University, Toronto*
December, 1989

# List of contributors

Lyn Y. Abramson, University of Wisconsin-Madison

Lauren B. Alloy, Northwestern University

John A. Bargh, New York University

Mitchell J. Cohen, Johns Hopkins University

J. Raymond DePaulo, Jr., Johns Hopkins University

John R. Debus, Southwestern Medical Center, University of Texas

Robert K. Elliott, University of Toledo

Norman S. Endler, York University

Lisa A. Feldman, University of Waterloo

Florence S. Foerster, York University

Ian H. Gotlib, San Diego State University

Leslie S. Greenberg, York University

Donald P. Hay, University of Wisconsin Medical School

Linda K. Hay, University of Wisconsin Medical School

E. Tory Higgins, Columbia University

Nicholas A. Kuiper, University of Western Ontario

Catherine M. Lee, University of Ottawa

Rod A. Martin, University of Western Ontario

Thomas W. McAllister, University of Pennsylavia

C. Douglas McCann, York University

Marlene M. Moretti, Simon Fraser University

L. Joan Olinger, London Psychiatric Hospital

Emmanuel Persad, London Psychiatric Hospital

Trevor R. P. Price, University of Pennsylvannia

A. John Rush, Southwestern Medical Center, University of Texas

Janusz K. Rybakowski, Medical Academy, Bydgoszcz, Poland

Paul G. Salmon, University of Louisville

Lisa A. Spielman, New York University

Jesse H. Wright, University of Louisville

# PART I

# PSYCHOSOCIAL FACTORS

Part I contains two chapters (Chapters 1–2) that are organized around the theme of Psychosocial Factors in Depression. Depression not only affects and is affected by the individual patient and his or her family, but is also influenced by the broader sociopolitical and historical context in which it occurs.

Endler (Chapter 1) discusses the historical meaning of stigma as a mark branded on a deviant and its current psychological meaning as a mark of disgrace. The chapter discusses the relevance of stigma for mental illness, particularly depression, both in terms of historical and current perspectives and in terms of the sociopolitical factors that have affected attitudes, behaviors, and treatments towards the mentally ill. It is noted that stigma attached to mental illness still exists at present.

Changing patterns of treatment during the nineteenth and twentieth centuries are described within a sociopolitical context, with examples from different countries. It is noted that the treatment of the mentally ill is not only affected by scientific factors, but also that social and political factors play an important role. Furthermore, the attitudes of the public and of mental health professionals towards depression affect both treatment and stigmatization.

Finally, suggestions are made for countering and reducing the stigmatizing of mentally ill persons. These include educational programs, direct contact with patients, the extension of self-help and social action groups, and the provision of additional funds for research and education aimed at reducing stigma and promoting mental health. In effect, this chapter focuses on the general social, psychological, and political context.

McCann (Chapter 2) focuses on more specific interpersonal and social mechanisms in depression and attempts to indicate how research and theory from both clinical and social psychology can be integrated in order to provide a more coherent perspective relevant to depression. After discussing both Lewinsohn's and Coyne's theories and research on interpersonal factors in depression, McCann discusses the role of interpersonal expectancies in depression. Using a behavioral perspective Lewinsohn focuses on social skills deficits associated with depression. Coyne's model of interpersonal factors was developed in reaction to the emphasis on intrapsychic mechanisms in etiological analyses of depression.

McCann then focuses on the role of normative expectations and deviations from these in terms of interpersonal factors and depression. He also discusses the relationships among expectancies, stereotypes, depression and interpersonal outcomes.

The major thrust of the McCann chapter is that integrating current research and theory in clinical and social psychology has heuristic value. McCann suggests that future advances in this area would be facilitated by more precise specification of the mechanisms underlying the interpersonal aspects of depression.

In summary, Part I focuses on the psychosocial factors relevant to both theory and treatment of depression and discusses factors at both a micro and macro level.

# 1

# Sociopolitical Factors and Stigma in Depression

Norman S. Endler
*York University*

KEY WORDS: depression, stigma, sociopolitical factors, mental
illness

During the 1988 USA Presidential campaign, it was rumored that Michael Dukakis, the nominee from the Democratic Party, had suffered from and had been treated for clinical depression. Although there was no evidence to support this rumor, the newspapers, radio and television presented major stories on this topic, many of which implied that a history of clinical depression should disqualify a person from being a candidate for the President of the USA. It was quite clear that had the rumors about Dukakis proven to be true he would have been *stigmatized* for his depression. As it was, the clamor died down and this rumor had no serious effect on the presidential campaign, nor was this a factor in the loss of Dukakis to Bush in the Presidential election of 1988. However, it should be noted that Senator Thomas Eagleton had to withdraw as a vice-presidential candidate in the 1972 USA Presidential Race, when it was revealed by the mass media that he had suffered from depression, and had received Electroconvulsive therapy as part of his treatment.

Stigma towards mental illness is not, however, just a contemporary development—it has a long historical basis. According to the 1982 edition of *The Concise Oxford Dictionary,* the archaic definition of stigma is a "mark branded on a slave, criminal, etc." The Greek meaning of stigma is a mark made by a pointed instrument or a brand: literally a *tattoo mark.* The medical meaning of stigma is a mark (e.g., a red spot on the skin) indicative of a history of some disease or abnormality, basically a characteristic feature of pathology. Generally, stigma is conceptualized as a token or mark of disgrace, infamy, or reproach.

In Victor Hugo's (1802–1885) classic novel *Les Miserables* (published in 1862), set in France in the first third of the nineteenth century, the hero Jean Valjean, after his release on parole following 19 years on the chain gang, is required to wear and display the "yellow ticket-of-leave," condemning him as an outcast. In 1555 Pope Paul IV issued a papal bull creating a seven-acre ghetto for Jews in Rome. Jews could not leave this ghetto, unless they wore a yellow identifying cap or scarf, an edict officially rescinded only in 1848. In Nathaniel Hawthorne's (1804–1864) novel *The Scarlet Letter* (published in 1850), the adulteress, Hester Prynne, is sentenced to wear the scarlet letter A on her bosom, in order to stigmatize her. The setting of the 17th century Hawthorne novel, Salem, Massachusetts, was also the scene of the infamous 1692 witchcraft trials. Perhaps the most well known historical example of stigma occurred during the Nazi regime in Germany, where Jews were required to wear a yellow "Star of David," an obvious sign of infamy. Although persons are not currently branded or burned at the stake, the various meanings of stigma still exist, at least symbolically, and characterize society's attitudes toward perceived deviants, including the mentally ill.

In the early 1990s, one recognizes that the civil rights of criminals, delinquents, and drug addicts are better protected in many jurisdictions than the civil rights of the mentally ill. There is a widespread aversion to mental illness; many prefer to perceive it as a personal weakness. Stigma is but one of many social attitudes and political factors that have shaped the diagnosis and treatment of the mentally ill. Let us review some of the historical and sociopolitical factors that have affected the attitudes, diagnoses, and treatments of mental illness, and then we will focus specifically on the role of stigma.

## EARLY ATTITUDES TOWARD MENTAL ILLNESS

In cases of physical illness, people have always been aware of and never doubted that they were sick. An ill person has always been aware of his or her pain. It was patients who initiated the need for doctors, as a result of their pain and suffering. Patients sought the help of friends, primitive priests, shamans, medicine men, and other potential healers to help them alleviate their pain somehow. The patient with physical complaints generally trusted and idealized his or her doctor.

With respect to mental illnesses, the development of the patient-doctor relationship is historically different. A mentally ill person, who was physically sound, was often feared rather than pitied, and in terms of the *zeitgeist* of primitive cultures with their emphasis on animistic properties, such a person was perceived as possessing supernatural powers. Initially, it was believed that the mentally ill were too sacred and too powerful for anyone to "treat" them. The field of medicine was not involved in the treatment of the mentally ill; even in ancient times, there were strong pressures against the scientific study of mental illness.

The belief that an evil being, i.e., the devil, could reside in a person and control his/her mind (the concept of demonology), although prevalent in the Middle Ages, originated during the Stone Age (Endler, 1988a). The Hebrews, during the era of Jesus Christ, believed that behavior could be controlled and directed by good or evil spirits that possessed a person (Endler, 1990). The demonological beliefs also existed during the times of the ancient Chinese, and Egyptians.

Both the Hindu and early Greek cultures also had profound effects on the attitudes towards and the treatment of mental illness. According to Zilboorg and Henry (1941), the Hindu medical system, which developed independently of the Greek system, was quite elaborate, with a high standard of medical ethics and a substantive and voluminous literature. Contributions and philosophies about mental illness are associated primarily with two Hindus, Susruta, who lived about 100 years before Hippocrates, and Charaka. Although many Hindus believed that mental illness was associated with demoniacal possession, Susruta had a more enlightened viewpoint. He proposed that strong emotions and passions were antecedents for mental illness and might even be responsible for some physical illnesses. According to the Hindus, the soul resides within the heart cavity and uses the body parts as its instruments. Mental illness was considered a mystery and a concept which did not belong to medicine, but rather to religion.

The Greeks were the first to consider mental illness from a scientific medical perspective, and Hippocrates and Galen were the chief proponents of the scientific view of mental illness. Both of them focused on the somatogenic hypothesis about mental illness. Although many physicians also believed in the possibility of demonic possession, Hippocrates suggested such treatments as sobriety, quietness, sexual abstinence, and care in selecting drink and food as treatments suitable for both body and brain.

## Stigma Through the Ages

The Greeks, as indicated earlier, were the first to attempt scientific studies of mental illness. In addition, they were also the first to use the term *stigma* to signify bodily signs as a marker for something bad or unusual about the moral status of the stigmatized individual (Goffman, 1963). A person who was disqualified from full social acceptance was a stigmatized individual.

The early Christians expanded the meaning of stigma to include: (1) a medical meaning with bodily signs serving as a marker for a physical disorder, and (2) a religious meaning indexing bodily signs of "holy grace" and marked by eruptive blossoms on the skins (Endler & Persad, 1988; Goffman, 1963). Currently, stigma is conceptualized in terms of discreditation and disgrace rather than in terms of any bodily evidence of a disorder.

In ancient times, during the Stone Age, *trephining,* a very crude surgical technique, was at times used to treat the mentally ill. The technique consisted of chipping holes in the skulls of mentally sick individuals. The belief was that this would allow the evil spirits, assumed to be causing the deviant behavior, to escape (Endler, 1988a).

Following the death of the Greek physician Galen in 200 A.D., there were very few advances in medicine during the Dark Ages. Roman physicians believed in both demonology and in superstitious explanations of illness. Furthermore, with the advent of Christianity, demonical possession by evil spirits was considered insulting to both the Church and to God (Endler, 1990). Medical treatment was strongly influenced by religious factors, and many of the healing procedures of the doctor were assumed by the priest.

During the period from 1000 to 1400 AD, the Middle Ages, the prime responsibility for treatment of the insane rested with the priests, who would pray for the mentally ill and also sprinkle them with holy water. During the first part of the Middle Ages, the religious establishment focused on two types of demonology. One type saw victims as people who had been involuntarily seized by the Devil as God's punishment for sinning—a personal misfortune. The second type involved the belief by the priests that a person had intentionally contracted with the devil, to become a witch with supernatural powers who did the devil's bidding, e.g., ruining crops, sickening cattle, striking down enemies, making men impotent, influencing the weather, destroying communities. Later on, beginning about the sixteenth century, the distinction between the two types of demoniacal possession became blurred, and many innocent individuals were labeled as heretics or witches and were held responsible for causing pestilence and floods (Endler, 1990).

During this period, especially during the fourteenth century, the mentally ill were seen as dangerous and thus became the targets for persecution. There may have been some relationship between the attitudes toward mental illness and the disappearance of leprosy between 1200 and 1400 (cf., Foucault, 1965). For example, in the middle of the twelfth century, there were 2000 leper houses in France and 220 in England and Scotland (to accommodate a population of one and one-half million). Due to the segregation of the lepers, leprosy began to disappear. The prior negative attitudes towards leprosy were thus transferred to the mentally ill.

Paradoxically, during the Middle Ages, laypersons held a more benign and enlightened attitude toward the insane than did the professionals. During the twelfth to fourteenth centuries, a good part of the populace believed that mental illnesses represented emotional problems and that they could be cured by psychological methods and by love. Whether mental illness was perceived to be caused by emotional problems or demoniacal possession, the care of the mentally ill was believed to be the responsibility of the community.

Bethlehem Hospital in London (later called "Bedlam"), an asylum for the insane, treated its inmates with compassion and concern when it was originally opened. When the patients were well enough to leave the hospital under familial supervision, they were provided with badges, enabling them to be readmitted to the hospital if they became ill again. Because of the attentive and sympathetic social support of the community, vagrants often counterfeited the badges in order to receive the same level of social support as that bestowed upon ex-patients of Bethlehem. Furthermore, Bartholomaeus Anglicus (c. 1480), the Franciscan monk, proposed rational therapy methods (e.g., baths, diets, and ointments) for the insane, even though he believed that the mentally ill were demoniacally possessed. Amidst the "snake pit"-like mental institutions, there were isolated humane methods—relics of the Greek and Judeo-Christian traditions and not developed in the Middle Ages.

The "norm" for treatment of the mentally ill during the Middle Ages revolved around theologically inspired witch hunts.

## Early Treatment of the Mentally Ill: Witches and Witch Hunts

The perception of the mentally ill as witches was reinforced and rationalized on the basis of a 1484 papal bull (*Summia Desiderantes*). Two Dominican monks, Johann Sprenger and Heinrich Kraemer, wrote the *Malleus Maleficarum* (The Witches' Hammer) in 1487, at the request of Pope Innocent VIII. This book was a manual that presented both technical instructions and a rationale for witch hunting. Signs of the "witch" included red spots or areas of skin sensitivity, thought to be made by the devil's claw in order to seal his pact with the possessed person. Any disease for which there was no discoverable reason was presumed to be due to the devil. "The Witches' Hammer" was believed to be divinely inspired, since it was created in response to a papal request, and in response to the *Malleus,* hundreds of thousands of mentally ill children, men, and women, over a 200-year period, were hunted down and captured, accused, and tortured. If found guilty, or if they confessed, these people were publicly executed. Witch hunting extended into the Renaissance period, and in the 1600s was exported to North America, with Salem, Massachusetts being the main perpetrator in 1692. Hundreds of people were arrested, 19 hanged, and one pressed to death in Salem; many of these people were mentally ill.

The first person to indicate that witchcraft was a superstition and that most of the alleged witches were mentally ill persons was Johann Weyer (1515–1588), a sixteenth century German physician born in Grave on the Meuse in Holland. Weyer was probably the founder of modern psychiatry and the first physician to specialize in mental illness. He proposed that the alleged witches should be treated by physicians rather than by the clergy since these persons were mentally ill and were not demoniacally possessed.

After studying the irrationalities of witchcraft for 12 years, Weyer published his rebuttal of the *Malleus* in his book *De Praestigiis Daemonum* (The Deceptions of Demons), published in 1563. Weyer postulated that the illnesses previously described as witchcraft and possession were due to natural causes. He attempted to prove that mental illnesses were neither supernatural nor sacred. Weyer's book, his theories, and he himself were all denounced by his Renaissance contemporaries (cf., Endler, 1990).

Two variables have usually characterized the methods used for treating mental illness over the centuries, namely: (a) the methods have been varied; and (b) they have usually been very unpleasant (cf., Deutsch, 1965; Endler & Persad, 1988; Zilboorg & Henry, 1941). Throughout the ages treatment methods for the mentally ill have included beatings, whippings and burnings, and other physical assaults; surgical techniques including the removal of parts of the intestines, castrations, hysterectomies, and pulling teeth; and, the removal of blood and the injection of animal blood (Alexander & Selesnick, 1966; Farina, 1982; Zilboorg & Henry, 1941). Lest we become too smug and proclaim that these treatments happened a long time ago, it should be noted that psychosurgery (cf., Valenstein, 1986) and Cameron's infamous experiments on psychic driving (Collins, 1988), which we will discuss later in this chapter, have occurred within the last quarter of a century. It should also be noted that although electroconvulsive therapy is the most efficacious method for treating depression, it also has been abused and overused in some instances (Endler, 1990; Endler and Persad, 1988).

Not only were the mentally ill treated as social outcasts during the Middle Ages and even during the Renaissance, they were also treated as physical outcasts. Many of them literally had no place to eat and sleep. Many of them wandered in the countryside, begging for their food and often sleeping in animal barns—basically the predecessors of beggars and vagrants of today.

Although there was some institutionalization of the mentally ill as early as the fourth century in Byzantium (now Istanbul) in a house called the "House of Lunatics," the number of mentally ill persons cared for in special institutions was very small until after 1850. When the mentally ill were housed in institutions, it was usually together with other deviants, including prisoners and lepers. Many were sheltered in monasteries. At times, one-person "asylums," seven by five feet in size, were built (Deutsch, 1965; Farina, 1982). Even after 1850, institutional care was primarily custodial and usually did not involve treatment.

## From Superstition to Reality

During the latter part of the Renaissance and the Age of Reason (during the 17th and 18th centuries), there was a general shift in the orientation of Western Civilization from superstition to reality. This was an age of reason and of objective observation. Science became public, communicable knowledge. To facilitate this, the Royal Society of London was founded in 1662, and the Academie Royale des Sciences was founded in Paris in 1666. Prominent scientists of that era included Boyle, Descartes, Galileo, Harvey, Kepler, Newton, and Pascal.

With respect to mental illness, Robert Burton, a clergyman, published his classic *Anatomy of Melancholy* in 1621, and there were five subsequent editions within a period of 30 years. This medical treatise discusses the etiology, symptoms, and cures for depression during the early seventeenth century. Robert Burton himself was probably a depressive, so he could relate to this topic from both an objective and a subjective viewpoint.

During the Age of Reason (late 17th and 18th centuries), there was an exponential increase of medical and scientific knowledge. In order to make sense of it, it became necessary to systematize and integrate all the new information. Nevertheless, the scientific and medical approach to mental illness was not accompanied by a more humane treatment of the mentally ill.

By 1800, however, there were a number of classification schemes of symptoms, developed by physicians. Philippe Pinel (1745–1826) of Paris, and Vincenzo Chiarugi (1759–1820) of Florence, two prominent clinicians, independently developed general nosologies and humane treatment methods, independent of the diagnostic classifications.

Philippe Pinel, in his classification of mental illness, categorized the psychoses into manias without delirium, manias with delirium, melancholia, and dementia. His classification was based on a systematic description of symptoms. Pinel was concerned with attention, memory, judgments, and the importance of emotions in mental illness. He adhered to the somatogenic hypothesis of mental illness and believed that the pathology was due to a lesion in the central nervous system. However, he proposed that mental illness was basically a natural phenomenon and a function of both heredity and life events, including emotional experience. Pinel, who focused on psychological aspects, was especially concerned with social reforms in the insane asylums. Because there were two major variables with respect to melancholy (a basic mental anomaly plus severe physical symptoms), Pinel recommended two kinds of treatment. *Remèdes simples* (ice cold showers, whippings with stinging nettles, etc.) were used for physical problems, and *traitement moral* (having the patients talk about their problems) for psychological problems (Endler, 1990, Endler & Persad, 1988).

Vincenzo Chiarugi, who developed a classification scheme of mental illness at about the same time as Pinel, was also a proponent and initiator of humane treatment methods for the mentally ill. Chiarugi proposed tact, understanding, and respect for the ill individual as a person, when treating the mentally ill. Chiarugi believed that mental illness was due to physical deterioration of the brain. Grand Duke Leopoldo of Tuscany (1747–1792) proposed the first liberal "law of the insane," and with the collaboration of Chiarugi, instituted hospital reform in Italy. Leopoldo built the Hospital of Bonifacio in Florence in 1788, a building now used as a police station. This was five years before Pinel became Director at Bicêtre in Paris, in 1793. In 1789, Chiarugi became director of Bonifacio and commenced to institute social reforms in the hospital.

Although Pinel and Chiarugi developed similar classification systems and similar treatment methods, they worked independently of one another and did not have a known direct influence on one another. Nevertheless, Pinel and Chiarugi represent one of the three major advances or revolutions in the treatment of the mentally ill—the more humane treatment and the unshackling of the inmates in the asylum in the 1790s. The second revolution was the advent of psychoanalysis as expounded by Sigmund Freud in the early 1900s; the third one was the biochemical revolution, including the advent of antidepressants, phenothiazines, tranquilizers, and lithium in the 1950s.

Nevertheless, except for the efforts of Pinel and Chiarugi, patients were usually treated harshly during the Enlightenment (late 17th and 18th centuries). The reasons for this include an almost complete ignorance of the causes of mental illness, a belief that mental illness was incurable, and a fear or dread of the insane—the deviant and the unknown.

## THE 19TH AND 20TH CENTURIES

### Psychiatric Treatment in the 19th and Early 20th Centuries

Tourney (1967), in reviewing the history of methods of psychiatry from 1800 to 1966, noted that: "The history of therapeutic modes in psychiatry reveals a general pattern in the waxing and waning of specific somatic and psychotherapeutic treatment methods" (p. 784). The initial step, when a new technique of psychiatric treatment is introduced, involves excitement and enthusiasm in the context of reports of cures and remarkable improvements. After this initial exuberance, reality ensues, the evaluation of results become more conservative, and the enthusiasm for the treatment diminishes. Finally, the treatment is either rejected or accepted, but *"with decidedly [more] limited applicability than its early proponents claims for it"* (Tourney, 1967, p. 784).

Many medicinal, psychotherapeutic, and surgical techniques have been developed since the early 1800s. Most of them were quickly forgotten (Tourney, 1967). Over 150 years ago, J.E.D. Esquirol, in commenting about psychiatric treatment, noted that at that time there was no *specific* treatment for mental illness, and since there were individual differences in the expression of mental illness, it would be necessary to combine, modify, and vary the different treatment methods available (Tourney, 1967). Esquirol's 1838 hypothesis about treatment is still highly relevant today, over 150 years later.

In France (e.g., Pinel) and in Italy (e.g., Chiarugi), in the late eighteenth century and early 19th century, humane treatment methods for the mentally ill were introduced primarily by physicians. In England, however, humane "moral" treatment methods manifesting trust and non-restraint were developed and executed by a group of religious Quakers. William Tuke (1732–1822), a Quaker tea merchant, opened the York Retreat in 1792. The techniques used included comfort and sympathy for the mentally ill, as well as a general benevolent ambience. William Tuke's son Henry (1755–1814) and grandson Samuel (1784–1857) continued his humanitarian orientation, undoubtedly influenced by both Pinel and Chiarugi.

In the USA, in the late 18th and early 19th centuries, both American physicians and Quakers were involved in instituting humanitarian treatments and reforms in mental hospitals and clinics. The Pennsylvania Hospital in Philadelphia, completed in 1757, admitted mental patients after 1752, and a special hospital was also built in Williamsburg, Virginia in 1775. In fact, the building of the Pennsylvania Hospital was actually proposed at the Quaker Monthly meeting in 1709 but was not built until the 1750s. Furthermore, the Quaker influence in its management decreased, and, for at least 50 years after the 1750s, very little was done with respect to humane treatments of the mentally ill.

In 1813, construction was started in the town of Frankford, Pennsylvania (and now part of Metropolitan Philadelphia) for an institution that would address many of the Quakers' worries and concerns. The institution, erected by a group of Quakers, was called the Friends Asylum. This institution "was one of the earliest hospitals in the United States devoted exclusively to the humane care and treatment of the insane" (Van Atta, 1980, p. 3). The founding father of Friends Asylum was Thomas Scattergood, a tanner and Quaker minister.

Whereas most hospitals felt their main responsibility was to keep the insane off the streets in order to protect the community, and whereas most of the religious leaders in the early 1800s "taught that insanity was a necessary evil and an integral part of the social hierarchy" (Van Atta, 1980, p. 11), the Quakers believed that it was necessary to find a cure for the mentally ill. Quakers assume "that in every man there is a 'divine principle' and nothing, be it slavery, poverty, or insanity, should prevent that man from obeying that principle, then insanity becomes merely another obstacle to be removed from the road to inward enlightenment and, like slavery and poverty, curable" (Van Atta, 1980, p. 11).

Because of this general belief, the Quakers felt more obligated to support Scattergood's proposal for an asylum. The Tukes' concept of "moral treatment" as proposed by Scattergood in Philadelphia, was a revolutionary concept at that time. What it basically stated was that an asylum could be built to (a) confine the mentally ill, and (b) to *cure* them. The notion of a hospital exclusively for Quakers served to solidify the group, and money for the construction of Friends Asylum (now Friends Hospital) was raised very easily, especially after Samuel Tuke published a book describing the York Retreat. Construction began in 1813, and in 1817 the first inmates were accepted.

The Friends Asylum influenced the development of other treatment centres and also provided an excellent training centre for physicians and other staff members, some of whom later became prominent psychiatrists. Some prominent visitors to the

Asylum were instrumental in the development of other similar institutions in New York, Maryland, Massachusetts, and even Scotland.

The revolutionary treatments proposed by Pinel, Chiarugi, Tuke, and Friends Hospital in Philadelphia created an atmosphere of positive enthusiasm both for workers in the mental health field and for patients. This had an impact and influence on 19th century treatments. As a function of the organization of mental hospitals, hospitalization of the insane, specialized hospital personnel, and the use of humanitarian and moral treatment methods, important therapeutic progress occurred. Pinel's introduction of statistical methods to psychiatry "led to the compilation of a great collection of data to prove the curability of insanity" (Tourney, 1967, p. 785).

Tourney (1967) summarized treatment results in psychiatric hospitals between the late 18th century until 1912. There are a number of limitations in this summary, as noted by Tourney (1967), including differing methodologies for data reported by different investigators and different time periods, differing patient populations, and different criteria for the various studies. However, Tourney's (1967) summary demonstrates some interesting and important statistical and substantive trends. Haslam reported a 35 percent rate of improvement or recovery for Bethlehem Hospital (1784–1794); Pinel reported a 47 percent improved or recovered rate for Salpêtrière (1803–1807). However, Esquirol reported a 61 percent success rate for Salpêtrière (1804–1814), and Hall reported a 91 percent success rate for the Hartford Retreat for 1827. Nevertheless, by 1844 the success rate had dropped to 41 percent. In 1859 the success rate of patients across all US asylums was 57 percent. After that, a gradual decline in therapeutic success was reported, "and by 1880 there was a retreat into custodialism and a breakdown of moral therapy" (Tourney, 1967, p. 786).

Therefore, by the end of the nineteenth century, many factors were operating to lower the base rates and change attitudes toward success rates with mentally ill patients. According to Tourney (1967), a mitigating factor "was a change in psychiatric leadership away from the early moral therapists to those who were strictly oriented towards insanity in terms of cerebral disease..." (p. 787). John P. Gray, the superintendent of the Utica State Hospital, New York and editor of the *American Journal of Insanity,* was one of the dominant figures in American psychiatry from 1855 to the 1880s, according to Tourney. Gray rejected the theory that emotions or moral factors were the causes of anxiety and instead "rightly proved through his statistics that the immediate causes of insanity were physical" (Tourney, 1967, p. 787).

Possible reasons for declining success rates can be attributed to rapid increases in hospital size (over 1,000 patients in some hospitals by the 1870s), population growth and immigration increases, and the hospitalization of more chronic patients and patients previously cared for in poor houses or by their own families, all of which led to deteriorating hospital care and alienation. Furthermore, as a result of this, the superintendent and other staff were overworked, there were serious budgetary problems, the mental hospitals became isolated from the general medical community, and the institutions for the insane became primarily centres of custodial care. Treatment became depersonalized, and by the 1920s, recovery rates were down to 10 percent. Until the advent of the somatotherapies of the 1930s, the tranquilizers, antidepressants, and phenothiazines of the 1950s, and a reintroduction of more humanitarian approaches in the 1950s (analogous in the humane approaches of the first part of the 19th century), the hospitals remained neglected and inhumane "holding operations," providing little more than custodial care.

## The Aims and Goals of 19th Century Psychiatry

Almost all 19th century psychiatrists worked as superintendents in public and semi-public institutions. Their reasons for collecting data—reams of data—were not because of an epidemiological approach to psychiatry, nor aimed at relating recovery from psychiatric illness to etiology or diagnostic classification. According to Grob (1985) there were four major goals or aims for collecting statistical data. (1) Statistics could be used to prove "curability" rates. (2) Psychiatrists believed that data collection would ultimately uncover laws relating health to disease. (3) Statistics could be used to advocate public policy (e.g., size of hospital). (4) Psychiatrists believed that "statistical data could be used to establish the legitimacy of public mental hospitals and build broad support among state officials and the public" (Grob, 1985, p. 229). Basically, statistical data were used by hospital superintendents (psychiatrists) primarily for political and social reasons. Part of the rationale was based on their religious commitments. "Virtually all nineteenth century American psychiatrists were Protestants who believed that inductive Baconian science would validate their religious faith" (Grob, 1985, p. 229).

In the 19th century, psychiatry in the USA was basically an administrative and managerial specialty which emphasized somatic interpretations of mental illness, although environmental interpretations about causality were accepted. Thus the emphases were on "moral treatment" and management. The assumption of most psychiatrists of that time was that institutionalization was essential for treating the mentally ill. This enabled one to create a new environment, quite different from the one at home or at work. Care was considered to be synonymous with treatment, and hence there was emphasis on developing beneficial environments within the asylums. As a result of this, the major roles for psychiatrists were managerial and administrative, and they spent little time on theoretical questions or epidemiological interpretations (cf., Grob, 1985).

With respect to outpatients, the early forms of psychotherapy were primarily of a "magico-religious" nature, but during the 19th century, psychotherapy became systematized and formalized (cf., Tourney, 1967). Hypnosis was a major form of psychotherapy, especially in the 1880s, primarily as a result of the work of Charcot, Liebault, and Bernheim. The enthusiasts of this procedure reported success rates as high as 90 percent for hysterical, psychosomatic, phobic, and depressive syndromes. However, after research was conducted in this area by Janet and others, a more realistic view prevailed, and by 1900 most people were skeptical about the therapeutic value of hypnotism (Tourney, 1967).

## The Aims and Goals of 20th Century Psychiatry

An important development in the direction of North American psychiatry was the founding of the National Committee for Mental Hygiene in the first decade of this century. Clifford W. Beers, a former patient, who published his autobiography, *A Mind That Found Itself* (1908), was one of the founders of the mental hygiene committee. His original aim was to improve conditions in mental hospitals, but he later broadened his concerns to include the promotion of mental hygiene. Thomas W. Salmon, the medical director of the National Committee from 1912 on, felt that psychiatry was too isolated and alienated from society. He wanted psychiatry to "reach beyond hospital confines and play a crucial part in the great movements for social betterment" (Grob, 1985, p. 232). Salmon encouraged psychiatrists to be involved in mental health research and policy for both prevention of illness and promotion of health.

In Canada, Clarence M. Hincks, a psychiatrist who also suffered from a mental disorder (cyclothymic personality, like Beers), was instrumental in founding the Canadian National Committee in Toronto in 1918. This organization is now called the Canadian Mental Health Association (cf., Griffin, 1982). Beers, who founded the National Committee for Mental Hygiene in New York in 1909 (now the National Mental Health Association), was hospitalized for a manic-depressive psychosis and was later public about his illness; Hincks, who was never hospitalized but had constant bouts of depression, was very secretive about his illness. Nevertheless, both mental health movements (Canadian and US) are still quite active today.

As a result of Salmon's initiatives in the US National Committee for Mental Hygiene, commencing in 1917, psychiatrists became active regarding various social problems. As a prerequisite to this, they became involved and immersed in statistical analyses. The American Medico-Psychological Association (later known as the American Psychiatric Association) through its committee on Statistics proposed (in 1917) that all mental hospitals use a uniform reporting system. This association, in cooperation with the National Committee for Mental Hygiene, introduced, in 1918, the first standard nomenclature for reporting and describing mental illness (cf. Grob, 1985).

In the late 1930s in North America there was a shift from a focus on institutions toward special attention to environmental and social factors. In Europe the shift was from custodial care to a more interventionist (and less funereal) psychiatry. Four somatic (biological) treatment techniques were developed between 1933–1938: insulin coma therapy, metrazol shock therapy, psychosurgery, and electroconvulsive therapy, with ECT still in existence today as a standard procedure (Endler, 1988b; Endler and Persad, 1988).

The North American "social shift" was to some extent a function of the dominance of environmentalism in psychology, sociology, and cultural anthropology (the social sciences). Ichheiser (1943), a psychologist, pointed out that the overestimation of the relevance of personal factors in personality research until the 1930s, *and* the underestimation of the relevance of situational factors were rooted in the ideology and social system of 19th-century liberalism. According to Ichheiser, this philosophy proclaimed that "our fate in social space depended exclusively, or at least predominantly, on our individual qualities—that we, as individuals, and not prevailing social conditions shape our lives" (1943, p. 152). During the 1930s and to a certain extent even up to the present, sociopolitical factors (e.g., World War II, The Cold War, the Depression of the 1930s, and recurrent recessions, unemployment, etc.) shifted the emphasis toward social factors in explaining behaviors.

After World War II, there were many epidemiological studies focusing on the role of environmental and social factors in mental illness (cf., Weissman & Klerman, 1978). Hollingshead and Redlich (1958) investigated mental illness, treatment, and social class, and demonstrated that social class was an important determinant of the incidence and treatment that mentally ill patients, especially schizophrenics, received. Myers and Bean (1968) replicated the original study and obtained basically the same results. One of the major conclusions was that schizophrenia was diagnosed more frequently in the lower classes. Another major conclusion was that treatment was more accessible to the upper classes.

The "social psychiatry" approach in North America overemphasized life experiences, economics, social class, and social stress as etiological factors in mental illness, and underemphasized genetics, nutrition, infections, birth defects, and biological factors. According to Weissman and Klerman (1978), "The unitary concept of mental illness in the United States was consistent with a concept of social causation of mental illness" (p. 707).

In North America in the 1980s and 1990s, there is certainly an emphasis on biological treatments in psychiatry and a resurgence of emphasis on hereditary factors in both intelligence and personality. Whether this merely represents a shift in the pendulum from an overemphasis on environmental factors and/or is rooted in a sociopolitical context is not clear. What is clear, however, is that after World War II, there were many community and demographic studies of the mentally ill, and psychoanalysis became the treatment of choice for many psychiatric outpatients, especially in the 1940s, 1950s, and early 1960s. By the mid-1960s, the main trend in psychiatric treatment was "Community Psychiatry," proclaimed as the third revolution by Hobbs (1964) or the "latest therapeutic bandwagon" by Dunham (1965).

However, what became and remained the third revolution (the first two being Pinel's & Chiarugi's humane treatments and Freud's psychoanalytic treatments) was the use of psychotropic drugs, commencing in the late 1950s. This led to a revolutionary shift in treatment from psychoanalysis to biological psychiatry—the current prevalent mode of treatment in most hospitals. In fact, since the 1970s, the heads of most departments of psychiatry have been biological psychiatrists rather than psychoanalysts (cf., Endler & Persad, 1988). In an ironic twist of fate, in Italy where electroconvulsive therapy (ECT) was first developed in 1938, ECT is rarely used, and from Vienna to New York to Rome there is a strong emphasis on psychoanalysis and family therapy.

## THE SOCIOPOLITICAL AMBIENCE AND PSYCHIATRIC TREATMENT

Psychiatric treatments and theories are not only based on scientific and practical considerations, but are also influenced by sociopolitical factors operating within the profession and within society. Endler and Persad (1988) have noted that "the general political climate of a society influences both the attitudes that society has towards mental illness, and the treatment methods that it uses" (p. 93).

There have been a number of extreme cases whereby society and the general political system have influenced the attitudes and practices regarding the mentally ill. Although occurring primarily in totalitarian states, there have been instances where questionable practices have taken place in North America.

## Psychoanalysis and Nazi Racism

The New German Society of Psychotherapy was organized in 1933 by an appointee of Hitler, M. H. Göring (a relative of Hermann Göring). Kretschmer, the president, soon resigned for political reasons, and Carl G. Jung became the president and editor of the Society's journal, *Zentralblatt für Psychotherapie*. The Society and its journal officially accepted the Nazi racial philosophy and Jung made concessions to this philosophy (Alexander & Selesnick, 1966). In the first issue under Jung's editorship Göring states that the Society's goal was to unify German physicians in the "spirit" of the Nazi government.

In the same issue Jung noted that "The factual and well known differences between German and Jewish psychology should no longer be blurred, which can only benefit science" (quoted in translation by Alexander & Selesnick, 1966, p. 407). Although Jung denied that he was either a Nazi or an anti-Semite, he did attack the "Jewish" Freudian and Adlerian theories, considered the Aryan psyche more creative and barbarian than the Jewish one, and believed that the Aryan unconscious had a higher potential. Jung's prime motivation for this was probably opportunistic rather than racist.

## The Nazis and the Medical Profession

Between the 1930s and the end of World War II, many physicians in Germany conducted research and clinical work in the service of the German state and its racist Nazi philosophy (Lifton, 1986). Members of the medical profession were active collaborators in the Nazi programme of genocide. They rationalized their behavior as attempts to "heal" the "racially diseased" body of the German nation. Furthermore, prisoners who were doctors sometimes also became involved in the "experiments" (in collaboration with the Nazi doctors) in the concentration camps such as Auschwitz. These "prisoners" were often socialized into the system, involving harmful studies, as a result of being pressured by the Nazi doctors (Lifton, 1986).

Both sterilization and euthanasia were basic parameters of the Nazi programme. The main targets were the crippled, the criminal, the insane, and the Jews. Although the Nazis were involved in *euthanasia,* (and the British scientist, Francis Galton, initiated and supported eugenics), the leader in sterilization of the mentally ill and criminally insane, against their will, in the 1930s, was the USA. By 1939, the USA had sterilized 30,000 "misfits" (Proctor, 1988), and the Danes (Denmark) performed sterilization operations before the Germans did. Proctor (1988) has noted that "The Society for Racial Hygiene" was founded in 1905. That is, the developments in Nazi Germany appeared in an intellectual climate that preceded Hitler.

Although countries other than Germany were involved in sterilization, when it came to euthanasia, the Nazis were in a class by themselves. In Germany, the mental hospitals became the vehicle for "consciousness raising" about *euthanasia.*

Various psychiatric institutions conducted courses for government officials, and after 1938, SS members, police, political leaders of the party, and the press. The euthanasia treatment program—was presented to the public as "putting the misfits to sleep." The Nazi genocide program was the ultimate in political interference with both scientific and medical practices. However, according to Proctor (1988), the physicians were never "ordered" to engage in the "euthanasia" programs—they had the authority to conduct them. According to Lifton (1986), many physicians, despite the Hippocratic oath, actively collaborated in genocide. Although they were trained as healers, many of them functioned as killers and mass murderers. Lifton (1986) interprets their behavior via the concept of "doubling." He believes that many physicians created a second, relatively autonomous self—a process justified and enhanced by the Nazi vision of a reborn German people. The rationalization was that mass murder helped heal the "racially diseased" German nation. Not all physicians participated. However, the social pressures of conformity and role playing induced behavioral and cognitive change in many physicians.

## The USSR and the Treatment of Mental Illness

The Western press and North American psychiatrists have frequently stated that Soviet psychiatry has been systematically used to suppress dissidents in the USSR, especially in the 1970s. Endler and Persad (1988) have noted that "In the USSR, political dissidents have often been labeled as mentally ill by the psychiatric establishment and sent to mental hospitals" (p. 95). This state of affairs goes back to the time of Stalin, but the situation seems to be improving—slowly—under the rule of Gorbachev.

Sergei Grigoryants, the editor of *Glasnost* (a USSR "dissent" magazine), in an article in *The New York Times* notes that in the USSR, "It's much easier to put people away in a psychiatric hospital than in prison... Anyone with some sort of standing in society or who simply knows doctors and psychiatrists can do it—and does do it" (Grigoryants, 1988, p. 31). He adds that "Those who have sent healthy people to psychiatric hospitals by a wave of their hands are keeping their posts" (Grigoryants, 1988, p. 31).

In a recent article (Nov. 19, 1988) by a Moscow psychiatrist, Mikhail I. Buyanov, in the teachers' newspaper *Uchitelskaya Gazeta* (cited in *The New York Times* by Felicity Barringer, 1988), it is asserted that "during the 1970s Soviet psychiatrists gave law enforcement officials "the idea that anyone opposed to anything was hiddenly or openly, a mental case" (Barringer, Nov. 22, 1988, p. 1). Buyanov's article (cf. Barringer, 1988) is the first paper published by a Soviet psychiatrist that supports the contention of Western critics and dissidents in pointing out "that Soviet psychiatrists systematically abused their profession to suppress dissent" (Barringer, Nov. 22, 1988, p. 1). Although this represents the current state of affairs in the Soviet Union, and official data indicate that almost five million persons are listed on the psychiatric register, the authorities state that by 1990, up to two million will be taken off the register (Grigoryants, 1988). In fact, during 1988 there has been a "steady, if not swift" series of releases of psychiatric prisoners who were arrested under the laws against defaming the state" (Barringer, Nov. 22, 1988, p. 6).

There have also been a number of critiques about the inadequate training many Soviet psychiatrists received. These changes reflect the desire of Soviet psychiatrists to be readmitted into the World Psychiatric Association as well as reflecting glasnost. In the past, the rationale for the Soviet strategy was that anyone who disagrees with the philosophy and the politics of the Soviet Union must ipso facto be mentally ill.

## North American Abuses of the Mentally Ill

The recent treatment of the mentally ill in North America has not always been kind and gentle. Henry A. Cotton, the superintendent of the Trenton State Hospital in New Jersey from 1907–1933, developed his own special brand of therapeutic methods for treating the mentally ill (cf., Collins, 1988). When Cotton became the hospital superintendent at Trenton State Hospital in New Jersey in 1907, most of the patients had been restrained, and the hospital had been run in a chaotic fashion. Cotton reorganized the administration of the hospital and of the wards, started an occupational therapy program and a training program for nurses, and instituted an after care program run by social workers. Furthermore, Cotton turned Trenton into a real hospital with clinical laboratories, an infirmary, and an operating room (Scull, 1987).

After nine years, however, the cure rate was no better in 1916 than it had been in 1907. In 1916, Cotton shifted tactics and began to extract patients' teeth, and "by 1917, Cotton had escalated to tonsils and thought he was on to something—the bacteriological or focal-infection theory of mental illness" (Collins, 1988, p. 78). Cotton then extended his "treatment for mental illness" by performing surgery on the stomach, the duodenum, the small intestine, the bladder, gall bladder, the colon, and the sexual organs. Cotton admitted to a 25 percent death rate from surgery, but rationalized this by stating that the patients had been too debilitated by disease to withstand the shock of the operation. During the 1920s Cotton was claiming an 85 percent recovery rate for patients treated via his interventionist methods. He believed that by surgically removing various organs, he could cure mental illness. This was the essence of Cotton's focal-infection theory of mental illness (cf., Collins, 1988).

By 1924, the hospital board was worried by professional criticism of Cotton's methods and asked Adolf Meyer (Cotton's mentor) to investigate the rates of cure at Trenton. Meyer sent Dr. Phyllis Greenacre (one of his former students and later a prominent New York psychoanalyst) to investigate Cotton's methods and results. She found a cure rate of 20 percent (rather than the 87 percent Cotton claimed) and a death rate close to 42 percent (rather than the 25 percent that Cotton had admitted to) (Scull, 1987).

Because Cotton was undergoing a public investigation by the New Jersey State Commission on financial waste and mismanagement, neither he nor the public were informed by Meyer about Greenacre's findings. Although the board was informed, it did nothing. During the public hearings, Cotton himself had a nervous breakdown, and the hearings were dropped. "Cotton had three dead and badly infected teeth removed and felt much better" (Collins, 1988, p. 81). Cotton resumed his duties with full support of the board but did not change his methods.

In fact, at a special meeting of the British Medical Association and Royal Medico-Psychological Association in Edinburgh in 1927, Cotton's focal infection theory was praised and Cotton felt vindicated. Meyer did not say anything against the theory, and in fact, when Cotton died suddenly in 1933, Meyer's obituary praised Cotton's achievements—procedures Meyer knew to be over 40 percent fatal (Scull, 1987). Not surprisingly, Trenton was later involved in lobotomy operations. In a touch of irony, Collins (1988) notes that after Cotton's death "an outstanding staff member was honored by the Cotton Award for kindness" (p. 77), yearly, in memory of the hospital's long-time superintendent.

A more recent misadventure has been described in a number of books, including Gillmor (1987) and Collins (1988). These books and others document the CIA brainwashing experiments, conducted by Ewan Cameron, during the 1950s and early 1960s at the Allan Memorial Institute, McGill University, in Montreal. During Cameron's "psychic driving" and "depatterning" experiments, patients were subjected to lengthy periods of sensory deprivation, drug administration (including LSD and curare), "shock" treatments (at higher doses than the usual ECT), and "psychic driving" i.e., continuous stimulation via taped messages, applied endlessly and repetitively while the patients were both asleep and awake. The aim was to "brainwash" the patients, to break down and "depattern" their personalities, and to help them develop new personalities. Patients were led to believe they were receiving standard treatment. In fact, they were unwitting, experimental guinea pigs in Cameron's poorly planned, poorly executed, and unethical research. Although Cameron really believed that his techniques had a therapeutic effect, the long-term effects on many of these patients were harmful.

Between 1957 and 1960, the CIA provided some of the funding for Cameron's project, because the agency was interested in brainwashing. This funding of about $60,000 US was supplied via a project code-named MKULTRA. Cameron died in 1967 (after resigning from McGill in 1964), and in the late 1970s (i.e., 1977), when the CIA connection became public, nine of Cameron's ex-patients sued, and the case dragged through the courts since 1981 until January 1988, when USA District Court Judge John Penn ordered the trial to begin. Finally in October 1988 (after both Gillmor's 1987 and Collins' 1988 books were published), eight of the patients and a widower were awarded a tentative $750,000 US collective settlement for damages, less than $100,000 US per patient.

The studies on patients by Cameron raised a number of ethical, clinical, and research questions. It is obvious that Cameron was not a very good research scientist, and his research was poorly designed. The results had no clinical efficacy and in fact the procedures were detrimental for many of the patients. Ethically, there was no informed consent and the patients and their families were misled. The money from the CIA was secretly "laundered" via "The Society for the Investigation of Human Ecology" under the project code-named MKULTRA. Furthermore, it is possible that Cameron was not aware of the link between the society and the CIA. Neither Gillmor (1987) nor Collins (1988) provide any clear evidence that Cameron was aware of any such link. Gillmor (1987) notes the irony of Cameron offering testimony on the sanity of Rudolf Hess during the Nazi War Criminal Trials in Nuremburg. The Nuremburg Code for experiments on human beings was proposed on the basis of these trials, and Cameron was involved with creating the code. Yet, his own research in the 1950s and early 1960s seems to have violated this code.

Although conditions have improved since Cameron's time and many jurisdictions now require informed consent for psychiatric treatment, the issue of consent is still being debated in the early 1990s and in some instances various treatments (e.g., ECT) are sometimes administered without the patient's (or a surrogate family member's) informed consent.

## Stigma, The Public, and Mental Health Professionals

The treatment of the mentally ill is influenced by sociopolitical factors within their society. In addition, treatment is also influenced by attitudes and values or the *zeitgeist* within the professions themselves. These factors influence and modify the scientific and professional practical training and experiences that mental health professionals receive.

Stigma related to mental illness is due to fear and ignorance about the causes, course, and treatment of mental illness. Because of this, one of the major goals of mental health workers is to educate both the general public and those whom they train. Nevertheless, because of a sense of mystique and secretiveness, mental health workers may at times inadvertently further contribute to the stigma regarding mental illness (cf., Endler & Persad, 1988).

## Negative Attitudes and the Mentally Ill

Prior to discussing the attitudes of professionals towards the mentally ill, let us discuss some general attitudes regarding deviancy and stigma. Farina (1982) has suggested that past attitudes regarding the mentally ill could influence present day attitudes. Nevertheless, they can also serve to assist us in taking corrective action and in avoiding the pitfalls and errors of the past. Attitudes towards the mentally ill have obviously changed remarkably since the Middle Ages. However, stigma towards mental illness still exists. Many people continue to have a conflict between feelings of fear and disgust towards the mentally ill, as opposed to a desire to help and assist people with emotional problems.

It is necessary to distinguish between attitudes toward patients and beliefs about the nature of mental illness (cf., Farina, 1982). "The term 'attitudes' refers to values and feelings, while 'beliefs' involve objectively verifiable information" (Farina, 1982, p. 308), two variables that may affect one another. Although beliefs about mental illness can be readily changed, it is much more difficult to change attitudes (Farina, 1982; Nunnally, 1961). There is also a difference between behavior and attitudes. Persons with negative attitudes towards the mentally ill may not always behave negatively when confronted with a mentally ill person, because of fear or because of the need to behave in a socially desirable and ethical manner. "As a consequence of these conflicting motivations—a fear and disdain on the one hand and an obligation to help those stricken by misfortune on the other—subtle differences in how research is done can produce dramatically different results" (Farina, 1982, p. 309). Despite this, the general conclusion is that the attitudes towards the mentally ill are primarily negative, and these attitudes frequently lead to negative behaviors towards the mentally ill.

Farina (1982) notes that the mentally ill are "refused jobs, they are not wanted as neighbors, and under some conditions they are treated more harshly because of their problems" (p. 356). Nevertheless, not everyone discriminates against the mentally ill, and at times they are even treated better because of their problems. Females are more accepting of the mentally ill than are males (cf., Farina, 1982).

### Variables that Affect Reactions to Stigmatized Persons

There are a number of characteristics of the mentally ill (stigmatized) person that affect our reactions to that person. Katz (1981) has discussed four classes of *differences* that affect our responses to a stigmatized deviant person, namely, visibility, threat, sympathy arousal, and perceived responsibility. Furthermore, he notes that the "perception of disadvantage" also affects our reactions. There are a number of aspects to *visibility,* beginning with the fact that it is often *evident* that a person is deviant (cf., Goffman, 1963). One important facet of visibility is "knowaboutness," i.e., whether the public's knowledge is based on present awareness, or merely on gossip, rumor, or past conditions that have changed over the course of time. *Obtrusiveness,* or the extent to which the stigma affects social interaction, and *perceived focus,* or the consequences of the deviation, are additional factors (cf., Goffman, 1963, Katz, 1981).

Often the stigmatized person represents a *threat* to us—a fear of the unknown. Serious, uncontrollable, and mysterious illnesses such as schizophrenia are more threatening than those where the patient's behavior is less disruptive and more subdued (e.g., depression). As well as negative feelings, the public also often feels sympathetic towards deprived and deviant groups such as the mentally ill. This *sympathy arousal* often takes the form of a belief that "the physically and mentally disabled should be treated well, a norm that finds concrete expression in a vast network of public and private helping agencies" (Katz, 1981, p. 4).

The degree of stigma is also related to the "victim's" *perceived responsibility* for her or his deviance. Stigmatization is a complex process, because marginal people are often perceived by the public not only as deviant, but also as disadvantaged. This *perception of disadvantage* may induce conflicting feelings of compassion and hostility in us towards the individual.

### Consequences of the "Mentally Ill" Label

Jones, Farina, Hastorf, Markus, Miller & Scott (1984) have suggested that our beliefs and labels strongly affect the manner in which we process incoming information. For example, once a person has been labeled as "mentally ill," it is difficult to remove this pejorative designation. In David Rosenhan's (1973) well-known and classic study, "On Being Sane in Insane Places," eight volunteers (including psychologists, a psychiatrist, a pediatrician) posed as patients and faked symptoms of mental illness and were admitted to mental hospitals in different parts of the USA.

The pseudopatients told the hospital staff that they had heard voices saying "thud," "empty," and "hollow," and all but one of the pseudopatients were diagnosed as schizophrenic.

"Immediately upon admission to the psychiatric ward, the pseudopatients ceased simulating any symptoms of abnormality" (Rosenhan, 1973, p. 251). After much hassling, they were eventually discharged, not as "normals," but with the diagnoses of "schizophrenia in recession." The average length of stay of the "pseudopatients" was 19 days, with a range of 7 to 52 days.

Although other patients recognized the "normality" of the pseudopatients, the staff did not. "Normal" behaviors were interpreted as pathological by the staff (e.g., pacing the hospital corridors due to boredom was interpreted as chronic tension by the staff). Jones et al. (1984), in commenting on the Rosenhan study, states that "The staff expected pathology, and if obvious pathology was not forthcoming, then more mundane behavior was apparently interpreted to fit the expectation" (p. 171).

Rosenhan (1973) in discussing the study points out that "Having once been labeled schizophrenic, there is nothing the pseudopatients can do to overcome the tag" (p. 253). "A broken leg does not threaten the observer, but a crazy schizophrenic?" (Rosenhan, 1973, p. 254). According to Rosenhan (1973), we perceive the mentally ill person in a quite different manner from the way we perceive the physically ill person. The perception in turn affects our attitudes and behaviors toward the mentally ill. Many of the attitudes Rosenhan described in 1973 are probably still prevalent today in the early 1990s.

## Attitudes of Professionals

To what extent do mental health workers inadvertently contribute to the stigmatization of the mentally ill? Rosenhan (1973) points out that like the public, mental health professionals also have ambivalent attitudes towards the mentally ill. Although mental health professionals are usually sympathetic and not overly hostile or avoidant of patients, negative attitudes still exist. Most frequently, patients are segregated from hospital staff on the basis of meeting places, bathrooms, dining facilities, living space, etc.

A fair number of the attitudes of the public—attitudes of stigma—stem from a lack of information about the causes, course, and treatment of mental illness. Mental health workers often, but not necessarily intentionally, create an aura of secretiveness and mystique. As members of society, professionals frequently reflect the attitudes of society. Often the professionals fail to educate themselves about the various facets of biological and psychological treatments available for the mentally ill, and focus only on their own sub-specialty.

Mental health professionals should provide a role model for the public, and some have done so by relating their own personal experiences with mental illness (e.g., Practicing Psychiatrist, 1965; Lehmann, 1982; Endler, 1990; Rippere & Williams, 1985). However, they often send a mixed message. Endler & Persad (1988) have noted this in their analysis of the edited book by Rippere and Williams (1985), entitled *Wounded Healers*. Basically, *Wounded Healers*, a very helpful, informative, and educational book, is a collection of essays by British mental health workers about their personal experiences with depression. The essays are written by experts who are quite open and frank about their personal experiences, and this increases the reader's understanding about depression. However, many of the "professionals hide behind a cloak of anonymity" (Endler & Persad, 1988, p. 109), and it is almost impossible to relate chapters to specific (usually anonymous) authors. Even the editors do not indicate which chapters they have written. Why do the authors fail to disclose what specific chapters they have written, and why do they usually fail to disclose their names? "Are they ashamed of the fact that they have been depressed; are they embarrassed; are they afraid that they might be stigmatized?" (Endler & Persad, 1988, p. 110). A similar double message is sent by *Practicing Psychiatrist* (1965), who presents his personal experiences with ECT in a frank and revealing manner, yet hides behind a cloak of anonymity. Maeder (1989) has noted that mental health professionals "appear to attract more than their share of the emotionally unstable" (p. 37) and that some of them have a "God complex." Perhaps this may partially account for the secretiveness and mystique of those professions.

### Stigma, Depression, and ECT

As another example of how the mental health professions may contribute to the stigma regarding mental illness, let us discuss depression and ECT. Obviously, mental illnesses involve complex, ambiguous, and multicausal disorders, not well understood by the public because of their complexity. Furthermore, many of the treatment modalities are not well understood, and some, primarily electroconvulsive therapy (ECT), are very controversial (Endler & Persad 1988). Many social workers and psychologists have negative attitudes towards ECT, often based on misinformation and myths. Most psychiatrists state that if they themselves were severely depressed, they would want ECT as the treatment of choice for them. The data indicate that ECT alleviates the symptoms for manic-depression in 85–90 percent of all cases, as compared to antidepressants, where the success rate is 65–70 percent.

Nevertheless, when a biological treatment is indicated, ECT is rarely the first treatment of choice. Endler and Persad (1988) have indicated that there are a number of "non-scientific" reasons for this. These include the following: (1) antidepressant drugs are less expensive; (2) it is easier and less time consuming to prescribe drugs; (3) ECT (even on an outpatient basis) necessitates a psychiatrist, a nurse, an anesthetist, equipment, a treatment room, and usually written consent; and (4) psychiatrists' concern and "worry" about the negative attitudes of the public towards ECT create a reluctance to prescribe it. As Endler (1990) has noted, psychiatrists try antidepressant drugs as the treatment of first choice; if that does not work, then they may use ECT. We believe there is also an additional reason. Nobody, including psychiatrists, likes the idea of having electricity applied to the brain. It is frightening, and furthermore the brain is considered the essence of the self, the core of "being." "Therefore, a depressed person who receives ECT may be doubly stigmatized: once for being mentally ill and then again for having undergone ECT..." (Endler & Persad, 1988, p. 108).

## COUNTERING AND REDUCING STIGMA

What can be done about countering and reducing the stigma regarding mental illness? Rosenhan (1973) has proposed two strategies for minimizing the stigmatization associated with labeling the mentally ill. In the first instance, society should not send the mentally ill to psychiatric hospitals but should perhaps emphasize community health facilities and crisis intervention centres—places where labeling is less likely to occur. However, this is not always feasible. In the second place, according to Rosenhan (1973), there is a "need to increase the sensitivity of mental health workers to the Catch-22 position of psychiatric patients" (p. 257). Education and publicity (e.g., relevant reading materials) and direct experience with the impact and influence of hospitalization can help achieve this goal. Endler and Persad (1988) have suggested a third strategy. "Awareness and sensitivity about mental illness and stigma can be facilitated by both public figures and mental health workers, who have been emotionally ill, publicly discussing their experiences" (Endler & Persad, 1988, p. 111) (e.g., Patty Duke's autobiography *Call Me Anna*).

Personal contacts with mentally ill patients could also counteract stigma and its negative consequences. Many of us react to the mentally ill in terms of *stereotypes*. Our attitudes towards the mentally ill are often based, not on direct contacts, but rather on what we have read and heard about mental illness from others and from the mass media. Seeing that mentally ill patients are not ogres and are not to be feared can reduce a fair amount of the stigma.

The concern regarding current attitudes towards the mentally ill is exemplified by the advertising campaigns that have been mounted in 1987 and 1988 by both the *American Mental Health Fund,* in cooperation with *The Advertising Council,* and the *Canadian Mental Health Association* (CMHA) (Ontario Division). Various advertisements aimed at combatting the stigmatization of mental illness and attempting to educate the public about mental illness have recently appeared in professional journals, on television, and in newspapers. Furthermore, the theme for the 1989 Annual meeting of the *American Psychiatric Association* was "Overcoming Stigma."

Mental health associations and various social action groups have been involved in efforts to convince the public that problems in adjustment are diseases. During the past few years, the National Institute of Mental Health (NIMH) has developed a Depression/Awareness, Recognition and Treatment program (D/ART) aimed at informing the public about the illness, hopefully lessening stigma, and facilitating support for research on depression.

Furthermore, since the mid to late 1970s, there has been a proliferation of self-help groups aimed at assisting mentally ill patients and their families. These groups consist of patients, ex-patients, their families, friends, and mental health professionals. The groups include the Manic-Depressive Association, Friends of Schizophrenics, and Neurotics Anonymous and serve important self-help, educational, and support functions. DRADA (the Depression and Related Affective Disorders Association), another group that offers social support, is made up of persons with affective disorders and their families, laypersons, and professionals. DRADA sponsors symposia jointly with the Johns Hopkins Affective Disorders Clinic, Department of

Psychiatry (Baltimore). "Fifteen years ago, not one clearing house existed to provide information about self-help groups or encourage the development of new ones" (Hurley, 1988, p. 64). At present, there are over 40 clearing houses. The National Alliance of the Mentally Ill (NAMI) also plays an important supportive and educational role. However, the patients' rights groups have not been as effective as they might be. This is partially due to the fact that their leadership often rests in the hands of disaffected individuals.

In addition to supporting (emotionally) patients and their families, the various self-help and social actions groups help educate the public, directly and indirectly, about mental illness. This should greatly assist in reducing the stigma surrounding mental illness. These groups can function as an important sociopolitical force. Furthermore, this will possibly encourage governments and granting agencies to provide additional research and educational funds toward the prevention and treatment of mental illness and the promotion of mental health.

## SUMMARY AND CONCLUSIONS

Stigma was discussed in terms of its historical meaning as a mark branded on a slave, criminal, etc., and in terms of its current psychological meaning as a token or mark of disgrace, infamy, or reproach. Its special relevance for mental illness was discussed in terms of historical and current perspectives and in terms of the sociopolitical factors that have affected attitudes and behaviors towards the mentally ill. Although these attitudes and behaviors have changed throughout the course of history, there is still a stigma attached to mental illness in the early 1990s. The mentally ill are no longer burned at the stake as witches, but even today physical illnesses are more socially acceptable than mental illnesses.

Changing treatment patterns during the nineteenth and twentieth centuries were discussed, and the relationship of the general sociopolitical system to the treatment of the mentally ill was presented, with examples cited from Nazi Germany, the USSR, and North America. It was pointed out that the treatment of the mentally ill is not only affected by scientific considerations, but also by social and political factors.

The attitudes of the public and of mental health professionals towards mental illness and the effects of these attitudes on stigmatization were discussed. Both the negative attitudes of the public and variables (relevant to perpetrators and victims) that affect reactions to stigmatized persons were described. The consequences of the "mentally ill" label were also discussed. It was indicated that to a certain extent, the stigma attached to mental illness was perpetrated by mental health professionals.

Finally, suggestions for countering and reducing stigma towards the mentally ill were presented. These included educational programs, direct contacts with patients, attempting more community approaches and less hospitalization of patients, the development and extension of more self-help and social action groups, and the provision of funds for research and education aimed at reducing mental illness and promoting mental health.

**Author's Note:** The writing of this chapter was supported by a Killam Research Fellowship, Canada Council, to the author.

The author wishes to thank Charlene Mahon for her helpful comments and James D. A. Parker for his suggestions and compiling the references. The chapter was written while the author held a Killam Research Fellowship from the Canada Council. A modified and condensed version was presented as an Invited Address to the 42nd Annual Convention of the Ontario Psychological Association (OPA) on February 17, 1989, Toronto, by the author, as the recipient of the 1988 OPA Award of Merit.

## References

Alexander, F. G. & Selesnick, S. I. (1966). *The history of psychiatry.* New York: Harper and Row.

Barringer, F. (1988, Nov. 22). Soviet article reports psychiatry was misused on dissidents in 70s. *New York Times,* Section A, pp. 1 and 6.

Collins, A. (1988). *In the sleep room: The story of the CIA brainwashing experiments in Canada.* Toronto: Lester & Orphen Dennys Limited.

Deutsch, A. (1965). *The mentally ill in North America* (2nd ed.). New York: Columbia University Press.

Dunham, H. W. (1965). Community psychiatry—The newest therapeutic bandwagon. *Archives of General Psychiatry, 12,* 303–313.

Endler, N. S. (1988a). Hassles, health and happiness. In M. P. Janisse (Ed.), *Individual differences, stress, and health psychology* (pp. 24–56). New York: Springer-Verlag.

Endler, N. S. (1988b). The origins of electroconvulsive therapy (ECT). *Convulsive Therapy, 4,* 5–23.

Endler, N. S. (1990). *Holiday of Darkness.* (Rev. Ed.). Toronto: Wall & Emerson, Inc.

Endler, N. S. & Persad, E. (1988). *Electroconvulsive therapy: the myths and the realities.* Toronto: Hans Hubers Publishers.

Farina, A. (1982). Stigma disorders. In A. G. Miller (Ed.), *In the eye of the beholder: Contemporary issues in stereotyping.* (pp. 305–363). New York: Praeger.

Foucault, M. (1965). *Madness and civilization.* New York: Random House.

Gillmor, D. (1987). *I swear by Apollo: Dr. Ewan Cameron and the CIA-brainwashing experiments.* Montreal: Eden Press.

Goffman, E. (1963). *Stigma: Notes on the management of spoiled identity.* Englewood Cliffs, N.J.: Prentice-Hall.

Griffin, J. D. (1982). *The amazing careers of Hincks and Beers.* Canadian Journal of Psychiatry, *27,* 668–671.

Grigoryants, S. (1988, February 23). Soviet psychiatric prisoners. *The New York Times,* Section A, p. 31.

Grob, G. N. (1985). The origin of American psychiatric epidemiology. *The American Journal of Public Health, 75,* 229–236.

Hobbs, N. (1964). Mental health's third revolution. *American Journal of Orthopsychiatry, 34,* 822–833.

Hollingshead, A. B. and Redlich, F. D. (1958). *Social class and mental illness.* New York: Wiley.

Hurley, D. (1988, January). Getting help from helping. *Psychology Today, 22,* 62–67.

Ichheiser, G. (1943). Misinterpretations of personality in everyday life and the psychologist's frame of reference. *Character and Personality, 12,* 145–160.

Jones, E. E., Farina, A., Hastorf, A. H., Markus, H., Miller, D. T. & Scott, R. A. (1984). *Social stigma: The psychology of marked relationships.* New York: W. H. Freeman.

Katz, I. (1981). *Stigma: A social psychological analysis.* Hillsdale, N.J.: Erlbaum.

Lehmann, H. E. (1982). A trouble in the brain-mind split: Self-description of a depressive episode. *Canadian Journal of Psychiatry, 27,* 216–217.

Lifton, R. J. (1986). *The Nazi doctors: Medical killing and the psychology of genocide.* New York: Basic Books.

Maeder, T. (1989, January). Wounded healers. *The Atlantic Monthly, 263,* 37–47.

Myers, J. K. & Bean, L. L. (1968). *A decade later: A follow-up of social class and mental illness.* New York: Wiley.

Nunnally, J. C. (1961). *Popular conceptions of mental health.* New York: Holt, Rinehart & Winston.

Practicing Psychiatrist (1965). The experience of electroconvulsive therapy. *British Journal of Psychiatry, 111,* 365–367.

Proctor, R. N. (1988). *Racial hygiene: Medicine under the Nazis.* Cambridge, Mass.: Harvard University Press.

Rippere, V. & Williams, R. (Eds.) (1985). *Wounded healers: Mental health workers' experiences of depression.* Chichester: Wiley.

Rosenhan, D. L. (1973). On being sane in insane places. *Science, 179,* 250–258.

Scull, A. (1987). Desperate remedies: A gothic tale of madness and modern medicine. *Psychological Medicine, 17,* 561–577.

Tourney, G. (1967). A history of therapeutic fashions in psychiatry, 1800–1966. *American Journal of Psychiatry, 124,* 784–796.

Valenstein, E. S. (1986). *Great and desperate cures: The rise and decline of psychosurgery and other radical treatments for mental illness.* New York: Basic Books.

Van Atta, K. (1980). *An account of the events surrounding the origins of Friends Hospital and a brief description of the early years of Friends Asylum 1817–1820.* Philadelphia: Friends Hospital.

Weissman, M. M. & Klerman, G. L. (1978). Epidemiology of mental disorders: Emerging trends in the United States. *Archives of General Psychiatry, 35,* 705–712.

Zilboorg, S. & Henry, G. W. (1941). *A history of medical psychology.* New York: Norton.

# Social Factors in Depression: The Role of Interpersonal Expectancies

C. Douglas McCann
*York University*

KEY WORDS: expectancies, stereotypes, self-fulfilling prophecy,
behavioral confirmation, social norms

One of the more curious observations that results from a consideration of much of the traditional work in the area of depression is the relative neglect of the role of interpersonal factors in its onset, maintenance, and exacerbation. This lack of emphasis on interpersonal and social factors is characteristic not only of research in depression; there has been a general tendency in clinical research to downplay the significance of interpersonal events. Recognition of the potential limitations of this general approach has led to repeated calls aimed at integrating research in clinical and social psychology within a framework of relevant social processes (e.g., Brehm, 1976; Carson, 1969; Frank, 1961). It is assumed that the work of social psychologists concerned with interpersonal processes could be used to inform clinical research in several areas. Further, it is believed that basic research in interpersonal processes could benefit from this transfer of knowledge.

Attempts to integrate clinical and social psychology have gained momentum in the last few years. Evidence for this is provided by the appearance of several journals and books devoted to this topic (e.g., Maddux, Stoltenberg & Rosenswein, 1987; Weary & Mirels, 1982; see Leary & Maddux, 1987, for a historical review, and the discussion by Endler & Edwards, 1988). Work in this area has been fueled by those formulations emphasizing interpersonal factors that are related to specific emotional and behavioral problems (e.g., Coyne, 1976a; Gotlib & Robinson, 1982; Higgins, 1987; McCann & Higgins, 1988; Strong & Claiborn, 1982).

Maddux and his colleagues (Leary & Maddux, 1987; Maddux, Stoltenberg, Rosenswein & Leary, 1987) have been vigorous proponents of the developing integration between social and clinical psychology. They have suggested that this work is proceeding in three directions: a) *Social-diagnostic psychology*, which focuses on an examination of the processes involved in classification and assessment of clinical disorders; b) *Social-therapeutic psychology*, which concentrates on the role of interpersonal processes in prevention and treatment; and c) *Social-dysgenic psychology*, which considers the role of interpersonal processes in the development (and maintenance) of behavior problems. It is this last orientation that is the focus of the present chapter. Two general assumptions of this orientation are especially relevant (see Leary & Maddux, 1987, for a more complete discussion). First, work on the integration of social and clinical psychology assumes that many psychological problems are essentially interpersonal in nature, in that interpersonal forces play an important role in their onset, maintenance, and exacerbation. Second, many dysfunctional behaviors are exaggerated manifestations or distortions of normal behavior. This latter point implies that the rules and structure of normal interaction can be useful in attempting to understand abnormal behavior patterns. These assumptions and their implications are discussed below in the context of examining the role played by social factors in depression.

## Overview

In this chapter, theory and research examining the role played by interpersonal and social factors in the maintenance and exacerbation of depression are considered. Two points are worthy of note in the context of this discussion. While some have claimed a primary causal role for interpersonal factors in the etiology of depression (e.g., Coyne, 1976a), the evidence on this point is equivocal. It is clear, however, that social factors do play an important role in the maintenance of depression. In addition, for much of the research, depression is identified by elevated scores on such measures as the Beck Depression Inventory (BDI; Beck, Ward, Mendelson, Mock & Erbaugh, 1961). In some cases, the implications of this work for clinical populations have yet to be systematically demonstrated.

This chapter is organized into several interrelated sections. First, some of the recent work in clinical psychology that has examined interpersonal processes in depression is briefly reviewed. Central here is the interactional model proposed by Coyne (1976a) and the research it has engendered. Second, the general nature of social interaction from a social psychological perspective is briefly considered, and some of the implications of this view for interactional models of depression are discussed. Finally, the role played by personal and interpersonal expectancies in the types of interactions characteristic of depressives are examined.

## SOCIAL INTERACTION AND DEPRESSION

Two recent models, that of Lewinsohn (1974) and Coyne (1976a), have emerged from clinical work on depression and have served to highlight the critical role of interpersonal factors in depression. Lewinsohn (1974), in his behavioral perspective, has focused on social skills deficits associated with depression. Lewinsohn suggested that a low rate of response-contingent positive reinforcement was critically implicated in the onset and course of depression. A low rate of response-contingent positive reinforcement was assumed to act as an unconditioned stimulus for depressive behaviors and symptoms, and was seen to be a function of: a) the number of potentially reinforcing events available to the individual; b) the availability of reinforcement in the individual's environment; and c) the instrumental behavior of the individual. All three sets of factors are considered important. However, much of the research has focused on detailing the social skills deficits associated with depression. These serve to limit the individual's ability to elicit positive reinforcement from the social environment.

Research conducted on this aspect of the model has generally taken the form of examining the differences in verbal and nonverbal behavior emitted by depressives and nondepressed individuals in interaction with others. The results of this work have supported the social skills deficit assumption of the model and have catalogued a number of behavioral differences between depressed and nondepressed individuals. Differences have been found on nonverbal indices such as eye-contact, speech rate, timing of interpersonal responses, smiling, and on verbal indices such as amount of self-disclosure, number of negative self-statements, and pleasantness of verbal content (e.g., Blumberg & Hokanson, 1983; Gotlib & Robinson, 1982; Hokanson, Sacco, Blumberg & Landrum, 1980; see Dryden, 1981, for a review).

Although this model has generated many behavioral differences, it has been criticized for its over-reliance on correlational techniques and because of equivocal results (e.g., Coyne, 1976b; Youngren & Lewinsohn, 1980). In addition, it would appear that there is some concern about the atheoretical manner in which predictions are generated for *specific indices* of social skill. Thus, there is little basic theoretical link between this formulation of depression and the nature and assessment of specific indices of social skill deficits. Finally, there is little work demonstrating that social skill deficits and depressive symptoms covary across the time course of a depressive episode. Although these are important concerns, it is also clear that several studies have demonstrated behavioral differences related to the concept of social skills between depressed and nondepressed individuals. This work deserves close consideration, because of its relevance to other interactional models of depression (e.g., Coyne, 1976a), and its clear treatment implications. More central to the present concerns is the interactional model proposed by Coyne (1976a).

Coyne's (1976a) model of depression was developed in reaction to Saccothe emphasis on intrapsychic mechanisms in etiological analyses of depression. He suggested that it was important to consider the nature of the depressed individual in his/her interpersonal environment. Thus, in terms of the social-dysgenic position described above, Coyne asserted that depression was partially an interpersonal phenomenon. Depressed persons and their interaction partners are interpersonally linked and the behaviors of each both influence, and are influenced by, the behaviors of the other. Therefore, a comprehensive understanding of the actors in such a system necessitates consideration of the nature of this influence *process*. One key feature of the model is the assumption that the behavior of the interaction partner serves to maintain, and perhaps, exacerbate the difficulties faced by the depressive.

Coyne (1976a) describes an interpersonal cycle in which the symptoms displayed by the depressive in an interpersonal context initially elicit reactions of sympathy and assistance. As the symptoms persist, however, those persons interacting with the depressed individual, experience an aversive reaction to the behavior of the depressive. The interaction partners begin to react negatively, feeling somewhat depressed and anxious themselves. These negative reactions are rarely presented explicitly to the depressive due to the partner's feelings of concern and/or guilt. Instead, the interaction partner tends to send mixed messages of support and rejection on verbal and nonverbal levels, respectively. In order to clarify this ambiguity, the depressive may then reassert the symptom display, thereby increasing the negativity and possible rejection by the other. The consequence of this cycle, of course, may entail a decision on the part of the other to leave the field, which would only increase the difficulties faced by the depressive. The model, as presented by Coyne (1976a; see Coates & Peterson, 1982, Coates & Wortman, 1980, and Gotlib & Whiffen, in press, for extensions) is based in systems theory and details the dynamic sources of influence inherent in such interpersonal systems. Empirical tests of the model, however, have tended to focus on specified aspects of the model without considering the system as a whole. Most often the interest has been in examining the effects on others due to interacting with depressives.

In Coyne's (1976b) first examination of the model, he had subjects converse on a telephone with depressed outpatients, non-depressed outpatients, or normal controls. Subjects interacting with the depressed outpatients reported feeling more depressed, hostile, and anxious as assessed by scores on the Multiple Affect Adjective Checklist (MAACL; Zuckerman & Lubin, 1965) than did subjects interacting with members of the other two groups. In addition, subjects interacting with members of the depressed outpatient group tended to reject the target more often than did subjects interacting with members of the other two groups. Thus, the predictions of the model regarding the *reactions of others* to interacting with depressives was strongly confirmed in this initial study. Coyne (1976b) also attempted to determine whether or not the behavior of the depressed targets differed from that of the other two groups. No differences were found on several indices of interpersonal behavior. Thus, no insight was provided as to what it was about the depressive's interpersonal behavior that resulted in the negative reactions of others observed in the study.

This initial study was the first in a large number of studies that were designed to address similar issues in the context of the model (e.g., Blumberg & Hokanson, 1983; Boswell & Murray, 1981; Gotlib & Beatty, 1983; Gotlib & Robinson, 1982; Hammen & Peters, 1977, 1978; Hokanson, Sacco, Blumberg & Landrum, 1980; Howes & Hokanson, 1979; Marks & Hammen, 1982; Robbins, Strack & Coyne, 1979; Strack & Coyne, 1983; Winer, Bonner, Blaney & Murray, 1981). Although an exhaustive review of this literature is beyond the scope of this chapter, a few other examples will suffice to convey the diversity of techniques employed, and a general sense of some of the main findings.

In a comprehensive study by Gotlib and Robinson (1982), forty nondepressed female university students engaged in a fifteen minute dyadic interaction with either a depressed or nondepressed university student. The interaction was purportedly arranged for the purposes of getting to know one another. Forty female students were recruited as targets and were categorized as depressed or nondepressed based upon elevated BDI scores. The interaction was videotaped and then coded for the presence of specific verbal and nonverbal behaviors. Following the interaction, subjects and targets were separated, and the subjects were asked to complete measures assessing their mood (MAACL subscales for Hostility, Depression and Anxiety) and willingness to engage in future interaction with the targets (i.e., an index relating to interpersonal rejection).

The behaviors of the subjects and the targets were coded from the videotapes and each verbal unit was categorized as examples of the following types of behavior: direct support, conversational maintenance—positive content, conversational maintenance—negative content, conversational maintenance—neutral content, direct negative, silences (no verbal response within five seconds), and total number of responses. Nonverbal behavior was assessed with respect to: smiling, facial expression—pleasantness and arousal, eye contact, and speech quality (e.g., loudness, monotony, etc.).

Both subject and target measures were analyzed in order to examine the assumptions of Coyne's (1976a) model about induced mood and rejection. Surprisingly, an analysis of subjects' *moods* revealed no differences between subjects who had interacted with depressives as compared to those interacting with nondepressed targets. There were, however, several differences in expressed verbal (e.g., fewer direct support statements, more conversational maintenance—negative) and nonverbal (e.g., less smiling and pleasantness) behaviors for those interacting with depressives as compared to those interacting with normals. In addition, it was also clear that these behavioral differences were evident from the first few minutes of the interaction. Analysis of target behaviors revealed complementary differences on the part of depressives on such indices as direct support (fewer for depressives) and conversational maintenance—negative content (more for depressives). Although the causal directions for the similarity observed in subject and target behavior are unclear, it was evident that subjects and targets tended to engage in similar behavior patterns. Thus, depressive interactions were marked by negative type behaviors on the part of both participants.

The results of these two studies provide general support for Coyne's (1976a) interactional model of depression in terms of induced mood and interpersonal rejection. It is also clear, however, that some inconsistency is evident when the results are compared across the two studies. The first (i.e., Coyne, 1976b) provides support for the assumptions regarding induced mood, but finds no evidence of behavioral differences between depressed and nondepressed individuals that might explain the induced mood effect. In contrast, the second (i.e., Gotlib & Robinson, 1982) provides evidence for behavioral differences without the predicted induced mood effects on those interacting with depressives. Of course, there are methodological differences that may account for these differing patterns of results. In addition, it is also important to note that Coyne makes no specific predictions regarding links between particular behaviors on the part of depressives and subsequent interpersonal rejection. Nonetheless, the lack of correspondence between the two studies has elicited some concern in this area. This issue is addressed more fully below.

However, the results of several investigations, taken together, do provide generally strong support for some aspects of Coyne's interactional model (see Gurtman, 1986). This level of general support is especially impressive given the diversity of methodological approaches that have been used in this research. These range from the use of actual interactions between depressives (i.e., mostly student samples) and their partners, to assessing reactions to depressives through the use of transcripts and confederates role-playing depressives (e.g., Boswell & Murray, 1981; Gotlib & Beatty, 1985; Howes & Hokanson, 1979). In addition, some researchers have extended the implications of the model in innovative ways. For example, Hokanson et al. (1980) had depressed and nondepressed university subjects engage in a modified Prisoner's Dilemma Game in which they manipulated the personal power of the players. They found that depressives in high-power roles tended to exhibit exploit-

ative and non-cooperative behavior which elicited non-cooperation and extra puni-
tiveness from their partners (see Blumberg & Hokanson, 1983, for an extension). In
sum, it is clear that this model has attracted considerable interest and has produced a
large body of results consistent with the model.

Taken together, the social skills orientation and the interaction model have both
highlighted the important role that interpersonal and social factors can have in
depression. They are innovative in the context of previous research orientations.
They also serve to provide a balance for approaches focusing more exclusively on
intrapsychic factors in depression. Each formulation, however, has been subjected
to criticism that suggests the need for further refinement. There is some concern
with regard to the social skills formulation and its implications for the interactional
model. Some data suggest that depressives are sometimes interpersonally rejected
by their partners in the absence of any evidence for behavior differences between
depressed and nondepressed individuals (e.g., Coyne, 1976a). This criticism is
based upon the assumption that it is the social skills deficits associated with depression that often lead to rejection of depressives by others. Coyne, Kahn & Gotlib
(1987) comment:

> The research we have reviewed has generally examined behaviors that can be
> reliably coded and that are likely to vary with mood. However, data demonstrating
> that these are socially significant behaviors have not yet been produced. It may be,
> for instance, that low-frequency but salient depressive verbalizations alienate others
> more than do the nonverbal and paraverbal behaviors that accompany them. Find-
> ings that depressed persons are negatively evaluated by partners and observers in
> the absence of differences on these behavioral measures suggests that critical be-
> haviors are not yet being assessed (p. 519).

Clearly relevant here is the suggestion that behavioral and social skills formulations would profit from theoretically derived meaningful behavioral indices in the
context of depression. Even more controversial, however, has been the research
conducted in the context of the interactional model proposed by Coyne (e.g.,
Burchill & Stiles, 1988; Coates & Wortman, 1980; Coyne, 1985; Doefler & Chaplin, 1985; Gurtman, 1986; King & Heller, 1984). The concerns expressed over the
status of the model and research have taken several forms.

First, some have questioned the degree of support for the model that actually
exists. As was illustrated above, it is possible to find examples in the literature
which, although providing general support for the model, nonetheless demonstrate
inconsistency at a more specific level (Coyne, 1976b; Gotlib & Robinson, 1982; see
also Burchill & Stiles, 1988). It is true, of course, that procedural variations preclude direct comparisons of some of this work. It is also true, however, that no
theoretically derived rationale has been generated to account for the equivocal
results in the context of the formulation. Further, concern has been expressed by
some who have failed even to reproduce the basic predictions of the model, using
very similar methodologies (e.g., King & Heller, 1984). Nonetheless, a fairly large
body of research has been amassed in support of the model (see Gurtman, 1986)
which suggests that its basic propositions have some validity, but are perhaps, in
need of further clarity.

A second type of criticism concerns the issue of whether the research discussed above is, in fact, really related to the model as outlined by Coyne (1976a). Doefler and Chaplin (1985) have suggested that much of the research generated by the model is *irrelevant* to it and represents what they term "Type 3 Errors." According to them, this error occurs in circumstances where inappropriate laboratory analogues are used to test theoretical formulations. In such contexts, it is important to ensure that "our laboratory operationalizations are relevant proxies for our theoretical assumptions" (p. 227). Doefler and Chaplin suggest that this criteria has not been met by much of the research reviewed above and thus, it provides only illusory support for the model. At issue here is the fact that although the interactional cycle described by Coyne (1976a) is typical of ongoing interactions with *significant* others, most of the research has employed *mildly* depressed college students in brief interactions with *strangers*. Doefler and Chaplin comment that the interactional model would seem to have little to say about the nature of interactions in such situations. Furthermore, the results taken in support of the interactional model are more consistent with the social skills formulation than with Coyne's model. Although this issue has not yet been systematically addressed, it is true that the limited research that does exist examining long-term interactions of clinical samples with significant others has revealed similar results (for reviews see Coyne, 1985; Coyne et al., 1987; Gotlib & Whiffen, in press). This research, however, has focused more on outcome variables in long term relationships (e.g., Burchill & Stiles, 1988; Hokanson, Lowenstein, Hedeen & Howes, 1986) than on examining the systemic mechanisms that are assumed in the model to lead to such outcomes. A related concern is that much of this research has relied exclusively on paper and pencil measures of depression (e.g., elevated BDI scores) which, in many cases, may be inadequate for a comprehensive assessment of depression.

A third limitation of this work is its failure to consider the potential implications of subtypes of depression and their relevance to interpersonal interaction. This may relate to the lack of consistency in results referred to above. Some suggestions have been made about subtypes of vulnerabilities for depression (for example, see Beck, 1983; McCann, in press) that have implications for the types of expected interpersonal behaviors enacted by different types of depressives (e.g., reactive vs. endogenous depression). It is possible that the types of interactional sequences discussed by Coyne may be more relevant to specific types of depressives and, thus, may not be characteristic of all depressed individuals. This issue remains to be addressed.

A final observation related to the status of the interactional models is that they appear to have entered a period of relative heuristic quiescence. That is, models such as that proposed by Coyne have generated an abundance of relatively supportive research attesting to the reality of the phenomena they describe (at least in the context of university samples). However, they appear to have provided little direction for additional research in the search for explanatory mechanisms. This is reflected in the comment by Coyne et al. (1987) that: "Results thus far clearly indicate the usefulness of further study but at the present we know little about what depressed people *do* that elicits a negative response from others or precisely how these others *become involved* in the perpetuation of depressed behavior" (p. 521, emphasis added). Few clues exist in the models themselves to suggest how to proceed in attempts to address these issues. It is possible that further insights may be gained by integrating this work with more basic formulations in the general area of social interaction. Consideration of work on the nature of social interaction may provide candidates for potential mediating mechanisms applicable to research on depressive interactions (see Cane & Gotlib, 1985, Coates & Wortman, 1980, Rosenblatt & Greenberg, 1988). The present chapter focuses on the relevance of one such mechanism.

In the next section of this chapter the implications of some of this more general work on social interaction are discussed. More specifically, the focus is on the potential role played by *interpersonal expectations*. Here, both the expectations held by depressives for themselves and the expectations and beliefs held by others about depressives and interaction more generally are considered. This necessitates consideration of expectations derived from individuals' knowledge of general social norms, expectations derived from the stereotypes that people hold of depressives, and the personal expectancies that depressives hold for themselves, based on their self-knowledge or self-concept. Expectancies derived from each of these sources may play a role in promoting the dysfunctional interaction patterns discussed above as being characteristic of depressives.

## EXPECTANCIES AND INTERPERSONAL INTERACTION

### The Role of Normative Expectations

Consideration of the nature and structure of interpersonal interaction has had a long history both in sociology and social psychology (e.g., McCann & Higgins, in press). This work has examined a variety of mechanisms and processes that are seen to be involved in interpersonal interactions. The focus in this section is on the potential role played by interpersonal expectancies in the dysfunctional interactions often experienced by depressives.

Athay and Darley (1981, 1982) have written extensively about the nature of social interaction from a social exchange viewpoint (Homans, 1961) as related to interaction-centered models of personality. They focus on the implications of the assumption that everyday interaction is primarily ego-centered. Individuals are assumed to engage in interpersonal interaction in an attempt to obtain important goals or personal objectives (see McCann & Higgins, 1988, for a discussion of the relevance of social goals to depression). These personal goals are of either the occasional, temporary sort, or may reflect more long-term, chronic personal orientations. Individuals, in pursuit of these goals, are faced by difficulties derived from the fact that the objectives of their interaction partners may diverge from, and conflict with, their own goals. Such divergence is seen to result from several sources, including experiential variables and social role membership. In such contexts conflict situations are established wherein the participants face the possibility of not obtaining what is important to them.

According to Athay and Darley (1981), this potential conflict leads to processes of instrumental manipulation on the part of the participants in their attempts to satisfy their needs. Thus, in order to obtain their personal objectives, individuals may require from others action sequences that these others might not ordinarily undertake. In such situations, Athay and Darley suggest the individual is placed in a position of manipulating or persuading the other to see that it is in their own best interests to do what is being requested of him or her. This type of interpersonal manipulation is seen to depend critically on the actor's "skillful exploitation of the normative principles of action recognized by interactants" (Athay & Darley, 1981, p. 286).

An individual's planning is dependent upon regularity in the actions of the other. This is assumed to be a function of the other's acknowledgment and adherence to shared normative principles of action. Thus, effective strategic planning is based on the actor's expectations regarding relevant normative principles of action and their implications for personally desired ends. In this context, personal goals can be achieved by getting the other individual to recognize the relevance of particular normative principles. Although there is much room for interpersonal negotiation in such matters, reliance on assumptions regarding the content and applicability of specific norms allows the actor to plan for movement toward personally desired outcomes. Normative principles of action imply *predictability* and serve as a basis for *expectations* about the behavior of the other. Failure to find such predictable regularity in the actions of others can be assumed to lead to confusion and irritation at first, and then perhaps to an increasing tendency on the part of the actor to abandon that particular interaction episode. Prolonged failure in this regard would most likely lead to a decision on the part of the actor to "leave the field."

Relevant here, of course, is the work discussed above regarding social skills deficits associated with depression (e.g., Gotlib & Robinson, 1982; Lewinsohn, 1974). This research has detailed the verbal and nonverbal behavioral differences that have been observed between depressed and nondepressed individuals in their interactions with others. The observed effects have ranged from differences in such things as the latency of responding to an utterance by another to differences in the verbal content emitted by depressed and nondepressed individuals.

What has not been clear in this area is how the various differences are related to the specific reactions of nondepressed interaction partners as discussed in the context of Coyne's (1976a) interactional model. One possibility, of course, is that the behaviors emitted by depressives are noxious in and of themselves. For example, the increased latency of response associated with depressives may prove irritating to those interacting with the depressive. Increased latency of response may serve to inhibit the smooth flow of the conversation which could serve to directly elicit negative reactions on the part of the other. This could lead to the types of negative reactions and interpersonal rejection effects discussed above.

Another possibility not yet considered in detail is that the negative reactions of the depressive's interactional partner are not due so much to the specific behaviors emitted by the depressive as to the fact that these behaviors are seen to be *non-normative* and as undermining the type of expectancy-based predictability outlined above. This may be especially true in the types of short-term, stranger interactions utilized in so much of this research. Thus, it may not be only the negativity of the utterances of the depressive that lead to negative reactions on the part of the other, but also the fact that this is non-normative in the context of brief interactions with strangers. This might suggest to the depressive's interaction partner that expectations based upon shared norms may not be useful in such situations.

Given that normatively-based expectations are important guides for action, the depressive's interaction partners may be faced with a situation of less than optimal predictability which could lead to confusion and rejection of the other. Our interactions with others, especially unfamiliar others, appear to be well scripted (e.g., Abelson, 1981) and are often of a routine nature. The topics and conversational sequencing are expected to follow a familiar pattern and typically lead to a situation of maximum predictability. Interacting with others who diverge dramatically from expected patterns, by definition, reduces the predictability of those others and may force the participants to delay, develop alternative paths to, or abandon the objectives they carried with them into the interaction.

When planning for and obtaining personal objectives, predictability based on adherence to typical or normative patterns of behavior is preferred. The different types of behavior enacted by depressives may be viewed as non-normative and as unpredictable in this context. Under most circumstances, such interpersonal contexts may be less rewarding and may ultimately result in interpersonal rejection.

This is clearly a speculative account of the potential role played by expectations in depressive interactions, but is one that is worthy of some consideration. An example of the effects of a specific type of non-normative behavior drawn from the literature in social psychology may serve to illustrate this point.

In an innovative program of research, Davis (e.g., Davis, 1982; Davis & Holtgraves, 1984) has considered the implications of normative expectations regarding "responsiveness" in interpersonal interactions. Communicative responsiveness is conceptualized as a general normative principle operative in social interactions. Responsiveness is a function of four types of contingencies between communicative participants: probability of response, response relevance, appropriateness of response latency, and appropriateness of response elaboration. According to Davis (1982), responsiveness is important in that to the extent that the other is responsive, his or her behavior is predictable and potentially controllable from the actor's viewpoint. Predictability is implicated in that one may expect: "1) that the other will respond, 2) that the response will address the content of the preceding communication, and 3) that it will be within a certain range of elaboration" (Davis, 1982, p. 87).

Responsiveness on the part of the other is assumed to reduce uncertainty (see McCann & Higgins, in press, for a review of the role of uncertainty in interpersonal interaction) and the frustration that stems from lack of a sense of control over the interaction. Unresponsiveness has been found to lead to general negative evaluations of the unresponsive other and unfavorable attributions with regard to competence and motivation. It can be assumed that repeated interactions characterized by unresponsiveness on the part of the other would lead to a decision by the actor to terminate the interaction episode and to avoid future interactions. There is a clear parallel between this formulation and the notions discussed above with regard to depressives and their interactional characteristics. It is likely that the behaviors associated with depressive social interactions may in fact lead to assessments of unresponsiveness. For example, the research discussed above has suggested that depressives tend to emit more negative content and inappropriate self-disclosure which, along with reduced eye-contact, smiling, and positive conversational-maintenance statements, may be taken by others as indicators of unresponsiveness.

Given the unpredictability associated with such non-normative behavior patterns and the uncertainty it introduces, it can be expected that the depressive's interaction partners may attempt to avoid further contact. The relationship between responsiveness and the types of interactional cycles described by Coyne (1976a), as characteristic of depressives, has not yet been examined empirically. It appears, however, that such formulations may have relevance to understanding some aspects of depressive interactions with others. The conclusions to be derived, however, go beyond just a consideration of norms relating to communicative responsiveness.

Because the behaviors of depressed individuals are often perceived to be nonnormative, the expectancies typically used by others to guide their behavior are less than maximally effective. The essential problem here may be one of a lack of predictability. Adherence to normative principles of actions guarantees a certain degree of predictability, potential control, and efficiency of social interaction. Given the high priority that individuals assign to such factors in their interactions with others, actions that appear to violate normative prescriptions may elicit perceived lack of control and a tendency to leave the field. This suggests one type of expectancy-based process that may be implicated in the types of dysfunctional interaction experiences typical of depressives. In the next section, the potential role played by another type of expectancy is considered. Non-normative behavior on the part of an individual may eventually lead to a judgment of him/her as abnormal or deviant. This type of categorization may carry with it other expectancies derived from stereotypic conceptions of deviant others. Especially relevant here are the possible implications of being categorized as mentally ill or depressed.

## Expectancies and Stereotypes of Depression

As is clear from the discussion presented above, students of social interaction often emphasize its strategic nature. It is described as a context in which individuals seek to obtain personally relevant social goals. Actors are dependent on the actions of others in order to obtain some types of objectives. Therefore, emphasis is placed on the predictability of those with whom one is interacting. In order to maximize predictability, actors often appeal to the behavioral prescriptions associated with general social norms to guide their behavior and plans.

Such general normative prescriptions are useful in many contexts. It is also true that most individuals recognize the fact that individual differences exist in behavior due to differences in such things as status, experience, and other important background variables. Thus, it is dysfunctional to rely exclusively on the prescriptions inherent in general social norms in anticipating the behavior of others. Accordingly, in order to maximize predictability, individuals often attempt to classify others as representing members of specific types of people from whom one can expect certain things. In fact, this categorization process is simply a continuation of the process described above. Here, instead of categorizing individuals as members of some large social group for whom certain norms apply, such as North Americans, the individuals may seek a more specific sub-categorization in order to generate more specific expectancies. Assignment of an individual to a specific type of person may allow for more specific judgments regarding attributes and behavior (e.g., Schneider, Hastorf & Ellsworth, 1979).

Research in social psychology has documented the range of linguistic and extra-linguistic cues used in such categorization processes (e.g., McCann, Ostrom, Tyner & Mitchell, 1985). Although potentially useful for the perceiver, these types of person-based expectancies often restrict the range of behavioral alternatives available to the target. That is, these types of expectancies have been found to result in self-fulfilling prophecy processes under certain conditions (e.g., Darley & Fazio, 1980; Merton, 1948; Miller & Turnbull, 1986; Snyder & Swann, 1978). Being categorized as deviant, mentally ill, or depressed, may elicit behavior patterns from others that constrain the actor from actions that would disconfirm the perhaps erroneous beliefs that others hold of people who are depressed. Before considering this issue, it will be instructive to review briefly some of the recent work examining the stereotypes and expectancies people have of depressives (see Endler, Chapter 1, this volume, for a more detailed review).

## Stereotypes of Depression

A great deal of attention has recently been devoted to an examination of the content and nature of stereotypes of various stigmatized groups including the mentally ill in general, and depressives in particular (e.g., Farina, 1982; Goffman, 1959; Jones, Farina, Hastorf, Markus, Miller & Scott, 1984; Rippere, 1977, 1980, 1981; Warren, 1983). Although an exhaustive review of this literature is beyond the purposes of the present chapter (see Cane & Gotlib, 1985, and Endler, Chapter 1, this volume), a brief discussion of some of the general findings is presented below.

Research on stereotypic conceptions of depression has been incorporated within a more general interest in peoples' conceptions of the mentally ill and has tended to confirm the notion that the mentally ill are negatively evaluated and are generally seen as unpredictable (e.g., Nunnally, 1961). Of particular interest here, is that literature devoted to understanding conceptions of depression and the depressed.

Cane and Gotlib (1985) have argued that our conceptions of depression are organized into cognitive prototypes. Prototypes have been shown, in other areas of research, to have profound effects on the ways in which individuals process information related to these types of cognitive structures (e.g., Kihlstrom & Cantor, 1984; Fiske & Taylor, 1984; Markus & Zajonc, 1985). Cognitive prototypes are used to classify and label persons as exemplars of particular types of persons. These individuals are then attributed the characteristics generally associated with this category of person. The attributes, or stereotypic information associated with depression, include information related to etiology, behavior, and effective modes of intervention. These characteristics are assumed to form the basis of expectancies regarding their likely behavior, and may be used to guide an actor's behavior in interaction with them.

For example, depressives are seen, among other things, as pessimistic, self-involved, socially isolated, preoccupied, different, and as expecting the worst (e.g.,

Horowitz, French, Lapid & Weckler, 1982). In addition, there is a tendency for perceivers to adopt the view that the depressives themselves should assume the primary responsibility for coping with the disorder, rather than having the responsibility fall on others (e.g., Rippere, 1977; see Cane & Gotlib, 1985). In general, it would appear that depressives are negatively evaluated. As a group, they are attributed various negative characteristics that might serve to interfere with smooth social interaction (e.g., McCann, in press).

As pointed out by Cane & Gotlib (1985), however, one of the limitations of research in this area is that much of it has failed to distinguish between characteristics attributed to depressives that are distinct from characteristics ascribed to the mentally ill in general. This problem is inherent in research that examines conceptions of depression without including control conditions in which subjects are also asked about their conceptions of the mentally ill in general, or some other specific disorder group.

In general, however, it is clear that many individuals seem to hold a relatively negative view of the mentally ill, including depressives. These negative prototypes may have implications for the nature of normal persons' interactions with depressives that are relevant to the interactional models discussed above. First, the type of stigma attributed to others appears to have important effects in terms of others' general reactions to them (see Endler, Chapter 1, this volume).

In a recent study, Weiner, Perry, and Magnusson (1988) found that physically based stigmas tended to be perceived as onset-uncontrollable (i.e., the individual has little control over the onset of the illness) and to elicit pity and helpful reactions. Mentally ill type stigmas, however, were more likely to be perceived as onset-controllable, and to elicit less pity, more anger, and more neglectful reactions. Second, as pointed out by several authors (e.g., Miller & Turnbull, 1986), these types of general expectancies may influence how we process information about target individuals leading to, for example, a tendency to increase the salience and memorability of confirming instances. In the case of depressives, the above may result in a tendency to more readily recall instances in which the depressives engage in self-derogation and dependent behavior at the expense of instances in which such behavior was not enacted. Third, our expectancies regarding the likely behavior of specific others will most likely impact on our own behavior toward them, leading to behavioral confirmation or self-fulfilling prophecy effects. This issue has been dealt with in general by several authors (e.g., Darley & Fazio, 1980).

Darley and Fazio (1980) have described the general interactional sequence involved in such situations as follows: 1) first, because of salient cues, emitted behavior, or information communicated by others, the perceiver categorizes and generates expectancies for the target; 2) these expectancies then guide the behavior of the actor that is directed toward the target; 3) the target interprets and responds to these actions on the part of the perceiver; 4) the perceiver encodes and interprets the actions of the target and re-enters the sequence beginning with step one. These interaction sequences often lead to the perceiver's initial expectations being confirmed. This may occur because the expectancy-based behaviors enacted by the perceiver constrain the actions of the target, and/or because of the effect of such expectancies on information processing biases (see Higgins & Bargh, 1987, and

Miller & Turnbull, 1986, for a review and discussion of limiting conditions).

Three types of problems are associated with these types of interaction sequences. First, the perceiver's preconceptions may be inaccurate, but may tend to be confirmed as outlined above. Second, even if generally accurate, the perceiver's expectancies make change on the part of the target more difficult and less likely. Third, the behavior enacted by the target in reaction to the perceiver may impact on his or her own self-concept. This can occur through processes such as those identified by Bem (1972). Thus, such interactions may elicit negative self-concept changes that may hinder the potential for future positive interactional experiences.

This formulation has clear relevance to the social interactional models of depression discussed above. To the extent that the depressive's interactional partners categorize them as mentally ill and/or depressed, this may lead to a host of negative expectancies for the interactions. These expectancies may be partially confirmed due to the types of processes outlined above. Once confirmed, these negative expectancies may lead to more general negative social judgments and interpersonal rejections characteristic of the interactions experienced by depressed individuals. In such contexts, the stigmatized individual may find few behavioral options open to him or her in any attempt to disconfirm such negative expectancies. Such processes may partially explain one way in which interaction partners become part of the negative interactional cycle described by Coyne (1976a).

Little research has systematically addressed the role of self-fulfilling prophecy processes in interaction with depressed individuals. We do know that the types of stereotypes and expectancies developed around the concept of depression are of the type that could conceivably set such processes in motion (Cane & Gotlib, 1985). This is clearly an area in which further research is needed. In addition, we do not yet know what aspects of the depressives interactional style might serve to elicit the initial categorization process as deviant, mentally ill, or depressed. It would seem, however, that the negativity of the depressive's verbal content and its generally non-normative nature might serve as salient cues for judgments of unpredictability and disturbance. In the next section the impact of such categorization on interactional expectancies, and the personal expectancies generated by depressives about their own behavior, are discussed.

### Personal Expectancies for Interpersonal Outcomes

The interactional expectancies that depressives hold for themselves are also relevant for promoting the dysfunctional interactional experiences, discussed by Coyne and others. Past research has documented the negative self-conceptions that depressives tend to have (e.g., Spielman & Bargh, Chapter 3, this volume; Kuiper, Olinger & Martin, Chapter 5, this volume; McCann, in press; Pietromonaco & Markus, 1985). For example, negative views of the self are a central aspect of the negative cognitive triad characteristic of depressives (cf., Beck, 1976). Depressives tend to see themselves as being, among other things, worthless, personally deficient, unlikable, and socially unskillful (e.g., Greenberg, Vazquez & Alloy, 1988; Lewinsohn, Mischel, Chaplin & Barton, 1980). Negative self-conceptions could play an important role in dysfunctional interactions (cf., Coyne, 1976a) in a variety of ways, including the initiation of self-verification processes, the generation of dysfunctional behavior patterns (see Curtis & Miller, 1986), and negative personal expectancies regarding interpersonal interactions. Each of these effects is discussed below.

Swann and his colleagues (e.g., Swann, 1983, 1987; Swann & Predmore, 1985; Swann, Griffin, Predmore & Gaines, 1987) have discussed how individuals tend to verify their conceptions of themselves in their interactions with others. They suggest that, analogous to self-fulfilling prophecy effects with regard to the expectations of others, individuals often engage in processes that serve to bring about confirmation of their own views of themselves. Individuals tend to preferentially solicit and value self-confirmatory feedback from others (e.g., Swann & Read, 1981a & b). They may develop interpersonal relationships in order to further such ends. Individuals appear to prefer as intimates others who hold congruent views about them (e.g., Swann & Pelham, 1987), and such intimates have been found to insulate them against self-discrepant feedback from other sources (e.g., Swann & Predmore, 1985). In addition, it seems that individuals often engage in such self-verification processes even when the self-discrepant feedback is *positive* (e.g., Swann et al., 1987).

Although such processes have not been investigated in the context of depressive interactions, the implications are clear. Given the types of negative self-views that appear to be characteristic of depressives, such processes would serve to reinforce the negative view of self held by depressed individuals. One way in which such negative self-views might be manifested in interpersonal contexts is by influencing the nature of the expectancies that depressives bring to their interpersonal interactions.

Several recent studies have been conducted to examine the expectations held by depressives for themselves (e.g., Alloy & Ahrens, 1987; Crocker, Alloy & Kayne, 1988; Hokanson & Meyer, 1984; Pyszczynski, Holt & Greenberg, 1987). Not surprisingly, this research has tended to confirm the assumption that, compared to nondepressed individuals, depressives hold generally negative expectations for themselves. From the present point of view, however, this research has been limited because of its tendency to focus on either *achievement* contexts or very *general interpersonal expectancies* (e.g., Hokanson & Meyer, 1984).

In a more recent study, Moretti and McCann (1986; see also McCann, in press) sought to examine the types of expectancies that depressed and nondepressed individuals held for one specific interactional context. As with other work in this area, depression was indexed by elevated (i.e., scores of nine and above) BDI scores. The evaluative nature of the expectancies that depressed and nondepressed university students had when asked to contemplate interacting with either an average or depressed student was assessed. Two target interaction partners were included in order to assess whether or not the types of expectancies generated by the subjects would generalize across target type and to examine the types of expectancies that nondepressed individuals would have in interacting with a depressed (i.e., stigmatized) other. All subjects were asked to complete the BDI and then were asked to think about interacting with a depressed or average university student. They were all asked to list all the thoughts that came to mind when imagining this interaction.

This type of thought-listing procedure has been used profitably in other research examining issues related to social interaction (e.g., Cacioppo, Glass & Merluzzi, 1979). The expectancies generated by the subjects were rated by two judges as reflecting either positive or negative interactional expectancies, and the proportion of positive expectancies were subjected to analysis.

Analysis of the interactional expectancies generated by the subjects indicated that depressed individuals produced more negative expectancies regardless of target type, and that the proportion of positive expectancies was equal in both conditions (i.e., 40% positive expectancies). The proportion of positive expectancies generated by nondepressed subjects varied with target type and indicated more positive expectancies in interacting with an average university student (i.e., 71%), and more negative expectancies when thinking about interacting with a depressed target (i.e., 42% positive expectancies).

The results suggested that the expectancies of the nondepressed subjects tended to be more *target-based*, whereas the expectancies of the depressed subjects seemed to be more *perceiver-based*. That is, nondepressed subjects anticipated a positive, rewarding, and smooth interaction with average students, but negative and uncomfortable interactions with a depressed individual. Clearly, such patterns of expectations are congruent with the research regarding the stigma associated with disorders such as depression. The depressed subjects, on the other hand, anticipated negative interpersonal experiences regardless of who they were interacting with. These types of negative expectancies are no doubt a reflection of these individuals' sense of self, relating to lack of skills and likability derived from past experiences. It is important to note, however, that the sample consisted primarily of mildly depressed university students. Further work is currently being conducted in order to assess the generalizability of these results to clinically depressed patient samples.

This line of research, along with those discussed previously in this section, suggest that the dysfunctional conceptions that depressives have of themselves may negatively impact on their relations with others. This occurs through the effects on such things as verification processes and the generation of interactional expectancies. Believing you are unliked and unlikable may elicit interpersonal events that serve to confirm these very views. Your behavior or information processing tendencies may serve to channel your behavior with others so that your negative views of self are not challenged. Such processes may be implicated in important ways in the types of interactional cycles described by Coyne and others. The relevance of these formulations may provide direction for future examination of these issues.

## SUMMARY AND IMPLICATIONS

Recent research and theory in clinical psychology have begun to consider the role of various social and interpersonal factors in the maintenance and exacerbation of depressive episodes. Notable here has been the work of Coyne (1976a) and others on an interactional model of depression. According to Coyne, depressives in their interpersonal interactions often experience negative reactions and rejection. The objective of the present chapter was to consider the relevance of one type of interpersonal factor derived from research in social psychology (i.e., interpersonal expectancies) in promoting dysfunctional interactional experiences.

The expectancy we develop for the behavior of others based upon our general knowledge of normative prescriptions for behavior was discussed. It was suggested that, especially with regard to social skills, the behaviors of depressives may appear to be non-normative. This may induce patterns of negative evaluations and rejection on the part of others due to the lack of predictability implied by non-normative (i.e., in particular contexts) behavior. Non-normative behavior may also result in *labeling* of the depressive as deviant, different, and disturbed. Because of self-fulfilling prophecy processes, this may exacerbate the tendency of dysfunctional interactions for depressives. The relevance of recent research on the personal expectancies of depressives for their own behavior and likely outcomes was discussed. It was suggested that because of past difficulties, depressives may anticipate negative outcomes, including rejection, in their interactions with others. These negative interpersonal expectancies may, through a variety of processes, lead to an eventual confirmation of interpersonal failure and rejection. This would serve to exacerbate the difficulties faced by the depressive.

One of the motivations underlying discussion of the issues mentioned above was the potential heuristic value of integrating current research and theory within and between clinical and social psychology. It would seem that future advance in this area would be enhanced by a more precise specification of the *mechanisms* underlying, what have been to date, largely *descriptive* accounts of depressive interactional experiences. Future work examining the types of interpersonal factors discussed in this chapter, *especially* in the context of patient samples, would be useful. This and other relevant phenomena may provide further insight into the dysfunctional interactional experiences characteristic of depressed individuals.

**Author's Note**: Preparation of this chapter and the research reported in it was partially supported by a Natural Sciences and Engineering Research Council of Canada Research Grant (#OPG0002016) awarded to the author. This chapter has benefited from the comments provided by Norman Endler and Alexander Mackenzie on a previous draft.

# References

Abelson, R.P. (1981). The psychological status of the script concept. *American Psychologist, 36*, 715–729.

Athay, M. & Darley, J.M. (1981). Toward an interaction-centered theory of personality. In N. Cantor & J.F. Kihlstrom (Eds.), *Personality, cognition and social interaction* (pp. 281–308). Hillsdale, N.J.: Erlbaum.

Athay, M. & Darley, J.M. (1982). Social roles as interaction competencies. In W. Ickes & E.S. Knowles (Eds.), *Personality, roles and social behavior* (pp. 55–83). New York: Springer-Verlag.

Alloy, L.B. & Ahrens, A.H. (1987). Depression and pessimism for the future: Biased use of statistically relevant information in predictions for self vs. others. *Journal of Personality and Social Psychology, 52*, 366–378.

Beck, A.T. (1983). Cognitive theories of depression: New perspectives. In P.J. Clayton & J.E. Barrett (Eds.), *Treatment of depression: Old controversies and new perspectives* (pp. 265–290). New York: Raven Press.

Beck, A.T., Ward, C.H., Mendelson, M., Mock, J. & Erbaugh, J. (1961). An inventory for measuring depression. *Archives of General Psychiatry*, *4*, 561–571.

Bem, D.J. (1972). Self-perception theory. In L. Berkowitz (Ed.), *Advances in experimental social psychology* (Vol. 6, pp. 27–44). New York: Academic Press.

Blumberg, S.R. & Hokanson, J.E. (1983). The effect of another person's response style on interpersonal behavior in depression. *Journal of Abnormal Psychology*, *92*, 196–209.

Boswell, P.C. & Murray, E.J. (1981). Depression, schizophrenia and social attraction. *Journal of Consulting and Clinical Psychology*, *49*, 641–647.

Brehm, S.S. (1976). *The application of social psychology to clinical practice*. Washington, D.C.: Hemisphere.

Burchill, S.A. & Stiles, W.B. (1988). Interactions of depressed college students with their roommates: Not necessarily negative. *Journal of Personality and Social Psychology*, *55*, 410–419.

Cacioppo, J.T., Glass, C.R. & Merluzzi, T.V. (1979). Self-statements and self-evaluation: A cognitive response analysis of heterosexual anxiety. *Cognitive Therapy and Research*, *3*, 249–262.

Cane, D.B. & Gotlib, I.H. (1985). Implicit conceptualizations of depression: Implications for an interpersonal perspective. *Social Cognition*, *3*, 341–368.

Carson, R.C. (1969). *Interaction concepts of personality*. Chicago: Aldine.

Coates, D. & Peterson, B.A. (1982). Depression and deviance. In G. Weary & H.L. Mirels (Eds.), *Integrations of clinical and social psychology* (pp. 154–170). New York: Oxford University Press.

Coates, D. & Wortman, C.B. (1980). Depression maintenance and interpersonal control. In A. Baum & J. Singer (Eds.), *Advances in environmental psychology* (Vol. 2, pp. 149–182). Hillsdale, N.J.: Erlbaum.

Coyne, J.C. (1976a). Toward an interactional description of depression. *Psychiatry*, *39*, 28–40.

Coyne, J.C. (1976b). Depression and the responses of others. *Journal of Abnormal Psychology*, *85*, 186–193.

Coyne, J.C. (1985). Studying depressed persons' interactions with strangers and spouses. *Journal of Abnormal Psychology*, *94*, 231–232.

Coyne, J.C., Kahn, J. & Gotlib, I.H. (1987). Depression. In T. Jacobs (Ed.), *Family interaction and psychopathology: Theories, methods and findings* (pp. 509–533). New York: Plenum Press.

Crocker, J., Alloy, L.B. & Kayne, N.J. (1988). Attributional style, depression and perceptions of consensus for events. *Journal of Personality and Social Psychology*, *54*, 840–846.

Curtis, R.C. & Miller, K. (1986). Believing another likes or dislikes you: Behaviors making the beliefs come true. *Journal of Personality and Social Psychology*, *51*, 284–290.

Darley, J.M. & Fazio, R. (1980). Expectancy confirmation processes arising in the social interaction sequence. *American Psychologist*, *35*, 867–881.

Davis, D. (1982). Determinants of responsiveness in dyadic interaction. In W. Ickes & E.S. Knowles (Eds.), *Personality, roles and social behavior* (pp. 85–139). New York: Springer-Verlag.

Davis, D. & Holtgraves, T. (1984). Perceptions of unresponsive others: Attributions, attraction, understandability, and memory of their utterances. *Journal of Experimental Social Psychology*, *20*, 383–408.

Doefler, L.A. & Chaplin, W.F. (1985). Type III error research on interpersonal models of depression. *Journal of Abnormal Psychology*, *94*, 227–230.

Dryden, W. (1981). The relationships of depressed persons. In S. Duck & R. Gilmour (Eds.), *Personal relationships: Personal relationships in disorder* (Vol. 3, pp. 127–160). New York: Academic Press.

Endler, N.S. & Edwards, J.M. (1988). Personality disorders from an interactional perspective. *Journal of Personality Disorders, 2,* 326–333.

Farina, A. (1982). The stigma of mental disorders. In A.G. Miller (Ed.), *In the eye of the beholder: Contemporary issues in stereotyping* (pp. 305–363). New York: Praeger.

Fiske, S.T. & Taylor, S.E. (1984). *Social cognition.* Reading, MA: Addison-Wesley.

Frank, J.D. (1961). *Persuasion and healing.* Baltimore, MD: Johns Hopkins University.

Goffman, E. (1959). *The presentation of self in everyday life.* New York: Doubleday-Anchor Books.

Gotlib, I.H. & Beatty, M.E. (1985). Negative responses to depression: The role of attributional style. *Cognitive Therapy and Research, 9,* 91–103.

Gotlib, I.H. & Robinson, L.A. (1982). Responses to depressed individuals: Discrepancies between self-report and observer-rated behavior. *Journal of Abnormal Psychology, 91,* 231–240.

Gotlib, I.H. & Whiffen, V.E. (in press). The interpersonal context of depression: Implications of theory and research. In D. Perlman & W. Jones (Eds.), *Advances in personal relationships.* Greenwich: JAI Press.

Greenberg, M.S., Vazquez, C.V., Alloy, L.B. (1988). Depression versus anxiety: Differences in self- and other-schemata. In L.B. Alloy (Ed.), *Cognitive processes in depression* (pp. 109–142). New York: Guilford Press.

Gurtman, M.B. (1986). Depression and the response of others: Re-evaluating the re-evaluation. *Journal of Abnormal Psychology, 95,* 99–101.

Hamilton, D.L. (1979). A cognitive-attributional analysis of stereotyping. In L. Berkowitz (Ed.), *Advances in experimental social psychology* (Vol. 12, pp. 72–97). New York: Academic Press.

Hammen, C.L. & Peters, S.D. (1977). Differential responses to male and female depressive relations. *Journal of Consulting and Clinical Psychology, 45,* 994–1001.

Hammen, C.L. & Peters, S.D. (1978). Interpersonal consequences of depression: Responses to men and women enacting a depressed role. *Journal of Abnormal Psychology, 87,* 322–332.

Higgins, E.T. (1987). Self-discrepancy: A theory relating self and affect. *Psychological Review, 94,* 314–340.

Higgins, E.T. & Bargh, J.A. (1987). Social cognition and social perception. *Annual Review of Psychology, 38,* 369–425.

Hokanson, J.E. & Meyer, B.E.B. (1984). Interpersonal expectancies and preferences for various types of social behaviors of depressed outpatients. *Journal of Personal and Social Relationships, 1,* 279–292.

Hokanson, J.E., Lowenstein, D.A., Hedeen, C. & Howes, M.J. (1986). Dysphoric college students and roommates: A study of social behaviors over a three-month period. *Personality and Social Psychology Bulletin, 12,* 311–324.

Hokanson, J.E., Sacco, W.P., Blumberg, S.R. & Landrum, G.C. (1980). Interpersonal behavior of depressive individuals in a mixed-motive game. *Journal of Abnormal Psychology, 89,* 320–332.

Homans, G.C. (1961). *Social behavior: Its elementary forms.* New York: Harcourt.

Horowitz, L.M., French, R., Lapid, J.S. & Weckler, D.A. (1982). Symptoms of interpersonal problems: The prototype as an integrating concepts. In J.C. Anchin & D.J. Kiesler (Eds.), *Handbook of interpersonal psychotherapy* (pp. 162–189). New York: Pergamon.

Howes, M.J. & Hokanson, J.E. (1979). Conversational and social responses to depressive interpersonal behavior. *Journal of Abnormal Psychology, 88,* 625–634.

Howes, M.J., Hokanson, J.E. & Lowenstein, D.A. (1985). Induction of depressive affect after prolonged exposure to a mildly depressed individual. *Journal of Personality and Social Psychology, 49,* 1110–1113.

Jones, E.E., Farina, A., Hastorf, A., Markus, H., Miller, D.T. & Scott, R.A. (1984). *Social stigma.* New York: Freeman & Co..

Kihlstrom, J.F. & Cantor, N. (1984). Mental representations of the self. In L. Berkowitz (Ed.), *Advances in experimental social psychology* (Vol. 17, pp. 30–62). New York: Academic Press.

King, D.A. & Heller, K. (1984). Depression and the responses of others: A re-evaluation. *Journal of Abnormal Psychology, 93,* 477–480.

Leary, M.R., Maddux, J.E. (1987). Progress toward a viable interface between social and clinical-counseling psychology. *American Psychologist, 42,* 904–911.

Lewinsohn, P.M. (1974). A behavioral approach to depression. In R.J. Friedman & M.M. Katz (Eds.), *The psychology of depression: Contemporary theory and research* (pp. 157–185). Washington, DC: Winston.

Lewinsohn, P.M., Mischel, W., Chaplin, W. & Barton, R. (1980). Social competence and depression: The role of illusory self-perceptions. *Journal of Abnormal Psychology, 89,* 203–212.

Maddux, J.E., Stoltenberg, C.D. & Rosenwein, R. (1987). *Social processes in clinical and counseling psychology.* New York: Springer-Verlag.

Maddux, J.E., Stoltenberg, C.D., Rosenswein, R., Leary, M.R. (1987). Social processes in clinical and counseling psychology: Introduction and orienting assumptions. In J.E. Maddux, C.D. Stoltenberg & R. Rosenwein (Eds.), *Social processes in clinical and counseling psychology* (pp. 1–13). New York: Springer-Verlag.

Marks, T. & Hammen, C.L. (1982). Interpersonal mood induction: Situational and individual determinants. *Motivation and Emotion, 6,* 387–399.

Markus, H. & Zajonc, R.B. (1985). The cognitive perspective in social psychology. In G. Lindzey & E. Aronson (Eds.), *The handbook of social psychology* (Vol. 1, 3rd Ed., pp. 137–230). New York: Random House.

McCann, C.D. (in press). The self and interpersonal relations. In J.M. Olson & M.P. Zanna (Eds.), *Self-inference processes: The Ontario symposium* (Vol. 6). Hillsdale, N.J.: Erlbaum.

McCann, C.D. & Higgins, E.T. (1988). Motivation and affect in interpersonal relations: The role of personal orientations and discrepancies. In L. Donahew, H.E. Sypher & E.T. Higgins (Eds.), *Communication, social cognition and affect* (pp. 53–79). Hillsdale, N.J.: Erlbaum.

McCann, C.D. & Higgins, E.T. (in press). Social cognition and communication. In H. Giles & W.P. Robinson (Eds.), *Handbook of language and social psychology.* Chichester & New York: Wiley.

McCann, C.D., Ostrom, T.M., Tyner, L.K. & Mitchell, M.L. (1985). Person perception in heterogeneous groups. *Journal of Personality and Social Psychology, 49,* 1446–1459.

Merton, R.K. (1948). The self-fulfilling prophecy. *Antioch Review, 8,* 193–210.

Miller, D.T. & Turnbull, W. (1986). Expectancies and interpersonal processes. *Annual Review of Psychology, 37,* 233–256.

Moretti, M.M. & McCann, C.D. (1986). *Interpersonal beliefs and expectancies in depression.* Paper presented at the 47th Annual Convention of the Canadian Psychological Association, Toronto, Canada.

Nunnally, J.C. (1961). *Popular conceptions of mental health.* New York: Holt, Rinehart & Winston.

Pietromonaco, P.R., Markus, H. (1985). The nature of negative thoughts in depression. *Journal of Personality and Social Psychology, 48*, 799–807.

Pyszczynski, T., Holt, K. & Greenberg, J. (1987). Depression, self-focused attention, and expectancies for positive and negative future life events for self and others. *Journal of Personality and Social Psychology, 52*, 994–1001.

Rippere, V. (1977). Commonsense beliefs about depression and antidepressive behavior: A study of social consensus. *Behavior Research and Therapy, 15*, 465–473.

Rippere, V. (1980). Some historical dimensions of commonsense knowledge about depressives and antidepressive behavior. *Behavior Research and Therapy, 18*, 373–385.

Rippere, V. (1981). How depressing: Another cognitive dimension of commonsense knowledge. *Behavior Research and Therapy, 19*, 169–181.

Robbins, B.P., Strack, S. & Coyne, J.C. (1979). Willingness to provide feedback to depressed persons. *Social Behavior and Personality, 7*, 199–203.

Rosenblatt, A. & Greenberg, J. (1988). Depression and interpersonal attraction: The role of perceived similarity. *Journal of Personality and Social Psychology, 55*, 112–119.

Schneider, D.J., Hastorf, A.H. & Ellsworth, P.C. (1979). *Person perception*. Reading, MA: Addison-Wesley.

Snyder, M. & Swann, W.B., Jr. (1978). Hypothesis testing processes in social interaction. *Journal of Personality and Social Psychology, 36*, 1202–1212.

Strack, S. & Coyne, J.C. (1983). Social confirmation of dysphoria: Shared and private reactions to depression. *Journal of Personality and Social Psychology, 44*, 798–806.

Strong, S.R. & Claiborn, C.D. (1982). *Change through interaction*. New York: Wiley-Interscience.

Swann, W.B. (1987). Self-verification: Bringing social reality into harmony with the self. In J. Suls & A.G. Greenwald (Eds.), *Psychological perspectives on the self* (Vol. 2, pp. 33–66). Hillsdale, N.J.: Erlbaum.

Swann, W.B. & Predmore, S.C. (1985). Intimates as agents of social support: Sources of consolation or despair. *Journal of Personality and Social Psychology, 49*, 1609–1617.

Swann, W.B. & Read, S.J. (1981a). Acquiring self-knowledge: The search for feedback that fits. *Journal of Personality and Social Psychology, 49*, 1609–1617.

Swann, W.B. & Read, S.J. (1981b). Self-verification processes: How we sustain our self-conceptions. *Journal of Experimental Social Psychology, 17*, 351–372.

Swann, W.B., Griffin, J.J., Predmore, S.C. & Gaines, B. (1987). Cognitive-affective crossfire: When self-consistency meets self-enhancement. *Journal of Personality and Social Psychology, 52*, 881–889.

Warren, L.W. (1983). Male intolerance of depression: A review with implications for psychotherapy. *Clinical Psychology Review, 3*, 147–156.

Weary, G. & Mirels, H.L. (1982). *Integrations of clinical and social psychology*. New York: Oxford University Press.

Weiner, B., Perry, R.P. & Magnusson, J. (1988). An attributional analysis of reactions to stigmas. *Journal of Personality and Social Psychology, 55*, 738–748.

Winer, D.L., Bonner, T.O., Jr., Blaney, P.H. & Murray, E.J. (1981). Depression and social attraction. *Motivation and Emotion, 5*, 153–166.

Youngren, M.A. & Lewinsohn, P.M. (1980). The functional relation between depression and problematic interpersonal behavior. *Journal of Abnormal Psychology, 89*, 333–341.

Zuckerman, M. & Lubin, B. (1965). *Manual for the multiple affect adjective checklist*. San Diego, CA: Education and Industrial Testing Service.

# PART II

# PSYCHOLOGICAL FACTORS

Part II contains six chapters (Chapters 3–8) that focus on the role played by a variety of psychological factors in the etiology and treatment of depression. The first four chapters provide a cognitive orientation and attempt to evaluate and extend current work examining social cognitive factors in depression and their treatment implications. The fifth chapter adopts a phenomenological/experiential orientation toward an analysis and treatment of depression, while the final chapter in this section reviews and evaluates current work examining the children of depressed parents.

Currently, one of the most dominant theoretical orientations in depression research is the cognitive approach, based largely on the early work of Aaron Beck. The first three chapters are similar in that they each involve a critical evaluation of the role of cognition in depression. They differ from each other, however, in the specific theoretical orientation adopted by the authors and in the aspects of cognition that they emphasize.

Kuiper, Olinger, and Martin (Chapter 3) consider the general question of whether or not cognitive approaches to depression are useful. They provide an extremely useful theoretical and empirical overview of cognitive models. They then consider some of the recent criticisms of this work, advanced by those working both within and outside of this general orientation. While recognizing the legitimacy of some of these criticisms, Kuiper et al. suggest that many of these comments are more applicable to the original cognitive formulations than to their more recent revisions and manifestations.

The authors of Chapter 3 review the evolution of cognitive models in general, and specify the ways in which most of the criticisms advanced are less applicable to the more recent models. Current models are seen to consider the demonstrated heterogeneity of the depressive disorders. They more specifically address the notion of subtypes of cognitive vulnerability for depression. In addition, the more recent models tend to adopt a diathesis-stress assumption in which it is suggested the pre-existent cognitive vulnerabilities or predispositions (i.e., the *diathesis*) interact with environmental events (i.e., the *stress*) in producing depression. The authors conclude by suggesting that cognitive models remain viable. Furthermore, these models are proving to be increasingly heuristic in terms of relevant research in this area.

These general themes are discussed and extended in the chapter by Abramson and Alloy (Chapter 4). The authors suggest that there is a need for theory-based taxonomic approaches to the classification of subtypes of depression, and proceed to present one such theory-based subtype of depression which they term the "negative cognition" subtype. After considering the causal status of various cognitive variables, the authors integrate previous work involving Beck's cognitive triad formulation with their own work on hopelessness depression. Abramson and Alloy suggest that the two models converge in identifying a subtype of depression which fits within a diathesis-stress framework. They review work consistent with this formulation and discuss its treatment implications. They conclude by outlining the necessary directions for future research designed to further examine this cognitive vulnerability subtype of depression.

The next chapter (Chapter 5), by Spielman and Bargh, focuses on one type of explanatory mechanism (i.e., the self-schema) which is often highlighted in cognitive models of depression. In their chapter, they attempt to answer whether or not the self-schema in depression really exists. The depressive self-schema is viewed, in this model, as an experientially based, cognitive vulnerability factor for depression. The schematic structure of the self is assumed to result in the negatively biased information processing that is so often characteristic of depressives. Spielman and Bargh review the general characteristics of schematic processing emerging from cognitive psychology. They then use this framework in an elaborate and cogent analysis to evaluate the evidence for self-schema processing in depression. They conclude by suggesting that the evidence is equivocal at this point, and that other cognitive formulations may prove to be more viable.

Moretti, Higgins, and Feldman (Chapter 6) continue this theme of the role of the self in depression, but from a different perspective. They adopt a novel approach to conceptualizing the nature of the self-system, and the ways in which it may be implicated in depression. Their chapter is based on earlier work by Higgins on his self-discrepancy theory.

The self-system is conceptualized as consisting of several distinct self-states, including the actual-self (an individual's representation of his or her actual attributes) and several self-guides, that serve as standards for the self. Discrepancies between the actual-self and various self-guides are assumed to produce dejection and depression-related affect. Moretti, Higgins, and Feldman consider the developmental antecedents of the self-system that may predispose individuals for the experience of depression. They then review support for this model. The authors discuss the structural and processing mechanisms inherent in this model of the self and indicate its relevance to considerations of the onset of depression. In the second part of their chapter, they explore the treatment implications of this formulation and relate them to existing intervention techniques. These techniques focus on changing the nature of an individual's actual-self or self-guides in an attempt to reduce self-discrepancy, thereby reducing depressed affect.

The theme of the centrality of the self in the etiology and treatment of depression is further continued in the chapter by Greenberg, Elliott, and Foerster (Chapter 7). The approach taken to the self here, however, is quite different from those discussed above. Greenberg et al. concern themselves with the phenomenal experience of the self. The self is here viewed as an organizing process, in which different self-organizations are continually merging and evolving in response to both person and situation influences. Hence, the view of the self adopted here is a much more fluid conceptualization than is evidenced in the other chapters in this section.

The authors' primary concern is with the role played by distinct types of self-organization in the therapeutic process. They consider and discuss the development and role played by the weak/bad self-organization, the self-critical organization, and the essential-self organization. More specifically, they emphasize the conditions under which these self-organizations emerge in psychotherapy, and how treatment interventions may be targeted at each of them. The authors focus their discussion of therapy on a variety of experimental techniques that may be useful in dealing with disordered self-organizations. They present both clinical transcripts, and the results of some of their own empirical research to underscore the potential inherent in this formulation.

The final chapter in this section by Gotlib and Lee (Chapter 8) is concerned with research examining the problems experienced by the children of depressed parents (most often maternal depression). The authors begin by presenting a comprehensive review of the literature assessing the adjustment and functioning of children of depressed parents. This discussion is presented in the context of a critical review in which the authors indicate quite clearly some of the limitations of work in this area. In particular, they suggest that much of the early work suffered from problems associated with faulty experimental designs, in which relevant control groups were not utilized.

Gotlib and Lee's review categorizes the relevant research, according to the age of the children assessed, making the point that the impact on children of depressed parents may differ depending upon the child's own cognitive and emotional developmental stage. The authors suggest that, in general, work in this area has indicated that the children of depressed parents are at considerable risk themselves for various disturbances in emotional, cognitive, and social functioning. There is, however, still some question as to the extent to which some of these problems are specific to children of depressed parents as opposed to children of parents suffering from various other forms of psychopathology. Gotlib and Lee indicate the format that future research must take to answer this question. They also suggest that future research must focus more specifically on an examination of processes that might lead to the observed increased risks of children of depressed parents.

In summary, the chapters in this section focus on an explication and evaluation of some of the mechanisms implicated in depression from a social-cognitive perspective. Although addressing this general theme, each chapter emphasizes the role played by distinct psychological processes.

# 3

# Are Cognitive Approaches to Depression Useful?

Nicholas A. Kuiper
*University of Western Ontario*

L. Joan Olinger
*London Psychiatric Hospital*

Rod A. Martin
*University of Western Ontario*

KEY WORDS: depression, cognitions, subgroups, self-worth, self-schema, type A

In the past two decades there has been an increasing emphasis on cognitive approaches to depression. Much of this interest can be traced back to Beck's seminal work in the 1960s on cognitive factors involved in the etiology, maintenance, and treatment of depression. In fact, in the last ten years this interest has produced a veritable explosion of cognitive research on depression. This explosion has resulted in a variety of models that utilize a number of different research paradigms to examine cognitive facets of depression in several populations, including community groups, university students, and clinical samples. This work has also integrated formerly diverse areas of psychology, such as cognitive and clinical approaches, and thus provided one means of bridging theoretical models and constructs across domains. Furthermore, in the past ten years we have seen the development of a large literature on the application and efficacy of cognitive therapy for depression.

Given this tremendous activity and interest, it is probably useful to step back and ask ourselves, "What is the current state of the field with respect to the utility of cognitive approaches to depression?" In other words, we might ask ourselves, "Are cognitive approaches to depression useful?" Proponents of cognitive models of depression have sometimes provided enthusiastic endorsements regarding the utility of their approaches. Conversely, the last five years have also witnessed the publication of several influential review articles which strongly question some of the fundamental assumptions underlying cognitive approaches to depression.

One strategy for assessing the utility of a cognitive approach to depression is to examine that approach in light of the more general aims of science, namely, description, explanation, and prediction. These aims can be arranged in a rough hierarchy of increasing sophistication and control. Thus, the first aim of science is to provide a more complete description of the phenomenon under investigation (in this case, depression). The second aim is closely aligned and builds upon the descriptive function by providing an explanation of the occurrence of the phenomena (in this case, why individuals may become depressed, and what factors might alleviate that depression). Finally, the predictive aim of science is often thought of as the acid test of any theory or approach. Here, the utility of an approach can be judged in terms of its success at predicting the occurrence of a phenomenon (e.g., who will become depressed and under what conditions). To the extent such predictions are successful, the approach demonstrates scientific control over the phenomenon. Using this framework, then, we would judge an approach useful if it allows us to significantly increase our understanding of the phenomena in a given domain. In the first instance, this would include more complete descriptions and explanations, followed, of course, by more precise and accurate predictions concerning behaviors in that domain.

In the present chapter we will comment on cognitive approaches to depression in terms of these aims of science. In addition to evaluating progress with respect to these aims, we will provide some specific observations and recommendations that may prove useful in incrementing the utility of cognitive approaches to depression. It should be noted at the outset that the purpose of this chapter is not to provide an exhaustive review of the cognitive depression literature. Rather, we will focus selectively on issues that could help clarify the utility of cognitive approaches to depression, and ultimately, may result in greater predictive capabilities for this approach.

## COGNITIVE APPROACHES TO DEPRESSION

### Overview of Cognitive Approaches

Considerable attention has been devoted to the possible role of cognitive factors in the onset, maintenance, and amelioration of negative emotions such as depression. A fundamental assumption of the cognitive approach is that attitudes or beliefs influence the way an individual interprets environmental events. In turn, these cognitive appraisals and evaluations then bear on the nature of emotional responses to events. At a general level, the cognitive approach suggests that individuals who maintain realistic, rational, and flexible attitudes or beliefs experience less extreme, inappropriate, or disturbed emotional responses than individuals who endorse unrealistic and dysfunctional cognitions.

Much of this interest in cognitive factors can be traced back to the influential work of two major theorists, Albert Ellis and Aaron Beck. Over the past quarter century, Ellis has promoted the view that the way people think has a profound impact on the way they feel (Ellis, 1962). In his work, Ellis has compiled a list of eleven irrational beliefs that are common in Western society (e.g., "One should be loved and approved by almost everyone in order to be a worthwhile person," "In order to be worthwhile, one should be competent in almost all respects"). Ellis maintains that individuals who endorse such beliefs have higher levels of negative emotions, including depression, anxiety, and anger. Similarly, Beck and his colleagues have provided a list of dysfunctional attitudes that may relate to the onset and maintenance of depressive symptoms (Beck, Rush, Shaw & Emery, 1979).

Examples of these attitudes include, "If I do not do well all of the time, people will not respect me," and, "If I do not perform as well as others, it means that I am an inferior human being." These attitudes can be thought of as a set of beliefs that delineate excessively rigid and perfectionist criteria for evaluations of self-worth. Since these criteria are so extreme, they are not often successfully met, resulting in a negative view of self and depressive affect (Kuiper & Olinger, 1986).

Even a quick perusal of the depression literature reveals the increased emphasis placed on cognitive approaches to depression. Several recent volumes have been written, either specific to cognitive elements of depression (Alloy, 1988), or including relevant chapters on cognition and depression (Beckham & Leber, 1985; Ingram, 1986). In addition, there has been a large number of recent theoretical/empirical review articles on cognitive components of depression. These articles range from critiques of cognitive approaches (Barnett & Gotlib, 1988; Segal, 1988) to the presentation of theoretical models emphasizing cognitive aspects of depression (Hyland, 1987; Kuiper & Olinger, 1986; Oatly & Bolton, 1985; Pyszczynski & Greenberg, 1987; Ruehlman, West & Pasahow, 1985; Swallow & Kuiper, 1988; Teasdale, 1988). Among other things, this work has focused on causal attributions and appraisals of life events (Abramson, Alloy & Metalksy, 1988; Hammen, 1988; Miller & Moretti, 1988), the role of negative self-schemata in depression (Kuiper & Olinger, 1986; Ruehlman et al., 1985; Segal, 1988), the precise delineation of cognitive vulnerability factors for depression (Beck, 1983; Janoff-Bulman & Hecker, 1988; Kuiper, Olinger & MacDonald, 1988; Robins & Block, 1988; Teasdale, 1988), cognitive assessment issues (Dobson & Shaw, 1986; Hammen & Krantz, 1985), and the extension of cognitive approaches to childhood depression (Cole & Kaslow, 1988; Hammen & Zupan, 1984).

One feature evident in this literature has been its bridging function, drawing together formerly diverse areas of psychology. To illustrate, our work on negative self-schemata in depression has drawn heavily from prior theorizing and research in both experimental cognitive psychology (Derry & Kuiper, 1981; Kuiper et al., 1988) and social psychology (Swallow & Kuiper, 1988). In a similar fashion, Ingram and Reed's (1986) work on encoding and retrieval processes in depression is also based strongly on the cognitive literature.

Recent approaches with a strong cognitive orientation have also helped bridge normally disparate areas of research within depression, encompassing the biological, cognitive, behavioral, and interpersonal domains. As one example, a recent integrative model of depression advanced by Lewinsohn and his colleagues has moved away from a strictly behavioral orientation to accord dysfunctional self-cognitions a prominent role (Lewinsohn, Hoberman, Teri & Hautzinger, 1985). Biological and cognitive orientations have also been integrated in a recent model examining attributional processes, personal vulnerabilities, and negative life events in conjunction with circadian dysrthymia (Healy & Williams, 1988). Finally, the interpersonal social support and coping literature in depression has been integrated with cognitive models focusing on attributional processes and stress appraisals (Billings & Moos, 1985; Kuiper & Olinger, 1989). Here, our own theoretical work has also integrated the depression role loss literature with perceptions and evaluations of self-worth, a central cognitive construct (Dance & Kuiper, 1987).

A further trend in this literature is the attempt to integrate various psychological theories of depression into a more unified approach with strong cognitive underpinnings. Perhaps most illustrative is the recent emphasis on control theories of depression (Hyland, 1987; Pyszczynski & Greenberg, 1987; Rehm, 1988). Based on negative feedback loop systems, these models generally propose that the individual's highest level of motivation is to maintain a positive view of self. Thus, when positive self-worth is disrupted, and the individual sees little possibility of reestablishing self-worth, depression may ensue (see also Kuiper & Olinger, 1986 and Oatley & Bolton, 1985 for earlier conceptually similar models not employing control terminology). Central cognitive elements in these models include such factors as aberrant standards for self-evaluation and a dysfunctional self-focus when depressed. As outlined previously, extreme self-standards relate to dysfunctional attitudes such as, "If I fail partly, it is as bad as being a complete failure." A dysfunctional self-focus refers to an exaggerated concern with inner thoughts and feelings. This enhanced level of private self-consciousness has a predominately negative orientation, consisting of ruminations of personal inadequacies and shortcomings (Kuiper, Olinger & Swallow, 1987).

A final trend evident in these theoretical models is their increasing refinement and sophistication. Whereas early cognitive models often stressed the primacy of dysfunctional cognitions (Beck, 1967, 1976), recent approaches have more carefully considered the complex relationships among cognitive factors, life stressors, and specific vulnerabilities. As will be considered in more detail shortly, this has resulted in the evolution of several cognitive theoretical models to incorporate additional components. One example is the recent hopelessness reformulation of the learned helplessness model (Abramson et al., 1988; Alloy, Hartlage & Abramson, 1988). A second illustration concerns more recent versions of Beck's model, which prominently emphasize such elements as the role of negative life events (Beck et al., 1979; Beck, 1983; Beck, 1984).

A strong cognitive orientation is also evident in the accumulating literature on therapeutic approaches to depression. In the past decade, cognitive therapy for depression has been advanced as a viable treatment approach (Beck et al., 1979; Beck, 1983; Beck, 1984; Hollon & Beck, 1986; Sacco & Beck, 1985), with its efficacy being endorsed in several examinations (e.g., Evans & Hollon, 1988). Recent work in this area has more closely examined such issues as the causal mediators of change in cognitive treatment of depression (Hollon, DeRubeis & Evans, 1987), and the relationship of cognitive treatment to biological factors such as circadian dysrthymia (Healy & Williams, 1988). Also evident is an increasing literature on the implications of cognitive depression research and theorizing on cognitive treatment approaches. Evans and Hollon (1988), for example, comment on the potential effects of depressive realism and self-schema research on cognitive therapies (see also Segal, 1988). A second example is Ingram and Hollon's (1986) work on cognitive information processing models and their implications for cognitive therapy. Finally, Pyszczynski and Greenberg (1987) have provided suggestions regarding cognitive treatment implications, based upon their self-awareness theory of depression.

In summary, although our overview is neither detailed nor comprehensive, it does serve to illustrate the tremendous amount of activity currently underway with respect to cognitive approaches to depression. Several investigators have commented on both the viability and utility of a cognitive approach, including the application of schema concepts (Derry & Kuiper, 1981; Ruhleman et al., 1985; Segal, 1988), and attributional models (Peterson & Seligman, 1984; Sweeney, Anderson & Bailey, 1986). Further indicators of a potentially healthy state of affairs are evident in recent cognitive models that attempt to integrate behavioral, biological, and interpersonal perspectives on depression, and thus attempt to account for other factors that may prove important in furthering our understanding of depression. Finally, the utility of a cognitive approach can also be assessed in terms of treatment efficacy, with cognitive therapy appearing to be a generally facilitative procedure. Overall, then, these indicators appear to provide initial evidence for the utility of a cognitive approach to depression and would certainly seem to suggest that this approach is worth further investigation.

## Concerns Regarding Cognitive Approaches

Tempering these optimistic conclusions, however, are a variety of concerns regarding cognitive approaches to depression. Some of these concerns are specific to given cognitive formulations, such as the attributional models, whereas other concerns are more broadly based. Starting at a general level, Coyne and Gotlib (1983) reviewed the status of the cognitive depression literature in the early 1980s. They examined five broad areas of functioning, including expectations and evaluations of performance, perceptions of environmental information, recall of information, cognitive biases, and attributional processes. At that time, their major conclusion was that neither Beck's cognitive model nor the learned helplessness model of depression received strong empirical support.

Turning more specifically to attributions, Coyne and Gotlib's concerns have been echoed in several more recent reviews. In 1985, for example, Hammen suggested that only global attributions appeared to be linked to depression (and not internal and stable dimensions as suggested by other researchers). Taking into account even more recent work, Hammen (1988) is more pessimistic and suggests that there is no consistent empirical support for a relationship between any type of causal attribution, be it internal, stable, or global, and depression. In a similar fashion, Brewin (1985) found only partial support for cognitive attributional models of depression, with the major evidence suggesting that attributions may only function to enhance or maintain an already existing depressive episode.

Cautionary notes have been advanced by other reviewers regarding cognitive attributional models. Miller and Moretti (1988), for example, offer a detailed and careful review of research on depressive attributional style. In their examination of attribution studies ranging from hypothetical events to achievement tasks, and from university students to clinical depressives, they conclude that a clear picture has not yet emerged regarding the relation between attributional patterns and etiological and maintenance aspects of depression.

Gotlib and his colleagues have provided several further insightful commentaries on cognitive approaches to depression. Although several of the specific concerns raised in these latter publications are new, the overall conclusions remain consistent. Coyne and Gotlib (1986), for example, in response to a commentary by Segal and Shaw (1986a), point out that they still remain convinced that cognitive approaches to depression face considerable conceptual, methodological, and empirical difficulties. In an even more recent paper, Barnett and Gotlib (1988) provide a detailed review of psychosocial variables relating to depression. These variables included attributional style, dysfunctional attitudes, personality, social support, marital distress, and coping style. With specific reference to the cognitive variables of attributional style and dysfunctional attitudes, Barnett and Gotlib (1988, p. 117) conclude, "there is little empirical evidence of a stable cognitive vulnerability to depression." This conclusion echoes comments of five years previous, in which Coyne and Gotlib (1983) suggested that the prominent cognitive models of depression at that time received little empirical support. Finally, it should be pointed out that other investigators have also offered general criticisms of cognitive approaches to depression. At the end of her detailed review of research on depressive cognitions regarding stressful life events, Hammen (1988, page 102) concludes, "This review points out that there are few specific cognitive contributions to understanding depression that have universal applicability."

## Responses to Concerns

As expected, the criticisms raised by various reviewers of cognitive approaches to depression have not been without response. Several responses detail specific concerns relating to the Coyne and Gotlib (1983) review article, including difficulties with both the studies selected for inclusion (Masters, Burish, Hollon & Rimm, 1987; Segal & Shaw, 1986a; 1986b) and the conclusions drawn from these studies (Robins, 1988). Other responses have been more general and highlight major concerns that we will elaborate on in this chapter. The first of these concerns relates to the issue of what cognitive model of depression is being evaluated. Segal and Shaw (1986a), for example, indicate that Beck's theory has evolved over the years from a simple cognitive model to an interactive diathesis-stress approach. In this approach, aberrant cognitions, such as dysfunctional attitudes, form the diathesis or personal vulnerability component for depression. Depression only ensues, however, if relevant life stressors impinge directly on this diathesis. Thus, cognitive elements alone are not sufficient for the expression of depressive symptomatology. Instead, depression results from the combination of a cognitive diathesis (e.g., dysfunctional attitudes) with impinging life stressors (see Olinger, Kuiper & Shaw, 1987 for an empirical test of this model). Given this more complex diathesis-stress model, Segal and Shaw (1986a) suggest that criticisms based on the original version of this model have only limited applicability and relevance. This evolution of cognitive models has also been pointed out by several other depression investigators (Abramson et al., 1988; Hammen, 1988), and we consider this issue to be one that has led to considerable confusion in the evaluation of cognitive approaches to depression. As such, we will outline this evolution and some of the resulting evaluative difficulties in subsequent sections of this chapter.

A second major concern is that reviewers of cognitive approaches have failed to consider the possible heterogeneity of depressive disorders, resulting in the possibility that cognitive models may only be applicable to a certain subset of depressed individuals. This argument has recently been pursued by Abramson and Alloy and their colleagues (Abramson et al., 1988; Alloy et al., 1988) who have suggested a subtype of negative cognition depression. This issue is also extremely important, and we will provide some further theoretical and empirical basis for this subtype distinction in subsequent sections of this chapter.

A third concern is that many reviewers of cognitive approaches to depression have made the assumption that all maladaptive cognitions must play an etiological role in this disorder, and thus must be evident during periods of remission (Segal & Shaw, 1986a). Thus, research which shows that remitted depressives do not display these aberrant cognitions is interpreted as evidence against cognitive models (e.g., Barnett & Gotlib, 1988). Unfortunately, this rationale is based primarily on Beck's early cognitive model, and thus ignores more fine-grained distinctions made over the years between maladaptive cognitions that play a role in the etiology of depression, and those which may be evident only after the onset of depressive affect (Beck & Epstein, 1982; Kuiper & Olinger, 1986; Segal & Shaw, 1986a; Teasdale, 1988). Again, this issue is of considerable importance, and we will return to it in more detail later.

Overall, then, the type of concerns outlined above have led many depression investigators to suggest that it is premature to make closure regarding the validity of cognitive approaches to depression (Abramson et al., 1988; Alloy et al., 1988; Miller & Moretti, 1988; Robins, 1988; Teasdale, 1988). We concur with this proposal and would suggest that a more detailed examination of the types of concerns outlined above will ultimately enhance the utility of these approaches.

## THE EVOLUTION OF COGNITIVE MODELS OF DEPRESSION

The evolution of theoretical models is certainly not unusual in science, and indeed, represents one typical process whereby new knowledge is incorporated into more comprehensive explanatory systems. This evolution is also evident in several cognitive models of depression. The learned helplessness approach, for example, was originally formulated in terms of animal research, then applied to depression, and then reformulated in the late 1970s to incorporate causal attributions. More recently, this model has undergone further evolution to consider more fully a diathesis-stress process whereby several contributing components ultimately lead to feelings of hopelessness and symptoms of depression. In this hopelessness model of depression, these components include the role of negative life events, situational cues for interpreting these events, social support difficulties, and a depressogenic attributional style (Abramson et al., 1988; Alloy et al., 1988). To take a concrete example, depression may ultimately ensue when a negative life event, such as failure on an important examination (the stressor), interacts with a depressogenic attributional style (the diathesis), to yield internal and stable attributions for the event (i.e., I failed because of a lack of ability). These cognitions may produce feelings of hopelessness, lower self-esteem, and ultimately, symptoms of depression. The lack of an adequate social support system may further contribute to these difficulties by isolating the individual during the stages of this hypothesized causal chain. This revised model also suggests the existence of a negative cognition subtype of depression relating to hopelessness.

Overall, then, this model has become more complex by considering a larger number of factors which may play a role in depression onset, maintenance, and remission. It should also be noted that several of these factors move the model away from the simple cognitive primacy notion (i.e., dysfunctional cognitions are the sole cause of depression) to a theoretical position that recognizes the complex interplay between cognitive and noncognitive compónents (Hammen, 1988). Finally, the evolving nature of this model is clearly acknowledged by Abramson et al. (1988), who suggest that the proposal for a cognitive subtype of depression be treated as an open concept, in which a construct validation approach is employed to refine theory as further empirical data is obtained.

A second illustration of the evolution of cognitive approaches to depression is provided by an examination of the changes in Beck's model over the past two decades. In much the same manner as the learned helplessness model, this approach has also moved away from a simple cognitive primacy notion (Hammen, 1988). Early versions of Beck's model certainly stressed the proposal that irrational cognitions cause depression (Beck, 1967; 1976). More recent versions, however, provide a more complex diathesis-stress orientation (Beck et al., 1979; Beck, 1984) which considers different types of vulnerabilities impinging on different life events (Beck, 1983; Robins & Block, 1988). This revised model also considers the possibility that only some dysfunctional cognitions may play a role in etiology (e.g., dysfunctional attitudes), whereas others are primarily concomitants of existing depressive episodes (e.g., automatic negative thoughts; Beck & Epstein, 1982; Rholes, Riskind & Neville, 1985).

A final example of the evolution of cognitive models of depression is provided by our own work. In the early 1980s, our primary emphasis was on documenting the nature of self-schema functioning in depression (Derry & Kuiper, 1981). This work drew heavily from cognitive psychology approaches, and provided an information-processing based description of the depressive self-schema at various levels of negative affect (see Kuiper, MacDonald & Derry, 1983 for a detailed account of this self-schema model of depression). More recently, our theoretical approach has evolved to consider etiological, maintenance, and remission issues, and has been presented as a self-worth contingency model of depression (see Kuiper & Olinger, 1986; and Kuiper, et al., 1988, for detailed presentations of this model and associated empirical evidence). The self-worth model integrates our earlier self-schema research, but also includes a number of additional factors relating to a diathesis-stress approach. Thus, as described earlier in the chapter, we have also begun to focus on stressful events that impinge negatively on dysfunctional attitudes (the diathesis). Our research has considered the effects of both the number of negative life events (Kuiper et al., 1988; Olinger et al., 1987) and the nature of these events (i.e., unresolved versus resolved; Kuiper & Olinger, 1989), on dysfunctional attitudes and depression. Thus, current versions of this model focus on the role of negative life events in depression, in addition to a broader variety of cognitive factors. These include a distinction between vulnerability and episodic cognitions in depression (Kuiper et al., 1985; Kuiper et al., 1988), the role of social comparison processes (Swallow & Kuiper, 1988), role loss and its relation to cognitive factors (Dance & Kuiper, 1987), and physiological factors and their relation to cognitive appraisals of stressful events (Kuiper, Olinger & Martin, 1988). Overall, we suggest that these factors ultimately relate to the individual's perception that a positive sense of self-worth has been lost and cannot easily be regained. Instrumental in these perceptions is the endorsement of dysfunctional attitudes specifying irrational contingencies for positive self-evaluation. The aberrant nature of these contingencies makes them extremely difficult to satisfy, leading to greater frequency of depressive affect. As suggested earlier, our approach is similar to other more recently presented models of depression emphasizing the central role of self-concept and self evaluation (Hyland, 1987; Janoff-Bulman & Hecker, 1988; Pyszczynski & Greenberg, 1987; Rehm, 1988). To summarize then, our approach is similar to the first two examples in that it has evolved from a primary focus on cognitions (i.e., describing the negative self-schema in depression) to an approach which attempts to understand and account for diverse factors relating to the etiology, maintenance, and remission of depressive symptoms.

## AIMS OF SCIENCE AND COGNITIVE APPROACHES TO DEPRESSION

In this section of the chapter we discuss cognitive approaches to depression in terms of the descriptive, explanatory, and predictive aims of science. Several of the issues discussed here follow from concerns outlined earlier. Thus, with respect to descriptive aims, we first consider the fundamental need to clarify which model we are evaluating (given the evolution of these models over time). A second important issue at this level is the need to consider which group of individuals the cognitive approach is attempting to describe. Here, we propose that the notion of a depressive cognition subgroup may be a viable avenue for further investigation. Next, at the explanatory level, we focus on the postulated role of cognitions in contemporary cognitive approaches to depression. Here, we suggest a need to clearly distinguish between those maladaptive cognitions that may play a role in the onset of depression (i.e., vulnerability cognitions), and those which may play a role only after the initial development of depressive affect (i.e., episodic cognitions). Vulnerability cognitions include dysfunctional attitudes that represent the diathesis component in a diathesis-stress approach. In contrast, episodic cognitions refer to maladaptive cognitions only evident after the onset of depressive affect. These include an extremely critical self-focus (as described previously), and the resulting emergence of a negative self-concept. At this level, we also consider the breadth of explanation apparent in cognitive approaches by outlining their application to other domains of interest. The Type A literature, for example, documents a well-established link between depression and Type A. In turn, we suggest that cognitive models originally developed in the depression domain may prove useful in furthering our understanding in these other domains. Finally, at the prediction level we comment on recent diathesis-stress cognitive approaches, and indicate possible refinements to these approaches which may increase our predictive capabilities.

## Descriptive Aims

### Clarifying Which Model is Being Evaluated

Over the years, a number of depression investigators have indicated that there is a strong need for greater clarity in defining theoretical constructs in cognitive models (Alloy et al., 1988; Coyne & Gotlib, 1986; Derry & Kuiper, 1981; Hammen, 1988; Segal, 1988). Such clarification is extremely important, with one prerequisite being the careful specification of which cognitive model is being considered and evaluated (Evans & Hollon, 1988).

One means of illustrating this concern is via reference to Beck's model of depression, which, as outlined earlier, has undergone considerable revision over the years. Some depression investigators have clearly acknowledged these changes (Alloy et al., 1988; Hammen, 1988; Kuiper & Olinger, 1986; Segal & Shaw, 1986a), whereas others seem to continue to focus on the old version of this model, along with its primary emphasis on dysfunctional cognitions as the cause of depression (Barnett & Gotlib, 1988; Cole & Kaslow, 1988; Segal, 1988).

Unfortunately, the perpetuation of this old model has sometimes resulted in confusion when trying to assess the possible role of cognitions in depression. One illustration can be drawn from the recent Barnett and Gotlib (1988) review paper. In this respect, Beck and Epstein (1982) provide a clear distinction between dysfunctional cognitions that may be involved in etiological aspects of depression (i.e., vulnerability cognitions relating to a sense of hopelessness, "Things just won't work out the way I want them"), and maladaptive cognitions which may be state dependent (i.e., automatic negative thoughts that only occur during a depressive episode, "I am a social failure"). It appears however, that this critical distinction has been blurred throughout much of Barnett and Gotlib's evaluation of the cognitive depression literature. One specific example is their consideration of the research reported by Rholes et al. (1985). Although not indicated in the review, Rholes et al. (1985) explicitly designed their two studies to test Beck and Epstein's (1982) distinction between vulnerability and state dependent cognitions in depression and anxiety. Thus, in Rholes et al., vulnerability cognitions refer to thoughts of hopelessness (e.g., "My future seems dark to me"), whereas state dependent cognitions refer to automatic negative thoughts, (e.g., "I can't do anything right," "No one will ever like me"). A further look at Rholes et al. indicates that the findings from both of their studies offer support for the hypothesized distinctions. Study 1, for example, found several predicted relationships between various automatic thoughts and specific negative emotional states. Threat cognitions (e.g., "Something awful is going to happen") were only evident for anxiety, whereas loss-related cognitions (e.g., "I'm worse off than they are") were evident for both emotions. Study 2 was a prospective design, and found, as predicted, that only hopelessness cognitions (e.g., "I might as well give up because I can't make things better for myself") predicted future depression (whereas loss cognitions, being state dependent, were hypothesized not to predict future depression). Thus, rather than being interpreted as only very limited support for a cognitive approach to depression (as appears to have been done by Barnett & Gotlib, 1988), a more appropriate interpretation seems to be that Beck and Epstein's cognitive formulations were generally supported by the findings from both studies. In essence, it appears that this research, explicitly conducted to evaluate a more recent and refined version of Beck's model, was assessed against the simple cognitive primacy assumptions of the original model (i.e., all maladaptive cognitions must play a causal role, therefore they should all be evident in remitted depressives and/or all be able to predict future depressive episodes). The perpetuation of this confusion is all the more perplexing as Barnett and Gotlib (1988) acknowledge the Beck and Epstein (1982) refinements in their article, and then go on to suggest that a concomitant role for some maladaptive cognitions may be both theoretically and empirically warranted.

In summary, this illustration suggests that cognitive depression investigators might achieve greater clarity in their theoretical-empirical approaches by very carefully delineating which specific cognitive model is being evaluated. The onus is on both the investigator and reviewer to clearly specify which model is being examined. Since the evolution of theoretical models is a normal, and indeed, healthy aspect of science, a reversion back to older models might only impede progress in this domain.

## Describing a Cognitive Depression Subgroup

As outlined earlier, one of the responses to critiques of cognitive approaches to depression was to carefully consider the possibility of a negative cognition subtype of depression. Given the demonstrated heterogeneity of the depressive disorders, several investigators have advanced the notion that vulnerability and/or episodic dysfunctional cognitions may be particularly relevant for certain theoretically identifiable subgroups (Abramson et al., 1988; Alloy et al., 1988; Beck, 1983; Kuiper, Olinger, MacDonald & Shaw, 1985; Miller & Norman, 1986; Norman, 1988; Teasdale, 1988). We reinforce this proposal by first providing an overview of some of the existing empirical evidence for a cognitive subtype of depression. Following this, we briefly consider the implications for evaluating research in this domain.

Several studies provide preliminary empirical support for the cognitive subtype proposal by indicating that only certain depressed individuals display negative cognitions. In our work, for example, we have found that only currently depressed individuals who also endorse a large number of dysfunctional attitudes (e.g., "If I fail partly, it is as bad as being a complete failure") display evidence of a negative content self-schema (Kuiper et al., 1985). In contrast, currently depressed individuals with few dysfunctional attitudes show a more positive view of self, being more closely aligned with the self-concept displayed by nondepressed controls. In a similar fashion, Teasdale and Dent (1987) employed a depressive mood induction procedure with two groups of subjects, recovered and never depressed. Recovered depressives had met Research Diagnostic Criteria for unipolar depression at some point in their lives, whereas the never depressed group had not. Engaging in a self-referent recall task once a depressed mood had been induced, it was found that the recovered depressives displayed stronger evidence of a negative self-schema.

Again, this finding converges on the subtype notion by indicating that a negative view of self may only be apparent in certain depressives.

Additional evidence for a negative cognition subtype comes from two studies conducted by Miller and Norman. The first study examined the persistence of dysfunctional cognitions across a nine-month time period in remitted depressives (Miller & Norman, 1986). For the subgroup of remitted depressives scoring low on a measure of cognitive distortion at Time 1 (when depressed), the persistence of negative cognitions during remission was minimal (14%). In contrast, the subgroup also scoring high on distortion when depressed showed much greater evidence of continuing distortion when remitted (54%). In a second study, Norman, Miller, and Dow (1988) divided a group of clinically depressed patients into high and low cognitive subgroups (on the basis of dysfunctional attitudes and cognitive biases). Compared to the low dysfunction subgroup, the high cognitive dysfunction subgroup was younger at both age of admission and depression onset, and with a greater number of previous episodes. The high dysfunction group also reported significantly poorer social skills functioning, and displayed a significantly higher frequency of both negative automatic thoughts (a postulated concomitant cognition) and hopelessness (a postulated vulnerability cognition). These distinctions led Norman et al. (1988) to conclude that the high dysfunction subgroup may have a unique set of problem areas and also a distinct course of illness. Furthermore, their review of the treatment literature indicates that high versus low dysfunction groups have a differential response to treatment.

In a further study examining depression and aberrant social comparison processes (Swallow & Kuiper, in press), we separated mildly depressed individuals into high and low dysfunction subgroups (on the basis of extreme dysfunctional attitudes). The high dysfunction subgroup reported a greater overall interest in social comparison, with this difference remaining quite evident for inappropriate comparisons with advantaged others. These comparisons with advantaged others may often be inappropriate as they inevitably place the self in an unfavorable light. From this pattern, we suggested that only high cognitive dysfunction depressives make inappropriate social comparisons, thus maintaining their negative view of self when depressed.

In sum, the preceding research is consistent with the proposal that only certain depressed individuals may display the dysfunctional cognitions associated with cognitive models of depression. Of central importance now is the further development of theory-based criteria generated from cognitive models of depression to identify these individuals prior to a depressive episode. The existing research also provides some rough estimates for the size of this subgroup. In their own work, Norman et al. (1988) report that approximately one-third of depressed patients were in the high cognitive subgroup. They also cite a number of studies that indicate that approximately 40–55% of depressives, when symptomatic, have elevated scores on measures of dysfunctional cognitions. In our research, using fairly stringent criteria to define high cognitive dysfunction (i.e., Dysfunctional Attitude Scale scores of 148 or more), we have found similar figures, with 35% of current depressives indicating high dysfunction (Swallow & Kuiper, in press). If we employ less stringent criteria (such as median splits of 115 to 125 on the Dysfunctional Attitude Scale, for example), the percentage of cognitive dysfunction in mildly depressed groups (BDI scores of 10 or above) increases considerably, being in the 70 to 80% range (Kuiper & McCabe, 1985; Kuiper, et al., 1985; MacDonald, Kuiper & Olinger, 1985). In addition, this research also suggests that approximately 36 to 48% of currently nondepressed samples (BDI scores of 0–9) obtain Dysfunctional Attitude Scale scores above the median, making them a sizable subgroup of nondepressed individuals at cognitive risk for depression. In summary, then, even if conservative grouping procedures are employed, this research would suggest that the cognitive dysfunction subgroup of depression is a substantial one and certainly worthy of further investigation.

Given this initial empirical support, the assumption of a cognitive depression subgroup also has implications for conducting and evaluating research in this domain. A major assumption made in many critiques of cognitive approaches is that aberrant cognitions should be evident in recovered depressives. Research findings inconsistent with this proposal are then interpreted as evidence against a cognitive approach (e.g., Barnett & Gotlib, 1988). Bolstered by the type of empirical evidence outlined above, however, the cognitive subgroup notion would suggest a great deal of caution in evaluating these findings in this manner. In particular, only a certain percentage of the originally depressed group would be expected to show dysfunction during remission. Thus, an overall analysis which does not distinguish subgroups may fail to show continued cognitive dysfunction, because of the masking effects of the low dysfunction group (and not because the approach lacks theoretical validity). This concern has been well-articulated by several depression researchers (Abramson et al., 1988; Alloy et al., 1988), with Norman et al., (1988) concluding that we can no longer assume that cognitive models of depression will be applicable to all depressed individuals.

## Explanatory Aims

### *The Precise Role of Cognitions in Depression*

In attempting to explain the phenomena of depression, contemporary cognitive models have increasingly delineated the role of cognitions. As part of this process, the simple cognitive primacy notion linked to early cognitive depression models has been displaced by more complex diathesis-stress models. In addition, these more refined models have increasingly recognized that dysfunctional cognitions may enter in at various stages in a depressive episode (i.e., etiology, maintenance, enhancement functions). One illustration, as outlined earlier, is Beck and Epstein's (1982) distinction between vulnerability and state dependent maladaptive cognitions (e.g., dysfunctional attitudes versus negative automatic thoughts). Also as described earlier, the failure to note this distinction may sometimes blur evaluations of cognitive depression research.

A further attempt to delineate more precisely the explanatory role of depressive cognitions is evident in the theoretical distinction between vulnerability and episodic cognitions (Kuiper et al., 1985; Kuiper et al., 1988). In this approach, vulnerability cognitions includes irrational beliefs and dysfunctional attitudes relating to self-evaluative standards and contingencies. Specific examples of these beliefs and attitudes have been presented throughout this chapter (e.g., "I cannot be happy unless most people I know admire me"). Episodic cognitions, in contrast, include an increase in negative self-focus (including ruminations of personal inadequacies and shortcomings) and the resulting emergence of a negative content self-schema. In this self-schema, the depressed individual would increasingly endorse such negative personal adjectives as "failure," "helpless," "inferior," "loser," "unlucky," and "unwanted." Thus, when applied to our self-worth model of depression, a negative content self-schema is viewed primarily as a concomitant or episodic aspect of depression, and not as a vulnerability factor. In this model, we suggest that negative content only becomes predominant in the self-concept as the vulnerable individual perceives that contingencies for self-worth are not being met. As long as these contingencies are being met, the vulnerable individual retains a positive self-concept (albeit fragile or poorly consolidated). Vulnerability cognitions play a role in our model by specifying the exact contingencies for self-worth. Since these contingencies are based on extreme dysfunctional standards for self-evaluation ("I am a failure unless everyone approves of me"), the vulnerable individual often encounters life circumstances that challenge positive self-evaluation. If these circumstances are extreme and/or persist over a long enough time period, a depressive episode may ensue, along with the emergence of a negative content self-schema. Across a number of studies we have provided empirical evidence for various facets of this model and the proposed distinction between vulnerability and episodic cognitions (Kuiper et al., 1985; Kuiper & Olinger, 1986; Kuiper et al., 1988; Kuiper & Olinger, 1989).

Other recent cognitive approaches to depression have also distinguished more closely between various types of maladaptive cognitions. Teasdale (1988), for example, has proposed a distinction between vulnerability to onset and vulnerability to persistence cognitions. In this approach, he suggests that certain negative cognitions and processes become activated only in the depressed state, with this state increasing the accessibility of negative interpretative categories and constructs (i.e., the differential activation hypothesis). Thus, even though vulnerability to persistence cognitions may not be evident in remitted depressives, they may still play an extremely important role in continuing and/or escalating a depressive episode once negative affect has been established. As one example, Teasdale proposes that extremely negative self-constructs (e.g., worthless, pathetic, no good) may contribute to the downward spiral of depression, whereas mildly negative self-constructs (e.g., thoughtless, inconsiderate, rude) may not.

In light of his proposed distinction, Teasdale (1988) suggests that a great deal of caution should be exercised in interpreting various cognitive findings in depression. In particular, findings which do not show the presence of maladaptive cognitions in remitted depressives should not be taken as general evidence against a cognitive approach. Instead, the possibility still remains that these cognitions may play a further causal role as vulnerability to persistence cognitions, but only once depressive affect is evident. Although this possibility has been acknowledged by some reviewers (Barnett & Gotlib, 1988), it seems thus far to have carried little weight in interpretations of the cognitive literature.

Some confusion relating to the proposed distinction between various types of maladaptive cognitions is also evident in Segal's (1988) recent review of the schema concept in depression. In presenting only the older version of Beck's model (1967; 1976), Segal appears to assume that a negative self-schema should be considered a vulnerability cognition for depression (see also Barnett & Gotlib, 1988, page 98 for a similar assumption). In addition, even though Segal cites several articles which have described the theoretical distinction between vulnerability and episodic cognitions (e.g., Kuiper et al., 1985; Kuiper et al., 1988), he does not bring this distinction to bear on his review of the self-schema depression research. Thus, his negative conclusion with respect to applying the self-schema construct to depression appears to be based on the old cognitive primacy assumption. In fact, in reviewing this literature, Segal arrives at the conclusion that a negative self-schema is more likely to be a concomitant feature of depression. This episodic conclusion also appears to be endorsed by several other depression investigators reviewing the self-schema literature (Barnett & Gotlib, 1988; Hammen, 1988; Kuiper & Olinger, 1986; Johnson & Magaro, 1987; Teasdale, 1988). We regard this conclusion as problematic only if evaluated against the cognitive primacy assumption of the older cognitive models of depression (i.e., that all dysfunctional cognitions must cause depression and therefore be evident in remission). More recent cognitive approaches, on the other hand, would view this conclusion as being entirely consistent with their general theoretical position that not all maladaptive cognitions must play an etiological role prior to the onset of depressive affect. Furthermore, the specific conclusion that negative self-schema content appears to be episodic in nature is particularly supportive of the theoretically generated predictions of our self-worth model.

## Breadth of Explanation and Cognitive Approaches

A further means of assessing the utility of cognitive approaches to depression is to consider their application to other domains that also involve depressive symptomatology. These might include such diverse domains as alcoholism, bulimia, and Type A personality. To the extent these applications increase our understanding of the psychological factors involved in these domains, they would seem to further enhance the utility of cognitive approaches.

In this section we focus on the relationship between Type A and depression, and suggest that such applications may indeed prove worthwhile. We have recently reviewed the Type A literature (Kuiper & Martin, 1989), and propose that, although Type A individuals may sometimes be more successful in academic and vocational pursuits than their Type B counterparts, this success is often attained at the cost of greater physical illness, increased levels of depression, anxiety, and hostility, and lower levels of life satisfaction and self-esteem. In addition, our review highlights the growing evidence that irrational cognitions may play a role in Type A behavior. These cognitions relate to such factors as irrational beliefs, anxious overconcern about the future, perfectionism, high self-expectations, unrealistic goal setting, and irrational standards for self-evaluation.

Theoretically, we have been developing a model to account for these cognitive, affective, and behavioral components of Type A (Martin, Kuiper & Westra, in press; Kuiper & Martin, 1989). This model is based closely on an extension of our self-worth model of depression, and suggests that many Type A behaviors can be viewed as a part of a maladaptive personality style relating to dysfunctional self-evaluative standards. In our model it is proposed that Type A individuals attempt to maintain a positive view of self by fulfilling their unrealistic performance demands through hard-driven, work-directed behaviors. Thus, in our theoretical approach, the compulsive and over-zealous work habits of the Type A individual are viewed as part of a maladaptive coping style employed to minimize negative self-evaluations. As long as they are able to meet their performance standards, Type A's will maintain a positive view of self and will experience positive affect. However, these self-worth contingencies are unrealistic and therefore very difficult to meet. Thus, the model predicts that Type A individuals will frequently perceive their actual performance as failing to meet standards, and as a result, will experience a threat to self-esteem. When this happens, it is predicted that they will engage in aggressive and hostile behavior in an attempt to overcome obstacles perceived to be thwarting attempts to achieve self-imposed goals. If such coping attempts are unsuccessful, the perceived failure to meet personal performance standards will result in diminution of self-esteem and increased depressive affect. Given the perfectionistic quality of Type A self-appraisal standards, it is likely that they will only rarely be met, and therefore Type A individuals are expected to frequently experience feelings of low self-esteem and depression.

In testing aspects of this theoretical model, our research to date has been aimed at examining various cognitive and affective variables which are hypothesized to relate to Type A personality (Martin et al., in press; Kuiper & Martin, 1989). Of initial interest are variables focusing on levels of self-esteem, negative affect, and the endorsement of dysfunctional attitudes tying perceptions of self-worth to unrealistic performance demands. Consistent with our theoretical proposals, it has been found that Type A individuals endorse a significantly greater number of dysfunctional attitudes, exhibit higher levels of perceived stress and depression, and lower levels of self-esteem. We have found further evidence for unrealistically high performance standards in the context of an academic examination, with Type A individuals indicating that they would require a higher mark in order to be satisfied with their performance, despite the fact that there was no difference in the mark they actually expected to attain, nor in their actual performance on the exam. In coping with stress, we have also found that Type A individuals, similar to depressives, generally make more use of maladaptive emotion-focused coping strategies than Type Bs (Martin et al., in press). Finally, preliminary research has indicated that the view of self displayed by Type A individuals is more depressive in content, less stable across time, and with greater real/ideal discrepancies than the view of self displayed by Type Bs (Kuiper & Martin, 1989).

Overall, we would suggest that the results of these studies support the utility of applying a cognitive model, originally developed in the depression domain, to help explain certain facets of Type A behavior. Interestingly, other cognitive depression models may also prove quite applicable. As one example, Janoff-Bulman and Hecker (1988) have recently described a set of dysfunctional beliefs which they postulate as cognitive vulnerability factors for depression. A further examination of these beliefs indicates that they converge closely on the maladaptive cognitions often postulated to relate to Type A (e.g., assumptions about the malevolence or benevolence of the world and the distribution of good and bad outcomes). Thus, the possible application of this cognitive depression approach to Type A would also appear warranted and useful.

## Predictive Aims

### *Diathesis-Stress Models and Beyond*

From our discussion thus far it is apparent that cognitive approaches to depression are becoming more refined and complex, taking into account a variety of factors that may relate to depression etiology, maintenance, and remission. Thus, the old notion that dysfunctional cognitions are the primary and only cause of depression has generally been replaced by diathesis-stress models that stress the interaction between individual vulnerability factors, various life circumstances, and other contributing variables. Several of these models have already been described throughout this chapter, with Beck's diathesis-stress model being one example. In this model, cognitive vulnerabilities relate to the endorsement of dysfunctional attitudes. Life events or circumstances which impinge on these attitudes in a negative fashion may then result in depression (Beck et al., 1979). With respect to this model, several studies have obtained the predicted increased levels of depression associated with the convergence of negative life events and dysfunctional attitudes (see Kuiper & Olinger, 1989 for a review). Several other studies, however, have not (see Barnett & Gotlib, 1988).

In turn, these negative findings have prompted greater specificity in diathesis-stress models. In our self-worth model, for example, we have specifically identified the type of negative events that might impinge on cognitive vulnerability for depression. These theoretically identified events are unresolved stressors that relate directly to the extreme self-evaluative contingencies specified in dysfunctional attitudes. In our research, we have found that this identification procedure enhances the prediction of depression, even across a three-month time span (see Kuiper & Olinger, 1989 for a detailed presentation).

Other approaches have also become more specific in terms of identifying individual elements of their diathesis-stress models. Beck (1983), for example, distinguishes between two forms of cognitive vulnerability, sociotrophic and autonomous achievement. Sociotrophic vulnerability refers to an extreme dependence on social approval, whereas autonomous achievement vulnerability relates to high goal attainment expectations. This distinction has received some empirical support in a recent study by Robins and Block (1988). Consistent with predictions, depression was related to the frequency of recent negative social events for sociotrophic individuals. Other findings in this study, however, did not support the specific matching hypothesis, with autonomous achievement not being related to depression. More generally, this pattern is similar to other findings which support only the sociotrophic or dependency aspect of this model (Hammen, Marks, Mayol & DeMayo, 1985; Zuroff & Mongrain, 1987).

In summary, although the general diathesis-stress models have received empirical support, this is not always the case. Similarly, the more specific diathesis-stress formulations have received mixed empirical support, with a precise matching not always being evident in tests of Beck's model. In examining this pattern, should we consider it an indictment against cognitive approaches? Probably not, as several further refinements may still increase the predictive utility of cognitive-based approaches. In moving beyond current diathesis-stress models, for example, Teasdale (1988) has proposed a differential activation hypothesis that suggests that the precise nature of the match is less important than the identification of specific factors which engage and maintain negative cognitions. In fact, this dynamic process orientation is also evident in other theoretical cognitive approaches to depression (Abramson et al., 1988; Hyland, 1987; Kuiper et al., 1988; Lewinsohn et al., 1985; Oatley & Bolton, 1985; Pyszczynski & Greenberg, 1987; Rehm, 1988), but does not appear to be as well represented in their research designs. Most of the current tests of diathesis-stress formulations, for example, are relatively static in the sense they do not really measure critical variables in an ongoing fashion. We would suggest that such ongoing measurement is of increasing importance and may help to distinguish more clearly why only certain diathesis-stress combinations may produce depression. Although beyond the scope of this chapter, it is interesting to note that general catastrophe theories have been applied to psychological stress research to account for sudden shifts in outcome variables, as a function of progressive changes on predictor variables (Neufeld, 1989). Catastrophe theories are based on underlying mathematical models that attempt to predict precisely when abrupt or discontinuous changes will become evident in the variables being studied. Furthermore, these models attempt to predict the exact magnitude of these changes. Thus, to the extent sudden shifts may also be evident in various aspects of depression (e.g., an abrupt downward spiral of depression, or remission), it may prove illuminating for future work to consider the predictive utility of catastrophe models.

## SUMMARY AND CONCLUDING COMMENTS

We began this chapter by posing the question, "Are cognitive approaches to depression useful?" Our answer to this question is yes, but it is not an unqualified yes. Rather, we have specified in detail several concerns relating to this approach and provided several possible avenues of further exploration. As one illustration, we have suggested that research and theorizing in this domain carefully consider the notion that cognitive dysfunction may be especially problematic for certain subgroups of depressed individuals. In addition, we have proposed that cognitive approaches must become increasingly sophisticated in terms of delineating the precise role of cognitions in various facets of depression. Whereas older models advocated the causal primacy of maladaptive cognitions, contemporary approaches offer a more illuminating perspective by integrating aberrant cognitions at various stages of depression with other relevant factors. Finally, we have suggested that cognitive approaches may have considerable utility in terms of furthering our understanding of potentially related phenomena, such as the maladaptive components of Type A personality.

A major theme of this chapter is that cognitive approaches can be quite useful in furthering our understanding of depression, but only if these approaches move away from the cognitive primacy assumption of a generation ago and towards a more balanced and integrated perspective on depression. We have overviewed this type of evolution in several contemporary cognitive models of depression, and we suggest that it represents the normal, and indeed, healthy progression of scientific theory building. Unfortunately, the failure to acknowledge the evolution of these models has sometimes produced a situation in which contemporary critiques are often directed at models which no longer exist. This difficulty is particularly evident in reviews of Beck's theoretical position and perhaps reflects the effects of undue perseveration on the radical paradigm shift evident in Beck's original thinking twenty years ago (from the prevailing view of depression as an affective disorder to a strong cognitive formulation).

Finally, it may be informative to close on a lighter note. On occasion we have heard critics of cognitive approaches to depression argue the superiority of a biological perspective. In general, this argument states that cognitive research in this domain is futile, as the only true advances will come from biologically based research. This argument is often presented in the context of the presumed eminence and superiority of the biological sciences. Some may be swayed by the ready appeal of this argument and thus begin to despair for cognitive approaches to depression. For those individuals, we supply a quote from a recent review of biological aspects of depression (Thase, Frank & Kupfer, 1985, pp. 877):

> A review of research conducted over the past two decades leads to few firm conclusions regarding the role of biological factors in the etiopathogenesis of major depression.

Just remember, then, the grass isn't really greener on the other side of the hill.

**Authors' Note**: This research was supported by a Social Sciences and Humanities Research Council Grant (410–88–0188) to the first and third authors. Address correspondence to N. Kuiper, Department of Psychology, University of Western Ontario, London, Ontario, Canada N6A 5C2.

# References

Abramson, L.Y., Alloy, L.B. & Metalsky, G.I. (1988). The cognitive diathesis-stress theories of depression: Toward an adequate evaluation of the theories' validities. In L.B. Alloy (Ed.). *Cognitive processes in depression* (pp. 3–30). New York: The Guilford Press.

Alloy, L.B. (Ed.). (1988). *Cognitive processes in depression*. New York: The Guilford Press.

Alloy, L.B., Hartlage, S. & Abramson, L.Y. (1988). Testing the cognitive-diathesis-stress theories of depression: Issues of research design, conceptualization, and assessment. In L.B. Alloy (Ed.). *Cognitive processes in depression* (pp. 31–73). New York: The Guilford Press.

Barnett, P. & Gotlib, I.H. (1988). Psychosocial functioning and depression: Distinguishing among antecedents, concomitants, and consequences. *Psychological Bulletin*, 104, 97–126.

Beck, A.T. (1967). *Depression: Clinical, experimental, and theoretical aspects*. New York: Harper & Row.

Beck, A.T. (1976). *Cognitive therapy and the emotional disorders.* New York: International Universities Press.

Beck, A.T. (1983). *Cognitive therapy of depression: New perspectives.* In P.J. Clayton & J.E. Barrett (Eds.), *Treatment of depression: Old controversies and new approaches* (pp. 265–290). New York: Raven Press.

Beck, A.T. (1984). Cognition and therapy. *Archives of General Psychiatry,* 411, 1112–1114.

Beck, A.T. & Epstein, N. (1982). *Cognitions, attitudes and personality dimensions in depression.* Paper presented at the annual meeting of the Society for Psychotherapy Research, Smuggler's Notch, Vermont.

Beck, A.T., Rush, A.J., Shaw, B.F. & Emery, G. (1979). *Cognitive therapy of depression.* New York: Guilford Press.

Beckham, E.E. & Leber, W.R. (Eds.). (1985). *Handbook of depression: Treatment, assessment, and research.* Homewood, Illinois, The Dorsey Press.

Billings, A.G. & Moos, R.H. (1985). Psychosocial stressors, coping, and depression. In E.E. Beckham & W.R. Leber (Eds.). *Handbook of depression: Treatment, assessment, and research* (pp. 940–976). Homewood, Illinois, The Dorsey Press.

Brewin, C.R. (1985). Depression and causal attributions: What is their relation? *Psychological Bulletin,* 98, 297–309.

Coyne, J.C. & Gotlib, I.H. (1983). The role of cognition in depression: A critical appraisal. *Psychological Bulletin,* 94, 472–505.

Coyne, J.C. & Gotlib, I.H. (1986). Studying the role of cognition in depression: Well-trodden paths and cul-de-sacs. *Cognitive Therapy & Research,* 10, 695–705.

Cole, P.M. & Kaslow, N.J. (1988). Interactional and cognitive strategies for affect regulation: Developmental perspectives on childhood depression. In L.B. Alloy (Ed.). *Cognitive processes in depression* (pp. 310–343). New York: The Guilford Press.

Dance, K.A. & Kuiper, N.A. (1987). Self-schemata, social roles, and a self-worth contingency model of depression. *Motivation and Emotion,* 11, 251–268.

Derry, P.A. & Kuiper, N.A. (1981). Schematic processing and self-reference in clinical depression. *Journal of Abnormal Psychology,* 90, 286–297.

Dobson, K.S. & Shaw, B.F. (1986). Cognitive assessment with major depressive disorders. *Cognitive Therapy and Research,* 10, 13–29.

Ellis, Albert (1962). *Reason and emotion in psychotherapy.* New York: Stuart.

Evans, M.D. & Hollon, S.D. (1988). Patterns of personal and causal inference: Implications for the cognitive therapy of depression. In L.B. Alloy (Ed.). *Cognitive processes in depression* (pp.344–373). New York: The Guilford Press.

Hammen, C. (1985). Predicting depression: A cognitive-behavioral perspective. In P.C. Kendall (Ed.). *Advances in cognitive-behavioral research and therapy* (Vol. 4, pp. 30–71). New York: Academic Press.

Hammen, C. (1988). Depression and cognitions about personal stressful life events. In L.B. Alloy (Ed.). *Cognitive processes in depression* (pp. 77–108). New York: The Guilford Press.

Hammen, C. & Krantz, S. (1985). Measures of psychological processes in depression. In E.E. Beckham & W.R. Leber (Eds.). *Handbook of depression: Treatment, assessment, and research* (pp. 408–444). Homewood, Illinois, The Dorsey Press.

Hammen, C., Marks, T., Mayol, A. & deMayo, R. (1985). Depressive self-schemas, life stress, and vulnerability to depression. *Journal of Abnormal Psychology,* 94, 308–319.

Hammen, C. & Zupan, B. (1984). Self-schemas, depression, and the processing of personal information in children. *Journal of Experimental Child Psychology,* 37, 598–608.

Healy, D. & Williams, J.M.G. (1988) Dysrhythmia, dysphoria, and depression: The interaction of learned helplessness and circadian dsyrhythmia in the pathogenesis of depression. *Psychological Bulletin,* 103, 163–178.

Hollon, S.D. & Beck, A.T. (1986). Cognitive and cognitive-behavior therapies. In S.L. Garfield & A.E. Bergin (Eds.). *Handbook of psychotherapy and behavior change: An empirical analysis* (3rd Ed., pp 443–482). New York: Wiley.

Hollon, S.D., DeRubeis, R.J. & Evans, M.D. (1987). Causal mediation of change in treatment for depression: Discriminating between nonspecificity and noncausality. *Psychological Bulletin,* 102, 139–149.

Hyland, M.E. (1987). Control theory interpretation of psychological mechanisms of depression: Comparisons and integrations of several theories. *Psychological Bulletin,* 102, 109–121.

Ingram, R.E. (Ed.). (1986). *Information processing approaches to clinical psychology.* New York: Academic Press.

Ingram, R.E. & Hollon, S.D. (1986). Cognitive therapy of depression from an information processing perspective. In R.E. Ingram (Ed.). *Information processing approaches to clinical psychology* (pp. 261–284). Academic Press, New York.

Ingram, R.E. & Reed, M.R. (1986). Information encoding and retrieval processes in depression: Findings, issues, and future directions. In R.E. Ingram (Ed.). *Information processing approaches to clinical psychology* (pp. 141–149). New York: Academic Press.

Janoff-Bulman, R. & Hecker, B. (1988). Depression, vulnerability, and world assumptions. In L.B. Alloy (Ed.). *Cognitive processes in depression* (pp. 177–192). New York: The Guilford Press.

Johnson, M.H. & Magaro, M.H. (1987). Effects of mood and severity on memory processes in depression and mania, *Psychological Bulletin,* 101, 28–40.

Kuiper, N.A. & Martin, R.A. (1989). Type A behavior: A social cognition motivational perspective. In G.H. Bower (Ed.). *The psychology of learning and motivation: Advances in research and theory* (Vol. 24, pp. 311–341). New York: Academic Press.

Kuiper, N.A., MacDonald, M.R. & Derry, P.A. (1983). Parameters of a depressive self-schema. In J.Suls & A.G. Greenwald (Eds.) *Psychological perspectives on the self* (Vol. 2, pp 191–217). Hillsdale, N.J.: Erlbaum.

Kuiper, N.A. & McCabe, S.B. (1985). The appropriateness of social topics: Effects of depression and cognitive vulnerability on self and other judgments. *Cognitive Therapy and Research,* 4, 371–379.

Kuiper, N.A. & Olinger, L.J. (1986). Dysfunctional attitudes and a self-worth contingency model of depression. In P.C. Kendall (Ed.). *Advances in cognitive-behavioral research and therapy* (Vol. 5, pp. 115–142). New York: Academic Press.

Kuiper, N.A. & Olinger, L.J. (1989). Stress and cognitive vulnerability for depression: A self-worth contingency model. In R.W.J. Neufeld (Ed.). *Advances in the investigation of psychological stress* (pp. 367–391). New York: Wiley.

Kuiper, N.A., Olinger, L.J. & MacDonald, M.R. (1988). Vulnerability and episodic cognitions in a self-worth contingency model of depression. In L.B. Alloy (Ed.). *Cognitive processes in depression* (pp. 289–309). New York: The Guilford Press.

Kuiper, N.A., Olinger, L.J., MacDonald, M.R. & Shaw, B.F. (1985). Self-schema processing of depressed and nondepressed content: The effects of vulnerability to depression. *Social Cognition,* 3, 77–93.

Kuiper, N.A., Olinger, L.J. & Martin, R.A. (1988). Dysfunctional attitudes, stress, and negative emotions. *Cognitive Therapy* and Research, 12, 533–547.

Kuiper, N.A., Olinger, L.J. & Swallow, S.R. (1987). Dysfunctional attitudes, mild depression, views of self, self-consciousness, and social perceptions. *Motivation and Emotion,* 11, 379–401.

Lewinsohn, P.M., Hoberman, H., Teri, L. & Hautzinger, M. (1985). An integrative theory of depression. In S. Reiss & R. Bootzin (Eds.). *Theoretical issues in behavior therapy* (pp. 351–359). New York: Academic Press.

MacDonald, M.R., Kuiper, N.A. & Olinger, L.J. (1985). Vulnerability to depression, mild depression, and degree of self-schema consolidation. *Motivation and Emotion, 9,* 369–379.

Martin, R.A., Kuiper, N.A. & Westra, H.A. (in press). Cognitive and affective components of the Type A behavior pattern: Preliminary evidence for a self-worth contingency model. *Personality and Individual Differences.*

Masters, J.C., Burish, T.G., Hollon, S.D. & Rimm, D.C. (1987). *Behavior Therapy: Techniques and empirical findings* (3rd Edition). New York: Harcourt Brace Jovanovich, Publishers.

Miller, D.T. & Moretti, M.M. (1988). The causal attributions of depressives: Self-serving or self-disserving? In L.B. Alloy (Ed.). *Cognitive processes in depression* (pp. 266–286). New York: The Guilford Press.

Miller, I.W. & Norman, W.H. (1986). Persistence of depressive cognitions within a subgroup of depressed inpatients. *Cognitive Therapy and Research,* 10, 211–225.

Neufeld, R.W.J. (1989). Methodological aspects of laboratory studies of stress. In R.W.J. Neufeld (Ed.). *Advances in the investigation of psychological stress* (pp. 71–132). New York: Wiley.

Norman, W.H., Miller, I.W. & Dow, M.G. (1988). Characteristics of depressed patients with elevated levels of dysfunctional cognitions. *Cognitive Therapy and Research,* 12, 39–52.

Oatley, K. & Bolton, W. (1985). A social-cognitive theory of depression in reaction to life events. *Psychological Review,* 92, 372–388.

Olinger, L.J., Kuiper, N.A. & Shaw, B.F. (1987). Dysfunctional attitudes and stressful life events: An interactive model of depression. *Cognitive Therapy and Research,* 11, 25–40.

Peterson, C. & Seligman, M.E.P. (1984). Causal explanations as a risk factor for depression: Theory & Evidence. *Psychological Review,* 91, 347–374.

Pyszczynski, T. & Greenberg, J. (1987). Self-regulatory perseveration and the depressive self-focusing style: A self-awareness theory of reactive depression. *Psychological Bulletin,* 102, 122–138.

Rehm, L.P. (1988). Self-management and cognitive processes in depression. In L.B. Alloy (Ed.). *Cognitive processes in depression* (pp. 143–176). New York: The Guilford Press.

Rholes, W.S., Riskind, J.H. & Neville, B. (1985). The relationship of cognitions and hopelessness to depression and anxiety. *Social Cognition,* 3, 36–50.

Robins, C.J. (1988). Attributions and depression: Why is the literature so inconsistent? *Journal of Personality and Social Psychology,* 54, 880–889.

Robins, C.J. & Block, P. (1988). Personal vulnerability, life events, and depressive symptoms: A test of a specific interactional model. *Journal of Personality and Social Psychology,* 5, 847–852.

Ruehlman, L.S., West, S.G. & Pasahow, R.J. (1985). Depression and evaluative schemata. *Journal of Personality,* 53, 46–93.

Sacco, W.P. & Beck, A.T. (1985). Cognitive therapy of depression. In E.E. Beckham & W.R. Leber (Eds.) *Handbook of depression: Treatment, Assessment, and Research* (pp. 3–38). Homewood, Illinois: Dorsey Press.

Segal, Z.V. (1988). Appraisal of the self-schema construct in cognitive models of depression. *Psychological Bulletin,* 103, 147–162.

Segal, Z.V. & Shaw, B.F. (1986a). Cognition in depression: A reappraisal of Coyne &

Gotlib's Critique. *Cognitive Therapy & Research,* 10, 671–693.

Segal, Z.V. & Shaw, B.F. (1986b). When Cul-de-Sacs are more mentality than reality: A rejoinder to Coyne & Gotlib. *Cognitive Therapy & Research,* 10, 707–714.

Swallow, S.R. & Kuiper, N.A. (1988). Social comparison and negative self-evaluations: An application to depression. *Clinical Psychology Review,* 8, 55–76.

Swallow, S.R. & Kuiper, N.A. (in press). Mild depression, dysfunctional cognitions, and interest in social comparison information. *Journal of Social and Clinical Psychology.*

Sweeney, P.D., Anderson, K. & Bailey, S. (1986). Attributional style in depression: A meta-analytic review. *Journal of Personality & Social Psychology,* 50, 947–991.

Teasdale, J.D. (1988). Cognitive vulnerability to persistent depression. *Cognition and Emotion,* 2, 247–274.

Teasdale, J.D. & Dent, J. (1987). Cognitive vulnerability to depression: An investigation of two hypotheses. *British Journal of Clinical Psychology,* 26, 113–126.

Thase, M.E., Frank, E. & Kupfer, D.J. (1985). Biological processes in major depression. In E.E. Beckham & W.R. Leber (Eds.). *Handbook of depression: Treatment, assessment, and research* (pp. 816–913). Homewood, Illinois, The Dorsey Press.

Zuroff, D.C. & Mongrain, M. (1987). Dependency and self-criticism: Vulnerability factors for depressive affective states. *Journal of Abnormal Psychology,* 96, 14–22.

# 4

# Search for the "Negative Cognition" Subtype of Depression

Lyn Y. Abramson
*University of Wisconsin—Madison*

Lauren B. Alloy
*Northwestern University*

KEY WORDS: attributional style, cognition, hopelessness,
hopelessness depression, negative cognition depression, negative
cognitive triad, negative cognitive triad depression, schemata,
subtype

Clinicians have long suggested that depression probably is not a single disorder but instead may be a group of disorders, heterogeneous with respect to symptoms, cause, course, therapy, and prevention (e.g., Abramson, Metalsky & Alloy, in press; Beck, 1967; Craighead, 1980; Depue & Monroe, 1978; Gillespie, 1929; Kendell, 1968; Kraepelin, 1913). Historically, a wide variety of nosological distinctions have been proposed to subdivide the depressive disorders, such as bipolar-unipolar, endogenous-neurotic, and so on. In the main, these classifications have arisen from insights gleaned in clinical practice or from numerical taxonometric procedures such as cluster analysis (Kendell, 1968; Skinner, 1981).

In this chapter, we present the hopelessness theory of depression (Abramson et al., in press) and Beck's theory (Beck, 1967; 1976)—two cognitive theories of depression. These theories complement clinical and taxonometric approaches and represent a *theory-based* approach to the classification of a subset of depressive disorders that is process-oriented rather than symptom-oriented. In essence, the cognitive theories postulate the existence in nature of an as yet unidentified subtype of depression—*negative cognition depression*—that may lurk among the various disorders currently called depression and perhaps even cut across other disorders (e.g., anxiety, personality disorders). We describe the hypothesized cause, symptoms, course, therapy, and prevention of negative cognition depression. We also discuss its relation to other types of depression as well as other forms of psychopathology. Finally, we discuss how to search for negative cognition depression to see if it exists in nature and conforms to its theoretical description.

At this point, a note on terms is in order. We use the phrase "hopelessness depression" to refer specifically to the cognitive subtype of depression postulated by the hopelessness theory and the phrase "negative cognitive triad depression" to refer specifically to the depressive subtype postulated by Beck's theory. However, we believe that these two hypothesized cognitive subtypes of depression are similar and overlapping and, for the most part, refer to the same group of individuals, although they may not be identical to each other. Thus, we will use the phrase "negative cognition depression" to refer to the cognitive subtype of depression postulated jointly by both cognitive theories.

## Preliminary Concepts

In presenting the hypothesized negative cognition depression subtype, it is useful to distinguish among the concepts of *necessary, sufficient,* and *contributory* causes of symptoms. A necessary cause of a set of symptoms is an etiological factor that must be present or have occurred in order for the symptoms to occur. The symptoms cannot occur if the etiological factor is absent or has not occurred. However, the symptoms need not occur when the necessary cause is present or has occurred (i.e., necessary but not sufficient). A sufficient cause of a set of symptoms is an etiological factor whose presence or occurrence guarantees the occurrence of the symptoms. An additional feature of a sufficient cause is that if the symptoms do not occur, then the etiological factor must not be present or must not have occurred. However, the symptoms may occur in the absence of the sufficient cause (i.e., sufficient but not necessary). A contributory cause of a set of symptoms is an etiological factor that increases the likelihood of occurrence of the symptoms but is neither necessary nor sufficient for their occurrence.

In addition to varying in their formal relation to the occurrence of symptoms (necessary, sufficient, or contributory), causes also vary in their sequential relation to the occurrence of symptoms. In an etiological chain culminating in the occurrence of a set of symptoms, some causes operate toward the end of the chain, proximate to the occurrence of symptoms, whereas other causes operate toward the beginning of the chain, distant from the occurrence of symptoms. The former are *proximal* causes, and the latter are *distal* causes.[1]

## THE COGNITIVE THEORIES OF DEPRESSION

The hopelessness theory, a revision of the reformulation of helplessness and depression (Abramson, Seligman & Teasdale, 1978), explicitly postulates the existence of hopelessness depression, and one interpretation (Abramson, Alloy & Metalsky, 1988a; Alloy, Clements & Kolden, 1985) of Beck's theory suggests the existence of negative cognitive triad depression. As noted earlier, we believe that these two hypothesized cognitive subtypes are similar and overlapping and, for the most part, refer to the same group of individuals. We use the phrase "negative cognition depression" to refer to the cognitive subtype of depression formed by combining hopelessness depression and negative cognitive triad depression. Below we present the hypothesized causes and symptoms of hopelessness depression and negative cognitive triad depression separately and then combine them to present the hypothesized cause and symptoms of negative cognition depression. We also pres-

---

[1] For simplicity of exposition, we have presented the proximal-distal distinction in terms of a dichotomy: Proximal versus distal. Strictly speaking, however, it is more appropriate to think in terms of a proximal-distal continuum.

ent the hypothesized course, remediation, and prevention of negative cognition depression as well as discuss its possible relationship to other categories of depression and psychopathology.

## Cause: Hopelessness Depression

In contrast to symptom-based approaches to the classification of the depressive disorders (see Kendell, 1968), *cause* figures prominently in the definition of hopelessness depression. Few would disagree that, when possible, classification of psychopathologies by etiology in addition to other factors is more desirable than classification by symptoms alone insofar as the former generally has more direct implications for cure and prevention than the latter (McLemore & Benjamin, 1979; Skinner, 1981). Overall, the hopelessness theory specifies a chain of distal and proximal contributory causes hypothesized to culminate in a proximal sufficient cause of the symptoms of hopelessness depression.

### A Proximal Sufficient Cause of the Symptoms of Hopelessness Depression: Hopelessness

According to the hopelessness theory, a proximal sufficient cause of the symptoms of hopelessness depression is an expectation that highly desired outcomes will not occur or that highly aversive outcomes will occur and that there is nothing one can do to change the situation.[1] We view this theory as a *hopelessness* theory because the common language term "hopelessness" captures the core elements of the proximal sufficient cause featured in the theory: Negative expectations about the occurrence of highly valued outcomes (a negative outcome expectancy) and expectations of helplessness about changing the likelihood of occurrence of these outcomes (a helplessness expectancy). Throughout the chapter, we use the term hopelessness to refer to this proximal sufficient cause. Abramson et al. used the phrase "generalized hopelessness" when people exhibit the negative outcome/helplessness expectancy about many areas of life. In contrast, "circumscribed pessimism" occurs when people exhibit the negative outcome/helplessness expectancy about only a limited domain. They suggested that cases of generalized hopelessness should produce severe symptoms of hopelessness depression, whereas circumscribed pessimism is likely to be associated with fewer and/or less severe symptoms. However, cases in which a person exhibits circumscribed pessimism about extremely important outcomes also may be associated with severe symptoms. According to the theory, hopelessness is a proximal sufficient, but not a necessary, cause of depressive symptoms. The theory therefore explicitly recognizes that depression may be a heterogeneous disorder and allows for the possibility that other factors such as genetic vulnerability, neurotransmitter aberrations, loss of interest in

---

[1] Abramson et al. (1978) cautioned that the problem of "current concerns" (Klinger, 1975) existed in their statement of the proximal sufficient cause of depression featured in the reformulated theory of helplessness and depression. People feel depressed about the occurrence of highly desired outcomes that they believe they cannot obtain only when the outcomes are "on their minds," "in the realm of possibility," "troubling them now," and so on. Although Abramson et al. found Klinger's concept heuristic, they felt it was not sufficiently well defined to be incorporated into the reformulation. We emphasize that the problem of current concerns still remains to be solved.

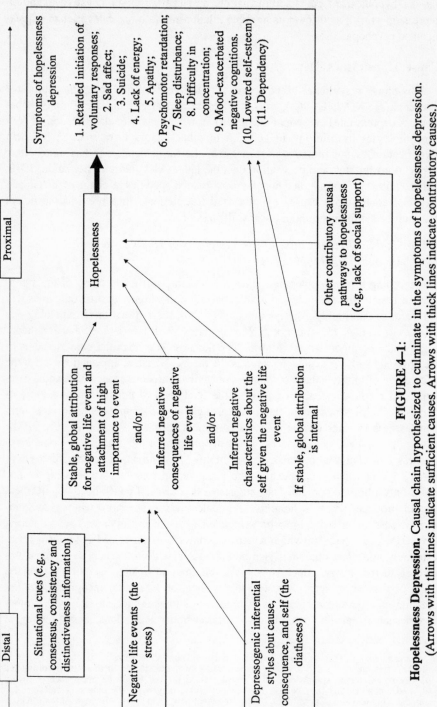

**FIGURE 4–1:**

**Hopelessness Depression.** Causal chain hypothesized to culminate in the symptoms of hopelessness depression. (Arrows with thin lines indicate sufficient causes. Arrows with thick lines indicate contributory causes.)

reinforcers, etc. also may be sufficient to cause depressive symptoms. Thus, the hopelessness theory presents an etiological account of one hypothesized subtype of depression, hopelessness depression, defined in part by its proximal sufficient cause.

## One Hypothesized Causal Pathway to the Symptoms of Hopelessness Depression

How does a person become hopeless and, in turn, develop the symptoms of hopelessness depression? As can be seen in Figure 4–1, the hypothesized causal chain begins with the perceived occurrence of *negative life events (or nonoccurrence of positive life events)*[1].. In the hopelessness theory, negative events serve as "occasion setters" for people to become hopeless. However, the relationship between life events and depression is imperfect: Not all people become depressed when confronted with negative life events (e.g., Brown & Harris, 1978; Lloyd, 1980a,b). According to the theory, there are at least three types of inferences people may make which modulate whether or not they develop hopelessness and, in turn, the symptoms of hopelessness depression in the face of negative life events: 1) Inferences about why the event occurred (i.e., inferred cause or causal attribution); 2) Inferences about consequences that might result from the occurrence of the event (i.e., inferred consequences); and 3) Inferences about the self, given that the event happened to the person (i.e., inferred characteristics about the self).

## Proximal Contributory Causes: Inferred Stable, Global Causes of Particular Negative Life Events and a High Degree of Importance Attached to These Events

The kinds of causal inferences people make for negative events and the degree of importance they attach to these events are important factors contributing to whether or not they develop hopelessness and, in turn, the symptoms of hopelessness depression. In brief, relatively generalized hopelessness and, in turn, the symptoms of hopelessness depression, are more likely to occur when negative life events are attributed to stable (i.e., enduring) and global (i.e., likely to affect many outcomes) causes and are viewed as important,than when they are attributed to unstable, specific causes and are viewed as unimportant. For understanding hopelessness depression, we focus on stable, global, as opposed to stable, specific attributions for negative life events, because only the former would be expected to contribute to relatively generalized hopelessness. The latter would be expected to contribute to relatively circumscribed pessimism. If causal inferences for negative events do modulate the likelihood of becoming hopeless, then it is important to delineate what influences the kinds of causal inferences people make. Over the past twenty years, social psychologists have conducted studies showing that people's causal attributions for events are, in part, a function of the situational information they confront (Kelley, 1967; McArthur, 1972). People tend to attribute an event to the factor or factors with which it covaries. According to this view, people would be predicted to

---

[1] For the sake of brevity, we will use the phrase "negative life events" to refer to both the occurrence of negative life events *and* the nonoccurrence of positive life events

make internal, stable, and global attributions for an event (e.g., failing a math exam) when they are confronted with situational information suggesting that the event is low in consensus (e.g., others do well on the math exam), high in consistency (e.g., typically failing exams in math), and low in distinctiveness (e.g., typically failing exams in other subjects as well as math; Kelley, 1967; Metalsky & Abramson, 1981). Thus, informational cues make some causal inferences for particular life events more plausible than others and some not plausible at all (see also Hammen and Mayol, 1982). Social psychologists have suggested a number of additional factors that also may guide the causal attribution process, including expectations for success and failure, motivation to protect or enhance one's self-esteem, focus of attention, salience of a potential causal factor, and self-presentational concerns, to name a few. Below we discuss a more distal factor that also influences what kind of causal inferences a person makes.

## Proximal Contributory Causes: Inferred Negative Consequences of Particular Negative Life Events

Hammen and her colleagues (e.g., Gong-Guy & Hammen, 1980; Hammen & Cochran, 1981; Hammen & de Mayo, 1982) have argued that the inferred consequences of negative events, independently of causal inferences for these events, may modulate the likelihood that people will become depressed when confronted with a negative life event. For example, a student may attribute his low scores on the Graduate Record Examination (GRE) to distracting noises in the testing room (an unstable, specific attribution) but infer that a consequence of his poor performance on the GRE is that he never will be admitted to a graduate program in mathematics, his preferred career choice. Abramson et al. (in press) suggested that inferred negative consequences moderate the relationship between negative life events and the symptoms of hopelessness depression by affecting the likelihood of becoming hopeless. Following the same logic as for causal attributions, inferred negative consequences should be particularly likely to lead to hopelessness when the negative consequence is viewed as important, not remediable, unlikely to change, and as affecting many areas of life. When the negative consequence is seen as affecting only a very limited sphere of life, relatively circumscribed pessimism rather than generalized hopelessness should result.

## Proximal Contributory Causes: Inferred Negative Characteristics About the Self-Given Negative Life Events

In addition to inferred consequences of negative events, Abramson et al. (in press) suggested that inferred characteristics about the self, given these events, also may modulate the likelihood of formation of hopelessness and, in turn, the symptoms of hopelessness depression. Inferred characteristics about the self refer to the inferences a person draws about his or her own worth, abilities, personality, desirability, etc. from the fact that a particular negative life event occurred. Such a concept appears to be central in Beck's (1967) description of cognitive processes and depression. For example, Beck (1976, pp. 99–100) reported the case of a depressed suicidal woman who previously had had a breach in her relationship with her lover Raymond and said, "I am worthless." When the therapist asked why she

believed she was worthless, she replie[d]                    love, I am worthless."
Again, following the same logic as f                    ferred negative characteristics about the self should be par[t]                    hopelessness when the
person believes that the negative chara[c]                    [a]ble or likely to change
and that possession of it will preclude                    important outcomes in
many areas of life. When the negative [c]                    een as precluding the
attainment of outcomes in only a very lim[i]                    life, relatively circumscribed pessimism rather than generalized hope[l]                    [wo]uld result. Inferred characteristics about the self, given negative events, n                    be independent of causal
attributions for these events, but it is useful to co..ceptualize and operationalize
them as distinct.

For the occurrence of a given negative life event, the three kinds of inferences (cause, consequence, and self-characteristics) may not be equally important in contributing to whether or not the person becomes hopeless and, in turn, develops the symptoms of hopelessness depression. For example, a young girl's inferences about the negative consequences of her mother's death, rather than about its cause or immediate implications for her view of herself, may be most important in contributing to whether or not she becomes hopeless.

## Distal Contributory Causes: Cognitive Styles

Complementing social psychologists' work on the situational determinants of causal attributions, Abramson et al. (1978) suggested a more distal factor that also may influence the content of people's causal inferences for a particular event: Individual differences in *attributional style* (see also Ickes & Layden, 1978). Some individuals may exhibit a general tendency to attribute negative events to stable, global factors and to view these events as very important whereas other individuals may not. We use the phrase "hypothesized depressogenic attributional style" to refer to this tendency.

Individuals who exhibit the hypothesized depressogenic attributional style should be more likely than individuals who do not to attribute any particular negative event to a stable, global cause and view the event as very important, thereby incrementing the likelihood of becoming hopeless and, in turn, developing the symptoms of hopelessness depression. However, in the presence of positive life events or in the absence of negative life events, people exhibiting the hypothesized depressogenic attributional style should be no more likely to develop hopelessness, and therefore the symptoms of hopelessness depression, than people not exhibiting this attributional style. This aspect of the theory is conceptualized usefully as a *diathesis-stress component* (Metalsky, Abramson, Seligman, Semmel & Peterson, 1982). That is, the hypothesized depressogenic attributional style (the diathesis) is a distal contributory cause of the symptoms of hopelessness depression that operates in the presence, but not in the absence, of negative life events (the stress; see also Alloy, Kayne, Romer & Crocker, 1989; Metalsky, Halberstadt & Abramson, 1987). The logic of the diathesis-stress component implies that a depressogenic attributional style in a particular content domain (e.g., for interpersonal-related events) provides *"specific vulnerability"* (cf. Beck, 1967) to the symptoms of hopelessness depression when an individual is confronted with negative life events in that same content domain (e.g., social rejection). This specific vulnerability hypothesis requires that there be a match between the content areas of an individual's depressogenic attributional style and the negative life events he or she encounters for the attributional diathesis-stress interaction to predict future symptoms of hopelessness depression (cf. Alloy, Hartlage & Abramson, 1988; Alloy et al., 1985; Anderson & Arnoult, 1985; Anderson, Horowitz & French, 1983; Hammen, Marks, Mayol & de Mayo, 1985; Alloy et al., 1989; Metalsky et al., 1987).

As with causal inferences, individual differences may exist in the general tendency to infer negative consequences and negative characteristics about the self, given the occurrence of negative life events. It is not known whether or not such cognitive styles are independent of the hypothesized depressogenic attributional style.

Abramson et al. (in press) suggested these two additional cognitive styles also are diatheses that operate in the presence, but not in the absence, of negative life events according to the specific vulnerability hypothesis. Abramson et al. referred to these three negative styles as *cognitive diatheses*. Beck's (Weissman & Beck, 1979) concept of dysfunctional attitudes and Ellis' (1977) concept of irrational beliefs appear to overlap, in part, with these cognitive diatheses. Abramson et al. (in press) suggested that cognitive styles probably are best conceptualized as continuua with some people exhibiting more negative styles than others. Similarly, it may be more appropriate to speak of a continuum of negativity of life events. The continuum view suggests a *titration* model (cf. Zubin & Spring, 1977) of the diathesis-stress component. That is, the less negative a person's cognitive style, the more negative an event needs to be in order to interact with that style and contribute to the formation of symptoms. Thus, although many cases of hopelessness depression will occur among cognitively vulnerable people when they are confronted with negative events, people who do not exhibit the cognitive diatheses also may develop hopelessness depression when they are confronted with events sufficient to engender hopelessness in many or most people (e.g., a person who is put in a concentration camp and repeatedly told by the guards that the only way to leave the camp is as a corpse). In a related vein, it is likely that although major negative life events often initiate the series of inferences hypothesized to culminate in the symptoms of hopelessness depression, they are not required to initiate the causal chain. The occurrence of more minor events, chronic stressors, or even daily hassles also may trigger the hypothesized depressogenic inferences among cognitively vulnerable people.

This discussion underscores the importance of the *causal mediation* component of the hopelessness theory: Each causal factor depicted in Figure 4–1 contributes to the next causal factor in the proximal direction.

In addition to the cognitive factors described above, interpersonal (e.g., lack of social support; Brown & Harris, 1978), developmental (e.g., death of mother during the child's early years; Brown & Harris, 1978), and even genetic factors also may modulate the likelihood that a person will develop hopelessness and, in turn, the symptoms of hopelessness depression (see Tiger, 1979 for an intriguing discussion of genetic and biological factors in the development of hope and hopelessness).

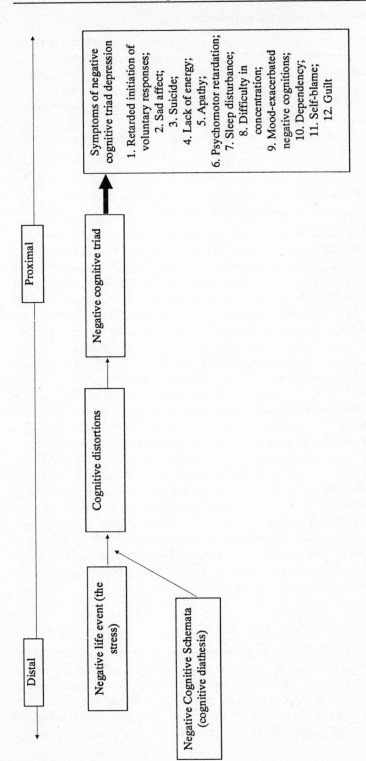

**FIGURE 4-2:**

**Beck's Cognitive Theory of Depression.** Causal chain hypothesized to culminate in the symptoms of negative cognitive triad depression. (Arrows with thick lines indicate sufficient causes. Arrows with thin lines indicate contributory causes.)

## Cause: Negative Cognitive Triad Depression

Although Beck's cognitive theory is less explicit than the hopelessness theory and recently has undergone revision (Beck, 1987), we have suggested that it can be interpreted as having a formal causal structure similar to that of the hopelessness theory (Abramson et al., 1988a; Abramson, Metalsky & Alloy, 1988b; Alloy, Clements & Kolden, 1985). Given this view, Beck's theory also can be understood as postulating a sequential causal pathway culminating in a proximal sufficient cause of the symptoms of a specific subtype of depression—negative cognitive triad depression.

### A Proximal Sufficient Cause of the Symptoms of Negative Cognitive Triad Depression: Negative Cognitive Triad

We suggest that Beck's theory may be interpreted as postulating that a negative view of the self, the world, and the future (i.e., the "negative cognitive triad") is a proximal sufficient cause of the symptoms of the negative cognitive triad subtype of depression (but see Abramson et al., in press for an alternative interpretation of Beck's theory and Beck, 1987 for a revision of his theory). The negative view of the self consists of the belief that one is deficient, inadequate, or unworthy. In the negative view of the world, one construes his or her experiences in terms of defeat, deprivation, or disparagement. The negative view of the future consists of the expectation that the future is bleak and appears to overlap greatly, if not completely, with the concept of hopelessness featured in the hopelessness theory.

Although Beck and his colleagues have discussed the heterogeneity that may exist among the depressive disorders (Beck, Rush, Shaw, and Emery, 1979), Beck has been less explicit about whether or not his theory postulates, as does the hopelessness theory, a distinct subtype of depression. Indeed, one of Beck's recent papers (Beck, 1987) can be interpreted as suggesting that he is not postulating a subtype (see Abramson et al., in press). Nevertheless, given the apparent formal structure of Beck's theory, we believe it is usefully construed as postulating a subtype of depression, defined in part by its cause: Negative cognitive triad depression. Unfortunately, the theoretical development of the concept of negative cognitive triad depression is more primitive than that of the concept of hopelessness depression. We think, however, that this hypothesized subtype overlaps greatly with the hypothesized subtype of hopelessness depression and that both theories are, for the most part, referring to the same group of individuals.

### Proximal Contributory Causes: Cognitive Distortions

According to Beck (1967), the negative cognitive triad and subsequent depressive symptoms are more likely to occur when negative life events are interpreted in a negatively distorted way. Beck argues that some (if not all) depression-prone people make inferences about themselves and their environments that are unrealistic, extreme, and illogical. These cognitive distortions are hypothesized to consist of the following kinds of logical "errors": 1) arbitrary inference, 2) selective abstraction, 3) overgeneralization, 5) personalization, and 6) absolutistic, dichotomous thinking (see Beck et al., 1979, for a more complete discussion of these hypothesized cognitive errors).

### *Distal Contributory Cause: Negative Cognitive Schemata*

Beck (1967) suggested that relatively consistent individual differences exist in the tendency to exhibit evaluatively negative cognitive distortions about the self, the world, and the future. Schemata with negative content about loss, failure, inadequacy, and so forth constitute the cognitive "diathesis" in Beck's theory of depression (Abramson et al., 1988a; Alloy et al., 1985; Beck et al., 1979; Kuiper, Olinger & MacDonald, 1988). In line with cognitive psychologists (e.g., Neisser, 1967), Beck defined a schema as an organized representation of prior knowledge that guides the processing of current information. Beck (1967) hypothesized that when activated by stress (negative life events), depressogenic schemata lead to negative cognitive distortions because incoming information is assimilated to the schemata. The cognitive distortions are viewed as relatively automatic and involuntary products of depressogenic schematic processing.

### Cause: Common Themes in the Hopelessness Theory and Beck's Theory

The hopelessness theory and Beck's theory present conceptual reorganizations of the phenomena typically associated with the concept of depression, giving some of the previously viewed "symptoms" causal status (e.g., hopelessness) while maintaining symptom status for others (e.g., sadness). They are *diathesis-stress* theories with negative cognitive styles and schemata serving as diatheses and life events as the stress. Moreover, insofar as the hopelessness theory (explicitly) and Beck's theory (given our interpretation) feature sufficient causes of depressive symptoms, they essentially posit the existence of a *subtype* of depression—*negative cognition depression*—defined, in part, by its causes.

### Symptoms: Hopelessness Depression

Hopelessness depression should be characterized by a number of symptoms. Two of these symptoms were described in the 1978 reformulation of helplessness and depression (Abramson, Seligman & Teasdale, 1978), and Abramson et al. (in press) retained them in the hopelessness theory: 1) retarded initiation of voluntary responses (motivational symptom); and 2) sad affect (emotional symptom). The motivational symptom derives from the helplessness expectancy component of hopelessness. If a person expects that nothing he or she does matters, why try? The incentive for emitting active instrumental responses decreases (Alloy, 1982; Bolles, 1972). Sadness derives from the negative outcome expectancy component of hopelessness and is a likely consequence of the expectation that the future is bleak. Abramson et al. no longer included the third symptom described in the 1978 reformulation, the cognitive symptom (associative deficit), because work on "depressive realism" (e.g., Alloy & Abramson, 1979, 1988) has not supported it.

Hopelessness depression should be characterized by other symptoms as well. Insofar as Beck and others have demonstrated that hopelessness is a key factor in serious suicide attempts and suicidal ideation, serious suicide attempts and suicidal ideation are likely symptoms of hopelessness depression (Beck, Kovacs & Weissman, 1975; Kazdin, French, Unis, Esveldt-Dawson & Sherick, 1983; Minkoff, Bergman, Beck & Beck, 1973; Petrie & Chamberlain, 1983). If lack of energy, apathy, and psychomotor retardation are, in part, concomitants of a severe decrease in the motivation to initiate voluntary responses (see Beck, 1967), then they should be symptoms of hopelessness depression. Abramson et al. (in press) hypothesized that to the extent that people brood about the highly desired outcomes they feel hopeless to attain, sleep disturbance (e.g., initial insomnia) and difficulty in concentration will be important symptoms of hopelessness depression. Based on work showing that mood affects cognition (e.g., Bower, 1981), Abramson et al. predicted that as individuals suffering from hopelessness depression become increasingly sad, their cognitions will become even more negative.

Although not necessarily symptoms of hopelessness depression, low self-esteem and/or dependency sometimes will accompany the other hypothesized symptoms. Lowered self-esteem will be a symptom of hopelessness depression when the event that triggered the episode was attributed to an internal, stable, global cause as opposed to any type of external cause or to an internal, unstable, specific cause. In contrast to the 1978 reformulation, then, the hopelessness theory postulates that attributing a negative life event to an internal cause does not, by itself, contribute to lowering self-esteem. The revision requiring internal, stable, global attributions for lowered self-esteem is based on a number of studies (e.g., Crocker, Alloy & Kayne, 1988; Dweck & Licht, 1980; Janoff-Bulman, 1979) showing that internal attributions per se are not maladaptive and, in some cases, may be very adaptive (e.g., attributing failure to lack of effort leads to increased trying). The link between internal, stable, global attributions for negative life events and lowered self-esteem is based on social psychological work showing that people's self-esteem is influenced by their comparisons with others (e.g., Festinger, 1954; Morse & Gergen, 1970; Rosenberg, 1965; Schachter, 1959; Tesser & Campbell, 1983). If people make internal, stable, global attributions, then they expect that others could attain the outcomes about which they feel hopeless and therefore would feel inadequate compared to others. In addition, lowered self-esteem should occur in cases of hopelessness depression when people have inferred negative characteristics about themselves which they view as important to their general self-concept and not remediable or likely to change. Finally, dependency frequently may co-occur with lowered self-esteem because the conditions that give rise to lowered self-esteem will leave the person feeling inferior to others and thereby increase the likelihood that s/he may become excessively dependent on them (Brewin & Furnham, 1987).

In general, circumscribed pessimism may not be associated with the full syndrome of the symptoms of hopelessness depression. Circumscribed pessimism is likely to produce fewer and/or less severe symptoms than generalized hopelessness except when the person is pessimistic about an extremely important outcome. Whereas the motivational deficit should occur in cases of circumscribed pessimism, sadness may be less intense or even absent. Similarly, people with circumscribed pessimism should be less likely to commit suicide or exhibit the other hypothesized symptoms of hopelessness depression. Thus, circumscribed pessimism should lead to an identifiable behavioral syndrome, but this syndrome should be characterized primarily by a motivational deficit in the relevant domain.

## Symptoms: Negative Cognitive Triad Depression

Because hopelessness is part of the negative cognitive triad, all of the hypothesized symptoms of hopelessness depression described above also should be manifestations of negative cognitive triad depression. In addition, based on Beck's writings, we suggest that negative cognitive triad depression also should include self-blame and guilt as symptoms resulting from the negative view of the self. Beck's (1967) writings suggest that negative cognitive triad depressives not only see themselves as inferior, but also blame themselves for their inadequacies and believe they could do or be otherwise (guilt). Note that because a negative view of the self is viewed as one of the *causes* of negative cognitive triad depression, in order to avoid tautology, low self-esteem should not be included as one of the symptoms of negative cognitive triad depression when testing the predictions of Beck's theory.

## Symptoms: Summary

Combining the hypothesized symptoms of hopelessness depression and negative cognitive triad depression, negative cognition depression should include 13 symptoms: 1) retarded initiation of voluntary responses, 2) sadness, 3) suicide attempts and suicidal ideation, 4) lack of energy, 5) apathy, 6) psychomotor retardation, 7) sleep disturbance, 8) difficulty in concentration, 9) mood-exacerbated negative cognitions, 10) low self-esteem (only for hopelessness depressives), 11) dependency, 12) self-blame (only for negative cognitive triad depressives because self-blame is an attribution and, therefore, a cause of hopelessness depression), and 13) guilt.

## Course of Negative Cognition Depression

In considering the course of a disorder, the concepts of *maintenance, recovery, relapse,* and *recurrence* need to be distinguished (Klerman, 1978). Maintenance refers to the duration of a given episode of a disorder, and recovery refers to its remission. Relapse is a return of clinically significant symptoms within a relatively short period following remission whereas recurrence is the onset of a new episode following a prolonged interval of remission.

### Duration of a Given Episode (Maintenance)

Insofar as hopelessness and/or the negative cognitive triad are hypothesized to be proximal sufficient causes of negative cognition depression, the duration of any given episode of negative cognition depression should be influenced by how long these beliefs are present. The longer the time over which an individual exhibits hopelessness and negative views of the self and world, the longer the duration of the episode of negative cognition depression triggered by these expectations.

What, in turn, influences the duration of hopelessness and negative views of the self and world? In hopelessness theory (Abramson et., in press), the chronicity of hopelessness is predicted by the relative stability of an individual's attributions for the negative life events or stressors he or she is experiencing. If an individual attributes the causes of negative life events to stable factors, he or she will expect those causes to again be present in the future and thus, to again produce negative events, hence, maintaining hopelessness. Although not a clear-cut prediction of hopelessness theory, it may be speculated that the globality (cross-situational generality) of individuals' attributions for stressful events would also influence the duration of hopelessness and hence, the duration of the episode of hopelessness depression. In Beck's theory, the duration of activity of biased and distorted personal inferences about negative life events (e.g., selective abstractions, arbitrary inferences, etc.) will predict the chronicity of people's negative views of the self, world, and future, and thus, the duration of an episode of negative triad depression. Similarly, the stability with which individuals infer negative consequences and negative characteristics about the self from the occurrence of negative life events should modulate the duration of negative self, world, and future expectations. More generally then, it is the duration of negatively biased (and plausible) personal and causal inferences that modulates the chronicity of negative expectations about the self, world, and future, and hence, the duration of an episode of negative cognition depression.

Finally, it is important to point out that the duration of hopelessness and the negative cognitive triad not only should be influenced by the duration of activity of negatively biased personal and causal interpretations of the *original* negative life events that "triggered" the onset of a given episode of negative cognition depression, but *also* by the chronicity of negatively biased inferences for *newly occurring* life stressors. Indeed, Lloyd, Zisook, Click, and Jaffe (1981) and Brown and Harris (1978) found that concurrent negative life events are important predictors of the course of an acute episode of depression. The cognitive theories would suggest that it is individuals' negatively biased interpretations for these concurrent events that modulate the course of negative cognition depression.

All of the above hypothesized predictors of the duration of a given episode of negative cognition depression follow directly from the logic of the hopelessness theory and Beck's theory. In addition, the possibility exists that once an individual becomes hopeless and/or develops the negative cognitive triad, some biological or psychological processes are triggered that need to run their course and do not dissipate as quickly as hopelessness or the negative cognitive triad. Such factors might maintain a negative cognition depression after hopelessness and/or the negative cognitive triad remit. Similarly, other factors such as lack of social support also may influence the duration of an episode of negative cognition depression after the proximal sufficient causes remit.

### Relapse and Recurrence

Given the logic of the cognitive theories, relapse or recurrence of negative cognition depression should be predicted by the reappearance of hopelessness and/or the negative cognitive triad because, by definition, a relapse or recurrence is a new onset of negative cognition depression. Thus, the etiological chains hypothesized to culminate in the onset of the symptoms of negative cognition depression also apply directly to the relapse or recurrence of these symptoms. Hence, people with cognitive diatheses will be more likely to have relapses or recurrences of negative cognition depression when confronted with negative life events than people who do not exhibit these diatheses.

## Remediation and Prevention of Negative Cognition Depression

Because the cognitive theories of depression specify etiological chains, each link suggests a point for clinical intervention. A major advantage of using the proximal-distal continuum to order the events that cause negative cognition depression is that it not only suggests points of intervention for reversing current episodes, but also suggests points for decreasing vulnerability to negative cognition depression.

Any therapeutic strategy that undermines hopelessness and the negative cognitive triad should be effective in remediating current symptoms of negative cognition depression. Hopelessness and/or the negative cognitive triad could be attacked directly. Alternatively, the proximal causes (e.g., stable, global attributions for particular negative life events) that contribute to a person's current hopelessness and/or negative cognitive triad could be attacked.

Insofar as negative events and situational information supporting depressogenic inferences contribute to the maintenance of hopelessness and/or the negative cognitive triad, therapeutic interventions aimed at modifying the hopelessness-inducing and/or negative cognitive triad-inducing environment should be helpful. Finally, if the person's own behavior is, to some degree, contributing to the depressogenic events and situational information he or she encounters, then personal behavior change would be an important therapeutic goal. Insofar as the hypothesized cognitive diatheses (negative cognitive styles and schemata) put people at risk for initial onset, relapse, and recurrence of negative cognition depression, modifying these diatheses is an important goal for prevention. Because the cognitive diatheses require negative life events to exert their depressogenic effects, prevention efforts also might be directed toward lessening the stressfulness of events in the environments of cognitively vulnerable people. Finally, primary prevention efforts could be aimed at building nondepressive cognitive styles and environments.

We do not present the strategies and techniques for achieving these therapeutic goals because we have detailed them elsewhere (Alloy et al., 1985; Beach, Abramson & Levine, 1981; Halberstadt, Andrews, Metalsky & Abramson, 1984). As with the other predictions about negative cognition depression, the clinical predictions can be corroborated or discorroborated only by empirical test.

## Hypothesized Relationship of Negative Cognition Depression to Other Categories of Depression and Psychopathology

With respect to DSM-III-R, it is possible to speculate that negative cognition depression constitutes a subset of unipolar major depressive disorder (particularly recurrent unipolar depression), dysthymic disorder, and adjustment disorder with depressed mood.

In addition, some everyday transient depressive mood reactions may constitute very mild forms of negative cognition depression. In addition to suggesting how negative cognition depression may map on to subsets of existing diagnostic categories of unipolar depression, it is useful to ask which diagnostic categories of unipolar depression, if any, involve different etiological processes, and perhaps symptoms and therapy, than those involved in negative cognition depression. Klein's (1974) concept of endogenomorphic depression may be fundamentally distinct from the concept of negative cognition depression. The hypothesized core process in endogenomorphic depressions is impairment in the capacity to experience pleasure leading to a profound lack of interest and investment in the environment (e.g., inability to enjoy food, sex, etc.). Klein's concept of endogenomorphic depression appears very similar to Costello's (1972) notion of reinforcer ineffectiveness and maps closely on to the DSM-III-R category of major depressive episode with melancholia. It is of interest for our purposes that Klein distinguishes endogenomorphic depressions, hypothesized to be responsive to imipramine drug therapy, from the categories of "acute dysphoria" and "chronic overreactive dysphoria," which he believes are fundamentally different depressive disorders. A close reading of Klein's paper suggests that the categories of acute dysphoria and chronic overreactive dysphoria correspond quite closely to our category of negative cognition depression.

This discussion and elaboration of the concept of negative cognition depression suggests that this category may not map directly in a one-to-one fashion on to any existing nosological category of depression. Instead, the category of negative cognition depression may cut across traditional categories of depression and perhaps even include psychological phenomena not previously covered by the existing nosologies of depression. For example, recent work on the co-morbidity of anxiety and depression suggests that many negative cognition depressives also may be suffering from anxiety (Alloy, Kelly, Mineka & Clements, in press). Also, it is tempting to speculate that a subset of individuals who exhibit personality disorders (e.g., borderline personality) are characterized by extremely negative cognitive diatheses that make them particularly susceptible to negative cognition depression (Rose & Abramson, 1987; Silverman, Silverman & Eardley, 1984).

A core question concerns the relation between the concept of negative cognition depression and general depression. We suggest that the relation of negative cognition depression to general depression is analogous to the relation between a subtype of mental retardation (e.g., phenylketonuria, cretinism) and mental retardation in general. Just as some symptoms of a particular subtype of retardation may be a general feature of retardation (e.g., low IQ), particular hypothesized symptoms of negative cognition depression are considered symptoms of general depression (e.g., sadness). Other hypothesized symptoms of negative cognition depression (e.g., retarded initiation of voluntary responses) may only partially overlap with the symptoms of general depression. Finally, still other symptoms of negative cognition depression (e.g., suicide and suicidal ideation) may not overlap at all with the symptoms of general depression. Thus, just as physicians do not define a particular subtype of retardation on the basis of symptoms alone because of potential overlap in some symptoms across subtypes, we do not define negative cognition depression on the basis of symptoms alone. Following the logic of workers in medicine more generally, we define negative cognition depression in terms of cause, symptoms, course, therapy, and prevention.

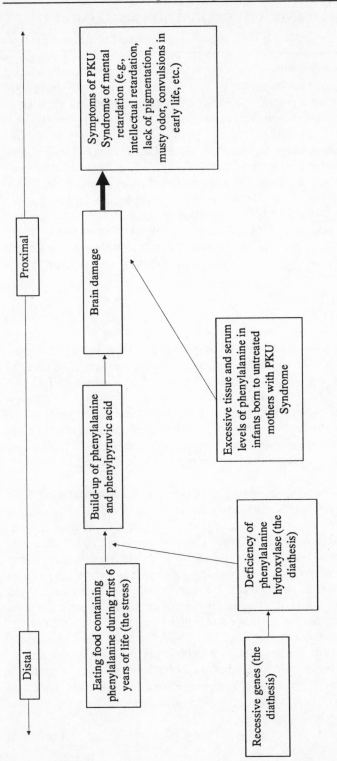

**FIGURE 4–3: PKU SYNDROME**

Causal chain specified in currently accepted account of PKU. (Arrows with solid lines indicate sufficient causes. Arrows with thin lines indicate contributory causes.)

## SEARCH FOR NEGATIVE COGNITION DEPRESSION

How might we search for negative cognition depression and delineate it from other subtypes of depression? At the outset we caution that a search for negative cognition depression raises some of the most basic and challenging questions facing any psychopathologist, such as: What is a useful category of psychopathology? How can one determine whether or not a hypothesized psychopathological entity exists in nature? How can one most meaningfully subdivide a heterogeneous disorder into its constituent subtypes?

Some of our colleagues have expressed puzzlement and even mystification about how one could determine whether or not a theory-based subtype of depression exists in nature or have suggested that a search for negative cognition depression involves "circular reasoning." In contrast to these colleagues, we suggest that at a conceptual level, the search for negative cognition depression is straightforward and doesn't involve anything spooky. To assert that negative cognition depressions exist in nature is simply to say that the hopelessness theory and Beck's theory are true (cf. Clark, 1983). We search for the negative cognition depression subtype by testing the cognitive theories.

### Search for the PKU Syndrome

To help illustrate how we can search for negative cognition depression or, for that matter, any theory-based subtype of a disorder (e.g., endogenomorphic depression, Klein, 1974), we make an analogy to a now relatively well-understood form of mental retardation, phenylketonuria (PKU). We choose the example of PKU because at a formal metatheoretical level, the causal pathway featured in the etiological account of this disorder is analogous in many important respects to the causal pathways featured in the cognitive theories: a proximal sufficient cause component and a relatively more distal diathesis-stress component. In making this analogy, we do not mean to imply that negative cognition depression, if it exists, is necessarily as rare as PKU.

According to Stanbury, Wyngaarden, Fredrickson, Goldstein, and Brown (1983), the causal sequence of events culminating in the PKU syndrome of retardation begins with a pair of recessive genes that leads to a deficiency of liver enzyme, phenylalanine hydroxylase, which is needed to convert phenylalanine, an amino acid of protein foods, to tyrosine (see Figure 4–3). If individuals with a deficiency of phenylalanine hydroxylase eat food containing phenylalanine during the first six years of life, it is almost inevitable that phenylalanine and phenylpyruvic acid build up in the body tissues and cause a particular form of brain damage which, in turn, causes mental retardation. On the other hand, if individuals with a deficiency of phenylalanine hydroxylase eat a restricted diet containing no phenylalanine during the first six or so years of life, phenylalanine and phenylpyruvic acid are unlikely to build up in the body tissues. Consequently, for vulnerable individuals, the particular type of brain damage and subsequent symptoms of mental retardation associated with PKU are unlikely to occur in the presence of a phenylalanine-restricted diet regime instituted early in life.

In the case of PKU, then, a particular form of brain damage is a proximal sufficient, but not a necessary, cause of mental retardation. The inability to metabolize phenylalanine (i.e., deficiency in phenylalanine hydroxylase) is a relatively distal cause of retardation that is best characterized as a diathesis in a diathesis-stress combination because the inability to metabolize phenylalanine contributes to the formation of a proximal sufficient cause of retardation (brain damage) in the presence, but not in the absence, of a particular stressor (eating foods containing phenylalanine in the first six years of life). The inability to metabolize phenylalanine, by itself, is not necessary, as well as not sufficient, to produce brain damage resulting from high tissue and serum levels of phenylalanine. For example, most of the infants born to untreated mothers with PKU exhibit brain damage due to excessive tissue and serum levels of phenylalanine, even when the infant itself does not display a deficiency of phenylalanine hydroxylase. In these cases, the fetal brain damage appears to result from the high levels of maternal blood phenylalanine.

Suppose that 50 years ago, a physician proposed the currently accepted etiological account of the PKU syndrome and suggested that the theory hypothesized the existence of an, as yet, unidentified subtype of mental retardation, the PKU syndrome, defined in part by its cause. It would seem to be a straightforward matter, conceptually, to determine whether or not the theory-based, hypothetical PKU syndrome exists in nature. We simply need to test the physician's theory.

A research design to "search" for the PKU syndrome would involve two groups of infants: one with a deficiency in phenylalanine hydroxylase and one without such a deficiency. The infants would be followed over time and subdivided further on the basis of whether or not they ate foods containing phenylalanine during the first six years of life. The physician's theory predicts that children who exhibit phenylalanine hydroxylase deficiency and eat foods containing phenylalanine during the first six years of life should develop the hypothesized manifest symptoms of the PKU syndrome (e.g., intellectual retardation, lack of pigmentation, musty odor, convulsions in early life, etc.). Children comprising the remaining three groups should be very unlikely to develop the hypothesized PKU symptoms.

In addition to testing the diathesis-stress component of the PKU theory, we also could examine the mediational processes component with this data-set. Does the occurrence of each causal factor in the hypothesized etiological chain increase the likelihood of the next most proximal cause? The mediation component predictions of the PKU theory are: 1) Children with a deficiency in phenylalanine hydroxylase who eat foods containing phenylalanine during the first six years of life should be more likely to develop a build-up of phenylalanine and phenylpyruvic acid than children with the same deficiency who do not eat such foods, as well as children without the deficiency who either do or do not eat foods containing phenylalanine; 2) A build-up of phenylalanine and phenylpyruvic acid should increase the likelihood of brain damage; and 3) Such brain damage should be sufficient for the manifest symptoms of PKU.

To further test the PKU theory, we could conduct a "prevention study" to determine if placing children with a deficiency in phenylalanine hydroxylase on a phenylalanine free diet dramatically decreases their chances of developing the manifest symptoms of PKU. Corroborative results from such a study combined with corroborative results from the prior research would point to the existence of the PKU syndrome in nature. Finally, we could determine the relationship of PKU to other subtypes of mental retardation. Evidence that PKU appeared to be a distinct entity taken with the above positive results would earn the once hypothetical PKU syndrome a place in classification systems of mental retardation.

Our search for the PKU syndrome was not spooky, circular, mystifying, or puzzling. The search simply involved standard scientific practices for testing theories. With the PKU analogy in mind, we now show how to search for negative cognition depression.

## Search for Negative Cognition Depression: Overview

A variety of possible methodological approaches exist for searching for negative cognition depressions and distinguishing them from other types of depression. For example, a symptom-based approach would involve determining if a subgroup of depressives exhibits the symptoms hypothesized to be associated with negative cognition depression (e.g., retarded initiation of voluntary responses, etc.) A symptom-based approach commonly has been utilized by workers in descriptive psychiatry, where categories of depression traditionally have been formed on the basis of symptom similarity. However, we believe a symptom-based approach alone would be unsatisfactory in the context of work on the cognitive theories. The basic problem is that some or all of the symptoms hypothesized to be characteristic of negative cognition depressions conceivably may be present in other types of depression as well (e.g., endogenomorphic depression; Klein, 1974). In contrast to a purely symptom-based approach and similar to the currently accepted theory of PKU, the cognitive theories of depression point to an additional strategy for searching for negative cognition depressions: a *process-oriented* approach.

## Search for Negative Cognition Depression: A Research Strategy

The way to search for negative cognition depression is to test the cognitive theories. We believe that a test of the cognitive theories of depression involves at least six components: 1) a test of the cognitive diathesis-stress component of the theories; 2) a test of the mediational processes specified by the theories to culminate in hopelessness or the negative cognitive triad; 3) a test of the symptom component of the theories; 4) a test of the cognitive theories' predictions about the course of negative cognition depression; 5) a test of the cognitive theories' predictions about the remediation and prevention of negative cognition depression; and 6) delineation of the place of negative cognition depression in the context of descriptive psychiatry. In describing what would constitute adequate tests of each of these components of the cognitive theories, we distinguish between tests that are necessary for evaluating the empirical validity of theoretical statements contained in the cognitive theories and tests that elaborate the theories where the theories currently make no explicit predictions.

### Necessary Test of the Diathesis-Stress Component.

The cognitive theories of depression explicitly predict that a negative attributional style or self-schema (cognitive diathesis) interacts with the occurrence of negative life events (stress) to increase the probability of onset of the symptoms of negative cognition depression. Hence, an adequate test of the diathesis-stress components of the cognitive theories involves at least two parts: (1) a demonstration that the interaction between the hypothesized cognitive diatheses and negative life events predicts future symptoms of negative cognition depression, over and above its association with past or current depression (cf. Alloy, Kayne, Romer & Crocker, 1989; Metalsky, Halberstadt & Abramson, 1987); and (2) a demonstration that the interaction between the hypothesized cognitive diatheses and negative life events predicts the complete constellation of symptoms hypothesized to constitute the negative cognition subtype of depression as opposed to only a subset of these symptoms or to symptoms that constitute other subtypes of depression.

In addition, the logic of the etiological sequences postulated by the cognitive theories implies that a depressogenic attributional style or self-schema in a particular content domain (e.g., for interpersonal events) provides "specific vulnerability" to the symptoms of negative cognition depression when an individual is confronted with negative life events in that same content domain (e.g., social rejection). This specific vulnerability hypothesis of the diathesis-stress component of the cognitive models requires that there be a match between the content areas of an individual's cognitive diatheses and the negative life events he or she encounters for the cognitive diathesis-stress interaction to predict future symptoms of negative cognition depression (Alloy et al., 1985; Hammen, Marks, Mayol & de Mayo, 1985; Riskind & Rholes, 1984).

### Elaborative Test of the Diathesis-Stress Component

One issue that is relevant to elaborating the cognitive theories of depression is the relative stability of the hypothesized depressogenic attributional style or self-schema. Although it is often assumed that the cognitive theories predict that the depressogenic attributional style or self-schema is traitlike, in fact, nothing in the logic of the theories requires that the cognitive diatheses be enduring. For example, even if the hypothesized depressogenic causal schema or self-schema is relatively statelike, as long as the interaction of this style and negative life events increases risk for the symptoms of negative cognition depression, the cognitive theories would be corroborated. Among the questions that need to be addressed in examining the stability of the depressogenic cognitive diatheses are the following: (1) In the natural course of negative cognition depression, does a depressogenic attributional style or self-schema persist beyond remission of a current depressive episode (cf. Eaves & Rush, 1984; Hamilton & Abramson, 1983; Persons & Rao, 1985)? (2) To what degree does a depressogenic attributional style or self-schema fluctuate over time in synchrony with environmental circumstances? That is, do challenges to an individual's cognitive system by environmental stressors (negative life events) "activate" or "prime" a depressogenic causal schema or self-schema (cf. Alloy et al., 1985; Riskind & Rholes, 1984)?

A second elaborative issue concerns the specific kinds of negative life events that contribute to negative cognition depression-proneness in interaction with the hypothesized cognitive diatheses. Although the cognitive models make no explicit predictions about particular types of negative events, some kinds may be especially likely to induce hopelessness or the negative triad in cognitively vulnerable individuals (e.g., uncontrollable events, exits from the social field, chronic stressors; cf. Alloy et al. 1985).

Finally, it would be useful to examine whether or not there is a feedback loop among the hypothesized cognitive diatheses, negative life events, and depression, such that current depression alone or current depression in interaction with stress predicts the development of a depressogenic attributional style or self-schema as well as the depressogenic causal schema or self-schema-stress interaction predicting the development of depression. Such an examination would significantly increase our understanding of the interplay among these factors in negative cognition depression (cf. Beck, 1967; Hamilton & Abramson, 1983).

## Necessary Test of the Mediational Processes Component

The cognitive theories of depression not only postulate distal diatheses-stress and proximal sufficient cause components but also specify a causal chain of events hypothesized to mediate these two components. Thus it is necessary to determine whether the probability linkages delineated in the theories actually obtain in nature. Is the likelihood of occurrence of each causal component in the hypothesized etiological chains increased by the occurrence of the next most distal causal component in the chains?

Specifically, an investigation of the empirical status of three probability linkages is required for an adequate test of the mediational processes component of the cognitive theories:

1. The interaction of the hypothesized cognitive diatheses and negative life events should increase the likelihood that individuals will make negative interpretations (e.g., internal, stable, and global attributions) for the particular negative events they encounter. Because in both theories cognitive diatheses and stress contribute to, but are not sufficient for, the particular interpretations a person makes, this probability linkage should be greater than 0 but less than 1.0 (Alloy et al., 1989; Metalsky et al., 1987).

2. The negative interpretations for particular negative life events (e.g., attributions) that a person makes should, in turn, increase the likelihood of forming hopelessness or the negative cognitive triad. Again, because the particular interpretations an individual makes for negative events are hypothesized to contribute to, but not be sufficient for, the formation of hopelessness or the negative cognitive triad, this probability linkage should also be greater than 0 but less than 1.0 (Alloy, 1982).

3. The occurrence of hopelessness or the negative cognitive triad should increase the likelihood of the development of the symptoms of negative cognition depression. Because hopelessness and the negative cognitive triad are hypothesized to be sufficient causes of depressive symptoms, this probability linkage should equal 1.0.

### Elaborative Test of the Mediational Processes Component

Although the cognitive theories clearly specify the probability linkages among the hypothesized causal components in the etiological chains, culminating in the symptoms of negative cognition depression, the theories are silent about the temporal intervals between pairs of these causal components (Cochran & Hammen, 1985; Alloy et al., 1989; Metalsky et al., 1987). That is, what is the time lag experienced by a cognitively vulnerable person between the occurrence of negative events and the occurrence of negative interpretations for these events, or between the occurrence of negative inferences for particular negative events and the formation of hopelessness or the negative cognitive triad? Consideration of the temporal issue is important, because attempts to test the probability linkages predicted by the theories could conclude mistakenly that the models are invalid if the relevant causal components are assessed with inappropriate time lags (Metalsky et al., 1987).

### Necessary Test of the Symptom Component

A necessary condition for the validity of the symptom component of the cognitive theories would include: (1) that the hypothesized symptoms of negative cognition depression be intercorrelated with one another (convergent validity) but not be as highly correlated with other symptoms found in depression and in other psychopathologies (divergent validity); (2) that this constellation of symptoms be correlated (in fact, perfectly correlated) with the hypothesized proximal sufficient causes of these symptoms (hopelessness, negative cognitive triad); and (3) that hopelessness and/or the negative cognitive triad not only be correlated with the hypothesized symptom complex, but that it temporally precede the formation of this symptom constellation.

### Elaborative Test of the Symptom Component

We (Abramson et al., 1988a) view the concept of negative cognition depression as open, and, therefore, exploratory work is needed in order to further characterize this subtype of depression. The symptom component of negative cognition depression could be elaborated more fully by a determination of whether other symptoms and clinical characteristics cohere with the predicted symptom constellation of negative cognition depression.

### Necessary Test of the Course Component

A basic prediction from the cognitive theories is that the duration of the proximal sufficient causes featured in these theories should predict the course or chronicity of the symptoms of negative cognition depression. In addition, the theories make predictions about what variables should influence the duration of the featured proximal sufficient causes. For example, a key prediction of the hopelessness theory is that the more stable a person's attribution for a negative life event, the longer the person will be hopeless and, consequently, depressed. The etiological chain hypothesized to culminate in the onset of the symptoms of negative cognition depression also should predict relapse and recurrence of this subtype of depression. Thus, an adequate test of the course component of the cognitive theories of depression involves the following: (1) examination of whether the duration of time over which individuals are hopeless and/or hold negative views of the self, world, and future determines the duration of an episode of negative cognition depression; (2) examination of whether the content (e.g., stable versus unstable attribution) and duration of the personal and causal inferences individuals make for the original negative life events that "triggered" an episode of negative cognition depression or for any newly occurring negative life events (i.e., events that occur after the events that "trigger" an episode) influence the duration of an episode of negative cognition depression; and (3) examination of whether the likelihood of and time to a relapse or recurrence of negative cognition depression is predicted by the reappearance of hopelessness and/or the negative cognitive triad (which, in turn, should be predicted by the entire etiological sequences featured in the cognitive theories of depression).

## Elaborative Test of the Course Component

The major issue relevant to elaborating the course component of the cognitive theories involves an investigation of whether there are additional predictors of the duration of an episode of negative cognition depression or of relapses or recurrences of negative cognition depression that do not follow directly from the logic of the cognitive theories. Additional predictors of the course of negative cognition depression may include prior episodes of depression (e.g., Klerman, 1978; Zis & Goodwin, 1979), family history of depression (Boyd & Weissman, 1982; Coryell & Winokur, 1982), and past or concurrent dysthymia (Keller & Lavori, 1984; Keller & Shapiro, 1982). An examination of whether some or all of these variables do, in fact, influence the course of negative cognition depression and whether they do so, in part, through the constructs featured in the cognitive theories of depression would serve to elaborate more fully these theories.

## Necessary Test of the Remediation and Prevention Component

A clear-cut prediction of the cognitive theories is that any therapy that undermines hopelessness and the negative cognitive triad should be effective in remediating current symptoms of negative cognition depression. Moreover, the theories predict that modification of the hypothesized cognitive diatheses (negative cognitive styles and schemata) should risk of future episodes of negative cognition depression.

## Elaborative Test of the Remediation and Prevention Component

An important clinical issue is which, if any, current treatments for depression (e.g., tricyclic drug therapy) are effective in treating negative cognition depression. Does negative cognition depression respond only to the interventions predicted by the cognitive theories or does it respond to other therapies as well?

## Negative Cognition Depression in the Context of Descriptive Psychiatry

By postulating the existence of a subtype of depression—negative cognition depression—the cognitive theories explicitly (the hopelessness theory) or implicitly (Beck's theory) recognize the heterogeneity of the depressive disorders. Thus, an important component of an adequate test of the cognitive theories is a determination of the relationship between negative cognition depression and other subtypes of depression. Before outlining research suggestions for placing the negative cognition subtype in the context of descriptive psychiatry, we note that negative cognition depression consists of at least two parts: the constellation of symptoms hypothesized to cohere by the cognitive theories (e.g., reduced initiation of voluntary responses, sad affect) and the causal chain of events postulated by the theories to culminate in this symptom complex. For example, the hypothesized symptom constellation may, in fact, cohere in nature but may not be caused by the chain of events specified in the theories. Alternatively, the etiological sequences described by the theories may produce an outcome that would be recognized as a case of depression but not the specific aggregate of symptoms hypothesized to constitute the negative cognition subtype of depression. Consequently, in delineating the issues involved in determining the place of negative cognition depression in descriptive psychiatry, we distinguish between the causal chain component and the symptom component. The nosological questions that need to be addressed include the following:

1. Does the concept of negative cognition depression (either the symptom or the causal chain component) map onto any nosological category of affective disorders that is currently diagnosed subtypes;dysthymic disorder (e.g., dysthymic disorder, unipolar major depression, intermittent depression)?

2. Does the concept of negative cognition depression (either the symptom or the causal chain component) cut across the various nosological categories of affective disorders that currently are diagnosed?

3. Does the concept of negative cognition depression (either the symptom or the causal component) include subsets or components of disorders not currently included among the affective disorders (e.g., generalized anxiety, personality disorders)?

## Empirical Validity of the Negative Cognition Subtype of Depression

Because the concept of negative cognition depression is new, the evidence about its validity is not in. However, we have conducted a number of studies to test it. Also, many of the studies conducted to test Beck's theory and the 1978 reformulation of helplessness and depression (Abramson et al., 1978), as well as other clinical and empirical work on depression, are relevant to evaluating the concept of negative cognition depression, although few provide a direct test. We now summarize this work.

Initial longitudinal tests of the proximal sufficient cause component have supported the temporal precedence of hopelessness in predicting change in depressive symptoms (Rholes, Riskind & Neville, 1985; Carver & Gaines, 1987; Riskind, Rholes, Brannon & Burdick, 1978). In addition, three cross-sectional studies have examined the relation between hopelessness and depressive symptoms as well as other forms of psychopathology (Abramson, Garber, Edwards & Seligman, 1978; Hamilton & Abramson, 1983; Beck, Riskind, Brown & Steer, 1988). Taken together, these studies suggest that hopelessness is specific to depression and not a general feature of psychopathology. Relatively powerful tests of the attributional diathesis-stress component have been conducted with supportive results (Metalsky et al., 1987; Alloy et al., 1989; Nolen-Hoeksema, Girgus & Seligman, 1986; Brown & Siegel, 1988; Alloy, Peterson, Abramson & Seligman, 1984; Sacks & Bugental, 1987). Similarly, Olinger, Kuiper & Shaw (1987) found that dysfunctional attitudes interacted with negative events impinging on subjects' cognitive vulnerability to predict current levels of depressive symptoms. Initial tests of the causal mediation component of the hopelessness theory have been supportive (Metalsky et al., 1987; Alloy et al., 1989). Finally, Evans et al. (1989) reported that in a study comparing cognitive therapy and pharmacotherapy for depression, posttreatment attributional styles predicted subsequent relapse of depression, consistent with the course component. Similarly, Rush, Weissenburger, and Eaves (1986) reported that the presence of dysfunctional attitudes at remission from depression predicted the presence of depression six months later. Although not statistically significant, a similar pattern was found for attributional style. A limitation of this study is the small sample size ($n = 15$).

## Future Directions in the Search for Negative Cognition Depression

On the basis of the aforementioned studies, the concept of negative cognition depression appears promising. However, further research is needed. For example, although powerful tests of the attributional diathesis-stress component have been conducted, no one has examined the cognitive diatheses of inferring negative consequences or characteristics about the self or whether the cognitive style diathesis-stress interaction predicts clinically significant depression. Moreover, it is crucial to determine if this interaction predicts the development of the hypothesized symptoms of negative cognition depression. More generally, an important limitation of the prior work is that it has not focused on the symptoms of negative cognition depression in particular and, instead, simply has examined the symptoms of depression in general. Future investigators need to test more fine-grained predictions about the hypothesized symptoms of negative cognition depression. The issue of the stability of the cognitive diatheses and negative schemata has not been resolved satisfactorily. We have only begun, in a preliminary way, to investigate the issues of specific vulnerability and mediational processes. Finally, further tests of the predictions about course, cure, and prevention are needed. We eagerly await this research.

Although straightforward conceptually, the search for negative cognition depression may involve difficult methodological issues. For example, the cognitive theories are silent about the time lag between formation of hopelessness and the negative cognitive triad (the hypothesized proximal sufficient causes) on the one hand and onset of the hypothesized symptoms of negative cognition depression on the other. If it is very short, then a major challenge will be to develop methods with sufficient temporal resolving power to determine if hopelessness and/or the negative cognitive triad indeed precede the occurrence of the hypothesized symptoms of negative cognition depression. The results of work to test the cognitive theories will determine if the concept of negative cognition depression needs to be revised. For example, perhaps the statement of the causal pathway is correct but it culminates in a different set of symptoms than those currently hypothesized to compose negative cognition depression. In this case, the symptom—but not the cause—component of the hopelessness theory would need to be modified.

In discussing how to search for negative cognition depression, we note the possibility that future work may not corroborate the existence of negative cognition depression as a bona fide *subtype* with characteristic cause, symptoms, course, treatment, and prevention. Instead the etiological chains featured in the cognitive theories may be one of many pathways to a final common outcome of depressive symptoms. In this case, it would be more compelling to speak of a negative cognition cause, as opposed to a negative cognition subtype, of depression.

## THEORETICAL AND CLINICAL IMPORTANCE OF PROVIDING A COMPLETE TEST OF THE COGNITIVE THEORIES OF DEPRESSION

It is important to provide a complete test of the cognitive theories of depression for at least five reasons. First, although depression long has been recognized as a major form of psychopathology, investigators only are just beginning to amass cumulative knowledge about its cause (Klerman, 1978). Thus, adequately testing *causal theories* of depression, such as the cognitive theories, may increase significantly our scientific understanding of this not yet well understood form of psychopathology.

Second, from the standpoint of clinical description, a search for the negative cognition *subtype* may prove fruitful in delimiting the heterogeneity of the depressive disorders.

A third reason for adequately testing the cognitive theories is that they have clear-cut *therapeutic and preventive implications* for depression. In addition, an adequate test of these theories may aid in understanding the causal mechanisms responsible for the success of cognitive therapy for depression.

Fourth, the hopelessness theory explicitly specifies *invulnerability* factors for depression. An accurate understanding of factors that protect against depression is crucial for a comprehensive theory of depression. Yet, little work has been conducted to uncover invulnerability factors for depression (but see Brown & Harris, 1978 for an exception).

A final reason for adequately testing the cognitive theories is that increases in understanding depression and nondepression from a cognitive perspective will help build a bridge between clinical and *experimental psychology*. Although researchers in several areas of psychology (e.g., neuropsychology and visual perception) have utilized the strategy of studying abnormal individuals as a means of developing principles of normal psychological functioning, clinical psychologists rarely have pursued this line of inquiry. Clinical investigators typically conduct research on depression simply to understand this disorder. Such research also can illuminate the functions of pervasive optimistic biases in normal cognition. These biases may be highly robust and have adaptive and/or evolutionary significance (e.g., Abramson & Alloy, 1981; Alloy & Abramson, 1979; Freud, 1917/1957; Greenwald, 1980; Martin, Abramson & Alloy, 1984; Tiger, 1979).

In this regard, a passage from Solzhenitsyn's (1973) writings on the destructive labor camps in the Gulag Archipelago is provocative. In discussing corruption of prisoners in the labor camps, Solzhenitsyn says he is not going to explain the cases of corruption. Why, he says, should we worry about explaining the house that in subzero weather loses its warmth? What needs to be explained, he goes on to say, is that there are houses which retain their warmth even in subzero weather. Analogously, perhaps what is to be explained by the depression researcher is not why certain people succumb to depression when confronted with the insults nature and our fellow humans deal to us all but rather why many people maintain a nondepressed state in what sometimes is the psychological equivalent of subzero temperatures. Work on the cognitive theories may illuminate not only how people may become depressed but also how they may maintain a positive state when confronted with adversity.

## SUMMARY

In summary, when integrated, the hopelessness theory and Beck's theory postulate the existence in nature of an as yet unidentified subtype of depression—negative cognition depression. Negative cognition depression is defined in terms of its hypothesized cause, symptoms, course, therapy, and prevention. Negative cognition depression may not map on to any currently diagnosed category of depression in a one-to-one fashion. Instead, this hypothesized subtype of depression may cut across existing categories of depression and, perhaps, even other types of psychopathology (e.g., anxiety disorders) and personality disorders (e.g., borderline personality disorder). The way to determine if negative cognition depression exists in nature is to test the hopelessness theory and Beck's theory. To say that negative cognition depression exists is simply to say that these theories are true. Preliminary tests of these theories are promising. We eagerly await further research to test whether negative cognition depression exists and conforms to its theoretical description.

**Authors' Note**: Preparation of this chapter was supported by a Romnes Fellowship from the University of Wisconsin, Biomedical Research Support Funds, and research grants from the University of Wisconsin and Northwestern University. We thank Rich Spritz for sharing his knowledge of medical disorders and the history of medicine with us. In addition, we thank Tony Ahrens, Ben Dykman, Laura Haack, Lucinda McClain, Doug Needles, Dan Romer, Donna Rose, and Carmelo Vazquez for many discussions about the concept of negative cognition depression.

### References

Abramson, L. Y. & Alloy, L. B. (1981). Depression, nondepression, and cognitive illusions: A reply to Schwartz. *Journal of Experimental Psychology: General, 110*, 436–447.

Abramson, L. Y., Alloy, L. B. & Metalsky, G. I. (1988a). The cognitive diathesis-stress theories of depression: Toward an adequate evaluation of the theories' validities. In L.B. Alloy (Ed.), *Cognitive processes in depression*. New York: Guilford.

Abramson, L. Y., Garber, J., Edwards, N. B. & Seligman, M.E.P. (1978). Expectancy changes in depression and schizophrenia. *Journal of Abnormal Psychology, 87*, 49–

74.

Abramson, L. Y., Metalsky, G. I. & Alloy, L. B. (in press). Hopelessness depression: A theory-based subtype of depression. *Psychological Review.*

Abramson, L. Y., Metalsky, G. I. & Alloy, L. B. (1988b). The hopelessness theory of depression: Does the research test the theory? In L.Y. Abramson (Ed.), *Social cognition and clinical psychology: A synthesis.* New York: Guilford.

Abramson. L. Y., Seligman, M.E.P. & Teasdale, J. (1978). Learned helplessness in humans: Critique and reformulation. *Journal of Abnormal Psychology, 87,* 49–74.

Alloy, L. B. (1982). The role of perceptions and attributions for response-outcome noncontingency in learned helplessness: A commentary and discussion. *Journal of Personality, 50,* 443–479.

Alloy, L. B. & Abramson, L. Y. (1979). Judgment of contingency in depressed and nondepressed students: Sadder but wiser? *Journal of Experimental Psychology: General, 108,* 441–485.

Alloy, L. B. & Abramson, L. Y. (1988). Depressive realism: Four theoretical perspectives. In L. B. Alloy (Ed.), *Cognitive processes in depression.* New York: Guilford.

Alloy, L. B., Clements, C. & Kolden, G. (1985). The cognitive diathesis-stress theories of depression: Therapeutic implications. In S. Reiss & R. Bootzin (Eds.), *Theoretical issues in behavior therapy.* New York: Academic Press.

Alloy, L. B., Hartlage, S. & Abramson, L. Y. (1988). Testing the cognitive diathesis-stress theories of depression: Issues of research design, conceptualization, and assessment. In L.B. Alloy (Ed.), *Cognitive processes in depression.* New York: Guilford.

Alloy, L. B., Kayne, N. T., Romer, D. & Crocker, J. (1989). Predicting depressive reactions in the classroom: A test of a cognitive diathesis-stress theory of depression with causal modeling techniques. Manuscript under editorial review.

Alloy, L. B., Kelly, K. A., Mineka, S. & Clements, C. M. (in press). Comorbidity in anxiety and depressive disorders: A helplessness/hopelessness perspective. In J.D. Maser & C.R. Cloninger (Eds.), *Comorbidity in anxiety and mood disorders.* Washington, D.C.: American Psychiatric Press, Inc.

Alloy, L. B., Peterson, C., Abramson, L. Y. & Seligman, M.E.P. (1984). Attributional style and the generality of learned helplessness. *Journal of Personality and Social Psychology, 46,* 681–687.

Anderson, C. A. & Arnoult, L. H. (1985). Attributional style and everyday problems in living: Depression, loneliness, and shyness. *Social Cognition, 3,* 16–35.

Anderson, C. A., Horowitz, L. M. & French, R. (1983). Attributional style of lonely and depressed people. *Journal of Personality and Social Psychology, 45,* 127–136.

Beach, S.R.H., Abramson, L. Y. & Levine, F. M. (1981). Attributional reformulation of learned helplessness and depression: Therapeutic implications. In J. F. Clarkin & H. I. Glazer (Eds.), *Depression: Behavioral and directive intervention strategies.* New York: Garland Press.

Beck, A. T. (1967). *Depression: Clinical, experimental, and theoretical aspects.* New York: Harper & Row.

Beck, A. T. (1976). *Cognitive therapy and the emotional disorders.* New York: International Universities Press.

Beck, A. T. (1987). Cognitive models of depression. *Journal of Cognitive Psychotherapy, An International Quarterly, 1,* 5–37.

Beck, A. T., Kovacs, M. & Weissman, A. (1975). Hopelessness and suicidal behavior: An overview. *Journal of the American Medical Association, 234,* 1146–1149.

Beck, A. T., Riskind, J. H., Brown, G. & Steer, R. A. (1988). Levels of hopelessness in DSM-III disorders: A partial test of content-specificity in depression. *Cognitive Therapy and Research, 12,* 459–469.

Beck, A. T., Rush, A. J., Shaw, B. F. & Emery, G. (1979). *Cognitive therapy of depression*. New York: Guilford.

Bolles, R. C. (1972). Reinforcement, expectancy, and learning. *Psychological Review, 79*, 394–409.

Bower, G. H. (1981). Mood and Memory. *American Psychologist, 36*, 129–148.

Boyd, J. H. & Weissman, M. M. (1982). Epidemiology. In E. S. Paykel (Ed.), *Handbook of affective disorders*. New York: Guilford Press.

Brewin, C. T. & Furnham, A. (1987). Dependency, self-criticism, and depressive attributional style. *British Journal of Clinical Psychology, 26*, 225–226.

Brown, G. W. & Harris, T. (1978). *Social origins of depression*. New York: The Free Press.

Brown, J. D. & Siegel, J. M. (1988). Attributions for negative life events and depression: The role of perceived control. *Journal of Personality and Social Psychology, 54*, 316–322.

Carver, C. S. & Gaines, J. G. (1987). Optimism, pessimism, and post-partum depression. *Cognitive Therapy and Research, 11*, 449–462.

Clark, A. (1983). Hypothetical constructs, circular reasoning, and criteria. *The Journal of Mind and Behavior, 4*, 1–12.

Cochran, S. D. & Hammen, C. L. (1985). Perceptions of stressful life events and depression: A test of attributional models. *Journal of Personality and Social Psychology, 1*, 48, 1562–1572.

Coryell, W. & Winokur, G. (1982). In E. S. Paykel (Ed.), *Handbook of affective disorders*. New York: Guilford Press.

Costello, C. G. (1972). Depression: Loss of reinforcers or loss of reinforcer effectiveness? *Behavior Therapy, 3*, 240–247.

Craighead, W. E. (1980). Away from a unitary model of depression. *Behavior Therapy, 11*, 122–128.

Crocker, J., Alloy, L. B. & Kayne, N. T. (1988). Attributional style, depression, and perceptions of consensus for events. *Journal of Personality and Social Psychology, 54*, 840–846.

Depue, R. A. & Monroe, S. M. (1978). Learned helplessness in the perspective of the depressive disorders. *Journal of Abnormal Psychology, 87*, 3–20.

Dweck, C. S. & Licht, B. G. (1980). Learned helplessness and intellectual achievement. In J. Garber and M.E.P. Seligman (Eds.), *Human helplessness: Theory and application*. New York: Academic Press.

Eaves, G. & Rush, A. J. (1984). Cognitive patterns in symptomatic and remitted unipolar major depression. *Journal of Abnormal Psychology, 93*, 31–40.

Ellis, A. (1977). The basic clinical theory of rational-emotive therapy. In A. Ellis and R. Grieger (Eds.), *Handbook of rational-emotive therapy*. New York: Springer.

Evans, M. D., Hollon, S. D., DeRubeis, R. J., Piasecki, J. M., Grove, W. M., Garvey, M. J. & Tuason, V. B. (1989). Differential relapse following cognitive therapy, pharmacotherapy, and combined cognitive-pharmacotherapy for depression: IV. A 2-year follow-up of the CPT project. Manuscript submitted for publication.

Festinger, L. A. (1954). A theory of social comparison processes. *Human Relations, 7*, 117–140.

Freud, S. (1917/1957). Mourning and melancholia. In J. Strachey (Ed. and trans.), *Standard edition of the complete psychological works of Sigmund Freud*. (Vol. 14). London: Hogarth Press.

Gillespie, R. D. (1929). Clinical differentiation of types of depression. *Guy Hospital Reports, 79*, 306–344.

Gong-Guy, E. & Hammen, C. (1980). Causal perceptions of stressful life events in depressed and nondepressed clinic outpatients. *Journal of Abnormal Psychology*, *89*, 662–669.

Greenwald, A. G. (1980). The totalitarian ego: Fabrication and revision of personal history. *American Psychologist*, *35*, 603–618.

Halberstadt, L. J., Andrews, D., Metalsky, G. I. & Abramson, L. Y. (1984). Helplessness, hopelessness, and depression: A review of progress and future directions. In N.S. Endler & J. Hunt (Eds.), *Personality and behavior disorders*. New York: Wiley.

Hamilton, E. W. & Abramson, L. Y. (1983). Cognitive patterns in major depressive disorder: A longitudinal study in a hospital setting. *Journal of Abnormal Psychology*, *92*, 173–184.

Hammen, C. & Cochran, S. (1981). Cognitive correlates of life stress and depression in college students. *Journal of Abnormal Psychology*, *90*, 23–27.

Hammen, C. & de Mayo, R. (1982). Cognitive correlates of teacher stress and depressive symptoms: Implications for attributional models of depression. *Journal of Abnormal Psychology*, *91*, 96–101.

Hammen, C., Marks, T., Mayol, A. & de Mayo, R. (1985). Depressive self-schemas, life stress, and vulnerability to depression. *Journal of Abnormal Psychology*, *94*, 308–319.

Ickes, W. & Layden, M. A. (1978). Attributional styles. In J. Harvey, W. Ickes & R. Kidd (Eds.), *New directions in attribution research* (Vol. 2). Hillsdale, NJ: Erlbaum.

Janoff-Bulman, R. (1979). Characterological versus behavioral self-blame: Inquiries into depression and rape. *Journal of Personality and Social Psychology*, 37, 1798–1809.

Kazdin, A. E., French, N. H., Unis, A. S., Esveldt-Dawson, K. & Sherick, R. B. (1983). Hopelessness, depression, and suicidal intent among psychiatrically disturbed inpatient children. *Journal of Consulting and Clinical Psychology*, *51*, 504–510.

Keller, M. B. & Lavori, P. W. (1984). Double depression, major depression, and dysthymia: Distinct entities or different phases of a single disorder? *Psychopharmacology Bulletin*, *20*, 399–402.

Keller, M. B. & Shapiro, R. W. (1982). "Double depression." Superimposition of acute depressive episodes on chronic depressive disorders. *American Journal of Psychiatry*, *139*, 438–442.

Kelley, H. H. (1967). Attribution theory in social psychology. In D. Levine (Ed.), *Nebraska symposium on motivation* (Volume 15). Lincoln: University of Nebraska Press.

Kendell, R. E. (1968). *The classification of depression illness*. London: Oxford University Press.

Klein, D. F. (1974). Endogenomorphic depression: Conceptual and terminological revision. *Archives of General Psychiatry*, *31*, 447–454.

Klerman, G. L. (1978). The evolution of a scientific nosology. In J.C. Shershow (Ed.), *Schizophrenia: Science and practice*. Cambridge, Mass.: Harvard University Press.

Klinger, E. (1975). Consequences of commitment to and disengagement from incentives. *Psychological Review*, *82*, 1–25.

Kraepelin, E. (1913). Manic-depressive insanity and paranoia. In *Textbook of psychiatry* (R.M. Barclay, trans). Edinburgh: Livingstone.

Kuiper, N. A., Olinger, L. J. & MacDonald, M. R. (1988). Vulnerability and episodic cognitions in a self-worth contingency model of depression. In L. B. Alloy (Ed.), *Cognitive processes in depression*. New York: Guilford Press.

Lloyd, C. (1980a). Life events and depressive disorder reviewed: I. Events as predisposing factors. *Archives of General Psychiatry*, *37*, 529–535.

Lloyd, C. (1980b). Life events and depressive disorder reviewed: II. Events as precipitating factors. *Archives of General Psychiatry*, *37*, 541–548.

Lloyd, C., Zisook, S., Click, M., Jr. & Jaffe, K. E. (1981). Life events and response to antidepressants. *Journal of Human Stress*, *7*, 2–15.

Martin, D., Abramson, L.Y. & Alloy, L. B. (1984). The illusion of control for self and others in depressed and nondepressed college students. *Journal of Personality and Social Psychology*, *46*, 125–136.

McArthur, L. A. (1972). The how and what of why: Some determinants and consequences of causal attributions. *Journal of Personality and Social Psychology*, *22*, 171–193.

McLemore, C. W. & Benjamin, L. S. (1979). Whatever happened to interpersonal diagnosis? A psychosocial alternative to DSM-III. *American Psychologist*, *34*, 17–34.

Metalsky, G. I., Abramson, L. Y., Seligman, M.E.P., Semmel, A. & Peterson, C. (1982). Attributional styles and life events in the classroom: Vulnerability and invulnerability to depressive mood reactions. *Journal of Personality and Social Psychology*, *43*, 612–617.

Metalsky, G. I., Halberstadt, L. J. & Abramson, L. Y. (1987). Vulnerability to depressive mood reactions: Toward a more powerful test of the diathesis-stress and causal mediation components of the reformulated theory of depression. *Journal of Personality and Social Psychology*, *52*, 386–393.

Minkoff, K., Bergman, E., Beck, A. T. & Beck, R. (1973). Hopelessness, depression and attempted suicide. *American Journal of Psychiatry*, *130*, 455–459.

Morse, S. & Gergen, K. (1970). Social comparison, self-consistency, and the concept of self. *Journal of Personality and Social Psychology*, *16*, 148–156.

Neisser, U. (1967). *Cognitive psychology*. New York: Appleton-Century-Crofts.

Nolen-Hoeksema, S., Girgus, J. S. & Seligman, M.E.P. (1986). Learned helplessness in children: A longitudinal study of depression, achievement, and explanatory style. *Journal of Personality and Social Psychology*, *51*, 435–442.

Olinger, L. J., Kuiper, N. A. & Shaw, B. F. (1987). Dysfunctional attitudes and stressful life events: An interactive model of depression. *Cognitive Therapy and Research*, *11*, 25–40.

Persons, J. B. & Rao, P. A. (1985). Longitudinal study of cognitions, life events, and depression in psychiatric inpatients. *Journal of Abnormal Psychology*, *94*, 51–63.

Petrie, K. & Chamberlain, K. (1983). Hopelessness and social desirability as moderator variables in predicting suicidal behavior. *Journal of Consulting and Clinical Psychology*, *51*, 485–487.

Rholes, W. S., Riskind, J. H. & Neville, B. (1985). The relationship of cognitions and hopelessness to depression and anxiety. *Social Cognition*, *3*, 36–50.

Riskind, J. H. & Rholes, W. S. (1984). Cognitive accessibility and the capacity of cognitions to predict future depression: A theoretical note. *Cognitive Therapy and Research*, *8*, 1–12.

Riskind, J. H., Rholes, W. S., Brannon, A. M. & Burdick, C. A. (1987). Attributions and expectations: A confluence of vulnerabilities in mild depression in a college student population. *Journal of Personality and Social Psychology*, *53*, 349–354.

Rose, D. T. & Abramson, L. Y. (1987). *Negative cognition depression: Preliminary results from a longitudinal study to test the cognitive theories of depression*. Paper presented at the meeting of the American Psychological Association, New York.

Rosenberg, M. (1965). *Society and the adolescent self-image*. Princeton University Press.

Rush, A. J., Weissenburger, J. & Eaves, G. (1986). Do thinking patterns predispose depressive symptoms? *Cognitive Therapy and Research*, *10*, 225–236.

Sacks, C. H. & Bugental, D. B. (1987). Attributions as moderators of affective and behavioral responses to social failure. *Journal of Personality and Social Psychology*, *53*, 939–947.

Schachter, S. (1959). *The psychology of affiliation.* Stanford, CA: Stanford University Press.

Silverman, J. S., Silverman, J. A. & Eardley, D. A. (1984). Reply to J. H. Riskind and R. Steer. *Archives of General Psychiatry, 41,* 112.

Skinner, H. A. (1981). Toward the integration of classification theory and methods. *Journal of Abnormal Psychology, 90,* 68–87.

Solzhenitsyn, A. I. (1973). *The Gulag Archipelago, 1918–1956.* New York: Harper & Row.

Stanbury, J. B., Wyngaarden, J. B., Fredrickson, D. S., Goldstein, J. L. & Brown, M. S. (1983). *The metabolic basis of inherited disease.* (5th Ed.) New York: McGraw-Hill.

Tesser, A. & Campbell, J. (1983). Self-definition and self-evaluation maintenance. In J. Suls and A. G. Greenwald (Eds.), *Psychological perspectives on the self* (Vol. 2). Hillsdale, N.J.: Erlbaum.

Tiger, L. (1979). *Optimism: The biology of hope.* New York: Simon & Schuster.

Weiner, B. (1985). An attributional theory of achievement motivation and emotion. *Psychological Review, 92,* 548–573.

Weissman, A. & Beck, A. T. (1979). The dysfunctional attitude scale. Paper presented at the Annual Meeting of the American Psychological Association, New York, N.Y.

Zis, A. P. & Goodwin, F. K. (1979). Major affective disorder as a recurrent illness: A critical review. *Archives of General Psychiatry, 36,* 835–839.

Zubin, J. E. & Spring, B. (1977). Vulnerability: A new view of schizophrenia. *Journal of Abnormal Psychology, 86,* 103–126.

# 5

# Does the Depressive Self-Schema Really Exist?

Lisa A. Spielman
*New York University*

John A. Bargh
*New York University*

KEY WORDS: self-schema, construct accessibility, distortion, encoding, memory, cognitive structure

Depression is one of the most well-researched conditions in the psychological literature. Much of the research emphasis lately has been on social-cognitive distortions associated with depression. For example, there is considerable evidence that depressives differ from nondepressed people in their attributional style. Taylor and Brown (1988) found that nondepressives tend to show self-enhancing effects when making attributions of causality for successes or failures, but depressives do not show this self-enhancing effect (see also Rhodewalt & Agustsdottir, 1986). Thus, nondepressives tend to make external attributions for a failure experience ("The test was too hard for anyone to do well"), but internal attributions for a success ("I did well because I'm smart;" e.g., Bradley, 1978). On the other hand, depressed individuals show the opposite attributional pattern, accepting responsibility for failure while downplaying their own influence in successful outcomes.

In accord with Beck's (1967) model of depression, there is also evidence that depressives have negative views of themselves, their world, and their futures (see reviews by Coyne & Gotlib, 1983; Segal, 1988). What researchers have only just begun to explore is why some people become depressed while others do not. Because some people can withstand numerous negative life events without showing signs of clinical depression, while others seem to become depressed without an obvious external cause, it seems that environmental factors alone (i.e., differential numbers or severity of negative life events) cannot supply a sufficient explanation. After all, if people *only* became depressed when terrible things happened to them, we probably would not consider the condition a mental illness, but rather an understandable, logical response to unfortunate circumstances.

Beck (1967, 1976; Beck, Rush, Shaw & Emery, 1979) hypothesized that there exists, in some individuals, a cognitive predisposition toward depression. That is, a vulnerability to depression may initially be acquired through painful early experiences, which form the basis of a latent cognitive structure or "schema" about the self. This latent structure becomes "activated," or triggered by some event later on in life. When this occurs, the latent structure is used to interpret incoming information, resulting in a negative assessment of the self.

Of course, all human information processing requires some process of interpretation or categorization to render the environmental stimulation comprehensible and meaningful to the person (see Bruner, 1957). The difference in the case of depressives, according to Beck (1967), is the negativity of the interpretative "frame" through which the environmental information concerning the self is filtered. Because this negative "self-schema" operates outside of the person's awareness to drive the interpretation of environmental events, the negative thoughts appear to the person as phenomenally immediate and derived naturally from the event. In short, the depressive is said to possess a long-term, stable, active cognitive structure that, when confronted by outside information, serves to direct automatically an interpretation of that information. The result is a negative assessment of oneself.

The speculation that there exists a particular cognitive structure, a "depressive self-schema" that differentiates people who are and who are not predisposed to become depressed, has generated a great deal of research (see reviews by Dobson, 1986; Segal, 1988). Why has the schema concept proven to be of such heuristic value to researchers? Certainly the possible identification of a predisposing factor for depression would be a valuable tool for the prevention and treatment of the disorder. Moreover, as clinicians have noted (e.g., Andersen & Lyon, 1987), no matter what the circumstances, no matter what the evidence, the depressive tends to remain resolutely negative in his evaluations of him or herself. The identification of a cognitive structure potentially capable of explaining the globality of depressive responding—its generalizability across all sorts of situations relating to the self—is very appealing indeed. Finally, as oftentimes depression does not seem to be the direct result of a negative life event, a cognitive structure that mediates the meaning drawn from life events is likely to be responsible for the dysphoric mood.

What is the nature of this hypothetical cognitive structure? As noted above, a great deal of research has centered around the concept of a *schema*, which is a particular type of cognitive structure. We will examine some of this research, and discuss some of the questions and problems that have arisen as a result of the findings. Then we will present an alternative to the schema hypothesis and present some preliminary research bearing on this alternative hypothesis. But before we examine the research, we must first be clear as to the precise theoretical nature and definition of a cognitive schema, and whether the characteristics of depressive thought are best represented in terms of a schematic structure.

## WHAT IS A SCHEMA?

Bartlett, who with Piaget was one of the originators of the schema notion, considered schematic functioning to be a nonconscious mental process; schemas were assumed to exert their processing effects outside of one's awareness, with the details of such processing not available to introspection (Bartlett, 1932). Schemas were described as highly organized and interconnected structures composed of representations of prior knowledge (that is, generic, abstract information), rather than of specific life events (episodic information; see Tulving, 1983). This last point highlights the difference between the schema notion and the associationist principles of the British Empiricist tradition, which held that all memories were exact traces of the incoming information (see Brewer & Nakamura, 1984).

This is not to say that episodic information had no place in Bartlett's theory. He argued that the act of recalling past events from memory was a joint function of the content of the abstract schema relevant to the event and some specific episodic information about the event itself. Thus, memory for any event is actually a reconstruction based on a combination of these two types of information. This "partial reconstructive memory theory" has been accepted in one form or another almost universally by modern memory theorists (see reviews by Brewer & Nakamura, 1984; Hastie, Park & Weber, 1984).

Modern schema theory is characterized by the assumption that certain phenomena cannot be accounted for by simple constructs, and require more complex mental entities comprised of interrelated constructs in order to represent higher levels of abstract thought (e.g., Minsky, 1975; Rumelhart & Ortony, 1977). In particular, modern theorists have begun to understand the necessary *structural* characteristics of a schema. The theoretical structure of a schema derives from the idea of associative networks, in which a specific feature represents a node, and various nodes linked together form the representation of some concept (Hebb, 1949). To use a very simple example, the representation of the concept *chair* would consist of various common features linked together: the features "seat," "back," and "legs" would constitute the nodes; the co-occurrence of these features in time and space would activate the links between them, and the identification of the object as a "chair" would be the end result.

The activation of a representation depends upon previous experiences with the concept in the environment, which serve to establish the links between features in the first place. These interrelated links between features (or constructs) form the basis of a schematic structure. Because of the interconnectedness of the constructs within the schema, the activation of any given element of a schema should, in turn, through spreading activation, increase the accessibility (i.e., the level of activation) of all other elements in the schema. That is, the activation of a given construct in the system spreads throughout the remainder of the system, because the activation travels along the links between the constructs. It is this spread of activation, resulting in all-or-none activation of the entire structure whenever any single element of it becomes active, that distinguishes a schematic structure from other types of cognitive structures (see Hayes-Roth, 1977).

Most of the recent research on schemas concerns their effects on encoding and memory processes. It is fairly well established that increased attention to a given stimulus results in better memory for that stimulus (e.g., Fisk & Schneider, 1984). However, it seems that less attention is often paid to schema-consistent information, as it corresponds to the usual and expected occurrences in the environment (i.e., what happens regularly in that situation). As this type of information can be processed relatively automatically (i.e., out of conscious awareness, and without requiring the use of attentional resources), there is less need for additional, conscious processing (see Bargh & Thein, 1985; Logan, 1980). Yet experimental results show that schema-consistent information is usually very well retained despite the paucity of active attention it usually receives (see reviews by Alba & Hasher, 1983; Hastie, 1981; Higgins & Bargh, 1987).

It would seem that the amount of attention an event receives is not the sole determinant of the probability that it will be accessible in memory and thus likely to be recalled, and thus that some other factor must be responsible for the superior recall of schema-consistent information. This factor is the organizational function of the schema, which operates to make information stored within the schema highly accessible during retrieval operations (Mandler, 1968). A schema serves as a framework by which new information can be integrated with existing knowledge (see Minsky, 1975; Neisser, 1976). This new information then is integrated with the existing knowledge in the schema, and the interaction between old and new information results in the formation of associative pathways that increase the likelihood of later retrieving the new information (Hastie, 1984; Srull, Lichtenstein & Rothbart, 1985). Subsequently, once the schema itself is accessed during the act of remembering (and it will be because it shares most of the abstract features of what is attempted to be remembered at the time), specific instances that are encoded in terms of the schema also become easily accessed (see Craik & Tulving, 1975).

Experimental evidence has shown that subjects given a recognition test containing both previously presented and unpresented information attempt to reconstruct what had been presented, rather than simply recalling the information directly (see review by Brewer & Nakamura, 1984). Apparently, the presented information is so well integrated into its relevant schema that direct access to the originally presented information becomes no longer possible. This integration effect also appears to become even stronger over time.

## THE DEPRESSIVE SELF-SCHEMA

How, then, does all of this apply to depression? First of all, the highly organized, relatively stable nature of a schema makes it a possible candidate for the latent predisposing cognitive structure proposed by Beck (1967). A schema is constructed from prior knowledge, just as Beck's hypothetical structure is derived from painful early experiences. The interconnected structure of a schema is consistent with the apparent globality of negative thinking in depression, in that the activation of any one portion of the schema should lead to activation of the rest of the structure. Thus, although incoming information may be relatively specific (e.g., failure at some task), the spread of activation may cause more overgeneralized effects (e.g., activation of all the other negative self-conceptions). Furthermore, one is unaware of the operation of a schema; the phenomenal experience is that no cognitive interpretation was necessary, and that the perceived features exist in the environment, not in the head (see Bargh, 1989; Bargh, Litt, Pratto & Spielman, 1989). This could explain the clinical observation that depressives not only come to negative interpretations about themselves based on their experiences, but that these perceptions are felt by the depressive to be inherently obvious and unquestionably valid (see Andersen & Lyon, 1987; Beck, 1967). The *perceptual fluency*, or ease with which perceptual interpretations are made, has been shown to be related to the degree of certainty with which the interpretation is held (see Jacoby & Kelley, 1987).

The process by which new information is integrated into a schema is also consistent with the phenomenology of depression. Because the schema provides the framework by which all new information is appraised, even supposedly conflicting evidence (e.g., success on some task) is colored by the content of the existing schema. Thus, the depressive might respond to a success by (nonconsciously) reinterpreting the event to be consistent with the existing negative self-knowledge, believing, for example, that "the task was too easy to be a valid test" (see Crocker, Hannah & Weber, 1983). Finally, schematic effects on retrieval allow the depressive to back up his or her claims with prior evidence, supporting the conclusion that "in the past, I have always done badly on tasks of this sort." Because new experiences are routinely reinterpreted at encoding to be in line with existing conceptions, recall of past experiences is necessarily colored by the interpretation given at the time of encoding. In this way, the original, unbiased information may not be available for recall, only the transformed, interpreted form of it (e.g., Higgins & McCann, 1984).

## INTERPRETATIONAL DIFFICULTIES WITH EXISTING RESEARCH EVIDENCE

### Self-Report Questionnaire Studies Cannot Assess Schematicity

What types of evidence would confirm the hypothesis that it is a schematic structure that either predisposes a person to depression, or at least has a hand in the maintenance of the cognitive distortions which accompany depression? First of all, several researchers have attempted to design questionnaires with which to measure the depressive self-schema (e.g., the Dysfunctional Attitude Scale; Weissman, 1979). These scales have been shown to correlate significantly with various cognitive-distortion measures (Blackburn, Jones & Lewin, 1987; Giles & Rush, 1983; Holland, Kendall & Lumry, 1986), leading researchers to conclude that evidence does exist for the presence of a depressive self-schema.

These questionnaire studies do provide evidence for the existence of valence differences between depressed and nondepressed subjects, by showing that depressives have negative thoughts whereas nondepressives do not. But valence differences in thought can as plausibly be considered a *consequence* of depression as a *cause*, and questionnaire studies do little to distinguish between the two. Further, because a schema is said to represent a stable, automatically activated structure, a paper and pencil measure is not an appropriate assessment technique for assessing the existence of a schema. Questionnaires require conscious, deliberate responding, and may not reflect automatic functioning, as it is clear that people often do not have introspective access to their own thought processes (Nisbett & Wilson, 1977), especially those involved in perceptual interpretation and categorization processes (e.g., Bargh, 1989; Posner, 1978). For example, the accessibility, or activation, of a given construct through priming has been shown to influence interpretations and judgments, even though subjects were unaware of the influence of priming (e.g., Higgins, Rholes & Jones, 1977). Thus, the questionnaire results can just as easily be explained by non-schematic cognitive processing. If constructs have become temporarily accessible (activated) through priming—that is, through reading and thinking about the ideas presented in the questionnaire—then the results cannot be taken as conclusive evidence for a long-term, automatic form of processing.

Moreover, differences in self-reported thought *content* alone is not conclusive evidence in favor of the existence of a specific schema. Many other types of cognitive structures or processes would also be expected to produce such content differences. What is distinctive about a schema is its structure, not its content. The key ingredient of a schema is the *interconnectedness* of its component constructs, not merely their presence. In a non-schematic account, a given construct may be active without necessarily causing the activation of other constructs, because of the lack of associative connections between them. This would be impossible in a schema conceptualization, because activation is said to spread along the links, resulting in an all-or-none activation of the entire schema (Hayes-Roth, 1977). Thus, the demonstration of spreading activation among component constructs is essential to demonstrate schematic processing.

## Defining a Long-Term Schema in Terms of Short-Term Symptoms

A second assessment technique has been widely used in a program of research by Kuiper and his colleagues: self-referential encoding (Derry & Kuiper, 1981; Dobson & Shaw, 1987; Kuiper & MacDonald, 1982, 1983; Kuiper & Olinger, 1986; Kuiper, Olinger, MacDonald & Shaw, 1985). In this paradigm, subjects classify each of a set of depressed-content and a set of nondepressed-content adjectives as to their self-descriptiveness. In addition to differential patterns of responses between depressives and nondepressives, the pattern of incidental recall of these adjectives is also assessed. Typically, depressives have been found to rate more negative content adjectives as self-descriptive than do nondepressives, and also show higher rates of incidental recall for these adjectives. The recall findings are especially important because one of the properties of a schematic structure is to facilitate the retrieval of schema-consistent information, even when subjects do not expect the memory task (e.g., Brewer & Nakamura, 1984; Hastie, 1981).

A difficulty with drawing conclusions about a depressive schema on the basis of these investigations has to do with the nature of the adjectives selected to assess self-referent encoding patterns. Of the set of positive content adjectives, the majority (23 of 30) were found to represent long-term, stable personality dispositions, as classified by Allport and Odbert (1936). The reverse is true in the case of the negative adjectives: only 7 were found to be dispositional terms; the majority were classified by Allport and Odbert (1936) as reflecting temporary states (Bargh, Panter, Pratto & Spielman, 1988; Spielman & Bargh, 1988). Since, by definition, depressed subjects in these studies were currently experiencing depressive affect, it is unremarkable that they showed high endorsement and recall rates for adjectives that describe their current mood at the time. As symptoms of depression are only manifested when one is in a depressive episode, the inclusion of symptom concepts in the self-concept should covary with the state of depression, and such concepts should not be contained within the self-schema when one is not currently depressed. A self-schema is generally considered to be more permanent than this, and to be constituted by long-term trait concepts instead of short-term state concepts such as those corresponding to symptoms of depression. This operationalization of the depressive self-schema in terms of symptom concepts instead of trait concepts may be one reason why prospective studies of the etiology of depression have failed to find any causal role for the depressive schema (e.g., Dobson & Shaw, 1987; Hammen, Marks, Mayol & de Mayo, 1985; Kuiper et al., 1985).

The repeated finding that depressive self-schema processing effects, as assessed by the self-referential encoding task, occur only when the individual is currently depressed has led to the conclusion that the differential processing of the negative content by depressives may be due to the congruency between the subject's current mood and the valence of the stimulus material (Hammen, Marks, Mayol & de Mayo, 1985). According to this interpretation, material in memory that matches the current mood becomes more accessible due to an apparent linkage between memory nodes sharing the same positive or negative valence (e.g., Isen, 1984; Isen, Shalker, Clark & Karp, 1978). This "mood congruency" hypothesis has gained the ascendancy in current thinking about depressive cognition (see Blaney, 1986; Segal, 1988), but our opinion is that the effects of a long-term, stable cognitive structure have not yet received a fair test because of the faulty operationalization of the structure in term of symptom concepts.

There does exist evidence that there is more than just a mood-accessibility effect going on in depressogenic cognition. Gotlib and McCann (1984) used a variation of the Stroop test to test for the presence of automatic processing by negative constructs in depression. This task requires subjects to name the color in which words are presented; the extent to which subjects unintentionally and uncontrollably (because it is irrelevant to their conscious task) process the meaning of the word causes them to take longer to name the color, as attentional resources are diverted from the color-naming task (e.g., Logan, 1980). Gotlib and McCann (1984) presented depressed and nondepressed subjects with sets of depressed, manic, and neutral trait terms for color-naming. Their essential findings were that nondepressives' showed approximately equal response latencies for all three types of words; depressives showed interference effects (slower response times) to depressed terms only.

In a second study, Gotlib and McCann (1984) manipulated the mood of nondepressed subjects to be either happy or sad, and found no differences in color-naming latencies across the three types of words as a function of the temporary mood state of the subjects. Whereas it appears that temporary mood effects can be ruled out in this study in favor of an account in terms of construct accessibility, one still cannot distinguish on the basis of the results between a schema model and a model in which the separate constructs related to depression are not associated in a single structure. We turn to this alternative model in more detail in the next section.

There are also findings from other literatures that call the existence of an interrelated self-schema into doubt. Fenigstein and Levine's (1984) work on the self, for example, has shown that specific parts of the self-concept can be activated in isolation (that is, independently from other content areas). They found that they could induce not only a general self-focus, but also a specific focus on taking causal responsibility for an event using a story-writing task. Subjects who were not in the self-focused condition indicated less responsibility for the events. The most interesting finding of this investigation was that subjects in the two focus conditions did not differ in domains other than that of responsibility. This lends support to the idea that the self-concept is not structured as a single, monolithic, thoroughly interrelated schema (see also Linville, 1985). If it were, one would expect activation to spread along the network and influence components of the self-concept other than responsibility, which Fenigstein and Levine (1984) found was not the case in their study.

## ALTERNATIVES TO THE SCHEMA EXPLANATION

What are the other types of structures or processes that might be implicated in depression? One possibility, already alluded to above, is that depressive cognition is characterized by a difference in the content of accessible social constructs. As we have noted above, a construct accessibility account is able to explain many of the findings that are taken as supportive of a depressive self-schema. In particular, it is possible that depressives possess a number of *chronically* accessible negative constructs—that is, constructs that are constantly activated and thus most likely to be called into service for the interpretation of social information (see Moretti & Shaw, 1989).

Higgins and his colleagues (Higgins & King, 1981; Higgins, King & Mavin, 1982) have identified two important individual differences with reference to chronically accessible constructs. First, people differ in the content of the constructs *available* to them—that is, the actual presence or absence of particular constructs— because of differences in the frequency with which they have experienced various kinds of social behavior in their interactions with others. For example, Amy may possess the interpersonal construct of *ruthlessness*, while Meg may not. Second, among those constructs one has available, there are differences in their accessibility, or their likelihood of being applied in the interpretation of environmental informational input. Thus, both Amy and Alison may possess the concept of *honesty* (i.e., have it available for application to input), but it may be chronically accessible (that is, at a higher constant level of activation and thus likelihood of use) only for one of them.

Thus, one possibility is that depressed individuals possess negative constructs that nondepressives do not (i.e., a difference in availability). Another possibility is that both depressives and nondepressives possess negative constructs, but these constructs are chronically accessible only for depressives, causing them to be used with much more frequency (see Bargh & Tota, 1988, for a further consideration of such possible models). How would this accessibility account explain depression? First of all, if environmental input is ambiguous, the accessibility of a given construct can affect its categorization and thus the meaning ascribed to it (Bruner, 1957; Higgins & King, 1981). That is, if the individual has negative constructs chronically accessible, it is therefore more likely that an ambiguous event will be seen as negative. Thus, like the self-schema hypothesis, the accessibility approach allows for an explanation of why depressives see "borderline" events as negative.

Because the accessibility of constructs determines the categorization and subsequent interpretation of an event, there is no need for an individual to consciously or effortfully interpret the event. The effortlessness of the negative interpretation is attributed by the individual to the qualities of the event, leading to the phenomenal experience of certainty (Bargh, 1989; Jacoby & Kelley, 1987). In other words, other possible interpretations of the event do not occur to the depressive, not even the possibility that alternatives do exist. The person thus experiences the feeling of certainty in the negative interpretation that, as noted above, characterizes depressive thinking.

One by-product of this categorization process may be the concurrent activation of similar past occurrences stored in memory to the extent they share features with the input, as predicted by Logan's (1988) retrieval account of automaticity effects. That is, once the event is recognized as a negative one, other negative events may also become accessible in memory (see Isen, 1984), thus leading to the globality, or overgeneralization, that is characteristic of depression. It can be derived from Logan's (1988) model that a single perceived negative event for the depressive can thus automatically call to mind many others from the past in a variety of life domains, forcing an immediate global negative evaluation of self and a diffused disconsolate affective reaction.

## A TEST OF SCHEMATIC STRUCTURE

Based on the above considerations, our position is that the question of the existence of the depressive self-schema is still open. One technique for assessing the structural characteristics of thought processes, the semantic priming paradigm, has been employed in several investigations in our laboratory. We now turn to a study (Spielman & Bargh, 1988) designed to directly test a schematic account versus an accessibility account.

In this experiment, depressed and nondepressed subjects were asked to decide whether or not a stimulus word, presented on a computer screen, was a real or a nonsense word. Subjects were selected on the basis of Beck Depression Inventory (BDI) scores. To guard against the improper categorization of the subjects into depression group, the BDI was administered twice: once at the beginning of the semester, and once at the end of the experimental session. It should be noted that, although subjects in this study were university students, BDI scores for our depressed group compared favorably with clinically depressed populations used in previous research (e.g., Derry & Kuiper, 1981; see Bargh & Tota, 1988, for a further discussion of these issues).

The lexical decision paradigm has been shown in previous research (e.g., Collins & Loftus, 1975; Meyer & Schvaneveldt, 1971) to detect links between highly associated constructs in semantic memory (e.g., BLACK—WHITE, DOCTOR—NURSE, etc.). Each target word is preceded by a prime word, with less than 350 msec between the two presentations. This very brief period between the prime and the target is so short that a conscious expectancy for what the target word will be has no time to develop (Neely, 1977).

If the prime and the target concepts are semantically associated in memory, the response latency for the target word is short, compared to the time it takes to judge the target member of a semantically unrelated word pair. This is because the activation of the prime concept automatically spreads to the target concept, so that when the target word is presented, less attention is needed to respond to the target (Logan, 1980).

For example, when the stimulus word "DOCTOR" appears, it activates its corresponding representation automatically in memory. This activation spreads along links between the concept of DOCTOR and other concepts in memory, resulting in the activation of the concept of NURSE. When the stimulus word "NURSE" appears for lexical judgment, its associated concept thus is already activated, and consequently requires less time to process the stimulus. Therefore, the time it takes to judge whether "NURSE" is a word when it is preceded by "DOCTOR" is less than the time it takes to judge "NURSE" when it is preceded by a semantically unrelated word (e.g., "TABLE").

Thus, if depressed content constructs are linked in memory, as in a schematic structure, the presentation of related prime-target pairs should result in shorter lexical decision response latencies than the presentation of unrelated pairs. In addition, because a schema is supposed to represent a long-term, stable cognitive structure, there should be differences in the priming effect between construct pairs that represent long-term traits, and those that represent short-term symptoms. One would not expect to find facilitation effects for pairs involving symptom terms, because the constructs corresponding to them are merely markers of the episode state of depression (e.g., Hammen et al., 1985; Kuiper et al., 1985) and so theoretically should not be part of the relatively permanent self-schema.

With this in mind, four sets of stimulus words were developed: depressed content trait terms, depressed content symptom terms, nondepressed content trait terms, and nondepressed content symptom terms. Six types of word pairs were presented for judgment: trait—trait, symptom—symptom, trait—symptom, symptom—trait, baseline—trait, and baseline—symptom. All of the pairs were content-consistent (that is, only depressed content words were presented with other depressed content words; and the same was the case for nondepressed content words). The baseline primes, for comparison purposes, consisted of repetitions of a letter (e.g., "BBBBB," "XXXXX"). In addition, several semantically related pairs were included as manipulation checks on the priming task (e.g., BREAD—BUTTER).

The prediction was that if a depressive self-schema does exist, one would expect to find facilitation effects (shorter response times to the target word) for depressed content trait pairs as compared to baseline—depressed trait pairs. This result, however, should only be true of depressed subjects. On the other hand, if the chronic accessibility account of depression outlined above is more reflective of depressive cognitive processing, one would not expect to find any facilitation effects due to the prime word preceding the target. This is because there should be no associative links between the prime and target concept over which activation could spread. Instead, one would simply expect to find faster response times in the depressed subjects to *any* depressed content target word, regardless of the prime, due to the greater accessibility and ease of activation of the target concept itself.

The results of the study were supportive of the chronic accessibility explanation. No reliable priming effects were obtained; all main effects and interactions involving the prime factor were nonsignificant at $p > .15$. Although this result does not technically conform to the $p > .25$ convention desirable to show support for the null hypothesis, these results indicate that the presence of a related prime word prior to the target word made no difference as to how quickly subjects could respond to the target. Importantly, such priming effects *were* obtained for the manipulation check pairs, demonstrating that the test was sensitive to the presence of structural interrelations, if they did exist. Instead, a significant Group X Content interaction was obtained ($F(1, 34) = 6.79, p = .02$). Simple effects within this interaction revealed that depressives were reliably faster than nondepressives in responding to both depressed symptom and depressed trait content adjectives ($Ms = 596$ versus $666$ milliseconds; $p < .05$), whereas the two groups did not differ in their latency of processing the positive content ($Ms = 568$ versus $595$ milliseconds; $p > .25$).

The lack of a significant priming effect strongly suggests that schematic structure—that is, interrelations among the constructs allowing for spreading activation—does not exist. On the other hand, the finding that depressives responded faster to depressed content than did nondepressives regardless of the type of prime that was presented before each instance of that content, supports the existence of accessible negative social-perceptual constructs in depression—as do the results of many other studies (see review by Segal, 1988).

## CONCLUSIONS

In the search for an individual difference variable that can help to explain why some people become depressed in the wake of negative life events and some do not, considerable research has focused on the concept of a cognitive structure that mediates the interpretation of those life events. People who are vulnerable to becoming depressed are presumed to derive more negative self-directed meanings from their interactions with others than do people who don't become depressed given equivalent provocation from the social environment. Moreover, these various negative conceptions about the self, across a variety of life domains (e.g., work, friends, health), are said to coalesce into a single cognitive structure, so that an event relevant to one of these negative beliefs necessarily results in a global negative evaluation of worthlessness.

There are two aspects of this cognitive mediational model that are of critical importance for understanding and treating depression: (1) whether negative self-beliefs across a variety of situations and significant others are interconnected in memory, such that the negative affective reaction to an instance relevant to one of these beliefs results in overgeneralization to other aspects of life, and is consequently much greater than would be appropriate given the setback in a single aspect of the individual's life, and (2) whether or not an individual's possession of a specific type of mental structure does indeed make him or her more vulnerable to depressive episodes than are other people faced with equivalent life stress or negative feedback. The former issue concerns whether a cognitive structure specific to depression is capable of explaining a significant feature of depressive cognition observed clinically (e.g., Beck, 1967; Beck et al., 1979); the latter issue concerns whether such a structure does in fact play a causal, mediational role in producing the disorder.

It is important to note that these two issues are orthogonal in that the answer to one of them does not determine the answer to the other. It is possible for there to be a schematic mental structure composed of interrelated negative concepts that comes into being as a *result* of the state of depression instead of predating it and playing a role in producing it; it is also possible for there to be a nonschematic depressive cognitive structure that does constitute a vulnerability to becoming depressed.

Our goal in this chapter was not only to examine the existing research evidence on both the schematicity and the vulnerability questions, but also to more sharply define the questions themselves. As others have noted recently as well (e.g., Segal, 1988), the hypothetical construct of a depressive self-schema has not been tested in such a way as to rule out other alternative models. The notion of a schematic structure carries with it several assumptions that distinguish it from other forms of mental structure; thus far the experimental evidence does not address these assumptions (i.e., of interrelations and all-or-none activation) and so does not permit conclusions as to the existence of a depressive schema as opposed to a set of distinct, unrelated accessible negative constructs (see Bargh & Tota, 1988). The experiment we (Spielman & Bargh, 1988) conducted to specifically test the structural assumption provided very clear evidence that while the negative constructs were certainly more accessible for depressives than for nondepressives, the depression-related constructs did not show any evidence of interrelatedness. Therefore, in response to our first question, we would conclude on the available evidence that the "depressive self-schema" does not exist as a schema—at least as it has been operationalized by researchers thus far.

Importantly, Higgins, VanHook, and Dorfman (1988), using a similar priming paradigm, also failed in three experiments to find any evidence of schematic structure among self-relevant constructs; their results call into question whether self-knowledge is organized schematically in general. In this light it is less surprising that self-concepts are not related schematically in depression as well. However, Higgins et al. (1988, Experiment 3) did find evidence of structure for subjects' self-constructs that were "problematic" issues in their lives. Although subjects in this study were not selected on the basis of current depression and so were presumedly nondepressed, it is possible that those individuals vulnerable to becoming depressed might show a greater number of such problematic constructs or an enhanced tendency to dwell on the corresponding life problems, or both. This would result in a difference relative to nonvulnerable individuals in the breadth of the negative self-structure, which thus would make it more likely to interpret the average event as negative, and to generalize beyond the single event to other aspects of the individual's life. Our concluding recommendation as to the search for the depressive self-schema is thus to move away from operationalizations in terms of general content presumed to apply to everyone, to more idiosyncratic descriptions of each individual's schematically-organized negative self-knowledge. This would appear to be a most promising area for future research into depressogenic cognition.

As to whether a cognitive structure exists that makes one more vulnerable to becoming depressed, it is our position that a fair test of this hypothesis has not yet been made. Prospective and longitudinal studies that have concluded the depressogenic cognition to be an episode marker and not a predisposing factor (e.g., Dobson & Shaw, 1987; Hamilton & Abramson, 1983; Hammen et al., 1985; Hollon et al., 1986; Kuiper et al., 1985; Lewinsohn, Steinmetz, Larson & Franklin, 1981) have not established the validity of their measures of long-term cognitive structure (see Bargh et al., 1988). As noted above, the two major problems with these studies are a reliance on self-report questionnaires and an operationalization of the depressive schemata in terms of symptoms instead of traits. Because of these problems, it remains an empirical issue whether a relatively permanent cognitive structure differentiates those vulnerable and those not vulnerable to depression. Careful attention to the construct validity of one's operational definition of the hypothetical depressive cognitive structure (e.g., not to be in terms of short-term symptoms) is first needed in order to provide conclusive evidence as to the causal role of cognition in depression.

Finally, our own data suggest that cognitive concepts other than the depressive self-schema, in particular chronic construct accessibility (Bargh & Tota, 1988; Moretti & Shaw, 1989; Segal, 1988) and self-concept discrepancy (Higgins, 1987; Higgins et al., 1988), might prove to be better explanatory and predictive vehicles in depression research. These alternatives to schematic functioning deserve to be seriously entertained. There is good reason to believe, on the basis of the current evidence, that the processes underlying the maintenance of depressive cognition can be identified. Once we understand these processes more clearly, and begin to investigate how they develop in the first place, we will have come a long way toward identifying possible predisposing cognitive factors in depression.

**Authors' Note:** Portions of the research presented in this chapter were supported by Grant BNS–8404181 from the National Science Foundation, and Grant MH43265 from the National Institute of Mental Health to John A. Bargh. We wish to thank Charles Hymes for his helpful comments on an earlier version of this chapter.

## References

Alba, J. W. & Hasher, L. (1983). Is memory schematic? *Psychological Bulletin, 93,* 203–231.

Allport, G. W. & Odbert, H. S. (1936). Trait-names: A psycholexical study. *Psychological Monographs, 47* (1, Whole No. 211).

Andersen, S. M. & Lyon, J. E. (1987). Anticipating undesired outcomes: The role of outcome certainty in the onset of depression. *Journal of Experimental Social Psychology, 23,* 428–443.

Bargh, J. A. (1989). Conditional automaticity: Varieties of automatic influence in social perception and cognition. In J.S. Uleman & J. A. Bargh (Eds.) *Unintended thought.* New York: Guilford.

Bargh, J. A., Litt, J., Pratto, F. & Spielman, L. A. (1989). On the preconscious evaluation of social stimuli. In K. McConkey & A. Bennett (Eds.), *Proceedings of the XXIV International Congress of Psychology* (Vol. 3). Amsterdam: Elsevier-North Holland.

Bargh, J. A., Panter, A. T., Pratto, F. & Spielman, L. A. (1988). *Traits versus symptoms as components of the depressive self-schema.* Unpublished manuscript, New York University.

Bargh, J. A. & Thein, R. D. (1985). Individual construct accessibility, person memory, and the recall-judgment link: The case of information overload. *Journal of Personality and Social Psychology, 49,* 1129–1146.

Bargh, J. A. & Tota, M. E. (1988). Context-dependent automatic processing in depression: Accessibility of negative constructs with regard to self but not others. *Journal of Personality and Social Psychology, 54,* 925–939.

Bartlett, F. C. (1932). *Remembering*. London: Cambridge University Press.

Beck, A. T. (1967). *Depression: Clinical, experimental, and theoretical aspects*. New York: Harper & Row.

Beck, A. T. (1976). *Cognitive therapy and the emotional disorders*. New York: International Press.

Beck, A. T., Rush, A. J., Shaw, B. F. & Emery, G. (1979). *Cognitive therapy of depression*. New York: Guilford.

Blackburn, I. M., Jones, S. & Lewin, R. J. P. (1987). Cognitive style in depression. *British Journal of Clinical Psychology, 25,* 241–251.

Blaney, P. H. (1986). Affect and memory: A review. *Psychological Bulletin, 99,* 229–246.

Bradley, G. W. (1978). Self-serving biases in the attribution process: A reexamination of the fact or fiction question. *Journal of Personality and Social Psychology, 36,* 56–71.

Brewer, W. F. & Nakamura, G. V. (1984). The nature and functions of schemas. In R. S. Wyer, Jr. & T. K. Srull (Eds.), *Handbook of social cognition* (Vol. 1). New Jersey: Erlbaum.

Bruner, J. S. (1957). On perceptual readiness. *Psychological Review, 64,* 123–152.

Collins, A. M. & Loftus, E. F. (1975). A spreading-activation theory of semantic processing. *Psychological Review, 82,* 407–428.

Coyne, J. C. & Gotlib, I. H. (1983). The role of cognition in depression: A critical appraisal. *Psychological Bulletin, 94,* 472–505.

Craik, F. I. M. & Tulving, E. (1975). Depth of processing and the retention of words in episodic memory. *Journal of Experimental Psychology: General, 104,* 268–294.

Crocker, J., Hannah, D. B. & Weber, R. (1983). Person memory and causal attributions. *Journal of Personality and Social Psychology, 44,* 55–66.

Derry, P. A. & Kuiper, N. A. (1981). Schematic processing and self-reference in clinical depression. *Journal of Abnormal Psychology, 90,* 286–297.

Dobson, K. S. (1986). The self-schema in depression. In L. M. Hartman & K. R. Blankstein (Eds.), *Perception of self in emotional disorder and psychotherapy: Advances in the study of communication and affect* (Vol. 11, pp. 187–217). New York: Plenum.

Dobson, K. S. & Shaw, B. F. (1987). The specificity and stability of self-referential encoding in clinical depression. *Journal of Abnormal Psychology, 96,* 34–40.

Fenigstein, A. & Levine, M. P. (1984). Self-attention, concept activation, and the causal self. *Journal of Experimental Social Psychology, 20,* 231–245.

Fisk, A. D. & Schneider, W. (1984). Memory as a function of attention, level of processing, and automatization. *Journal of Experimental Psychology: Learning, Memory, and Cognition, 10,* 181–197.

Giles, D. E. & Rush, A. J. (1983). Cognitions, schemas, and depressive symptomatology. In M. Rosenbaum, C. M. Franks & Y. Jaffe (Eds.) *Perspectives on behaviour therapy*, New York: Springer-Verlag.

Gotlib, I. H. & McCann, C. D. (1984). Construct accessibility and depression: An examination of cognitive and affective factors. *Journal of Personality and Social Psychology, 47,* 427–439.

Hamilton, E. W. & Abramson, L. Y. (1983). Cognitive patterns and major depressive disorder: A longitudinal study in a hospital setting. *Journal of Abnormal Psychology, 92,* 173–184.

Hammen, C., Marks, T., Mayol, A. & de Mayo, R. (1985). Depressive self-schemas, life stress, and vulnerability to depression. *Journal of Abnormal Psychology, 94,* 308–319.

Hastie, R. (1981). Schematic principles in human memory. In E. T. Higgins, C. P. Herman & M. P. Zanna (Eds.), *Social cognition: The Ontario symposium* (Vol. 1, pp.

39–88). Hillsdale, NJ: Erlbaum.

Hastie, R. (1984). Causes and effects of causal attribution. *Journal of Personality and Social Psychology, 46,* 44–56.

Hastie, R., Park, B. & Weber, R. (1984). Social memory. In R. S. Wyer, Jr. & T. K. Srull (Eds.), *Handbook of social cognition* (Vol. 2, pp. 151–212). Hillsdale, NJ: Erlbaum.

Hayes-Roth, B. (1977). Evolution of cognitive structures and processes. *Psychological Review, 84,* 260–278.

Hebb, D. O. (1949). *Organization of behavior.* New York: Wiley.

Higgins, E. T. (1987). Self-discrepancy: A theory relating self and affect. *Psychological Review, 94,* 319–340.

Higgins, E. T. & Bargh, J. A. (1987). Social cognition and social perception. *Annual Review of Psychology, 38,* 369–425.

Higgins, E. T. & King, G. A. (1981). Accessibility of social constructs: Information-processing consequences of individual and contextual variability. In N. Cantor & J. F. Kihlstrom (Eds.), *Personality, cognition, and social interaction.* Hillsdale, NJ: Erlbaum.

Higgins, E. T., King, G. A. & Mavin, G. H. (1982). Individual construct accessibility and subjective impressions and recall. *Journal of Personality and Social Psychology, 43,* 35–47.

Higgins, E. T. & McCann, C. D. (1984). Social encoding and subsequent attitudes, impressions, and memory: "Context-driven" and motivational aspects of processing. *Journal of Personality and Social Psychology, 47,* 26–39.

Higgins, E. T., Rholes, W. S. & Jones, C. R. (1977). Category accessibility and impression formation. *Journal of Experimental Social Psychology, 13,* 141–154.

Higgins, E. T., Van Hook, E. & Dorfman, D. (1988). Do self-attributes form a cognitive structure? *Social Cognition, 6,* 177–206.

Hollon, S. D., Kendall, P. C. & Lumry, A. (1986). Specificity of depressotypic cognitions in clinical depression. *Journal of Abnormal Psychology, 95,* 52–59.

Isen, A. M., Shalker, T. L., Clark, M. & Karp, L. (1978). Affect, accessibility of material in memory, and behavior: A cognitive loop? *Journal of Personality and Social Psychology, 36,* 1–12.

Isen, A. M. (1984). Toward understanding the role of affect in cognition. In R. S. Wyer, Jr. & T. K. Srull (Eds.), *Handbook of social cognition* (Vol. 3). New Jersey: Erlbaum.

Jacoby, L. L. & Kelley, C. M. (1987). Unconscious influences of memory for a prior event. *Personality and Social Psychology Bulletin, 13,* 314–336.

Kuiper, N. A. & MacDonald, M. R. (1982). Self and other perception in mild depressives. *Social Cognition, 1,* 223–239.

Kuiper, N. A. & MacDonald, M. R. (1983). Schematic processing in depression: The self-based consensus bias. *Cognitive Therapy and Research, 7,* 469–484.

Kuiper, N. A. & Olinger, L. J. (1986). Dysfunctional attitudes and a self-worth contingency model of depression. In P.C. Kendall (Ed.), *Advances in cognitive-behavioral research and therapy.* Orlando, FL: Academic Press.

Kuiper, N. A., Olinger, L. J., MacDonald, M. R. & Shaw, B. F. (1985). Self-schema processing of depressed and nondepressed content: The effects of vulnerability to depression. *Social Cognition, 3,* 77–93.

Lewinsohn, P. M., Steinmetz, J. L., Larson, D. W. & Franklin, J. (1981). Depression-related cognitions: Antecedent or consequence? *Journal of Abnormal Psychology, 90,* 213–219.

Linville, P. W. (1985). Self-complexity and affective extremity: Don't put all of your eggs in one cognitive basket. *Social Cognition, 3,* 94–120.

Logan, G. D. (1980). Attention and automaticity in Stroop and priming tasks: Theory and data. *Cognitive Psychology, 12*, 523–553.

Logan, G. D. (1988). Toward an instance theory of automatization. *Psychological Review, 95*, 492–527.

Mandler, G. (1968). Organization and memory. In K. W. Spence & J. T. Spence (Eds.), *The psychology of learning and motivation* (Vol. 1, pp. 327–372). New York: Academic Press.

Meyer, D. E. & Schvaneveldt, R. W. (1971). Facilitation in recognizing pairs of words: Evidence of a dependence between retrieval operations. *Journal of Experimental Psychology, 90*, 227–234.

Minsky, M. (1975). A framework for representing knowledge. In P. H. Winston (Ed.), *The psychology of computer vision*. New York: McGraw-Hill.

Moretti, M. M. & Shaw, B. F. (1989). Unintended and uncontrolled thought processes: Implications for clinical interventions. In J. S. Uleman & J. A. Bargh (Eds.), *Unintended thought*. New York: Guilford.

Neely, J. H. (1977). Semantic priming and retrieval from lexical memory: Roles of inhibitionless spreading activation and limited-capacity attention. *Journal of Experimental Psychology: General, 106*, 226–254.

Neisser, U. (1976). *Cognition and reality*. San Francisco: Freeman.

Nisbett, R. E. & Wilson, T. D. (1977). Telling more than we can know: Verbal reports on mental processes. *Psychological Review, 84*, 231–259.

Posner, M. I. (1978). *Chronometric explorations of mind*. Hillsdale, NJ: Erlbaum.

Rhodewalt, F. & Agustsdottir, S. (1986). Effects of self-presentation on the phenomenal self. *Journal of Personality and Social Psychology, 50*, 47–55.

Rumelhart, D. E. & Ortony, A. (1977). The representation of knowledge in memory. In R. C. Anderson, R. J. Shapiro & W. E. Montague (Eds.), *Schooling and the acquisition of knowledge*. Hillsdale, NJ: Erlbaum.

Segal, Z. V. (1988). Appraisal of the self-schema construct in cognitive models of depression. *Psychological Bulletin, 103*, 147–162.

Spielman, L. A. & Bargh, J. A. (1988). *In search of the depressive schema: The absence of structural interrelatedness among depressed-content concepts*. Unpublished manuscript, New York University.

Srull, T. K., Lichtenstein, M. & Rothbart, M. (1985). Associative storage and retrieval processes in person memory. *Journal of Experimental Psychology: Learning, Memory, and Cognition, 11*, 316–345.

Taylor, S. E. & Brown, J. D. (1988). Illusion and well-being: A social psychological perspective on mental health. *Psychological Bulletin, 103*, 193–210.

Tulving, E. (1983). *Elements of episodic memory*. New York: Oxford University Press.

Weissman, A. N. (1979). The dysfunctional attitude style: A validation study. (Doctoral dissertation, University of Pennsylvania, 1978). *Dissertation Abstracts International, 40*, 1389B–1390B.

# The Self-System in Depression: Conceptualization and Treatment

Marlene M. Moretti
*Simon Fraser University*

E. Tory Higgins
*Columbia University*

Lisa A. Feldman
*University of Waterloo*

KEY WORDS: accessibility, availability, actual-self, automatic processes, ideal-self, self-discrepancy, self-system (development of, structure of), parental socialization practices (effect on development of self-system), relational thought (effect of development on self-system)

The self has been associated with psychological adjustment and adaptive functioning by psychologists of many persuasions (Allport, 1955; Cooley, 1902; Erikson, 1950, 1968; Freud, 1952/1920; Horney, 1950; James, 1890; Rogers, 1965; Sullivan, 1953). Psychotherapists, particularly those from Neo-Freudian and non-Freudian schools, have consistently maintained that changes in the self-system are central to therapeutic improvement. For example, Seward (1962) interviewed a group of 65 analysts including Freudians, Neo-Freudians, Horneyians, Jungians, Sullivanians, and Existentialists, and encouraged them to spontaneously discuss the general goals they set for therapy and the changes they anticipated occurring during therapy. He found that personal integrity and insight into self-dynamics were common goals of all therapeutic schools. In addition, most psychotherapists viewed self-realization and self-expression as common goals of therapy and anticipated that therapy produced changes in self-acceptance and self-expression. From a Horneyian perspective, the most important therapeutic changes occurred within the self-system, allowing the patient to achieve the "ability to accept himself as he is, together with the awareness that he now can grow further and realize his potentials without having to beat himself down for not having achieved perfect goals" (Seward, 1962, p. 144).

Sullivan (1953) and Rogers (1965) have explicitly discussed the changes that are expected to occur in the self-system during therapy. Sullivan suggested that therapy needed to include "complexly organized, rather prolonged, therapeutic operations by which we gradually build up a series of situations which require the self-system to expand—that is, to take in experience which had previously, because of selective attention or otherwise, had no material effect on the patient's susceptibility to anxiety…" (p. 192). Rogers noted that, in successful therapy, a movement from "symptoms to self," from "environment to self," and from "others to self" was expected to occur. Successful therapy produced a fundamental move toward greater acceptance of the self in which the individual's self-evaluative standards were self-selected rather than introjected from significant others or cultural pressures. More recently, Guidano and Liotti (1983) have suggested that the modification of one's attitude toward oneself and the restructuring of personal identity are central to changes that occur as a result of successful psychotherapy.

The self has also been implicated in the development and maintenance of many types of psychopathology (Guidano & Liotti, 1983), including depression (Beck, 1967, 1976; Freud, 1952/1920, 1957/1917). Current models of the role of the self in the etiology and treatment of depression have adopted a distinctively cognitive perspective (e.g, Beck, 1967, 1976; Derry & Kuiper, 1981; Kuiper & Derry, 1982; Teasdale, 1983). Other theorists and psychotherapists have emphasized the affective and motivational aspects of the self that are important in depression (e.g., Guidano & Liotti, 1983; Leventhal, 1980).

A theoretical model that integrates the cognitive, affective, and motivational aspects of the self that are central in the etiology of depression may provide a useful framework for directing therapeutic intervention. In the first section of the chapter we present a structural and developmental model of the self-system in depression that emphasizes the interactive role of cognitive, affective, and motivational factors. In subsequent sections we examine self-system processes that contribute to the onset and maintenance of depression, and intervention strategies.

## SELF-DISCREPANCY AND DEPRESSION

Several contemporary theories suggest that discrepancies between the actual-self and valued self-states are associated with psychological distress (e.g., Ogilvie, 1987; Pyszczynski & Greenberg, 1987). Self-discrepancy theory (Higgins, 1987) also proposes that discrepancies within the self-system are associated with psychological distress, and in addition identifies the types of self-system disorders that are specifically associated with vulnerability to depression. A fundamental assumption of self-discrepancy theory is that various self-state representations act as important guides or standards for self-evaluation and self-regulation. Individuals may evaluate their *actual-self* (i.e., the traits or characteristics they actually believe they possess) in relation to either their *ideal-self* representation (i.e., the traits or characteristics they wish or hope to possess), or their *ought-self* representation (i.e., the traits or characteristics they believe they have a duty or obligation to possess). Furthermore, the actual-self may be evaluated in relation to self-state representations that embody either one's *own* perspective (e.g., ideal-own, ought-own), or the inferred perspective of a significant *other* (e.g., ideal-other, ought-other).

When individuals perceive their actual-self as discrepant from a self-guide, they are likely to experience psychological distress. The type of distress they experience depends on the type of self-discrepancy they perceive. When the actual-self is perceived as discrepant from the hopes and wishes that individuals hold for themselves (*ideal-own*), or from the hopes and wishes that they believe others hold for them (*ideal-other*), they may view themselves as unable to attain positive goals in their lives. This psychological situation is specifically associated with depression and other dejection-related emotions (e.g., disappointment; discouragement). In contrast, when the actual-self is perceived as discrepant from the duties and obligations that individuals hold for themselves (*ought-own*), or from the duties and obligations that they believe others hold for them (*ought-other*), they may view themselves as unable to avoid punishment and associated negative events in their lives. This psychological situation is specifically associated with anxiety and other agitation-related emotions (e.g., fear; worry).

Self-discrepancy theory assumes that self-knowledge is organized in memory, and that the *relation* between each actual-self attribute and its corresponding ideal-self attribute becomes interconnected in memory as a cognitive structure (for a discussion of the definition of cognitive structure, see Brewer & Nakamura, 1984; Fiske & Taylor, 1984; Greenwald & Pratkanis, 1984; Higgins, 1989b; Wyer & Gordon, 1984). The cognitive structures that represent the relation between actual-self and ideal-self attributes are stable internal representations of self-knowledge that guide information processing and facilitate efficient encoding, identification, interpretation, appraisal, and memory of self-related information (Higgins & Moretti, 1988; Higgins, Strauman & Klein, 1986).

There may be several levels of informational organization within the self-system. At the simplest level, the relation between *each* attribute of the actual-self and a corresponding attribute of the ideal-self may form a cognitive structure. Because of the formation of this cognitive structure, the activation of one element of the cognitive structure (e.g., a specific actual-self attribute) will result in the activation of its corresponding element (e.g., the corresponding ideal-self attribute). In other words, when attention is directed to a specific attribute of the actual-self, the corresponding attribute of the ideal-self will automatically become activated. Alternatively, when attention is directed to a specific attribute of the ideal-self, the corresponding attribute of the actual-self will automatically become activated. It is important to note that individuals need not be aware of the activation of attributes within the self-system for the activation to influence self-evaluation and affect (Higgins, 1989b).

When there is a discrepant relation between an actual-self and an ideal-self attribute, chronic or momentary activation of the discrepancy should produce dejection-related emotions. Correlational and experimental investigations have provided strong support for this hypothesis. Higgins, Klein, and Strauman (1985) found that discrepancy between the actual-self and the ideal-self as measured on their Selves questionnaire was related to self-reports of depression, but not to self-reports of other types of psychological distress. They also found that the magnitude of discrepancy between the actual-self and ideal-self was associated with the degree of dejection reported by subjects. Subsequent studies have also demonstrated that the presence of actual-ideal discrepancy is predictive of whether or not individuals will experience depression in the future (Higgins, Klein & Strauman, 1987; Strauman & Higgins, 1988).

Studies examining the effects of momentary activation (i.e., contextual priming) of subjects' self-discrepancies have indicated that activation of actual-ideal discrepancies produces dejection-related emotions, but does not produce other types of emotional distress. For example, Higgins, Bond, Klein, and Strauman (1986) asked subjects to imagine either a positive event (receiving a grade of "A" in a course; spending the evening with someone they admired) or a negative event (receiving a "D" in a course; finding out a lover has just left them). Subjects suffering from actual-ideal discrepancy experienced significantly greater dejection and more psychomotor retardation when they imagined a negative event than did subjects suffering from other types of self-discrepancy (i.e., actual-ought) or subjects who imagined a positive event. Similar results were reported by Strauman and Higgins (1987) in a study that asked subjects to complete a series of sentences ("An 'x' person is...") that contained either discrepant or nondiscrepant self-attributes. Subjects demonstrated significantly greater psychomotor retardation (i.e., longer verbalization times, reduced skin conductance amplitude) when they completed sentences that contained actual-ideal discrepant traits than when they completed sentences that contained actual-ought discrepant or nondiscrepant traits. These results have been replicated with a sample of clinically depressed subjects (Strauman, 1989).

This research indicates that the activation of actual-self attributes alone, or ideal-self attributes alone, produces psychological consequences associated with the automatic activation of self-discrepancies composed of the relation between actual-self and ideal-self attributes. These findings suggest that actual-self and ideal-self attributes are *structurally* interconnected. It may also be the case that priming actual-self attributes activates other actual-self attributes. This effect would occur if *actual-self attributes were also structurally interconnected with other actual-self attributes.* The implication of this type of structural connectedness within the self-system is that the activation of any single self-attribute within the self-system might activate the entire self-system (see Higgins, 1989b for a discussion of horizontal and vertical activation patterns).

To test this hypothesis, Higgins, Van Hook, and Dorfman (1988, Study 3) presented subjects with a series of slides of target words printed in different colored inks and asked them to name the color of each word as quickly as possible. Each target word was preceded by the presentation of a prime. Targets and primes included self-related or self-unrelated trait words. Higgins et al. (1988) predicted that if self-attributes were structurally interconnected, then greater interference in a color naming task should occur when self-related targets were preceded by self-related primes than when they were preceded by self-unrelated primes. This effect was not found. However, results indicated that there was greater interference in color naming when either the prime or the target was a *discrepant* self-attribute (i.e., an actual-self attribute that was discrepant from a self-evaluative guide). These results suggest that *discrepant self-attributes are structurally interconnected* such that the activation of one discrepant self-attribute leads to the activation of other discrepant self-attributes.

If depression is associated with a greater number of actual-ideal discrepant attributes and discrepant self-attributes are structurally interconnected, then depressed individuals should demonstrate greater structural interconnectedness within the self-system than should nondepressed individuals. Few studies have investigated the self-system organization of depressed individuals. The research of Segal, Hood,

Shaw, and Higgins (1988), however, provides preliminary evidence of greater structural interconnectedness within the self-systems of clinically depressed individuals than within those of nondepressed individuals. Frequent activation over an extended period of time may produce chronically accessible discrepant self-attributes that are activated in the absence of triggering stimuli (i.e., environmental or contextual cues).

The findings of Higgins et al. (1988) and Segal et al. (1988) suggest that individuals who possess actual-ideal self-discrepancies are vulnerable to depression not only because they possess individual discrepant self-attributes, but also because the activation of one discrepant self-attribute results in the activation of other discrepant self-attributes. The greater the number of discrepant traits that individuals possess, the more frequently all discrepant traits will be activated and the more accessible (i.e., readily accessed during processing) they will be during the processing of self-relevant information.

How might the structural relatedness of self-discrepant attributes in memory contribute to the maintenance of depression? It is well established that the development of an organized representation of information in memory *automatically* directs information processing with little demand on limited attentional capacity (Bryan & Harter, 1899; James, 1890; Logan, 1980; Shiffrin & Schneider, 1977). Automatic information processing may be triggered without an individual's awareness and, once initiated, may be difficult to inhibit even when individuals are aware of the triggering stimuli. If we assume that the influence of discrepant self-attributes on information processing is similar to that of other cognitive representations, then it is likely that discrepant self-attributes will automatically influence self-relevant information processing without an individual's awareness. In addition, an individual may experience difficulty inhibiting the influence of discrepant self-constructs on information processing even when he or she is aware of triggering stimuli (Bargh & Pratto, 1986; Higgins & King, 1981; Strauman & Higgins, 1987; Strauman, 1989).

Self-relevant information processing in depression may be overly determined by automatic processes because discrepant self-attributes are related in memory. Because automatic processing is predominantly directed by internalized cognitive representations, encoding, identification, and interpretation of information may be biased. Therefore, automatic processing is likely to *sustain stability within a cognitive representation rather than promote change.* As a consequence, the self-system in depression may be highly negative, rigid, and unchanging. This view of depression is consistent with clinical observations offered by Beck and his colleagues (Beck, 1967, 1976; Beck et al., 1979; Moretti & Shaw, 1989).

If automatic processing in depression leads to psychological distress and maintains dysfunction within the self-system, why don't depressed individuals simply interrupt these processes? It may be that although depressed individuals are aware of the *outcomes* of automatic processing (e.g., negative self-evaluations, feelings of dejection and disappointment), they are not aware of the operation of automatic processes. Moreover, the negative self-evaluations and negative feelings that occur as a consequence of automatic processes may go unquestioned because they are consistent with the negative view that depressed individuals hold of themselves. Finally, the highly negative emotional state that characterizes depression may reduce attentional resources that are necessary to interrupt dysfunctional automatic processes and engage in corrective controlled processes (Moretti & Shaw, 1989).

## THE SELF-SYSTEM IN DEPRESSION: DEVELOPMENTAL CONSIDERATIONS

Up to this point, we have considered the types of self-system deficits that are associated with depression. To fully understand and treat depression it is important that we also consider the etiology of vulnerability within the self-system. The importance of early childhood experiences in the development of the self-system and vulnerability to depression has been emphasized by many theorists. Psychoanalytic approaches to depression have emphasized the role of early experiences of loss (Abraham, 1985/1911; Freud, 1957/1917), feelings of helplessness regarding discrepancies between aspirations and expectancies (Rapaport, 1985), and child-parent relationships and parental attitudes (Cohen, Baker, Cohen, Fromm-Reichmann & Weigert, 1985/1954). Sullivan (1953) believed that the self-system frequently exerted a negative impact on psychological functioning, but that the degree of negative impact depended on the type of socialization practices that individuals experienced as children. Once established, the self-system had "nothing less than stupendous importance in personality" (Sullivan, 1953, p. 169) because it was resistant to change even when experiences were incongruous with its organization and functional activity.

More recent cognitive theories (Beck, Rush, Shaw & Emery, 1979; Guidano, 1987; Kovacs & Beck, 1985) also suggest that early interpersonal experiences have an impact on vulnerability to depression. Early experiences become organized, integrated, and cognitively represented in schemas about the self, the world (including interpersonal relationships), and the future. Once established, these cognitive representations operate as a filter or guide for the interpretation of self-relevant experiences.

While many theories acknowledge the importance of childhood experience as a distal cause of depression (see Alloy, Abramson, Metalsky & Hartlage, 1988, for a discussion of the notion of distal versus proximal causes in psychopathology), most do not specify the mechanisms by which these early events influence later experience, particularly with respect to the role of the self-system. A model that specifies the conditions that give rise to the development of vulnerability within the self-system and the effects of the self-system on subsequent experiences would assist psychotherapists in effectively targeting aspects of the self for therapeutic intervention. Higgins and his colleagues (Higgins, 1989a; Moretti & Higgins, in press-a) have recently formulated a developmental model that traces the development of discrepancies between self-beliefs to the interaction between the development of relational thought in children and parental socialization practices.

The development of relational thought (Case, 1985; Fischer, 1980; Selman, 1980) is a fundamental precursor to the development of the self-system. In order for children to develop different perspectives on the self that can be used for self-evaluation, they must be capable of representing the relation between their behavior and the responses of others to them (self-other contingencies). At the earliest level of development (sensorimotor level), infants have the capacity to experience the presence or absence of both positive and negative events. Even though infants at this level are able to anticipate positive or negative events, they lack the capacity to relate these events to their own behavior. However, to the extent that children anticipate either the absence of positive events or the presence of negative events, they may withdraw or respond negatively to the approaches of others. These responses may have a negative impact on the self at a later stage of development since withdrawal and/or rejection of others can increase the probability that negative interpersonal events will occur in the future and will be related to the self when infants have reached a level of cognitive maturity to be able to do so.

As early as two years of age, children develop the ability to represent events symbolically (Bruner, 1964; Case, 1985; Fischer, 1980; Piaget, 1951; Werner & Kaplan, 1963) and they begin to consider bidirectional relations between objects. At this age children can represent the relation between themselves, or their actions, and the responses of another individual to them (e.g., their mother or father). They are also able to represent the psychological impact of others' responses to them on their own psychological state (e.g., feelings of happiness, sadness, fear, contentment).

The ability to understand and represent the impact of self-features or behaviors on the responses of others provides the basis for children to represent self-other contingencies—that is, representations of the types of self-aspects or behaviors that lead to acceptance or rejection by others. This has an important impact on the development of the self-system and the emergence of self-regulation. Because children at this level can represent the relation between their behavior and the responses of others, as well as the impact of others responses on their own psychological state, they are motivated to monitor their behavior to ensure the presence of positive psychological events and to avoid the presence of negative psychological events.

During the period of development between the ages of 4–6 years (late interrelational and early dimensional development), children are capable of viewing their behavior from the perspective of others, and they are able to adopt these perspectives or viewpoints as standards for self-evaluation (for a discussion of the development of perspective taking, see Case, 1985; Feffer, 1970; Fischer, 1980; Flavell, Botkin, Fry, Wright & Jarvis, 1968; Higgins, 1981; Piaget, 1965; Selman & Bryne, 1974; Werner, 1957). Because these children can *simultaneously* consider and compare their own behavior with the standards that they believe others hold for them, they can determine the extent to which they are discrepant. At this point of self-development, children become vulnerable to experiencing discrepancies between their self-features or behaviors, and the self-features or behaviors that they believe others would like them to possess. If they believe that they have not behaved as others would ideally wish them to behave (ideal-self; other-perspective), then they may feel sad and humiliated. If children believe that they have not behaved as others thought they should or ought to (ought-self; other perspective), then they may feel fearful and guilty.

Between the ages of 9 and 11 years (late dimensional development), children's inferences of how others view them become organized in terms of generalized traits rather than specific behaviors (Harter, 1983). These changes in self-representation are associated with changes in self-evaluations and self-regulation. Children at this stage are more likely to make general self-evaluations when they compare themselves to the standards that they believe others hold for them. If children experience discrepancies during this comparison process, then they are confronted with the task of altering themselves to reduce the discrepancies. This may be problematic because the discrepancies now reflect dispositional characteristics rather than behaviors. It is no longer a question of children changing *what they do* in order to meet important self-standards, but rather altering *who they are*.

The final level of cognitive development (vectorial development) occurs during early adolescence (ages 13–16) and is marked by the ability to simultaneously consider and integrate information from multiple perspectives (Case, 1985; Fischer, 1980; Inhelder & Piaget, 1958; Selman & Byrne, 1974). The ability of adolescents to simultaneously consider themselves from many different perspectives may lead to a more complex and differentiated view of the self. This may have positive consequences (Linville, 1985, 1987), but it may also carry risks for psychological distress. Adolescents may experience themselves as discrepant from several important self-evaluative standards and they may feel pulled between conflicting self-guides. As a result, adolescents may suffer from problems in self-regulation and from feelings of conflict, confusion, and rebelliousness (see Van Hook & Higgins, 1988).

Not all children develop vulnerable self-systems. Parental socialization practices are an important factor in the development of children's self-systems. These practices influence both the *type* and the *strength* of self-evaluative guides that are acquired by children. When parents are oriented toward identifying and responding to their children's features that *match* their hopes and wishes, their relationships with their children are likely to be dominated by the presence of positive outcomes—that is, they are likely to reinforce and praise their children's behaviors. Parental interactions that consistently, clearly, and significantly highlight matches of children's features with parental wishes and hopes are likely to result in children's acquisitions of strong *ideal* self-guides. When parents are oriented toward identifying and responding to their children's features that match the duties and obligations that they have prescribed for them, their relationships with their children are likely to be dominated by the absence of negative outcomes (i.e., an absence of the need to punish their children). Parental interactions that consistently, clearly, and significantly highlight matches of children's features with the duties and obligations that parents have prescribed for their children are likely to result in children's acquisitions of strong *ought* self-guides.

Children exposed to either of these parental interaction styles are likely to develop self-concepts characterized by congruence rather than by discrepancy between the actual-self and self-evaluative guides. The perception of congruence between the actual-self and self-evaluative guides is more likely to be associated with positive emotional states than is the perception of discrepancy. When parents are oriented toward identifying and responding to their children's features that are *discrepant* from their hopes and wishes for them, their relationships with their children are likely to be dominated by the absence of positive outcomes—that is, parents may feel disappointed or dissatisfied with their children and they may withdraw support and acceptance. When parents are oriented toward identifying and responding to their children's features that are discrepant from the duties and obligations that they have prescribed for them, their relationships with their children are likely to be dominated by the presence of negative outcomes—that is, parents may feel angry and resentful, and criticize, reprimand, or punish their children. Parental socialization practices that focus on mismatches between children's features and parental guides are likely to produce vulnerability and discrepancy within children's self-systems.

Of course, these descriptions are simplified prototypes of parental socialization orientations. For most parents, socialization practices may vary across time, circumstances, and types of behavior enacted by their children. Variability in socialization practices across and within parents is likely to produce significant individual differences in degree and type of self-discrepancy within the self-system.

## PSYCHOTHERAPY AND THE SELF-SYSTEM IN DEPRESSION: GENERAL ISSUES

We have suggested that depression is associated with discrepancy between the actual-self and ideal-self guides. Self-discrepancies develop as a result of parental socialization practices that emphasize the mismatch between parental ideals for a child and the child's self-attributes or behaviors. Once established, actual-ideal discrepancies form a cognitive structure that is automatically activated during self-referent information processing. There is evidence to suggest that when attention is directed toward one element of a discrepant cognitive structure (e.g., an actual-self attribute), the corresponding element of the structure is automatically activated (e.g., an ideal-self attribute). Moreover, preliminary findings suggest that when attention is directed toward one element of a discrepant cognitive structure (e.g., an actual-self attribute), the entire structure of discrepant self-attributes may be automatically activated (e.g., all discrepant actual-self and corresponding ideal-self attributes). The structural interconnectedness between discrepant self-attributes within the self-system may lead to frequent activation of the entire system and chronic accessibility of discrepant self-constructs during information processing.

Despite the importance of the self-system in the onset and maintenance of depression, the process by which therapeutic interventions alter the self-system and lead to improvement is not well understood. Few studies have evaluated self-system changes as a function of psychotherapy, with the exception of the research of Rogers and his colleagues. According to Rogers (1954), psychotherapy produced a movement toward more realistic and achievable self-ideals, and greater congruence between the actual-self and the ideal-self. He believed that the role of the therapist is to provide the patient with a nonevaluative, accepting, and nondirective reflection of the self—"a genuine alter ego in an operational and technical sense" (p. 40). The reflection of the self by the therapist provided patients with the opportunity to fully understand their own feelings and attitudes, promoting acceptance and reorganization of the self.

Several studies were completed by Rogers and his colleagues to evaluate self-system changes that occurred as a function of psychotherapy. Although many of these studies suffer from methodological and statistical flaws (see Wylie, 1979, for a review), they provide some indication of the types of changes that might be expected to occur in the self-system as a function of client-centered psychotherapy. The standard design in this research was to evaluate the correlation between the actual-self and ideal-self prior to and following psychotherapy. Actual-ideal discrepancy was typically measured with a version of Butler and Haigh's (1954) Q-sort instrument consisting of up to 100 self-referent statements (e.g., "I am likable," "I really am disturbed"). Patients were asked to sort the items twice: once to describe their actual-self and once to describe their ideal-self. Both times, subjects sorted the items into 9 piles ranging from least descriptive to most descriptive.

Haigh and Butler (1954) predicted that psychotherapy would produce changes in the actual-self rather than in the ideal-self because the actual-self was idiosyncratic to the individual whereas the ideal-self was primarily based on general societal norms. Results indicated that the mean congruence between the actual-self and ideal-self across subjects increased from a pre-therapy correlation of approximately zero to a post-therapy and follow-up correlation of 0.34. These results were similar to those reported by other researchers using the Q-sort measure (Fairweather, Simon, Gebhard, Weingarten, Holland, Sanders, Stone & Reahl, 1960; Harrow, Lox, Markus, Stillman & Hallowell, 1954; Rogers & Dymond, 1954; Rudikoff, 1954). Unfortunately, most of these researchers did not report whether increased congruence was due to changes in the actual-self or in the ideal-self.

Rudikoff (1954), however, did evaluate changes both in the actual-self and in the ideal-self over the course of client-centered therapy. Patients completed the Q-sort measure twice prior to therapy, once immediately following therapy, and once at follow-up six months later. Rudikoff's results indicated that the correlation between the two pre-therapy *actual-self* Q-sorts was significantly higher than the correlation between the pre-and post-therapy actual-self Q-sorts. In contrast, the correlation between the two pre-therapy *ideal-self* Q-sorts was not significantly different from the correlation between the pre- and post-therapy ideal-self Q-sorts. Finally, the Q-sorts of the ideal-self were significantly more stable than the Q-sorts of actual-self over all periods.

There are several possible explanations of Rudikoff's (1954) finding that the actual-self, but not the ideal-self, changed over the course of client-centered therapy. First, the range of scores for ratings of the ideal-self using the Q-sort may be more restricted than the range of scores for the actual-self. Second, the Q-sort measure may not identify actual-self or ideal-self attributes that are personally significant for patients. Changes may have occurred in the ideal-self that were not detected with the Q-sort measure. The use of an idiographic measure of the actual-self and ideal-self may ensure that changes in both the actual-self and the ideal-self are adequately assessed (Moretti & Higgins, in press-b). Third, as previously noted, client-centered therapy is designed to facilitate unconditional acceptance of the self. It may be that client-centered techniques are more likely to produce changes in the ratings of the actual-self than in ideal-self standards.

The research of Rogers and his colleagues highlights the role of the self-system in psychopathology, and suggests that psychotherapy produces positive changes within the self. Rogers did not, however, identify specific types of interventions that would lead to specific types of changes within the self-system. Rather, he suggested that therapeutic techniques were secondary to therapists adopting the general attitude that an "individual has a sufficient capacity to deal constructively with all those aspects of his life which can potentially come into conscious awareness" (p. 24). Furthermore, Rogers believed that therapists interventions should be directed toward conveying an understanding of the client's attitudes and feelings rather than achieving direct changes within the self-system. Changes within the self were assumed to occur as consequence of the patients increased awareness and understanding of their feelings and attitudes. Thus, although Rogers did emphasize the self in psychopathology and psychotherapy, he neither provided a framework for understanding how specific interventions produce change in the self, nor advocated that the self should be the immediate target of therapeutic intervention.

The understanding and organization of existing therapeutic techniques according to the effects they may have on the self during therapy may be valuable for several reasons. A framework that organizes existing therapeutic techniques according to the effects that they may have on the self is unlikely to suffer from the limitations of any single therapeutic approach (e.g., behavioral, cognitive, interpersonal, and psychodynamic). By identifying the self as the target and *integrating theme* of therapy, a framework of self-system therapeutic interventions cuts across the rigid boundaries of major psychotherapeutic models and encourages therapists to determine the course of treatment as a function of the changing needs of patients. It may be that some patients are more likely to benefit from therapeutic techniques designed to alter the actual-self, while others are helped by therapeutic techniques designed to alter the ideal-self. In addition, the types of problems and therapeutic needs presented by a patient may change over the course of therapy: patients may work on changing their actual-self and their ideal-self at different points in therapy. A framework of self-system therapeutic interventions could guide the use of therapeutic techniques that alter specific aspects of vulnerability within the self-system and offer a wide range of treatment options to clinicians and their patients.

In the final section of this chapter we present a framework that organizes existing therapeutic interventions according to the effects that they may have on the self-system. This framework integrates therapeutic techniques from several major psychotherapy models (Beck, Rush, Shaw & Emery, 1979; Lewinsohn, Sullivan & Grosscup, 1982; Rounsaville, Klerman, Weissman & Chevron, 1985; Sacco & Beck, 1985; Strupp, Sandell, Waterhouse et al., 1982; Weiss & Sampson, 1986; Zaiden, 1982) in an attempt to achieve a "pragmatic blending" (Halgin, 1985) of therapeutic techniques with the goal of changing the self-system. In addition, we have included several innovative therapeutic techniques that are suggested from research in the area of social cognition. This review does not provide an exhaustive description of therapeutic techniques that may lead to self-system changes, but rather a selection of examples of therapeutic techniques that may be useful in changing specific self-related problems. It should also be noted that although some therapeutic interventions may be more effective in treating some types of self-related problems, there is probably not a one-to-one correspondence between specific types of therapeutic interventions and specific types of self-system problems: similar techniques may be used to alter a variety of self-system problems.

Before discussing specific self-system interventions, it is important to consider general therapeutic issues that may arise during the treatment of depression. Persistent negative thoughts about the self and intense feelings of sadness, despair, and hopelessness are common complaints of individuals who are depressed. Patients often feel immobilized by intrusive and uncontrollable thoughts of personal inadequacy, worthlessness, and self-reproach. Psychotherapists may adopt a variety of approaches in treating these symptoms. Regardless of the specific approach or technique adopted by clinicians, however, the effectiveness of many therapeutic interventions for depression may rest on the patients' awareness of dysfunctional processes, and on their capacity to temporarily inhibit these automatic processes in order to utilize the therapeutic process. Many depressed persons have difficulty developing an awareness of dysfunctional processes and inhibiting automatic processes because of their intense emotional distress. As we have noted, intense emotional arousal may limit attentional resources that are available for monitoring and inhibiting automatic processes. This may be most problematic during the early phases of psychotherapy when psychological distress is intense, and during periods in which patients are dealing with highly emotional issues. At these times, clinicians need to be sensitive to patients' difficulties in identifying and inhibiting dysfunctional automatic processes and to their reduced capacity to immediately benefit from therapeutic interventions. Even if patients are unable to identify and interrupt dysfunctional processes "on-line," they can often review their thoughts, feelings, and behaviors shortly thereafter. This often brings relief from negative feelings and thoughts, and provides patients with an opportunity to consider alternative perspectives on the self.

## SELF-SYSTEM THERAPEUTIC INTERVENTIONS

Our model of the self-system in depression suggests that therapeutic interventions may be aimed at several targets within the self-system: the actual-self, the ideal-self, and the structural relations between the actual-self and ideal-self. For each target, interventions may produce changes by altering patterns of self-knowledge activation. Changes in patterns of self-knowledge activation include changing the *availability* of self-related constructs (i.e., creating new self-related constructs in memory) or the *accessibility* of self-related constructs (i.e., increasing or decreasing the readiness with which existing self-related constructs are activated). In the following sections we summarize the types of interventions that may be helpful in altering different targets within the self-system by changing patterns of self-knowledge activation.

### Changing the Actual-Self

Several existing psychotherapeutic techniques are likely to alter the actual-self in depression. The techniques discussed below share the common goal of either increasing congruency (i.e., match) or decreasing discrepancy (i.e., mismatch) between the actual-self and the ideal-self.

## Making New Information Available Within the Actual-Self Representation.

Considerable research suggests that positive attributes are less frequently represented in the actual-self representations of depressed than nondepressed individuals (see Moretti & Shaw, 1989). Rogers (1954) suggested that the structure of the self often precludes the intrusion of inconsistent information. This may occur because of conscious denial of feedback that is inconsistent with the actual-self, or because of the failure to symbolize and internalize experiences that are incongruent with beliefs about the self. For example, depressed patients may deny or fail to accept positive feedback from others, or they may fail to acknowledge and fully experience their successes. This observation is consistent with research indicating that individuals fail to attend to and encode information that is inconsistent with their structure of self-knowledge (Bargh, 1989; Fiske & Taylor, 1984; Higgins & Bargh, 1987).

Several therapeutic techniques may effectively introduce new information into the actual-self representation of depressed patients. These include behavioral techniques or group therapy processes that provide patients with new experiences. Patients may come to believe that they are assertive, friendly, or capable of tackling new challenges once they have engaged in behaviors that were previously avoided or were not experienced because of lack of opportunity. The therapists' knowledge of patients' ideal guides may be helpful in determining what types of behavioral experiences are most important to patients and most likely to lead to the creation of actual-self/ideal-self matches.

Cognitive techniques that actively encourage patients to attend to particular types of experiences may also successfully introduce new information into the actual-self. For example, therapists may encourage patients to identify and attend to experiences of mastery and pleasure to promote the development of a balanced rather than negative view of the self (Beck et al., 1979). Again, knowledge of patients' ideal-self guides may be helpful to therapists in determining *which* attributes and experiences patients should pay attention to, thus maximizing the likelihood of creating increased congruence between the actual-self and ideal-self.

Finally, patients may hold beliefs about the type of individual they actually are, or can be, based on their early experiences with significant others. Exploration of these beliefs and how they might lead to constriction of individuals' current views of the self may be beneficial in removing unconscious constraints on self-definition. As a consequence of this process, patients may begin to consider new definitions of their actual-self and try out behaviors that were previously viewed as inconsistent with the self.

## Increasing or Decreasing the Accessibility of Specific Types of Information Within the Actual-Self Representation

Depression has also been associated with the heightened accessibility of negative information and the attenuated accessibility of positive information that is represented in the self-system (Gotlib & Cane, 1987; Gotlib & McCann, 1984; Higgins & King, 1981). Particular contexts may temporarily prime the accessibility of actual-self attributes that either match or are discrepant from the ideal-self. Indeed, therapy in itself can act as a context that primes different types of actual-self information.

Several behavioral, cognitive, and psychodyanmic techniques may alter patterns of self-knowledge accessibility. Therapists may encourage patients to make particular behavioral changes in their lives to increase the accessibility of actual-self attributes that match an ideal-self guide (e.g., changing jobs or pursuing long term goals they have put on hold). Other techniques, such as helping patients leave destructive relationships or living conditions by offering alternative living arrangements (e.g., homes for battered women) may also temporarily reduce the accessibility of actual-self attributes that do not match ideal-self standards (e.g., the perception of oneself as unloved and worthless). Similarly, helping patients to inhibit problematic behavioral patterns may temporarily reduce the accessibility of actual-self attributes that do not match ideal-self standards because of the consequent lack of contextual cues. From a cognitive perspective, identifying and drawing attention to patients' attributes that match ideal-self standards can temporarily increase the accessibility of those particular traits.

Therapeutic techniques that temporarily alter the accessibility of actual-self information may have limited effectiveness, because, outside therapy, patients can encounter cues that prime the accessibility of actual-self/ideal-self mismatches, and/or not encounter cues that prime the accessibility actual-self/ideal-self matches. The long-term effectiveness of interventions designed to alter the temporary accessibility of actual-self information may depend on the patients' ability to adopt self-regulatory strategies to help themselves provide their own source of contextual priming of actual-self attributes (e.g., keeping a diary of experiences associated with actual-self attributes that match ideal-self guides, making sure that they control their environment and avoid situations that are associated with actual-self attributes that mismatch ideal-self guides).

Interventions that alter the temporary accessibility of actual-self information may also be effective if they occur frequently over a long period of time and result in fundamental changes in chronic patterns of accessibility. As previously noted, chronic accessibility of actual-self knowledge develops when experiences frequently prime certain types of self-knowledge over an extended period of time. Depressed patients often report chronic negative self-perceptions that are resistant to change. Techniques that can be utilized to temporarily alter patterns of self-knowledge accessibility may also be used to change patterns of chronic accessibility of actual-self information if they are used repeatedly and over an extended period of time. Some therapeutic interventions, however, may be more effective than others in altering patterns of chronic self-knowledge accessibility. For example, if patients' memories of significant events in their lives act as chronic sources of self-knowledge activation, then psychodynamic interpretations may be used to alter patterns of self-knowledge accessibility by changing patients' understanding of early experiences and the meanings that they have attached to these experiences. By changing the meanings that are attached to significant memories, therapists can alter the types of self-knowledge that are primed by these memories.

## Changing the Extent to which Actual-Self Attributes are Believed to Exist

Depressed individuals may believe that they do possess actual-self attributes that they value (i.e., attributes that are represented in their ideal-self guide), but they may also believe that the extent to which they possess such attributes falls short of their hopes and wishes (i.e., fails to meet their ideal-self guide). For example, depressed individuals may complain of not being well-liked by others despite the fact that they report having many close friends. When questioned further, they may claim to be "tolerated" and perhaps even "liked a little," but still maintain that they are not really well-liked. It may become clear that their standard for being well-liked entails being well-liked by everyone.

Therapists may adopt one of two strategies in dealing with patients' perceptions that they do not possess actual-self attributes to the extent that they desire. One strategy is to target the patients' ideal-self standards. We will explore this option when we discuss therapeutic interventions that may change the ideal-self. An alternative strategy is to target the actual-self and to work with patients to change the extent to which they believe that they actually do possess actual-self attributes. Behavioral techniques designed to increase patients' desired behavior (e.g., assertiveness training, social skills training) may lead to changes in patients' actual-self perceptions. Cognitive therapy techniques such as encouraging patients to attend to the friendly behaviors of others toward them, and to reevaluate their negative interpretations of interpersonal events, may also lead to changes in patients' beliefs about the extent to which they possess desired actual-self attributes. Similarly, reviewing memories of significant events that have had a profound effect on their self-definitions may lead patients to reinterpret these events in such a way that the memories no longer suggest that they fail to possess adequate levels of desired actual-self attributes.

Altering the extent to which individuals believe that they possess actual-self attributes can lead to a more positive self-view. These interventions can be useful in cases of depression where patients underestimate their abilities and the attractiveness of their personality characteristics. However, therapists should carefully consider whether the goals that depressed patients' set for themselves (i.e., ideal-self guides) are realistic and attainable. Research suggests that depressed patients may evaluate their performance more negatively than is appropriate given the feedback that they receive (DeMonbreun & Craighead, 1977; Dobson & Shaw, 1981; Golin & Terrell, 1977; Hammen & Krantz, 1976). Negative self-evaluation may result when depressed patients compare their performance to extremely high ideal standards. If this is the case, attempting to reduce actual-ideal discrepancies by increasing the extent to which individuals believe they possess actual-self attributes may be impossible, and it may support patients' use of unrealistic ideal standards.

## Changing the Certainty of Beliefs Regarding the Existence of Actual-Self Attributes

Depressed patients often believe that they possess unacceptable actual-self attributes. As Beck (1967, 1976) has pointed out, negative beliefs about the self can exist despite the lack of confirming evidence, and even in the presence of disconfirming evidence. For example, depressed individuals may claim with absolute certainty that they are selfish despite their desire to be unselfish. They may support their belief with one or two ambiguous examples and discount counterevidence presented by therapists or other individuals.

Several therapeutic techniques may be helpful in altering the certainty with which patients' believe that they possess actual-self attributes. From a cognitive perspective, therapists can help patients to assess the validity of their beliefs in light of confirmatory and contradictory evidence. Tendencies toward "black and white" thinking and selective attention to current or past experiences may also be pointed out to the patient. Psychodynamic interpretations may alter the meaning of previous experiences so that they no longer serve as evidence of undesirable actual-self attributes. Such interventions could be directed both to decreasing the certainty of patients' beliefs about actual-self attributes that are discrepant from the ideal-self, and increasing the certainty of their beliefs about actual-self attributes that are congruent with the ideal-self.

### Changing the Perceived Importance and Consequences of Possessing Actual-Self Attributes

Individuals do not suffer from psychological distress simply because they possess actual-self attributes that are discrepant from their ideal-self: they suffer because they believe that the consequences of possessing such attributes are extremely negative (see Higgins, 1987). As previously noted, children learn that their parents respond differentially to their various behaviors and traits. Some of their behaviors and traits are responded to with praise and reward, while others elicit disappointment or punishment. The beliefs that individuals adopt regarding the probable consequences associated with possessing actual-self attributes that are discrepant from ideal-self guides (i.e., self-other or interpersonal contingency beliefs) exert a tremendous influence over their emotional well-being.

Depressed individuals often anticipate that extremely negative events will occur as a consequence of their possessing particular actual-self attributes. For example, they may be concerned that others will discover that they are sometimes envious, unfriendly, or irritable. They believe that they will be abandoned when these "flaws" are discovered. When asked how they know this to be the case, it is often clear that they have worked diligently to avoid the possibility of others discovering their perceived flaws. Consequently, they have provided themselves with few opportunities to "check out" their interpersonal contingency beliefs (see Beck, 1976; Beck et al., 1979).

Psychotherapists may utilize a variety of techniques, alone or in combination, to address this problem. Behavior therapists might encourage patients to engage in rather than avoid interpersonal interactions. These experiences may lead to changes in patients' beliefs about the self and the interpersonal consequences of their actual-self attributes. Cognitive interventions can also help patients identify the existence of catastrophic beliefs and understand the impact of beliefs on current interpersonal functioning. Patients are encouraged to evaluate the validity of their beliefs in light of available evidence and to check out their beliefs by experimenting with new interpersonal behaviors. Psychodynamic techniques that explore the early experiences that led to the development of dysfunctional interpersonal contingency beliefs can also be helpful in promoting patients' awareness of the unconscious beliefs that continue to influence interpersonal relationships. In both psychodynamic and interpersonal therapies, the therapeutic relationship becomes an important arena where patients play out their interpersonal beliefs. Interpretation and analysis of the therapeutic relationship can increase patients' awareness and understanding of their interpersonal beliefs and self-related attitudes. The therapeutic relationship may also provide a context for the patient to experience a "corrective interpersonal experience" that produces change in beliefs about the self in relation to others.

## Changing the Ideal-Self

The actual-self is only one component of the self-system that may require therapeutic attention. As previously noted, depressed patients may hold unattainable ideal-self standards that lead to negative self-perceptions. Several existing therapeutic techniques may be effective in changing the ideal-self standards of depressed patients. These interventions are similar to those utilized for altering the actual-self, but attempt to alter the ideal-self rather than the actual-self in order to achieve greater actual-self/ideal-self congruence. As with actual-self interventions, the goal of ideal-self interventions is to increase congruence (i.e., maximize matches), or decrease discrepancy (i.e., minimize mismatches) between the actual-self and the ideal-self.

### Making New Information Available Within the Ideal-Self Representation

Few therapeutic techniques have been developed to introduce new information into the ideal-self representation. If the ideal-self does not contain information about attributes that match the actual-self, depressed patients may fail to value their experiences and achievements. Encouraging patients to value their experiences and achievements (i.e., identifying these experiences and achievements as highly desirable and ideally wished for) may create new ideal-self attributes. Knowledge of patients' actual-self representations may be helpful to therapists in determining *which* attributes and experiences patients fail to value, and may maximize the likelihood of creating actual-self/ideal-self matches.

Behavioral techniques, such as encouraging individuals to participate in activities in which their undervalued actual-self attributes will be recognized and praised, may be effective in introducing new information into the ideal-self representation. For example, a patient who is artistically talented may not value his abilities because his ideal-self does not contain attributes related to these abilities. This patient could be encouraged to join an art class in which he may have the opportunity to receive praise and recognition for his undervalued artistic abilities. If artistic abilities came to be valued and represented in his ideal-self, the congruence between his actual-self and ideal-self would be increased as a function of the increased number of matches between the two self-state representations.

Cognitive techniques that actively encourage patients to attend to undervalued actual-self attributes may also be effective in altering ideal-self guides. Depressed patients often dwell on the standards that they have failed to achieve rather than the goals they have attained. Cognitive therapy techniques such as recording experiences of mastery and pleasure may help patients become aware of their successes and encourage them to value these experiences. As a consequence, these interventions may introduce new information into the ideal-self representation. Finally, depressed patients may hold beliefs about the types of attributes that are valuable or worthless based on their early experiences with significant others. These experiences may lead to constriction of the ideal-self and to the reduced capacity of patients to derive enjoyment from their attributes or abilities. Psychodynamic exploration of the meanings that patients have attached to early experiences and the effects of these experiences on their current capacity to value themselves may help to remove unconscious constriction of the ideal-self.

### Increasing or Decreasing the Accessibility of Particular Types of Information Within the Ideal-Self Representation

Particular contexts may prime the accessibility of ideal-self attributes that are either congruent with or discrepant from the actual-self. Therapy may act as a context that primes specific types of ideal-self knowledge in the same way that it may prime specific types of actual-self information. If therapy increases the accessibility of patients' ideal-self standards that match actual-self attributes it can temporarily increase actual-self/ideal-self congruency.

Behavioral techniques such as encouraging patients to include activities in their lives that are highly valued or pleasurable may increase the accessibility of ideal-self standards that are congruent with actual-self attributes. For example, a patient for whom creativity is both an actual-self attribute and an ideal-self standard might be encouraged to engage in activities where creativity is an important component.

As previously noted, therapeutic techniques that alter the temporary accessibility of self-related information may not produce enduring changes. The long-term effectiveness of these interventions depends on patients' abilities to adopt self-regulatory strategies to help themselves provide their own contextual priming of ideal-self attributes (e.g., making sure they are engaged in activities that are highly valued and consistent with actual-self attributes). Interventions that temporarily alter patterns of construct accessibility may also produce long-lasting effects if they are repeatedly introduced over an extended period of time and result in fundamental changes in the chronic accessibility of ideal-self standards.

Interventions may also focus on reducing the chronic accessibility of ideal-self standards that are discrepant from actual-self attributes. This may be difficult to achieve because the activation of chronically accessible ideal-self standards may automatically inhibit the activation of other less accessible ideal-self standards. Cognitive therapy techniques, such as encouraging patients to identify *when* ideal-self standards have been automatically activated (e.g., using negative feelings as a "cue" to examine whether or not they are evaluating themselves in relation to a chronically accessible ideal-self standard) and whether the application of ideal-self standards is *reasonable*, may help patients reduce the chronic accessibility of ideal-self standards (see Moretti, Feldman & Shaw, in press; Moretti & Shaw, 1989).

Memories of significant events may serve as a chronic source of activation for discrepant ideal-self standards in the same way that they serve as a chronic source of activation for discrepant actual-self attributes. Psychodynamic interpretations of significant experiences may be effective in altering the meanings that patients have attached to these experiences and reducing or eliminating the extent to which memories prime discrepant ideal-self standards.

## Changing the Extent to which Ideal-Self Attributes are Desired

It is not uncommon to find that depressed individuals hold extremely high standards for themselves. Performance that falls anything short of these standards is seen as evidence of personal inadequacy and failure. As previously noted, therapists may attempt either to increase the degree to which patients actually possess significant attributes, or to modify patients' ideal-self standards. Attempts to modify actual-self attributes so that they are not discrepant from the extremely high ideal-self standards that some depressed individuals hold for themselves may be impossible and destructive. Identifying and altering unreasonable ideal-self standards is often more productive.

Unreasonably high ideal-self standards may be identified and altered by encouraging depressed patients to consider whether they would negatively evaluate a peer using the same standards that they apply to themselves. This intervention is suggested from research on self and other perception (e.g., Bargh & Tota, 1988; Kuiper & MacDonald, 1982; Moretti & Shaw, 1989; Tabachnik, Crocker & Alloy, 1983) indicating that negative evaluations are restricted to the self in depression. Often patients realize that their ideal-self standards are quite unreasonable when they are asked to apply them to others. Patients may be encouraged to consider the types of standards that are reasonable to apply to others to generate alternative standards for the self.

The desire to achieve very high ideal-self standards is often based on beliefs about negative consequences that may occur if one fails to live up to these standards. Therefore, reducing ideal-self standards may involve altering the beliefs that individuals have associated with achieving or failing to achieve ideal-self standards. Therapeutic techniques that alter the perceived importance and consequences of achieving ideal-standards are considered in a section to follow.

## Changing the Certainty with which Ideal-Self Attributes are Desired

Depressed patients may wish to possess a number of ideal-self attributes that they perceive as positive and socially desirable. This may arise from the tendency of depressed individuals to unfavorably compare themselves to others and to believe that others possess positive attributes that they themselves lack (Tabachnik, Crocker & Alloy, 1983). It may be helpful for therapists to encourage depressed patients to evaluate the assumptions that underlie their beliefs that they need to achieve particular ideal-self standards. Cognitive therapy techniques may help patients to evaluate the validity of their beliefs that others possess many positive qualities that they themselves lack, and that others do not suffer from stress or concerns about self-worth. Patients might also be encouraged to explore the costs and benefits of striving to achieve extremely high standards. As they review the costs and benefits associated with achieving these standards they may become less certain that they desire to do so.

### Changing the Perceived Importance and Consequences of Possessing Ideal-Self Attributes

Individuals do not suffer from psychological distress simply because they wish to achieve an ideal-self standard, but because of the negative consequences that they believe will occur if they fail to live up to these standards. We have suggested that some children learn that their failure to live up to parental standards leads to parental disappointment or disapproval. Once established, beliefs about the consequences of failing to live up to standards can strongly influence the motivation to reach self-evaluative standards and the emotional consequences of believing that one has failed to do so.

It is important for therapists to determine depressed patients' beliefs about the consequences of failing to live up to high ideal-self standards. Patients may report that they believe their failure to live up to these standards will result in catastrophic events (e.g., "everyone will reject me," "they will see that I'm no good"), yet they do not know that this actually is the case because they have worked hard to prevent such an event from occurring. Behavioral techniques that encourage patients to "try out" moderate levels of performance that fall short of their ideal-self standards may provide patients with the opportunity to learn that the catastrophic outcomes they have imagined do not actually occur. Psychodynamic techniques may also help patients to alter unrealistic ideal-self standards by exploring the meaning they have attached to past experiences that are associated with beliefs about the consequences of failing to meet ideal-self standards. Patients may come to realize that the standards that they hold for themselves are not their own standards, but the standards that they believe that their parents or significant others hold for them. The consequences that they believe will occur if they fail to meet these standards may be based on their childhood interpretations of early experiences. Working through these beliefs from an adult perspective may result in patients changing the nature and extent of their ideal-self standards.

## Changing Actual-Self/Ideal-Self Relations

The most straightforward approach to intervening in the self-system in order to increase actual/ideal congruency or decrease actual/ideal discrepancy is to work directly on either the actual-self or the ideal-self as specific targets of intervention. This is the approach that we have discussed thus far. It should be noted that because actual/ideal congruency and discrepancy concern *relations* between the actual-self and the ideal-self, interventions that alter the availability and accessibility of actual-self attributes or of ideal-self guides also alter the availability and accessibility of actual-self/ideal-self relations. In this approach, however, the targets of intervention are the actual-self or ideal-self attributes per se. It is worth considering, if only briefly, how therapists might directly alter actual-self/ideal-self relations. For the purposes of illustration, consider the following two possibilities:

### Changing the Relative Accessibility of Actual-Self/Ideal-Self Discrepancies

Consider the following case. A female patient is suffering from depression and is found to possess a highly discrepant relation between her actual-self and the ideals that she believes her parents hold for her. The therapist observes that the patient becomes especially distressed when she discusses the views she believes her parents have of her. On the other hand, when the patient discusses alternative viewpoints on herself (e.g., her spouse's, her children's, her best friends', her own) she does not become distressed, and, indeed, the relations between the patient's actual-self and ideal-self associated with these other standpoints are found to be congruent.

When the patient evaluates herself, she can do so from any of these alternative self-guide standpoints (see Higgins, Strauman & Klein, 1986). At the beginning of therapy, it is likely that the self-guide standpoint of the patient's parents predominates and thus determines her self-evaluative processes. Her preoccupation with ideals she believes her parents hold for her may have led the attributes represented in the patient's actual-self to become strongly interconnected with the attributes represented in the parents' ideal-self for her. Thus, the "actual-self/ideal-parents" structure is likely to predominate and determine how the patient feels about herself. When an actual-self attribute is activated, it is this structure that is most likely to be activated. Given that this structure reflects an actual/ideal discrepancy, the patient is vulnerable to depression. How might one alter the likelihood that this structure will be activated?

The likelihood that any knowledge structure will be activated and used to process input decreases when the accessibility of an alternative structure that is equally applicable to input is increased. If the excitation level of the alternative structure is increased beyond the level of the discrepant structure, the alternative structure should begin to predominate and perhaps even inhibit activation of the discrepant structure (see Higgins, 1989b). Actual/ideal structures involving any self-guide standpoint are equally applicable for self-evaluation. Therefore, increasing the accessibility of an actual/ideal structure involving a self-guide standpoint that is an alternative to the standpoint of the patient's parents should decrease the likelihood that the "actual-self/ideal-parents" structure will be activated. This could be accomplished by having the patient frequently discuss and think about the viewpoint of some alternative person, such as the patient's own view of herself or the viewpoint of the patient's spouse. As a consequence of such frequent priming, the alternative actual/ideal structure might eventually predominate and even inhibit activation of the "actual-self/ideal/parent" structure. Given that the alternative structure reflects an actual/ideal congruency, the patient should then experience less psychological distress and greater self-satisfaction.

The critical feature of this intervention is to increase the accessibility of an alternative, competing self-guide standpoint that is known to involve an actual/ideal congruency (or, at least, a substantially smaller actual/ideal discrepancy). In this example, increased accessibility of the alternative self-guide standpoint was accomplished by frequent priming. But there are many sources of accessibility and activation other than frequent priming (see Higgins, 1989b; Higgins & King, 1981). For example, a patient's living conditions or life style might be altered so that the likelihood of contextual activation (i.e., recent priming) of an alternative self-guide standpoint is increased. Increasing the actual or perceived importance or applicability of an alternative self-guide standpoint might also increase its accessibility and the likelihood that it will be used. Thus, there are many specific techniques by which this type of intervention could be accomplished.

### Changing the Automatic Activation of Actual-Self/Ideal-Self Discrepancies

A major characteristic of actual-self/ideal-self discrepancies as a vulnerability factor is the fact that they can be automatically activated outside of awareness and cause emotional suffering (see Higgins, 1989b). Indeed, as discussed earlier, when people possess an actual-self/ideal-self discrepancy, mere exposure to a positive attribute (even an attribute characterizing other people) that is contained in their ideal-self can be sufficient to produce depressive symptoms if there is a mismatch between the actual-self attribute and that ideal-self attribute (see Strauman & Higgins, 1987).

The likelihood that an accessible knowledge structure will automatically influence responses decreases when people are actively oriented or consciously directed toward an alternative structure (see Neely, 1977; Posner, 1978). According to Posner (1978), when conscious attention is directed toward one kind of knowledge, processing input related to that knowledge is facilitated, but processing input unrelated to that knowledge is inhibited. Higgins et al., (1982) found evidence suggesting that such inhibition can also occur in relation to chronically accessible constructs, such that an active orientation to evaluate a target person in a particular way can inhibit automatic effects of chronically accessible constructs on judgment.

Actual-self/ideal-self discrepancies are chronically accessible knowledge structures. Therefore, if patients actively orient themselves to self-evaluative processes that are incompatible with these knowledge structures, then the automatic effects of such structures should be inhibited, thereby reducing suffering. This could be accomplished by training the patient to focus on their strengths and pay attention to their successes. Indeed, it is possible that one source of the "power of positive thinking" is the inhibition of the depressing effects of chronically accessible actual-self/ideal-self discrepancies. An active orientation to positive self-evaluations may have two beneficial effects. First, it would momentarily inhibit the negative consequences of automatic activation of actual-self/ideal-self discrepancies. Second, if such momentary inhibition occurs repeatedly, the excitation level of the discrepant structure would be given a chance to decay. By thus decreasing the chronic accessibility of the actual-self/ideal-self discrepancy structure, this structure might lose its predominance in the self-evaluative process. This technique, then could be combined with the previously described techniques to make alternative, actual-self/ideal-self congruency structures predominate as the automatic source of self-evaluation.

## The Need for a Holistic Approach to Self-System Intervention

This section has described self-system interventions aimed at multiple targets within the self-system: the actual-self, the ideal-self, and actual-self/ideal-self relations. Although two of these targets—the actual-self and the ideal-self—are elements of actual-self/ideal-self discrepancies, it is important to recognize that self-system interventions are not conceptualized as altering one aspect of the self (e.g., actual-self) independently of other aspects of the self (e.g., ideal-self). In addition, these interventions are exclusively focused on attributes that are currently involved in actual-self/ideal-self discrepancies (i.e., mismatches), or attributes that are currently or potentially involved in actual-self/ideal-self congruencies (i.e., matches). Moreover, self-system interventions may not alter actual-self or ideal-self attributes in an absolute way, but rather increase the representation of actual-self/ideal-self matches and minimize the representation of actual-self/ideal-self mismatches within the self-system. That is, all interventions that have been discussed, regardless of the target of intervention, have actual-self/ideal-self *relations* in mind. Thus, they reflect a holistic rather than elementistic approach to treatment.

At this point, the reader might well ask why not treat targets within the self-system in an elementistic fashion? Is it just a matter of theoretical preference not to do so or are there disadvantages to taking an elementistic approach? Cognitive-behavioral approaches to therapeutic intervention have tended to emphasize the importance of changing people's negative or irrational beliefs, cognitions, and attitudes (Beck et al., 1979). Such beliefs, cognitions, and attitudes are typically treated, both conceptually and therapeutically, as independent units. This elementistic approach is certainly effective, but it may have its drawbacks.

First, focusing on the negativity of independent self-beliefs rather than on negative relations between self-beliefs may be inefficient. For example, not all negative actual-self attributes are psychologically significant. Moretti and Higgins (in press-b) found, for instance, that individuals' negative actual-self attributes predicted low self-esteem only when these attributes were also discrepant from the individuals' ideal-self. Thus, interventions may be more effective if they focus on self-beliefs involved in actual-self/ideal-self discrepancies rather than simply on negative self-beliefs. In addition, it would be reasonable to concentrate on self-beliefs involved in actual-self/ideal-self discrepancies when patients suffer primarily from dejection-depression syndromes, and to concentrate on self-beliefs involved in actual-self/ought-self discrepancies when patients suffer primarily from agitation syndromes. By distinguishing between these and other specific types of self-belief relations (e.g., actual-self/ideal-*own* discrepancies versus actual-self/ideal-*other* discrepancies), interventions may be utilized with even greater precision and efficiency.

Second, identifying functional and dysfunctional self-beliefs in terms of their positivity and negativity as independent elements could even lead to errors in intervention. Imagine, for example, a male patient who is depressed about his past accomplishments but has not yet lost confidence in his capabilities and potential. From a strict cognitive-behavioral perspective, this patient's positive view of his capabilities might be seen as a positive indicator that could be strengthened and used to improve his condition. For example, the patient might be reminded of his own positive view of his high potential in order to provide evidence against his current claim that he is totally worthless and will never accomplish anything.

Such an approach would be reasonable when considering each of the patient's self-beliefs independently. But when the relations among his self-beliefs are considered, the pattern that emerges might suggest a very different therapeutic strategy should be implemented. It may be, for example, that this patient's beliefs about his capabilities or potential—his *Can* self—is part of a pattern in which his actual-self is discrepant from both his ideal-self and his can-self, but his can-self matches his ideal-self. He believes he can live up to the ideals he holds for himself, but he is actually failing to do so. Higgins, Tykocinsky, and Vookles (in press) have found that when the actual-self is discrepant from the ideal-self and the can-self, but the can-self matches the ideal-self, individuals are likely to report depressive symptoms. Moreover, they found that this self-belief pattern involving a belief in one's positive potential (i.e., the can-self is congruent with the ideal-self) was *more* predictive of later depressive symptoms than a self-belief pattern involving the belief that one's potential is limited (i.e., the can-self is discrepant from the ideal-self), even though both patterns involve an actual-self/ideal-self discrepancy.

The results of the Higgins et al. (in press) studies suggest that a self-belief pattern reflecting "chronic failure to meet one's positive potential" is more problematic than a self-belief pattern reflecting "fulfillment of limited potential." Thus, a patient's belief in his or her potential it is not necessarily a positive sign. In the case of our male patient, it may be advantageous to focus interventions on how he might ensure that he actually carries through and fulfills the potential that he possesses (e.g., behavioral strategies), or on understanding the underlying reasons that may have impeded his fulfillment of his potential.

By considering how a particular self-belief is related to other self-beliefs, it is possible to determine its true psychological significance for a patient. The key question for intervention is whether the self-belief is an element in a pattern that *as a whole* has negative psychological significance, rather than whether the self-belief by itself is negative. Indeed, without considering the role of a particular self-belief within a patient's self-system as a whole, there is the risk of strengthening a positive self-belief element only to produce a more negative self-belief pattern that increases the patient's suffering. And given that patients can have multiple *and* conflicting self-guides (see Van Hook & Higgins, 1988), one might intervene to change a patient's actual-self in order to reduce an actual-self/ideal-self discrepancy only to increase some other actual-self/self-guide discrepancy. Thus, self-system interventions need to adopt a holistic rather than elementistic approach precisely because *the self is a system.*

## SUMMARY AND CONCLUDING REMARKS

If changes in the self-system are central to therapeutic improvement, as many psychotherapists believe, then the first step toward producing such changes is to understand the nature of the self-system. Surprisingly, more attention has been paid to developing therapeutic methods than to understanding the nature of the target of these interventions. The self has received more conceptual attention recently in social, personality, and developmental psychology. Even here, however, the attention has been mostly restricted to the self-concept. Before dramatic progress can be made in developing therapeutic methods, there is a need to understand more fully not just the self-concept, but the self-system as a whole.

There are, of course, many possible perspectives on the self-system that can contribute to this fuller understanding. The present chapter began by reviewing one such recent perspective—self-discrepancy theory. According to self-discrepancy theory (see Higgins, 1987; 1989a), the key element in the self-system is the self-guide rather than the self-concept. Self-guides are valued end-states, self-directive standards. Both self-regulation and self-evaluation occur in relation to self-guides. And self-regulation and self-evaluation, in turn, are a major determinant of the self-concept.

In the first section of this chapter, the relation between the self-system and vulnerability to depression was discussed in detail. According to self-discrepancy theory, the people who are especially likely to suffer from depression are those who self-regulate and self-evaluate in relation to the ideal-self, and who believe that their actual-self (i.e., their self-concept) is discrepant from the hopes, wishes, and aspirations that they or others hold for them. Research evidence was described that supports the theory's proposal that symptoms of depression increase as the magnitude of actual-self/ideal-self discrepancies increase and as the accessibility of discrepancies increase.

The second section discussed the development of the self-system in general and of self-guides in particular. According to self-discrepancy theory, the critical precursor of self-guides is children's representations of the relations between their attributes and significant others' responses to them. Two major factors that influence children's acquisition of such self-other contingency knowledge are developmental changes in children's representational capacity, and different modes of caretaker-child interaction. This section also discussed how children's acquisition of self-other contingency knowledge and self-guides could increase some children's vulnerability to depression.

The model of the self-system provided by self-discrepancy theory provides a framework for utilizing therapeutic interventions with the common goal of altering the self-system. The logic of the model suggests three basic self-system targets—the actual-self, the ideal-self, and actual-self/ideal-self structural relations. The logic of the model also suggests that the major goal of intervention for each target is to reduce the magnitude and accessibility of actual-self/ideal-self discrepancies. To illustrate the application of this logic, possible therapeutic interventions for each target were discussed.

The purpose of this chapter was to examine the relation between the self-system and depression, and, by examining this relation, to identify therapeutic techniques that may be effective in treating depression. Self-discrepancy theory was used to fulfill this purpose. But self-discrepancy theory is not restricted to providing a model of the relation between the self-system and depression. The theory has also proposed relations between the self-system and both agitation-related symptoms (e.g., social anxiety) and confusion-related symptoms, and these proposed relations have received empirical support (see Higgins, 1987). Indeed, one of the distinct advantages of applying self-discrepancy theory to the treatment of depression is its ability to differentiate self-system vulnerability to depression from self-system vulnerability to other types of emotional/motivational problems, and its ability to suggest interventions that may be particulary effective for the treatment of depression.

**Authors' Note:** This chapter was written with the support of a Social Sciences and Research Council of Canada Grant to the first author (SSHRC 410–88–0908). We would like to thank Ian McBain for his helpful comments during the preparation of the manuscript.

# References

Abraham, K. (1985). Notes on the psychoanalytic investigation and treatment of manic-depressive insanity. In J. C. Coyne (Ed.), *Essential papers on depression*. New York: New York University Press. (Original work published 1911)

Alloy, L. B., Abramson, L. Y., Metalsky, G. I. & Hartlage, S. (1988). The hopelessness theory of depression: Attributional aspects. *British Journal of Clinical Psychology, 27*, 5–21.

Allport, G. W. (1955). *Becoming*. New Haven: Yale University Press.

Bargh, J. A. (1984). Automatic and conscious processing of social information. In R. S. Wyer Jr. & T. K. Srull (Eds.), *Handbook of social cognition, Vol.3*. Hillsdale, N.J.: Lawrence Erlbaum Associates.

Bargh, J. A. (1989). The power behind the throne of judgement: Varieties of automatic influence in social perception and cognition. In J. S. Uleman & J. A. Bargh (Eds.), *Unintended thought: Limits of awareness, intention, and control*. New York: Guilford.

Bargh, J. A. & Pratto, F. (1986). Individual construct accessibility and perceptual selection. *Journal of Experimental Social Psychology, 22*, 293–311.

Bargh, J. A. & Tota, M. E. (1988). Context-dependent processing in depression: Accessibility of negative constructs with regard for self but not others. *Journal of Personality and Social Psychology, 54*, 924–939.

Beck, A. T. (1967). *Depression: Clinical, experimental and theoretical aspects*. New York: Harper and Row.

Beck, A. T. (1976). *Cognitive therapy and the emotional disorders*. New York: Guilford Press.

Beck, A. T. (1986). Cognitive approaches to anxiety disorder. In B. F. Shaw, Z. V. Segal, T. M. Vallis & F. E. Cashman (Eds.), *Anxiety disorders: Psychological and biological perspectives*. New York: Plenum Press.

Beck, A. T., Rush, A. J., Shaw, B. F. & Emery, G. (1979). *Cognitive therapy of depression*. New York: Guilford.

Brewer, W. F. & Nakamura, G. V. (1984). The nature and function of schemas. In R. S. Wyer Jr. & T. K. Srull (Eds.), *Handbook of social cognition, Vol. 1*. Hillsdale, N.J.: Lawrence Erlbaum Associates.

Bruner, J. S. (1957). On perceptual readiness. *Psychological Review, 64*, 123–152.

Bruner, J. S. (1964). The course of cognitive growth. *American Psychologist, 19*, 1–15.

Butler, J. M. & Haigh, G. V. (1954). Changes in the relation between self-concepts and ideal concepts consequent upon client-centered counseling. In C. R. Rogers & R. Dymond (Eds.), *Psychotherapy and personality change*. Chicago: University of Chicago Press.

Bryan, W. L. & Harter, N. (1899). Studies of telegraphic language: The acquisition of a hierarchy of habits. *Psychological Review, 6*, 345–375.

Case, R. (1985). *Intellectual development: Birth to adulthood.* New York: Academic Press.

Cohen, M. B., Baker, G., Cohen, R. A., Fromm-Reichmann, F. & Weigert, E. V. (1985). An intensive study of twelve cases of manic-depressive psychosis. In J. C. Coyne (Ed.), *Essential papers on depression.* New York: New York University Press. (Original work published 1954)

Cooley, C. H. (1902). *Human nature and the social order.* New York: Scribner.

DeMonbreun, B. F. & Craighead, W. E. (1977). Distortion of perception and recall of positive and neutral feedback in depression. *Cognitive Therapy and Research, 1,* 311–330.

Derry, P. A. & Kuiper, N. A. (1981). Schematic processing and self-reference in clinical depression. *Journal of Abnormal Psychology, 90,* 286–297.

Dobson, K. S. & Shaw, B. F. (1981). The effects of self-correction on cognitive distortions in depression. *Cognitive Therapy and Research, 5,* 391–403.

Erikson, E. H. (1950). *Childhood and society.* New York: Norton.

Erikson, E. H. (1968). *Identity: Youth and crisis.* New York: Norton.

Fairweather, G. W., Simon, R., Gebhard, M. E., Weingarten, E., Holland, J. L., Sanders, R., Stone, G. B. & Reahl, J. E. (1960). Relative effectiveness of psychotherapeutic programs: A multicriteria comparison of four programs for three different patient groups. *Psychological Monographs: General and Applied, 74,* (5, Serial No. 492).

Feffer, M. (1970). Developmental analysis of interpersonal behavior. *Psychological Review, 77,* 197–214.

Fischer, K. W. (1980). A theory of cognitive development: The control and construction of hierarchies of skills. *Psychological Review, 87,* 477–531.

Fiske, S. T. & Taylor, S. E. (1984). *Social cognition.* New York: Random House.

Flavell, J. H., Botkin, P. T., Fry, C. L., Wright, J. W. & Jarvis, P. E. (1968). *The development of role-taking and communication skills in children.* New York: John Wiley and Sons.

Freud, S. (1952). *A general introduction to psychoanalysis.* New York: Washington Square Press. (Original work published 1920)

Freud, S. (1957). *Mourning and Melancholia.* Collected papers (Volume 4). London: Hogarth Press. (Originally work published 1917)

Gotlib, I. H. & Cane, D. B. (1987). Construct accessibility and clinical depression: A longitudinal investigation. *Journal of Abnormal Psychology, 96,* 199–204.

Gotlib, I. H. & McCann, C. D. (1984). Construct accessibility and depression: An examination of cognitive and affective factors. *Journal of Personality and Social Psychology, 47,* 427–439.

Greenwald, A. G. & Pratkanis, A. R. (1984). The self. In R. S. Wyer Jr. & T. K. Srull (Eds.), *Handbook of social cognition, Vol. 3.* Hillsdale, N.J.: Lawrence Erlbaum Associates.

Guidano, V. F. (1987). *Complexity of the self: A developmental approach to psychopathology and therapy.* New York: Guilford.

Guidano, V. F. & Liotti, G. (1983). Cognitive processes and emotional disorders: A structural approach to psychotherapy. New York: Guilford Press.

Halgin, R. P. (1985). Teaching integration of psychotherapy models to beginning therapists. *Psychotherapy, 22,* 555–563.

Hammen, C. L. & Krantz, S. (1976). Effect of success and failure on depressive cognitions. *Journal of Abnormal Psychology, 85,* 577–586.

Harrow, M., Lox, D. A., Markus, K. L., Stillman, R. & Hallowell, C. B. (1968). Changes in adolescents' self-concepts and their parents' perceptions during psychiatric hospitalization. *Journal of Nervous and Mental Disease, 147,* 252–259.

Harter, S. (1983). Developmental perspectives on the self-system. In P. H. Mussen (Ed.), Handbook of child psychology. Volume IV: Socialization, personality, and social development. (pp. 275–385). New York: Wiley.

Higgins, E. T. (1981). Role-taking and social judgement: Alternative developmental perspectives and processes. In J. H. Flavell & L. Ross (Eds.), *Social cognitive development: Frontiers and possible futures.* Cambridge: Cambridge University Press.

Higgins, E. T. (1987). Self-discrepancy: A theory relating self and affect. *Psychological Review, 94,* 319–340.

Higgins, E. T. (1989a). Continuities and discontinuities in self-regulatory and self-evaluative processes: A development theory relative self and affect. *Journal of Personality, 52,* 407–444.

Higgins, E. T. (1989b). Knowledge accessibility and activation: Subjectivity and suffering from unconscious sources. In J. S. Uleman & J. A. Bargh (Eds.), *Unintended thought: The limits of awareness, intention,* and control. New York: Guilford Press.

Higgins, E. T., Bond, R.N., Klein, R. & Strauman, T. (1986). Self-discrepancies and emotional vulnerability: How magnitude, accessibility and type of discrepancy influence affect. *Journal of Personality and Social Psychology, 51*(1), 5–15.

Higgins, E. T. & King, G. (1981). Accessibility of social constructs: Information processing consequences of individual and contextual variability. In N. Cantor & J. Khilstrom (Eds.), *Personality, cognition, and social interaction.* Hillsdale, N.J.: Lawrence Erlbaum Associates.

Higgins, E. T., King, G. A. & Mavin, G. H. (1982). Individual construct accessibility and subjective impressions on recall. *Journal of Personality and Social Psychology, 43,* 35–47.

Higgins, E.T., Klein, R. & Strauman, T. (1985). Self-concept discrepancy theory: A psychological model for distinguishing among different aspects of depression and anxiety. *Social Cognition, 3,* 51–76.

Higgins, E. T. & Moretti, M. (1988). Standard utilization and the self-evaluative process: Vulnerability to types of aberrant beliefs. In T. F. Oltmanns & B. A. Maher (Eds.), *Delusional Beliefs.* New York: Wiley.

Higgins, E. T., Strauman, T. & Klein, R. (1986). Standards and the process of self-evaluation: Multiple affects from multiple stages. In R. M. Sorrentino & E. T. Higgins (Eds.), *Handbook of motivation and cognition: Foundations of social behavior.* New York: Guilford.

Higgins, E. T., Tykcinsky, O. & Vookles, J. (in press). Patterns of self-beliefs: The psychological significance of relations among the actual, ideal, ought, can, and future selves. In J. M. Olson & M. P. Zanna (Eds.). *Self-inference processes: The Ontario symposium (Volume 6).* Hillsdale, N. J.: Erlbaum.

Higgins, E. T., Van Hook, E. & Dorfman, D. (1988). Do self-attributes form a cognitive structure? *Social Cognition, 6*(3), 177–207.

Horney, K. (1950). *Neurosis and human growth.* New York: Norton.

Inhelder, B. & Piaget, J. (1958). *The growth of logical thinking from childhood to adolescence.* New York: Basic.

James, W. (1890). *The principles of psychology.* New York: Holt.

Kovacs, M. & Beck, A. T. (1978). Maladaptive cognitive structures in depression. *American Journal of Psychiatry, 135,* 525–533.

Kuiper, N. A. & Derry, P. (1982). Depressed and non-depressed content self-reference in mild depressives. *Journal of Personality, 50,* 67–80.

Kuiper, N. A. & MacDonald, M. R. (1982). Self and other perception in mild depression. *Social Cognition, 1,* 223–239.

Lewinsohn, P. M., Sullivan, J. M. & Grosscup, S. J. (1982). Behavioral therapy: Clinical applications. In A. J. Rush (Ed.), *Short-term psychotherapies for depression.* New York: Guilford.

Leventhal, H. (1980). Toward a comprehensive theory of emotion. In L. Berkowitz (Ed.), *Advances in experimental social psychology* (Volume 13). New York: Academic Press.

Linville, P. W. (1985). Self-complexity and affective extremity: Don't put all of your eggs in one cognitive basket. *Social Cognition, 3,* 94–120.

Linville, P. W. (1987). Self-complexity as a cognitive buffer against stress-related illness and depression. *Journal of Personality and Social Psychology, 52,* 663–676.

Logan, G. D. (1980). Attention and automaticity in Stroop and priming tasks: Theory and data. *Cognitive Psychology, 12,* 523–553.

Moretti, M. M., Feldman, L. F. & Shaw, B. F. (in press). Cognitive therapy: Current issues in theory and practice. In V. J. Giannetti (Ed.), *The Handbook of Brief Psychotherapies.* New York: Plenum Press.

Moretti, M. M. & Higgins, E. T. (in press-a). The development of self-system vulnerabilities: Social and cognitive factors in developmental psychopathology. In R. J. Sternberg & J. Kolligian (Eds.), *Perception of competence and incompetence across the lifespan.* New Haven, CT: Yale University Press.

Moretti, M. M. & Higgins, E. T. (in press-b). Relating self-discrepancy to self-esteem: The contribution of discrepancy beyond actual-self ratings. *Journal of Experimental Social Psychology.*

Moretti, M. M. & Shaw, B. F. (1989). Automatic and dysfunctional cognitive processes in depression. In J. S. Uleman & J. A. Bargh (Eds.), *Unintended thought: The limits of awareness, intention, and control.* New York: Guilford Publications.

Neely, J. H. (1977). Behavior implications of information presented outside conscious awareness: The effects of subliminal presentation of trait information on behavior in the prisoner's dilemma game. *Social Cognition, 6,* 207–230.

Ogilvie, D. M. (1987). The undesired self: A neglected variable in personality research. *Journal of Personality and Social Psychology, 52,* 379–385.

Piaget, J. (1951). *Play, dreams, and imitation in childhood.* New York: Norton.

Piaget, J. (1965). *The moral judgment of the child.* New York: Free Press. (Original work published 1932)

Posner, M. I. (1978). *Chronometric explorations of the mind.* Hillsdale, N.J.: Erlbaum.

Pyszczynski, T. & Greenberg, J. (1987). Self-regulatory perseveration and the depressive self-focusing style: A self-awareness theory of reactive depression. *Psychological Bulletin, 102*(1), 122–138.

Rapaport, D. (1985). Edward Bibring's theory of depression. In J. C. Coyne (Ed.), *Essential papers on depression.* New York: New York University Press.

Rogers, C. R. (1954). Changes in the maturity of behavior as related to therapy. In C. R. Rogers & R. F. Dymond (Eds.), *Psychotherapy and personality change.* Chicago: University of Chicago Press.

Rogers, C. R. (1965). *Client-centered therapy.* Boston: Houghton Mifflin.

Rogers, C. R. & Dymond, R. F. (1954). *Psychotherapy and personality change.* Chicago: University of Chicago Press

Rounsaville, B. J., Klerman, G. L., Weissman, M. M. & Chevron, E. S. (1985). Short-term interpersonal psychotherapy (IPT) for depression. In E. E. Beckham & W. R. Leber (Eds.), *Handbook of depression: Treatment, assessment, and research.* Homewood, Illinois: Dorsey.

Rudikoff, E. C. (1954). A comparative study of the changes in the concepts of the self, the ordinary person, and the ideal in eight cases. In C. R. Rogers & R. Dymond (Eds.), *Psychotherapy and personality change*. Chicago: University of Chicago Press.

Sacco, W. P. & Beck, A. T. (1985). Cognitive therapy of depression. In E. E. Beckham & W. R. Leber (Eds.), *Handbook of depression: Treatment, assessment, and research*. Homewood, Illinois: Dorsey.

Segal, Z. V., Hood, J. E., Shaw, B. F. & Higgins, E. T. (1988). A structural analysis of the self-schema construct in major depression. *Cognitive Therapy and Research, 12,* 471–485.

Selman, R. L. (1980). *The growth of interpersonal understanding: Developmental and clinical analyses*. New York: Academic Press.

Selman, R. L. & Bryne, D. F. (1974). A structural-developmental analysis of levels of role-taking in middle childhood. *Child Development, 45,* 803–806.

Seward, G. H. (1962). The relation between psychoanalytic school and value problems in therapy. *American Journal of Psychoanalysis, 22,* 138–152.

Shiffrin, R. M. & Schneider, W. (1977). Controlled and automatic human information processing: II: Perceptual learning, automatic attending, and a general theory. *Psychological Review, 84,* 127–190.

Strauman, T. J. (1989). Self-discrepancies in clinical depression and social phobia: Cognitive structures that underlie emotional disorders? *Journal of Abnormal Psychology, 98*(1), 14–22.

Strauman, T. J. & Higgins, E. T. (1987). Automatic activation of self-discrepancies and emotional syndromes: When cognitive structures influence affect. *Journal of Personality and Social Psychology, 53*(6), 1004–1014.

Strauman, T. J. & Higgins, E. T. (1988). Self-discrepancies as predictors of vulnerability to distinct syndromes of chronic emotional distress. *Journal of Personality, 56,* 685–707.

Strupp, H. H., Sandell, J. A., Waterhouse, G. J., O'Malley, S. S. & Anderson, J. L. (1982). Psychodynamic therapy: Theory and research. In A. J. Rush (Ed.), *Short-term psychotherapies for depression*. New York: Guilford.

Sullivan, H. S. (1953). *The interpersonal theory of psychiatry*. New York: Norton.

Tabachnik, N., Crocker, J. & Alloy, L. B. (1983). Depression, social comparison, and the false consensus effect. *Journal of Personality and Social Psychology, 45,* 688–699.

Teasdale, J. D. (1983). Negative thinking in depression: Cause, effect, or reciprocal relationship. *Advances in Behavior Research and Therapy, 5,* 3–25.

Van Hook, E. & Higgins, E. T. (1988). Self-related problems beyond the self-concept: Motivational consequences of discrepant self-guides. *Journal of Personality and Social Psychology, 55,* 625–633.

Weiss, J. & Sampson, H. (1986). *The psychoanalytic process: Theory, clinical observations, and empirical research*. New York: Guilford.

Werner, H. (1957). *Comparative psychology of mental development*. New York: International Universities Press.

Werner, H. & Kaplan, B. (1963). *Symbol formation*. New York: Wiley.

Wyer R. S. & Gordon, S. E. (1984). The cognitive representation of social information. In R. S. Wyer Jr. & T. K. Srull (Eds.), *Handbook of social cognition, Vol. 2*. Hillsdale, J.: Lawrence Erlbaum Associates.

Wylie, R. C. (1979). *The self concept*. (Volume 2, revised edition). Lincoln, Nebraska: University of Nebraska Press.

Zaiden, J. (1982). Psychodynamic therapy: Clinical applications. In A. J. Rush (Ed.), *Short-term psychotherapies for depression*. New York: Guilford.

# 7

# Experiential Processes in the Psychotherapeutic Treatment of Depression

Leslie S. Greenberg
*York University*

Robert K. Elliott
*University of Toledo*

Florence S. Foerster
*York University*

KEY WORDS: depression, emotion, experiential, self, therapy

There are several existing theories of depression, each particularly concerned with specific types of depressogenic processes—biological, psychodynamic, cognitive, interpersonal, and behavioral. Despite their different emphases, these theories have in common that they give little consideration to the adaptive role of affect (Greenberg & Safran, 1987) in therapeutic change or to the organismic tendency[1] toward survival and growth (Rogers, 1959; Perls, Hefferline & Goodman, 1951). The omission of these processes in theorizing about depression and its treatment is unfortunate. After all, depression is primarily an affective disorder characterized by discouragement, a deadening of the will to live, a dampening of excitement or the life force, and stagnation in the tendency to growth. The adaptive role of affect and the organismic thrust towards growth are important in humanistic and experiential views of human functioning. Experiential therapies therefore should have something important to contribute in discussing this disorder.

Drawing on observations of the psychotherapeutic treatment of depression, we identify certain recurrent features of depressive information processing and discuss these as patterns of self-organization which leave people vulnerable to depression. Based on these observations we suggest that treatment, in addition to dealing with negative cognition (Beck, Rush, Shaw & Emery, 1979), requires accessing biologically adaptive primary emotional responses and associated self-organizations in order to remobilize the growth tendency and increase the person's ability to attend to and process new information (Greenberg & Safran, 1987, 1989).

---

[1] Organism is used here to represent the whole functioning person combining physiological and psychological functioning into an integrated view of the human system.

## THEORIES OF DEPRESSION

Although various theories of depression have been proposed, each with some support, no theory has proved definitively superior in understanding or predicting depression. Most research has examined particular variables which vary with levels of depression. Correlations have been found, but etiology is still unclear. What is clear is that a number of variables do covary with depression. An affective variable, dysphoria, is central in depression, although behavior, cognition, and biochemical functioning, in addition to affective functioning, are clearly impaired. In addition to feeling bad, depressed people are less active (Libet & Lewinsohn, 1973), have a negative social impact (Coyne, 1976, Hammen & Peters, 1978), have higher expectation of negative outcomes (Lewinsohn, Larson & Munoz, 1982), are self blaming (Beck, 1967; Semmel, Abramson, Seligman & von Baeyer, 1978), and recall more negatively affectively toned information (Kuiper, 1978).

Depression, as most clinicians recognize, is clearly not a uniform specific condition, nor are depressed clients uniform in their response to treatment. Rather, depression is a complicated multifaceted disorder, often diffuse in character, involving a broad spectrum of feelings, moods, and behaviors. Individuals' depressions are not only multidimensional, but are also highly idiosyncratic. The different phenomenological aspects of depression may have their own causes and patterns of etiology (Craighead, 1980), and each depressed person has a partially individual configuration of depressive features and experience.

Of the existing unidimensional theories of depression, biological theories hypothesize that depression occurs when there is an imbalance in the concentration or intake of certain neurotransmitters in certain areas of the brain. The biological framework also includes theories regarding the genetic transmission of depression. Intrapersonal theories, which see depression as a problem within the person, include the psychodynamic view of depression as predominantly a function of loss. In this view, individuals who are too dependent on others for maintaining a sense of self-esteem feel rage when the object of dependence is lost, through death or rejection. This rage cannot be directly expressed because of the dependence but is rather turned "inward" and becomes the self-blame and self-hatred characteristic of depression. Another intrapersonal view conceptualizes depression as a product of distorted thinking. In Beck's cognitive therapy of depression (Beck et al., 1979), emotions are seen as the consequence of thoughts. If one is depressed, it is because one is thinking in negative and unrealistic ways.

Interpersonal theories view depression as a reflection of the social system of which the individual is a part. The central hypothesis is that depression arises primarily from depressogenic relationship patterns. A recent treatment conceptualization (Kelman, Rounsaville, Chevron, Neu & Weissman, 1984) sees depression as occurring as a function of interpersonal and social problems. In this view, depression can be alleviated by bringing about improvement of the patient's current interpersonal functioning in such defined areas as grief, interpersonal disputes, role transitions, and interpersonal deficits. Behavioral theories regard depression as due to a decrease in response contingent positive reinforcement and/or a high rate of aversive experience, where reinforcement is defined in terms of the quality of interaction with the environment. This lack of reinforcement is postulated as occurring for several possible reasons, including the person's lack of social skills in obtaining positive reinforcers or in coping effectively with aversive events (Lewinsohn, Biglan & Zeiss, 1976; Nezu, 1986).

In contrast, our contention is that *self* processes are important in the generation of depression and that emotional self-regulation is important in the psychotherapeutic treatment of depression. We believe that a focus on self-organizational processes (Greenberg & Johnson, 1988; Guidano 1987, Horowitz, 1979; Kaplan & Kaplan, 1982; Markus & Nurius, 1986) and emotional processing (Greenberg & Safran, 1984, 1987, 1989; Foa & Kozak, 1986; Safran & Greenberg, 1986) can enhance the understanding of depression.

Before discussing our approach to depression, we need to address the issue of the taxonomy of depression. As we have said, depression is a complex and heterogeneous syndrome with the adequacy of DSM-III-R categorization for treatment as yet undetermined. It appears that alternate subtyping of depression will be useful to enhance the differential treatment of depression. Currently, attempts at subtyping based on factors such as self-esteem and dependence (Arieti & Bemporad 1980; Blatt, Quinlan, Chevron, McDonald, Zuroff, 1982; Beck et al., 1979) and on severity and functional impairment (Elkin, Shea, Imber, Pilkonis, Stoskey, Glass, Watkins, Leber & Collins, 1986) seem promising for making differential treatment decisions. Our discussion will focus on mild to moderate depression of either self-esteem or dependence type, but will exclude endogenous depressions and more severe and functionally impaired patients.

## ASSUMPTIONS REGARDING THE SELF AND EMOTION

Our understanding of the nature of the self and emotional experience in depression includes a number of assumptions. First of all, the self is an *organizing process* in which different self-organizations are continually forming in response to the changing situation. The self is a field event, that is, the self forms or emerges as a product of the interaction between person variables (beliefs, affects, actions) and environmental variables. The self comes into existence every moment as an organization for making contact with the environment (Greenberg & Johnson, 1988; Kaplan & Kaplan, 1982; Perls et al., 1951). This is a process-constructive conception of human functioning which views the person as a dynamic self-organizing system (Guidano, 1987; Greenberg & Johnson, 1988; Mahoney & Liddon, 1988; Markus & Nurius, 1986) in which the self is organized or constructed at each moment at the organism/environment contact boundary as a function of all the influences operating on it at that moment. This process-constructive view can be contrasted with a more structural psychodynamic view (Shapiro, 1965) which emphasizes an ingrained character structure, and gives primacy to early childhood in determining this structure. Rather, the process-constructive view emphasizes organizational processes as coping devices and pathology as occurring when these processes become too rigid to be adaptive.

The internal factors of most significance in the formation of self are cognitive/affective information processing structures or schemas. These schemas organize incoming information and provide the expressive motor and affective valence to experience. Thus, they are cognitive/affective action structures built over time by abstracting generic representations of stimulus features of events, appraisals of the events, specific expressive motor responses, and patterns of autonomic arousal in response to these events (Lang, 1985; Leventhal, 1979). Schemas organize incoming information by orienting perception and encoding in a schema-consistent direction. In addition, they provide the expressive motor and affective valence to experience and organize the person for action (Greenberg and Safran, 1987). Schemas change or develop over time by the admission of new experience.

Self-organizations are the activation of particular schemas or sets of schemas in response to internal or external cues. Each self-organization is a synthesis of a set of schemas. When activated, or more accurately, when synthesized, the schemas and associated self-organizations produce particular views of self, world, and others. Recent empirical work (Epstein, 1984; Greenwald & Pratkanis, 1984; Kihlstrom & Cantor, 1984; Markus, 1983) supports the idea of early self theorists that these self structures are among the most important factors in the psychological field that organize the person's experience and interpretation of the world (Allport, 1943; Kelly, 1955; Snygg & Combs, 1949). In our view, a vulnerable self-organization, for example, is based on the synthesis of a particular set of schemas, including feelings of fear or anxiety, a need for contact/comfort, a perception of others as aggressive or uncaring, a view of the world as hurtful or dangerous, and a sense of the future as insecure or unsure. On the other hand, an assertive self-organization includes feelings of self-confidence, a view of oneself as having legitimate needs, of others as receptive, and of the future as hopeful. Thus, a person can at any one time be organized as vulnerable, at another time as assertive, at yet another time as playful, and yet another as self-critical. In our view, recurrent self-organizations (Markus & Nurius, 1986; Higgins & King, 1981; McCann & Higgins, 1988) are recurring syntheses of the same or a similar set of schemas. Recurrent self-organizations are not reified internal structures or sub-selves but are, rather, the product of repeated syntheses of sets of schemas.

This view of self-organizations is similar in a number of ways to the Markus & Nurius view of possible selves. In both views, the self is viewed as a system of affective cognitive schemas that lend structure and coherence to the individual's self-relevant experiences, shape the perceiver's expectations, and guide information processing in particular domains. Both suggest that when a negative possible self is activated, it brings with it associated negative affect which influences behavior.

Differences in the two views centre on the degree to which these self-structures are aspects of a self-concept on which people are easily able to reflect. Markus and Nurius see possible selves as conscious self-representations which can act as incentives and essentially are motives. In our view, self-organizations are not self-concepts at all; rather, they are the fundamental automatic processing units which organize information and create self-experience. They are not conscious aspects of self-knowledge. Self-organizations are the self-in-process, creating self-experience in the world. Our self-organizations are agents rather than self-concepts and in this way differ somewhat from possible selves, which in fact appear to mix these two conceptions of the self.

The second assumption in our view is that primary emotions play an adaptive role in human functioning (Greenberg & Safran, 1984, 1987; Izard, 1979) and produce the motivation inherent in self-organization. Primary emotion is a biologically based action tendency which organizes us for action. Thus, anger organizes the individual for fight, and fear, for flight. It is important at this point to distinguish the organismic response pattern of depression from sadness. Sadness/distress is an adaptive primary emotion that occurs in response to loss and pain. The experience of sadness/distress motivates the individual to attempt to recover that which is *lost* directly or through replacement, or to act to relieve the distress. The expression of sadness/distress is also an important signalling system which promotes bonding and social cohesiveness by evoking nurturing caretaking responses in others.

Thus, sadness/distress informs us of our response to an environmental event that is one of loss or pain to us as biological organisms (Greenberg & Safran, 1987; Safran & Greenberg, 1988). This type of internal feedback organizes the individual to act in a fashion to recover the lost object, compensate for it, or to engage in action to relieve the distress. Sadness is a motivational source that induces the individual to remedy the effects of adverse events. When the remedy is found, the sorrow or grief work is completed and the sadness diminishes greatly or disappears. In contrast, the depressed individual lacks the capacity for the sorrow work (Arieti and Bemporad, 1980), gives up, no longer tries to repair the damage or recover the lost object, and so enters a state of hopelessness. In our view, psychological problems often arise when people are organized to avoid, block, or interrupt potentially adaptive primary emotional experience and the associated action tendency. This blocking of emotional processing results in particular self-organizations being disclaimed or their formation prevented.

A final assumption in our view is that emotional experience, if fully allowed and processed, is transient in nature, and that the complete processing of emotional experience leads to a *shift* in emotional state (Greenberg & Safran, 1987) and the emergence of new self-organizations. In contrast, chronic, unchanging, maladaptive emotional states result from interruption or incomplete processing of primary biologically adaptive emotions and result in static, dysfunctional, self-organization.

## SELF-ORGANIZATIONS IN THE THERAPY OF DEPRESSION

Psychotherapy is a potential laboratory for studying the different experiential states and psychological phenomena involved in human dysfunction and in change. In therapy, one can observe the emergence of different psychological states, the processes involved in generating and maintaining these states, and the changes in these processes correlated with in-session alleviation of problematic states (Greenberg, 1986; Greenberg & Pinsof, 1986; Rice & Greenberg, 1984). These observations can and should be used to shed light on the nature of maladaptive states and their "cure."

The therapeutic process has been sorely neglected as a source of data for understanding depression. Rather than attempting to define general characteristics of depressed people, it seems far more profitable to look at the depressed processes people manifest in the therapeutic situation and then describe these as person-situation variables for further study. The study of a *depressive process* in the therapy hour provides a lens for identifying the cognitive/affective and interactional factors that accompany mood swings in the hour. Therapy thus provides us with an in-depth "process" laboratory for studying depressive processes and their changes.

Luborsky, Singer, Hartke, Crits-Christoph & Cohen (1984) for example, drew upon the therapy setting to demonstrate that shifts into *depressive states* in psychotherapy, as well as the states preceding this shift, can be reliably identified. Thus, it appears that depressive states in therapy may be responses to prior experiential states. In the intensive analysis of a single case, Luborsky and his coworkers showed that a variety of state indicators, including those of helplessness and hopelessness, reliably preceded the shift into a depressive state in therapy. Viewing depression as a state which can be evoked in therapy, we can begin to ask questions not only about the nature of the in-therapy state, but also about the antecedents that evoke this state and the processes involved in changing this state.

Below we will describe four aspects of depression that we have observed in therapy and the processes associated with their emergence and alleviation. The four aspects are the *weak/bad self-organization*, the *self-critical organization*, *hostility toward the self* and the *withdrawn or hidden essential self*. We will extrapolate from these in-therapy observations to attempt to explain certain depressive processes that are not fully captured by psychological theories which do not focus on the self and self-organizational processes.

## The Weak/Bad Self-Organization

Based on our observations of depressive states in therapy, we hypothesize that a common feature among many people prone to depression is the emergence of a particular self-state, which we will call the weak/bad self-organization, characterized by a feeling of weakness and a desire to withdraw, close down, give up, and disengage from contact. This weak/bad self state is distinguished by feelings of weakness and unremitting fear and distress. This self-organization is marked by an extreme lack of self-confidence and a perception of oneself as fragile and unable to cope.

In addition to feeling fragile, this state is experienced as intolerable because the person is in unbearable pain. In depression, people feel ashamed of this weak state; thus it is felt not only to be a weak, but also to be a bad and undesirable state. This self-devaluation stems from the person's intense fear of feeling weak and helpless; these feelings are experienced as a threat to self-coherence. When this weak/bad self-organization is evoked, the person desires to withdraw, close down, give up, and disengage from contact. The person becomes depressed because, from this state, they perceive their efforts to be futile and their world to be hopeless. In this helpless, hopeless state, the depressed person becomes passive and breaks contact with new information about self and the world by allocating attention to depressive content rather than attending to what occurs at the organism/environment contact boundary. This state appears largely to be based on learned helplessness (Seligman, 1974, 1975). People have learned to expect that bad outcomes will occur (Abramson, Garber & Seligman, 1980). This has led to beliefs that actions are doomed to failure, and this in turn leads to depressed affect.

The following transcript shows the client's experience of the weak/bad self with its characteristic aspects of powerlessness and helplessness. This self-organization developed in response to the emergence in the session of the client's own self-criticisms and memories of criticism from her father.

C1: Yeah, like there's no purpose in trying. I'll never make up my mind. I'm a mess, I'll never make it, what's the use.

T1: Uh-huh, feeling like a failure. What is this feeling of being a failure? What is it that you're never going to make?

C2: I'm 50 years old, I'm alone, no money, no man. I'll end up on the heap (complaining tone). I'll never make it.

T2: You feel finished.

C3: Yeah.

T3: Say this. I'm finished.

C4: (30 seconds.) I don't know if I can say it.

C5: I'm finished. (Cries 20 seconds.)

* * *

The therapist picks up in T9 by asking the client to breathe and to symbolize her experience.

T9: Breathe. What's happening?

C10: I just feel like what's the use. It's no good trying. (7 seconds silence.)
(A few minutes later in the session the client again enters the hopeless, helpless state.)

C24: I go through life feeling like I'm going to be hammered. That's what it is; just this awful feeling like I'm crouching in a corner afraid of being hammered.

T25: What do you feel now?

C25: Torn to pieces. I don't know what to do... I feel what's the use. I don't know what to do.

In this segment, the client begins to experience feelings of failure and worthlessness associated with the dreaded weak/bad self-organization. The expression of "I'm finished" (C 5) "What's the use. It's no good trying" (C10) expresses the core of this experience of defeat and futility. In C24 and C25, the weak/bad self is clearly expressed.

Thus, we see this clients' weak/bad self-organization emerge in the process of therapy. It is a complex dreaded self-organization involving feelings of helplessness, hopelessness, failure, and worthlessness. The organization of the weak/bad self is evidently a complex one involving a number of information processing levels (Greenberg & Safran, 1987). It includes processing at the conceptual level with beliefs about failure, at the level of schematic emotional memory with episodic memories of failure and the feelings associated with it, and processing at the sensorimotor level, expressed in the crouching, hiding posture and other internal physiological reactions.

Earlier experiences of physical and emotional injury or loss, in which the devastating outcomes were uncontrollable, often appear, as in the case above, to be factors which lead people to form or internalise a weak, powerless self-organization (Brown, Harris & Copeland, 1977). This helpless sense of self probably emerges from some form of developmental experience in which healthy striving, enthusiasm, orientation to growth, and surgency were impaired, either through trauma, lack of environmental support, temperamental factors, or interactions of these. This sense of self is internally represented in a set of affective/cognitive schemes which, when activated, produce the weak/bad experience. The internalization and activation of the schematic representation of weak/bad self contributes to the vulnerability to depression. All people have internal representations of some of this weak/bad self-experience, but some have schemas which are much more readily accessible than others (Higgins and King, 1981) and/or representations that contain much more overwhelming experiences of powerlessness and helplessness. It is important to note that, in our view, not all depression is a function of developmental deficit, but this type of deficit can make a person more vulnerable to depression.

## Development of the Self

Daniel Stern's (1985, 1977) work on development of the self has implications for understanding the role of constitutional and interpersonal factors in the development of the weak/bad self-organization and *vulnerability to depression*. Drawing upon extensive observation of infants and young children, Stern has made inferences about the different ways the child may experience him or herself. He describes four clusters of self-experience which he calls senses of self: the senses of emergent self, core self, subjective self, and verbal self. He indicates that these organizations of self are achieved sequentially during early development, and once achieved, continue to be available throughout life. In this view, all infants experience these senses of self, yet each self-organization contains unique experiences for each person. The child's temperament and experiences with significant others are factors which can significantly affect how each of the organizations of self is experienced.

During development of the core self-organization, for example, between two and six months of age, the infant and significant others participate in the regulation of the child's overt self-experience. One aspect is regulation of excitement and stimulation. Each child has a range of excitement, below which boredom is experienced and above which unpleasurable overstimulation is experienced. Normally, the child seeks stimulation in the upper part of the range and will break away from contact which exceeds the upper threshold. However, Stern has observed caregivers who attempt to maintain stimulating contact beyond the child's upper limit. The caregiver might chase the child back and forth when the child starts averting his of her head in an obvious attempt to avoid the caregiver's previously enjoyable funny faces and sounds. In response to overstimulation like this, a plucky, determined child attempts, through many such interactions, to regulate the situation, perhaps resorting to tantrums, and to turn away the persistent other. A less strong willed child may give up regulating attempts much earlier. It seems that this child concludes that his or her inner needs have little impact upon the interpersonal situation; the child gives up, resorting to compliant, subdued behavior and forms a weak, ineffective self-organization.

In the later development of subjective and verbal senses of self, the child begins to enjoy and seek interpersonal sharing of internal states, such as intention, feeling states, or focus of attention. Depending upon the child's temperament, the response of the significant other will have a measure of influence upon how the child experiences him or herself as an intersubjective partner. According to the nature of the other's responses, the child learns which inner states are valued and which are likely to break the desired intersubjective union. Responses of disgust or disappointment, or a lack of any response at all, to the child's enthusiasm or desire for attention, introduces a "badness-tinged" feeling into the child's experience of him or herself. Upon acquiring language, the child becomes aware that certain self-experiences can be expressed verbally; other experiences, such as feelings of anger, perhaps, are so unacceptable that the child disavows or closes these out as "not me" experiences. The child who is more sensitive to this feedback will feel more keenly and react more intensely to the experience of parts of the self as unacceptable. This child is more likely to block or deny those unacceptable inner experiences, essentially giving up attempts to express them. The child has now begun to form a weak/bad self-organization.

Over and above traumatic losses or failures, we hypothesize that it is the self-experience made weak or bad in this way which can lead to a resigned, helpless, depressive response. Constitutionally vulnerable children may learn outward compliance and passivity rather than persistent efforts to regulate interactions, engage the other, or explore and master particular aspects of the environment. Repeated experiences of this kind—the initial self thrust, the unsupportive or the disapproving response, the subsequent experience of self as disempowered or bad, and withdrawal or resignation—are integrated, stored in schematic emotional memory, and re-activated when cued. The repeated occurrence of similar experiences broadens the range of cues which will activate the memory, making the person increasingly vulnerable to the experience of self as helpless, weak, or bad and the subsequent depressive response. Depression is thus characterized by the attribution of bad outcomes to the internal stable and global factors that have been shown to accompany learned helplessness (Abramson, Garber & Seligman, 1980).

## Self-Critical Organization

In addition to the weak/bad self, many depressed clients manifest a strong, internal, self-critical organization. They attribute failures to themselves and suffer from low self-esteem that characterizes one type of depression (Blatt et al., 1982). It appears as though negative, critical, unsupportive interactions with significant others has led the person to form a strong, internal, self-persecutory critic along with the weak, hopeless self-organization. Gestalt therapy (Perls et al., 1951) describes these criticisms as introjects; client-centered therapy (Rogers, 1959), as conditions of worth.

Because of the ready accessibility and self-disparaging quality of negative cognitions, they are often mistaken as a sufficient cause precipitating the depressive experience. It is interesting, however, that people can often voice negative self-views and not be precipitated into depressive episodes. While negative views of self, world, and future are characteristic and symptomatic of depression, we hypothesize that the more critical factor in depression is the *degree of negative affect* toward the self associated with these cognitions. Depressed people consistently show a large degree of hostility toward themselves when they are being critical. They are not just evaluating themselves negatively, they are furious at themselves for their perceived failings and are often very self-punishing. Depressed people say such things to themselves as "You stupid thing, why don't you think," or "You're disgusting and weak," or "You're a driveling slob. You don't deserve anything." However, this anger is not the anger at the lost attachment object turned inward, as postulated by psychodynamic theorists. Rather, it appears to be more like the internalized perceived hostility of the other toward the self. Certainly in some depressions, being able to express anger outward is a helpful change process, but this does not mean that depression is anger turned inward. This is too simple and linear an explanation of a far more complex process.

These extremely self-persecutory, punitive statements often occupy centre stage in depressions involving loss of esteem or failure. In depressions involving loss of love or loss of relationships, the hostility and negative cognitions are not initially as apparent. Negative views of the self, world, and future, such as "no one will ever like or love me," as well as negative affect, anger at the self, and blaming oneself for the loss are operating, however. In general, these negative voices are not always fully conscious initially, but are readily accessible and can be easily articulated with a little therapeutic probing.

The following transcript of a twenty-six-year old depressed female client shows the punitive, relentless nature of a depressed client's internal critic. In this example, the client is engaged in a two-chair dialogue between two aspects of self—the critic and the experiencing self (Greenberg, 1984). The client's experiencing self responds to the critic, not with anger or self-assertion, but by agreeing with the critic. In the face of the relentless critic, the client essentially collapses or gives up into hopelessness.

C1: I'm depressed all the time and I don't know why. People tell me, "You have everything that a girl could want," or whatever and I just ... you know ... I don't feel happy. What I don't have—you know—is the energy to create, the brains.

T1: So tell her this. (Indicating an imaginary self in an empty chair.)

C2: You don't have any creativity. You don't have any understanding. You don't have the mind. You don't have any brains. You are not sensitive; you're selfish ... (pause) ... you are immature, I know that. I know for sure you are immature. You don't work hard. You deserve whatever marks you get. Forties, fifties, failure ...

The client continues a few moments later.

C8: You don't have any patience. You always give up easy. You have no motivation. You always will be lazy. You are always giving up. You will always be like that. You are never going to be the person you want to be. You will never be the person who is active, thinks clearly, enjoys, is happy. Never, you'll never be like that.

T8: Change.

C9: Maybe what you say is true. I am a lazy bum. I don't do the work. I don't study hard. Maybe it is true. I don't have guts ... courage. Nobody trusts me any more. It is true. I know what you say is true and I'll always be like that.

Initially, the client describes feeling depressed. As she more fully experiences her critical self, the harshness and punitive sting of the critic is opened: "You don't have any brains..." in C2. In her response, the client's vulnerability to the harsh criticisms is evident. Her previous attempts to speak about the hurt collapse, and she agrees with the critic in C9. "Maybe it is true. I don't have guts and courage." It is this helpless internal response to the hostile criticism, the inability to combat the negative cognition (Greenberg & Safran 1987), that appears to be critical in generating depression.

## The Essential Self-Organization

Even though the weak, bad organization and self-critical organizations are well formed and dominate attentional allocation in depression, they do not completely obliterate the natural strivings of the core self and organism. This core sense of self is the essential self-organization—the earliest natural capacities integrated into the sense of self. This sense of self includes the organismic tendency to survive and to grow (Rogers, 1959; Perls et al., 1951) and the interpersonal tendency to be with others (Sullivan, 1953; Fairbairn, 1962; Bakan, 1966), in addition to the primary emotional responses (Eckman, Friesen & Ellsworth, 1972; Greenberg & Safran, 1987) and needs, such as needs for stimulation, contact/comfort, mastery, and security (McLelland, 1985). These organismic responses can only be experienced by attending to them. Even when attended to, they will emerge for the depressed client, initially, only in a very tentative, cautious form of self-organization and only if the environment appears safe.

In depression, it appears that the client's essential self, with the thrust towards growth and connectedness, has often in the past been met with harsh, severe, or otherwise unsupportive responses. The essential self withdrew, afraid of further hurt and trauma. It appears safer to the depressed person to put away the feelings and needs of the essential self and hold them apart from interpersonal contact and attempts to satisfy them. Clients in fact, often talk about self-organizations that are separate, isolated, or hidden and refer to closing off or closing down parts of the self, of putting part of themselves in closets or boxes, or shutting them in back rooms or drawers so that they won't be troubled by these aspects of themselves. Other times, people refer to parts of themselves as hiding, seeking protection, being in a cocoon, or being hidden away in some safe place, free of the "slings and arrows of outrageous fortune." It is as though some aspect of the self has withdrawn for safety and is closed off for fear of pain and turmoil. Depressive ways of responding in the world, such as resigning and giving up, mask the essential self, which lies hidden beneath, possibly hurt and angry, but still longing for warmth and contact and to be able to come out and grow. The essential self described here is similar to the hidden self described by object relations theorists (Fairbairn, 1962; Guntrip,

1969; Winnicott, 1965) and the archaic self described by Kohut (1977).

At the end of the section on the weak/bad self, we drew upon a session with a depressed client to show the organization of the weak/bad self. Further along in that session, after some intense emotional processing of the fear of being hammered and the feeling of being useless, we see the emergence of the client's essential self-organization.

T2: What's happening? Are you feeling sleepy?

C3: Yeah, like I'd like to curl up with a hot water bottle and just go to sleep.

T3: Yeah, just cozy, away from all this, which feels so overwhelming. It would be nice to just curl up into a ball, nice and protected.

C4: Yeah.

T4: Just all protected.

C5: Away from all this pressure.

T5: Yeah, can you speak from that position? What's it like for you inside, wanting to curl up? Do it actually—curl up and speak from there.

C6: (Curls up in the chair.) Well, I feel safe ... just away from the barrage, like I need to do this to wall myself off from all the criticisms and demands.

T6: So kind of protecting yourself by walling off your harsh side, other people's criticism, pressures, just the whole lot.

C7: Yeah, I wish she (her harsh side) would leave me alone.

T7: Say this to her.

C8: Leave me alone ... lay off.

T8: What do you want from her?

C9: Just to give me some space to breathe!

A few minutes later ...

T16: What you are feeling now?

C16: I feel sad, but I feel calmer sort of, like all that turmoil inside over the past weeks somehow isn't there now. Kind of makes more sense, all that turmoil. I have just been feeling so hopeless.

T17: Difficult to make a decision to feel like you can carry something through.

C17: Yeah.

Below is a second example from another client of the essential self-organization. First we see the experience of giving up and resignation (C1, T1, C2), then we see the gradual renewal and resurgence of the life force of the essential self (C8, C11, C16, C17).

C1: (Crying—emotional voice). I just want (crying) so bad to just (crying) to just rest (T: yes) and enjoy life, to go dancing, to laugh and walk along the beach ... and then I feel, just feel I'm too tired (crying), too depleted, or too, too far sunk inside (sigh) to just be here (sniff) (T: uh-huh). It's like I feel like I've sort of gone past sadness—about two weeks ago—and past the snarkiness, past fighting, to just (sigh)—giving up (T: uh-huh).

T1: I'd like you to give up now. Yeah. Stay with it.

C2: (Cries—sobbing for 50 seconds)

T2: Let yourself shake

C3: (Cries—sobbing for 50 seconds—then breathes deeply for 20 seconds more.)

T3: There is more?

C4: (Cries—sobbing for about 30 seconds more, deep breathing afterward.)

* * *

T6: Uh-huh. What happens now?

C7: I just want to breathe. To be loose (T: uh-huh) and just breathe. (Breathes deeply.) I've been ... so tight and so (T: uh-huh) just hanging on (sighs), struggling to keep the pieces together for a long time (T: uh-huh). I'm at the bottom, feels good.

T7: Uh-huh, uh-huh. (Inaudible phrase sounding gently inquiring.)

C8: There's just, there's fresh air (T: uh-huh) (deep breathing). Like I'm breathing back, just some clarity (T: uh-huh) some easiness.

T8: Yeah, some more.

C9: (Deep sighs.) Yeah.

T9: You smile.

C10: Like I'm still here (T: uh-huh), I've just been so buried for so long.

T10: Uh-huh, uh-huh. So be this "here." Describe it. What happens (inaudible)? (C: several deep breaths) What do you want (inaudible)?

C11: So (inaudible) (deep breathes) I'm here (deep breath) (inaudible), I really am here (T: uh-huh) Trust me (T: uh-huh). Don't go; just trust me.

* * *

C13: I'm (sighs) ... I'm here, I'm, I'm deep within you.

T13: I haven't left.

C14: And I haven't left (T: again). I haven't left (T: right) sighs) (T: what is that like?) I feel like I'm still deep inside (T: uh-huh); not some kind of trap (T: uh-huh, uh-huh); somehow some of the lid is off ... (T: right) but I feel really deep down now ...

T14: Yeah, I understand what you're saying.

C15: But I'm O.K. (T: yeah) I'm strong and (T: uh-huh) and just—I'm here. My experience is I'm strong and I'm replenishable (T: uh-huh). I can breathe again ... I can, I am building, I'm building a base, or I'm rebuilding.

T16: Say this again.

C17: I'm rebuilding; I'm replenishing.

## DEPRESSION—A COMPLEX PATTERN OF STATES

As we have mentioned, while patterns of negative depressive cognitions do indeed co-occur with dysphoria and are thus clearly concomitants of depression, there is increasing evidence that this style of thinking is not present either before or after a depressive episode (Lewinsohn, Steinmetz, Larson & Franklin, 1981; Peterson, Schwartz & Seligman, 1981; Wilkinson & Blackburn, 1981) and is probably not causal. Thus, we hypothesize that it is not simply negative thoughts which are involved in depression, as some theories hold, but a complex pattern of feeling and thinking that constitutes a vulnerability to depression. We have discussed self-organizations in addition to the negative, self-critical organization, which contribute to this vulnerability: organizations involving intense self-punitiveness, collapse into the weak/bad, helpless, hopeless sense of self and the fearfulness of the hidden, essential self. These aspects leave a person less able to combat the negative cognitions and more vulnerable to depression. This complex, depressogenic system of self-organizations is not readily accessible in laboratory situations, and this may be part of the reason why investigators have been unable to identify depressogenic schemas prior to or after depression.

Based on our clinical observation, it appears that depression is much more likely if the person's weak/bad, hopeless, self-organization is triggered, than if the critical self and the negative cognitions alone are activated. It is much more the person's response to the negative cognitions and their inability to cope with the self-criticisms, than the cognitions and criticisms alone, that lead to depression. People are unable to counter or combat the negative cognitions when the weak/bad helpless state has been evoked. This is when depressed affect emerges.

It is thus the combination of the hostility of the critic and the activation of the weak/bad self which constitutes an experiential vulnerability to depression, and it may well be that the hostility is the crucial variable in evoking the weak/bad organization. The weak/bad organization, although it is a recurrent, possible self-organization and therefore possesses some degree of structuralization, does not predominate in the person's everyday functioning and is not necessarily accessible under normal circumstances. Other forms of self-organization develop and help the person function in the world. In therapy, it is only when the weak/bad state is evoked that the depressive complex becomes visible and amenable to change. In addition, because these schemas were developed and elaborated in situations that were often highly traumatic or carried strong survival related meanings, and because they may represent internalizations of strong repetitious parental modeling, they tend to remain relatively unchanged and often inaccessible to contradictory experience in everyday life. This kind of refractoriness to change compounds the usual conservative tendency of schemas to remain unchanged due to their confirmatory tendencies. These schemas therefore, tend to remain isolated from new experience and disconfirming information.

To reiterate our main argument, based on our observations of the therapeutic process of depressed clients, we hypothesize that depression involves four experiential processes: negative or distorted thinking, associated hostile or punitive affect toward the self, such as anger or disgust, a weak/bad helpless self organization unable to counter the negativity and an unattended to, often fearful, hidden aspect of the self which is the essential, adaptive, organismic striving towards life and growth. Because this life force is not available, the essential, life sustaining, core self-organization is disengaged and when the helpless state is evoked, dysphoria ensues.

## THERAPY

The experiential treatment of depression involves, not only modifying the negative cognitions as in cognitive therapy, but more importantly, evoking and changing the weak/bad helpless, hopeless state. The evocation of this state in therapy allows for fuller emotional processing of the pain associated with it, and enhances access to and provision of support and comfort to the vulnerable, withdrawn, essential aspect of self. Experiential treatment mobilizes internal support by accessing the essential self-organization and by attending to the biologically adaptive emotions, such as sadness at loss, or anger at violation, that are associated with it. In this way, the person, strengthened from within, is more able to combat negative cognitions (Greenberg & Safran, 1987; Greenberg, Safran & Rice, in press). It is the response of the self to the negative cognitions, as much as the cognitions themselves, that requires modification. Thus, treatment involves, not only working with self-criticism and negative cognitions, but also accessing the weak/bad self and supporting the emergence of the essential self-organization and the creation of new self-organizations to replace the weak/bad self-organization. The self needs to be reorganized as well as cognitions modified. This is done, as we have said, both by mobilising primary affect and the biologically adaptive tendency toward survival and growth, embodied in them, and by providing support for the essential self by means of an affirming, empathic relationship to encourage the withdrawn, protected aspect of the self to emerge. These processes are at the core of our treatment of the self in depression.

### Theory of Intervention

This treatment entails both the establishment of a supportive, empathic relationship plus the facilitation of specific types of emotional processing and restructuring to achieve schematic processing changes. The former aspect we refer to as the provision of the primary relationship conditions of the treatment, the latter, the task facilitative aspect of the treatment (Greenberg & Rice, 1988; Rice & Greenberg, 1988; Rice, 1984). The primary relationship conditions involve an attitude of acceptance and empathy plus a focus on the client's current experience. These conditions enhance the development of a good therapeutic working alliance, an important contributor to change. As the client experiences the empathic attitude (Rogers, 1959) and the encouragement and acceptance of inner experience, he or she, as well as being willing to collaborate in the tasks of therapy, comes to internalize the therapist's optimistic and accepting view as an alternative to the self-rejection involved in depression. In addition to producing a safe, trusting, present-centered relationship, the therapist is process directive, guiding the client to engage in particular modes of processing at particular times. A specific set of therapeutic tasks which deal with specific types of in-therapy problems and involve different modes of processing in order to achieve resolution are also specified.

In this process-directive, experientially oriented view of therapeutic treatment, we suggest that mild to moderate reactive type depressions without melancholia are best viewed as a complex response to a variety of different underlying schematic processing difficulties that influence self-organization. This type of depression is treated by identifying the particular schematic processing difficulties involved in generating depression.

Treatment is viewed as proceeding best when the therapist engages in an ongoing "process diagnosis" of what current schematic processing difficulty is involved in generating the immediate manifestation of the disorder. This focus on the client's present experience and construction is the best way of accessing an individual's pathogenic information processing structures. This process diagnostic approach to therapy identifies which structures are currently operating and determining the person's immediate experience and then implements interventions in a fashion designed to produce change in that structure. In this treatment, the therapist is continually attending to in-session, client performance indicators of underlying processes or process "markers" (Rice & Greenberg, 1984) in making diagnoses of experiential states that currently need therapeutic attention and are amenable to intervention. The therapeutic judgment is concerned less with a particular theory of psychopathology, and more with assessment of the client's present processing style. We are thus proposing a process diagnostic, process directive, "marker driven," differential intervention approach to therapy and to the treatment of depression. (Greenberg & Rice, 1988; Rice & Greenberg, 1988).

Depressed clients in therapy present a number of recurrent in-session markers of different affective problems. They often refer to: (a) painful or confusing feelings which are experienced as coming from within and as either intruding on the client or being avoided; (b) strong emotional or behavioral reactions, such as depressive reactions, to external situations, which the person finds puzzling or unwanted (e.g., crying for no apparent reason); (c) unexpressed and unresolved grief and anger toward significant others regarding loss, either leftover from the past or stemming from current interpersonal conflicts; (d) internal conflicts between parts or aspects of the person involving self-criticism or a blaming and blamed parts of self; and, (e) apathy and an inability to satisfy needs, feeling resigned, powerless, and constrained in efforts to express and satisfy needs, desires, or wishes.

In response to these problems and the cognitive/affective information processing difficulties which underlie them, we have devised an integrated treatment (Greenberg & Rice, 1988), consisting of five therapeutic tasks. These tasks, described in Table 1, are focusing (Gendlin, 1981) and systematic evocative unfolding (Rice & Saperia, 1984; Rice 1984) from client-centered therapy, and two-chair dialogue (Perls, 1970; Greenberg & Safran, 1987), two-chair enactment (Greenberg & Minden, 1988) and empty chair dialogue (Perls, 1970; Greenberg & Safran, 1987), from gestalt therapy. Each intervention focuses on a specific processing difficulty and promotes resolution of that difficulty in a specific fashion. In addition, all are combined and enhanced by the provision of the overarching primary relationship conditions.

It is our contention that this "process diagnostic" approach is more sensitive than a subtyping approach (Blatt et al., 1982; Beck, 1984), to the particular processing difficulties that are involved in each person's experience of depression, and that each difficulty is best addressed by an intervention appropriate to the particular processing difficulty involved.

**TABLE 7–1: Therapeutic Tasks in Experiential Therapy of Depression**

| Technique Resolution | Task | Markers | Intervention | Resolution |
|---|---|---|---|---|
| Focusing | Clarify painful, present, felt sense | Strong, vague or confusing feelings reported; evidence of lack of involvement (e.g., superficial repetition) | C directs attention to specific felt sense; differentiates felt sense | C reports sense of newness, relief |
| Systematic Evocative Unfolding | Clarify sources of problematic personal reaction (usually recent) | Report of a personal reaction to a situation reported as problematic (puzzling or painful) | C, T reconstruct scene of reaction; alternate between exploring stimulus, feeling sides | C becomes aware of own mode of functioning |
| Two-Chair Dialogue for Self-evaluative Splits | Resolve internal conflict (of wishes or possible actions) | Description of two tendencies, reported as contradictory and causing current discomfort | C enacts conflict, alternating roles; specifies criticisms, feelings | C becomes more self accepting and integrated |
| Empty chair Work | Resolve negative feelings toward Significant Other | Description of blocked but lingering anger, hurt toward important person (complaining, resentful) | C enacts conversation with other; T pushes for emotional expression | C accepts and understands the other |
| Two-Chair Enactment for Self-Interruption | Expression of feelings and needs | Report of resigned, hopeless feelings; Sense of being squeezed, blocked, overcontrolled | C focuses attention upon self-interrupting process, reconnects interrupted feeling to relevant situation and learns to express it in constructive fashion | C expresses self and reports sense of empowerment |

| TABLE 7–2: Two Levels of Theory | |
|---|---|
| *Theory of Dysfunction* | *Theory of Intervention* |
| Latent self organizations | Manifest Process markers of dysfunctional aspects of information processing |
| 1. Weak/bad self (helpless, hopeless feelings) | • Self evaluative splits |
| 2. Self critical organizations (negative cognitions) | • Unfinished business |
| 3. Negative affect toward self (hostility, disgust) | • Self interruption |
| 4. Essential self organization (survival/growth & connectedness, primary affects.) | • Problematic reactions |
| | • Being on the surface |

## Theory of Intervention in Relation to Theory of Dysfunction

The therapeutic approach, based on assessing performance markers of underlying processing difficulties, is a theory of intervention as to how to best facilitate change in therapy. The previously stated theory of experiential processes in depression identifies common depressogenic self-organizations but does not specify how to access or modify these in therapy. Thus, we have two levels of theory, as outlined in Table 7–2: a theory of dysfunction outlining four aspects of self-organization which constitute vulnerability to depression, and a theory of intervention which suggests that depression in any particular client can be treated best by identifying a variety of schematic processing difficulties in the individual that result from underlying depressive self-organizations. Because depression is not a unidimensional, homogeneous disorder, (Craighead, 1981; Lewinsohn, Larson & Munoz, 1982), we have found that therapy often needs to deal with different processing difficulties in different people or different processes at different times in the same individuals. As we pointed out above, depressed people in therapy talk about painful feelings, problematic reactions, conflicts, unfinished business, and their inability to satisfy needs. This is the level at which the therapist must intervene to access the depressogenic process.

We will now briefly look at how each of these processing difficulties is treated, bearing in mind that individuals are unique meaning constructing beings and that therapy involves working within each individual's meaning framework and working with each client's current experience. Table 7–1 summarizes the five therapeutic tasks in the experiential treatment of depression. It identifies the purpose of each task, the client behaviors or "markers" that indicate readiness to engage in the task, the way the task is carried out, and the indicators of resolution or completion of the task.

## THERAPEUTIC TASKS

### Two-Chair Dialogue at Self-Evaluative Splits

In therapy, clients often present conflicts between two aspects of the self. In depression, these often contain, implicitly or explicitly, self-criticisms such as "I'm bad," "I'm too selfish," or "I've failed miserably." These can be worked with as two manifestations of an internal dialogue, with one part of the self criticising the other part. Initially, the second part responds either by agreeing with the criticism or becomes passive in response to it.

In working with these self-evaluative splits (Greenberg, 1979, 1984), the two aspects of the self or different self-organizations, a harsh "critical" self and an experiential reaction to the criticism, are clearly separated, often spatially, in two chairs. A dialogue between them is instigated with the therapist promoting the active expression of each side of the split and encouraging a confrontation between them. The depressive processes become readily apparent. In the critical chair, after first berating themselves for being depressed and possibly coaching themselves on how to improve, clients move to more concrete and specific types of criticism. In response to the punitive criticism, the depressed person's experiencing self initially complies with the critic, saying "You're right, I'm dumb; I've never achieved anything" or "I should try harder." Both of these responses then shift to the depressed sense of futility, "It's no use" and to the depressed, bad feeling, "I'm useless; I'm bad" and to an ultimate sense of hopelessness and helplessness.

Change occurs by supporting and mobilizing affect in the essential self which has withdrawn from the critical self-organization. The mobilized, strong, essential sense of self is then able to combat the negative cognitions from a position of strength. Research has shown that this process of emergence of new aspects of the self leads to a softening of the critic and to greater self-acceptance (Greenberg, 1979, 1984). Thus, accessing of this survival and growth force occurs paradoxically, by exposing the negative self-statements, stimulating the hostility toward the self, and by allowing the weak and the hopeless response of the weak/bad sense of self to be experienced fully within an accepting and prizing environment. The person generally expends a lot of attentional effort and emotional energy in trying to stave off the helpless, hopeless feelings from conscious experience or feels overwhelmed by them and out of control. In contrast, full awareness and experience of these feelings in a safe environment and with an appropriate sense of control over them allows them to be fully processed and accepted. This leads to a change in these feelings. Fully embracing them decreases their bad quality for no longer are they alien, "not me" experiences; now the person feels "It is me who feels helpless and powerless" or "*I* feel finished." This acceptance and ownership of one's bad feelings gives them a previously denied legitimacy. In allowing and accepting these previously disavowed feelings, a shift in emotional organization takes place (Greenberg & Safran, 1987). New emotional responses and self-organizations emerge.

It is important to emphasize that it is not the critical, depressive, "I'm bad; I'm no good" which is heightened and more deeply experienced, but rather, it is the fundamental pain and distress—the wounded, hurt, self-experience at the core of the depression—which is being experienced and allowed and consequently embraced and comforted. Acceptance of the disowned experience brings a relief similar to that which occurs in allowing oneself to cry and be accepted and comforted by another. However, in accepting the pain (Greenberg & Safran, 1987), one is recognising and allowing the loss and sadness in oneself and comforting oneself while experiencing it. This is the "sadness work" (Arieti & Bemporad, 1980) of grieving which the depression has prevented.

## Empty Chair Dialogue and Unfinished Business

In addition to reconnecting with the emotion of sadness, depressed clients often experience biologically adaptive anger en route to change. This is particularly apparent when people work on unfinished business related to the depression (Daldrup, Beutler, Engle & Greenberg, 1988; Greenberg & Safran, 1987). For example, people often have a lot of unexpressed anger toward a parent or an ex-spouse. In therapy, an "empty chair" dialogue with the imagined parent leads to the expression of resentment and anger which could not be expressed directly when the person was younger or more dependent. Earlier, the person came to feel hopeless and apathetic and just gave up. Being able to remobilise these unexpressed feelings in a supportive environment empowers the person and gives them a sense of the legitimacy of their needs. This greater sense of entitlement helps overcome the depression. Unfinished grieving can also be facilitated by this type of dialogue which helps activate the interrupted grieving process and allows the person to work through the loss and separate in a healthy fashion.

It is the purpose of intervention to allow the person to express their feelings fully to the imagined significant other (such as an alcoholic parent) in an empty chair. The intervention involves the *arousal* of emotion and the *expression* of what was previously restricted until the expression is completed. The process of intense expression leads to a *relief and recovery* phase and then to a *restructuring* of the schema of the other. This occurs by the development of a new view of the significant other, based on a greater understanding of the other and the incorporation of the good and bad features of the other into a single more unified representation (Greenberg & Safran, 1987). This results in the development of a feeling of closure about the unfinished business and relief of depressive symptoms and mobilization of the resources of essential self. Beutler and his group (Beutler, 1986; Daldrup et al., 1988) have shown that the use of empty chair work, for the expression of constricted anger, has led to improvement on some measures of depression and subjective aspects of pain, for patients, with arthritis and depression.

## Two-Chair Enactment for Self-Interruption

In addition to carrying unfinished business, many depressed people display a chronic process of self-interruption and self-punishment in which primary feelings or needs are prohibited from expression in a punitive way which leaves the person feeling helpless and passive. The distinguishing characteristic of this type of split (Greenberg 1979, 1984) is the *interruption or suppression of self-expression* as opposed to the negative evaluation of an aspect of the self as in conflict splits. The prototypic state is one in which an angry or assertive response to an environmental impingement is restricted and literally "held back" by muscular squeezing, clenching of the jaw, or tensing of the body. Thus, healthy assertive expressions, such as anger at violation or requests for support when vulnerable, are interrupted, resulting in apathy and/ or tension and a passive, helpless, or hopeless sense of self. Awareness by the person that "It is I who am interrupting myself" rather than a view that it just happens, or that others are doing it to me, plus an awareness of the blocked emotion and action tendency begins to give the person a greater sense of control of the experience. When the previously automatic processing involved in the interruption is slowly transformed into controlled processing by the enactment procedures (Greenberg & Safran, 1981, 1987), people are able to bring the interruptive processing under greater control. They can then become aware of the interrupted feeling, can connect it to the relevant situation, and begin to learn how to express it in a constructive fashion. This experience *empowers* the client and enables him or her to engage more actively in the world. Thus, a person who feels hopeless after a setback can mobilize anger to deal with the world, or a person who feels overwhelmed by the demands of others can reassert his or her own boundaries.

## Systematic Evocative Unfolding at Problematic Reactions

A fourth in-therapy state, frequently involved in the therapy of depression, addresses a class of schematic processing difficulties that govern one's interactions with other people and situations. Clients often report feeling inexplicably depressed at some time or in response to some situation. The client is puzzled by his or her reaction, and the awareness of a discrepancy between his/her expected and actual reaction makes the client amenable to examine the problematic reaction (Rice 1974; Rice & Saperia, 1984).

At this marker, the therapist encourages the client to describe the incident as vividly as possible, thus re-evoking the situation and feelings experienced at the time. The therapist then facilitates the client in getting in touch with the edges of his/her affectively-toned experience and thus discovering and synthesizing crucial elements of the experience that had not been fully processed in awareness. The assumption underlying this process is that if the incident can be vividly re-evoked under conditions of safety, the incident can be reprocessed by the client more slowly and completely. It is this new, self-discovered information that will force reorganization of the inadequate or distorted self-in-the-world schemas that are involved in the depressive reaction.

## "Being on the Surface" and Focusing

The final task in this approach is most general in use and involves focusing of attention on the preverbal, bodily felt sense underlying the depressed state. This intervention can be used early in treatment and subsequently to help clients clarify experiences underlying depression. The technique seems especially useful when the client is experiencing confusion or lack of meaning, or is unable to articulate a feeling she or he knows is there. It is also a good method for teaching the client about many of the basic concepts and assumptions of the treatment, such as experiencing.

Using the intervention, the therapist engages the client in a series of steps designed to facilitate movement from a surface or confused level of experience to an internal focus. The steps involve: clearing one's mind and bringing attention to bear upon the bodily felt referent; characterizing this bodily felt referent by a word or image; checking this symbol, either word or image, against the bodily felt sense: "Does it convey the felt sense?"; and, exploring what it is about the whole problem that produced this particular quality or felt sense. This technique has been manualized in detail (Gendlin, 1981).

This process is essentially a method of accessing tacit schematic level processing. These schemata are the basis of bodily felt meaning, and their activation is the required baseline level of process in a experiential therapy. Working at this level of personal meaning helps the client to feel more aware of and accepting of their feelings and needs—important steps in breaking the hopeless, powerless cycle of depression. Focusing helps the depressed client achieve a higher level of experiencing and to sense the authenticity and validity of that inner reality which is not easily wiped out by punitive self-criticism. This is a powerful antidote to the feelings of powerlessness and futility of depression.

## RESEARCH ON THE EXPERIENTIAL THERAPY OF DEPRESSION

Despite a potential fit between depression and experiential therapy, its effectiveness with moderately depressed clients is just beginning to be investigated. This is largely an accident of history—early researchers used the now defunct diagnostic category of "neurotic" to describe their client populations. The success of client-centered therapy with "neurotic" clients suggests that experiential therapy is likely to be effective with a Major Depressive disorder, formerly subsumed under the "neurosis" label (Rogers and Dymond, 1954; Shlien, Mosak & Dreikurs, 1962; Smith, Glass & Miller, 1980). In addition, there is already some adventitiously obtained evidence from two studies from the cognitive therapy literature which suggest that experiential therapy can be a somewhat effective treatment for depression (Fuchs and Rehm, 1977; Shaw, 1977). In both studies, weak forms of client-centered therapy groups, used as so-called "attention placebo" controls, outperformed wait-list controls; in one study (Fuchs and Rehm, 1977), client-centered therapy was equal in effectiveness to a cognitive self-control treatment.

The process-experiential treatment for depression described above, combining the primary relationship conditions of the client-centered approach and the specific tasks for working on different processing difficulties, is currently being investigated as a treatment for depression (Elliot, Clark, Kemeny, Wexler, Mack & Brinkerhoff, 1988). This treatment shows promise in alleviating depression. In addition to evaluating treatment effects, Elliott and his group have concentrated on investigating client reports of the therapeutic process. The process and outcome results of the study to date are discussed briefly below.

Ten clients involved in this study have so far completed treatment. All were

TABLE 7–3: Change Measure Data for First
Ten Cases: Means and SDs

| Measure | Initial Screening | Pre-treatment | Mid-treatment | Post-treatment | 6-month Follow-up |
|---|---|---|---|---|---|
| BDI Mean: | 22.4 | 21.6 | 15.0 | 8.7 | 7.8 |
| (SD): | (6.1) | (8.3) | (9.0) | (9.6) | (9.4) |
| n: | 10 | 10 | 10 | 10 | 4 |
| Hamilton | 19.4 | — | 13.8 | 7.3 | 5.4 |
| | (4.9) | | (3.8) | (4.6) | (6.5) |
| | 6 | | 6 | 6 | 4 |
| MCMI D | 111.9 | 103.7 | 89.8 | 74.6 | 69.3 |
| | (15.2) | (17.2) | (14.8) | (15.8) | 7.4 |
| | 10 | 10 | 10 | 10 | 4 |
| SCL–90 | 1.47 | 1.19 | .90 | .68 | .42 |
| | (.39) | (.31) | (.52) | (.61) | (.51) |
| | 10 | 10 | 9 | 9 | 3 |
| HSRS | — | 60.4 | 66.8 | 71.0 | 81.3 |
| | | (6.0) | (7.9) | (13.0) | (4.3) |
| | | 6 | 8 | 10 | 6 |

Note: BDI=Beck Depression Inventory (cut-off=11). Hamilton=Hamilton Depression Scale (cut-off=14). MCMI D = Millon Clinical Multiaxial Inventory, Dysthymia Scale (BR score; cut-off=75). SCL–90=Symptom Checklist–90 Global Symptom Index (cut-off=1.0). HSRS=Health Sickness Rating Scale (cut-off=75).

diagnosed as depressed on at least two of the following three instruments: a) Hamilton Depression Scale; b) the Beck Depression Inventory; or c) a diagnosis on DSM-III of either Major Episode of Depression or dysthymia. Clients were treated for sixteen sessions of experiential therapy. None of the clients was on any medication for depression or other psychological disorders.

Treatment effects were evaluated in a number of ways. The first indication of effects were the outcome results on a number of measures of symptomatology. Table 7–3 shows client performance on these measures. These results can be summarized in terms of the number of clients passing the five clinically significant threshold values on the Beck Depression Inventory (Beck, Ward, Mendelson, Mock & Erbaugh, 1961), Hamilton Depression Scales (Hamilton, 1960), Millon Clinical Multixial Inventory (Millon, 1983), Symptom Checklist–90 (Derogatis, Rickels &

Roch, 1976), and the Health Sickness Rating Scale (Luborsky, 1962). At the end of therapy, all ten clients bettered the threshold value on at least one of these five change measures; six out of ten clients passed the cut-offs on a majority of measures; and three clients passed all five. At a six-month follow-up, eight out of nine clients scored at below clinical levels on a majority of the five measures; but only one passed on all five.

Averaging change effect sizes across measures provides another way to summarize treatment effects. At midtreatment, clients had changed an average of 1.04 standard deviations; at posttreatment, this value reached 1.71 standard deviations; while at six-month follow-up, it improved still further to 2.47 standard deviations.

The results for the Beck allow comparison to the no-treatment control group data meta-analyzed by Nietzel, Russell, Hemmings & Gretter (1987). The outcome data for these ten clients compare quite favorably with the average effects found for 31 studies of psychotherapy of depression (pre-to posttreatment BDI: 25 to 11 vs. 22 to 9 for the present data). Based on this, it appears reasonable to infer that clients treated with the integrated experiential therapy changed more than if they had gone untreated.

In studying the change process further, Elliott (Elliott et al., 1988) probed the clients' self-reports of what had changed for them in therapy. Grounded theory analysis of the changes over treatment reported by clients in a posttreatment interview led to the identification of three major domains of change: improvements within the self, improvements in dealing with others, and improvements in the client's environment. Consistent with the intrapersonal nature of experiential therapy, all clients described improvements within the self. Clients reported three different types of improvements in self: enhanced positive feelings, action-related changes, and closer contact with the self. This third sub-category, closer contact with the self, is particularly relevant to the experiential model of therapy. Clients ratings of session impacts and most helpful events gave highest ratings to being understood and supported, becoming closer to the therapist and more involved in the therapy, and gaining increased awareness. The above results were obtained from client ratings on predetermined scales. In addition, clients were asked to describe in their own words the most helpful or hindering events within each session. These reports were categorised by raters. "Awareness of self" was by far the most common impact described, occurring at a rate of almost forty percent in the events described. These data are all consistent with the experiential model in placing the locus of the change process firmly in the therapeutic relationship and the process of enhanced self-awareness.

This continuing research is investigating the impacts of an experiential therapy of depression at both "macro" (outcome) and "micro" (events and sessions) levels. The picture from each is a predominately positive one. It seems that experiential therapy does what it purports to do—brings a person into better relationship with him or herself. Furthermore, this process was perceived as helpful by all clients seen in this study to date.

## SUMMARY AND CONCLUSIONS

Although evidence has begun to demonstrate that treatments such as cognitive therapy (Beck, et al., 1979) and interpersonal therapy (Klerman et al., 1982) are effective for moderate depression (Elkin et al., 1986), the process by which clients change in therapy is still not clear. A process analysis of the experience of depression in therapy is needed to provide a true understanding of the manner in which psychotherapeutic treatments help alleviate depression. We have, in this paper, given an initial description of the major experiential processes that we have observed in the treatment of depression and have reported the initial results of a study of the process and outcome of this therapeutic approach to depression. Further research on the process of change (Greenberg, 1986) in the psychotherapy of depression is needed for a true understanding of the curative agents in this treatment.

We have suggested four aspects of self-organization that emerge in the treatment of depression: the weak/bad self, the critical self, hostility toward the self, and the essential growth/survival oriented self. In addition, we specified five therapeutic tasks important in overcoming depression: the resolution of conflict, the completion of unfinished business, the understanding of problematic reactions, the clarification of painful and confusing feelings, and the mobilization of affect to overcome the suppression of self-expression. These tasks are facilitated by active interventions designed to deal with the specific affective information-processing difficulties involved in the different affective problems. The active intervention tasks are embedded in an overarching relationship involving empathic responsiveness to, and a genuine prizing of, the individual's ongoing experience. This combination of a supportive relationship with active interventions that address particular affective information processing problems appears promising in the psychotherapeutic treatment of depression.

## References

Abramson, L.Y., Garber, J. & Seligman, M.E.P. (1980). Learned helplessness in humans: An attributional analysis. In M.J. Garber & M.E.P. Seligman (Eds.), *Human helplessness.* (pp. 3–34). New York: Academic.

Allport, G.W. (1943). *Becoming: Basic considerations for a psychology of personality.* New Haven, CT: Yale University Press.

Arieti, S. & Bemporad, J.R. (1980). The psychological organization of depression. *American Journal of Psychiatry, 137,* 1360–1365.

Bakan, D. (1966). *The duality of human existence.* Chicago: Rand McNally.

Beck, A.T. (1967). *Depression: Clinical, experimental, and theoretical aspects.* New York: Harper & Row.

Beck, A.T. (1984). Cognition and therapy. *Archives of General Psychiatry, 41,* 1112–1125.

Beck, A.T., Rush, A.J., Shaw, B.F. & Emery, G. (1979). *Cognitive therapy of depression.* New York: Guilford.

Beck, A.T., Ward, C.H., Mendelson, M., Mock, J. & Erbaugh, J. (1961). An inventory for measuring expression. *Archives of General Psychiatry, 4*, 561–571.

Beutler, L.E. (1986). An efficacy study of experiential therapy among depressed patients. Unpublished manuscript, University of Arizona, Tuscon, Arizona.

Blatt, S.J., Quinlan, D.M., Chevron, E.S., McDonald, C. & Zuroff, D. (1982). Dependency and self-criticism: Psychological dimensions of depression. *Journal of Consulting and Clinical Psychology, 50*, 113–124.

Brown, G.W., Harris, T. & Copeland, J.R. (1977). Depression & loss. *British Journal of Psychiatry, 130*, 1–18.

Coyne, J.C. (1976). Toward an international description of depression. *Psychiatry, 39*, 28–40.

Craighead, W.E. (1980). Away from a unitary model of depression. *Behavior therapy, 11*, 112–118.

Daldrup, R.J., Beutler, L.E., Engle, D. & Greenberg, L.S. (1988). *Focused expressive psychotherapy; Freeing the overcontrolled patient*. New York: Guilford.

Derogatis, L.R., Rickels, K. & Roch, A.F. (1976). The SCL–90 and the MMPI. A step in the validation of a new self report scale. *British journal of Psychiatry, 128*, 280–289.

Eckman, P., Friesen, W.V. & Ellsworth, P. (1972). *Emotion in the human face*. New York: Pergamon.

Elkin, I., Shea, T., Imber, S., Pilkonis, P., Stoskey, S., Glass, D., Watkins, J., Leber, W. & Collins, J. (1986). NIMH treatment of depression collaborative research program: Initial outcome findings. Paper presented to the American Association for the Advancement of Science, May, 1986.

Elliot, R., Clark, C., Kemeny, V., Wexler, M.M., Mack, C. & Brinkerhoff, J. (1988). The impact of experiential therapy on depression: The first ten cases. Paper presented at International Conference on Client-centered and Experiential Psychotherapy, Leuven, Belgium, September, 1988.

Elliot, R., Greenberg, L.S., Rice L.N. & Clarke, C. (1988). Experiential psychotherapy of depression. Unpublished manuscript, University of Toledo, Ohio.

Epstein, S. (1984). The self-concept: A review and the proposal of an integrated theory of personality. In E. Staub (Ed.), *Personality: Basic issues and current research* (pp.81–132). Englewood Cliffs, N.J: Prentice-Hall.

Fairbairn, W.R.D. (1962). *An object relations theory of the personality*. New York. Basic Books.

Foa, E.B. & Kozak, M.J. (1986). Emotional processing of fear: Exposure to corrective information. *Psychological Bulletin, 99*, 20–35.

Fuchs, C.Z. & Rehm, L.P. (1977). A self-control behaviour therapy program for depression. *Journal of Consulting and Clinical Psychology, 45*, 206–215.

Gendlin, E.T. (1981). *Focusing*. New York: Bantam.

Greenberg, L.S. (1979). Resolving splits: The two-chair technique. *Psychotherapy: Theory, Research and Practice, 16*, 310–318.

Greenberg, L.S. (1984). A task analysis of intrapersonal conflict resolution. In L.N. Rice and L.S. Greenberg (Eds.). *Patterns of change: Intensive analysis of psychotherapy process*. New York: Guilford.

Greenberg, L.S. (1986). Change process research. *Journal of Consulting and Clinical Psychology, 54*, 4–11.

Greenberg, L.S. & Johnson, S. (1988). *Emotionally focused couples therapy*. New York: Guilford.

Greenberg, L.S. & Minden, R.R. (1988). Manual for three specific marker-driven interventions drawn from Gestalt therapy. Unpublished manuscript, York University, Ontario, Canada.

Greenberg, L.S. & Pinsoff, W.M. (1986). *The psychotherapeutic process: A research handbook.* New York: Guilford.

Greenberg, L.S. & Rice, L.N. (1988). Change Processes in Experiential Psychotherapy. Unpublished manuscript, York University.

Greenberg, L.S. & Safran, J.D. (1981). Encoding and cognitive therapy: Changing what clients attend to. *Psychotherapy: Theory, Research and Practice, 18* 163–169.

Greenberg, L.S. & Safran, J.D. (1984). Integrating affect and cognition: A perspective on the process of therapeutic change. *Cognitive therapy and research, 8,* 559–578.

Greenberg, L.S. & Safran, J.D. (1987). *Emotion in psychotherapy.* New York: Guilford.

Greenberg, L.S. & Safran, J.D. (1989). Emotion in psychotherapy. *American Psychologist, 44,* 19–29.

Greenberg, L.S., Safran, J.D. & Rice, L.N. (in press). Experiential therapy: Its relation to cognitive therapy. In M.A. Freeman, L. Beuter, H. Arkowitz (Eds.), *Handbook of cognitive therapy.* New York: Plenum.

Greenwald, A.Y. & Pratkanis, A.R. (1984). The self. In R.S. Wyer & T.K. Skrull (Eds.). *Handbook of social cognition* (pp. 129–178). Hillsdale, N.J.: Erlbaum.

Guidano, V.F. (1987). *Complexity of the self: A developmental approach to psychopathology and therapy.* New York. Guilford

Guntrip, H. (1969). *Schizoid phenomena, object relations and the self.* New York: International Universities.

Hamilton, M. (1960). A rating scale for depression. *Journal of Neurology, Neurosurgery & Psychiatry, 23,* 56–62.

Hammen, C.L. & Peters, S.D. (1978). Interpersonal consequences of depression: Responses to men and women enacting a depressed role. *Journal of Abnormal Psychology, 87,* 322–332.

Higgins, E.G. & King, G.A. (1981). Accessibility of social constructs: Information-processing consequences of individual and contextual variability. In N. Cantor & J. Kihlstrom (Eds.), *Personality, cognition, and social interaction.* Hillsdale: Erlbaum.

Horowitz, M. (1979). *States of mind: Analysis of change in psychotherapy.* New York: Plenum.

Izard, C.E. (1979). *Emotion in personality and psychopathology.* New York: Plenum.

Kaplan, M.L. & Kaplan, N.R. (1982). Organization of experience of family members in the immediate present: A Gestalt systems integration. *Journal of Family and Marital Therapy, 8,* 5–14.

Kelly, G.A. (1955). *The psychology of personal constructs (Vols. 1 & 2).* New York: Norton

Kihlstrom, J.R. & Cantor, N. (1984). Mental representations of the self. In M.L. Berkowitz (Ed.), *Advances in experimental social psychology,* Vol. 15, (pp. 1–47). New York: Academic Press.

Kelman, G., Rounsaville, B., Chevron, E., Neu, C. & Weissman, M. (1984). *Manual for short-term interpersonal therapy for depression.* New York: Basic.

Kohut, H. (1977). *The restoration of the self.* New York: International Universities.

Kuiper, N.A. (1978). Depression and causal attributions for success and failure. *Journal of Personality and Social Psychology, 36,* 236–246.

Lang, P.J. (1979). The cognitive psycho-physiology of emotion: Fear and anxiety. In A.H. Tuma & J.D. Maser (Eds.), *Anxiety and the anxiety disorders* (pp. 130–170). Hillsdale, NJ: Erlbaum.

Leventhal, H. (1979). A perceptual-motor processing model of emotion. In P. Pliner, K. Blankstein & I.M. Spigel (Eds.), *Perception of emotion in self and others, Vol.5* (pp. 1–46). New York: Plenum.

Lewinsohn, P.M., Biglan, A. & Zeiss, A.M. (1976). Behavioral treatments of depression. In P.O. Davidson (Ed.), *The behavioral management of anxiety, depression & pain*. New York: Bruna/Mozel.

Lewinsohn, P.M., Larson, D.W. & Munoz, R.F. (1982). Measurement of expectancies and other cognitions in depressed individuals. *Cognitive Therapy & Research*, *6*, 437–446.

Lewinsohn, P.M., Steinmetz, J., Larson, D. & Franklin, J. (1981). Depression related cognitions: Antecedent or consequence? *Journal of Abnormal Psychology*, *90*, 213–219.

Libet, J.M. & Lewinsohn, P.M. (1973). The concept of social skills with special reference to the behavior of depressed persons. *Journal of Consulting and Clinical Psychology*, *40*, 304–312.

Luborsky, L. (1962). Clinicians' judgements of mental health. *Archives of General Psychiatry*, *7*, 407–417.

Luborsky, L., Singer, B., Hartke, J., Crits-Christoph, P. & Cohen, M. (1984). In L.N. Rice & L.S. Greenberg (Eds.), *Patterns of Change: Intensive analysis of psychotherapeutic process*. New York: Guilford.

Mahoney, M.J. & Lyddon, W.J. (1988). Recent developments in cognitive approaches to counseling and psychotherapy. *Counseling Psychologist*, *16*, 190–234.

Markus, H. (1983). Self-knowledge: An expanded view. *Journal of Personality*, *51*, 543–565.

Markus, H. & Nurius, P. (1986). Possible selves. *American Psychologist*, *41*, 954–969.

McCann, C.D. & Higgins, E.T. (1988). Motivation and affect in interpersonal relations: The role of personal orientations and discrepancies. In L. Donohew, H.E. Sypher & E.T. Higgins (Eds.), *Communication, social cognition & affect* (pp. 53–80). Hillsdale, NJ: Erlbaum.

McClelland, D.G. (1985). *Human Motivation: A book of reading*. Morristown, N.J.: General Learning Press.

Millon, T. (1983). *Millon Multiaxial Clinical Inventory Manual*. Minneapolis: National Computer Systems.

Nezu, A.M. (1986). Efficacy of a social problem-solving therapy approach for unipolar depression. *Journal of Consulting and Clinical Psychology*, *54*, 196–202.

Nietzel, M.T., Russell, R.L., Hemmings, K.A. & Gretter, M.L. (1987). Clinical significance of psychotherapy for unipolar depression. A meta-analytic approach to social comparison. *Journal of Consulting and Clinical Psychology*, *55*, 150–160.

Perls, F. (1970). Four Lectures. In J. Fagan and L.L. Sheperd (Eds.), *Gestalt Therpay Now*. New York: Harper & Row.

Perls, F., Hefferline, R. & Goodman, P. (1951). *Gestalt Therapy*. New York: Dell.

Peterson, C., Schwartz, S. & Seligman, M.E.P. (1981). Self-blame and depressive symptoms. *Journal of Personality and Social Psychology*, *41*, 253–259.

Rice, L.N. (1974). The evocative function of the therapist. In D. Wexler & L.N. Rice (Eds.), *Innovations in client-centered therapy*. New York: Interscience.

Rice, L.N. (1984). Client tasks in client-centered therapy. In R.F. Levant and J.M. Shlien, (Eds.) *Client-centered therapy and the person-centered approach: New directions in theory research and practice*. New York: Praeger.

Rice, L.N. & Greenberg, L.S., (Eds.) (1984). *Patterns of Change: Intensive analysis of psychotherapeutic process*. New York: Guilford.

Rice, L.N. & Greenberg, L.S. (1988). Fundamental dimensions in experiential therapy: New directions in research. Paper presented at International Conference on Client-centered and Experiential Psychotherapy, Leuven, Belgium, September, 1988.

Rice, L.N. & Saperia, E. (1984). Task analysis of the resolution of problematic reactions. In L.N. Rice & L.S. Greenberg (Eds.), *Patterns of change: Intensive analysis of psychotherapy process*. New York: Guilford.

Rogers, C.R. (1959). A theory of therapy, personality and interpersonal relationships, as developed in the client-centered framework. In S. Koch (Ed.), *Psychology: A Study of science (Vol. 3)*. New York: McGraw-Hill.

Rogers C.R. & Dymond, R.F. (1954). *Psychotherapy and personality change*. Chicago: University of Chicago Press.

Safran, J.D. & Greenberg, L.S. (1986). Hot cognition and psychotherapy process: An information processing /ecological approach. In P.C. Kendall (Ed.), *Advances in cognitive-behavioral research and therapy (Vol. 5)*. New York: Academic.

Safran, J.D. & Greenberg, L.S. (1988). The treatment of anxiety and depression from an affective perspective. In P.C. Kendal & P. Watson (Eds.), *Negative affective conditions*. New York: Academic.

Seligman, M.E.P. (1974). Depression and learned helplessness. In R.J. Friedman & M.M. Katz (Eds.), *The Psychology of depression: Contemporary theory and research* (pp. 83–120). Washington, DC: Winston.

Seligman, M.E.P. (1975). *Helplessness*. San Francisco, CA: W.H. Freeman

Semmel, A., Abramson, L.Y. Seligman, M.E.P. & vonBaeyer, C. (1978). A scale for measuring attributional style. Unpublished manuscript, University of Pennsylvania.

Shapiro, David (1965). *Neurotic styles*. New York: Basic.

Shaw, B.F. (1977). Comparison of cognitive therapy and behaviour therapy in the treatment of depression. *Journal of Consulting and Clinical Psychology, 31*, 557–563.

Shlien, J.M., Mosek, H.M. & Dreikurs, R. (1962). Effect of time limits: A comparison of two psychotherapies. *Journal of Counselling Psychology, 9*, 31–34.

Smith, M.L., Glass, G.V. & Miller, T.I. (1980). *The benefits of psychotherapy*. Baltimore: John Hopkins University.

Snygg, D. & Combs, A.W. (1949). *Individual behavior: A new frame of reference for psychology*. New York: Harper & Row.

Stern, D.N. (1977). *The first relationship: Infant and mother*. Cambridge, Mass: Harvard University Press.

Stern, D. (1985). *The interpersonal world of the infant*. New York: Basic.

Sullivan, H.S. (1953). *The interpersonal theory of psychiatry*. New York: Norton.

Wilkinson, I.M. & Blackburn, I.M. (1981). Cognitive style in depressed and recovered depressed patients. *British Journal of Clinical Psychology, 20*, 283–292.

Winnicott, D.W. (1965). *The maturational process and the facilitating environment*. New York: International Universities Press.

# 8

# Children of Depressed Parents: A Review and Directions for Future Research

Ian H. Gotlib
*San Diego State University*

Catherine M. Lee
*University of Ottawa*

KEY WORDS: depression, children, parents, infants, mothers

Depression is by far the most common of all the psychiatric disorders, accounting for 75 percent of all hospitalizations. Each year, more than 100 million people worldwide develop clinically recognizable depression, an incidence ten times greater than that of schizophrenia. Furthermore, during the course of a lifetime, it is estimated that 20 percent of the general population will experience at least one clinically significant episode of depression (Weissman, Myers & Harding, 1978).

Over the last decade, researchers examining psychological antecedents, concomitants, and consequences of depression have given increasing attention to interpersonal aspects of this disorder (e.g., Brown & Harris, 1978; Coyne, Kahn & Gotlib, 1987; Gotlib & Whiffen, in press; Youngren & Lewinsohn, 1980). Much of the empirical work in this area has focused on the marital relationships of depressed persons (e.g., Hinchliffe, Hooper & Roberts, 1978; Ruscher & Gotlib, 1988; Weissman & Paykel, 1974). In general, the results of these studies indicate that the marriages of depressed persons are characterized by high levels of conflict, negative communication, tension, and hostility. In fact, in a recent review of this literature, Gotlib and Hooley (1988) concluded that the poor quality of the marriages of depressed persons may play a significant role in the onset and prognosis of this disorder.

The relationships between depressed persons and their children have received less theoretical and empirical attention, although results of the studies that have been conducted indicate that these relationships, too, are problematic. Before we discuss these studies, however, it is important to note that there are also other reasons for examining the interactions of depressed women and their children. Epidemiological investigations, for example, consistently report that depression afflicts a greater number of women than men, and in particular, women who are living at home and raising children (Brown & Harris, 1978; Gotlib, Whiffen, Mount, Milne & Cordy, 1989; Weissman, 1983; Weissman & Klerman, 1977). There is also evidence to indicate that depressed women find it difficult to be warm and consistent parents (McLean, 1976; Weissman & Paykel, 1974) and that they are less positive in their assessments both of their mothering capabilities and of their enjoyment of being mothers (Bromet & Cornely, 1984). Given these findings, it is not surprising that there is a growing body of evidence suggesting that the children of depressed parents are at increased risk for a variety of psychological and social difficulties (Beardslee, Bemporad, Keller & Klerman, 1983).

The purpose of this chapter is to examine research assessing the adjustment and functioning of children whose parents (typically the mother) are depressed. In conducting this assessment, we will first discuss briefly the historical context of the study of children of depressed parents. Next, we will describe results of recent controlled investigations that have examined the adjustment of children of depressed parents. Following this review, we will present a number of key issues in the study of the offspring of depressed parents, and will describe in some detail the methodology and results of a longitudinal investigation that was conducted in our laboratory in order to address a number of these issues. Finally, we will conclude with our assessment of the status of our knowledge in this area, and will identify what we believe are important directions for future research.

Before we begin our presentation, we should outline three general criteria that we used in selecting the studies for inclusion in this review. First, given our limited space in this chapter, we will review only those studies that have included samples of unipolar, as opposed to bipolar, depression. There is a considerable literature assessing the effects of bipolar depression on infant and child behavior (e.g., Decina et al., 1983; Klein, Depue & Krauss, 1986; Kuyler, Rosenthal, Igel, Dunner & Fieve, 1980; Zahn-Waxler, McKnew, Cummings, Davenport & Radke-Yarrow, 1984), and the interested reader is referred to these articles.

The second criterion used in selecting studies for review involves the investigators' operationalization of "depression." A number of investigators have examined the effects on the child of "elevated depressive symptoms" in the mother (e.g., Forehand et al., 1988; Lyons-Ruth, Zoll, Connell & Grunebaum, 1986; Pannacione & Wahler, 1986), or of induced or simulated depressed mood (e.g., Cohn & Tronick, 1983; Zekoski, O'Hara & Wills, 1987). Typically, these researchers have defined depression on the basis of elevated levels of depressed mood on such self-report measures as the Beck Depression Inventory (BDI; Beck, Ward, Mendelson, Mock & Erbaugh, 1961) and the Center for Epidemiological Studies Depression Scale (CES-D; Radloff, 1977). Although the results of these investigations are important, several researchers have questioned the generalizability to clinically diagnosed depression of results obtained with mildly depressed or dysphoric individuals (cf. Depue & Monroe, 1978; Gotlib, 1984; Gotlib & Cane, 1989; Kendall, Hollon, Beck, Hammen & Ingram, 1987). Consequently, for the purposes of this review, we will focus primarily on those studies that have used either a clinical population or a clinical diagnosis to define depression. Nevertheless, because in some research areas there is a notable lack of investigations using a clinical population, studies using samples of women demonstrating elevated depressive symptomatology will be presented where appropriate.

Finally we have selected for review only those studies employing control groups that have been published subsequent to the review conducted by Beardslee et al. (1983).

## HISTORICAL CONTEXT

The study of the offspring of affectively disordered parents represents a relatively recent endeavor. The first studies of children of parents suffering from psychiatric disorders were conducted in an attempt to gain a better understanding of the etiology of schizophrenia. Researchers in this area observed that schizophrenia was characterized by clear patterns of familial incidence. A significant proportion of the offspring of schizophrenic parents, for example, were found to become schizophrenic themselves, and high concordance rates for this disorder were obtained for siblings. Thus, groups of young children who were at risk for schizophrenia by virtue of having a schizophrenic parent were identified and followed longitudinally in order to chart the emergence of symptoms of the disorder.

Early studies in this area assessed children of schizophrenic parents on a number of constitutional and physiological variables, psychological tasks and inventories, and compared these children with offspring of normal parents (e.g., Mednick & Schulsinger, 1968). Not surprisingly, the results of these investigations indicated that children of schizophrenic parents performed more poorly on these tasks and inventories than did the children of normal parents. However, because these initial studies did not include psychiatric control groups (i.e., children of parents exhibiting other types of psychiatric symptomatology), it was not possible to examine the specificity of obtained deficits to schizophrenia, or to make statements concerning early or causal factors unique to the development of this disorder. It is possible, for example, that the difficulties manifested by the offspring of schizophrenics were a function of global psychopathology, rather than deficits specific to schizophrenia per se.

As more investigations in this area were initiated, the inclusion of psychiatric control groups became more common. Although many studies included control groups composed of children of a heterogeneous group of psychiatric patients with a variety of diagnoses (cf. McNeil & Kaij, 1980), several investigations used psychiatric control groups composed exclusively of patients diagnosed as depressed, or as demonstrating major affective disorders. It is out of this research base that the first studies of children of depressed parents were conducted. Among the most notable of these investigations are the Stony Brook High Risk Project (e.g., Neale & Weintraub, 1975; Weintraub, Liebert & Neale, 1978; Weintraub, Prinz & Neale, 1975), the Massachusetts Mental Health Center Project (e.g., Cohler, Gallant & Grunebaum, 1977; Cohler, Gallant, Grunebaum & Kauffman, 1983), the Rochester Longitudinal Study (e.g., Sameroff & Zax, 1973; Sameroff, Seifer & Zax, 1982), and the University of Rochester Child and Family Study (e.g., Fisher, 1980; Harder, Kokes, Fisher & Strauss, 1980). Interestingly, and contrary to the predictions of these investigators, the results of these projects indicate that not only do children of depressives demonstrate social and cognitive deficits that are similar to those exhibited by children of schizophrenics, but further, that children of depressed parents often demonstrate *greater* impairment than do children of schizophrenic parents.

In the Stony Brook High Risk Project, children of schizophrenic mothers and unipolar or bipolar depressed mothers were compared with children of nonpsychiatric mothers. Both the children of the schizophrenic mothers and the offspring of the depressed mothers in this project were found to be impaired on a number of indices. For example, few differences were found between school-aged children of depressed and schizophrenic mothers with respect to both peer ratings (Weintraub et al., 1975) and teacher ratings (Weintraub et al., 1978) of adjustment, with both groups of children receiving lower ratings than did children of well mothers. In a subsequent report, Winters, Stone, Weintraub, and Neale (1981) found that the children of depressed parents were also often more deviant than were the control children with respect to their performance on a number of cognitive and attentional tasks. Moreover, the children of depressed parents were indistinguishable on these tasks from the children of schizophrenic parents.

In the Massachusetts Mental Health Center Project, Cohler and his associates examined the young children of schizophrenic, psychotically depressed, and normal mothers over a period of about ten years. Gamer, Gallant, Grunebaum, and Cohler (1977) reported that when these children were about three years old, offspring of psychotically ill parents were found to have poorer cognitive functioning on the Wechsler Intelligence Scale for Children than were offspring of well parents. As in the findings reported from the Stony Brook Project, no differences were found between children of schizophrenics and children of depressed mothers. Based on these findings, Gamer et al. suggested that living with a mother who is generally mentally disordered may adversely influence the cognitive development of their young children. As the children from this project grew older, however, this pattern of findings seemed to change. Cohler et al. (1977) reported that, at five years of age, the children of the depressed mothers showed greater intellectual impairment and greater impairment on measures of both sustained and selective attention than did the children of the schizophrenic or of the well mothers. Furthermore, these depression-associated deficits were maintained up to seven years later. Grunebaum, Cohler, Kaufman, and Gallant (1978) reported that, when the children were 8–12 years of age, the depressed mothers rated their children as less cooperative at home, as exhibiting a greater number of symptoms characteristic of a behavioral disorder, and as less involved with the family.

A similar pattern of results was reported by Sameroff and his colleagues in the Rochester Longitudinal Study, in which children of mothers who had received a diagnosis of schizophrenia, neurotic depression, personality disorder, or no mental illness were examined. Sameroff and Zax (1973) reported early results from this investigation indicating that the infants of the depressed women demonstrated greater perinatal deficits than did infants in any of the other groups. Moreover, these early deficits, which appeared to be specific to the offspring of the depressed mothers, continued to be noted as these children were assessed at 4, 12, 30, and 48 months of age. For example, Sameroff, Baracos, and Seifer (1984) found that at the age of 4 months, the children of the depressed mothers were the least responsive to people. Similarly, Seifer, Sameroff, and Jones (1981) reported that at 30 and 48 months of age, the children of the depressed mothers were rated as least cooperative in the family and with others, more whiny, and were found to engage in more imaginary play than were the control children, leading the investigators to suggest that maternal depression is more detrimental to the behavior of the child than are other maternal psychiatric disturbances. As Sameroff et al. (1982) conclude, "To summarize these diagnostic comparisons, if one were to choose a diagnostic group where children were most at risk, it would be neurotic depression rather than schizophrenia" (p. 58).

Finally, Fisher and his colleagues reported results from the University of Rochester Child and Family Study, in which four groups of patients and their male children were assessed: narrow band schizophrenia, broad band schizophrenia, affective psychosis (largely manic and bipolar patients), and nonpsychotic (largely neurotic depression) patients. These investigators examined the relationships among such variables as peer- and teacher-ratings of the children's academic and social competence, family functioning, family communication, severity of parent psychopathology, and gender of patient. The results of this project suggest that, in general, there are few significant differences between the sons of schizophrenic parents and the sons of depressed parents. In fact, as Fisher, Harder, and Kokes (1980) note, where differences were obtained it was the sons of psychotic mothers, both schizophrenic and bipolar, who were rated by their teachers as *more* competent than were the sons of the nonpsychotic, or neurotically depressed mothers. Consistent with this finding, Harder et al. (1980) reported that the severity of the impairment of parental functioning appeared to be a separate and more important variable in determining the child's level of academic competence than was parental diagnosis.

Considered collectively, the results of these four projects indicate that, compared with children of schizophrenics, offspring of depressed parents are at equal, if not greater, risk for psychopathology. These initial serendipitous findings represented promising leads for a better understanding of depression, and provided the impetus for investigations explicitly designed to study the children of depressed parents. As will become apparent, however, these investigations are clearly not as impressive as the high-risk schizophrenia projects. They do not typically have as large a sample of subjects, nor are they as sophisticated with respect to the use of both psychiatric and nonpsychiatric control groups. Finally, and perhaps most importantly, there are no large-scale longitudinal studies of the children of depressed parents that have been designed with this population as the group of primary interest. Although one can refer to results of the longitudinal schizophrenia risk projects that have used children of depressives as controls, it is important to bear in mind that the depressed patients in such studies were not typically carefully chosen or well-described, and the measures used in these studies were chosen on the basis of their theoretical and empirical relationship to schizophrenia. It is certain that different measures would have been selected had these studies been designed to assess the disorder of depression. With these caveats in mind, we now turn to the investigations of children of depressed parents.

## CHILDREN OF DEPRESSED PARENTS

Not only do children differ psychologically from adults, but they differ from one another, at different periods of development, with respect to their behavioral, affective, and cognitive functioning (cf. Digdon & Gotlib, 1985; Kendall, Lerner & Craighead, 1984). Therefore, it is likely that the relation between maternal depression and child adjustment is also different at various stages of child development. In this context, the symptoms of maternal depression may have a differential impact on developmental tasks the child faces in cognitive, affective, social, and physiological domains at different ages. Consequently, we have organized the studies in this section according to the ages of the children assessed in the investigations. We begin with infants and pre-school-age children of depressed parents, and then turn to studies that have examined the functioning of school-age and adolescent children of depressed parents.

## Infants and Pre-school Age Children

With a few notable exceptions, studies of the relationships between mothers and their infants under six months old have examined the interactions of women who report elevated levels of depressive symptoms and their infants. Livingood, Daen, and Smith (1983), for example, examined a group of symptomatic (Beck Depression Inventory scores of greater than 9) and nonsymptomatic mothers with respect to the level and quality of stimulation they provided for their newborn infants during an in-hospital feeding session. The symptomatic mothers were found to shift their positions more frequently during feeding, interrupting the smooth flow of their rocking movements, and to gaze less often at their infants. As Livingood et al. note, the finding that the symptomatic mothers gaze less often may reflect withdrawal from their infants, which may interfere with the development of both mutual visual regard and a strong attachment bond.

Field and her colleagues (e.g., Field, 1984; Field et al., 1985) also examined the interactions of symptomatic and nonsymptomatic mothers and their infants. These investigators found that, compared with the nonsymptomatic women, the symptomatic mothers were rated by observers as more depressed and anxious during the interactions, as less active and playful, and as less contingently responsive to their infants' behavior. The infants of these women were rated as more drowsy or fussy, and as less relaxed or content than were the infants of the nondepressed controls. In a similar study, Bettes (1988) examined speech latency, length of pauses, and vocal intonation of symptomatic and nonsymptomatic mothers. Bettes reported that the symptomatic mothers took longer to respond to their infants' vocalizations and failed to modify their own speech after their infants had vocalized. In contrast, the nonsymptomatic mothers were quicker to respond and uttered shorter phrases after their infants had vocalized.

Considered collectively, these studies demonstrate that with young infants, the interactions of mothers reporting elevated levels of depressive symptomatology are characterized by withdrawal and a lack of engagement with and responsiveness to their infants. Moreover, infants of symptomatically depressed mothers themselves tend to be rated as more passive than are infants of nonsymptomatic mothers. Indeed, findings from other studies also suggest that the infants of depressed mothers may be temperamentally difficult. Cutrona and Troutman (1986) and Whiffen (1988) both found depressive symptomatology to be correlated with maternal reports of infant crying and unsoothability. Preliminary results from our own laboratory confirm and extend these findings. Whiffen and Gotlib (1989) assessed the effects of a diagnosable episode of postpartum depression on infant cognitive and socio-emotional development. Initial analyses indicate that at two months postpartum, the depressed mothers perceive their infants as more temperamentally difficult than do the nondepressed mothers. Observers' ratings of the infants' behavior provide convergent validity for the mothers' perceptions. Observers rated the infants of the depressed mothers as more tense and less happy, and as showing less tolerance for the test procedures, that is, as deteriorating more quickly under the stress of testing. Thus, although further research using psychiatric control groups is clearly required, the results of the interactional and observational studies converge to suggest that the infants of depressed mothers are both more passive and less content than are the infants of nondepressed mothers.

One of the earliest longitudinal studies of the adjustment of the infants of depressed women was conducted in England by Ghodsian, Zayicek, and Wolkind (1984). These investigators assessed a random sample of women with young children on the Present State Examination (Wing, Cooper & Sartorius, 1974). Mothers were asked to rate their children at age 14 months, 27 months, and 42 months. Although at 14 months there were no differences between the ratings of depressed and nondepressed women, at both 27 and 42 months depressed women rated their children as having a greater number of behavior problems than did nondepressed mothers.

Radke-Yarrow and her colleagues have also conducted a number of studies examining the relationship between maternal depression and child adjustment. One of the important indicators of infant adjustment is attachment behavior, which is assumed both to reflect the quality of the mother-child relationship (cf. Ainsworth, Blehar, Waters & Wall, 1978) and to provide an important link to the child's later interpersonal competence. Indeed, it is possible that the increased risk of affective disorders among offspring of depressed mothers has its roots in insecure attachment of the infant. Using the Strange Situation developed by Ainsworth (Ainsworth & Wittig, 1969; Ainsworth et al., 1978), Radke-Yarrow, Cummings, Kuczynski, and Chapman (1985) evaluated attachment status among two- to three-year-old children whose mothers had a previous diagnosis of bipolar, unipolar-major, or unipolar-minor affective disorder. The authors reported that the rates of insecure attachment were highest among the children of the bipolar and unipolar-major mothers.

Other reports from Radke-Yarrow's laboratory describe the interactions of depressed mothers with their children, beginning at the age of two. The earliest reports focused on the two-year-old children of 23 mothers who met Research Diagnostic Criteria (RDC; Spitzer, Endicott & Robins, 1978) for lifetime unipolar depression, but who had not been hospitalized during the child's lifetime (Zahn-Waxler, Cummings, Iannotti & Radke-Yarrow, 1984). Observations of these children suggested two general tendencies that distinguished the children of depressed mothers from the children of nondepressed controls. First, the children of depressed mothers were more maladaptively empathic, such that their own activity was disrupted when distress was experienced by other people. Second, the children of depressed mothers showed greater emotional containment by being more likely to suppress the expression of affect. Of particular interest were the findings that these children were more likely than were the control children to attempt to appease a frustrating adult, and were less likely to become physically aggressive across a variety of situations. Zahn-Waxler et al. hypothesized that the children of depressed mothers are overly sensitive to their mothers' negative affect, while being unable to seek or accept comfort for their own emotional distress. It is likely that children of depressed mothers have learned to suppress aspects of their own emotional experience because the expression of certain affects (such as aggression) has not been accepted by their mothers. Similarly, the greater empathy of the children of depressed mothers reported in the study of Zahn-Waxler et al. may be due to the reinforcement they have received from their mothers for their displays of concern.

Subsequent studies have attempted to delineate the specific characteristics of depressive mothering. Breznitz and Sherman (1987), for example, reported that in a non-threatening situation, depressed mothers of two- to three-year-old children spoke less than did nondepressed mothers. When placed in a more stressful situation, however, they increased their speech rate and decreased their response latency, a speech pattern indicative of anxiety. On the basis of these findings, Breznitz and Sherman proposed that the children of depressed mothers are socialized to respond to stress with exaggerated emotionality. Depressed mothers also appear to have difficulty negotiating conflict situations with their children. Kochanska, Kuczynski, Radke-Yarrow, and Welsh (1987) compared the interactions of depressed and control mothers in situations in which the mother initiated an attempt to control or influence the child's behavior. Overall, the depressed mothers were more likely than were the well mothers to terminate the attempt before resolution, and were less likely to reach a compromise solution. Kochanska et al. proposed that the premature termination of control attempts may be due to the depressed mother's fear of confrontation, a hypothesis consistent with the results of studies demonstrating that depressed adults cope by avoiding stressful situations (e.g., Coyne, Aldwin & Lazarus, 1981).

It is clear, therefore, that the infants and pre-school-age children of depressed mothers are characterized by deficits in their social and cognitive functioning. Moreover, in several investigations depressed and nondepressed mothers have been found to differ with respect to their parenting behaviors. Despite the causal statements offered by some of these researchers, however, it is important to note that mother behaviors and child functioning were measured concurrently. Therefore, appealing as it may be to postulate causal links between these two variables, the data reported in these investigations do not support such a position. We will return to a discussion of this issue in the following section, in which the functioning of school-age children of depressed parents is examined.

## School Age Children

Billings and Moos (1983) conducted a large-scale study of the relation between parental unipolar depression and child adjustment. Depressed parents and matched nondepressed community control parents completed a battery of questionnaires on various aspects of their daily lives, family functioning, and their children's adjustment. Billings and Moos found that the depressed parents described their families as less cohesive, less expressive, and higher in conflict than did the nondepressed parents. Moreover, the depressed parents reported a greater number of physical and psychological problems in their children than did nondepressed parents.

In a one-year follow-up, Billings and Moos (1986) compared the children of remitted and nonremitted depressed parents with children of their nondepressed controls. Interestingly, despite the abatement of their own depressive symptoms, parents in the remitted group continued to report more dysfunction in their children than did the control parents. As expected, the nonremitted depressed group reported the highest incidence of dysfunction in their children. These families also reported a greater number of stressors and conflict, and less cohesion and expressiveness than did the remitted families. This pattern of results suggests that it may not be depressive symptomatology per se through which the depressed parents adversely affect their children.

In a similar study, Weissman et al. (1984) interviewed depressed parents and nondepressed community controls about their children's adjustment. According to the parents' reports, 34 percent of the children of the depressed parents had psychiatric symptoms or had received psychological treatment, compared with only 16 percent of the children of the controls. Furthermore, 24 percent of the children of the depressed parents were diagnosable by DSM-III criteria, compared with only 8 percent of the control children. Differences between the two groups of children were also noted for the use of psychotropic medication and the incidence of problems in school. Finally, Weissman et al. found that children with both parents depressed were at greater risk for a diagnosis of a psychiatric disorder than were children with one depressed parent. On the basis of these findings, Weissman et al. concluded that children of depressed parents are at increased risk for psychological symptoms, treatment for emotional problems, school problems, suicidal behavior, and multiple DSM-III diagnoses.

The results of these studies indicate that school-age children of depressed parents function more poorly than do children of nondepressed parents. Although provocative, it is important to bear in mind that these data are based on parental reports, rather than on direct observations of the children. Unfortunately, depressed parents' reports may be biased by a tendency to see both their parenting and their children's behavior in a negative light (cf. Gotlib, 1983; Rickard, Forehand, Wells, Griest & McMahon, 1981). Compounding this problem is an issue raised by data reported by Yarrow, Campbell, and Burton (1970) indicating that normal (i.e., nondepressed) subjects recall parenting events to be more *positive* after even a short time span than they did while the event was occurring. Given these two sources of bias, it is critical that the functioning of children of depressed parents be assessed more directly.

Addressing this issue, Hirsch, Moos, and Reischl (1985) directly examined a group of adolescent children of unipolar depressed parents, and compared them to both a community group and to a group of adolescent offspring of arthritic patients. Hirsch et al. found that although the children of depressed parents reported more symptoms than did the normal group, there were no significant differences between the children of the depressed and the arthritic patients. However, these authors failed to provide information concerning the psychological adjustment of the arthritic parents. Given the high incidence of reactive depression in rheumatoid arthritis patients (Anderson, Bradley, Young, McDaniel & Wise, 1985), it is possible that the lack of differences between the children of depressed and arthritic parents was attributable to undiagnosed depression in the arthritic parents rather than to the effects of general disability.

Orvaschel, Walsh-Ellis, and Ye (1988) examined prevalence of psychological problems in the school-age children of parents with recurrent major depression and in children of parents with no history of depression. Relying on both maternal and child responses to the Schedule for Affective Disorders and Schizophrenia for School-Age Children—Epidemiologic Version (Kiddie-SADS-E; Orvaschel, Puig-Antich, Chambers, Tabrizi & Johnson, 1982), these investigators found that 41 percent of the children with affectively disordered parents met criteria for at least one episode of diagnosable psychiatric disturbance at some time in their lives, whereas the rate for children of nondepressed parents was only 15 percent.

Similar findings were reported by Beardslee, Schultz, and Selman (1987), who assessed the adjustment of adolescent offspring of affectively disordered and normal parents using parental and adolescent reports on the Diagnostic Interview for Children and Adolescents. Beardslee et al. reported that 38 percent of the adolescents in the high-risk group received a diagnosis of past or current affective disorder, whereas only two percent of the adolescents in the low-risk group received such diagnoses. In another report from the same project, Kaplan, Beardslee, and Keller (1987) found that the 7- to 19-year-old children of affectively disordered parents demonstrated cognitive impairment, in the form of subtest variability on the WISC-R.

Finally, Hops, Biglan, and their colleagues (e.g., Hops et al., 1987; Biglan, Hops & Sherman, in press) conducted home observations of clinically depressed mothers and their families. Compared to normal mothers, depressed mothers emitted higher rates of dysphoric affect and lower rates of happy affect than did nondepressed mothers. Across groups, mothers did not differ in their rates of caring behaviors towards their spouses or children. Hops et al. found that children of depressed mothers differed from children of normal mothers only with respect to displaying more irritated affect. Furthermore, such irritated affect was evident only in families where there was concomitant marital distress. Interestingly, conditional probability analyses revealed that maternal dysphoric behavior was effective in suppressing aggressive behavior in both spouses and children.

## ISSUES

It appears, therefore, that children of depressed parents are at risk for a full range of psychological symptoms, behavioral problems, and diagnosable disorder. Moreover, this pattern of results has been found in assessments utilizing parental reports, child self-reports, and teacher, peer and clinician ratings. Combining results across studies, it appears that 30 to 40 percent of the children of depressed parents (compared with less than 20 percent of unselected children) experience diagnosable psychiatric disorder, both affective diagnoses and attentional deficits/conduct disturbance. Moreover, the nature and severity of problems found in children of depressed parents appears to be similar to that observed among offspring of schizophrenics. Indeed, some investigators have posited that difficulties in child functioning may be due not to depression or schizophrenia per se, but rather, to parental psychopathology (e.g., Fisher, 1980; Harder et al., 1980; Rutter, 1966). Despite this formulation, however, research to date has not fully examined the specificity to depression of observed child adjustment difficulties. It is unclear, for example, whether child problems are associated only with parental psychological disorders, or whether they are related to parental disturbance in general, including physical disorders.

It is critical that investigators address the important issue of the specificity of observed child difficulties to parental depression. The studies reviewed thus far have yielded equivocal results. The findings of the high-risk projects described earlier, for example, suggest that depression and schizophrenia in mothers are both associated with difficulties in child functioning, indicating that maternal distress may be an important factor mediating this relationship. In contrast to these findings, however, Radke-Yarrow and her group found that diagnostic status was a significant predictor of child adjustment status, but that self-reported maternal distress was not. These studies clearly indicate that the general effects of psychological distress versus major depression should be examined by the inclusion of a nondepressed psychiatric patient control group. In addition, they also highlight the need for assessment not only of diagnostic status, but also of severity of psychological disturbance.

Two recently published studies shed light on this issue. Hammen et al. (1987) assessed the children of four groups of mothers: mothers suffering from recurrent unipolar depression, mothers with a bipolar affective disorder, chronically medically ill mothers, and normal mothers. Hammen et al. found that children of unipolar depressed and bipolar depressed mothers had high rates of psychiatric diagnoses compared to children of normal mothers. Although children of medical patient mothers had moderate rates of psychiatric diagnosis, these were lower than the rates in children of affectively disordered parents. Hammen and her colleagues noted that several medical patient mothers had experienced depressive or other reactions to life circumstances. Consequently, it is unclear whether the rates of diagnosis in children of medical patient mothers were attributable to the effects of maternal disability or to concomitant maternal psychological distress.

In the second study, Turner, Beidel, and Costello, (1987) examined the offspring of anxiety disorder patients, dysthymic disorder patients, and community control parents. Turner et al. found a greater number of internalizing problems in the children of psychiatric parents than in children of community parents. Nevertheless, the greatest impairment was found in the children of anxiety disordered parents. It is important to note that in this study, the anxiety disorder group was composed of agoraphobic and obsessive-compulsive disorder parents. These disorders likely reflect the severe end of the anxiety disorder spectrum; in contrast, the dysthymic group consisted of parents whose disturbance represents a less severe type of affective disorder. In light of other findings indicating that severity of parental psychopathology is related to child adjustment (e.g., Harder et al., 1980; Keller et al., 1986), it is possible that in both studies the severity of impairment in children was related to the severity of parental impairment rather than to parental diagnostic status. However, because Turner et al. do not provide severity ratings for parents, an assessment of this hypothesis in their study is precluded. In future research, it will be important to compare parents with different diagnoses who are equated in terms of the severity of their psychopathology.

In addition to the issue of specificity to parental depression of problematic in child functioning, it is important to note that few studies have examined the stability of the relation between maternal depression and child difficulties. Coyne's (1976) conceptualization of depression contends that negative responses to the depressed person are maintained by demonstrations of depressive symptomatology. This model leads to the prediction that an amelioration of maternal depressive symptomatology would be associated with a resumption of normal functioning in the child. Consistent with this prediction, Weissman (1983) reported improvements in the behavior of adolescent children following the alleviation of their mothers' depression. It is not clear, however, that this pattern of results would be evident with younger children. It is possible, for example, that maternal depression interferes with the younger child's mastery of developmentally salient tasks. If this is the case, alleviation of maternal symptomatology may not be sufficient to remedy the child's difficulties. Consistent with this reasoning, Weissman and Paykel (1974) noted residual mother-child difficulties following symptomatic improvement of the mother. Billings and Moos (1986) similarly found that remitted parents continued to rate their young children as having problems. Keitner, Miller, Epstein, Bishop, and Fruzetti (1987) found that, although family functioning was improved when parents were no longer depressed, these families remained at a level of functioning below that of families without a depressed parent. Finally, Cox, Puckering, Pound, and Mills (1987) recently reported that the two-year-old children of depressed mothers continued to demonstrate emotional and behavioral disturbance even after the mothers were no longer depressed.

In a recent study in our laboratory, we examined child adjustment in families in which the mother was diagnosed as suffering from a nonpsychotic, unipolar depression (Lee & Gotlib, 1989a, 1989b). Two major questions were examined. First, the specificity to depression of adjustment difficulties was measured by assessing 20 children of depressed psychiatric patient mothers, 13 children of nondepressed psychiatric patient mothers, 8 children of nondepressed medical patient mothers, and 30 children of nondepressed community mothers. The inclusion of these control groups permitted an evaluation of the "depression-specificity" hypothesis, the "psychological distress" hypothesis, and the "general disability" hypothesis. The depression-specificity hypothesis (e.g., Beardslee et al., 1983) predicted that child adjustment problems would be demonstrated only by children of depressed patients, and that the other three nondepressed groups would not differ from one another. In contrast, the psychological distress hypothesis (e.g., Gotlib, 1982; Hammen et al., 1987) predicted that child difficulties would be related to general psychopathology in the mothers. Thus, children in the two psychiatric groups would not be predicted to differ from one another, but would be expected to demonstrate poorer adjustment than would children in both nonpsychiatric control groups (i.e., nondepressed medical patients and community mothers). Finally, the general disability hypothesis (e.g.,

Hirsch et al., 1985) predicted that child problems would be associated with having a parent whose general functioning was impaired. This hypothesis would be supported if children in all three patient groups (depressed psychiatric, nondepressed psychiatric, and nondepressed medical) demonstrated adjustment difficulties.

The second issue addressed in this study involved the stability of the relation between maternal depressive symptomatology and child adjustment difficulties. In order to examine this issue, two complete evaluations were conducted for each dyad: the first, early in the patient's treatment, and the second, eight to ten months later. The acute impairment hypothesis (e.g., Weissman, 1983) predicted that an alleviation in maternal depressive symptomatology would be associated with a resumption of normal child functioning. The prolonged impairment hypothesis (e.g., Cox et al., 1987; Keitner et al., 1987) predicted that even when mothers were symptomatically improved, there would be residual difficulties in child adjustment.

Families in the outpatient groups were recruited through various treatment facilities in the London, Ontario area. Group assignment for the psychiatric patients was based on a DSM-III diagnosis of depression, and on scores on the Hamilton Rating Scale for depression (HRSD; Hamilton, 1960). The nondepressed psychiatric outpatients were diagnosed as manifesting symptoms of anxiety disorder, personality disorder, and adjustment disorder subtypes;major depressive disorder(without depressed mood). Criteria for inclusion for the medical outpatient mothers, who were diagnosed with rheumatoid arthritis, included (a) no reported current or past treatment for a psychiatric disorder, (b) failure to meet DSM-III criteria for a diagnosis of Major Affective Disorder, and (c) an HRSD score of 10 or less. Community subjects were recruited via local newspaper advertisements, and were accepted into the study if they (a) had no history of psychiatric disorder, (b) obtained a score of less than 10 on the BDI, and (c) were not medically impaired. To be included in the study, the mother and child must have lived together for at least a year, and there had to be no evidence of maternal alcoholism, psychotic ideation, or brain damage. Finally, because we were interested in examining the stability of the relation between maternal and child adjustment, mothers and children could not be currently involved specifically in family therapy or in child management training.

Child functioning was assessed by means of both an interview with the child and maternal ratings. Children were interviewed using the Child Assessment Schedule (CAS; Hodges, 1983), a semi-structured protocol designed for the clinical assessment of children seven years and older. The CAS assesses fears and anxieties, worries and concerns, self-image, mood disturbance, physical complaints, and conduct problems. In the present study, inter-rater reliability was determined by having a second rater code audiotapes of 15 of the CAS interviews. Kappa coefficients calculated on the total symptom scores for each subscale of the CAS ranged from 0.96 to 1.0, indicating a high degree of reliability between raters. All mothers also completed the Child Behavior Checklist (CBCL; Achenbach & Edelbrock, 1983), on which behavior problems are rated in terms of aptness in describing the child's behavior over the previous six months.

A multivariate analysis of variance conducted on mothers' age, income, years of education, number of children, and age of child indicated that mothers in the four groups did not differ significantly with respect to demographic variables. The mean age of the children in this study was nine years. At the first session, mothers in the depressed group reported moderate to severe levels of depression, whereas women in the other three groups reported BDI scores in the nondepressed range.

To compare the rates of child disturbance in the four groups, we examined the proportions of children in each group whose behavior, as rated by their mothers on the CBCL, exceeded an empirically established clinical cut-off score. Children's scores were defined as "clinical" or "non-clinical" on the basis of T-scores on the CBCL that indicated problems at the 90th percentile. Chi-square analyses indicated that the groups differed significantly with respect to the proportions of children whose behavior was rated within the clinical range. For both internalizing and externalizing problems, the highest proportions of clinical range scores were found for the children of the depressed mothers. Indeed, two-thirds of these children were placed in the clinical range on the CBCL; approximately one-third of the children of nondepressed psychiatric patient mothers scored in the clinical range. No child of a medical patient mother was rated as functioning in the clinical range, and the rates for children of community mothers were 23 percent (internalizing) and 13 percent (externalizing). Consistent with the maternal ratings, interviewers identified a greater number of symptoms and poorer overall adjustment in the children of both the depressed and the nondepressed psychiatric patient mothers than they did in the children of the community mothers; children of the medical patient mothers did not differ significantly from children in the other three groups with respect to their CAS scores. Using the mean ratings on the CAS presented by Hodges, McKnew, Cytryn, Stern, and Kline (1982), it is apparent that the children of both the depressed and nondepressed psychiatric patient mothers were functioning at a level comparable to a group of behaviorally disordered outpatient children.

At the follow-up, eight to ten months after the initial assessment, our sample was reduced. Attrition occurred for a variety of reasons, including loss of custody of the child, move from the area/phone disconnected, and mother no longer interested in participating. Because of the small number of medical patients remaining in the study, this group was excluded from the follow-up analyses. Thus, the follow-up analyses were conducted on 12 initially depressed women, 9 nondepressed psychiatric patient women, and 23 nondepressed community women. At the second session, women in all three groups reported BDI scores in the nondepressed range. Despite this reduction in reported depressive symptomatology, women in both psychiatric groups continued to describe their children as having a higher number of internalizing problems than did the community mothers. With respect to externalizing problems, depressed mothers described their children as having a greater number of problems than did community mothers; nondepressed psychiatric patient mothers' ratings of their children's externalizing problems did not differ from those of mothers in the other two groups. Finally, interviewer ratings on the CAS indicated that children of nondepressed psychiatric patient mothers had lower self-esteem than did children of community mothers; children of depressed mothers did not differ from children in the other two groups with respected to clinician-rated self-esteem. Children of both the depressed and the nondepressed psychiatric patient mothers were rated as having a greater number of mood symptoms and somatic complaints than were children of the community mothers.

Thus, children of both depressed and nondepressed mothers demonstrated problematic adjustment, even when their mothers were no longer overtly symptomatic, indicating that there may be a substantial lag between alleviation of maternal symptomatology and improvement in child functioning. These findings not only corroborate Billings and Moos' (1986) observations that remitted depressed parents continue to report adjustment difficulties in their children, but further, replicate these results with ratings by clinicians. It seems clear, therefore, that alleviation of maternal symptomatology should not be taken as a signal that all family members are functioning adequately. Indeed, these results indicate that greater attention must be paid to systemic factors that may render the family prone to further problems (cf. Gotlib & Colby, 1987).

Considered collectively, the present data on child adjustment corroborate previous findings of impairment in the children of depressed parents. Consistent with these findings, child difficulties spanned a range of adjustment difficulties but were most prominent in terms of internalizing problems. Moreover, consistent with the "psychological distress" hypothesis (e.g., Gotlib, 1982; Hammen et al., 1987) outlined earlier, impairments were also observed in this study in the children of the nondepressed psychiatric patient mothers, calling into question the specificity to maternal depression of problematic child adjustment. Furthermore, there was no evidence to support the hypothesis that child adjustment difficulties are related to general maternal disability. Indeed, despite the relatively small sample, children of the medical patient mothers differed significantly from children of the depressed mothers on most indices.

## CONCLUSIONS

Given the current state of the literature, firm conclusions about the offspring of depressed parents may be premature. Nevertheless, a tentative summary of the findings to date would be appropriate as a guide to future research. There is some indication that, as early as birth, children of depressed parents manifest difficulties (Sameroff & Zax, 1973). Throughout infancy and early childhood, these children demonstrate deficiencies in cognitive, emotional, and social development that persist and may worsen over time (e.g., Cohler et al., 1977; Sameroff et al., 1985; Seifer et al., 1981). In primary school years, children of depressed mothers have been found to have lower IQ scores and to perform poorly in school (Cohler et al., 1977), and to receive lower peer and teacher ratings (Fisher et al., 1980; Neale & Weintraub, 1975; Weintraub et al., 1975, 1978) than have children of psychiatric and community controls. In adolescence, children of unipolar depressed persons have been found to demonstrate lower self-esteem, more psychological and physical symptoms, and to participate less in school activities than have community and medical controls (Hirsch et al., 1985; Lee & Gotlib, 1989a, 1989b).

Findings of similarities in the problems in the children of schizophrenic, depressed, and other-psychiatrically disturbed parents caution against any assumption at the present time that there are factors specific to having a depressed parent that produce child problems. There is a clear need to give further attention to social impairments of the parents, as distinct from psychiatric symptomatology (e.g., Gotlib & Lee, 1989), as well as to the possible deleterious effects of both parental hospitalization and children remaining in the care of a severely disturbed parent.

Findings that children of unipolar or neurotically depressed parents may be at greater risk than the children of schizophrenic parents also needs clarification. The unipolar and neurotically depressed parents in such studies typically have been neither carefully selected nor well described. Concurrent findings that these parents may have been more socially impaired, and for a longer period than the schizophrenic parents, are somewhat surprising. Given our current state of knowledge, however, it is not clear whether these results reflect the nature of difficulties associated with ostensibly less severe depression, with features of the children's family environments, or with selection biases in the studies that obtained these findings. In any case, it should be noted that much of the research that we have reviewed in this chapter has been conducted in University hospitals and other tertiary care settings. There is a pressing need to study the child problems associated with the less severely depressed and first-episode parents who are more likely to be found at outpatient clinics and other primary care settings, as well as with untreated depression in community samples. In the absence of such research, we must be cautious about generalizing from the findings discussed here.

As we have noted, there is great variability in the methods and samples of these studies, and this contributes to the tentativeness of these summaries. One recurring methodological issue is the comparability of interview and self-reports of parents and children. The results of a number of studies suggest that parents are not accurate reporters of their children's affective disturbance. Orvaschel et al. (1982), for example, found that the parents of depressed children under-report their children's symptoms. In a more complex study, Moretti, Fine, Haley, and Marriage (1985) found that parents overestimate depression in children with conduct or dysthymic disorder, and underestimate depression in children with major depressive disorder. Although the parents' reports in this study were significantly correlated with each other, they were not highly correlated with their children's reports. Similarly, Kashani, Orvaschel, Burk, and Reid (1985) found that depressed parents under-report depression in their children, but over-report oppositional and attentional problems. Further research is needed to elucidate the sources of discrepancies between child and parental reports, as well as their relationship to evaluations by professionals who have had sufficient time to observe the children. Clearly, reports by depressed parents about the symptomatology ought not be dismissed as mere distortions. Furthermore, the issue of dyadic interactions with parents as a context for observing children needs investigation in instances where parents appear to overestimate their children's difficulties. However, it should be noted that the trend in the study of child psychopathology is toward greater reliance on structured interviews with children, although this is often preceded by an interview with a parent in the case of prepubertal children (cf. Puig-Antich, Chambers & Tabrizi, 1983). In the interest of comparison and comparability of findings, researchers examining the children of depressed parents would do well to include such an approach.

In concluding, we believe that we are nearing (if not standing on) the point of diminishing returns with respect to simple demonstrations that the offspring of depressed or psychiatric parents exhibit difficulties in their psychosocial functioning. It is now time that we focus our efforts on elucidating the *processes* underlying the relationship between maternal psychiatric disturbance and child dysfunction. In this context, there are a number of promising directions for study. First, several investigators have found that individuals experiencing unipolar depression are characterized by a heightened state of self-focused attention (e.g., Ingram, Lumry, Cruet & Seiber, 1987; Lewinsohn, Hoberman, Teri & Hautzinger, 1985; Pyszczynski & Greenberg, 1987). One obvious effect of an increased self-focus in depressed parents would be a relative lack of awareness and responsivity of the parents to the emotional needs of their children. Prolonged parental self-focus, therefore, and the consequent unavailability of the parent may be one mechanism through which difficulties in children's adjustment are established (cf. Lee & Gotlib, in press). Second, as we noted earlier, recent direct observations of families with depressed parents suggest that depressive symptoms may be functional in reducing aversive exchanges between family members (e.g., Hops et al., 1987; Kochanska et al., 1987). If this is in fact the case, children's mastery of appropriate conflict-resolution and affect-regulation skills would be disrupted, leading to problems in adjustment. Third, the results of several investigations suggest that the exposure of the children to parental marital discord and hostility, or to a chronic personality disorder in a parent, may result in child difficulties (e.g., Cox et al., 1987; Emery, Weintraub & Neale, 1982; Quinton & Rutter, 1985). As a final caution, however, Quinton and Rutter (1985) correctly point out that even though different psychiatric disorders seem to carry similar psychiatric risks for the children, they may do so for different reasons. The fact that parental diagnosis is not a strong predictor of adjustment difficulties in the children, for example, does not mean that all forms of parental disturbance necessarily give rise to psychiatric risks for the children in the same way. Thus, while it remains for future studies to examine more explicitly the viability of these explanations in accounting for the significant association of maternal psychiatric disorder and child dysfunction, we must remain cognizant of the possibility that there may be more than one path linking these two constructs.

**Authors' Note:** Preparation of this chapter was facilitated by Grants #977–87–89 from the Ontario Mental Health Foundation and #6606–3465–51 from Health and Welfare Canada to the first author. Catherine Lee is now at the University of Ottawa.

## References

Achenbach, T.M. & Edelbrock, C. (1983). *Manual for the Child Behavior Checklist and Revised Child Behavior Profile.* Burlington Vermont: University of Vermont.

Ainsworth, M., Blehar, M., Waters, E. & Wall, S. (1978). *Patterns of attachment.* Hillsdale, N.J.: Erlbaum.

Ainsworth, M.D.S. & Wittig, B.A. (1969). Attachment and exploratory behavior of one-year-olds in a strange situation. In B.M. Foss (Ed.), *Determinants of infant behavior, Vol. 4.* (pp. 111–136). London: Methuen.

Anderson, K.O., Bradley, L.A., Young, L.D., McDaniel, L.K. & Wise, C.M. (1985). Rheumatoid arthritis: Review of psychological factors related to etiology, effects, and treatment. *Psychological Bulletin, 98,* 358–387.

Beardslee, W.R., Bemporad, J., Keller, M.B. & Klerman, G.L. (1983). Children of parents with major affective disorder: A review. *American Journal of Psychiatry, 140,* 825–832.

Beardslee, W.R., Schultz, L.H. & Selman, R.L. (1987). Level of social-cognitive development, adaptive functioning, and DSM-III diagnoses in adolescent offspring of parents with affective disorders: Implications for the development of the capacity for mutuality. *Developmental Psychology*, *23*, 807–815.

Beck, A.T., Ward, C.H., Mendelson, M., Mock, J. & Erbaugh, J. An inventory for measuring depression. (1961). *Archives of General Psychiatry*, *4*, 561–571.

Bettes, B.A. (1988). Maternal depression and motherese: Temporal and intonational features. *Child Development 59*, 1089–1096.

Biglan, A., Hops, H. & Sherman, L. (in press). Coercive family processes and maternal depression. In R.D. Peters & R.J. McMahon (Eds.), *Marriage and families: Behavioral-systems approaches*. New York: Brunner Mazel.

Billings, A.G. & Moos, R.M. (1983). Comparisons of children of depressed and non-depressed parents: A social-environmental perspective. *Journal of Abnormal Child Psychology*, *11*, 463–486.

Billings, A.G. & Moos, R.H. (1986). Children of parents with unipolar depression: A controlled one year follow-up. *Journal of Abnormal Child Psychology*, *14*, 149–166.

Breznitz, Z. & Sherman, T. (1987). Speech patterning of natural discourse of well and depressed mothers and their young children. *Child Development*, *58*, 395–400.

Bromet, E.J. & Cornely, P.J. (1984). Correlates of depression in mothers of young children. *Journal of the American Academy of Child Psychiatry*, *23*, 335–342.

Brown, G.W. & Harris, T. (1978). *Social origins of depression*. New York: Free Press.

Burbach, D.J. & Borduin, C.M. (1986). Parent-child relations and the etiology of depression: A review of methods and findings. *Clinical Psychology Review*, *6*, 133–153.

Cohler, B.J., Gallant, D.H., Grunebaum, H.U. (1977). Disturbance of attention among schizophrenic, depressed and well mothers and their five-year-old children. *Journal of Child Psychology and Psychiatry*, *18*, 115–136.

Cohler, B.J., Gallant, D.H., Grunebaum, H.U. & Kaufman, C. (1983). Social adjustment among schizophrenic, depressed, and well mothers and their school-aged children. In H.L. Morrison (Ed.), *Children of depressed parents: Risk, identification, and intervention* (pp. 65–98). New York: Grune & Stratton.

Cohn, J. & Tronick, E.J. (1983). Three-month-old infants' reaction to simulated maternal depression. *Child Development*, *54*, 185–190.

Cox, A.D., Puckering, C., Pound, A. & Mills, M. (1987). The impact of maternal depression in young children. *Journal of Child Psychology and Psychiatry*, *28*, 917–928.

Coyne, J.C. (1976). Toward an interactional description of depression. *Psychiatry*, *39*, 28–40.

Coyne, J.C., Aldwin, C. & Lazarus, R.S. (1981). Depression and coping in stressful episodes. *Journal of Abnormal Psychology*, *90*, 439–447.

Coyne, J.C., Kahn, J. & Gotlib, I.H. (1987). Depression. In T. Jacob (Ed.), *Family interaction and psychopathology* (pp. 509–533). New York: Plenum.

Cutrona, C.E. & Troutman, B.R. (1986). Social support, infant temperament, and parenting self-efficacy: A mediational model of postpartum depression. *Child Development*, *57*, 1507–1518.

Decina, P., Kestenbaum, C.J., Farber, S., Kron, L., Gargan, M., Sackeim, H.A. & Fieve, R.R. (1983). Clinical and psychological assessment of children of bipolar probands. *American Journal of Psychiatry*, *140*, 548–553.

Depue, R.A. & Monroe, S.M. (1978). Learned helplessness in the perspective of the depressive disorders: Conceptual and definitional issues. *Journal of Abnormal Psychology*, *87*, 3–20.

Digdon, N. & Gotlib, I.H. (1985). Developmental considerations in the study of childhood depression. *Developmental Review*, *5*, 162–199.

Emery, R., Weintraub, S. & Neale, J.M. (1982). Effects of marital discord on the children of schizophrenic, affectively disordered, and normal parents. *Journal of Abnormal Child Psychology, 10*, 215–228.

Field, T.M. (1984). Early interactions between infants and their postpartum depressed mothers. *Infant Behavior and Development, 7*, 517–522.

Field, T., Sandberg, D., Garcia, R., Vega-Lahr, N., Goldstein, S. & Guy, L. (1985). Pregnancy problems, postpartum depression and early mother-infant interactions. *Developmental Psychology, 21*, 1152–1156.

Fisher, L. (1980). Child competence and psychiatric risk. I. Model and method. *Journal of Nervous and Mental Disease, 168*, 323–331.

Forehand, R., Brody, G., Slotkin, J., Fauber, R., McCombs, A. & Long, N. (1988). Young adolescent and maternal depression: Assessment, interrelations, and family predictors. *Journal of Consulting and Clinical Psychology, 56*, 422–426.

Gamer, E., Gallant, D., Grunebaum, H., Cohler, B.J. (1977). Children of psychotic mothers. *Archives of General Psychiatry, 34*, 592–597.

Ghodsian, M., Zayicek, E. & Wolkind, S. (1984). A longitudinal study of maternal depression and child behavior problems. *Journal of Child Psychology and Psychiatry, 25*, 91–109.

Gotlib, I.H. (1982). Self-reinforcement and depression in interpersonal interaction: The role of performance level. *Journal of Abnormal Psychology, 91*, 3–13.

Gotlib, I.H. (1983). Perception and recall of interpersonal feedback: Negative bias in depression. *Cognitive Therapy and Research, 7*, 399–412.

Gotlib, I.H. (1984). Depression and general psychopathology in university students. *Journal of Abnormal Psychology, 93*, 19–30.

Gotlib, I.H. & Cane, D.B. (1989). Self-report assessment of depression and anxiety. In P.C. Kendall & D. Watson (Eds.), *Anxiety and Depression: Distinctive and overlapping features* (pp. 131–169). New York: Academic Press.

Gotlib, I.H. & Colby, C.A. (1987). *Treatment of depression: An interpersonal systems approach*. New York: Pergamon Press.

Gotlib, I.H. & Hooley, J.M. (1988). Depression and marital distress: Current status and future directions. In S. Duck (Ed.), *Handbook of Personal Relationships* (pp. 543–570). Chicester, England: Wiley.

Gotlib, I.H. & Lee, C.M. (1989). The social functioning of depressed patients: A longitudinal assessment. *Journal of Social and Clinical Psychology, 8*, 223–237.

Gotlib, I.H. & Whiffen, V.E. (in press). The interpersonal context of depression: Implications for theory and research. In D. Perlman & W. Jones (Eds.), *Advances in Personal Relationships*. Greenwich: JAI Press.

Gotlib, I.H., Whiffen, V.E., Mount, J.H., Milne, K. & Cordy, N.I. (1989). Prevalence rates and demographic characteristics associated with depression in pregnancy and the postpartum. *Journal of Consulting and Clinical Psychology, 57*, 269–274.

Grunebaum, H., Cohler, B.J., Kaufman, C. & Gallant, D. (1978). Children of depressed and schizophrenic mothers. *Child Psychiatry and Human Development, 8*, 219–228.

Hamilton, M. (1960). A rating scale for depression. *Journal of Neurology, Neurosurgery, and Psychiatry, 23*, 56–62.

Hammen, C., Gordon, D., Burge, D., Adrian, C., Jaenicke, C. & Hiroto, D. (1987). Maternal affective disorders, illness, and stress: Risk for children's psychopathology. *American Journal of Psychiatry, 144*, 736–741.

Harder, D.W., Kokes, R.F., Fisher, L. & Strauss, J. (1980). Child competence and psychiatric risk IV. Relationships of parent diagnostic classifications and parent psychopathology severity to child functioning. *Journal of Nervous and Mental Diseases, 168*, 343–347.

Hinchliffe, M., Hooper, D. & Roberts, F.J. (1978). *The melancholy marriage*. New York: John Wiley.

Hirsch, B.J., Moos, R.H. & Reischl, T.M. (1985). Psychosocial adjustment of adolescent children of a depressed, arthritic, or normal parent. *Journal of Abnormal Psychology*, *94*, 154–164.

Hodges, K.K. (1983). *The Child Assessment Schedule*. Unpublished manuscript. University of Missouri.

Hodges, K.K., McKnew, D., Cytryn, L., Stern, L. & Kline, J. (1982). The Child Assessment Schedule (CAS) Diagnostic Interview: A report on and validity. *Journal of the American Academy of Child Psychiatry*, *21*, 468–473.

Hops, H., Biglan, A., Sherman, L., Arthur, J., Friedman, L. & Osteen, V. (1987). Home observations of family interactions of depressed women. *Journal of Consulting and Clinical Psychology*, *55*, 341–346.

Ingram, R.E., Lumry, A., Cruet, D. & Seiber, W. (1987). Attentional processes in depressive disorders. *Cognitive Therapy and Research*, *11*, 351–360.

Kaplan, B.J., Beardslee, W.R. & Keller, M.B. (1987). Intellectual competence in children of depressed parents. *Journal of Clinical Child Psychology*, *16*, 158–163.

Kashani, J.H., Orvaschel, H., Burk, J.P. & Reid, J.C. (1985). Depressed children of depressed parents. *Canadian Journal of Psychiatry*, *30*, 265–268.

Keitner, G.I., Miller, I.W., Epstein, N.B., Bishop, D.S. & Fruzetti, A.E. (1987). Family functioning and the course of major depression. *Comprehensive Psychiatry*, *28*, 54–64.

Keller, M.B., Beardslee, W.M., Dorer, D.J., Lavori, P. W., Samuelson, H. & Klerman, G.R. (1986). Impact of severity and chronicity of parental affective illness on adaptive functioning and psychopathology in children. *Archives of General Psychiatry*, *43*, 930–937.

Kendall, P.C., Hollon, S.D., Beck, A.T., Hammen, C.L. & Ingram, R.E. (1987). Issues and recommendations regarding use of the Beck Depression Inventory. *Cognitive Therapy and Research*, *11*, 289–299.

Kendall, P.C., Lerner, R.M. & Craighead, W.E. (1984). Human development and intervention in childhood psychopathology. *Child Development*, *55*, 7119682.

Klein, D.N., Depue, R.A. & Krauss, S.P. (1986). Social adjustment in the offspring of parents with bipolar affective disorder. *Journal of Psychopathology and Behavioral Assessment*, *8*, 355–366.

Kochanska, G., Kuczynski, L., Radke-Yarrow, M. & Welsh, J.D. (1987). Resolutions of conflict episodes between well and affectively ill mothers and their young children. *Journal of Abnormal Child Psychology*, *15*, 441–456.

Kuyler, P.L., Rosenthal, L., Igel, G., Dunner, D.L. & Fieve, R.R. (1980). Psychopathology among children of manic depressive patients. *Biological Psychiatry*, *15*, 589–597.

Lee, C.M. & Gotlib, I.H. (1989a). Clinical status and emotional adjustment of children of depressed mothers. *American Journal of Psychiatry*, *146*, 478–483.

Lee, C.M. & Gotlib, I.H. (1989b). Maternal depression and child adjustment: A longitudinal analysis. *Journal of Abnormal Psychology*, *98*, 78–85.

Lee, C.M. & Gotlib, I.H. (in press). Family disruption, parental availability, and child adjustment: An integrative review. In R.J. Prinz (Ed.), *Advances in the behavioral assessment of children and families*. Greenwich: JAI Press.

Lewinsohn, P.M., Hoberman, H., Teri, L. & Hautzinger, M. (1985). An integrative theory of depression. In S. Reiss & R. Bootzin (Eds.), *Theoretical issues in behavior therapy* (pp. 331–359). New York: Academic Press.

Livingood, A.B., Daen, P. & Smith, B.D. (1983). The depressed mother as a source of stimulation for her infant. *Journal of Clinical Psychology*, *39*, 369–375.

Lyons-Ruth, K., Zoll, D., Connell, D. & Grunebaum, H.U. (1986). The depressed mother and her one-year-old infant: Environmental context, mother-infant interaction and attachment, and infant development. In E. Tronick & T. Field (Eds.), *Maternal depression and infant disturbance: New directions in child development* (pp. 61–82). San Francisco: Jossey Bass.

McLean, P.D. (1976). Parental depression: Incompatible with effective parenting. In E.J. Mash, C. Handy & L.A. Hammerlynck (Eds.), *Behavior modification approaches to parenting* (pp.209–220). New York: Brunner/Mazel.

McNeil, T.F. & Kaij, L. (1980). *Offspring of women with nonorganic psychoses: Progress report, February 1980*. Paper presented at the Risk Research Consortium Plenary Conference, San Juan.

Mednick, S.A. & Schulsinger, F. (1968). Some premorbid characteristics related to breakdown in children with schizophrenic mothers. In D. Rosenthal & S.S. Kety (Eds.), *The transmission of schizophrenia*. Oxford: Pergamon.

Moretti, M.M., Fine, S., Haley, G. & Marriage, K. (1985). Childhood and adolescent depression: Child-report versus parent-report information. *Journal of the American Academy of Child Psychiatry, 24*, 298–302.

Neale, J.M. & Weintraub, S. (1975). Children vulnerable to psychopathology: The Stony Brook high-risk project. *Journal of Abnormal Child Psychology, 3*, 95–113.

Orvaschel, H., Puig-Antich, J., Chambers, W.J., Tabrizi, M.A. & Johnson, R. (1982). Retrospective assessment of child psychopathology with the K-SADS-E. *Journal of the American Academy of Child Psychiatry, 4*, 392–397.

Orvaschel. H., Walsh-Allis, G. & Ye, W. (1988). Psychopathology in children of parents with recurrent depression. *Journal of Abnormal Child Psychology, 16*, 17–28.

Panaccione, V.F. & Wahler, R.G. (1986). Child behavior, maternal depression, and social coercion as factors in the quality of child care. *Journal of Abnormal Child Psychology, 14*, 263–278.

Puig-Antich, J., Chambers, W.J. & Tabrizi, M. (1983). The clinical assessment of current depressive episodes in children and adolescents: Interviews with parents and children. In D.P. Cantwell & G.A. Carlson (Eds.), *Affective disorders in childhood and adolescence: An update*. New York: Spectrum Publications.

Pyszczynski, T. & Greenberg, J. (1987). Self-regulatory perseveration and the depressive self-focusing style: A self-awareness theory of reactive depression. *Psychological Bulletin, 102*, 122–138.

Quinton, D. & Rutter, M. (1985). Family pathology and child psychiatric disorder: A four-year prospective study. In A.R. Nicol (Ed.), *Longitudinal studies in child psychology and psychiatry* (pp. 91–134). Chichester: Wiley.

Radke-Yarrow, M., Cummings, E.M., Kuczynski, L. & Chapman, M. (1985). Patterns of attachment in two- and three-year olds in normal families and families with parental depression. *Child Development, 56*, 884–893.

Radloff, L.S. (1977). The CES-D Scale: A self-report depression scale for research in the general population. *Applied Psychological Measurement,1*, 385–401.

Rickard, K.M., Forehand, R., Atkeson, B.M. & Lopez, C. (1982). An examination of the relationship of marital satisfaction and divorce with parent-child interactions. *Journal of Clinical Child Psychology, 11*, 61–65.

Ruscher, S.M. & Gotlib, I.H. (1988). Marital interaction patterns of couples with and without a depressed partner. *Behavior Therapy, 19*, 455–470.

Rutter, M. (1966). *Children of sick parents: An environmental and psychiatric study*. Maudsley Monograph No. 16. Oxford: Oxford University Press.

Sameroff, A.J., Barocas, R. & Seifer, R. (1984). The early development of children born to mentally ill women. In N.F. Watt, E.J. Anthony, L.C. Wynne & J. Rolf (Eds.), *Children at risk for schizophrenia*. New York: Cambridge University Press.

Sameroff, A.J., Seifer, R. & Zax, M. (1982). Early development of children at risk for emotional disorder. *Monographs of the Society for Research in Child Development*, *47*, (7, Serial No. 199).

Sameroff, A.J. & Zax, M. (1973). Perinatal characteristics of the offspring of schizophrenic women. *Journal of Nervous and Mental Disease*, *157*, 191–199.

Seifer, R., Sameroff, A.J. & Jones, F. (1981). Adaptive behavior in young children of emotionally disturbed women. *Journal of Developmental Psychology*, *1*, 251–276.

Spitzer, R.L., Endicott, J. & Robins, E. (1978). Research Diagnostic Criteria: Rationale and reliability. *Archives of General Psychiatry*, *36*, 773–782.

Turner, S.M., Beidel, D.C. & Costello, A. (1987). Psychopathology in the offspring of anxiety disorder patients. *Journal of Consulting and Clinical Psychology*, 229–235.

Weintraub, S., Liebert, D. & Neale, J.M. (1978). Teacher ratings of children vulnerable to psychopathology. In E.J. Anthony (Ed.), *The child and his family (Vol.4), Vulnerable children* (pp. 335–346). New York: Wiley.

Weintraub, S., Prinz, R. & Neale, J.M. (1975). Peer evaluations of the competence of children vulnerable to psychopathology. *Journal of Abnormal Child Psychology*, *6*, 461–473.

Weissman, M. M. (1983). The depressed mother and her rebellious adolescent. In H.L. Morrison (Ed.), *Children of depressed parents: Risk, identification, and intervention* (pp. 99–113). New York: Grune & Stratton.

Weissman, M.M. & Klerman, G.L. (1977). Sex differences in the epidemiology of depression. *Archives of General Psychiatry*, *34*, 98–111.

Weissman, M. M., Myers, J.K. & Harding, P.S. (1978). Psychiatric disorders in a U.S. urban community: 1975–1976. *American Journal of Psychiatry*, *135*, 259–262.

Weissman, M.M. & Paykel, E.S. (1974). *The depressed woman: A study of social relationships*. Chicago: University of Chicago Press.

Weissman, M.M., Prusoff, B.A., Gammon, G.D., Merikangas, K.R., Leckman, J.F. & Kidd, K.K. (1984). Psychopathology in the children (ages 6–18) of depressed and normal parents. *Journal of the American Academy of Child Psychiatry*, *23*, 78–84.

Whiffen, V.E. (1988). Vulnerability to postpartum depression: A prospective multivariate study. *Journal of Abnormal Psychology*, *97*, 467–474.

Whiffen, V.E. & Gotlib, I.H. (1989). Infants of postpartum depressed mothers: Temperament and cognitive status. *Journal of Abnormal Psychology*, *98*, 274–279.

Wing, J.K., Cooper, J.E. & Sartorius, N. (1974). *Measurement and classification of psychiatric symptoms: An instruction manual for the PSE and CATEGO program*. Cambridge, MA: Harvard University Press.

Winters, K.C., Stone, A.A., Weintraub, S. & Neale, J.M. (1981). Cognitive and attentional deficits in children vulnerable to psychopathology. *Journal of Abnormal Child Psychology*, *9*, 435–453.

Yarrow, M.R., Campbell, J.D. & Burton, R.V. (1970). Recollections of childhood: A study of the retrospective method. *Monographs of The Society for Research on Child Development*, *35*, No. 5.

Youngren, M.A. & Lewinsohn, P.M. (1980). The functional relationship between depression and problematic behavior. *Journal of Abnormal Psychology*, *89*, 333–341.

Zahn-Waxler, C., Cummings, E.M., McKnew, D.H. & Radke-Yarrow, M. (1984). Altruism, aggression and social interactions in young children with a manic-depressive parent. *Child Development*, *55*, 112–122.

Zahn-Waxler, C., McKnew, D.H., Cummings, E.M., Davenport, Y.B. & Radke-Yarrow, M. (1984). Problem behaviors and peer interactions of young children with a manic-depressive parent. *American Journal of Psychiatry*, *141*, 236–240.

Zekoski, E.M., O'Hara, M.W. & Wills, K.E. (1987). The effects of maternal mood on mother-infant interaction. *Journal of Abnormal Child Psychology*, *15*, 361–378.

# PART III

# PSYCHOBIOLOGICAL FACTORS

Part III contains two chapters (Chapters 9 and 10) that focus on psychobiological analyses of depression. In both of these chapters, the authors attempt to integrate biological and psychological orientations regarding theory and research in depression.

Wright and Salmon (Chapter 9) review and evaluate the research examining learning and memory deficits associated with depression. They argue that there are two distinguishable types of cognitive deficits associated with depression. The first, which is discussed extensively in the chapters in Part II, is the tendency of depressed individuals to distort cognitively (in a negative fashion) information they are exposed to concerning themselves, their world, and their future. The second, which is the focus of this chapter, concerns the nature of learning and memory deficits characteristic of depressed individuals.

In their chapter (Chapter 9), Wright and Salmon consider three basic issues: 1) the evidence for a link between depression, and learning and memory deficits; 2) identification of the modes of functioning that suffer the most profound dysfunction; and 3) the specific stages in information processing that are implicated in the learning and memory deficits observed. The authors begin by reviewing our current knowledge regarding the psychological, neuropsychological, and biological bases of learning and memory. They then discuss and examine cognitive deficits in depression, including work examining the effects of antidepressants and electroconvulsive therapy. Their review suggests that depressed individuals tend to manifest short-term memory deficits, slowed responses to memory and psychomotor tasks, along with *state-dependent* recall distortions. They conclude that multiple stages in information processing are implicated in the observed deficits. Finally, in addition to this review of basic research in this area, Wright and Salmon consider the treatment implications of the relevant research and theory.

In his chapter on Treatment-Resistant Depression and Rapid Cycling Affective Disorders, Persad (Chapter 10) takes a clinician's perspective on both the etiology and treatment for these types of depressive disorders. In the first major section of his chapter, Persad considers the extent and characteristics of truly treatment-resistant depressives. He then reviews the types of sociodemographic, clinical, and biochemical characteristics linked to unfavorable treatment responses (i.e., patient characteristics). Next, he considers therapist variables (e.g., prescribing habits, etc.) that may also be implicated in less than maximal treatment effectiveness. Persad concludes this section by indicating directions for the effective management of such patients.

In the second section of his chapter, Persad discusses the nature of Rapid-Cycling Affective Disorders. These disorders are characterized by frequent mood shifts and significant failures to benefit from lithium therapy. Patients characterized by this type of disorder have proven to be extremely difficult to treat. Persad reviews the features of this problem and integrates current empirical work in this area, as well as detailing potentially effective treatment modes. These include combining pharmacological and psychosocial intervention techniques. Persad illustrates these techniques by presenting a case study of one of his patients who suffered from a rapid-cycling disorder. He makes the point that biological and psychological interventions need to be systematically combined in order to alleviate this disorder.

In summary, Part III focuses on current attempts to integrate biological and psychological research, theory, and treatment relevant to depression. The chapters address both clinical and theoretical issues, and should serve to promote future advances in this area.

# 9

# Learning and Memory in Depression

Jesse H. Wright and Paul G. Salmon
*University of Louisville*

KEY WORDS: learning, memory, cognitive deficits, mood and
memory, antidepressant drugs

"Pluck from the memory a rooted sorrow,
Raze out the written troubles of the brain
And with some sweet oblivious antidote
Cleanse the stuff'd bosom of that perilous stuff..."
*Macbeth*, William Shakespeare

The depressed patient is plagued with disordered cognitive functioning in two major areas. One of these is negative biasing of cognitions, a process that influences memories for past events, evaluations of present circumstances, and expectations for the future (Beck, Rush, Shaw & Emery, 1979; Wright & Beck, 1983; Wright, 1988). Cognitive distortion may initiate or aggravate depressive syndromes (Wright & Beck, 1983; Wright, 1988). However, if one of the modern-day "antidotes" such as cognitive therapy, antidepressants, or electroconvulsive therapy is successful, the predominantly negative valence of thinking gives way. Ruminations cease, errors of the past are less important, and possibilities for the future seem more promising (Wright, 1988).

The second area of cognitive dysfunction, impaired learning and memory, has received somewhat less attention, but also appears to be a significant component of the depressive syndrome. It has been known for some time that patients with depression have a decreased ability to concentrate and remember. This form of cognitive impairment is considered to be one of the core symptoms of major depression (American Psychiatric Association, 1987). Also, pseudodementia (i.e., memory decline without organic cause) is a well-recognized sequela of severe depression in the elderly (Miller & Lewis, 1977). Learning and memory have been studied intensively in depressed patients, but the implications of this work have not been integrated into clinical practice as effectively as have findings concerning distorted thought content.

In this chapter we examine the contribution of learning and memory research to understanding the psychopathology and treatment of depression. Basic questions addressed in this review are: (1) Is there firm evidence for learning and memory impairment in depression? (2) What functions are most severely affected? and (3) What stages or processes of memory are involved? Other areas discussed include the effects of antidepressants and electroconvulsive therapy on learning and memory, and the relationship between mood and memory. These topics link learning and memory research with both biological and psychological models of depression. Finally, treatment procedures are suggested for modifying cognitive dysfunction in depressed patients.

Current concepts of learning and memory have been derived from somewhat disparate, yet related, fields of study. We first summarize predominant theories of learning and memory (e.g., information processing, developmental, neuropsychological, and biochemical). This provides a background for the evaluation of learning and memory research in depression.

## THEORIES OF LEARNING AND MEMORY

### Information Theory and Information Processing

The term "information processing" (IP) refers to an analogy between the characteristics of computers and humans in solving problems and performing other cognitive tasks. The concept of information, which is defined as an entity which reduces uncertainty, was developed in reference to communication technology (Shannon & Weaver, 1949). The characterization of information as data capable of being "processed" evolved in conjunction with the development of digital computers.

As applied to depression, an IP model could be used to specify the characteristic manner in which information is encoded, manipulated, and retrieved (Ingram, 1984). The IP perspective may be of heuristic value in the future, but as yet it has not added significantly to an understanding of learning and memory in depression (Pribram, 1980; Wexler, 1986). IP concepts derived from current digital computer analogies have significant limitations because they are based on sequential, or serial, processing operations. Human mental activity is considerably more complex and thus may be better analyzed in terms of simultaneous, or parallel, processing (Thompson, 1986).

### Social and Developmental Influences on Cognitive Processes

Psychologists such as Piaget (1976) and Bowlby (1985) have described cognitive development as an active process by which symbolic, representational capabilities are acquired. Milestones, including attachment, object permanence, motor skills, and language, have been linked not only to the evolution of adult thought processes, but to their stunting and impairment as well (Bowlby, 1969; Flavell, 1976; Ault & Vinsel, 1980; Guidano & Liotti, 1983).

Contemporary analyses of cognitive development stress that schemata (cognitive templates, or rules for information processing) determine which of a myriad of incoming stimuli become the object of focus (Guidano & Liotti, 1983; Bowlby, 1985). These structures filter out information to reduce input to a manageable level and thereby have a major influence on perception and memory. Schemata can be either adaptive or maladaptive (Wright & Beck, 1983). With respect to depression, the developmental perspective suggests that schemata may selectively distort cognitions in a negative direction, thereby reducing the nature and amount of information available for processing. Such restrictive schemata may form the basis for the development of an overly personalized, self-referent bias in decision-making (Kuiper & MacDonald, 1983).

## Neuropsychology of Learning and Memory

Current neuropsychological theories are based on the concept of a flexible, organizational hierarchy of the neural processes underlying learning and memory. The involvement of both cortical and subcortical structures in cognitive tasks has been proposed by researchers including Hebb (1949), Luria (1973), Pribram (1980), and Squire (1986a), who have stressed the functional integration of the central nervous system. The idea that a unified system of structures underlies behavioral and cognitive responses represents a significant departure from early models of localization in which functions were ascribed discrete anatomic loci. Although these older models may be valid for some reflexive, lower-order motor and affective functions (Flor-Henry, 1979), they are less useful in describing the broadly-based, neural representation of more complex mental capabilities.

Because the encoding of objects and experiences in memory is an analytical process, there needs to be a mechanism through which memories are retrieved in a unified fashion. Recent work by Bower (1981) and Shaw, Silverman & Pearson (1985) has built upon Hebb's (1949) concept that memory traces are mediated by neuronal networks that connect multiple areas of the brain. Once a network is formed, individual elements can be triggered when related neuronal groups are stimulated. According to this model, the perceptual and sensory correlates of objects—a car, for instance—become integrated in such a way that the evocation of a specific attribute, such as a steering wheel, triggers images of other associated features. Bower has suggested that emotional states play a major role in organizing memory networks (Bower & Cowen, 1982). The activation of an emotional state can "prime" the individual to retrieve memories linked to the affect at the time information was acquired. In analyzing the impact of depressed mood states on memory and learning, Bower (1981) hypothesized that memory nodes are developed when depressed affect is associated with specific experiences. A return of depressed mood then leads to selective retrieval of these memories.

Memory is usually viewed as having three discrete stages: iconic, short-term, and long-term (Atkinson & Shiffrin, 1968). Iconic memory consists of literal representations of perceptual stimuli, and is the first stage in coding information subsequently stored in short- and long-term memory. Research on iconic memory has focused on the early stages of perception (Neisser, 1967). Deficient performance by depressed subjects has been presumed to reflect processing deficits associated with subsequent stages of encoding and retrieval, though the issue has yet to be put to an empirical test.

Short-term memory (STM) is a temporary storage system of limited capacity (Squire, 1986a). The storage duration of STM has been rather loosely defined as anywhere from a few seconds to a few minutes (Baddeley, 1984). STM content depends on the focus of attention. Early theorists (e.g., Broadbent, 1957) proposed that attention acted like a filter to exclude all but a limited amount of information from awareness and memory. Triesman (1969) and others (e.g., Kahneman, 1973) suggested that focus of attention attenuates—rather than eliminates—the transfer of irrelevant information from iconic memory to STM.

According to Estes (1972), STM operates like a temporary reverberating loop involving both memories and "control elements." Specific memories are associated with control elements which represent contextual cues, the activation of which cause the memory to be evoked. Information in STM is thus held in reverberating circuits which mediate the transition from sensory memory into more permanent storage. The transfer of information from STM to long-term memory (LTM) is affected by the nature of the material being processed.

In general, information related to knowledge of skills and procedures is stored in LTM more effectively than factual material. Squire (1986a) has termed these two types of information "procedural" and "declarative" knowledge. Thus far, studies of memory and depression have focused more on declarative than on procedural knowledge. Baddeley (1984) has proposed a further division of declarative knowledge into "semantic" and "episodic" types to emphasize the distinction between formally acquired material (semantic) and personalized or autobiographical memory (episodic). Vocabulary skills, for example, make extensive use of semantic knowledge. Episodic memories are based more on contextual and emotional cues than are their semantic counterparts (Tulving, 1983). Research on state-dependent learning in depression has examined both semantic and episodic memory.

## The Biological Basis of Memory

Recent neurobiological models of learning and memory have incorporated research findings concerning the relationships between neurotransmitters, post-synaptic events, and neuronal networks. It is generally accepted that experience modifies neuronal and synaptic morphology (Squire, 1986a; Thompson, 1986). Neurotransmitters are thought to play an important role in the formation of memory by participating in the construction of reverberating neural circuits and initiating the process of intracellular structural transformation (Black et al., 1987).

Studies with experimental animals such as *Aplysia*, the marine snail, have contributed significantly to understanding the biochemical basis of learning and memory (Kandel & Schwartz, 1982; Woody, 1986; Thompson, 1986). Kandel & Schwartz have shown that learning in *Aplysia* is dependent on serotonin and "second messengers" (e.g., phosphorylated proteins), both of which control ionic channels. It is assumed that short-term memory does not require synthesis of new protein macromolecules, but that long-term memory is probably dependent upon conformational or structural changes (Kandel & Schwartz, 1982; Woody, 1986).

Although alterations in intracellular processes are of considerable interest, research on neurotransmitter modulation has greater relevance for current biochemical theories of depression. Noradrenergic agents such as amphetamine have usually been found to facilitate memory, while antiadrenergic agents (e.g., alpha-methylparatyrosine, 6-hydroxydopamine) have impaired memory (Stein, Belluzzi & Wise, 1975; Hunter, Zornetzer, Jarvik & McGaugh, 1977; Alpern & Jackson, 1978; Dunn, 1980). Lesions of noradrenergic tracts such as the locus coeruleus have also been shown to have disruptive effects (Hunter et al., 1977). Results of such studies, however, have not been entirely uniform. Noradrenergic agonists have in some cases been found to interfere with memory (Hunter et al., 1977).

Anticholinergic drugs (e.g., atropine, scopolamine) have usually reduced memory performance, but physostigmine, a cholinergic agonist, has facilitated cognitive functioning in some instances (Hunter et al., 1977; Weingartner, Sitaram & Gillin, 1979; Dunn, 1980; Davies, 1985; Nissen, Knopman & Schacter, 1987). Neurohumoral agents such as ACTH and other steroids have also been studied. Both ACTH and vasopressin have stimulated memory, perhaps through elevation of norepinephrine and dopamine levels (Dunn, 1980). In other research, ACTH treatment has been associated with no appreciable effects on memory (Frederiksen, d'Elia & Holsten, 1985).

Changes in neurotransmitter regulation or other biological processes that underlie learning and memory functioning offer one possible explanation for cognitive deficits in depression. At the present time there is limited evidence that such mechanisms are involved. However, studies of antidepressant effects and neuroendocrine influences to be reviewed in this chapter provide some insights into the biochemistry of learning and memory dysfunction in depression.

## LEARNING AND MEMORY RESEARCH

### Overview

The bulk of research performed on learning and memory in depression has been centered on the identification of *cognitive deficits*. Despite 25 years of work in this area, the nature of learning and memory dysfunction in depression is still not well understood. Methodological problems have been an important limiting factor. For example, variables which affect learning and memory, such as electroconvulsive therapy and psychotropic drugs, have usually not been adequately controlled, and diagnostic categorization procedures have not always been rigorous. Yet, a wealth of data from studies of learning and memory suggests that depressed patients do have significant cognitive impairment. These investigations are reviewed with a focus on two primary issues: research design adequacy and evidence for specific patterns of cognitive dysfunction.

*Antidepressant effects* on learning and memory provide another avenue for studying information processing in depression. Several antidepressants such as amitriptyline, imipramine, and nortriptyline have been used. The varied actions of these drugs have made it possible to study the effects of modulation of different neurotransmitter systems on learning and memory. In addition, drug studies have examined response to treatment and thus have yielded information on whether cognitive deficits persist or resolve as depression improves. Generally, antidepressants have stimulated cognitive functioning, but this effect has not been uniform.

Learning and memory have also been examined in patients who have received *electroconvulsive therapy* (ECT). Bilateral ECT has usually impaired memory, but in some cases unilateral ECT has had the reverse effect. This research is discussed briefly here in relation to other findings on cognitive deficits in depression. The reader is referred to reviews by Strömgren (1973), Fromm-Auch (1982), and Squire (1986b) for comprehensive information concerning ECT and memory.

**TABLE 9–1: Learning and Memory Test Performance of Depressed Patients**

| STUDY | CATEGORI-ZATION | DRUG CONTROL | E.C.T. CONTROL | CONTROL SUBJECTS | MEASURES | RESULTS |
|---|---|---|---|---|---|---|
| Cutting 1979 | 20 depressed subjects. Criteria of Wing and Present State Exam. | Not controlled. | No E.C.T. within one year. | 40 neuro-psychiatric patient controls and 20 schizophrenics. Matched on Short-Form I.Q. Test. | Associate Learning Test. Recognition of histological slides. | Acute schizophrenics > depressed > brain lesions > dementia. |
| Breslow, Kocsis, & Belkin 1980 | 21 depressed subjects met R.D.C. | 5 patients were taking antidepressants. | No data. | 21 subjects matched on age, education. | Wechsler Memory Scale. | Normals > depressives. |
| Weingartner et al. 1981 | 10 unipolar depressed subjects met R.D.C. | On placebo but extent of drug washout unclear. | No data. | 10 subjects matched on age, sex, education. | Learning words with acoustic or semantic cues. | Acoustic cues: normals = depressed. Semantic cues: normal > depressed. |
| Cohen et al. 1982 | 11 unipolar and bipolar depressed subjects met R.D.C. | No drugs for 3 weeks. | No data. | 11 subjects "roughly" matched on educational level. | Memory for 30 trigrams. Dynamometer motor task. | Expenditure of effort on psychomotor task correlated positively with performance on memory tasks. |

| Study | Subjects | Drug-free | E.C.T. | Controls | Memory test | Results |
|---|---|---|---|---|---|---|
| Calev et al. 1986 | 10 depressed patients met DSM-III, 10 euthymic depressives. | "Drug-free" for 14 days. | No E.C.T. within one year. | 53 normal controls matched on age, sex, education. | Word and visual design memory. | Normals > depressives. Verbal = visual. |
| Roy-Byrne et al. 1986 | 10 unipolar and bipolar subjects met R.D.C. | None. | No data. | 10 control subjects matched on age, sex, education. | Word pair memory. | Normals > depressives for more difficult tasks. |
| Watts, Morris, & MacLeod 1987 | 21 subjects depressed on Levine-Pilowsky Questionnaire. | None. | No E.C.T. within 3 months. | 21 subjects matched on vocabulary test. | Signal detection analysis of word list memory. | Normals > depressives. Defect not due to response bias. |
| Watts & Sharrock 1987 | 21 subjects depressed on Levine-Pilowsky Questionnaire. | None. | No E.C.T. within 3 months. | 21 subjects matched on vocabulary test. | Recall of book passage. | Normals > depressives. |
| Wolfe et al. 1987 | 21 unipolar, 12 bipolar subjects met DSM-III | "Drug-free" 6 days. | No E.C.T. in lifetime. | 20 control subjects matched on age and education, 10 Huntington's disease patients. | Rey Auditory Verbal Learning. Verbal fluency. | Normal > unipolar and bipolar on Rey Test. |

(Table adapted from Wright, 1986.)

The relationship between *mood and memory* has been the subject of several important recent studies. These investigations have concentrated on state-dependent effects because recollections of past events by depressed individuals appear to be selectively biased toward situations associated with dysphoric mood states. Although this is a promising area of research, most studies of mood and memory have utilized experimental subjects who were not clinically depressed.

## Cognitive Deficits in Depression

The first major study of learning and memory in depression was reported by Friedman (1964). A comprehensive battery of cognitive tests was administered to a group of patients with mixed depressive disorders, but no diagnostic criteria were given. Variables that might affect cognitive functioning, such as psychotropic drugs and previous ECT treatment, were not controlled. Because performance was impaired in only six of the 33 tests, it was concluded that there was minimal evidence for cognitive deficit in depression. Complaints of decreased ability to concentrate were attributed to subjective distortions about intellectual capacity.

The methodological problems associated with Friedman's study recurred frequently in subsequent investigations. Of 23 nontreatment investigations reported, only nine meet a set of minimal criteria chosen to allow meaningful comparisons among studies. These criteria are: (1) inclusion of a control group with some attempt at matching; and (2) use of a diagnostic system that gives reasonable assurance that patients were depressed. Reports that meet these criteria are compared and contrasted in Table 9–1.

All studies in which the diagnosis of depression was firmly established by recognized criteria have found evidence for learning and memory impairment in depression. For example, Cutting (1979), who used the Present State Exam and the criteria of Wing to choose depressed subjects and patient control groups, described results that contrasted sharply with those reported earlier by Friedman (1964). Depressed patients performed as poorly as organic patients on measures of verbal and visual memory (Cutting, 1979). In another study, Breslow, Kocsis & Belkin (1980) found that depressed patients categorized by the Research Diagnostic Criteria (RDC) had clear and widespread deficits on the Wechsler Memory Scale (WMS).

A research group from the National Institute of Mental Health performed a series of small-scale studies that examined the impact of task difficulty on performance in depression (Weingartner, Cohen, Murphy, Martello & Gerdt, 1981; Cohen, Weingartner, Smallberg, Pickar & Murphy, 1982; Roy-Byrne, Weingartner, Bierer, Thompson & Post, 1986). The basic research methodology in these studies was to use procedures that tested memory for groups of words. In one study, depressed individuals accurately recalled word lists grouped into sets, but had difficulty remembering unrelated words. Depressed patients also performed poorly in attempts to learn words associated with complex semantic cues. Conversely, words with acoustic cues (an easier task involving rhyming) were remembered equally well by both groups (Weingartner et al., 1981). Subsequent studies confirmed this group's hypothesis that depressed patients have impaired memory for complex tasks or those that require considerable effort, but do reasonably well with easy or "automatic" procedures (Cohen et al., 1982; Roy-Byrne et al., 1986).

Various procedures to measure memory for words have been employed by other investigators. Calev, Korin, Shapira, Kugelmass & Lerer (1986) used a word recognition test to study depressed patients who met DSM-III criteria. As expected, depressed patients did less well than control subjects. Memory for visual designs was also impaired. Watts, Morris & MacLeod (1987) and Watts & Sharrock (1987) used the Levine-Pilowski Questionnaire to classify depressed patients who were tested for memory of word lists (Watts et al., 1987) and recall of a book passage (Watts & Sharrock, 1987). Depressed subjects had impaired scores relative to controls on both procedures.

A rigorously controlled study of learning and memory in depression was reported recently by Wolfe, Granholm, Butters, Saunders & Janowsky (1987). Depressed patients (unipolar and bipolar) were categorized according to DSM-III criteria, had been drug-free for six days, and had never received ECT. Compared to matched controls, they performed significantly worse on the Rey Auditory Verbal Learning Test, but achieved comparable levels on a measure of verbal fluency.

Results of studies that did not use control groups or lacked adequate diagnostic criteria must be interpreted with caution. However, they provide additional information about learning and memory in depression. One such investigation (Raskin, Friedman & DiMascio, 1982) used a diverse array of measures including WAIS subtests, finger-tapping speed, and the Stroop Test to document cognitive dysfunction in a large sample of depressed patients. Evidence for learning and memory impairment has been found by most other investigators. Studies that failed to find deficits have employed inadequate screening criteria for depression or have studied patients when they were not depressed (Davis & Unruh, 1980; Koh & Wolpert, 1983; Gass & Russell, 1986).

Findings of other investigations have been consistent with the Weingartner et al. (1981) conclusion that depressed patients have difficulty when they encounter challenging memory tasks. Examples include Donnelly, Dent & Murphy's (1972) report that depressed subjects performed as poorly as epileptics on the Halstead-Reitan Battery, and Braff & Beck's (1974) observation that depressed patients had intermediate performance between normal control subjects and schizophrenics on tests that required abstract thinking (Shipley Institute of Living Abstraction Test and Gorham Proverbs). Digit span and visual scanning were normal in depressed patients studied by Rush, Weissenburger, Vinson & Giles (1983), but trail-making scores were lower in those with endogenous depression. Also, Kopelman (1986) found that control subjects outperformed depressed patients on tests including Difficult Word Associations and WMS Logical Memory. In another study, Calev & Erwin (1985) found that depressed patients performed better on word recognition than on recall.

Speed of information processing has been studied by several investigators (Brand & Jolles, 1987; Glass, Uhlenhuth, Hartel, Matuzas & Fischman, 1981) who have reported that depressed patients perform more slowly than control subjects on digit recognition and reaction time procedures. In a well-controlled study, Breslow et al. (1980) noted that depressed subjects had slowed responses on timed tests from the Wechsler Memory Scale (WMS). This finding was later replicated by Wright (1986) in an investigation of antidepressant drug effects.

Two additional reports are of interest because of their attempt to correlate learning and memory functioning with neurohumoral changes. Rubinow, Post, Savard & Gold (1984) found that high urinary cortisol levels were associated with poor performance on the Halstead Categories Test, a measure of concept-recognition ability. In contrast, Caine, Yerevanian & Bamford (1984) did not find a significant relationship between nonsuppression on the Dexamethasone Suppression Test and scores from a broad range of memory tasks. These investigations are important because they have broken ground for the study of relationships between biological and cognitive components of depression.

In summary, the results of studies of cognitive deficits in depression suggest that patients with a clear diagnosis of depressive disorder have substantive impairment in learning and memory functioning. However, these deficits are not global. In almost all of the investigations cited in this review, some measures were performed equally well by both patients and controls. The most consistent pattern emerging from these studies is that complex or effortful mental operations are more likely than relatively easy tasks to present problems for depressed patients.

A plausible means of clarifying the deficient performance of depressed patients on difficult encoding tasks can be found in the levels of processing (LOP) model originally formulated by Craik & Lockhart (1972). These investigators observed that memory retrieval accuracy is influenced by the depth at which information is originally encoded. Superficial encoding is associated with rapid forgetting, while deep-level encoding enhances memory acquisition and storage. To illustrate, the word "car" could be encoded as a "three-letter word" (shallow level—physical properties), a word that rhymes with "far" (mid level—rhyming properties), or "a means of transportation, a necessity if you live in the suburbs" (deep level—semantic attributes). Although semantic features are most commonly cited as indicative of deep levels of processing, Baddeley (1984) has discussed other correlates including: (1) the degree to which the information is associated with one's current knowledge; (2) the extent to which information is consistent with existing knowledge; and (3) the degree of self-relevance of the information.

Depressed patients appear not to encode information effectively at deep levels. The specific reasons for this processing selectivity have not been systematically investigated, but Weingartner, et al. (1981) have proposed that lowered cortical arousal may inhibit complex processing. Other mechanisms were suggested by Ellis, Thomas & Rodriguez (1984), who found that expenditure of effort and ability to organize material influenced depth of encoding in subjects who had induced depressed mood. Ellis et al. (1984) also noted that the opportunity to employ semantic encoding processes aided performance. This finding raises the possibility that depressed individuals may be able to improve learning and memory functioning if they are taught strategies designed to maximize recall.

Most studies of cognitive deficits in depression were not designed to examine stages of memory. Iconic memory has not yet been investigated. The great majority of reports appear to have measured only short-term memory. Results from three studies of drug effects on long-term memory that will be reviewed in detail later gave contradictory results (Henry, Weingartner & Murphy, 1973; Sternberg & Jarvik, 1976; Wright, 1986). Thus, currently there is strong evidence for short-term memory impairment in depression, but the influence of depression on long-term memory remains unclear.

Observations on speed of information processing have corroborated the long-held clinical view that depression is associated with psychomotor retardation. However, little is known about the meaning or significance of these findings. Is slowing of information processing a compensatory mechanism to account for deficiencies in other aspects of cognitive functioning, or is it a pathological process with deleterious effects? What specific functions are slowed at what rate? It should be possible with further investigation to identify characteristic changes in speed of information processing in depressive syndromes.

Learning and memory research has not clearly delineated the processes by which depressed patients encode memories. Impaired performance on test outcome measures could be explained by inefficiencies in several phases of information processing including: inattention at the time of learning, response bias, deficient encoding, interference with rehearsal, or inaccurate retrieval. Available studies of depression suggest that problems could occur at all of these steps. Investigation of these processes has been difficult because they are so closely interrelated. However, several studies employing procedures based on Signal Detection Theory (SDT) have attempted to measure effects of response bias.

Signal Detection Theory, a general theory of decision-making processes in perception, provides a means of distinguishing between subjects' perceptual acuity and response bias (Swets, Tanner & Birdsall, 1961). SDT was first employed in research concerning the detection of sensory signals, and has since been found to be a valid technique for studying recognition memory as well (Healy & Kubovy, 1978). Results have been somewhat inconsistent when this methodology has been applied to depression. A study by Miller & Lewis (1977) of elderly depressed patients found a pattern of response bias that impaired recall performance. In contrast, Dunbar & Lishman (1984) and Watts et al. (1987) reported differences in performance accuracy but not response bias in comparisons of depressed and non-depressed subjects.

## The Effect of Antidepressants on Learning and Memory

Although it is generally assumed that antidepressants can reverse core symptoms of depression, including impaired concentration (Group for Advancement of Psychiatry, 1975), there has been little investigation of drug effects on learning and memory in depressed patients. Studies in which learning and memory functioning was assessed in patients treated with antidepressants are compared in Table 9–2. The first major study of antidepressants and cognitive functioning was reported by Henry et al. (1973). A mixed group of bipolar (manic phase) and unipolar depressed patients were treated with diverse medications including imipramine, L-dopa, L-tryptophan, alpha-methyl-paratyrosine, and lithium carbonate. Details about drug washouts, placebo administration, order of medication dosing, and ECT history were not given.

Henry et al. (1973) considered the first trial of a word learning task to be a measure of short-term memory, while subsequent trials (which followed immediately) were described as measuring long-term memory. It is unclear whether they

## TABLE 9–2: Antidepressant Effects on Learning and Memory of Depressed Patients

| STUDY | CATEGORI-ZATION | DRUG CONTROL | E.C.T. CONTROL | CONTROL SUBJECTS | DRUG TREATMENT | MEASURES | RESULTS |
|---|---|---|---|---|---|---|---|
| Henry et al. 1973 | 11 unipolar and 14 bipolar patients. No formal diagnostic criteria. | Unclear. | No data. | None | Imipramine, L-dopa, L-tryptophan, alpha-MPT, and lithium. | Serial learning, free recall of word lists. | No significant improvement with imipramine and lithium. L-dopa improved serial learning and free recall. |
| Sternberg & Jarvik 1976 | 26 depressed subjects. Diagnosis by symptom checklist. | Unclear. | No data. | 26 subjects matched on age, sex, education. | Imipramine or amitriptyline. | Chrönholm-Molander Tests. | Controls > depressed. Antidepressants improved memory. |
| Glass et al. 1981 | 32 depressed subjects met R.D.C. | Tested prior to starting antidepressants. No data on other drugs. | No data. | 31 subjects matched on age, sex, education. | Imipramine or placebo. | Tapping speed, lift off reaction time, short-term memory for digits. | Reaction time: controls < depressed. Other tests: controls = depressed. Imipramine improved performance. |

| Study | Subjects | Drug Status | ECT | Controls | Drug | Tests | Results |
|---|---|---|---|---|---|---|---|
| McNair et al. 1984 | 20 depressed subjects met R.D.C. | Not stated. | No data. | None | Amitriptyline (AMI), Amoxapine (AMOX) | Continuous Performance Test, short-term retrieval, long-term verbal memory. | AMI increased CPT speed but decreased accuracy. Initial negative, then positive effect of AMI on LTM. AMOX had little effect. |
| Lamping et al. 1984 | 40 depressed subjects met DSM-III criteria. | No antidepressants for 28 days. Other drugs not controlled. | No ECT for 28 days. | None | Amitriptyline, Clovoxamine (CLO) | Signal Detection Memory; Benton Visual Memory; WMS Logical Memory. | AMI impaired SDM. CLO facilitated SDM. AMI and CLO impaired BVM. No effect on Logical Memory. |
| Wright 1986 | 42 depressed subjects met DSM-III criteria. | Free of C.N.S. active drugs. | No ECT in lifetime. | 19 controls matched on age, sex, education. Controls treated with nortryptyline. | Nortriptyline | WMS, 30-Figure Test. Shipley Abstraction Test. | Controls > depressed on difficult tests. Treatment improved learning and memory. |

(Table adapted from Wright, 1986.)

were actually studying long-term memory because of the short delay between trials. The authors concluded that depressed patients had normal short-term, but impaired long-term memory. Relatively few subjects (samples of 6–12) received each of the drugs, so results were not analyzed separately for bipolar (manic phase) and unipolar (depressed) patients. L-dopa and L-tryptophan were found to improve some aspects of learning and memory, but lithium carbonate, alpha-methyl-paratyrosine, and imipramine did not.

The use of small groups of patients with mixed diagnoses makes it difficult to interpret the results of this study. However, Henry et al. (1973) proposed an intriguing hypothesis that warrants further investigation: excessively heightened (manic) or lowered (depressed) arousal are both associated with cognitive impairment because of a U-shaped arousal and learning curve. A similar relationship between performance efficiency and arousal was proposed earlier by Yerkes & Dodson (1908) and Broadhurst (1957). Henry et al. (1973) also suggested that medications could reverse learning and memory deficits by regulating the state of arousal, while not necessarily affecting the level of depressive symptomatology.

Sternberg & Jarvik (1976) utilized the Chrönolm-Molander Test Battery to assess word association memory, visual memory, and organization of data into new associations. The immediate recall of items from these tests was treated as a measure of short-term memory. Responses after a three-hour interval were used to assess long-term memory. Depressed patients were selected using a depression checklist similar to the RDC and were then treated with either imipramine or amitriptyline, 150–300 mg. per day. A matched control group did not receive medication. Results of this study contradicted the earlier work of Henry et al. (1973). Depressed patients had impaired short-term memory but performed as well as control subjects after a three-hour delay (long-term memory). After 26 days of treatment, memory was significantly enhanced in those subjects who demonstrated clinical improvement. Unfortunately, data from patients treated with amitriptyline and imipramine were not analyzed separately.

A salutary effect of tricyclic antidepressants on short-term memory was also found by Glass et al. (1981), who studied depressed outpatients treated with imipramine. Before treatment, depressed patients had equivalent scores to control subjects on psychomotor tests and short-term memory for digits, but took significantly longer to perform the tasks. Imipramine improved memory accuracy in the depressed patients without slowing reaction time. It was concluded that depressed patients compensated for memory difficulties by taking longer to perform mental operations.

Amitriptyline, the tricycle antidepressant with the strongest anticholinergic effects, has been associated with both positive and negative influences on cognition in depressed patients. McNair, Kahn, Frankenthaler & Faldetta (1984) noted that amitriptyline increased Continuous Performance Test response speed but reduced accuracy. Speed of performance was also improved for short-term memory tasks. However, long-term memory (recall of trigrams after a 45-minute delay) was initially impaired but then facilitated after three weeks of treatment with amitriptyline. Since a control group was not used, it is not known whether performance was actually impaired on any of the measures prior to treatment. Amoxapine, an antidepressant with low anticholinergic potency, was also used in the study. There was little evidence that this drug affected response time.

Differences between drugs with high and low anticholinergic effects were studied by an additional research group (Lamping, Spring & Gelenberg, 1984), who noted that amitriptyline interfered with performance of depressed outpatients on a signal detection task. Conversely, clovoxamine, an experimental antidepressant with limited anticholinergic effects, facilitated responses. A control group was not employed in this study.

The only investigation to date that administered a tricyclic antidepressant to both depressed patients and matched controls was conducted by Wright (1986), who examined the effects of nortriptyline on a variety of measures of short- and long-term memory. Subjects were drug-free before testing and had never had electroconvulsive therapy. Comparisons before treatment revealed that depressed patients had significant cognitive deficits. Difficult Wechsler Memory Scale subtests for short-term memory (Logical Memory, Hard Word Associations), timed measures, and Shipley-Hartford Institute of Living Abstraction scores discriminated the two groups. Long-term memory for Hard Word Associations was also impaired in depression. Treatment with nortriptyline led to recovery of most of these deficits.

Effects of antidepressants on learning and memory in control subjects contrast sharply with results obtained from depressed patient groups. Generally, single doses or short-term treatments have impaired memory and psychomotor performance (Thompson & Trimble, 1982). This has been true for a variety of antidepressants including imipramine, nortriptyline, and amitriptyline (DiMascio, Henninger & Klerman, 1964; Wittenborn, Flaherty, McGough, Bossange & Nash, 1976; Sepplälä, 1977; Crome & Newman, 1978; Thompson & Trimble, 1982; Branconnier, Devitt, Cole & Spera, 1982). In a longer-term trial, Wright (1986) found little evidence for either disruption or facilitation of cognitive functioning in control subjects treated with nortriptyline. Another research group described interference with word association memory after 14 days of nortriptyline (Liljequist, Linnoila & Mattila, 1974). The results of these studies indicate that antidepressants are probably not general stimulants of memory. Instead, their favorable influences appear to be limited to depressed patients who have impaired learning and memory before treatment.

Studies of antidepressant influences on learning and memory have contributed to understanding cognitive functioning in depression in three major ways. First, they provide further evidence that learning and memory deficits of depressed patients are greatest for complex, effortful, or timed tasks. Research with antidepressants has also helped answer questions about the permanence of information processing deficits in depression. Evidence to date strongly suggests that impaired learning and memory is largely reversed with successful treatment (Sternberg & Jarvik, 1976; Glass et al., 1981; Wright, 1986). Similar results have been observed with unilateral ECT (Strömgren, 1973; Fromm-Auch, 1982).

The third contribution of tricyclic antidepressant investigations concerns the relationship of different neurotransmitters to information processing. Drugs that have noradrenergic activity (imipramine, nortriptyline) have been found to promote learning and memory (Sternberg & Jarvik, 1976; Glass et al., 1981; Wright, 1986). Conversely, amitriptyline, an antidepressant with strong anticholinergic effects, has in some cases interfered with performance (Lamping et al., 1984; McNair et al., 1984). In other situations, amitriptyline has facilitated cognitive functioning (Sternberg & Jarvik, 1976; NcNair et al., 1984).

Most tricyclic antidepressants have a mixture of actions on norepinephrine, serotonin, and acetylcholine. Furthermore, active metabolites of antidepressants may have a different pattern of effects than do parent compounds. Thus, it is not surprising that varied results have been observed. Definitive studies have not yet been done, but the development of newer antidepressants with more specific actions and use of bioassays to measure the activity of neurotransmitter systems could help facilitate this area of research.

## Electroconvulsive Therapy and Learning and Memory

A number of studies of ECT effects have been reported (Strömgren, 1973; Fromm-Auch, 1982; Squire, 1986b), but little additional information about basic learning and memory processes in depression has been uncovered. Recurrent design problems such as lack of categorization criteria for depression, use of groups with varied diagnoses, and failure to include control groups have been very common. Also, studies have been designed primarily to measure side effects of treatment, not to identify the nature of learning and memory dysfunction in depression.

The major findings of ECT research have been as follows: (1) learning and memory is impaired before treatment; (2) bilateral ECT usually causes anterograde and retrograde amnesia; (3) unilateral ECT causes much less amnesia and may actually improve cognitive functioning by relieving depression; and (4) brief pulse treatment is less likely to cause cognitive dysfunction than is sine wave ECT (Strömgren, 1973; Fromm-Auch, 1982; Squire, 1986b; Malloy, Small, Miller, Milstein & Stout, 1982; Warren & Groome, 1984; Weiner, Rogers, Davidson & Squire, 1986; Schuster, Opgenoorth, Gabriel, Presslich & Sowinetz, 1986).

Several authors have interpreted findings from ECT research to suggest that depression is predominantly a right cerebral hemisphere disorder (Goldstein, Filskov & Weaver, 1977; Kronfol, Hamsher, Digre & Waziri, 1978; Flor-Henry, 1976, 1979; Fromm-Auch, 1982). For example, Goldstein et al. (1977) noted that Halstead-Reitan scores, which are presumed to measure right hemispheric function, were impaired before ECT. Fromm-Auch (1982) has argued that clinical improvement after non-dominant, unilateral ECT indicates that depression is associated with right-hemisphere pathology. However, Wexler (1986) critiqued these findings and presented convincing evidence, including studies of regional blood flow and metabolic activity, that both cerebral hemispheres are involved in the neurobiology of depression. Thus, there are no current grounds for localizing neuroanatomical sites either for depression or for the learning and memory deficits observed with this disorder.

## Mood and Memory: State-Dependent Effects

The concept of state-dependent memory (SDM) was originally used to account for the behavior of alcoholics, who when sober were unable to locate possessions they had hidden while intoxicated but successfully located them when they became intoxicated again (Glass, Holyoak & Santa, 1979). Although early research on SDM and alcoholism was generally inconclusive (e.g., Parker, Birnbaum & Noble, 1976), SDM effects have also been reported for states including hyperactivity (Swanson & Kinsbourne, 1976), depression (Weingartner, Miller & Murphy, 1977; Clark & Teasdale, 1982), and even cigarette smoking (Peters & McGee, 1982). The work of Bower (1981) on network theory has been especially influential in formulating a contemporary model of SDM.

One of the first studies of SDM and depression was that of Lloyd & Lishman (1975), in which depressed patients were asked to recollect personal experiences evoked by stimulus words at two different times in the course of their depression. They reported that the severity of depression was positively related to the speed with which memories of unpleasant events associated with stimulus words were retrieved. Memories for events matching the patient's emotional tone at the time of recall were more likely to be evoked than were those associated with a different emotional tone.

Weingartner, Sitaram & Gillin (1979) examined eight patients with bipolar disorder who were asked to recall free associations to stimulus words presented during the various phases of their mood cycle. Depressed subjects performed best when retrieval occurred during the same mood state in which the associations were originally produced. In a similar vein, Clark & Teasdale (1982) evaluated patients' recall patterns of previous life events during different phases of depression. Subjects were given cue words to which they responded with associated memories drawn from their life histories, as well as ratings on a happiness dimension. Higher levels of depression were associated with retrieval of the most negative memories, while more positive mood states led to reports of less negative experiences. In addition, ratings of happiness attributed to each experience were affected by patients' mood state at the time of rating. Interpreting these results, Bourne, Dominowski, Loftus & Healy (1986) concluded that depressed mood influences both the selection of retrieved material and the emotional valence attributed to that material once it has become conscious.

The studies by Lloyd & Lishman (1975), Weingartner et al. (1977), and Clark & Teasdale (1982) provide some support for SDM effects in depression. However, a problem with the interpretation of these studies is that it is difficult to verify the accuracy of episodic memories. Because these memories are autobiographical in nature, their evocation is related to the image an individual holds of oneself at a particular time. Neisser (1981, 1985) has concluded that episodic memory retrieval involves an active reconstruction of prior events and experiences according to what a person believes ought to have happened. In a like manner, Kuiper & MacDonald (1983) suggested that the self-schemata of depressed patients affect their assessment of the likelihood that they have acted in a particular way in the past.

With respect to depression, it may be as reasonable to conclude that depressed patients generate mood-congruent associations to stimulus words in keeping with their overall self-assessment as it is to infer that information retrieval is state-dependent. Mood states may provide contextual cues for emotionally concordant memories (Johnson & Magaro, 1987), but these states may also stimulate the reconstruction of memories that, at the time of initial encoding, may have had far different emotional connotations.

Studies of SDM using semantic information could help in assessing the impact of depression on recall. One such investigation, by Breslow, Kocsis & Belkin (1981), tested recall of thematic information for brief stories from a Wechsler Memory Scale subtest. They found that, compared to a group of non-depressed subjects, depressed individuals recalled fewer memories overall, and were less likely to recall memory items with positive themes. Comparable results were reported in a subsequent study by Fogarty & Hemsley (1983), in which recall of stimulus words and associated memories was assessed. These results suggest caution in ascribing to depressed patients the capacity to accurately recall detailed past memories. The "recollection" of episodic events may be hampered by the same type of processing deficits that appear to impair the recall of semantic information.

There have also been a series of reports in which the influence of induced depressive mood on episodic memory was studied. An investigation by Teasdale, Taylor & Fogarty (1980) is representative of this methodological approach. Findings were consistent with results from studies of clinically depressed individuals: extremely unhappy memories were more commonly retrieved when subjects were in a depressed mood than when they were elated. A subsequent study by Teasdale & Russell (1983) investigated the effect of induced depressed mood on recall of semantic (as opposed to episodic) information, and reported comparable results.

To summarize, results of studies on SDM and depression suggest that mood exerts a major influence on information retrieval, and that depressed individuals tend to preferentially recall memories with sad or depressive emotional connotations (Johnson & Magaro, 1987). From an evolutionary standpoint, the integration of emotional cues with sensory and motor correlates of experiences stored in episodic memory is highly adaptive. Intense affective arousal, such as that which is associated with fear, heightens the significance of cues associated with dangerous situations. The effect of this can be to promote very rapid, even one-trial, learning. For example, escaping from a dangerous animal leads to highly salient encoding of emotional cues as well as semantic or procedural knowledge. Subsequent confrontations with the same dangerous animal result in rapid activation of state-dependent procedural memories mediating escape behavior patterns without the necessity of intervening practice and rehearsal.

The significance of the association between emotional cues and other facets of experience lies in their capacity to serve as filters which restrict or attenuate information available for recall. In depression, the inhibitory effect tends to be maladaptive, preventing the individual from maintaining a balanced perspective by restricting the amount of information available for consideration. On the other hand, in situations where one is physically threatened, rapid access to information needed to deal with the situation is needed, and emotional cues appear to aid in accessing that information.

## DIRECTIONS FOR LEARNING AND MEMORY RESEARCH

Learning and memory is clearly a psychobiological process. Both psychological and biological factors are involved in the complex mechanisms by which memories are encoded, stored, and retrieved. The interrelationship between multiple variables makes learning and memory a challenging area for scientific study. For example, an investigator may be primarily interested in biochemical manipulations, but other variables such as attention, environmental cues, or mood may contribute to the outcome of the experiment. Most studies with depressed patients have been directed toward either neuropsychological or biological parameters rather than the investigation of learning and memory as an integrated psychobiological phenomenon. Interestingly, Kandel & Schwartz (1982) have taken a more comprehensive stance in their work with *Aplysia*. Specific synaptic and intracellular changes have been determined for habituation and sensitization, processes that are somewhat analogous to environmentally induced learning in humans.

There are several areas in which an integration of theoretical viewpoints might advance this field of research. One initiative in this direction was made by Rubinow et al. (1984) and Caine et al. (1984), who examined relationships between neurohumoral function and parameters of learning and memory. The effects of antidepressant medications on cognitive processes have also been investigated, although the focus of most such studies has been rather narrow. The typical methodology has been to employ cognitive test batteries to measure the impact of hormones or drugs on learning and memory deficits. State-dependent effects and processes such as attention, response bias, and environmental cues have rarely been considered. Comprehensive studies that take such variables into account, while investigating biological elements of cognitive functioning, have the potential for improving our understanding of the psychobiology of depression and learning and memory. Newer biological techniques that could be applied to this field of research include: (1) measures of regional central nervous system activity, such as brain electrical mapping or positron emission tomography; (2) new antidepressants or other drugs that have specific neurotransmitter influences; and (3) biochemical markers.

The interaction between pharmacotherapy and psychotherapy is another area in which learning and memory functioning is of theoretical interest. It has been proposed that pharmacotherapy might facilitate psychotherapy by improving the patient's ability to concentrate, learn, and remember (Group for Advancement of Psychiatry, 1975). Trials of combined pharmacotherapy and psychotherapy of depressed patients have not tested this hypothesis in a systematic manner. Studies of learning and memory as a facet of the interface between pharmacotherapy and psychotherapy could enhance efforts to combine these treatments efficiently in clinical practice.

Learning and memory research could also be used to develop a much more detailed picture of how depressed patients characteristically manage information. To date, the levels of processing hypothesis has yielded the most useful information, but additional work is needed to fully understand the manner in which information is encoded and accessed in depression. Applications of information processing and developmental models of learning and memory might be considered for broadening the investigative effort on cognitive dysfunction. State-dependent effects on schemata for interpreting and managing information could be studied with computer modeling. Another possibility would be to devise computer-assisted learning technologies which could be used to uncover and potentially influence maladaptive information processing styles.

## TREATMENT IMPLICATIONS

Based on the preceding analysis, we hypothesize that disturbances of learning and memory inhibit recovery from depression and that they do so for the following reasons. First, depressed patients do not manage information efficiently, and thus have difficulty performing occupational, social, and familial roles. Second, learning of new information (e.g., educational material, problem-solving strategies, insight from psychotherapy) that could contribute to recovery is impaired. Third, state-dependent effects are self-perpetuating. Depressed mood causes biases toward negatively distorted recall, which in turn maintains mood at a depressed level. Finally, cognitive deficits reinforce the depressed person's low self-esteem, hopelessness, and helplessness. These observations emphasize the importance of recognizing the impact of learning and memory deficits in depression, and making them a target for systematic therapeutic intervention.

The cause of cognitive dysfunction in depression is still unknown. Possibilities include factors such as interference with neurobiological mechanisms, response bias, reduced cognitive capacity, or excessive reliance on self-referent experiences in making decisions (Kuiper & MacDonald, 1983). Delineation of the relative contribution of these elements awaits further research. Yet, enough is known about the nature of learning and memory deficits in depression to suggest methods for improving cognitive functioning.

The major finding that has direct implications for treatment is that depressed patients have particular difficulty with "deep-level" information processing. Complex or abstract psychotherapy material may overload the patient, be poorly understood and remembered, or even contribute to a sense of hopelessness and helplessness. Therapies that emphasize structure, clarity of communication, and learning enhancement would appear to offer advantages in the treatment of depression. This viewpoint is compatible with increasing evidence that short-term, focused interventions including cognitive and psychopharmacologic approaches to therapy are highly effective (Morris & Beck, 1974; Baldessarini, 1977; Wright & Beck, 1983; Hollon & Najavitis, 1988). Both are direct, straightforward, and emphasize education about treatment.

Attempts at improving learning and memory deficits can also be made. Many depressed patients have the capacity for performing at higher levels if they are given assistance in doing so (Ellis et al. 1984; Wright, 1986). Techniques that might be considered include providing written instructions, and asking patients to write notes during treatment sessions. Writing can reinforce memory at the time of encoding and also serve as a reminder of concepts learned during therapy. Diagrams or pictorial representations may have a higher likelihood of being remembered than verbal material because they are more elaborately encoded (Craik, 1979). The therapist can also make an effort to provide coherent strategies for organizing information, give repeated feedback during sessions, and stop frequently to check for understanding (Wright, 1985, 1988). In addition, awareness of state-dependent effects on memory can guide the therapist to use procedures which enhance more accurate memory retrieval. Educating the patient about this phenomenon can help counteract negatively biased recall.

## SUMMARY

Depression has generally been considered to be a mood disorder. Yet, there is substantial evidence that this syndrome is also a cognitive disorder. Distortions in thought content and significant changes in learning and memory functioning have been consistently observed. Studies reviewed in this chapter have revealed that depressed patients are likely to have short-term memory deficits, slowed responses to psychomotor and memory tasks, and state-dependent distortions in recall of information.

Memory encoding that requires deep-level processing or considerable effort is particularly difficult for depressed patients. However, relatively easy procedures are usually done well. The effect of depression on long-term memory—and processes such as attention, rehearsal, and retrieval—has not been well-delineated. The possibility of response bias has been investigated with signal-detection analysis, but results are still inconclusive. Studies to date suggest that there are deficits in multiple stages and components of memory.

Investigations of the influence of antidepressant medication on cognitive functioning have found that learning and memory skills improve following treatment. However, some biological therapies, such as drugs with strong anticholinergic potency and bilateral electroconvulsive therapy, appear to have deleterious effects on cognition. Treatment with noradrenergic drugs has been associated with improved learning and memory.

It is concluded that learning and memory impairment is a central feature of depression, and that this form of cognitive dysfunction contributes to the evolution and maintenance of the depressed state. Learning and memory processes thus offer opportunities for therapeutic change. Further developments in theory and practice can be expected from investigations of the psychobiological processes involved in learning and memory in depression.

## REFERENCES

Alpern, H. P. & Jackson, S. J. (1978). Stimulants and depressants: Drug effects on memory. In M. A. Lipton, A. DiMascio & K. F. Killam (Eds.), *Psychopharmacology: A generation of progress* (pp. 663–675). New York: Raven Press.

American Psychiatric Association. (1987). *Diagnostic and Statistical Manual of Mental Disorders* (3rd ed., revised). Washington, DC: American Psychiatric Association.

Atkinson, R. C. & Shiffrin, R. M. (1968). Human memory: A proposed system and its control processes. In K. W. Spence & J. T. Spence (Eds.), *The psychology of learning and motivation* (Vol. 2, pp. 90–195). New York: Academic Press.

Ault, R. L. & Vinsel, A. (1980). Piaget's theory of cognitive development. In R. L. Ault (Ed.), *Developmental perspectives* (pp. 1–47). Santa Monica: Goodyear Publishing Co.

Baddeley, A. D. (1984). Memory theory and memory therapy. In B.A. Wilson & N. Moffat (Eds.), *Clinical management of memory problems* (pp. 5–27). Rockville,

MD: Aspen Systems Corporation.

Baldessarini, R. J. (1977). *Chemotherapy in psychiatry.* Cambridge, MA: Harvard University Press.

Beck, A. T., Rush, A. J., Shaw, B. F. & Emery, B. (1979). *Cognitive therapy of depression.* New York: Guilford Press.

Black, I. B., Adler, J. E., Dreyfus, C. F., Friedman, W. F., LaGamma, E. F. & Roach, A. H. (1987). Biochemistry of information storage in the nervous system. *Science,* 236, 1263–1268.

Bourne, L. E., Dominowski, R. L., Loftus, E. F. & Healy, A. F. (1986). *Cognitive processes* (2nd ed). Englewood Cliffs, NJ: Prentice-Hall.

Bower, G. H. (1981). Mood and memory. *American Psychologist,* 36, 129–148.

Bower, G. H. & Cowen, P. R. (1982). Emotional influences in memory. Data and theory. In S. Fiske & M. Clark (Eds.), *Affect and social cognition* (pp. 291–331). Hillsdale, NJ: Lawrence Erlbaum.

Bowlby, J. (1969). *Attachment and loss* (Vol. 1). New York: Basic Books.

Bowlby, J. (1985). The role of childhood experience in cognitive disturbance. In M. J. Mahoney & A. Freeman (Eds.), *Cognition and psychotherapy* (pp. 181–200). New York: Plenum Press.

Braff, D. L. & Beck, A. T. (1974). Thinking disorder in depression. *Archives of General Psychiatry,* 31, 456–459.

Branconnier, R. J., Devitt, D. R., Cole, J. O. & Spera, K. F. (1982). Amitriptyline selectively disrupts verbal recall from secondary memory of the normal aged. *Neurobiology of Aging,* 3, 55–59.

Brand, N. & Jolles, J. (1987). Information processing in depression and anxiety. *Psychological Medicine,* 17, 145–153.

Breslow, R., Kocsis, J. & Belkin, B. (1980). Memory deficits in depression: Evidence utilizing the Wechsler Memory Scale. *Perceptual and Motor Skills,* 51, 541–542.

Breslow, R., Kocsis, J. & Belkin, B. (1981). Contribution of the depressive perspective to memory function in depression. *American Journal of Psychiatry,* 138, 227–230.

Broadbent, D. E. (1957). A mechanical model for human attention and immediate memory. *Psychological Review,* 64, 205–215.

Broadhurst, P. L. (1957). Emotionality and the Yerkes-Dodson Law. *Journal of Experimental Psychology,* 54, 345–352.

Caine, E. D., Yerevanian, B. I. & Bamford, K. A. (1984). Cognitive function and the dexamethasone suppression test in depression. *American Journal of Psychiatry,* 141, 116–118.

Calev, A. & Erwin, P. G. (1985). Recall and recognition in depressives: Use of matched tasks. *British Journal of Clinical Psychology,* 24, 127–128.

Calev, A., Korin, Y., Shapira, B., Kugelmass, S. & Lerer, B. (1986). Verbal and non-verbal recall by depressed and euthymic affective patients. *Psychological Medicine,* 16, 789–794.

Clark, D. M. & Teasdale, J. D. (1982). Diurnal variation in clinical depression and accessibility of memories of positive and negative experiences. *Journal of Abnormal Psychology,* 91, 87–95.

Cohen, R. M., Weingartner, H., Smallberg, S. A., Pickar, D. & Murphy, D. L. (1982). Effort and cognition in depression. *Archives of General Psychiatry,* 39, 593–597.

Craik, F. I. M. (1979). Human memory. *Annual Review of Psychology,* 30, 63–102.

Craik, F. I. M. & Lockhart, R. (1972). Levels of processing: A framework for memory research. *Journal of Verbal Learning and Verbal Behavior,* 11, 671–684.

Crome, P. & Newman, B. (1978). A comparison of the effect of single doses of mianserin and amitriptyline on psychomotor tests in normal volunteers. *Journal of International Medical Research*, 6, 430–434.

Cutting, J. (1979). Memory in functional psychosis. *Journal of Neurological and Neurosurgical Psychiatry*, 42, 1031–1037.

Davies, P. (1985). A critical review of the role of the cholinergic system in human memory and cognition. *Annals of New York Academy of Sciences*, 444, 212–217.

Davis, H. & Unruh, W. R. (1980). Word memory in non-psychotic depression. *Perceptual Motor Skills*, 51, 699–705.

DiMascio, A., Henninger, G. & Klerman, G. L. (1964). Psychopharmacology of imipramine and desipramine: A comparative study of their effects in normal males. *Psychopharmacologia*, 5, 361–371.

Donnelly, E. F., Dent, J. K. & Murphy, D. L. (1972). Comparison of temporal lobe epileptics and affective disorders on the Halstead-Reitan test battery. *Journal of Clinical Psychology*, 28, 61–62.

Dunbar, G. C. & Lishman, W. A. (1984). Depression, recognition-memory and hedonic tone: A signal detection analysis. *British Journal of Psychiatry*, 144, 376–382.

Dunnn, A. J. (1980). Neurochemistry of learning and memory: An evaluation of recent data. *Annual Review of Psychology*, 31, 343–390.

Ellis, H. C., Thomas, R. L. & Rodriguez, I. A. (1984). Emotional mood states and memory: Elaborative encoding, semantic processing, and cognitive effort. *Journal of Experimental Psychology: Learning, Memory, and Cognition*, 10, 470–482.

Estes, W. K. (1972). An associative basis for coding and organization in memory. In A. W. Melton & E. Martin (Eds.), *Coding processes in human memory* (pp. 161–190). Washington, DC: Winston.

Flavell, J. H. (1976). *Cognitive development*. Englewood Cliffs, NJ: Prentice-Hall.

Flor-Henry, P. (1976). Lateralized temporal-limbic dysfunction and psychopathology. *Annuals of New York Academy of Sciences*, 280, 777–795.

Flor-Henry, P. (1979). On certain aspects of the localization of the cerebral systems regulating and determining emotion. *Biological Psychiatry*, 14, 677–698.

Fogarty, S. J. & Hemsley, D. R. (1983). Depression and the accessibility of memories. *British Journal of Psychiatry*, 142, 232–237.

Frederiksen, S., d'Elia, G. & Holsten, F. (1985). Influence of ACTH 4–10 and unilateral ECT on primary and secondary memory in depressive patients. *European Archives of Psychiatry and Neurological Sciences*, 234, 291–294.

Friedman, A. S. (1964). Minimal effects of severe depression on cognitive functioning. *Journal of Abnormal Sociology and Psychology*, 69, 237–243.

Fromm-Auch, F. (1982). Comparison of unilateral and bilateral ECT: Evidence for selective memory impairment. *British Journal of Psychiatry*, 141, 608–613.

Gass, C. S. & Russell, E. W. (1986). Differential impact of brain damage and depression on memory test performance. *Journal of Consulting and Clinical Psychology*, 54, 261–263.

Glass, A. L., Holyoak, K. J. & Santa, J. L. (1979). *Cognition*. Reading, MA: Addison-Wesley.

Glass, R. M., Uhlenhuth, E. H., Hartel, F. W., Matuzas, W. & Fischman, M. W. (1981). Cognitive dysfunction and imipramine in outpatient depressives. *Archives of General Psychiatry*, 38, 1048–1051.

Goldstein, S. G., Filskov, S. B. & Weaver, L.A. (1977). Neuropsychological effects of electroconvulsive therapy. *Journal of Clinical Psychology*, 33, 798–806.

Group for Advancement of Psychiatry—Committee on Research. (1975). *Pharmacotherapy and psychotherapy: Paradoxes, problems, and progress*. New York: Brunner/Mazel.

Guidano, V. F. & Liotti, G. (1983). *Cognitive processes and emotional disorders*. New York: Guilford Press.

Healy, A. F. & Kubovy, M. (1978). The effects of pay-offs and prior probabilities on indices of performance and cut-off location in recognition-memory. *Memory and Cognition*, 6, 544–553.

Hebb, D. O. (1949). *The organization of behavior*. New York: Wiley.

Henry, G. M., Weingartner, H. & Murphy, D. L. (1973). Influences of affective states and psychoactive drugs on verbal learning and memory. *American Journal of Psychiatry*, 130, 966–971.

Hollon, S. D. & Najavitis, L. (1988). Review of empirical studies on cognitive therapy. In A. J. Francis & R. E. Hales (Eds.), *American Psychiatric Press Review of Psychiatry* (Vol. 7, pp. 643–666). Washington, DC: American Psychiatric Press.

Hunter, B., Zornetzer, S. F., Jarvik, M. E. & McGaugh, J. L. (1977). Modulation of learning and memory. In S. D. Iverson & S. H. Snyder (Eds.), *Principles of behavioral pharmacology: Handbook of pharmacology* (pp. 531–577). New York: Plenum Press.

Ingram, R. E. (1984). Toward an information processing analysis of depression. *Cognitive Therapy and Research*, 8, 443–478.

Johnson, M. H. & Magaro, P. A. (1987). Effects of mood and severity on memory processes in depression and mania. *Psychological Bulletin*, 101, 28–40.

Kahneman, D. (1973). *Attention and effort*. Englewood Cliffs, NJ: Prentice-Hall.

Kandel, E. R. & Schwartz, J. H. (1982). Molecular biology of learning: Modulation of transmitter release. *Science*, 218, 433–443.

Koh, S. D. & Wolpert, E. A. (1983). Memory scanning and retrieval in affective disorders. *Psychiatry Research*, 8, 289–297.

Kopelman, M. D. (1986). Clinical tests of memory. *British Journal of Psychiatry*, 148, 517–525.

Kronfol, Z., Hamsher, K. des., Digre, K. & Waziri, R. (1978). Depression and hemispheric functions: Changes associated with unilateral ECT. *British Journal of Psychiatry*, 132, 560–567.

Kuiper, N. A. & MacDonald, M. R. (1983). Schematic processing in depression: The self-based consensus bias. *Cognitive Therapy and Research*, 7, 469–484.

Lamping, D. L., Spring, B. & Gelenberg, A. J. (1984). Effects of two antidepressants on memory performance in depressed outpatients: A double-blind study. *Psychopharmacology*, 84, 254–261.

Liljequist, R., Linnoila, M., & Mattila, M. J. (1974). Effect of two weeks' treatment with chlorimipramine and nortriptyline, alone or in combination with alcohol, on learning and memory. *Psychopharmacologia*, 39, 181–186.

Lloyd, G. G. & Lishman, W. A. (1975). Effect of depression on the speed of recall of pleasant and unpleasant experiences. *Psychological Medicine*, 5, 173–180.

Luria, A. R. (1973). *The working brain*. New York: Basic Books.

Malloy, F. W., Small, I. F., Miller, M. J., Milstein, V. & Stout, J. R. (1982). Changes in neuropsychological test performance after electroconvulsive therapy. *Biological Psychiatry*, 17, 61–67.

McNair, D. M., Kahn, R. J., Frankenthaler, L. M. & Faldetta, L. L. (1984). Amoxapine and amitriptyline: Specificity of cognitive effects during brief treatment of depression. *Psychopharmacology*, 83, 134–139.

Miller, E. & Lewis, P. (1977). Recognition memory in elderly patients with depression and dementia. *Journal of Abnormal Psychology*, 36, 84–86.

Morris, J. B. & Beck, A. T. (1974). The efficacy of antidepressant drugs: A review of research (1958–1972). *Archives of General Psychiatry*, 30, 667–674.

Neisser, U. (1967). *Cognitive psychology*. Englewood Cliffs, NJ: Prentice-Hall.

Neisser, U. (1981). John Dean's memory: A case study. *Cognition, 9*, 1–22.

Neisser, U. (1985). Toward an ecologically oriented cognitive science. In T. M. Shlechter & M. P. Toglia (Eds.), *New directions in cognitive science* (pp. 17–32). Norwood, NJ: Ablex Publishing Corp.

Nissen, M. J., Knopman, D. S. & Schacter, D. L. (1987). Neurochemical dissociation of memory systems. *Neurology, 37*, 789–794.

Parker, E. S., Birnbaum, I. M. & Noble, E. P. (1976). Alcohol and memory: Storage and state dependency. *Journal of Verbal Learning and Verbal Behavior, 15*, 691–702.

Peters, R. & McGee, R. (1982). Cigarette smoking and state-dependent memory. *Psychopharmacology, 76*, 232–235.

Piaget, J. (1976). *The grasp of consciousness*. Cambridge, MA: Harvard University Press.

Pribram, K. H. (1980). Mind, brain, and consciousness: The organization of competence and conduct. In J. M. Davidson & R. J. Davidson (Eds.), *The psychobiology of consciousness* (pp. 47–63). New York: Plenum Press.

Raskin, A., Friedman, A. S., DiMascio, A. (1982). Cognitive and performance deficits in depression. *Psychopharmacologic Bulletin, 4*, 196–202.

Roy-Byrne, P. P., Weingartner, H., Bierer, L. M., Thompson, K. & Post, R. M. (1986). Effortful and automatic cognitive processes in depression. *Archives of General Psychiatry, 43*, 265–267.

Rubinow, D. R., Post, R. M., Savard, R. & Gold, P. W. (1984). Cortisol hypersecretion and cognitive impairment in depression. *Archives of General Psychiatry, 41*, 279–283.

Rush, A. J., Weissenburger, J., Vinson, D. B. & Giles, D. E. (1983). Neuropsychological dysfunctions in unipolar nonpsychotic major depressions. *Journal of Affective Disorders, 5*, 281–287.

Schuster, P., Opgenoorth, E., Gabriel, E., Presslich, O. & Sowinetz, B. (1986). Results of learning experiments in the course of treatment of endogenomorphic depression. *Psychopathology, 19*, 116–130.

Seppläla, T. (1977). Psychomotor skills during acute and two-week treatment with mianserin (ORG GB 94) and amitriptyline, and their combined effects with alcohol. *Annals of Clinical Research, 9*, 66–72.

Shannon, C. E. & Weaver, W. (1949). *The mathematical theory of communication*. Urbana, IL: University of Illinois Press.

Shaw, G. L., Silverman, D. J. & Pearson, J. C. (1985). Model of cortical organization embodying a basis for a theory of information processing and memory recall. *Proceedings of the National Academy of Sciences, 82*, 2364–2368.

Squire, L. R. (1986a). Mechanisms of memory. *Science, 232*, 1612–1619.

Squire, L. R. (1986b). Memory functions as affected by electroconvulsive therapy. *Annals of New York Academy of Sciences, 462*, 307–314.

Stein, L., Belluzzi, J. D. & Wise, C. D. (1975). Memory enhancement by central administration of norepinephrine. *Brain Research, 84*, 329–335.

Sternberg, D. E. & Jarvik, M. E. (1976). Memory functions in depression: Improvement with antidepressant medication. *Archives of General Psychiatry, 33*, 219–224.

Strömgren, L. S. (1973). Unilateral versus bilateral electroconvulsive therapy. *Acta Psychiatrica Scandinavica (Suppl.), 240*, 8–26.

Swanson, J. & Kinsbourne, M. (1976). Stimulant-related state-dependent learning in hyperactive children. *Science, 192*, 1354–1357.

Swets, J. A., Tanner, W. C. & Birdsall, T. G. (1961). Decision processes in perception. *Psychological Review, 68*, 301–340.

Teasdale, J. D. & Russell, M. L. (1983). Differential effects of induced mood on the recall of positive, negative, and neutral words. *British Journal of Clinical Psychology*, 22, 163–171.

Teasdale, J. D., Taylor, R. & Fogarty, S. J. (1980). Effects of induced elation-depression on the assessibility of memories of happy and unhappy experiences. *Behavior Research and Therapy*, 18, 339–346.

Thompson, P. J. & Trimble, M. R. (1982). Non-MAOI antidepressant drugs and cognitive functions: A review. *Psychological Medicine*, 12, 539–548.

Thompson, R. F. (1986). The neurobiology of learning and memory. *Science*, 233, 941–947.

Triesman, A. M. (1969). Strategies and models of selective attention. *Psychological Review*, 76, 282–299.

Tulving, E. (1983). *Elements of episodic memory*. New York: Oxford University Press.

Warren, E. W. & Groome, D. H. (1984). Memory test performance under three different waveforms of ECT for depression. *British Journal of Psychiatry*, 144, 370–375.

Watts, F. N., Morris, L. & MacLeod, A. K. (1987). Recognition memory in depression. *Journal of Abnormal Psychology*, 96, 273–275.

Watts, F. N. & Sharrock, R. (1987). Cued recall in depression. *British Journal of Clinical Psychology*, 26, 149–150.

Weiner, R. D., Rogers, H. J., Davidson, J. R. T. & Squire, L. R. (1986). Effects of stimulus parameters on cognitive side effects. *Annals of New York Academy of Sciences*, 462, 315–325.

Weingartner, H., Cohen, R. M., Murphy, D. L., Martello, J. & Gerdt, C. (1981). Cognitive processes in depression. *Archives of General Psychiatry*, 38, 42–47.

Weingartner, H., Miller, H. & Murphy, D. L. (1977). Mood-state-dependent retrieval of verbal associations. *Journal of Abnormal Psychology*, 86, 276–284.

Weingartner, H., Sitaram, N. & Gillin, J. C. (1979). The role of the cholinergic nervous system in memory consolidation. *Bulletin of the Psychonomic Society*, 13, 9–11.

Wexler, B. E. (1986). A model of brain function: Its implications for psychiatric research. *British Journal of Psychiatry*, 148, 357–362.

Wittenborn, J. R., Flaherty, C. F., McGough, W. E., Bossange, K.A. & Nash, R. J. (1976). A comparison of the effect of imipramine, nomifensine and placebo on the psychomotor performance of normal males. *Psychopharmacology*, 51, 85–90.

Wolfe, J., Granholm, E., Butters, N., Saunders, E. & Janowsky, D. (1987). Verbal memory deficits associated with major affective disorders: A comparison of unipolar and bipolar patients. *Journal of Affective Disorders*, 13, 83–92.

Woody, C. D. (1986). Understanding the cellular basis of memory and learning. *Annual Review of Psychology*, 37, 433–493.

Wright, J. H. (1985). The cognitive paradigm for treatment of depression. In P. Pichot, P. Berner, R. Wolf, K. Thau (Eds.), *Psychiatry* (Vol. 4, pp. 31–36). New York: Plenum Publishing Corporation.

Wright, J. H. (1986). Nortriptyline effects on cognition in depression. *Dissertation Abstracts International*, 47(Section B), 2667.

Wright, J. H. (1988). Cognitive therapy of depression. In A. J. Francis & R. E. Hales (Eds.), *American Psychiatric Press Review of Psychiatry* (Vol. 7, pp. 554–570). Washington, DC: American Psychiatric Press.

Wright, J. H. & Beck, A. T. (1983). Cognitive therapy of depression: Theory and practice. *Hospital and Community Psychiatry*, 34, 1119–1127.

Yerkes, R. M. & Dodson, J. D. (1908). The relation of strength of stimulus to rapidity of habit-formation. *Journal of Comparative Neurology and Psychology*, 18, 459–482.

# Treatment-Resistant Depression and Rapid Cycling Affective Disorder

Emmanuel Persad
*London Psychiatric Hospital*

KEY WORDS: depression, treatment-resistant, chronicity, pharmacotherapy, rapid cycling, antidepressant, mood stabilisers

Depression is said to be an eminently treatable disorder. Response rates to treatment have been given as 65–70%, or as high as 80%, depending on the adequacy of the treatment schedule. However, approximately 10–15% of depressed patients do not appear to respond to conventional treatment. This chapter is an examination of this phenomenon, and it reviews current pharmacologic approaches in dealing with this so-called treatment-resistant group. The treatment of rapid cycling mood disorders will be briefly addressed as well.

Unipolar depression has been referred to as the most widespread, most extensively studied, and best understood of the major psychiatric disorders (Keller 1988). Yet, some studies indicate that less than one-third of those with major depression receive any kind of treatment (Kupfer & Freedman 1986). As well, it is not an uncommon experience to find that those depressed patients who are in treatment receive less than comprehensive care. Keller, Klerman, Lavori, Fawcet, Coryell and Endicott (1982) found that of 217 depressed patients referred for non-response to treatment, 67% had received psychotherapy alone, 55% anti-anxiety medication, and 34% had been treated with antidepressant medication. Schatzberg, Cole, Cohen, Altesman and Sniffin (1983) have reported that in their study of non-response in 110 depressed patients, 69% had received at least one antidepressant, but only 39% of 170 antidepressant trials had met their criteria of adequacy of treatment (2/3rd of the manufacturer's recommended dose of the antidepressant for three weeks). The result of treatment of the 24 patients who were considered truly treatment-resistant (two trials of antidepressants) was reported as 50% "markedly" improved, and a third remained nonresponsive. The extent of the problem of true non-response is not known with accuracy but some (Ananth & Raskin 1974) have suggested that 10–20% of depressives are treatment resistant. Remick (1988) feels that absolute treatment-resistant depression (TRD) is a rare entity. In his study of 114 patients referred to his clinic as TRD, only eight exhibited absolute TRD. These eight patients were characterized as older and having other concurrent diagnoses (personality disorder and alcoholism). Schatzberg and colleagues (1983) emphasized the increasing awareness that non-responsiveness may not be limited to atypical, non-endogenous or characterologic depressions, but may include patients with endogenous depression as well. The factors in dealing with the problem of treatment non-response can be considered under two headings: patients' variables and therapists' variables.

## PATIENT VARIABLES

Certain sociodemographic, clinical, and biochemical features of a depressed patient may, at the outset, predict an unfavourable response to treatment. The demographic factors which predict poor response to pharmacotherapy include the elderly, lower social classes, and marital discord. Himmelhoch, Auchenbach and Fuchs (1982) suggest that the elderly do less well on drugs because of a combination of a decline in physical health and severe social stressors (loss and loneliness). Marital disharmony and lower social class status appear to predict chronicity in depression (Akiskal 1983), as well as resistance to treatment, but in both instances the explanation may have to do more with the persistence of severe stress as well as non-compliance. It is generally accepted that treatment response to any modality will be significantly augmented by a supportive social network that promotes the integrity of the patient.

The following factors affect treatment outcome:

1. Chronicity

2. Clinical features: High levels of anxiety and atypical neurovegetative symptoms

3. Characterological features

4. Concurrent medical illnesses

5. Biological features

### Chronicity

An important feature of major depression is a clinical course of remission and recurrences. Lehman (1983) has suggested that a depressive episode lasts for 5–9 months and then goes into remission. The non-responders tend to follow an unremitting course of several years. Schatzberg and colleagues (1983) found, in their sample, that 54% had been depressed for more than one year and 16% had been continuously depressed for more than 10 years. Others (Keller & Lavori, 1984) have described a subtype of depression called double depression. This is characterized by a chronic course of dysphoria (dysthymic disorder) complicated by episodes of worsening (major depression). This group tend to benefit from pharmacotherapy for the acute episodes. In a discussion of chronic depression, Keller and Lavori (1984) have described five forms of depressive subtypes, all characterized by a chronic course. These are: major depression with residual chronicity; chronicity following multiple episodes of major depression; "double depression," acute episodes of depression superimposed on a dysthymic disorder; subaffective dysthymia, in which characterological problems may predominate; and, chronic secondary dysphoria.

## The Clinical Features

The clinical features which predict responsiveness have been extensively studied, but no consistent pattern has emerged. The current thinking is that the symptom profile may be of help in selecting a particular treatment approach. For example, psychomotor agitation accompanied by subjective anxiety and panic may resist most approaches, and may require a combination of two or more modalities. Monoamine oxidase inhibitors (MAOIs) and sedating tricyclics (TCAs) (amitriptyline) may be effective, but some TCAs (imipramine group) may cause worsening of symptoms. On the other hand, psychomotor retardation may be more responsive to imipramine and its related agents. Some patients experience reverse neurovegetative symptoms (e.g., hypersomnia and hyperphagia) with weight gain. These do less well on TCAs.

Severity of depression may also bear upon response. The mildly depressed may also be the group that experiences a chronic course and for whom psychosocial treatments are indicated. The moderately severe group is said to be best suited for antidepressant pharmacotherapy, whereas the very severe group may benefit preferentially from ECT (Abou-Selah & Coppen 1983).

## Characterological Features

Depressed patients with certain personality traits tend to do poorly with conventional treatment modalities, and they have been classified in various ways, such as atypical depression (West & Dally 1959), hysteroid dysphorias, and secondary depression. These terms create confusion as they tend to be used merely for those depressed patients without the typical features of melancholia.

It is now generally believed that there is a subtype of depression in which the core of the disorder is characterized by the presence of a mood reactivity to environmental stimuli, reversed neurovegetative symptoms, and hypersensitivity to rejection (Leibowitz, Quitkin, Stewart, McGrath, Harrison, Tricamo, Markowitz & Klein 1984). Akiskal (1983) has also described a group of chronic depressed patients whom he has called subaffective dysthymia, and these may benefit from MAOI.

Patients with psychotic symptoms, especially those with mood incongruent delusions, do not respond to the usual treatment approach. Spiker, Perel and Hanin (1986) recommend that such patients are better treated with a combination of a neuroleptic and an antidepressant.

One of the major difficulties in the treatment of depressed patients with drugs is the problem of compliance. The chief reason for non-compliance is the emergence of troubling side effects; lack of information about the drugs and patient's natural inclination to rely on time may also contribute to low levels of compliance.

## Concurrent Medical Problems

There are a number of medical problems which are known to mimic the symptoms of depression. These are well described by Cassem (1988). In that review Cassem also notes that certain medical illnesses can be associated with depressive symptoms. For example, carcinoma of the pancreas may present with depression.

Similarly cerebrovascular accidents (strokes) may induce episodes of depression. Perhaps the best documented relationship between depression and a physical disorder occurs with Cushing's Disease. The pathophysiology between an organic-based disorder and an affective disorder provides an intriguing area of study. It is important in the assessment of a patient with depression to rule out the possibility of an organic disorder in order to provide meaningful treatment.

## Biochemical Features

Leonard (1988) has suggested that there are biochemical differences in non-responders as compared with responders. For example, the delusional depressive patient tends to have greater activity of the hypothalamic-pituitary-adrenal axis. In these patients, enhancement of the serotonergic system may prove therapeutically beneficial.

## THERAPIST VARIABLES

Physicians tend to prescribe medication largely on the basis of their familiarity with particular drugs. As noted in the foregoing, non-response may be attributed to features in the patient, but several studies indicate that a significant reason for non-response may be due to the prescribing habits of the clinician. Current diagnostic systems may be deficient in helping with a specific treatment schedule.

For example, patients who are depressed may present with predominant symptoms of panic, obsessions, phobias, and/or somatic symptoms. Such patients may receive treatment dealing with the most obvious signs and symptoms, for example, benzodiazepines for anxiety and panic. The assessment of a patient with a mood disorder should include a longitudinal history as well as corroborative information.

The question of adequacy of treatment is not a simple one. Some studies (Bridges 1983, Keller et al., 1982) suggest that undertreatment is a significant reason for non-response. Quitkin, Rifkin and Klein (1985) suggest that patients should receive at least 300 mg of imipramine or equivalent, or 90 mg phenelzine or equivalent before being considered refractory. It is also felt that the duration of these trials should exceed 4–6 weeks. It should be noted that for most drugs the relationship between dosage, plasma level, and response tends to be linear. A curvilinear relationship is said to exist for nortriptyline, that is, a plasma level in excess of the therapeutic window may contribute to worsening of symptoms.

Kupfer and Freedman (1986) do not feel there is any justification for inadequate treatments, though others state the obvious in that the main reason for low dosages is the emergence of intolerable side effects.

Keller, Lavori, Klerman, Andersen, Endicott, Coryell, Fawcett, Rice and Hirschfeld (1986) found that after eight weeks of treatment, 67% of 338 depressed patients had not yet recovered, and 38% still had marked symptoms. This study was done using academic centres where it was expected that there would be strict adherence to treatment standards. The author concluded that inadequate treatment was the chief reason for this poor outcome. In their commentary on the Keller study, Kupfer and Freedman (1986) state that the prevailing "ethos" of the treatment centre is important in understanding outcome studies. They propose that, in addition to high quality methodology, it is also important to find methods to capture the "real transactions" between the patient and the therapist during an experimental treatment protocol. A "gold standard" for drug treatment of depression does not yet exist.

## MANAGEMENT OF THE INTRACTABLE PATIENT

It appears that the depressed patients who are most likely to be "intractable" are those who are inadequately treated (Keller et al., 1986, Schatzberg et al., 1983). However, there is a group of depressed patients who are truly treatment resistant. As noted earlier, they may be identified at the outset on the basis of demographic, clinical, and biochemical features. This group usually require non-conventional approaches in the management of their disorders.

Patients who fulfill the criteria for a major depression, uncomplicated by medical problems, should benefit from antidepressants, and indeed 60–70% do after one trial. A further 10–15% respond following a course of ECT or an alternative antidepressant (Leonard 1988). The management of the non-responders should follow a carefully planned treatment protocol that should begin with a period (5–10 days) of drug-free observation. This may have to be carried out in hospital, especially if the patient is suicidal or is severely dysfunctional.

During the assessment a detailed treatment history should be obtained to decide whether one is dealing with a case of absolute intractability or one of relative non-response. Both Ayd (1983) and Shaw (1977) have provided criteria for separating the two groups. A true intractable depression is considered to be a disorder which has not responded to what is felt to be adequate treatment. The latter is usually defined in terms of somatotherapy e.g., non-response after adequate trials of TCAs, MAOIs, and ECT (Shaw 1977). Such a definition is usually too narrow and does not allow for consideration of psychosocial interventions.

Assuming that the patient is considered truly intractable, the following pharmacotherapeutic strategies may be considered. It must be emphasized that adequate attention should also be paid to the relative merit of other interventions, such as cognitive therapy, marital therapy, and other psychosocial therapies, concurrent with pharmacotherapy.

## Trial #1

Montigny, Greenberg, Mayer and Deschenes (1981) have proposed the addition of lithium to potentiate the TCA response. A similar lithium potentiation to MAOIs may be tried, but the latter combination may lead to severe side effects, including a serotonergic syndrome with confusion and shock. A trial with lithium should not be continued after three weeks. Even though Montigny et al. (1981) have elicited a response within 48 hours, others (Heninger, Charney & Steinberg 1983) have felt that the combination may require at least one to two weeks for maximum benefit. This regime may provide the added benefit of preventing a hypomanic or manic swing in susceptible patients.

## Trial #2

Combination of TCA and MAOIs is avoided in current practice because of the concern of severe side effects. Sethna (1984) has reviewed this approach and concluded that it is a relatively safe procedure so long as there is strict adherence to certain safeguards, dietary controls, starting with low dosages, increasing dosages slowly, avoidance of other drugs such as central nervous system stimulants, and frequent monitoring of vital signs. The usual practice is to start the patient on the TCA (usually amitriptyline or imipramine) and gradually build the dose up to 75–100 mg in 5 days; then the MAOI (usually phenelzine) is added and also built up gradually. Thereafter there may be weekly dosage changes. The TCA should always be started first. If the patient had been on an MAOI, there should be a 14-day interval after going off the MAOI before commencing the TCA. Feighner, Herbstein and Damlouji (1985) have reported on a study of 16 treatment-resistant patients in which they utilized a regime of TCA, an MAOI, and a psychostimulant drug. Eight patients were given the three simultaneously. In their sample of 5 males and 11 females, the mean duration of depression was 7 years. Most patients were reported to have benefitted, and there were no significant side effects. They recommended that the increments of the stimulants must be very low (2.5 mg methylphenidate).

## Trial #3: The Use of Thyroid Hormone

Prange, Wilson and Wabon (1969) reported on the use of l-Triiodothyronine (25 microgram) as a potentiating agent to TCAs. They found that this combination appears to work best in psychomotor-retarded female patients who did not benefit from conventional treatment. The relationship between thyroid function and affective disorder is an area of current investigative interest. Some (Gold & Potash 1983) suggest that a subclinical auto-immune thyroiditis may exist in some patients who are clinically depressed. Nemeroff, Simon, Haggerty and Evans (1985) have demonstrated that 20% of depressed patients have thyroid antibodies.

## Trial #4: The Use of Precursors

On the basis of the amine hypothesis of depression, it has been suggested that substances such as tryptophan may have a role to play in the treatment of depression. There is no convincing evidence of this though tryptophan may be considered as an adjunctive drug to another combination, e.g., lithium plus a TCA. It is not recommended that it be added to any combination with an MAOI. Tryptophan has been licensed in Canada as an adjunctive medication to lithium for intractable mania. The recommended dose is 8–14 grms (Chouinard, Jones, Young & Annable 1979).

## Trial #5: The Newer Antidepressants

The newer antidepressants have not had an easy time. Nomifensine, and Zimelidine have been withdrawn. Others such as Bupropion (seizures), Trazodone (priapism), and Amoxapine (tardive dyskinesia) are being carefully scrutinized.

L-Deprenyl and Fluoxetine are too new to judge. Cole (1988) makes a plea for the continued availability of these newer drugs in spite of their apparent problems. It is his view that drug companies and the governmental regulatory bodies are over-reacting and thereby depriving the difficult-to-treat group of depressed patients of possible relief. "It is the individual patient who counts" (Cole 1988).

Measures such as psychosurgery do merit serious consideration in patients who are truly intractable and who have not benefitted from anything else.

## RAPID CYCLING AFFECTIVE DISORDERS (RCAD)

Within the spectrum of Mood or Affective Disorders there is a clinical group referred to as Rapid Cyclers. The group is characterized as having frequent shifts in moods and a significant failure to benefit from therapy with lithium (Dunner & Fieve, 1974). It is also common clinical experience that, in addition to the failure to benefit prophylactically from lithium or from any mood stabilizer, the condition is also difficult to manage in the acute phase.

The condition receives only a brief mention in current systems of classification, and it is a relatively rare occurrence. RCAD is more frequent in bipolars than in unipolars; female bipolars cycle more frequently in the postpartum or menopausal period. RCAD may exhibit early onset, with the illness displaying cycling from the start, or late onset, with cycling occurring only after a period (years) of conventional recurrences. Both early and late onset may require an age threshold, suggesting life-cycle change initiation. RCAD may be spontaneous, without identifiable external precipitants, or may be induced by pharmacological agents. Cycle periodicity may range from ultrarapid (less than 48 hours) to classical (days to weeks) durations.

If bipolar illness is difficult to treat, RCAD patients present an even greater challenge. As a first approach, Roy-Byrne, Joffe, Uhde and Post (1984) recommended: (1) charting the relationship between drug use and cycle frequency; (2) assessment of thyroid status; (3) neurological evaluation to rule out multiple sclerosis, seizure disorder, or gross brain pathology; (4) assessment of the reproductive endocrine system to establish how mood cycles are affected by use of oral contraceptives or other gonadal steroids and by menstruation or the postpartum period.

### Management of RCAD

Since the etiology of RCAD remains in doubt, effective preventive measures are not readily available.

The following procedure is recommended in the management of this condition (Behesnilian 1988). The first step is to discontinue any medications that might contribute to rapid cycling. These may include antidepressants, steroids, and even Lithium.

The second step is the gradual introduction of medications which have been found helpful. These include the following options:

(a) Carbamazepine alone or in combination with lithium.

(b) A neuroleptic by itself or in combination with Carbamazepine or lithium.

(c) Hypermetabolic doses of Thyroxine (Stancer & Persad, 1982). This regimen was found useful in an open study of ten RCAD patients. Seven patients who were female and had had a postpartum onset experienced either complete or partial remission.

(d) Sodium Valproate. There is a hypothesis that mania represents a central Gamma amino butyric acid (GABA) dysfunction and that increasing CNS levels of GABA may be effective in the treatment of mania. Valproic acid is known to be a potent inhibitor of amygdala kindling. Recently, there was a report of the use of Valproic Acid (VPA) in the prophylactic treatment of six RCAD patients who had failed to benefit from the traditional mood stabilizers.

McElroy, Keck, Pope and Hudson (1988) postulate that the finding that VPA may be helpful with RCAD may support the relationship between GABA and RCAD. VPA enhances the inhibitory effects of GABA. There is also a direct link between GABA and the desynchronization of circadian rhythm.

(e) Repetitive Sleep Deprivation. Roy-Byrne et al. (1984) have reviewed the literature, which is mainly about open trial case reports, on this mode of intervention. They could not confirm a beneficial effect in their own studies.

(f) Finally, the psychosocial aspects of the case must be addressed. It might be necessary to offer a variety of interventions such as combined pharmacotherapy, environmental manipulation, and conjoint or family therapy.

## A Case Report

This report describes a case of a patient with a rapid-cycling affective disorder (RCAD), from the onset of the illness in 1956 to the present time. The many points of interest in the case include the diagnostic uncertainties which tend to accompany this condition and the impact of various interventions. Since this patient's clinical history has paralleled the major developments in pharmacotherapy, she was exposed to trials of drugs in the very early stages of their availability, e.g., Chlorpromazine in 1956, Lithium in 1970, and the anticonvulsants in 1982. The following is a personal account of the illness (RCAD) of the patient:

I had my first psychotic episode in August 1956. I was 24 years of age. It came without any warning. I had been working at Ayerst, McKenna and Harrison (a Montreal drug company) at the time and had quite a demanding job in the research department working on trying to find new anti-Parkinsonian drugs. The psychotic episode took the shape of weird thoughts and ideas and much agitation and not sleeping at all. My parents were away at the time and I had a girl friend staying with me. I talked incessantly through the night—all of it not making much sense and really frightened my girlfriend (of my age) who, of course, had had no dealings with mental illness before. As ill as I was, I went to work as usual (I didn't realize what was happening to me either) and it was very fortunate that, on staff in the Research Department of Ayerst McKenna and Harrison, there was a man who had psychology training and he recognized what was wrong with me and alerted my boss who got in touch with my family doctor who arranged for a psychiatrist to see me at the Montreal General and also arranged to have me admitted to a private room (although it was not on the psychiatric wing). The psychiatrist (Dr. M) gave me an injection and for the next 48 hours I slept. When I awoke, I was completely sane again and I remember very clearly thinking "What will my friends think?" To this day I can remember some of my unusual thoughts of that first psychotic episode. All my friends were, indeed, shocked that I should have mental illness, because I had always been such a normal, well-adjusted person. Dr. M gave me a very large dose of Chlorpromazine (very new in those days and not much work had been done on correct dosage)—1000 mg daily. I became paralysed from the drug so he had to discontinue it. I was kept in hospital for three weeks and at my insistence I was discharged. No sooner had I got home than I became psychotic again and my father got in touch with Dr. M and he arranged to have me put in Verdun Protestant Hospital (now the Douglas Hospital). As you can imagine, my family were deeply distressed. At Verdun I was on a locked ward and given again Chlorpromazine (usually called Largactil). I was in Verdun for five weeks and was in good shape when I was discharged. I went back to Dr. M and he advised me to go back to work at Ayerst, so I went. In the meantime, depression had set in and I found it extremely difficult to work. I struggled on for two months until finally Dr. M thought since I was having such a hard time, I should stop working. That was in November 1956. After that, I continued to be very depressed and I had serious thoughts of suicide (the only time I have had thoughts of suicide). I was on a daily dose of Largactil. All through the winter of 1957, I continued to be depressed and in April 1957 (I did not see Dr. M on a regular basis), I decided on my own without telling anyone to stop taking my Largactil. Immediately there was a big improvement in my feelings—the depression went away and I was my normal self again.

Between the years 1957 to 1967, the patient continued to experience frequent swings in mood which were treated symptomatically and usually in hospital. In 1969 a new substance was on the horizon in Canada—Lithium Carbonate.

All this time I was on Tofranil and Stemetil. Then in January of 1969 I had another psychotic attack and had to be hospitalized in the Allan Memorial Institute. This is when Dr. M told me that she could no longer keep me on at work. That was a terrible blow to me. In 1969 I was hospitalized twice again, both times for psychosis, once in the Allan Memorial Institute again, and once in the Herbert Reddy Memorial Hospital. I fell into a very deep depression but because it was felt that Tofranil was causing my psychotic episodes, it was decided that it was too dangerous to give me Tofranil. In May of 1970 I became manic again. My friends, who felt that Dr. P was not helping me, drove me down to Sherbrooke to see Dr. D who hospitalized me in St. Vincent de Paul Hospital in Sherbrooke. For the first three weeks of my hospitalization there, I have no memory. It was then that I went on Lithium. All through 1970 and until March 1971 I would commute to Sherbrooke to see Dr. D. I still continued to be very depressed. In March 1971, I felt it was too much for me to commute to Sherbrooke so Dr. D recommended me to Dr. V of the Montreal General Hospital. I started seeing Dr. V and in November 1971, he recommended I should start to work again. In January 1972 I started a new job, also in research in the Montreal General Hospital. No longer was I in the job (two weeks) than I became manic again and had to be hospitalized in the Montreal General. (My usual stay in hospital was three months.) Between May 1972 and September 1974 I was hospitalized twice more in the Montreal General Hospital, both times for mania. I was now diagnosed as a chronic schizophrenic. In between my fits of mania I would have deep depressions. During one of my hospitalizations at the Montreal General, I received a series of six electroshock treatments. Dr. V tried literally every type of neuroleptic on me that was on the market. I continued to

**FIGURE 10–1:**
**Case of Rapid-Cycling Affective Disorder**
**(CPZ: Chlorpromazine; CBMZ: Carbamazepine)**

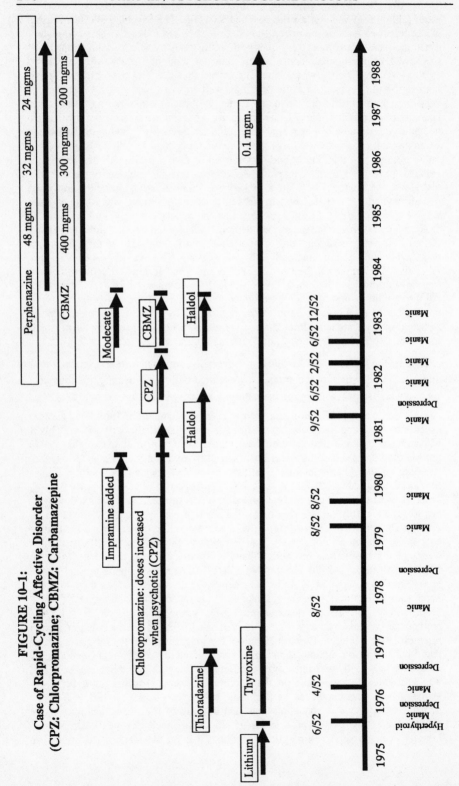

suffer from depression. In September 1974 a good friend phoned me and offered me a job and I was too embarrassed to say I didn't want it because I was depressed, so from September 1974 to September 1975 I worked four days a week from 10:00 a.m. to 4:00 p.m. looking after the library at the C.D. Howe Research Institute. It was a terrible struggle because I was depressed, although I managed to do a good job and no one at work there knew of my depression. In September 1975, I came to Toronto and met with Dr. Persad (who had been recommended to me by Dr. V).

While I was connected with the Montreal General Hospital (at one point I was on their Day Care Programme which was excellent), I had extensive group therapy sessions (for a period of two years). I found them especially helpful and learned in those sessions how to express my innermost feelings, which now, because of those sessions, I have no trouble in expressing. One last remark I would like to make is that I feel one of the reasons I am so well now is that I have gone through menopause. Another friend of mine who lives in Vancouver and who, after the birth of her baby back in the 1950s, suffered as badly as me from manic depression, has now recovered, also since she went through her menopause. She is working and very happy and even travelling with her husband (an unheard of thing when she was younger and afflicted with manic depression).

What I also would like to point out is that I had no problems as a child or teenager. I had a very happy childhood and uneventful adolescence. I was always a very happy individual that had lots of friends. I lived abroad in England from 1953 to '55 with no problem. I have always been a well-rounded, well-adjusted person with many interests. I realize I am very fragile. One reason for my continuing good health is that I try to avoid situations of great stress as much as I can. At work, which I enjoy immensely, I do very simple work—nor do I feel capable of doing anything more than simple work. My brain just does not function well enough (could that be a result of my electroshock treatment?). I am quite content to do simple jobs. My work is very important to me. Actually it is good therapy. At the moment, I am extremely content with my life—I feel I have evolved a lifestyle that suits me extremely well. You can certainly see why I enjoy life so much—to have recovered so well after having been so ill for so many years is like a miracle to me—let me tell you, every day seems like a gift. One last remark of interest is that I can remember many of my manic episodes vividly even to remembering the weird thoughts I had.

This author became involved with the patient's care in 1975. Her hospitalization history since 1975 is summarized in Figure 10–1. Her clinical course was characterized by rapid fluctuations of mood marked by episodes of severe (psychotic) decompensation until 1983.

This patient's affective disorder has gone into an impressive remission over the last five years. It is possible, though not very likely, that this remission could have been spontaneous or a postmenopausal phenomenon as the patient suggests. What is more likely, however, is that the combination of Carbamazepine (CBMZ) a neuroleptic (Perphenazine), and Thyroxine may have succeeded where other prior pharmacotherapeutic attempts failed. The CBMZ was first introduced in April 1982 during a manic episode and had been added to Haldol. The patient developed leucopenia and the CBMZ was discontinued.

In 1983, when it was clear that her moods were fluctuating rapidly, she agreed to another trial of CBMZ. Again leucopenia occurred, but the patient opted to remain on the drug to see whether it could improve attempts to curtail the frequency and severity of the episodes. Since 1983 she has been maintained on a regime of CBMZ 300 mg/day, Thyroxine 0.1 mg/day, and Perphenazine now at 24 mg/day. There have been no fluctuations of mood in the past five years. She is seen monthly for supportive psychotherapy and for blood tests.

This patient benefitted from a combination of Carbamazepine and a neuroleptic.

## SUMMARY

This has been a discussion of treatment-resistant depression (TRD) and rapid cycling affective disorder (RCAD). TRD accounts for up to 20% of depressed patients, but that represents a heterogeneous group characterized by differences in clinical and biochemical features. A distinction must be made between relative and absolute TRD. Management strategies emphasize the value of accurate diagnostic assessment, study of clinical course, and the merits of adequate pharmacotherapy. Depression is not merely a disease but an illness in the true sense of the word. Even though this paper emphasized pharmacotherapy, other interventions, including psychotherapy, family therapy, and social interventions, form a necessary part of any management for all types of depression—the illness.

Rapid Cycling Affective Disorder (RCAD) has been discussed with special reference to a clinical case (Figure 10–1). The latter is graphically described by the patient herself. The many points of interest in this condition, as exemplified by the case, include the diagnostic uncertainties, the erratic course, and the difficulty of management. However, in the case described, the patient experienced a significant remission, which is now into its fifth year, after 30 years of a disabling illness.

### References

Akiskal, H. S. (1983). Dysthymic disorder: Psychopathology of proposed chronic depressive subtypes.*American Journal of Psychiatry* 140, pp. 11–20.

Abou-Selah, M. T. & Coppen, A. (1983). Classification of depression and response to antidepressive therapies. *British Journal of Psychiatry* 143, pp. 601–603.

Ananth, J. & Raskin, R. (1974). Treatment of intractable depression. *International Pharmacopsychiatry* 9, pp. 218–229.

Ayd, F. J. (1983). Treatment-resistant depression: Therapeutic strategies in affective disorders reassessed. In F. J. Ayd, I. J. Taylor & B. J. Taylor (Eds.), *Ayd Medical Communications* (pp. 115–125), Baltimore, MD.

Behesnilian, K. (1988). Rapid-cycling affective disorders. *Clinical Psychopharmacology: Bulletin #11. Clarke Institute of Psychiatry publication, May 1988.*

Bridges, P. K. (1983). Point of view. *British Journal of Psychiatry* 142, pp. 676–687.

Cassem, E. H. (1988). Depression secondary to medical illness. In A. J. Frances & Robert E. Hales (Eds.), *Review of Psychiatry* (Vol. 7., pp. 256–273). Washington, DC: American Psychiatric Press.

Chouinard, G., Jones, B. D., Young, S. N. & Annable, L. (1979). Potentiations of lithium by Tryptophan in a patient with bipolar illness. *American Journal of Psychiatry* 136, pp. 719–720.

Cole, J. O. (1988). Where are those new antidepressants we were promised? *Archives of*

General Psychiatry 45, pp. 193–194.

Dunner, D. L. & Fieve, R. (1974). Clinical factors in Lithium Carbonate prophylaxis failure. Archives of General Psychiatry 30, pp. 229–233.

Feighner, J. P., Herbstein, J. & Damlouji, M.D. (1985). Combined MAOI, TCA and Direct Stimulant Therapy of treatment-resistant depression. Journal of Clinical Psychiatry 46, pp. 206–209.

Gold, M. S. & Pottash, A. L. C. (1983). Thyroid dysfunction or depression? In Affective Disorders Reassessed. In F. J. Ayd, I. J. Taylor & B. T. Taylor (Eds.), Ayd Medical Communication (pp. 179–191). Baltimore, MD.

Heninger, G. R., Charney, D. S. & Steinberg, D. E. (1983). Lithium augmentation of antidepressant treatment. Archives of General Psychiatry 40, pp: 1135–1142.

Himmelhoch, J., Auchenbach, R. & Fuchs, C. Z. (1982). The Dilemma of Depression in the Elderly. Journal Clinical Psychiatry 43, Sec. 2, pp. 25–32.

Keller, M. B. (1988). Unipolar depression. In Allen J. Francis & R. E. Hales (Eds.), Foreword in review of psychiatry (pp. 147–148), Washington: American Psychiatric Press Inc.

Keller, M. B., Klerman, G. L., Lavori, P. W., Fawcett, J. A., Coryell, W. & Endicott, J. (1982). Treatment received by depressed patients. Journal American Medical Association 248, pp. 1845–1855.

Keller, M. B. & Lavori, P. W. (1984). Double depression, major depression and dysthymia: Distinct entities or different phases of a single disorder. Pychopharmacology Bulletin Vol. 20, No. 3, pp. 399–402.

Keller, M. B., Lavori, P. W., Klerman, G. L., Andersen, N. C., Endicott, J., Coryell, W., Fawcett, J., Rice, J. P., Hirschfeld, R. M. A. (1986). Low levels and lack of predictors of somatotherapy and psychotherapy received by depressed patients. Archives General Psychiatry 43, pp. 458–466.

Kupfer, D. J. & Freedman, D. X. (1986). Treatment for Depression. Archives General Psychiatry Vol. 43, pp. 509–511.

Lehman, H. (1983). Clinical evaluation and natural course of depression. Journal Clinical Psychiatry 44: 5, Sec. 2, pp. 5–10.

Leibowitz, M. R., Quitkin, F. M., Stewart, J. W., McGrath, P. J., Harrison, W., Tricamo, E., Markowitz, J. S. & Klein, D. S. (1984). Phenelzine versus Imipramine in atypical depression. Archives of General Psychiatry 41, pp. 669–677.

Leonard, B. E. (1988). Biochemical aspects of therapy-resistant depression. British Journal of Psychiatry 152, pp. 453–459.

McElroy, S. L., Keck, P., Pope, H. G. & Hudson, J. I. (1988). Valproate in the treatment of rapid-cycling bipolar disorder. Journal of Clinical Psychopharmacology 8, pp. 275–279.

Montigny, C., Greenberg, F., Mayer, A. & Deschenes, J. P. (1981). Lithium induces rapid relief of depression in tricyclic drug nonresponders. British Journal of Psychiatry 138, pp. 252256.

Nemeroff, C. B., Sanar, J. S., Haggerty, J. J. & Evans, D. L. (1985). Antithyroid antibodies in depressed patients. American Journal of Psychiatry 142, pp. 840–843.

Pitts, F. N. (1951). Combination Drug therapy in Depression. Editorial. Journal of Clinical Psychiatry 46, p. 205.

Prange, A., Wilson, I. & Wabon, A. (1969). Enhancement of Imipramine activity by thyroid hormone. American Journal of Psychiatry 126, pp. 38–51.

Quitkin, F., Rifkin, A. & Klein, D. (1985). The importance of dosage in prescribing antidepressants. British Journal of Psychiatry 147, pp. 593–597.

Remick, R. D. (1988). Paper presented at the Canadian Consensus Conference on Depression, September 8–10, 1988, Ottawa.

Roy-Byrne, P. P., Joffe, R., Uhde, T. W. & Post, R. (1984). Approaches to evaluation and treatment of rapid-cycling affective disorder. *British Journal of Psychiatry* 145, pp. 543–550.

Schatzberg, A. F., Cole, J., Cohen, B., Altesman, R. I. & Sniffin, C.M. (1983). Survey of depressed patients who have failed to respond to treatment. In D. Davis & J. Maas (Eds.), *The Affective Disorders.* Washington, DC: American Psychiatric Association Press.

Sethna, E. (1974). A study of refractory cases of depressive illness and their response to combined antidepressant treatment. *British Journal of Psychiatry* 124, pp. 265–272.

Shaw, D. M. (1977). The practical management of affective disorders. *British Journal of Psychiatry* 130, pp. 432–451.

Spiker, D. G., Perel, J. M. & Hanin, I. (1986). Pharmacological treatment of delusional depression, part II. *Journal Clinical Psychopharmacology* 6, pp. 339–342.

Stancer, H. & Persad, E. (1982). Treatment of intractable rapid cycling manic-depressive disorder with Levo-thyroxine: Clinical observation. *Archives General Psychiatry* 39, pp. 311–312.

West, E. D. & Dally, P. J. (1959). Effects of Iproniazide in depressive syndromes. *British Medical Journal* 1, pp. 1491–1493.

# PART IV
# BIOLOGICAL FACTORS

Prior to the 1930s, there were few interventionist techniques available to psychiatrists for the treatment of inpatients. Therapists could do little other than provide social support and custodial care. However, during the 1930s, four major biological therapies were developed: insulin coma therapy, metrazol therapy, psychosurgery, and electroconvulsive therapy (ECT). Of these four, only ECT is still used as a standard procedure for treating depression.

Part IV contains six chapters (Chapters 11–16) that focus on biological factors in depression.

Hay and Hay (Chapter 11) discuss the historical origins and indices for ECT for treating depression and other clinical disorders. In addition, they focus on the controversies surrounding ECT and the clinical and research issues regarding the theories and treatments relevant to ECT. The authors discuss the pathophysiology of depression and the physiological effects of ECT. Major advances have been made with respect to treatment procedures and knowledge about biochemical factors involved in the efficacy of ECT. Legal and ethical issues surrounding ECT are also discussed. Of all the treatments available for depression, ECT is efficacious in terms of alleviating symptoms in 85–90 percent of cases. However, because of the controversies, stigma, and the social and political factors surrounding ECT, it is not used as frequently as antidepressant drugs or the various psychological therapies.

Whereas ECT was developed during the 1930s, no new somatic treatments appeared until the 1950s. In fact, the third revolution in the treatment of depression and other clinical disorders (the other two being the unshackling of inmates by Pinel and Pussin in France and Freudian psychoanalysis, commencing in the early 1900s) was the development and use of antidepressant drugs (tricyclic and monoamine oxidase inhibitors) in the 1950s. In fact, the discovery that tricyclic antidepressants (TCA) and monoamine oxidase (MAO) inhibitors were effective in treating depression was to some extent serendipitous.

McAllister and Price, in their first chapter in this part (Chapter 12), note that the use of psychopharmacological techniques for treating depression is a broad and complex topic. The authors review the basic principles of psychopharmacotherapy and the standard classes of antidepressant drugs: TCA, MAO inhibitors, and the "second generation" antidepressants (which came to fruition during the 1980s). McAllister and Price also discuss research aimed at treating resistant or refractory depressive syndromes. They note that the evidence is quite conclusive that the antidepressant drugs alleviate depressive symptoms to clinically and statistically greater degrees than placebos, especially for the endogenomorphic symptoms cluster. McAllister and Price point out that the antidepressant drugs induce alterations in predictable monoamine systems in the central nervous system (CNS). They also discuss the theoretical and clinical implications regarding the various antidepressant drugs.

In 1949 John F. Cade of Australia discovered that lithium was a useful therapeutic agent for treating mania (also a somewhat serendipitous discovery), and in 1954 Mogens Schou of Denmark conducted the first double blind treat study using lithium. The first systematic research on lithium in the USA was initiated in 1958 by Ronald R. Fieve and Shervert Frazier. However, during the 1960s lithium was illegal in the United States (because of its toxic effects in high doses) except for research purposes. In 1970 the USA Federal Drug Administration (FDA) finally approved lithium as a prescription drug for mania, and in 1971 it was approved for maintenance use in manic depression.

Rybakowski (Chapter 13) and Cohen and DePaulo (Chapter 14) discuss the role of lithium in the treatment of the recurring affective disorders. Rybakowski, in his chapter, notes that lithium is beneficial for treating a large proportion of patients who suffer from a unipolar or bipolar affective disorder. It is suggested that lithium is the drug of first choice for the prevention of depressive episodes of both unipolar and bipolar disorders. A major conclusion is that lithium acts as a pharmacological prophylaxis for most patients with endogenous depression and is very effective in treating mania. Rybakowski also notes that the prophylactic treatment is related to significant reductions in suicide risks for endogenously depressed patients.

Cohen and DePaulo (Chapter 14) focus on lithium salts as an empirical medical treatment for recurrent affective illness. They note that lithium has revolutionized the treatment of episodic (recurring) affective disorder, and that the therapist should use it with sensitivity to the symptoms and sequelae of a disorder which affects not only motivated behaviors, perceptions, cognitions, and moods, but also affects interpersonal relationships, especially with respect to family life. They discuss the need for and existence of self-help groups (some in collaboration with clinicians) in order to educate and support patients and their families. Cohen and DePaulo also discuss bipolar disorders as a disease entity and emphasize the genetic contributions to this illness. The possible side effects of lithium are also presented. Whereas Rybakowski (Chapter 13) focuses primarily on its therapeutic effects, Cohen and DePaulo (Chapter 14) provide a theoretical background for the bipolar affective disorders, suggest implications for future research, and attempt to integrate the therapeutic effects of lithium with the theoretical bases of the affective disorders.

Debus and Rush (Chapter 15) discuss the abnormalities of the sleep electroencephalogram (EEG) occurring in the affective disorders. They note that psychiatrists and others have aimed at discovering various "windows on the brain" in order to better understand the underlying pathophysiology of various disorders. Although neuroendocrine measures and metabolites of various neurotransmitters assessed via urine, blood stress, or cerebral spinal fluid samples have been investigated as indices of depression for quite some time, it is only in the last decade that sleep EEG has been used to assess depression. Debus and Rush review the various methodologies used to describe characteristics of normal sleep, then discuss findings with respect to sleep patterns in depression, including the various subtypes and other psychiatric disorders, and then attempt to clarify the relationships of these findings to other biological indices of depression. The clinical and theoretical implications of the various findings are also presented. The authors note that sleep EEG disturbances are useful in differentiating among the various types of depression, and in discriminating between depression and both dementia and anxiety disorders. They also suggest that there is prognostic utility in the assessment of sleep EEG patterns. Finally, they conclude that understanding of the underlying neuroanatomy and neurochemistry that account for abnormalities in sleep EEG patterns will lead to improved diagnosis and treatment techniques for depressed patients.

McAllister and Price, in their second chapter in this part (Chapter 16) discuss depression in the brain-injured. They note that depressive syndromes frequently occur in the context of various types of neurological disorders. Thus, these depressive sequelae present a major complication and potential block for rehabilitating patients with central nervous system (CNS) disorders. In Chapter 16, McAllister and Price discuss the role of lesion location in depression, the relationship of the laterality of the injury to depression, and the effect of the lesion on the phenomenology or expression of the depressive syndrome. The relationships between various CNS disorders (e.g., dementing disorders, traumatic brain injury, Parkinson's disease, multiple sclerosis, Huntington's disease, and epilepsy) and depression are also discussed. The final section is concerned with treatment issues, including the uses of antidepressants and ECT. The authors note that although depressive syndromes are eminently treatable, it is important to understand the implication of brain disorders for the evaluation, treatment procedures (psychopharmacological and ECT), and the assessment of responses to treatment.

It should be noted that in the 1950s, 1960s, and early 1970s there was heavy emphasis on psychoanalytic theories and treatments for major clinical disorders. During the last 15 years the focus has been on biological psychiatry. Part IV reflects the biological factors prevalent in the theory and research, as well as the treatment of the various affective disorders.

# 11

# The Role of ECT in the Treatment of Depression

Donald P. Hay and Linda K. Hay
*University of Wisconsin Medical School*

KEY WORDS: electroconvulsive therapy, convulsive therapy, seizure induction, depression, endogenous depression, biological depression, major depressive disorder, bipolar disorder, manic depressive disorder, schizophrenia, history

## THE HISTORY OF ECT: THE FIRST 50 YEARS

Electroconvulsive Therapy (ECT) is a leading biological treatment for major depressive disorder, bipolar disorder, and certain forms of schizoaffective disorder, which although effective and on the cutting edge of modern psychiatry and technology, still evokes the image of being primitive, punitive, and destructive. This paradox can best be explained in terms of the history of ECT. An understanding of the controversies surrounding the use of ECT is dependent upon an awareness of its development and the nature of mental illness.

The use of electric current in the treatment of mental illness had been thought of as early as Roman times (Abrams, 1988; Endler & Persad, 1988; Endler, 1988), but state-of-the-art ECT as used today bears little resemblance in theory or practice to those early concepts. The initial attempts at using electricity were based on vague notions of catharsis in the form of gross shock delivered by electric eels to alleviate undesired symptoms, and as such, were very different from today's conceptualization and methodology in the use of a well-controlled electrical stimulus to induce therapeutic changes in neurotransmission in the brain through seizure induction.

The actual basis for the use of electricity to initiate a seizure for the treatment of mental disorders was preceded by the use of chemical convulsion-inducing agents. As early as 1785, there were reports of a case study involving the use of camphor to treat a mentally ill patient (Kalinowsky, 1982; Endler, 1988).

Insulin coma therapy was developed by Manfred Sakel (1900–1957) and was used from 1927 to 1933. While using insulin to treat a variety of symptoms, such as irritability, insomnia, and morphine withdrawal, Sakel observed the induction of seizures in some patients and the subsequent reduction of schizophrenic symptoms (Fink, 1979). The use of insulin coma for induction of a seizure became an important treatment for schizophrenia even though it presented problems of unpredictability and variable efficacy and was subsequently shown to be effective only in nonspecific ways.

Laszlo Von Meduna (1896–1964), a Hungarian psychiatrist, has been credited with the development of modern convulsive therapy. His research in the neuropathology of schizophrenia led him to speculate that the epileptic seizure could be used to treat schizophrenia (Fink, 1979, 1984). His determination was supported in part by reports of the rarity of finding individuals with schizophrenia who also had a history of epilepsy. He interpreted this to mean that the seizure of epilepsy had a curative effect upon the schizophrenic process.

Meduna treated his first patient with camphor to induce a convulsion in 1934 and reported improvement. The use of camphor to induce seizures was replaced by pentylenetetrazol (Metrazol, Cardiozol). It was Meduna's understanding that the convulsions in his patients created change in the chemical constituents of the brain and promoted the cure for schizophrenia.

Convulsive therapies were accepted as appropriate and effective treatments for dementia praecox or schizophrenia by the end of the 1930s. Eventually this treatment spread to other mental illnesses, and the positive effects of convulsive therapy were reported for patients with psychotic depressions, involutional depression, and mania (Fink, 1979). Much interest developed in the mode of action and the theories were varied and numerous.

The introduction of electric current to induce seizures was instituted by Ugo Cerletti and Lucio Bini in 1938 (Abrams, 1982; Endler, 1988; Endler & Persad, 1988; Fink, 1979). Their intention was to replace the use of Metrazol, as they observed many patients who experienced pain and trauma while undergoing this treatment. In 1938 Cerletti and Bini reported their success in treating a 39-year-old man who had exhibited schizophrenic symptoms. Subsequent to 11 electrically induced seizures, the patient was noted to be working regularly at his former job. Cerletti and Bini maintained that the epileptiform convulsive seizure was the causative factor in reduction of symptoms, and that the minimum stimulus to produce that seizure was the most important aspect.

ECT became widely used after World War II, with a focus on ways to improve its delivery, through control of current and increased comfort to the patient by means of muscle paralysis and anesthesia. Its proponents were steadfast in their claims of the efficacy of ECT, but its widespread use gave rise to concerns. There was fear that the widespread use of ECT might impact adversely on the acceptance of psychotherapy, and this, along with the revolutionary introduction of pharmacotherapy in the early 1950s, led to the decline of the use of convulsive therapy (Fink, 1979).

One of the prevailing myths surrounding ECT is that it is a form of behavioral modification, conditioning, or control. This has consistently been reinforced by the media in such memorable moments as the punishment of the character Jack Nicholson portrayed in "One Flew Over The Cuckoos Nest" or of Francis Farmer in "The Francis Farmer Story." In reality, ECT has been used in a variety of situations, sometimes inappropriately. It is most important, then, that the correct use of ECT be understood and educational information be conveyed to the public as a way of dispelling the myths.

Today with increasing public concern for consumer safety, ECT remains under scrutiny as to its appropriate use in the treatment of the mentally ill. In part, these concerns arise from the original perception of ECT as unclear in its reason for application and as having been painful for the patient. In reaction to these concerns, an American Psychiatric Association Task Force, made up of the foremost researchers in the field of ECT, is presently addressing the issue of the use of ECT. By 1990, they hope to release an intensive report detailing most current issues and concerns regarding ECT.

No doubt, on occasion ECT was used inappropriately and excessively during its early years. However, the procedure continues to be employed frequently throughout the world, and its usefulness, efficacy, safety, and acceptance by the medical community, as well as the appreciation by those who have benefited from its frequent success, appears to be increasing.

## INDICATIONS FOR ECT

Rigorous studies have confirmed that ECT is an effective treatment for depressive illness (major depression), mania, and acute schizophrenic episodes with an affective component (Abrams, 1988; Endler & Persad, 1988).

The use of ECT for situational sadness, unhappiness, dysthymic disorder, personality or characterological disorders is generally not considered to be appropriate or justified.

In addition, there are some rare situations where ECT is also indicated. These include other medical disorders, only after trials of standard treatment alternatives have been considered. Some of these are catatonia, intractable seizure disorder, neuroleptic malignant syndrome, and Parkinson's Disease.

### Depressive Illness: Major/Endogenous/Biologic Depression

Depression may be conceptualized from the perspective of both situational sadness and endogenous (biological) depression. It is important to distinguish these perspectives when evaluating the indications for ECT. Situational sadness, "unhappiness," or dysthymic disorder, in and of itself, does not require biologic psychiatric treatment, and this form of depression appears to respond best to psychotherapy. It is the endogenous form of depression which is perceived to be a chemical imbalance in the central nervous system and which is the type most responsive to biological treatments such as ECT.

Major depression is defined by DSM-III-R criteria as the presence of at least five of the following nine symptoms lasting for at least two weeks. At least one of the five must include the first or second symptoms:

1. depressed mood most of the day nearly every day

2. markedly diminished interest or pleasure in all or almost all activities most of the day

3. significant weight loss or weight gain

4. insomnia or hypersomnia nearly every day

5. psychomotor agitation or retardation nearly every day

6. fatigue or loss of energy nearly every day

7. feelings of worthlessness or excessive or inappropriate guilt

8. diminished ability to think or concentrate

9. recurrent thoughts of death, suicidal ideation, or a suicide attempt (American Psychiatric Association, 1987).

A simple clinical guide for diagnosis of endogenous depression is a depression check list developed by the authors called "Cease Sad" (Hay, 1988). The list differs only slightly from DSM-III criteria and has not been validated, but it serves as a useful reminder to mental health professionals and general practitioners when assessing patients for symptoms of depression. This acronym delineates the most critical symptoms of biologic depressive disorder. There appears to be a positive relationship between an individual exhibiting a greater number of these symptoms and the existence of major depressive disorder.

Concentration: diminished

Energy: diminished

Anxiety: agitation or restlessness

Spontaneous crying: inappropriate crying or not being able to cry

Early morning awakening: insomnia in the early morning hours

Suicidal thoughts: thoughts of self-harm

Appetite disturbance: diminished with weight loss

Deprecatory thoughts: self-reproach or guilt

If these symptoms persist for at least two weeks without any apparent precipitating event, they are strong indicators for the possibility of endogenous depression (major depressive disorder). It is important to note that in some cases the most predominant symptom may not be the feeling of sadness, which is more commonly associated with the term " depression." The individual may be crying without knowing why or be restless and agitated without feeling particularly sad. In this type of situation, major depression, rather than dysthymia, should be considered as the etiological explanation. Correct diagnosis is critical since the diagnosis of a major depressive disorder requires consideration of antidepressant medication and/or ECT, whereas the diagnosis of a dysthymic disorder might require only psychotherapy. Mistaking one for the other could result in the withholding of necessary medical intervention.

It is also important to note that this delineation of situational versus endogenous depression is best understood in terms of a continuum, with biologic aspects located at one end and situational aspects at the other.

Each individual presenting with symptoms falls somewhere on this continuum with varying proportions of each type of depression. No individual exists without situational events having an effect on mood. With respect to this fact, ECT and other medical treatments for depressive illness are usually initiated in conjunction with appropriate psychotherapy and educational support, focused on the entire individual.

Based on the theory that the biological type of depression is a physical illness to which an individual may be genetically predisposed and is often precipitated by situational stressors, such as physical or emotional trauma, it follows that the treatment be based primarily on a biologic model and supplemented by psychological and social support treatments. The usual treatment of choice is that of antidepressant medication such as tricyclics, heterocyclics, or monoamine oxidase inhibitors (MAOIs). Traditionally, ECT has been considered when medication was found to be either ineffective, too delayed in onset of action, or contraindicated as a result of dangerous side effects.

In certain situations, the patient does not respond to the anti-depressant medication. This may occur when an individual has a very severe form of depression which is resistant to psychopharmacological intervention. In some cases, in which an individual is suicidal or experiencing severe physical debilitation due to the process of the depression, the antidepressant medication may be too slow, often requiring several weeks or more to exert a therapeutic effect. Anti-depressant medication may be contraindicated for a variety of reasons, such as anticholinergic and/or cardiovascular side effects. In all of these situations, ECT might become the treatment of choice.

Although memory loss may occur to varying degrees, the use of ECT has not been shown in the literature to produce any significant lasting deleterious side effects (Abrams, 1982; Endler & Persad, 1988) and has been shown to be relatively safe, and thus is supported by research as being the indicated treatment in these clinical situations. ECT is probably the most effective clinical treatment for severe depressive disorders, especially those involving hallucinations, delusions, psychomotor retardation, and suicidal ideation (Taylor, 1982).

## Mania

ECT is a very effective treatment in the acute manic phase of bipolar (manic-depressive) disorder. Bipolar disorder is distinguished from unipolar depression in that, in addition to the depressed phase, the individual occasionally manifests symptoms characterized by impulsiveness, distractibility, rapid speech, and exaggerated mood swings, including irritability, euphoria, and expansiveness. In these situations the patient is usually brought to the attention of the practitioner by family members or peers because of the often bizarre and uncontrollable behavioral consequences of this phase. If medication does not adequately diminish the agitation and thought disorder that may typify this phase of the illness, hospitalization may be necessary for the safety and protection of the individual and others.

ECT has been shown to be effective in quickly reducing the symptoms of mania, as well as shortening the course of treatment. However, it is frequently difficult to convince a manic individual that he/she is indeed suffering from an emotional illness resulting in distorted thinking and behavior, much less to sign informed consent and agree to be treated with ECT. Acceptance to proceed with ECT usually requires that the patient has received prior treatment for the depressed phase of the illness and furthermore, has received adequate information about the illness and the various options for its treatment. Usually it is only under these circumstances that an individual in a manic phase will agree to proceed with a series of ECT.

## Schizophrenia

ECT was the main treatment modality for schizophrenia until the advent of psychotropic medications in the 1950s. Concern developed, however, in the 1970s over the side effects of neuroleptic medication, such as severe extrapyramidal symptoms and tardive dyskinesia. Extrapyramidal side effects include extreme restlessness (akathisia) and stiffness of neck or extremities (dystonia), and tardive dyskinesia usually appears initially as uncontrollable movements of tongue and mouth. ECT was turned to once again as a reasonable alternative treatment. Today ECT is indicated in the treatment of certain types of schizophrenia (acute, catatonic, and with an affective component) and may be utilized when medication is ineffective or contraindicated.

The efficacy of ECT in schizophrenia has been difficult to assess due to a variety of variables. First, differences and discrepancies in the diagnosis of schizophrenia, usually based on the duration of symptoms as chronic or acute, have led to difficulties in assessing the effectiveness of ECT for this illness. Second, the variables of electroconvulsive therapy, such as number of treatments and type of seizures, are important in assessing the efficacy of ECT in schizophrenia. Usually, in schizophrenia, more seizures, more frequently induced (12–20) are needed than in the treatment of depression (Fink, 1979). Third, it has been difficult to differentiate the depressed psychotic symptoms of some schizophrenic patients from those suffering from pure depression. There has been a resurgence of interest in recent years as to the effectiveness of ECT for schizophrenic illnesses, especially those with an acute psychotic course with either a catatonic or delusional component.

# PATHOPHYSIOLOGY OF ECT

As there is no completely satisfactory explanation for the origins of depression, there is yet to be a totally satisfactory understanding of the pathophysiology of the treatment of ECT for depression. The various theories posed are based on the prevailing theories for the etiology of depression. These include structural theories, psychological theories, electrophysiologic theories, and biochemical theories.

The structural theories were the first concepts involved in insulin coma techniques for seizure induction. Included were a variety of concepts such as the protection of the oversensitive abnormal brain cells by coma and the restoration of glucagon, a form of sugar utilized by brain cells. Other theorists believed that the increased permeability of the blood-brain barrier promoted excretion of toxic brain substances supposedly implicated in mental diseases (Fink, 1979).

The psychological theories of the effect of ECT have to do with repression, punishment, and amnesia. In the case of denial and punishment, the reduction of symptoms was believed to be produced by the trauma and the fear of the treatment. This has been significantly reduced with modern ECT and the use of anesthesia and muscle relaxers so that these theories have lost their credence. The amnesia theory had to do with development of memory loss as a way of repressing painful experiences which may have had a role in the development of the disease (Endler, 1982). Modified ECT produces minimal memory loss making this theory inaccurate in terms of contemporary procedures.

The electrophysiological theories followed the development of electroencepha-lography, which demonstrated similar EEG patterns between spontaneous epileptic seizures and ECT-induced seizures. This relationship has been known to be solely associative and not direct.

The biochemical theories are widely accepted as the explanation of the etiology of depression and its treatments, both chemical and electroconvulsive. The bio-chemical theory of depression is that there is inadequate effect of an implicated neurotransmitter (norepinephrine) in the central nervous system, and it is possible that several neurotransmitters may be involved. Thus in the treatment of depression the transmission is enhanced with anti-depressant medications by either preventing re-uptake of norepinephrine or preventing monoamine oxidase from breaking down the neurotransmitters (Fink, 1979).

There are many biochemical changes in the body subsequent to ECT, including the enhanced receptor sensitivity to norepinephrine. Other neurotransmitters impli-cated in theories of depression are also increased following ECT, including seroto-nin and dopamine. It is difficult to define any single cause because of the multiplicity of effects of ECT on different neurotransmitter systems.

## TECHNIQUES AND PROCEDURES

### Pre-ECT Work-up

Modern day modified ECT is always given under general anesthesia.

This is achieved through the administration of an anesthetic such as methohexital (Brevital), and succinylcholine, which totally relaxes the voluntary muscles. As with all situations requiring general anesthesia, a complete history and physical examina-tion is initiated by the primary care physician. The following laboratory tests are done routinely: complete blood count, urinalysis, fasting blood sugar, blood chemis-tries, serum electrolytes, chest X-ray, and electrocardiogram.

Some additional tests may be indicated depending on the individual situation. X-rays of the spine were traditionally taken before the introduction of succinylchol-ine. The X-rays were needed to assess any spinal fractures which might be worsened by seizure induction. With the use of total muscle relaxation there is rarely any significant jarring of the spine. However, spinal x-rays may be helpful in providing the treating psychiatrist with information as to the state of the spine. (It is helpful beforehand to know if there are spinal fractures, how many, where, and how severe.) Occasionally, cases of calcified abdominal aortic aneurysms are discovered during the pre-ECT spinal x-rays, and this may result in a change in plans as to whether or not to proceed, and if so, with what precautions.

Some practitioners prefer to obtain an EEG before ECT to help in obtaining a baseline of brainwave electrical functioning prior to the ECT. It is said not to be as helpful in assessing abnormality of brain function, given its low level of specificity. A CT brain scan is usually obtained only in the presence of abnormal findings on basic physical and neurological examinations.

In addition to a thorough history and physical examination by the primary care physician, medical consultation by a cardiologist or neurologist is initiated whenever it seems appropriate. ECT is routinely and safely done in patients with medical illnesses when proper consultation is obtained.

## Treatment Plan

ECT in the United States and Canada is usually given three times weekly as it is felt to be best to allow a nontreatment day between each treatment day. Recent research has shown that it is the total number of treatments that results in reduction of symptoms and that this may be achieved more rapidly in a three-day-a-week schedule (Shapira, Kindler & Lerer, 1989). The number of treatments in each series is individualized, depending on the patient's response and reduction of symptoms. An average series consists of from 6 to 9 treatments for major depressive disorder, and upwards of 12 or more for schizoaffective disorders.

The patient has no food or liquids after 12 midnight prior to the treatment. This is to keep the stomach empty in order to prevent any aspiration during anesthesia, as is routine for all situations requiring general anesthesia. Atropine or glycopyrrolate (Robinul, a synthetic anticholinergic) is administered 45 minutes before the treatment to prevent excess secretions and to reduce activity of the vagus nerve. Atropine may also administered intravenously at the time of the anesthetic induction.

All psychotropic drugs which may raise the seizure threshold are discontinued, especially the benzodiazapines. Typically, antidepressants may be continued during the series. Many practitioners prefer to lower the dose during the ECT series and thereby lower the anticholinergic load on the patient. Similarly, it is felt to be inadvisable to suddenly discontinue anticholinergic antidepressants since this may pose a significant change in functional response of the cardiovascular system. Neuroleptics may be continued if necessary, and in fact may be helpful in lowering the seizure threshold for seizure-resistant individuals. Theophylline preparations, used for asthma, should be discontinued if possible since there have been cases of post-ECT status epilepticus reported. Lithium should also be discontinued since cases of organic brain syndrome or acute confusion and disorientation following ECT with lithium coadministration have been reported. Until relatively recently it had been said that to give ECT with coadministration of monoamine oxidase inhibitors could result in a potentially dangerous interaction with the anesthesia, more for phenelzine (Nardil), which blocks monoamine oxidase for up to two weeks, than tranylcypromine (Parnate), which blocks MAO for about 24 hours (Jenike, 1984). However, recent studies have shown that one can proceed with ECT and MAOIs, if necessary, without concern for adverse effects.

The actual ECT treatment is administered in an area which is safe for administration of anesthesia, which often is the recovery room of the hospital near the surgical suite. Once an intravenous catheter is in place, the anesthesiologist administers the anesthesia—methohexital sodium is preferred over thiopental sodium as a result of lesser cardiac side effects (Pitts, Desmarias, Stewart & Shaberg, 1965). Next, succinylcholine is injected to produce total muscle relaxation, and the patient is ready to be treated when all fasciculations have ceased. At this stage the patient is asleep and totally relaxed. With the muscles of respiration totally relaxed, along with the rest of the muscles of the body, the anesthesiologist uses an Amboue bag, a type of breathing bellows operated by hand, and an airway to provide adequate ventilation for the patient. By keeping the patient well oxygenated, cardiovascular compromise and side effects are prevented, and the procedure may be facilitated with a reduction in seizure threshold as well as a reduction in any potential for memory loss. Caffeine has been found to lower the seizure threshold as well, and might be administered at this point.

The electrode placement may be either bilateral or unilateral. There have been many studies as to the therapeutic differences between these two positions, but the reports are unclear due to mitigating variables such as stimulus intensity, distance between unilateral electrodes, and the symptoms and age of the patients in the studies (Abrams, 1986; Weiner & Coffey, 1986; Sackeim, 1986).

Most clinicians prefer to proceed with the unilateral position on the non-dominant hemisphere, which is usually on the right, as the initial approach. The unilateral electrode position usually results in less, if any, memory loss or confusion (Squire, 1986). On some occasions it may be found that a unilateral approach, even using the d'Elia position, with one electrode on the temple and the other at the vertex, just lateral to the midline, which allows for greater curvature of the head included in the treatment area, will not illicit a seizure. Then it may be necessary to use a bilateral position, encompassing both hemispheres. Often it is more difficult to induce a seizure in an older individual, especially as the series proceeds, and bilateral ECT may become necessary. Some studies have also shown that individuals suffering from bipolar manic depressive disorder appear to have an improved response to bilateral ECT as compared with unilateral.

The electrical stimulus can be delivered as either a sine wave or a brief pulse current. Sine wave stimulus has been used since the introduction of ECT. Recent studies have indicated that the brief pulse stimulus, which uses less than one-third the total energy as the sine wave, is associated with less confusion and memory loss (Weiner, Rogers, Davidson & Squire, 1986).

Frontally recording EEG electrodes may also be employed as a way of obtaining evidence of a seizure since the overt signs of the seizure, such as tonic-clonic movements, may be totally eliminated by the succinylcholine. Some psychiatrists prevent blood flow to one of the patient's limbs with a blood pressure cuff as a way of providing visual evidence of the seizure since the cuffed-off limb will show tonic-clonic movements during the seizure, resulting from lack of circulation of the succinylcholine in this limb.

At this point, oxygen is administered to the patient at a rate of 20–30 respirations per minute as it is known that cerebral oxygen requirements are increased during a seizure (Abrams, 1982). The actual administration of the electric current for a few seconds is initiated by the psychiatrist. The EEG shows the activity of the brain seizure, which may be the only visible evidence due to the absence of muscle movements or convulsions. The brain seizure is the necessary element for the therapeutic effect of the treatment.

The length of the seizure is variable, depending on the stimulus intensity, the higher intensity producing longer seizures (Welch, 1988), and other variables related to individual patients. The average length of the seizure is one minute. Studies have shown that less than twenty-five seconds is usually found to be sub-therapeutic, whereas seizures lasting longer than two minutes are typically aborted by the administration of either more of the anesthetic agent or of a benzodiazepine such as diazepam.

After the seizure the patient continues to be ventilated by the anesthesiologist and then awakens a few minutes later following the termination of the anesthesia. Routine post-anesthesia care ensues with pulse and blood pressure checks and reorientation of the patient. In most cases the patient is oriented within several minutes and is kept in the recovery area for less than an hour for routine post-anesthesia care.

In some cases, as does with 5–10% of all patients receiving general anesthesia, an emergence delirium may occur, or extreme agitation, restlessness, and a delirious state (Abrams, 1982). In this case, diazepam, a tranquilizer, is administered and can be given at all subsequent treatments immediately following the seizure.

ECT may be administered while the patient is an inpatient in the hospital, as a series of 6–12 treatments every other day, or as an outpatient procedure, usually as a follow-up treatment subsequent to the initial series. The advantage of outpatient ECT is that the individual avoids the inconvenience of a hospitalization and may continue with work and family activities. As long as the ECT work-up is updated every six months, outpatient ECT is as safe and effective as inpatient ECT, so long as the individual is medically stable.

Maintenance ECT is an outpatient program of treatments which follow the initial series in intervals designed to meet the individual needs of the patient. The program is designed to prevent relapse, and treatments can be spaced in weekly or monthly intervals, depending on the reemergence of symptoms. Maintenance ECT may continue as long as symptoms persist or may be discontinued during symptom-free periods.

## CLINICAL ISSUES IN THE USE OF ECT

### Prediction of Response

Many investigators have found a favorable response to ECT to be associated with a variety of variables. These include increasing age, shorter duration of illness, better results in women than men, bipolar versus unipolar depression, among others (Abrams, 1988). The variables that have been looked at include physiological, psychological, and clinical, the last being the most significant.

The physiological variables include blood pressure levels after injection of adrenalin or methacholine, sedation threshold or point at which a patient shows symptoms of blurred vision and slurred speech after receiving sodium amylobarbitone, dexamethasone nonsuppression or higher blood levels of dexamethasone 12 hours after a loading dose, and prolactin release after ECT with a greater release predicting a poorer response (Hamilton, 1982; Abrams & Swartz, 1985). There has been no evidence to clearly support the use of these variables as predictors; however, research continues especially in the area of prolactin.

The relationship between personality characteristics and response to ECT has been looked at in a variety of ways. Feldman developed a subscale of the Minnesota Multiphasic Personality Inventory (MMPI) that included 52 items which showed a positive relationship between recovery after ECT (Feldman, 1951). Unfortunately, subsequent research was unable to reproduce his results.

The Rorschach was found to be useful in predicting good responders to ECT (Kahn & Pollack, 1959; Kahn & Fink, 1960).

Early experience with ECT has shown that depressive disorders do better than any other illness in terms of reduction of symptoms. Clinical experience also shows that the major depressive disorders of the melancholic type, as opposed to the situational type, do better with ECT.

In practice, it is generally the patients who are clearly suffering from major depressive disorders who do best with ECT. The patients who present with the symptoms which have been previously mentioned, such as early morning awakening, spontaneous crying, and suicidal ideation, are more likely to respond well to ECT treatment than those with personality disorders or long-standing anxiety from childhood.

## Effects of ECT

One effect of ECT which has received the most notice is memory loss. The literature in this area is affected by a variety of variables. Subject selection, assessment techniques, treatment protocols, time intervals used, and choice of terms such as memory, recall, forgetting, and learning are diverse and inconsistent. Although memory may be impaired by ECT, the duration and extent of this memory loss has yet to be totally understood.

The type of amnesia experienced during ECT may be described as being both retrograde and anterograde. Retrograde amnesia is memory loss of past events and anterograde includes difficulty retaining newly learned material.

Memory is also affected by number of treatments. The loss of memory is greatest immediately following the seizure but improves afterwards, with continuing improvement after termination of the series. Memory is also affected by the frequency of seizures. In multiple ECT, in which the patient experiences three to eight seizures during one treatment, there is little evidence supporting greater memory loss as compared to just one seizure per treatment (Fink, 1979).

It has been shown that placement of electrodes affects the extent of memory loss. There is less memory loss with unilateral placement as opposed to bilateral (Squire, 1977). Current intensity also affects memory loss as brief stimulus currents such as pulsed square waves have resulted in less memory loss than sine wave current (Abrams, 1988).

Ultimately it has been found that memory of events prior to the illness are usually completely restored once the series is terminated. Any memory loss that occurs can be minimized by the use of proper placement of electrodes, maximum spacing of treatments, and brief pulse current.

Another effect of ECT is increased consumption of oxygen during each seizure. It has been found that by hyperoxygenation and restriction of muscle activity, there is a minimalization of lactate and carbon dioxide build-up.

There are several biochemical effects of ECT which have been noted. These include an increase in blood-brain barrier permeability, some brain enzyme changes, a brief increased production of adrenal cortical steroids, and, of course, the increase of the neurotransmitters norepinephrine, serotonin, dopamine and acetylcholine.

The cardiovascular system is also affected by ECT. Arrhythmias may occur, and bradycardia and tachycardia are also noted on occasion. Atropine, succinylcholine, anesthesia, and blocking agents can reduce arrhythmias.

There is also a brief increase in blood pressure during ECT, and this can be controlled if necessary by the use of various agents.

## Medical Considerations

There have been many studies supporting the safety of ECT. It has been reported that there are two deaths per 100,000 treatments (Kramer, 1985). This mortality rate is even lower than that of childbirth and at the bottom range for anesthesia alone (Abrams, 1988). Most of these deaths have been related to the cardiovascular effects of ECT, which can be minimized with proper management. In fact, due to the advanced monitoring techniques which enable the practitioner to prevent and correct most potentially dangerous side effects, ECT has become routine for a population of patients previously believed to be too ill or too old. Thus ECT is not a high-risk procedure, but certain medical situations require special consideration during a treatment regimen.

There have been substantial reports in the literature concerning the high-risk patient, including the areas of central nervous system disease, anticoagulant therapy, neuroleptic malignant syndrome, osteogenesis imperfecta, glaucoma, cerebralangioma, pregnancy, post-stroke depression, ventriculoatrial shunt, Parkinson's disease, monoamine oxidase inhibitors, skull prostheses, burns, osteoporosis, and multiple sclerosis (Elliot et al., 1982; Weiner, 1983; Gerring & Shields, 1982; Regestein & Reich, 1985; Hay, 1989). An entire volume of *Convulsive Therapy*, guest edited by Richard Abrams, was devoted to the topic of the high-risk patient, delineating two target areas, including cardiovascular and central nervous systems, and ECT in the medically ill elderly patient (Abrams, 1989).

## LEGAL AND ETHICAL ISSUES

### Informed Consent

Informed consent for ECT is required in most states and provinces. This involves an extensive process of education for the patient and the patient's family. It is especially important to include the family members in the educational process (with the patient's permission of course) and the signing of the consent form, in situations in which the depression is so severe that the patient may be cognitively impaired or psychotic and not totally able to judge the significance of the treatment.

There exists a paradoxical situation within the consent process for ECT as it exists today. Whereas an individual is considered technically and legally to be "competent" in the eyes of the law until adjudged incompetent, when an individual is being considered for ECT, he/she is often not able to think clearly as a result of the depressive illness. Even though the patient in this situation is requesting to proceed with the ECT, one could call into question the validity of the informed consent process. In cases such as these, further in-depth discussions with the patient and his/her family may become essential to insure adequate understanding by all, and it is recommended to obtain full informed consent from as many of the patient's close relatives as can be located. If any one, patient or family member, should not be in favor of proceeding, it may be wise not to proceed unless the illness is felt to be life threatening, and then to go ahead only with a court order.

It is important to note that "informed consent" means just that: the form itself should include information regarding the indications for the treatment, what the treatment entails, the potential risks, potential benefits, as well as the possible alternatives to the treatment. Any modern day ECT that does not include full informed consent (often augmented with the educational written materials and recorded videotapes made for the patient and family just for this purpose) is not adequate informed consent.

In extreme cases in which the patient is not able to give consent or is refusing treatment for the depression, it may become necessary to obtain a court order to be able to proceed with ECT. This is sometimes necessary when the patient is extremely suicidal or physically debilitated to the point such that if treatment is not initiated to alleviate the symptoms, he/she might die as a result of uncontrollable behavior (suicide) or medical complications (intestinal shutdown, malnutrition, dehydration, cardiac arrhythmia, myocardial infarction, cardiac arrest).

## The Right to Treatment and the Right to Refuse Treatment

A closely related issue to informed consent is that of right to treatment and the right to refuse treatment. These issues have been defined by the courts in various legal decisions and must be addressed in order to better understand the principals involved in the administration of ECT.

First, associated with informed consent is the issue of right to refuse treatment. Administration of ECT without the consent of the patient may be legally defined as a battery. For this reason the informed consent is imperative.

The question of competency to sign an informed consent plays an important legal role at this point. Competency is a legal decision but often based on psychiatric or psychological advice. In the question of competency for ECT, the issue is confounded by the process of the illness for which the treatment is sought. Depression can result in cognitive impairment and psychosis, and studies have suggested that individuals suffering from confusion and psychosis may not be able to make informed decisions. This makes it important to involve as many family members as possible in the informed consent proceedings.

Finally, when the right to refuse treatment is exercised by an individual suffering from depression, it is wise to consider the effect that the symptoms of hopelessness, helplessness, and suicidal ideation might be exerting on this decision. This again reinforces the need to involve family members in the decision process.

In addition, the courts have always upheld the right to treatment of a person as a constitutional right. The Rouse v. Cameron decision in 1966 established precedent for a bona fide effort to provide an individualized treatment program with periodic evaluation for persons confined due to mental illness (Frankel, 1982). More specific attention was paid to the criteria for adequate treatment in subsequent rulings, and it was clear that the court was concerned with the use of ECT as a mode of treatment. It was described by one court as an extraordinary and dangerous treatment (Frankel, 1982).

There are many implications of this legal definition of adequate treatment as opposed to the medical and scientific definitions. There is no lack of evidence as to the efficacy and safety of ECT, and yet there are legal precedents defining it as dangerous and extreme. The question arises as to the ethical dilemma for the practitioner who must provide the best treatment possible for the patient and yet may be reluctant to do so based on legal precedent.

Although the legal and ethical issues for ECT include those for any medical intervention, there are additional concerns due to the variety of issues unique to ECT. The nature of the illness itself can interfere with the judgment of the patient, the mechanisms of the treatment are poorly understood, the providers of the treatment are mistrusted, and the context of civil commitment and forced treatment connote fear.

## SOCIAL AND POLITICAL ISSUES

### Patient Attitudes

Various studies have been devoted to assessing the attitude of patients toward ECT. Of several hundred patients interviewed, most had positive views about ECT and reported little fear, pain, or unpleasant feelings associated with their treatment (Abrams, 1988). In spite of this there is a widespread public image which depicts ECT as an extremely fearful and drastic treatment. The issues contributing to this attitude are the abuse of ECT, the vocal groups who protest ECT on a regular basis, inadequate consent procedures, misrepresentation of ECT in the media, and fears of memory loss.

The present Task Force on ECT, sponsored by the American Psychiatric Association, is addressing the issue of abuse of ECT by clarifying and delineating the recommended guidelines for its use based on the most current research. When these clear guidelines are available to practitioners, they will be more likely to use ECT appropriately and safely.

Again, the issue of informed consent is paramount in dispelling misunderstandings concerning the use of ECT. A thorough educational process for patient and family can do much to reduce the fear of the unknown and to eliminate the aura of ECT as a punishment or mind control.

The groups which often lobby against ECT, referred to as the vocal minority, include many lay organizations such as Mental Patient Law Project, the Citizen's Commission on Human Rights (Sponsored by the Church of Scientology), and the Network Against Psychiatric Assault, among others. It is notable that these groups are seldom opposed by advocate groups, whereas there are an estimated 50,000 to

100,000 patients receiving ECT each year with positive results. The pro-ECT patients are generally too busy with their activities of life and fearful of stigma to speak out (Abrams, 1988).

There is a lack in the public media of a positive portrayal of ECT, and as the media serves as educator for a majority of the public, they see only one side of the issue. Although high quality journalistic endeavors, such as Barbara Walters on "20–20," have presented a factual representation of ECT, most television, radio, and movie depictions capitalize on the sensational aspects of ECT. Basically, it is not interesting or entertaining to hear about the successful, routine treatment of depression by the induced seizure.

The Association for Convulsive Therapy (ACT) is an international group dedicated to the dissemination of correct information about ECT.

## The Stigma of Mental Illness and Its Treatments

The stigma towards the mentally ill stems from the misunderstandings as to the etiology of mental illness and therefore, the treatments employed and the caregivers themselves. In the past, causality of disease was ascribed to the supernatural, and the victims were shunned and feared as bearers of uncontrollable forces. This was especially true in the case of mental illness, which is often translated into bizarre behavior not unlike primitive conceptions of demonic possession. Our present understanding of disease process is based on more tangible and less fearful theories, but still not well understood by the public, due to the complexities involved and the multicausality (Endler, 1988). Although there is greater understanding of the disease process, there is still a tendency to fear and avoid the behavior of the mental patient.

In the case of the caregivers of the mentally ill, the stigma of the disease is transferred to those who treat the disease and to the treatments they utilize. ECT specifically evokes all the negative images of primitive mechanisms of disease exorcism. Unmodified ECT produces a convulsion by means of mysterious looking machinery, and without an understanding of the scientific rationale, it evokes an emotional response similar to that of Dr. Frankenstein creating a monster.

In their book, *Electroconvulsive Therapy: The Myths and the Realities*, Endler and Persad dispel the misunderstandings about ECT as a way of lessening the stigma. They encourage education as the best way to deal with the fear and mystery surrounding ECT. They emphasize that there is no conclusive evidence that ECT causes permanent brain damage and that memory loss may be reduced with proper techniques (Endler & Persad, 1988).

## RESEARCH ISSUES IN ECT

Given the premise that education and information reduce fear and misunderstanding, it follows that research is necessary to provide more knowledge. As yet, the exact mechanisms involved in the process of ECT are not totally understood, leaving room for speculation as to its rationale. The future of ECT as a viable treatment for depression depends on research, which must keep up with the rapidly advancing technology of our era.

Furthermore, research promotes an optimistic viewpoint for the future of ECT. With improved techniques of treatment and better understanding of the indications for ECT, the treatment will become even safer. In addition, the research in ECT is an important contribution to the general understanding of brain functioning and its relationship to behavior (Fink, 1979).

The research in ECT has to do with a variety of aspects. These include the mechanisms of depression and how this is related to ECT, the parameters of the delivery, including medications and electrical technology, the effects on body systems, including the central nervous system, and the expanded use of ECT in tardive dyskinesia and other related diseases.

In a recent issue of *Convulsive Therapy* (1989), the areas of new citations included among many: stimulus wave form (Andrade & Gangadhar, 1988; Andrade, Gangadhar, Subbakrishna, Channabasavanna & Pradhan, 1988); receptor site functioning (Buckholtz, Davies, Rudorfer, Golden & Potter, 1988); leukoencephalopathy in elderly depressed patients (Coffey et al., 1988); a comparison of anesthetic agents (Dwyer, McCaughey, Lavery, McCarthy & Dundee, 1988; Konarzweski, Milosavljevic, Robinson, Banham & Beales, 1988); monitoring response to ECT with polysomnographic recordings (Grunhaus et al., 1988); and ECT in obsessive compulsive disorders (Kjhanna, Gangadhar, Sinha, Rajendra & Channabasavanna, 1988).

## SUMMARY AND CONCLUSIONS

The issues surrounding ECT are complex and multifaceted, which contributes to the difficulty with its acceptance as an appropriate treatment for depression and other illnesses. Throughout its history ECT has been fraught with controversy due to misinformation as to its indications, mechanisms, efficacy, and safety. In addition, ECT is subject to the stigma associated with the entire science of mental illness, including patients, practitioners, and treatments.

The evidence supports the fact that ECT is a safe and effective treatment for certain psychiatric illnesses. The positive effects of ECT outweigh the negative effects, which may be minimized through proper management.

There is much experimental data available for the student and practitioner interested in developing a greater knowledge and understanding of ECT. Those who practice ECT and those patients who have been treated with it have clearly benefited from this information.

The treatment of ECT is safe and efficacious. The science of ECT is comparable to any medical procedure. The treatment itself is not controversial for those who are aware of its scientific underpinnings. The hope for the future is that ECT will be replaced by more effective medications and more advanced techniques of prevention, but at present it remains the most effective treatment for selected patients with severe depression, particularly those with melancholic or psychotic features.

# References

Abrams, R. (1988). *Electroconvulsive Therapy*. New York: Oxford University Press.

Abrams, R. & Essman, W. B. (Eds.). (1982). *Electroconvulsive therapy: Biological foundations and clinical applications*. New York: Spectrum.

Abrams, R. & Swartz, C. M. (1985). ECT and prolactin release: Effects of stimulus parameters. *Convulsive Therapy*, 1, 115–119.

Abrams, R. (1989). ECT in the high-risk patient. *Convulsive Therapy*, 5, 1–2.

Andrade, C., Gangadhar, B.N., Channabasavanna, S. M. & Pradhan, N. (1988). Does ECT stimulus wave from influence rate of recovery in endogenous depression? *NIMHANS J*,6, 121–126.

Andrade, C., Gangadhar, B. N., Subbakrishna, D. K., Channabasavanna, S. M. & Pradhan, N. (1988). A double-blind comparison of sinusoidal wave and brief-pulse electroconvulsive therapy in endogenous depression. *Convulsive Therapy*, 4, 297–305.

Buckholtz, N. S., Davies, A. O., Rudorfer, M. V., Golden, R. N. & Potter, W. Z. (1988). *Biologic Psychiatry*, 24, 451–457.

Coffey, C. E., Rigiel, G. S., Djang, W.T., Cress, M., Saunders, W. B. & Weiner, R. D. (1988). Leukoencephalopathy in elderly depressed patients referred for ECT. *Biol Psychiatry*, 24, 143–161.

Coffey, C. E., McCall, W. V., Hoelscher, T. J., Carroll, B., Hinkle, E. E., Saunders, W. B., Erwin, C. W., Marsh, G. R. & Weiner, R. D. (1988). Effects of ECT on polysomnographic sleep: a prospective investigation. *Convulsive Therapy*, 4, 269–279.

*Diagnostic Criteria from DSM-III-R*. (1987). Washington D.C.: American Psychiatric Association.

Dwyer, R., McCaughey, W., Lavery, J., McCarthy, G. & Dundee, J. W. (1988). Comparison of propofol and methohixitone as anaesthetic agents for electroconvulsive therapy. *Anesthesia*, 43, 459–462.

Elliot, D. R., Linz, D. H. & Kane, J.A. (1982). Electroconvulsive therapy: pretreatment medical evaluation. *Arch. Int. Med.*, 142, 979–981.

Endler, N.S. (1988). The origins of electroconvulsive therapy (ECT). *Convulsive Therapy*, 4, 5–23.

Endler, N.S. & Persad, E., (1988). *Electroconvulsive Therapy: The myths and the realities*. Toronto: Hans Huber Publishers.

Feldman, M. J. (1951). A prognostic scale for shock therapy. *Psychol. Monogr.* No. 327.

Fink, M., (1979). *Convulsive Therapy: Theory and practice*. New York: Raven Press.

Fink, M., (1984). Meduna and the origins of convulsive therapy. *American Journal of Psychiatry*, 144, 1034–1041.

Frankel, F. H. (1982). Medicolegal and ethical aspects of treatment. In R. Abrams & W. Essman (Eds.), *Electroconvulsive therapy: Biological foundations and clinical applications*. New York: Spectrum.

Gerring, J. P. & Shields, H. M. (1983). The identification and management of patients with a high risk for cardiac arrhythmias during modified ECT. *J. Clin. Psychiatry*, 43, 140–143.

Grunhaus, L., Tiongco, D., Pande, A., Eiser, A., Haskett, R. F., Grenen, J. F. & Shipley, J. E. (1988). Monitoring of antidepressant response to ECT with polysomnographic recordings and the dexamethasone suppression test. *Psychiatry Res.*, 24, 177–185.

Hamilton, M. (1982). Prediction of the response of depressions to ECT. In R. Abrams & W. Essman (Eds), *Electroconvulsive therapy: Biological foundations and clinical applications*. New York: Spectrum.

Hay, D. P. (1988). Trends in care for the elderly in Geriatric Psychiatry. *Wis. Med. J.,* Dec. 1988.

Hay, D. P. (1989). Electroconvulsive therapy in the medically ill elderly. *Convulsive Therapy,* 5, 8–16.

Jenike, M. (1984). The Use of Monoamine Oxidase Inhibitors in the Treatment Of Elderly, Depressed Patients. *Journal of the American Geriatrics Society,* Vol. 32, #8, pp 571–575.

Kahn, R. L. & Fink, M. (1960). Prognostic value of Rorschach criteria in clinical response to convulsive therapy. *J. Neuropsychiatry,* 1, 242–245.

Kahn, R. L., Pollack, M. (1959). Prognostic application of psychological techniques in convulsive therapy. *Dis Nerv. Syst.,* 20, 180–184.

Kalinowsky, L. B. (1982). The history of electroconvulsive therapy. In R. Abrams & W. Essman (Eds.), *Electroconvulsive therapy: Biological foundations and clinical applications* (pp. 1–5). New York: Spectrum.

Kjhanna, S., Gangadhar, B. N., Sinha, V., Rajendra, P. N. & Channabasavanna, S. M. (1988). Electroconvulsive therapy in obsessive-compulsive disorder. *Convulsive Therapy,* 4, 314–320.

Kramer, B. A. (1985). Use of ECT in California. *Am. J. Psychiatry,* 142, 1190–1192.

Pitts, F. N., Desmarias, G. M., Stewart, W. & Shaberg, K. (1965). Induction of anesthetic with methohexital and thiopental in electroconvulsive therapy. *N. Engl. J. Med.,* 273, 353–360.

Regestein, Q. R. & Reich, P. (1985). Electroconvulsive therapy in patients at high risk for physical complications. *Convulsive Therapy,* 1,101–114.

Sackeim, H.A. & Mukherjee, S. (1986). Neurophysiological variability in the effects of the ECT stimulus. *Convulsive Therapy,* 2, 267–276.

Squire, L. R. (1986). Memory functions as affected by electroconvulsive therapy. *Ann NY Sci,* 4672, 307–314.

Squire, L. R. (1987). ECT and memory loss. *Am. J. Psychiatry,* 134, 997–1001.

Taylor, M. A. (1982). Indications for electroconvulsive treatment. In R. Abrams & W. Essman (Eds.), *Electroconvulsive therapy: Biological foundations and clinical applications* (pp. 7–40). New York: Spectrum

Weiner, R. D. (1983). ECT in the physically ill. *J. Psychiatr. Treat. Eval.,* 5, 457–462.

Weiner, R.D. & Coffey, C.E.(1986). Minimizing therapeutic differences between bilateral and unilateral nondominant ECT. *Convulsive Therapy,* 2, 261–265.

Weiner, R.D., Rogers, H.J., Davidson, J.R.T. & Squire, L.R. (1986). Effects of stimulus parameters on cognitive side-effects. *Ann NY Acad. Sci,* 462, 315–325.

Welch, C. (1988). Electroconvulsive therapy. *Manual of Psychiatric Treatment,* American Psychiatric Association.

# 12

# Psychopharmacology and Depression

Thomas W. McAllister and Trevor R.P. Price
*University of Pennsylvania*

KEY WORDS: psychopharmacology, antidepressants, monamine oxidase inhibitors, refractory depression

## INTRODUCTION

The use of psychopharmacologic agents to treat depressive syndromes is a broad and complex topic. The fact that there are such agents capable of inducing remission in all but the most refractory depressive disorders has resulted in a great deal of attention directed towards the molecular mechanisms underlying depressive syndromes. This search has proved to be a more complex one than perhaps originally anticipated. Yet the history of what has been learned and almost certainly that which will come to be better understood has been and will be closely linked to a better understanding of the molecular mechanisms of these agents. It should go without saying that the psychosocial context in which any medication is administered must be understood and appreciated if one is to have a complete understanding of "mechanisms of action."

In an attempt to present an update on new developments in the area of the psychopharmacology of depression, this chapter will review basic principles of antidepressant therapy and the standard classes of agents (tricyclic or first generation antidepressants and monoamine oxidase inhibitors), as well as the so-called "second generation" antidepressants. Examination of recent efforts directed towards treatment resistant or refractory depressive syndromes and the theoretical as well as clinical implications raised by these agents and approaches will also be discussed.

## MECHANISMS OF ACTION

Theories about the mechanisms of action of the antidepressants are important not only because of what they reveal about the medications themselves, but also because of what they reveal about the underlying pathophysiology of depressive disorders. Furthermore, better understanding of the presumed mechanisms of action may lead to more rational clinical practice, such as appropriate sequencing of antidepressant trials, and defensible combination approaches in patients with more treatment resistant depressive syndromes.

## Monoamine Deficiency Theory

Like many theories of the etiology of depressive disorders, this one originated in the observation that specific agents with obvious effects on monoamine metabolism could produce dramatic changes in patients with depressive symptoms. Specifically, imipramine (because of certain structural similarities to chlorpromazine) was evaluated for its antipsychotic properties and was observed to have thymoleptic (mood altering) properties (Kuhn, 1958). In addition, the use of drugs with monoamine oxidase inhibiting properties for the treatment of tuberculosis and the observation of their thymoleptic properties (Bloch, Dooneief, Buchberg & Spellman, 1954; Crane, 1957; Selikoff, Robitzek & Ornstein, 1952; Zeller, Barsky, Fouts, Kirchheimer & Van Orden, 1952) resulted in their application to patients with primary depressive disorders (Crane, 1957; Kline, 1958). As more tricyclic antidepressants were developed, the common pharmacologic effect most focused on was the ability to block the pre-synaptic re-uptake of various monoamines, in particular norepinephrine and serotonin. This, in combination with the observed efficacy of MAO inhibitors, led to the general theory of a monoamine deficiency state as the fundamental cause of depression (Schildkraut, 1965). This was further supported by the tendency of Reserpine (which effectively depletes pre-synaptic neurons of catecholamine and indoleamine stores) to induce significant depressive syndromes (Bernstein, 1984).

Unfortunately, study of a variety of measures of monoamine levels, including norepinephrine, dopamine, epinephrine, serotonin, and their primary metabolites in both cerebrospinal fluid and urine have failed to show a consistent "deficit" state (Heninger & Charney, 1987). In fact, monoamine "hyperactivity" has been shown and suggests that the relationship between the monoamine alteration and mood disturbance is likely to be a complex one, more consistent with an imbalance in various monoamine systems interacting with age, sex, menopausal status, and clinical phenomenology as well as other factors rather than a simple deficit (Koslow, Maas, Bowden, Davis, Hanin & Javaid, 1983).

In addition, the significant difference between the time of pharmacological onset versus clinical onset of action, the fact that several potent monoamine re-uptake inhibitors are poor long-term antidepressants (cocaine, amphetamines), and the observation that several of the second generation antidepressants are not re-uptake blockers, add further evidence that the deficit theory is unsatisfactory (Frazer & Brunswick, 1989; Heninger & Charney, 1987; Koslow et al., 1983).

## Monoamine Receptor Alteration Theories

With the elucidation of the problems inherent in a simple "monoamine deficit" theory of depressive illness, attention has turned to potential alterations in monoamine or neuropeptide receptor sensitivity and number. The neurotransmitters thought to be prominently involved in the regulation of mood and affect are numerous and include the catecholamines (norepinephrine and epinephrine), the indoleamine serotonin, acetylcholine, the neuropeptide gamma-aminobutyric acid, and possibly beta-endorphin and its derivatives. Each neurotransmitter has a distinct receptor type, through which the initial step in communication of information between neurons is initiated. Not uncommonly, a given neurotransmitter will actually have two or more subpopulations of receptors which can differ in their location in the brain (e.g., frontal cortex vs brain stem), synaptic location ("pre-synaptic vs post-synaptic"), and specificity for the neurotransmitter or various structural relatives. For example the dominant catecholaminergic receptors (the alpha and beta adrenoreceptors) each have at least two subtypes designated as the alpha1, alpha2, and beta1, beta2 receptors. Alpha1 and alpha2 receptors differ with respect to their affinity for certain agonists and antagonists, as well as their synaptic distribution, with alpha1 receptors occurring almost exclusively postsynaptically, and alpha2 receptors occurring both pre- and postsynaptically. Functional differences are apparent as well, with the presynaptic alpha2 receptors functioning primarily as "autoreceptors," regulating the further release of norepinephrine, and the functions of the other subpopulations being less clear cut (Janowsky & Sulser, 1987). Similar kinds of subpopulations and subtle differences exist as well for many of the other prominent neurotransmitter receptor systems mentioned (see Watson, Roeske & Yamamura, 1987; Creese, 1987; Enna & Mohler, 1987; Green, 1987; Pasternak, 1987; Peroutka, 1987). Alterations in several of these systems are felt to be possibly involved in the mechanism of action of various antidepressants and will be commented on here. (See Charney, Menkes & Heninger, 1981; Frazer & Brunswick, 1989; Frazer & Conway, 1984; Heninger & Charney, 1987, for a more in-depth treatment.)

The generalizations that follow are based largely on evidence from three general models: alteration in norepinephrine induced Cyclic-Adenosine-Monophosphate production in brain slices, single-unit electrophysiologic studies, and alterations in various neurotransmitter binding kinetics. It is helpful to keep in mind that the effect on these systems of any given psychopharmacologic agent is often very different depending on the duration of exposure (i.e., acute vs. chronic administration), as well as whether the receptors are "pre-synaptic" or "post-synaptic" in location.

## Beta Adrenergic Receptor Changes

A variety of observations suggest that Beta adrenergic receptor changes are closely associated with depressive disorders. Reduction of norepinephrine induced Cyclic-Adenosine-Monophosphate production, which is felt to be at least in part a Beta receptor function, has been demonstrated to occur in whole brain slices and shown to be associated with administration of a variety of antidepressant regimens including ECT (Frazer & Conway, 1984; Heninger & Charney, 1987). In addition to Beta receptor mediated physiological effects, Beta receptor density has been shown to be reduced in response to administration of a variety of antidepressants but not most other psychotropic agents (Frazer & Brunswick, 1989; Frazer & Conway, 1984; Heninger & Charney, 1987). Of note is that the time course of these changes is much more consistent with the time course of antidepressant effect in the clinical context than the monoamine re-uptake blockade which of course occurs with the initial dose. Of some interest is that this "down-regulation" of the Beta-adrenergic receptor system appears (in some models) to be at least in part dependent on a functionally intact serotonergic system (Frazer & Conway, 1984; Heninger & Charney, 1987; Janowsky, Okada, Manier, Applegate, Sulser & Steranka, 1982). This suggests a beginning point for understanding the multi-system nature of mood regulation, dysfunction, and treatment. In addition, the observations that *several* antidepressants, in particular those with primarily serotonin uptake blocking properties, do not appear to significantly alter Beta receptor function (Frazer & Brunswick, 1989; Heninger & Charney, 1987) suggest that changes in the Beta adrenergic system cannot account for all the facts.

## Alpha Adrenergic Receptor Changes

Similarly interesting yet less than straightforward findings have been reported with respect to the alpha adrenergic system. From a physiological standpoint, acute administration of many antidepressants results in reduced firing rate of the primary central adrenergic neurons located in the locus ceruleus, almost certainly due to the norepinephrine uptake blockade and subsequent stimulation of an $alpha_1$ type autoreceptor. As with the other receptor systems, longer term exposure to most of the antidepressants attenuates this initial effect, assumably on the basis of alterations in alpha receptor sensitivity. This does not appear to be associated with consistent changes in the number or density of $alpha_1$ or $alpha_2$ receptors (Charney et al., 1981; Frazer & Brunswick, 1989; Frazer & Conway, 1984).

## 5HT (Serotonin) Receptor Changes

Alterations in the 5HT system are again variable depending on the population of receptors studied, the length of exposure to drug, and the experimental model being used. Thus, $5HT_1$ receptor density seems only inconsistently altered. $5HT_2$ receptors (localized mainly in cortical regions), however, are fairly consistently decreased with long-term exposure to most antidepressants (except ECT). Despite this, neurophysiological response to 5HT appears overall to be enhanced by chronic exposure to most antidepressant drugs. The net effect of chronic exposure may be to facilitate 5HT mediated transmission by a combination of pre-synaptic "down-regulation" of 5HT autoreceptors and to a somewhat lesser degree a concomitant decrease in post-synaptic sensitivity (Charney et al., 1981; Frazer & Brunswick, 1989; Frazer & Conway, 1984; Heninger & Charney, 1987).

## Opiate System Changes

Changes in various aspects of the endogenous opioid system also suggest some potential involvement in the mechanisms of antidepressant action and depressive pathophysiology. Although less research has been directed to this area, it appears that certain opiate derivatives have thymoleptic properties (apart from the usual short-term euphorogenic effects) and some depressives show evidence of opiate receptor subsensitivity (Emrich, Gunther & Dose, 1983). Various changes associated with ECT, including changes (decreased sensitivity) of opioid receptors (Emrich et al., 1983; Heninger & Charney, 1987), also suggest that the opiate system may play a role in the pathophysiology of affective disorders and their treatment.

## Gamma Aminobutyric Acid (GABA) System Changes

Evidence for alterations in GABA systems is less forthcoming. However, the demonstration that several antidepressants, as well as ECT, are associated with an increase in GABA receptor number or sensitivity in certain animal models has stimulated further interest (Heninger & Charney, 1987; Lloyd, Thuret & Pilc, 1985). Furthermore, the "anti-manic" effects associated with certain medications (Propranolol, Lithium, Valproic acid) may be related in part to their stimulation of the GABA system (Emrich et al., 1983).

### Other Receptor Changes

In addition to the changes summarized so far, a variety of other systems are significantly influenced by a variety of antidepressant interventions including the cholinergic, histaminic and dopaminergic systems. The potent cholinergic and $H_1$ histamine receptor antagonist properties of most of the first generation antidepressants have been considered to be related to the generation of side effects rather than any thymoleptic effect (Baldessarini, 1985; Frazer & Brunswick, 1989) . The role of the dopaminergic system remains unclear, with down-regulation of pre-synaptic dopamine receptors occurring with longer term administration of several antidepressants and ECT, and inconsistent findings with regard to changes in receptor density (Heninger & Charney, 1987).

Work is also ongoing evaluating the potential roles of various neuropeptides including Substance P and Thyrotropin Releasing Hormone (TRH) (Heninger & Charney, 1987).

### Summary

As should be clear from the foregoing discussion, the many pharmacotherapeutic agents capable of effecting alleviation of depressive symptoms have provided exciting glimpses into the molecular mechanisms involved in depressive disorders. However, it is clear that the story is a complex one, and quite inconsistent with conceptual schemes involving only single "deficit states." It is probably safe to summarize the current conceptual schemes as follows:

- At this time there is no single mechanism which all effective antidepressant regimens share in common.
- Alterations in monoamine transmission (through a variety of mechanisms including changes in receptor sensitivity, receptor density, or effects on a "second messenger") is a final common pathway in virtually all effective antidepressant agents.
- There is no single monoamine system which can be shown to be consistently altered by all effective antidepressant agents.
- Alterations in Beta adrenergic receptor sensitivity (pre-synaptic down-regulation), alpha adrenergic receptor sensitivity, and serotonergic receptor sensitivity (post-synaptic enhancement) appear to be the most consistent changes associated with antidepressant administration and occur over a time course consistent with that seen clinically.

## Table 12–1: First Generation Antidepressants

| Names | Absorption/ Metabolism | Most Common Clinically Significant Side Effects |
|---|---|---|
| Imipramine<br>Desipramine<br><br>Amitriptyline<br>Nortriptyline<br><br>Protriptyline<br><br>Doxepin<br>Trimipramine | • Rapid from G.I. tract<br><br>• Significant and variable<br>• Hepatic "first pass" effects<br><br>• Demethylation & hydroxylation in liver<br><br>• Excretion in Urine<br><br>• Some active metabolites<br><br>• Elimination half-life varies significantly | *Anti-Muscarinic*<br>• dry mouth<br>• blurred vision<br>Tachycardia<br>• constipation<br>• urinary retention<br><br>*Anti-Histaminic*<br>• sedation<br><br>*Cardiovascular*<br>• orthosatatic hypotension<br>• prolongation of P-R interval<br>• tachycardia<br><br>*Other*<br>• lowered seizure threshold<br>• altered sexual function<br>• precipitation of manic episode |

## PSYCHOPHARMACOLOGIC AGENTS

### First Generation ("Tricyclic") Antidepressants

In addition to the various effects that these agents have on important CNS neurotransmitter systems, it is worth briefly outlining some other characteristics of these agents (See Frazer & Brunswick, 1989), especially as they relate to clinical practice.

As mentioned previously, Imipramine, which in many ways is the prototypic TCA, was synthesized in an attempt to find a new antipsychotic agent. As such it shares certain structural features in common with the phenothiazines, having a central seven-member ring attached to two benzene rings and a tertiary amine side chain attached to the central ring. The other six first generation antidepressants in common practice (Amitriptyline, Trimipramine, Doxepin, Desipramine, Nortriptyline, Protriptyline) are very similar, varying primarily in the structure of the side chain. Of particular note clinically is that Desipramine and Nortriptyline are demethylated metabolites of Imipramine and Amitriptyline respectively.

These agents are associated with a number of potentially troublesome side effects (see Table 12-1). Again, because of the immense inter-individual differences in metabolic rate, these side effects can be seen across a very wide range of dosing schedules. In addition, certain populations such as the elderly and those with pre-existing cerebral dysfunction are particularly susceptible to all of these side effects even at very low doses.

One of the most consistently shared characteristics among the first generation antidepressants are the anti-muscarinic and antihistaminic (acetylcholine and Histamine $H_1$ receptor blocking) effects. Though apparently unrelated to antidepressant capabilities, these properties are responsible for the most common side effects.

Though the intensity of antimuscarinic effects does vary from agent to agent, all of the commonly used agents are capable of producing clinically meaningful anticholinergic side effects such as dry mouth, blurred vision, tachycardia, constipation and urinary hesitancy or even acute urinary retention. Desipramine and Nortriptyline are less likely to produce as intense anticholinergic effects as the other first generation agents.

Sedation is another common side effect, due probably to the antihistaminic properties of these agents. Amitriptyline and Doxepin are particularly likely to be associated with significant sedation, whereas Protriptyline is often described as an "activating" antidepressant.

From a cardiovascular standpoint, orthostatic hypotension (probably related to $alpha_1$ adrenergic receptor blocking properties) and alterations in cardiac conductivity are the most prominent side effects. The latter is at least largely dose related in that in the usual antidepressant doses (and serum levels) these agents have an *antiarrhythmic* profile similar to Quinidine and other similar antiarrhythmics. At higher serum levels prolongation of the P-R interval, other conduction disturbances, and ventricular irritability are seen (Glassman, Roose, Giardina & Bigger, 1987; Jackson, Roose & Glassman, 1987).

## Monoamine Oxidase Inhibitors (MAOIs)

In the past five to ten years there has been a resurgence of interest in the MAOIs based on the growing recognition of several factors (Pare, 1987). First, that higher than initially recommended doses, at least sufficient to achieve 85% inhibition of platelet MAO activity, are necessary for a full therapeutic effect. Second, these drugs are safe, even in the elderly and medically ill, when appropriate dietary restrictions are observed and potentially dangerous drug-drug interactions are avoided. Third, that they may be effective in certain patients when other antidepressant treatments, including ECT, have failed.

Placebo-controlled studies have most consistently demonstrated the high degree of efficacy of MAOIs in patients with "atypical" depressions, especially those with associated panic disorder or prominent anxiety symptoms. Variable efficacy has been reported in patients with endogenomorphic depressions, and their role in these disorders has not as yet been clearly nor fully delineated. Recent comparative studies have suggested that first generation antidepressants and MAOIs probably have equivalent antidepressant effects, while the MAOIs are significantly more effective against anxiety symptoms (Murphy, Sunderland & Cohen, 1984A). Other studies using crossover designs have suggested that some depressed patients respond specifically and preferentially to first generation antidepressants or MAOIs but not to both. Further, a majority of patients who have failed to respond to first generation antidepressants, ECT, and even the newer second generation antidepressants, do respond to MAOIs (Pare, 1985).

### Mechanism of Action

All of the MAOIs are believed to have antidepressant activity by virtue of their

| TABLE 12–2: Monoamine Oxidase Inhibitors | | |
|---|---|---|
| Categories/Names | Absorption/Metabolism General | Clinical Points General |
| Hydrazine<br><br>Phenelzine (Nardil)<br>Isocarboxazid (Marplan)<br><br><br><br><br>Non-Hydrazine<br>  Tranylcypromine<br>    (Parnate)<br>  Pargyline (Eutonyl)<br><br>Selective MAO A<br>Inhibition<br>  Clorgyline<br><br>Selective MAO B<br>Inhibition<br>  Pargyline (Eutonyl)<br>  L-Deprenyl<br><br>Non-Selective<br>  Pehnelzine<br>  Tranylcypromine<br>  Isocarboxazid | • Rapid GI Absorption<br><br>• Peak Plasma levels<br>  60-120 minutes<br>• Rapid Elimination<br>  half-life (2 hours)<br>• Irreversible binding to<br>  intra-cellular MAO | • Sometimes require doses<br>  in excess of usual<br>  recommended range<br><br>• Use requires strict<br>  adherence to tyramine<br>  free diet and avoidance<br>  of sympathomimetics<br><br>• Can be cautiously used<br>  in combination with<br>  TCA's or Li |

ability to inhibit the inactivation of critical CNS biogenic monoamines, including serotonin, dopamine, and norepinephrine. This effect rapidly and acutely leads to increased levels of these biogenic amines in the brain. However, the usual delay of two to three weeks in the appearance of a clinically significant antidepressant response suggests that this response is related, not to the acute changes in monoamine levels, but rather to delayed, adaptive biochemical effects resulting from them.

As Murphy et al. (1984) note, these effects are believed to be related primarily to delayed down-regulation (a decrease in number and/or functional activity of the receptors involved) of central alpha and beta noradrenergic receptors. Thus, the weight of currently available evidence suggests that the antidepressant effect of MAOIs results from secondary, delayed reduction in central noradrenergic activity rather than acute, primary increases in catecholamine levels in the CNS.

## General Pharmacology

There are two general types of MAOIs currently available for clinical use in the U.S. They are the hydrazine and non-hydrazine MAOIs. The former include phenelzine (Nardil) and isocarboxazid (Marplan); the latter, tranylcypromine (Parnate) and pargyline (Eutonyl). (see Table 12-2)

There are two kinds of MAO enzymes, Type A and Type B. They differ with respect to where they occur in the body, the biogenic amine substrates on which they act, and the types of drugs which specifically inhibit their biochemical activity. In humans, MAO in the intestinal tract is predominantly Type A, that in platelets is Type B, while brain MAO is of both types, though 75% is believed to be Type B (Pare, 1985; Robinson & Kurtz, 1987). Type A MAO preferentially inactivates norepinephrine, serotonin, and tyramine; while Type B preferentially inactivates phenylethylamine, benzylamine, and dopamine (Dowson, 1987; Silver & Yudofsky, 1988; Tollefson, 1983). The major antidepressant effect of MAOIs in en-dogenomorphic depressions has been suggested to be associated with Type A MAO inhibition (Murphy et al., 1981), while it has been suggested that Type B MAO inhibition (Mann, Frances, Kaplan, Kocsis, Peselow & Gershon, 1982) may mediate the antidepressant effect in non-endogenous depression.

### Pharmacokinetics and Pharmacodynamics

Following oral administration, MAOIs are, in general, rapidly absorbed with peak plasma levels occurring between 60 and 120 minutes. They are also rapidly cleared from plasma, having a half-time of elimination of less than two hours (Robinson & Kurtz, 1987). There are no predictable nor clinically meaningful rela-tionships between the biological and pharmacological effects of the MAOIs and their plasma levels. In the past it had been suggested by some (Johnstone, 1976) that fast or slow "acetylator status" might have a significant relationship to the relative efficacy of these drugs, but recent data suggesting that MAOIs such as phenelzine are metabolized principally via oxidative metabolism rather than acetylation, argues strongly against this (Robinson & Kurtz, 1987).

### Dosage

While plasma or serum levels of MAOIs do not correlate with therapeutic re-sponse, doses of phenelzine sufficient to inhibit from 80–85% of platelet MAO (Type B) activity in *in vitro* laboratory assays produce significant antidepressant and anti-anxiety effects; whereas, doses that produce 60% or less of platelet MAO inhibition are associated with poor antidepressant and anti-anxiety. It is important to emphasize that this is not a general phenomenon with all MAOIs. It has only been clearly established for phenelzine.

In clinical practice, it has been found that initially recommended doses of MAOIs frequently have not achieved optimal results in some patients, and that larger doses often are both necessary and well-tolerated (Pare, 1985; Quitkin, Rifkin & Klein, 1979; Guze, Baxter & Rego, 1987).

### Side Effects—Minor

There are side effects which though unpleasantly symptomatic are generally neither serious nor life threatening (see Table 12-3). In fact, they usually subside during the first two to four weeks of treatment. The most common of these is orthostatic hypotension (sudden lowering of blood pressure in response to postural changes) which usually develops slowly and often reaches its maximum severity only after two or more weeks of treatment. (See table)

| TABLE 12–3: Monoamine Oxidase Inhibitors | |
|---|---|
| "Minor" Side Effects | "Major" Side Effects |
| • Arousal & insomnia<br><br>• REM Suppression<br><br>• REM Rebound<br><br>• Dry Mouth<br><br>• Constipation<br><br>• Sexual Dysfunction<br><br>• Weight gain/hyperphagia<br><br>• Peripheral edema<br><br>• Orthostatic Hypotension<br><br>• Precipation of Manic Episode | • Hepato-Cellular Damage<br><br>• Hypertensive Crisis<br><br>• Drug-Drug Interactions<br>  • Sympathomimetics (e.g. "diet pills")<br><br>• Accentuation of Anti-hypertensives<br>  • CNS Depressants<br>  • Anticholinergic Agents<br>  • Oral Hypoglycemics<br><br>• Overdose<br>  • high lethality<br>  • toxicity appears up to 12 hrs. after<br>    ingestion |

### Side Effects—Major

As Sheehan et al. (1980–81), Tollefson (1983) and Murphy et al. (1984) suggest, the major side effects which can be seen include: hepatotoxicity, the tyramine-mediated hypertensive crises (the so-called "cheese reaction"), and other serious drug-drug interactions, each of which will be discussed in turn.

### Hepatotoxicity

Unlike the cholestatic jaundice that occurs with TCAs, the hepatotoxicity with the MAOIs, especially with iproniazid before its abandonment, was associated with hepato-cellular damage and a high degree of lethality. This hepatotoxicity is believed to be due to the free hydrazine group, and thus, liver complications are likely to be seen more frequently in hydrazine as opposed to non-hydrazine MAOIs (Sheehan et al., 1980–81).

### Hypertensive Crisis—"The Cheese Reaction"

When patients who are taking MAOIs ingest foods rich in tyramine, a sympathomimetic pressor amine, which is present in a variety of foods and beverages in significant amounts, they may experience a number of alarming and potentially dangerous symptoms. These include: a severe, throbbing headache, nausea and vomiting, flushing, photophobia, profuse sweating, markedly elevated blood pressure, palpitations, cardiac arrhythmias, and elevated temperature. These symptoms come on suddenly, usually within a few minutes to an hour or two, after the ingestion of fermented, overly ripe, or aged foods, such as cheeses (hence the colloquial name of the reaction), which are rich in tyramine, progress rapidly in severity, and may last as long as several hours. Caused by the unimpeded absorption of tyramine as a result of the inhibition of intestinal and liver MAO enzymes which would normally break tyramine down and prevent its absorption and the occurrence of such symptoms, such hypertensive crises can cause cerebrovascular accidents (CVAs), cardiovascular complications, and death.

There have been a small number of well-documented "spontaneous," i.e., non-dietary-tyramine-precipitated hypertensive episodes reported in the literature (Fallon, Foote, Walsh & Roose, 1988).

### Drug-Drug Interactions

MAOIs inhibit the activity of a number of other enzymes involved in the metabolism of a variety of drugs in addition to MAO. Thus, many different kinds of drug-drug interactions involving the MAOIs are possible. An in-depth discussion of this is beyond the scope of this chapter but relevant reviews are available (Gaultieri & Powell, 1978; Zisook, 1985).

## Second Generation Antidepressants

Numerous agents have been developed and tested for antidepressant efficacy which differ from the traditional tricyclic antidepressants and monoamine oxidase inhibitors in numerous ways including putative mechanisms of action, chemical structure and side effect profiles (see Table 12-4). Although usually considered together and referred to as "atypical" or "second generation" antidepressants, they are not a homogeneous group and differ in important ways not only from the "first generation" agents but from each other as well. (See Asberg, Eriksson, Martensson, Traskman-Bendz & Wagner, 1986; Awad, 1987; Cole, 1988; Frazer & Brunswick, 1989; Mendels, 1987; Pi & Simpson, 1985; Schatzberg, Dessain, O'Neil, Katz & Cole, 1987, for recent discussions.)

### Serotonin Re-uptake Inhibitors

Much attention has been directed to the role of serotonin in the etiology of mood disorders. This interest follows from several observations, including aforementioned changes in the primary serotonin metabolite 5HIAA, differences in regional brain serotonin levels between suicide victims and controls, changes in platelet serotonin transport in depressives compared with controls, as well as the known effects of standard first generation tricyclic antidepressants on serotonin re-uptake as discussed earlier (Asberg et al., 1986; Awad, 1987; Cochran, Robins & Grote, 1976; Lapin & Oxenkrug, 1969; Lloyd, Farley, Deck & Hornykiewicz, 1974; Pare, Yeung, Price & Stacey, 1969).

The psychopharmacological fallout of this interest in serotonin's putative role in affective disorders has been the development of several compounds with relatively pure effects on inhibition of serotonin re-uptake. The relative therapeutic efficacy in depressive illness and the side effect profiles of these agents are quite similar and are thus considered together.

Of the numerous agents in this class (which include Zimelidine, Citalopram, Sertraline, Fluvoxamine, Paroxetene, Fluoxetine) only Fluoxetine is currently clini-

| TABLE 12–4: Second Generation Antidepressants | | | |
|---|---|---|---|
| *Category/Name* | *Therapeutic Efficacy* | *Common Side Effects* | *Other* |
| *Sertonin-Re-Uptake Inhibitors*<br>• Zimelidine<br>• Setraline<br>• Citalopram<br>• Fluoxetine<br>• Fluvoxamine | Probably Same As First Generation Agents | •Insomnia/ "Activation"<br>• Headache<br>• Nausea<br>• Anorexia/Weight Loss<br>• Very Little Anticholinergic Effect<br>• Very Little Cardiotoxicity | • Rapid GI Absorption<br>• Less "First Pass" effect<br>• Once Daily Dosing |
| *Other*<br><br>Trazodone | Probably Same As First Generation Agents | • Sedation<br>• Priapism<br>• Very Little Anticholinergic Effect | • Dose Range Approximately Twice That of Imipramine |
| Maprotiline | Probably Same As First Generation Agents | • Sedation<br>• Probable Higher Risk of Seizure Development or Exacerbation | • Fairly Selective Noradrenergic Re-uptake Inhibition<br>• Long Half-Life |
| Amoxapine | Probably Same As First Generation Agents | • Concern About Typical Neuroleptic Side Effects | • Neuroleptic ($D_2$ Doramine Receptor Blocking) Activity |

cally available in the United States.

From a structural standpoint, these agents are quite variable, with Fluvoxamine being a "unicyclic"; Fluoxetine and Zimelidine bicyclics; and Sertraline, Citalopram, and Paroxetene being tricyclics. Despite this structural heterogeneity, all are relatively pure serotonin re-uptake inhibitors.

With respect to relative antidepressant efficacy, these agents have been studied in a variety of settings and study designs. The most common interpretation of the data would suggest that there is no significant difference between these agents and the "first generation" antidepressants, with expected antidepressant response rates in the 50–75% range in both groups, and both groups showing a consistent statistically and clinically significant advantage with respect to placebo (Asberg et al., 1986; Awad, 1987; Mendels, 1987; Schatzberg et al., 1987).

Probably in large measure related to their relatively little known effects on other major neurotransmitter systems, these agents do differ significantly from first generation antidepressants with respect to their side effect profile. In particular, they have a marked absence of antimuscarinic mediated effects such as dry mouth, blurred vision, and constipation. They have little in the way of cardiotoxicity and as such may be somewhat safer in an overdose setting. Statistically significant, though probably not clinically significant, decreases in heart rate have been reported (Asberg et al., 1986; Mendels, 1987). In addition, they have less propensity to induce clinically significant orthostatic hypotension, which can be of great importance in certain medically ill patients and the elderly.

The major side effects encountered with the serotonin uptake inhibitors are insomnia, headache, nervousness or agitation ("activation"), diarrhea, nausea, and vomiting. Perhaps related to these last two effects, several of these agents have been associated with weight loss and in fact are being studied as potential adjunctive anorectic agents in the management of obesity.

## Other Second Generation Antidepressants

These agents represent, if anything, an even more heterogeneous group of drugs whose major common point is simply that they were developed subsequent to the first generation antidepressants and MAOIs. They do not have a similar spectrum of effects on the major neurotransmitter systems, nor do they inhibit monoamine oxidase. The three clinically available agents Trazodone, Amoxapine, and Maprotiline will be considered separately.

### Trazodone

Trazodone, a phenylpiperazine derivative, is frequently included in discussions of Serotonin Re-uptake inhibitors because it does in fact have this effect in vitro. However, Trazodone may also function as a serotonin antagonist (at least in certain concentrations) and as such the net effect on serotonergic transmission may be somewhat variable (Awad, 1987; Fuller & Wong, 1985; Wander, Nelson, Okazaki & Richelson, 1986). In addition, it appears to have some affinity for $alpha_1$ and $alpha_2$ adrenergic receptors, which may account for some of the common side effects mentioned below.

Efficacy studies have been reviewed by Schatzberg et al. (1987) and Asberg et al. (1986) and once again suggest in aggregate that Trazodone does not differ significantly from first generation antidepressants if used in appropriate doses (approximately twice the usual dose for such agents as Imipramine and Amitriptyline).

Trazodone has a rather unique side effect profile with little of the anticholinergic effects of the first generation TCAs, and little of the gastrointestinal effects of the serotonin re-uptake inhibitors. It is usually markedly sedating and also can cause priapism (Scher, Krieger & Juergens, 1983).

### Maprotiline

Maprotiline shares much in common with the first generation antidepressants from a variety of perspectives. Structurally, it is usually referred to as a tetracyclic compared with the three rings of the latter group (Frazer & Brunswick, 1989).

Maprotiline is widely regarded as having fairly selective and potent noradrenergic re-uptake inhibitory effects (Pi & Simpson, 1985; Pinder, Brogden, Speight & Avery, 1977), though as pointed out earlier this is not necessarily how it exerts its antidepressant effects. It has nonetheless been used in several studies contrasting relatively pure serotonin re-uptake inhibitors with Maprotiline, representing a "pure" noradrenergic re-uptake inhibitor (Benkelfat, Poirier, Leouffre, Gay & Loo, 1987; Bouchard et al., 1987; Nystrom & Hallstrom, 1987; Nystrom, Ross, Hallstrom & Kelder, 1986; Timmerman et al., 1987).

From a clinical standpoint, as with the other second generation antidepressants, there appears to be no significant difference in efficacy between Maprotiline and other agents. It is also well absorbed from the gastrointestinal tract and has a fairly long half-life, ranging as high as 100 hours (Frazer & Brunswick, 1989).

Perhaps, because of the relatively pure noradrenergic profile, it has less anticholinergic effects but can be somewhat sedating and appears to carry a somewhat higher risk of seizure development, especially in the context of relative or absolute overdosing or in patients with pre-existing irritative features on EEG (Dessain, Schatzberg, Woods & Cole, 1986; Frazer & Brunswick, 1989).

*Amoxapine*

Amoxapine is perhaps most notable for being a structural relative of Loxapine, a compound with significant dopamine receptor blocking capability and used clinically as an antipsychotic agent. Amoxapine does have neuroleptic-like activity in vivo (due to its $D_2$ dopamine receptor blocking capability), being associated with elevated serum prolactin levels and galactorrhea, as well as other clinical side effects usually associated with neuroleptic agents or dopamine insufficiency such as akathisia, dystonic reactions, Parkinsonism, and reversible cognitive impairment (Burns & Tune, 1987; Luna, Jayatilaka & Walker, 1984; Sunderland, Orsulak & Cohen, 1983). In addition, a withdrawal dyskinesia has been described with Amoxapine, leading to the very real concern that its prolonged use could result in the development of tardive dyskinesia (Lesser, 1983).

In addition, although some depressed patients may show alleviation of some antidepressant symptoms within only a few days of initiation of treatment with Amoxapine, this is not generally the case. It may even be that patients treated with Amoxapine are more likely to suffer recurrence of some depressive symptoms in their course of treatment than is true with other agents (Cole, 1988).

## Choice of Agent

Given the similarity in therapeutic efficacy between the major classes of agents, choice of antidepressant agent is usually governed by the clinician's choice as to which side effect profile is likely to be best tolerated in a given patient, past history of response or lack thereof to given agents, or even a family history of such response. A patient's willingness to tolerate the necessary dietary restrictions with MAOIs is also an important factor.

In general, once it is determined that a given agent is not effective, alternate agents from other classes should be tried in an orderly, sequential fashion.

## GENERAL QUESTIONS RELATING TO
## PHARMACOTHERAPY AND DEPRESSION

### Who Gets Better?

It is quite clear from an array of studies over the last 20–30 years that the various pharmacologic agents discussed in this chapter are significantly more effective than placebo in alleviating the symptoms of depressive illness. (See Brotman, Falk & Gelenberg, 1987; Davis, Klerman & Schildkraut, 1968; Kessler, 1978.) However, one of the more consistent findings in this field is that, depending on the definition chosen for antidepressant response, anywhere from 25% to 50% of depressives *do not* respond to an antidepressant trial. Thus, it becomes important clinically and theoretically to identify factors which are closely associated with response or non-response. Unfortunately, most of the studies in this area have addressed the question of what predicts response to tricyclic (almost exclusively first generation) antidepressants, and in fact primarily the tertiary amine agents. Much less work has been done on the MAOIs, and even less on the second generation agents.

### Demographic Factors

A variety of very basic demographic variables have been examined as predictors of first generation antidepressants. (For a thorough review, see Bielski & Friedel, 1976.) Based on their review of the relevant studies, Bielski and Friedel suggested that higher socioeconomic status was associated with tricyclic response. Surprisingly, such basic variables as age and sex are not thoroughly studied. A more recent study controlling for variables such as socioeconomic status, and excluding patients with delusional or other psychotic symptoms (see below) found that patients over age 50 had a poorer response rate than their younger colleagues, despite a longer medication trial (Brown, Sweeney, Frances, Kocsis & Loutsch, 1983).

### Clinical Presentation

Several associated clinical features have emerged as being helpful predictors of response to at least the first generation antidepressants.

### *Duration of Episode*

The duration of depressive symptoms has been found to be inconsistently associated with patterns of response, with some finding that short duration is a good predictor of AD response and others finding much the opposite (Downing & Rickels, 1973; Paykel, Prusoff, Klerman, Haskell & DiMascio, 1973). Conclusions about this question are confounded by studies which used different definitions of long or short duration, questions of diagnosis, and whether the populations studied were inpatients or outpatients (Bielski & Friedel, 1976). Looking at more extreme ends of this dichotomy, it would appear that patients with either very short (a few weeks) or very long (two years or more) duration of symptoms (Bielski & Friedel, 1976; Brotman et al., 1987) appear to respond less well to medications. This appears to be particularly true of those patients who develop the picture of a major depressive episode in the context of a virtual life-long history of low grade depressive symptoms (Akiskal, Rosenthal, Haykal, Lemmi, Rosenthal & Scott-Strauss, 1980; Extein, Gold & Pottash, 1984).

## Associated Symptoms

Another area which is of great clinical importance are those individuals who in addition to the "core" symptoms of depression, suffer from a variety of associated clinical phenomena or personality styles. Once again, issues of definition are most difficult to sort through and the literature contains lots of characterizations such as "atypical," "neurotic," "exogenous," "hysterical," etc., all of which can have significantly different meanings while being difficult to measure or operationalize. However, there remains a fairly strong sense in the literature that the greater the preponderance of hypochondriacal, "neurotic," "hysterical," or "atypical" features manifested, the less likely a full antidepressant response is to occur. What is less clear is whether this is because the persistence of these more chronic, usually trait-related features is masking a genuine response in the core depressive symptoms (Bielski & Friedel, 1976; Brotman et al., 1987).

## "Core" Symptoms

In addition to the above described associated factors, it is important to consider the core symptoms of the depressive syndromes and ask whether specific symptoms, or symptom clusters can assist in prediction of response to pharmacotherapy. The answer would appear to be a qualified yes.

As was implied in the observation that those with atypical, "reactive," or "neurotic" features had a lower percentage response, those with a more "endogenous" picture are more likely to respond. This term is usually meant to describe those patients with more pronounced neurovegetative signs and symptoms (change in weight, sleep pattern, libido, energy level, etc.). Although the term implies an emphasis on the absence of a clear precipitating event (from a psychological standpoint), this is of much less importance than some of the neurovegetative symptoms from the standpoint of predicting antidepressant response. Specifically, sleep disturbance (especially mid-cycle and late cycle awakenings), psychomotor disturbances (either retardation or agitation), as well as increasing global severity of symptoms (to a point) are predictive of better response to the first generation antidepressants (Abou-Selah & Coppen, 1983; Bielski & Friedel, 1976; Brotman et al., 1987; Extein et al., 1984; Rama Rao & Coppen, 1979).

Perhaps of greatest significance from the standpoint of predicting response to antidepressants alone is the presence or absence of associated delusions. The observation that depressed patients with mood congruent delusions ("delusional depression," "psychotic depression") respond very poorly to antidepressants alone and require ECT or combination antidepressant and antipsychotic regimens is one of the most consistent findings in this area in the past ten years (Brown, Frances, Kocsis & Mann, 1982; Charney & Nelson, 1981; Clower, 1983; Glassman, Kantor & Shostak, 1975; Hirschfeld & Cross, 1987; Kantor & Glassman, 1977; Minter & Mandel, 1979; Nelson & Bowers, 1978; Spiker et al., 1985).

## Rate of Response

In addition to specific symptoms and symptom clusters which appear to predict antidepressant benefit, it would appear that early response to medication may well predict final outcome in many depressives. The usual teaching has been to consider four to six weeks an adequate duration before concluding whether a given agent is efficacious in a given individual. Further, as discussed previously, clinical response to an antidepressant was felt to take at least 10–14 days. This in fact was an important part of the rejection of the monoamine re-uptake blockade theory as the sole mechanism of antidepressant action. Quitkin, Rabkin, Ross, and McGrath (1984) suggested, from a review of the literature and their own clinical experience, that a significant percentage of patients on a variety of antidepressants, who are rated as unimproved after four weeks of medication, will show important clinical improvement subsequent to that (weeks 4–6) compared with placebo treated patients.

However, Coryell, Coppen, Zeigler, and Biggs (1982) reported that, at least in certain groups of depressives, significant improvement in symptoms at the end of two weeks of treatment was predictive of overall response at the end of four weeks. Furthermore, a recent report from the National Institute of Mental Health (NIMH) collaborative study on depression (Katz, Koslow, Maas, Frazer, Bowden, Casper, Croughn, Kocsis & Redmond, 1987) strongly suggests that in severely ill, hospitalized depressives, significant improvement in certain core depressive symptoms (sleep disturbance, anxiety, depressed mood, cognitive impairment, disturbed affect) occurs in the first week of treatment and that *some* of these changes are strongly predictive of response at the end of four weeks. In addition to the important clinical implications of this data, significant questions about the timing of antidepressant action and thus putative mechanisms of action of these agents are raised.

## Laboratory Tests For Antidepressant Response

Although much interest has been directed towards the finding of laboratory tests which might aid in prediction of response to antidepressants, there are none which have clearly emerged which add significantly to the clinical predictors discussed above. (See Bielski & Friedel, 1976; and Brotman et al., 1987, for discussion.)

### Serum Antidepressant Levels

For obvious reasons, attempts have been made to correlate serum levels of antidepressants and their active metabolites with clinical response. This remains an area of some controversy, especially given the increasingly widespread practice of frequent monitoring of serum drug levels.

Although "therapeutic" levels have been reported for virtually all of the first and second generation agents, these are, with the exception of Nortriptyline, and probably Desipramine and Imipramine, largely meaningless. (See American Psychiatric Association [APA] Task Force Report (APA Task Force on the Use of Laboratory Tests in Psychiatry, 1985) for extensive review.)

From a clinical standpoint these levels are best used in patients who are experiencing significant side effects at seemingly low doses, not achieving a clinical response after an appropriate period of time at usually therapeutic doses, and perhaps in certain instances to monitor compliance.

## Neuroendocrine Tests

The most carefully studied of these tests are of course the Dexamethasone Suppression Test (DST) and the Thyrotropin Releasing Hormone infusion test. Consistent abnormalities have been described in significant percentages of depressed patients for both tests. The implications of an abnormal response to either test, however, for likelihood of response to drug therapy, or particular class of drug, have been disappointing.

With respect to the DST, there is some evidence to suggest that depressives who do not suppress (abnormal DST) prior to treatment have a greater likelihood of medication response (Brotman, Falk, Gelenberg, 1987). However, the evidence is certainly not robust enough to make DST status a significant factor in deciding whether or not a given individual should have a medication trial (Brotman, Falk, Gelenberg, 1987; Simon, Evans & Nemeroff, 1987).

Of further interest are the studies addressing whether the DST might be important with regard to which antidepressant agent to choose. It has been suggested that DST non-suppression might be secondary to a relative noradrenergic deficiency state, and that patients with abnormal DSTs might be more likely to respond to noradrenergic enhancing agents relative to "serotonergic" agents. Although initial evidence suggested this might be true, subsequent studies do not appear to have borne this out (Benkelfat, Poirier, Leouffre, Gay, Loo, 1987; Brown, Haier & Qualls, 1980; Steardo, Barone, Monteleone, Iovino & Cardone, 1987).

Although a "blunted" (diminished) TSH response to an injection of TRH occurs in probably 25–30% of those with a major depressive disorder (Loosen & Prange, 1982), the implications for treatment are not clarified. Early relapse and a slower response have been reported (Brotman et al., 1987), and implications for combination antidepressant and thyroid supplementation are being studied.

## Neurotransmitter System Markers

Another strategy used to identify subgroups of depressive drug responders has been to attempt to correlate pretreatment levels of various monoamines and their primary metabolites in urine, serum, or CSF. This has of course been closely connected in its theoretical underpinnings with assumed mechanisms of antidepressant action, and the results are essentially as tantalizing as they are consistently unclear.

Initial work (Maas, 1975) suggested fairly consistently that there might be two major "biochemical" subgroups of depressives, corresponding to either norepinephrine or serotonin deficit states respectively. The former group was characterized by low or normal urinary MHPG levels, initial affective response to stimulant challenge paradigms, and a good response to antidepressants such as Imipramine and Desipramine, which have prominent norepinephrine re-uptake blocking capabilities. The latter group tended to have normal or high urinary MHPG levels, little or no response to stimulant challenge, and be less likely to respond to Imipramine or Desipramine, but tended to respond to Amitriptyline. Some of the studies were not placebo controlled, did not account for some of the clinical factors (already described) which are predictive of response, and did not adequately address diet and activity levels, both of which can affect the pertinent biochemical factors (Bielski & Friedel, 1976).

Subsequent studies have failed to show a significant relationship between urinary MHPG levels and drug response in general, or specific noradrenergic spectrum vs. serotonergic spectrum agents, except perhaps in bipolar patients (Brotman et al., 1987; Loo et al., 1986A). This has also been the case with CSF metabolites (Timmerman et al., 1987). More recent attempts to correlate response to maprotiline and the serotonin re-uptake blocker Indalpine to serum norepinephrine metabolite levels have also been unsuccessful (Loo et al., 1986B).

Different methods for assessing subtle changes in specific neurotransmitter systems, including inhibition of $C^{14}$ labeled serotonin and ($^{14}C$–5-HT) $^{3}H$ labeled norepinephrine accumulation in rat synaptosome preparations in the presence of patient serum are being investigated. One such recent study suggests that, at least in depressed women, changes in $^{14}C$–5-HT might correlate with clinical response to a serotonin re-uptake blocking agent (Nystrom et al., 1986).

Other potential markers, including certain changes in sleep architecture and various stimulant challenge paradigms, have also been proposed as potential predictors of medication response. (See Brotman et al., 1987.)

## ISSUES IN THE MANAGEMENT OF RESISTANT AND REFRACTORY DEPRESSION

### Identification

An important problem in the drug treatment of depression is that of refractory depression, i.e., a major depressive disorder, refractory to treatment trials with standard antidepressant drugs, given in adequate doses, for adequate periods of time. The consensus in the literature considers a fully adequate trial as being the administration of an antidepressant in doses equivalent to 250–300 mgm. per day of imipramine, over a period of at least four, and preferably six, weeks with at least two weeks at the maximal dose attained. Patients who fail to respond to such regimens should be considered treatment resistant but not necessarily truly treatment refractory.

There are a large number of important clinical factors that can contribute to treatment resistance. The clinician who is treating an apparently treatment-resistant or refractory depressed patient should carefully consider each. The first and foremost is inaccurate diagnosis. Mistaking a characterologic or psychosocially-based disorder, which might respond better to psychotherapeutic or environmental interventions, for a major depressive disorder, may lead to one or more unsuccessful trials of antidepressant treatment. Likewise, failure to recognize a specific organic etiology for a depressive syndrome, such as occult thyroid dysfunction, the etiologic role that depressogenic medications like Beta blockers or reserpine may be playing, or the presence of CNS disorders like multiple sclerosis, temporal lobe epilepsy, or normal pressure hydrocephalus, may lead not only to failures to respond to antidepressant drug treatment regimens, but to harmful delays in the application of specific medical or surgical treatment approaches.

The second factor is the nature and the adequacy of prior drug treatment trials. This requires determining, through careful history-taking and obtaining all available old clinical records, the kind(s) of drugs given, the doses administered, the duration of treatment, and blood levels of the drugs involved where they may be helpful. Without such detailed information, it is impossible to know whether the patient is really treatment resistant or refractory, or has just received inadequate prior treatment trials. Further treatment approaches obviously hinge critically on this determination.

Likewise it is important to know in patients who have received inadequate treatment courses, why this has occurred (whether it was a result of inadequate treatment prescription by the physician, or a result of patient intolerance of side effects of one or more of the antidepressant agents). Similarly, non-compliance with prescribed treatment regimens may be an important but difficult to identify factor in apparent treatment resistance.

When these and other related clinical issues have been addressed and appropriately rectified, a large proportion of putatively treatment-resistant or refractory depressed patients respond to relatively standard treatment regimens. Nonetheless, various estimates suggest that from 10–15% of patients with major depressive disorders may truly be relatively treatment-resistant and require one or more alternative treatment approaches before getting better. In addition, there does appear to be a sub-population, of uncertain size, which is truly refractory to all currently available therapeutic interventions. This refractory group is generally believed to be much smaller than the treatment-resistant group, and this should lead the clinician to pursue the various alternative treatment approaches that follow.

## Treatment

At present there are a number of different ways of proceeding with the treatment of antidepressant-resistant depressions. A number of authors have reviewed the relatively sparse and, for the most part, uncontrolled pharmacologic literature on the efficacy of various (alternative) single or combination drug regimens (Gerner, 1983; Mitchell, 1987; Paykel & Van Woerkom, 1987; Stern & Mendels, 1981; White & Simpson, 1987), and several have suggested specific sequential treatment paradigms. However, at present there is neither compelling scientific evidence nor consensual agreement among clinicians as to which approach is likely to be most effective and best tolerated with the fewest complications and side effects.

The following represents an amalgam of approaches to antidepressant resistant depression based on the authors' own clinical experience, in conjunction with that reported by others (Gerner, 1983; Mitchell, 1987; Paykel & Van Woerkom, 1987; Silver & Yudofsky, 1988; Stern & Mendels, 1981; White & Simpson, 1987).

If dose, duration of treatment, blood level, and/or patient compliance during the course of treatment with the initially-selected standard antidepressant have been in any way sub-optimal, the clinician's next steps are clear. He should take action to assure full patient compliance and increase the dose of the antidepressant until the patient achieves a fully therapeutic blood level or side effects become intolerable, and then continue treatment at that level for a full four to six weeks or until a full therapeutic response has been achieved. If, despite appropriate conservative management, side effects are significant enough to prevent the administration of doses of a standard antidepressant such as Imipramine, high enough to achieve a full clinical response, switching to a secondary amine TCA such as desipramine or nortriptyline or one of the second generation antidepressants, which have diminished anticholinergic side effects and are less likely to cause significant orthostatic hypotension as well as other side effects, may be effective.

If, after four to six weeks of treatment, there has been no or sub-optimal improvement, the clinician might consider initiating another four-to-six-week trial with an antidepressant of a different type (e.g., a secondary amine TCA if the initial agent was a tertiary amine, or vice versa), or an amitriptyline-type TCA (amitriptyline or nortriptyline) if the initial drug was an imipramine type (imipramine or desipramine) or vice versa.

If there still is no response, Lithium Carbonate may be added to the antidepressant as an adjunctive agent. Frequently, the addition of Lithium Carbonate converts a TCA non-responsive patient to a responder. This can occur in some cases quite rapidly, i.e., in two to four days, though it may take as long as one to three weeks. Alternatively, adjunctive thyroid hormone either with the TCA alone or the TCA/lithium combination, may improve the antidepressant response, especially in female patients and particularly in those with clinical or sub-clinical thyroid hypofunction as revealed by standard thyroid function tests ($T_4$, $T_3$ uptake, and TSH) or by TRH stimulation testing.

A number of patients who have failed to respond to one or more first generation TCAs and/or second generation antidepressants will respond to MAOIs, and these should probably be considered next. They can be instituted as or even before the TCAs have been discontinued. In fact, combination treatment with TCAs and MAOIs (as long as they are started and increased together or the TCA started first, but not vice versa) is safe and may be effective in some patients with treatment resistant depression (Ananth & Luchins, 1977; White & Simpson, 1981).

## Antidepressants and Adjunctive Agents

If a therapeutic trial of MAOIs alone is ineffective, then similarly to the first or second generation antidepressants, combination treatment with Lithium and/or thyroid hormone may be effective (Fein, Paz, Rao & LaGrassa, 1988).

Patients who have failed to respond to these therapeutic approaches will often be considered appropriate candidates for ECT. Of course, depending on the severity and degree of dysfunction and suicidality associated with the depression, ECT may be indicated much sooner than this. Additional trials of antidepressant medication, which may not have been effective before ECT, may be effective following it (Shapira, Kindler & Lerer, 1988).

Other combinations of antidepressants with adjunctive agents have been reported effective in selected treatment-resistant patients. These have included: TCAs and stimulants (amphetamines, methylphenidate, etc.); TCAs and reserpine; TCAs and antipsychotics, especially in psychotic/delusional depressions; and MAOIs and tryptophan.

Other novel drug treatments in otherwise treatment-resistant patients have included: stimulants alone, especially in secondary depressions with associated medical or neurological illnesses; carbamazepine, though it appears to be more effective acutely against mania; sex hormones (testosterone in males, estrogens in females), either combined with TCAs or given singly, though these agents may be associated with dangerous side effects; salbutamol, a beta receptor agonist; combinations of yohimbine with TCAs; combinations of Lithium with the "newer generation" antidepressants; or cautious use of very high dose treatment regimens with careful monitoring with such standard agents as TCAs and MAOIs.

Experience with these novel approaches is not extensive and there are no solid guidelines indicating which patients will be likely to respond to which treatment approaches. Thus, in the absence of any clear guidance from a substantial body of solid empirical data, the clinician should be persistent in the careful and systematic application of sequential pharmacological trials, which should be closely supervised and monitored with respect to efficacy and safety. With patience, persistence, and the willingness to approach treatment-resistant patients as open empirical therapeutic trials with an "N" of one, the careful clinician will more often than not find an effective pharmacological intervention, thereby sparing the patient unnecessary pain, chronic dysfunction, and disability.

## CONTINUATION AND PROPHYLACTIC TREATMENT

Once control of the presenting symptoms has been achieved with a given medication regimen, there remains the theoretically and clinically important question of how long to continue on the particular regimen which has brought relief from symptoms. In addition to the obvious clinical implications, it would seem important from a theoretical perspective if the antidepressants could bring about relief of symptoms, without terminating a given affective episode. This in fact appears to be the case, in that patients switched from active medication to placebo have a significantly higher relapse rate than those continued on active regimens, even though both groups were symptom free at the time of the change (Prien, 1987; Prien & Kupfer, 1986). This has led to the distinction between "continuation" treatment and long-term prophylactic treatment. (See Prien, 1987; Prien & Kupfer, 1986, for discussion.)

### Continuation Treatment

It is quite clear that medication should not be discontinued at the time of relief of symptoms. Studies suggest that the relapse rate of untreated depressives is about 50% (29–73% range) in the first year following alleviation of initial symptoms. This percentage falls to about 20% for those with ongoing or continuation treatment (Prien & Kupfer, 1986; Schou, 1979). This would appear to be true across a wide array of demographic, illness characteristic, and biological variables (Prien, 1987). Of interest is that once a patient has been symptom free for at least 16 weeks, it would appear that continuation treatment does not significantly change the relapse rate (Prien & Kupfer, 1986). This suggests that active treatment should continue for at least four to five months beyond the time at which the affective symptoms have fully and continuously resolved.

Several studies have examined the efficacy of various treatment regimens in preventing relapse, though most have looked at lithium, first generation antidepressants (usually imipramine or amitriptyline), or the combination of lithium and first generation antidepressant (Glen, Johnson & Shepherd, 1984; Kane, Quitkin, Rifkin, Ramos-Lorenzi, Nayak & Howard, 1982; Maj, Del Vecchio, Starace, Pirozzi & Kemali, 1984; Prien & Kupfer, 1986; Prien et al., 1984; Schou, 1979). The consensus from these studies strongly suggests that both lithium and the first generation antidepressants are effective in reducing relapse rates to the 20–30% range, that lithium would appear to be a better choice in bipolar patients, and that there is no significant advantage gained by the combination approach. Whether there are significant differences between rapid cyclers and other bipolar patients remains largely unexplored to date. In the above studies, lithium levels were maintained at the usual therapeutic serum levels, and the antidepressant dosages usually were 100–150 mg. of Imipramine or its equivalent.

Of note is the marked lack of studies addressing the efficacy of second generation antidepressants and monoamine oxidase inhibitors. Two studies suggest lithium to be more effective than maprotiline and mianserin (Coppen, Ghose, Rao, Bailey & Peet, 1978; Coppen, Montgomery, Gupta & Bailey, 1976;) and there are no MAOI studies that we are aware of.

## Prophylactic Treatment

There is even less data available to guide the practitioner in deciding who should receive long-term treatment (i.e., beyond continuation treatment). Clearly the risk of recurrent episodes is very high for both unipolar (50%) and bipolar patients (80%) (Prien, 1987). However, the interval between episodes can vary immensely, and thus until some clue as to cycle length is given, it is probably prudent to not commit a patient to chronic prophylactic treatment. On the other hand, there is data suggesting that the interval between recurrences tends to shorten over time, and that the more frequently episodes occur, the greater the risk for subsequent early relapse (Prien, 1987).

From a treatment standpoint, the issues and conclusions remain essentially the same as for continuation treatment.

## SUMMARY

As noted in the beginning of this chapter, much of the knowledge of the biochemistry of depression is linked to observations about the complex relationship between various chemotherapeutic agents and changes in the symptoms of depressive illness. These observations and the hypotheses they generate have had a certain cyclical nature of their own (not unlike the disorder they struggle to explain), and have at times seemed somewhat contradictory or confusing. Yet there are several consistent observations which are remarkably robust and thus provoke investigation into the nature of depressive illness and the impact that chemotherapeutic agents can have on it. The overwhelmingly consistent finding that various classes of agents alleviate depressive symptoms to clinically and statistically greater degrees than placebo, the consistent relationship between the "endogenomorphic" symptom cluster and drug responsivity, the common denominator that effective agents have with respect to alterations in predictable monoamine systems in the CNS, the clinically and statistically significant changes in relapse rate in the presence of these agents, as well as many other such observations, when taken together, suggest strongly that from a theoretical perspective, the relationship between pharmacotherapy and depression will continue to be critical to our further understanding of the biochemical underpinnings of depressive illness. From a clinical perspective, these observations make appropriate medication treatment the gold standard against which any other interventions must be measured.

## Specific Conclusions

1. At this time there is no single mechanism which all effective antidepressant regimes share in common.

2. Alterations in monoamine transmission (through a variety of mechanisms including changes in receptor sensitivity, receptor density, or effects on a "second messenger") is a final common pathway in virtually all effective antidepressant agents.

3. Alterations in Beta adrenergic receptor sensitivity (pre-synaptic down-regulation), alpha adrenergic receptor sensitivity and serotonergic receptor sensitivity (post-synaptic enhancement) appear to be the most consistent changes associated with antidepressant administration and occur over a time course consistent with that seen clinically.

4. First and second generation agents, and MAO Inhibitors have comparable efficacy profiles, and vary primarily in side effect profiles, and putative mechanisms of action.

5. Gradual onset of symptoms, preponderance of neurovegetative signs and symptoms, absence of delusions, and significant improvement in the first one to two weeks of treatment predict a good overall response to medication.

6. Chronic (greater than two years) or acute (less than two weeks) symptoms, the presence of delusions, and "atypical" features predict a poor overall response to medication.

7. A variety of adjunctive agents ($T_4$, Lithium, methylphonidate) and combination approaches can be effective in the refractory depressed patient, though matching patient with regimens is not possible in advance.

8. When effective, medication regimens should be continued 16–20 weeks beyond the episode to reduce otherwise high relapse rates.

# References

Abou-Selah, M.T. & Coppen, A. (1983). Classification of depression and response to antidepressive therapies. *British Journal of Psychiatry, 143*, 601–603.

Abrams, R. (1988). Unilateral electroconvulsive therapy. Chapter 8 in *Electroconvulsive therapy* (pp. 157–167). New York: Oxford University Press.

Akiskal, H.S., Rosenthal, T.L., Haykal, R.F., Lemmi, H., Rosenthal, R. H. & Scott-Strauss, A. (1980). Characterological depressions: Clinical and sleep EEG findings separating "subaffective dysthymias" from "character spectrum disorders." *Archives of General Psychiatry, 37*, 777–783.

American Psychiatric Association [APA] Task Force on the Use of Laboratory Tests in Psychiatry. (1985). Tricyclic antidepressants—Blood level measurements and clinical outcome: An APA Task Force report. *American Journal of Psychiatry, 142*, 155–162.

Ananth, J. & Luchins, D. (1977). A review of combined tricyclic and MAOI therapy. *Comprehensive Psychiatry, 18*(3), 221–230.

Asberg, M., Eriksson, B., Martensson, B., Traskman-Bendz, L. & Wagner, A. (1986). Therapeutic effects of serotonin uptake inhibitors in depression. *Journal of Clinical Psychiatry, 47*(4) (Supplement), 23–35.

Awad, A.G. (1987). New antidepressants—The serotonin reuptake inhibitors. *Psychiatric Journal of the University of Ottawa, 12*(1), 2–5.

Baldessarini, R.J. (1985). *Chemotherapy in psychiatry* (2nd ed.). Cambridge, MA: Harvard University Press.

Benkelfat, C., Poirier, M.F., Leouffre, P., Gay, C. & Loo, H. (1987). Dexamethasone suppression test and the response to antidepressant depending on their central monoaminergic action in major depression. *Canadian Journal of Psychiatry, 32*(3), 175–178.

Bernstein, J.G. (1984). Neurotransmitters and receptors in pharmacopsychiatry. In J.G. Bernstein (Ed.), *Clinical Psychopharmacology* (2nd ed.) (pp. 59–76). Boston: John Wright-PSG.

Bielski, R.J. & Friedel, R.O. (1976). Prediction of tricyclic antidepressant response: A critical review. *Archives of General Psychiatry, 33*, 1479–1489.

Bloch, R.G., Dooneief, A.S., Buchberg, A.S. & Spellman, S. (1954). The clinical effect of isoniazid and iproniazid in the treatment of pulmonary tuberculosis. *Annals of Internal Medicine, 40*, 881–900.

Bouchard, J.M., Delaunay, J., Delisle, J.P., Grasset, N., Mermberg, P.F., Molczadzki, M., Pagot, R., Richou, H., Robert, G., Ropert, R., Schuller, E., Verdeau-Pailles, J., Zarifian, E. & Hopfner Petersen, H.E. (1987). Citalopram versus maprotiline: A controlled, clinical multicentre trial in depressed patients. *Acta Psychiatrica Scandinavica, 76*, 583–592.

Brotman, A.W., Falk, W.E. & Gelenberg, A.J. (1987). Pharmacologic treatment of acute depressive subtypes. In Meltzer, H.Y. (Ed.), *Psychopharmacology: The third generation of progress* (pp. 1031–1040). New York: Raven Press.

Brown, R.P., Frances, A., Kocsis, J.H. & Mann, J.J. (1982). Psychotic vs. nonpsychotic depression: Comparison of treatment response. *The Journal of Nervous and Mental Disease, 170*(10), 635–637.

Brown, R.P., Sweeney, J., Frances, A., Kocsis, J.H. & Loutsch, E. (1983). Age as a predictor of treatment response in endogenous depression. *Journal of Clinical Psychopharmacology, 3*(3), 176–178.

Brown, W.A., Haier, R.J. & Qualls, C.B. (1980). Dexamethasone suppression test identifies subtypes of depression which respond to different antidepressants. *Lancet, 1*, 928–929. Burns, A. & Tune, L. (1987). Amoxapine-induced cognitive impairment in two patients. *Journal of Clinical Psychiatry, 48*(4), 166–167.

Charney, D.S., Menkes, D.B. & Heninger G.R. (1981). Receptor sensitivity and the mechanism of action of antidepressant treatment. *Archives of General Psychiatry, 38,* 1160–1180.

Charney, D.S. & Nelson, J.C. (1981). Delusional and nondelusional unipolar depression: Further evidence for distinct subtypes. *American Journal of Psychiatry, 138*(3), 328–333.

Clower, C.G. (1983). Recurrent psychotic unipolar depression. *Journal of Clinical Psychiatry, 44*(6), 216–218.

Cochran, E., Robins, E. & Grote, S. (1976). Regional serotonin levels in brain: A comparison of depressive suicides and alcoholic suicides with controls. *Biological Psychiatry, 11,* 283–294.

Cole, J.O. (1988). The drug treatment of anxiety and depression. *Medical Clinics of North America, 72*(4), 815–831.

Coppen, A., Ghose, K., Rao, R., Bailey, J. & Peet, M. (1978). Mianserin and lithium in the prophylaxis of depression. *British Journal of Psychiatry, 133,* 206–210.

Coppen, A., Montgomery, S.A., Gupta, R.K. & Bailey, J. E. (1976). A double-blind comparison of lithium carbonate and maprotiline in the prophylaxis of the affective disorders. *British Journal of Psychiatry, 128,* 479–485.

Coryell, W., Coppen, A., Zeigler, V.E. & Biggs, J.T. (1982). Early improvement as a predictor of response to amitriptyline and nortriptyline: A comparison of 2 patient samples. *Psychological Medicine, 12,* 135–139.

Crane, G.E. (1957). Iproniazid (Marsilid) phosphate, a therapeutic agent for mental disorders and debilitating diseases. *Psychiatric Research Reports of the American Psychiatric Association, 8,* 142–152.

Davis, J.M., Klerman, G.L. & Schildkraut, J.J. (1968). Drugs used in the treatment of depression. In Efron, D.H., Cole, J.O., Levine, J. & Wittenborn, J.R. (Eds.), *Psychopharmacology: A review of progress 1957–1969* (pp. 718–748). Washington, D.C.: United States Government Printing Office.

Dessain, E.C., Schatzberg, A.F., Woods, B.T. & Cole, J.O. (1986). Maprotiline treatment in depression: A perspective on seizures. *Archives of General Psychiatry, 43,* 86–90.

Downing, R.W. & Rickels, K. (1973). Predictors of response to amitriptyline and placebo in three outpatient treatment settings. *The Journal of Nervous and Mental Disease, 156,* 109–129.

Dowson, J.H. (1987). MAO inhibitors in mental disease: Their current status. *Journal of Neural Transmission, 23* (Supplement), 121–138.

Emrich, H.M., Gunther, R. & Dose, M. (1983). Current perspectives in the pharmacopsychiatry of depression and mania. *Neuropharmacology, 22*(3B), 385–388.

Extein, I., Gold, M.S. & Pottash, A.L.C. (1984). Psychopharmacologic treatment of depression. *Psychiatric Clinics of North America, 7*(3), 503–517.

Fallon, B., Foote, B., Walsh, T. & Roose, S.P. (1988). "Spontaneous" hypertensive episodes with monoamine oxidase inhibitors. *Journal of Clinical Psychiatry, 49*(4), 163–165.

Fein, S., Paz, V., Rao, N. & LaGrassa, J. (1988). The combination of lithium carbonate and an MAOI in refractory depressions. *American Journal of Psychiatry, 145*(2), 249–250.

Frazer, A. & Brunswick, D.J. (1989). Antidepressant drugs. In, (Ed.), *Drill's Textbook of Pharmacology.* In Di Gregorio, J., Di Palma, J.D. (Eds.), *Basic Pharmacology in Medicine.* New York: McGraw-Hill.

Frazer, A. & Conway, P. (1984). Pharmacologic mechanisms of action of antidepressants. *Psychiatric Clinics of North America, 7*(3), 575–586.

Fuller, R.W. & Wong, D.T. (1985). Effects of antidepressants on uptake and receptor systems in the brain. *Progress in Neuro- psychopharmacology and Biological Psychiatry, 9*, 485–490.

Gaultieri, C.T. & Powell, S.F. (1978). Psychoactive drug interactions. *Journal of Clinical Psychiatry, 39*(9), 62–71.

Gerner, R.H. (1983). Systematic treatment approach to depression and treatment resistant depression. *Psychiatric Annals, 13*(1), 37–49.

Glassman, A.H., Kantor, S.J. & Shostak, M. (1975). Depression, delusions, and drug response. *American Journal of Psychiatry, 132*(7), 716–719.

Glassman, A.H., Roose, S.P., Giardina, E.-G. V. & Bigger, J.T., Jr. (1987). Cardiovascular effects of tricyclic antidepressants. In Meltzer, H.Y. (Ed.), *Psychopharmacology: The third generation of progress* (pp. 1437–1442). New York: Raven Press.

Glen, A.I.M., Johnson, A.L. & Shepherd, M. (1984). Continuation therapy with lithium and amitriptyline in unipolar depressive illness: A randomized, double-blind, controlled trial. *Psychological Medicine, 14*, 37–50.

Guze, B.H., Baxter, L.R., Jr. & Rego, J. (1987). Refractory depression treated with high doses of a monoamine oxidase inhibitor. *Journal of Clinical Psychiatry, 48*(1), 31–32.

Heninger, G.R. & Charney, D.S. (1987). Mechanisms of action of antidepressant treatments: Implications for the etiology and treatment of depressive disorders. In Meltzer, H.Y. (Ed.), *Psychopharmacology: The third generation of progress* (pp. 535–544). New York: Raven Press.

Hirschfeld, R.M.A. & Cross, C.K. (1987). Clinical psychopathology and diagnosis in relation to treatment of affective disorders. In Meltzer, H.Y. (Ed.), *Psychopharmacology: The third generation of progress* (pp. 1021–1029). New York: Raven Press.

Jackson, W.K., Roose, S.P. & Glassman, A.H. (1987). Cardiovascular toxicity of antidepressant medications. *Psychopathology, 20* (Supplement 1), 64–74. Janowsky, A., Okada, F., Manier, D.H., Applegate, C.D., Sulser, F. & Steranka, L.R. (1982). Role of serotonergic input in the regulation of the beta-adrenergic receptor-coupled adenylate cyclase system. *Science, 218*, 900–901.

Johnstone, E.C. (1976). The relationship between acetylator status and inhibition of monoamine oxidase, excretion of free drug, and antidepressant response in depressed patients on phenelzine. *Psychopharmacologia, 46*, 289–294.

Kane, J.M., Quitkin, F.M., Rifkin, A., Ramos-Lorenzi, J.R., Nayak, D.D. & Howard, A. (1982). Lithium carbonate and imipramine in the prophylaxis of unipolar and bipolar II illness: A prospective placebo-controlled comparison. *Archives of General Psychiatry, 39*, 1065–1069.

Kantor, S.J. & Glassman, A.H. (1977). Delusional depressions: Natural history and response to treatment. *British Journal of Psychiatry, 131*, 351–360.

Katz, M.M., Koslow, S.H., Maas, J.W., Frazer, A., Bowden, C.L., Casper, R., Croughan, J., Kocsis, J. & Redmond, E. (1987). The timing, specificity and clinical prediction of tricyclic drug effects in depression. *Psychological Medicine, 17*, 297–309.

Kessler, K.A. (1978). Tricyclic antidepressants: Mode of action and clinical use. In Lipton, M.A., DiMascio, A. & Killam, K.F. (Eds.), *Psychopharmacology: A generation of progress* (pp. 1289–1302). New York: Raven Press.

Kline, N.S. (1958). Clinical experience with iproniazid (Marsilid). *Journal of Clinical and Experimental Psychopathology and Quarterly Review of Psychiatry and Neurology, 19* (Supplement 1), 72–78.

Koslow, S.H., Maas, J.W., Bowden, C.L., Davis, J.M., Hanin, I. & Javaid, J. (1983). CSF and urinary biogenic amines and metabolites in depression and mania. *Archives of General Psychiatry, 40*, 999–1010.

Kuhn, R. (1958). The treatment of depressive states with G 22355 (imipramine hydrochloride). *American Journal of Psychiatry, 115*, 459–464.

Lapin, I.P. & Oxenkrug, G.F. (1969). Intensification of the central serotoninergic processes as a possible determinant of the thymoleptic effect. *Lancet*, *1*, 132–136. Lesser, I. (1983). Case report of withdrawal dyskinesia associated with amoxapine. *American Journal of Psychiatry*, *140*, 1358–1359.

Lloyd, K.G., Farley, I.J., Deck, J.H.N. & Hornykiewicz, O. (1974). Serotonin and 5-hydroxyindoleacetic acid in discrete areas of the brainstem of suicide victims and control patients. *Advances in Biochemical Psychopharmacology*, *11*, 387–397.

Lloyd, K.G., Thuret, F. & Pilc, A. (1985). Upregulation of gamma-aminobutyric acid (GABA) B binding sites in rat frontal cortex: A common action of repeated administration of different classes of antidepressants and electroshock. *Journal of Pharmacology and Experimental Therapeutics*, *235*(1), 191–199.

Loo, H., Benkelfat, C., Poirier, M.F., Vanelle, J.M., Olie, J.P., Dennis, T. & Scatton, B. (1986A). Plasma 3,4—dihydroxyphenylethyleneglycol and therapeutic response to maprotiline and indalpine in major depression. *Neuropsychobiology*, *15*, 62–67.

Loo, H., Benkelfat, C., Vanelle, J.M., Dennis, T., Poirier, M.F., Olie, J.P. & Scatton, B. (1986B). Urinary 3-methoxy, 4-hydroxyphenylethylene glycol and therapeutic response to maprotiline and indalpine in major depression. *Journal of Neural Transmission*, *66*, 47–58.

Loosen, P.T. & Prange, A.J. (1982). Serum thyrotropin response to thyrotropin-releasing hormone in psychiatric patients: A review. *American Journal of Psychiatry*, *139*(4), 405–416.

Luna, O.C., Jayatilaka, A. & Walker, V. (1984). Amoxapine and extrapyramidal symptoms [Letter]. *Journal of Clinical Psychiatry*, *45*(9), 407.

Maas, J.W. (1975). Biogenic amines and depression: Biochemical and pharmacological separation of two types of depression. *Archives of General Psychiatry*, *32*, 1357–1361.

Maj, M., Del Vecchio, M., Starace, F., Pirozzi, R. & Kemali, D. (1984). Prediction of affective psychoses response to lithium prophylaxis: The role of socio-demographic, clinical, psychological and biological variables. *Acta Psychiatrica Scandinavica*, *69*, 37–44.

Mann, J.J., Frances, A., Kaplan, R.D., Kocsis, J., Peselow, E.D. & Gershon, S. (1982). The relative efficacy of L-deprenyl, a selective monoamine oxidase Type B inhibitor, in endogenous and nonendogenous depression. *Journal of Clinical Psychopharmacology*, *2*(1), 54–57.

Mendels, J. (1987). Clinical experience with serotonin reuptake inhibiting antidepressants. *Journal of Clinical Psychiatry*, *48*(3) (Supplement), 26–30.

Minter, R.E. & Mandel, M.R. (1979). The treatment of psychotic major depressive disorder with drugs and electroconvulsive therapy. *The Journal of Nervous and Mental Disease*, *167*(12), 726–733.

Mitchell, P. (1987). The pharmacological treatment of tricyclic-resistant depression: Review and management guidelines. *Australian and New Zealand Journal of Psychiatry*, *21*, 442–451.

Murphy, D.L., Lipper, S., Pickar, D., Jimerson, D., Cohen, R.M., Garrick, N.A., Alterman, I.S. & Campbell, I.C. (1981). Selective inhibition of monoamine oxidase Type A: Clinical antidepressant effects and metabolic changes in man. In Youdim, M.B.H. & Paykel, E.S. (Eds.), *Monoamine oxidase inhibitors—The state of the art* (pp. 189–205). Chichester: John Wiley & Sons.

Murphy, D.L., Sunderland, T. & Cohen, R.M. (1984). Monoamine oxidase-inhibiting antidepressants: A clinical update. *Psychiatric Clinics of North America*, *7*(3), 549–562.

Nelson, J.C. & Bowers, M.B. (1978). Delusional unipolar depression: Description and drug response. *Archives of General Psychiatry*, *35*, 1321–1328.

Nystrom, C. & Hallstrom, T. (1987). Comparison between a serotonin and a noradrenaline reuptake blocker in the treatment of depressed outpatients: A cross-over study. *Acta Psychiatrica Scandinavica 75*, 377–382.

Nystrom, C., Ross, S.B., Hallstrom, T. & Kelder, D. (1986). Comparison between a serotonin and a noradrenaline reuptake blocker in the treatment of depressed outpatients: Biochemical aspects. *Acta Psychiatrica Scandinavica, 73*, 133–138.

Pare, C.M.B. (1985). The present status of monoamine oxidase inhibitors. *British Journal of Psychiatry, 146*, 576–584.

Pare, C.M.B. (1987). Monoamine oxidase inhibitors in the treatment of affective disorders. *Psychiatric Annals, 17*(5), 309–315.

Pare, C.M.B., Yeung, D.P.H., Price, K. & Stacey, R.S. (1969). 5-Hydroxytryptamine, noradrenaline and dopamine in brainstem, hypothalamus and caudate nucleus of controls and of patients committing suicide by coal-gas poisoning. *Lancet, 2*, 133–135.

Paykel, E.S., Prusoff, B.A., Klerman, G.L., Haskell, D. & DiMascio, A. (1973). Clinical response to amitriptyline among depressed women. *The Journal of Nervous and Mental Disease, 156*, 149–165.

Paykel, E.S. & Van Woerkom, A.E. (1987). Pharmacologic treatment of resistant depression. *Psychiatric Annals, 17*(5), 327–331.

Pi, E.H. & Simpson, G.M. (1985). New antidepressants: A review. *Hospital Formulary, 20*, 580–588.

Pinder, R.M., Brogden, R.N., Speight, T.M. & Avery, G.S. (1977). Maprotiline: A review of the pharmacological properties and therapeutic efficacy on mental depressive states. *Drugs, 13*, 321–352.

Price, T.R.P., McAllister, T.W., Peltier, D. & Kraft, A. (1986). Positive response to bilateral sinusoidal ECT in unilateral and bilateral brief-pulse "ECT-resistant" depressive illness. *Convulsive Therapy, 2*, 277–284.

Prien, R.F. (1987). Long-term treatment of affective disorders. In Meltzer, H.Y. (Ed.), *Psychopharmacology: The third generation of progress* (pp. 1051–1058). New York: Raven Press.

Prien, R.F. & Kupfer, D.J. (1986). Continuation drug therapy for major depressive episodes: How long should it be maintained? *American Journal of Psychiatry, 143*(1), 18–23.

Prien, R.F., Kupfer, D.J., Mansky, P.A., Small, J.G., Tuason, V.B., Voss, C.B. & Johnson, W.E. (1984). Drug therapy in the prevention of recurrences in unipolar and bipolar affective disorders: Report of the NIMH collaborative study group comparing lithium carbonate, imipramine, and a lithium carbonate-imipramine combination. *Archives of General Psychiatry, 41*, 1096–1104.

Quitkin, F., Rifkin, A. & Klein, D.F. (1979). Monoamine oxidase inhibitors: A review of antidepressant effectiveness. *Archives of General Psychiatry, 36*, 749–760.

Quitkin, F.M., Rabkin, J.G., Ross, D. & McGrath, P.J. (1984). Duration of antidepressant drug treatment: What is an adequate trial? *Archives of General Psychiatry, 41*, 238–245.

Rama Rao, V.A. & Coppen, A. (1979). Classification of depression and response to amitriptyline therapy. *Psychological Medicine, 9*, 321–325.

Robinson, D.S. & Kurtz, N.M. (1987). Monoamine oxidase inhibiting drugs: Pharmacologic and therapeutic issues. In Meltzer, H.Y. (Ed.), *Psychopharmacology: The third generation of progress* (pp. 1297–1304). New York: Raven Press.

Schatzberg, A.F., Dessain, E., O'Neil, P., Katz, D.L. & Cole, J.O. (1987). Recent studies on selective serotonergic antidepressants: Trazodone, Fluoxetine, and Fluvoxamine. *Journal of Clinical Psychopharmacology, 7*(6), 44S–49S.

Scher, M., Krieger, J.N. & Juergens, S. (1983). Trazodone and priapism. *American*

*Journal of Psychiatry, 140*(10), 1362–1363.

Schildkraut, J.J. (1965). The catecholamine hypothesis of affective disorders: A review of supporting evidence. *American Journal of Psychiatry, 122,* 509–522.

Schou, M. (1979). Lithium as a prophylactic agent in unipolar affective illness: Comparison with cyclic antidepressants. *Archives of General Psychiatry, 36,* 849–851.

Selikoff, I.J., Robitzek, E.H. & Ornstein, G.G. (1952). Toxicity of hydrozine derivatives of isonicotinic acid in the chemotherapy of human tuberculosis: A preliminary report. *Quarterly Bulletin of Sea View Hospital, 13,* 17–51.

Shapira, B., Kindler, S. & Lerer, B. (1988). Medication outcome in ECT-resistant depression. *Convulsive Therapy, 4*(3), 192–198.

Sheehan, D.V., Claycomb, J.B. & Kouretas, N. (1980–81). Monoamine oxidase inhibitors: Prescription and patient management. *International Journal of Psychiatry in Medicine, 10*(2), 99–121.

Silver, J.M. & Yudofsky, S.C. (1988). Psychopharmacology and electroconvulsive therapy. In Talbott, J.A., Hales, R.E. & Yudofsky, S.C. (Eds.), *The American Psychiatric Press Textbook of Psychiatry* (pp. 767–853). Washington, D.C.: American Psychiatric Press.

Simon, J.S., Evans, D.L. & Nemeroff, C.B. (1987). The dexamethasone suppression test and antidepressant response in major depression. *Journal of Psychiatric Research, 21*(3), 313–317.

Spiker, D.G., Cofsky Weiss, J., Dealy, R.S., Griffin, S.J., Hanin, I., Neil, J.F., Perel, J.M., Rossi, A.J. & Soloff, P.H. (1985). The pharmacological treatment of delusional depression. *American Journal of Psychiatry, 142*(4), 430–436.

Steardo, L., Barone, P., Monteleone, P., Iovino, M. & Cardone, G. (1987). Is the dexamethasone suppression test predictive of response to specific antidepressant treatment in major depression? *Acta Psychiatrica Scandinavica, 76,* 129–133.

Stern, S.L. & Mendels, J. (1981). Drug combinations in the treatment of refractory depression: A review. *Journal of Clinical Psychiatry, 42*(10), 368–373.

Sunderland, T., Orsulak, P.J. & Cohen, R.M. (1983). Amoxapine and neuroleptic side effects: A case report. *American Journal of Psychiatry, 140*(9), 1233–1235.

Timmerman, L., De Beurs, P., Tan, B.K., Leijnse-Ybema, H., Sanchez, C., Hopfner Petersen, H.E. & Cohen Stuart, M.H. (1987). A double-blind comparative clinical trial of Citalopram vs. Maprotiline in hospitalized depressed patients. *International Clinical Psychopharmacology, 2,* 239–253.

Tollefson, G.D. (1983). Monoamine oxidase inhibitors: A review. *Journal of Clinical Psychiatry, 44*(8), 280–288.

Wander, T.J., Nelson, A., Okazaki, H. & Richelson, E. (1986). Antagonism by antidepressants of serotonin $S_1$ and $S_2$ receptors of normal human brain in vitro. *European Journal of Pharmacology, 132,* 115–121.

White, K. & Simpson, G. (1981). Combined MAOI-tricyclic antidepressant treatment: A reevaluation. Journal of *Clinical Psychopharmacology, 1*(5), 264–282.

White, K. & Simpson, G. (1987). Treatment-resistant depression. *Psychiatric Annals, 17*(4), 274–278.

Zeller, E.A., Barsky, J., Fouts, J.R., Kirchheimer, W.F. & Van Orden, L.S. (1952). Influence of isonicotinic acid hydrazide (INH) and 1-isonicotinyl-2-isopropyl hydrazide (IIH) on bacterial and mammalian enzymes. *Experientia, 8,* 349–350.

Zisook, S. (1985). A clinical overview of monoamine oxidase inhibitors. *Psychosomatics, 26,* 240–251.

# 13

# The Role of Lithium in the Treatment of Depression

Janusz K. Rybakowski
*Medical Academy, Bydgoszcz, Poland*

KEY WORDS: lithium, F.J. Cade, potentiation, augmentation, somatic side effects

## LITHIUM AND DEPRESSION

Depression is a frequent psychopathological phenomenon that may result from the interplay of a variety of factors: stressful life events, biological predisposition, somatic conditions, maladaptive learning, etc. However, when considering the role of lithium in the therapy of depression, the term "depression" refers to the endogenous depressive syndrome occurring in the course of a major affective disorder. The name "endogenous" points to the prevalent contribution of genetic and metabolic factors in its pathogenesis. Two types of affective illness are presently recognized: 1) unipolar affective illness with periodic recurrent depressions and 2) bipolar affective illness where, in addition to depressions, their phenomenological opposites (manias) also periodically occur; however, on the average, the number of depressive episodes in bipolar illness exceeds by 4–5 times, that of manias. Clinical and genetic data provide evidence that unipolar and bipolar illnesses are separate nosological entities (Leonhard, 1957; Perris, 1966). Remarkable discoveries have been made concerning a possible link of a genetic predisposition to the bipolar illness with chromosome X (Mendlewicz & Fleiss, 1974) and recently with DNA markers on chromosome 11 (Egeland, 1988). Several groups of drugs such as tricyclic antidepressants, MAO inhibitors, or so-called "atypical" antidepressants, as well as electroconvulsive therapy, have been proven to be effective treatment modalities in endogenous depressions occurring in the course of affective illnesses.

The invalidism of patients with endogenous depressions is caused, on the one hand, by the severity of depressive episodes, which are to a great extent disabling and also life-threatening, due to the suicidal tendencies of depressive patients. The severity often necessitates psychiatric hospitalization which may last for several months. On the other hand, the disablement of affective patients is also due to the recurrent nature of the episodes, disrupting the patient's pattern of life and social functioning. Future episodes of depression are awaited by patients with anxious anticipation. Thus, it is important both to treat the current depressive syndrome and to prevent the future ones. The role of lithium in these two areas will be outlined in this chapter.

Lithium as a chemical element was discovered in the beginning of the 19th century and introduced to medicine in the middle of that century. Lithium urate was found to be the most soluble urate salt, and the administration of lithium at that time was recommended for treating metabolic disorders such as gout or other rheumatic conditions where an excess of urate deposits was thought to occur. Interestingly enough, some investigators (e.g., Carl Lange in Denmark) regarded periodic depression as a variant of "uric acid diathesis" and suggested using lithium as a therapeutic agent in this condition (Lange, 1896). This preceded the modern lithium therapy for affective illness by more than half a century.

The "uric acid" connection was also the reason for experimenting with lithium forty years ago by John Cade of Australia, who is regarded as the founder of contemporary lithium therapy. Cade speculated on the possible toxic properties of urine of manic patients and gave urea and lithium urate to guinea pigs. He observed that after administering lithium urate, the animals became lethargic, as they did with other lithium salts. Apparently, the psychotropic activity was caused by the lithium ion. This prompted Cade to use lithium in the treatment of manic excitement with surprisingly good results (Cade, 1949). Following that, lithium was introduced to psychiatry as an antimanic drug. The advent of modern psychotropic drugs in the fifties reduced the number of lithium investigations. This reduction was also influenced by the fact that in the late forties in the USA lithium was tried as salt substitute in sodium-free diets, with some fatal complications (Corcoran, Taylor & Page, 1949). However, a revival of interest in lithium occurred in the sixties when the prophylactic activity of lithium was observed, and this interest has continued up to the present time. In addition to John Cade, another great investigator of lithium should be mentioned, namely Mogens Schou of Denmark, whose experimental and clinical work, as well as indefatigable promotion of lithium, set the stage for the increased use of this drug all over the world.

At present, the psychopharmacological spectrum of lithium action in affective illness can be best described as "normothymic," i.e., providing therapeutic effectiveness at both psychopathological poles (mania and depression). This means it provides both acute antimanic and antidepressant efficacy, as well as prophylactic action against both manias and depressions. There is still controversy as to whether this lithium action is "asymmetrical," or more effective against mania than against depression. As both a psychotropic substance and monovalent action (positive ion), lithium possesses specific pharmacokinetic properties different from other drugs. It was also the first psychotropic drug whose administration was paralleled by the routine monitoring of plasma level. In addition to this, lithium has a specific spectrum of somatic side effects, and special knowledge and experience is needed to use this drug properly for therapeutic purposes.

Three aspects of the contribution of lithium to the therapy of endogenous depressions will now be discussed: (1) the antidepressant effect in acute depressive episodes; (2) the potentiation by lithium of other antidepressant treatments; and (3) the prevention of depressive recurrences in both unipolar and bipolar affective illnesses.

## ANTIDEPRESSANT EFFECT OF LITHIUM IN ACUTE DEPRESSIVE EPISODES

Early anecdotal observations of the therapeutic action of lithium in endogenous depression when used during acute depressive episodes gave rise to studies using larger numbers of patients, as well as to studies incorporating placebo or double-blind designs. One of the largest of those was presented by Czechoslovakian authors (Nahunek, Svestka & Rodova, 1970) who studied 98 patients. They found beneficial effects of lithium in 54% of endogenously depressed patients, both unipolar and bipolar, which was slightly less than the average level of improvement obtained with tricyclic antidepressants. The authors concluded that lithium had definite antidepressant properties, but may not be the first choice drug for acute antidepressant treatment because of its lower overall efficacy than conventional antidepressants.

Our own study (Rybakowski, Chlopocka, Lisowska & Czerwinski, 1974) included 39 patients with endogenous depression. Marked improvement, as measured after 14 days, was observed in 23 (59%) patients. We did not find any relationship between the therapeutic effect of lithium and the nomological (unipolar, bipolar) or syndromological (retardation, agitation) type of depression, nor with lithium dose or plasma lithium level. Patients who showed better response to lithium had slightly less intense symptoms of depression.

Ten controlled studies of acute antidepressant effects of lithium were summarized by Mendels (1976). The majority of these studies, conducted with a total of 152 patients, showed the marked antidepressant effect of lithium in certain subgroups of affective patients (mostly bipolar). In three of the papers, the results were equivocal.

A number of studies attempted to find the specific clinical or biochemical features of lithium responders in acute depressive episodes. These studies indicated some tendency for patients with a diagnosis or family history of bipolar illness to respond more favorably than patients with unipolar depression or without a family history of affective illness (Baron, Gershon, Rudy, Jonas & Buchsbaum, 1975). Another clinical characteristic related to good therapeutic reaction to lithium may be the existence of a typical affective endogenous symptom pattern, as well as the occurrence of depressive episodes that are not linked to environmental events (Noyes, Dempsey, Blum & Cavanaugh, 1974). An altered lithium transport (increased erythrocyte lithium ratio) (Mendels & Frazer, 1973), and biogenic amine metabolism—lower MHPG excretion (Beckmann, St-Laurent & Goodwin, 1975), and lower CSF 5-HIAA level (Goodwin, Post & Dunner, 1973) were also expected in patients showing a more favorable antidepressant response to lithium.

The course of therapeutic action of lithium in depression, in most cases, has resembled that of classical antidepressants, with a gradual effect occurring within two to four weeks. However, in selected cases, a dramatic improvement of depression within several days has also been observed. The issue has still not been settled regarding the plasma lithium level for optimal antidepressant action. In most studies, a standard therapeutic lithium concentration of 0.6–1.2 mmol/l was used, but some investigators recommend keeping the lithium level within an upper or lower limit of this range while treating depression (Friedel, 1976).

It seems that lithium may have acute antidepressant effects. Also, recent controlled studies (Worall, Moody, Peet, Dick, Smith, Chambers, Adams & Naylor, 1979; Khan, Wickham & Reed, 1987) confirm this conclusion. This is of both theoretical and practical value. Theoretically, it may point to some common pathophysiological and biochemical features of mania and depression in bipolar illness, despite their opposite phenomenological manifestations. It may also give rise to the question as to whether only bipolar affective depression is responsive to lithium. In fact, some unipolar depressed patients who respond well to lithium could be considered "pseudo-bipolar" because of their family history, cyclothymic personality traits, or drug-induced hypomanic episodes. However, it cannot be denied that lithium does not help all bipolar depressions, and that it also has spectacular effects in some clearly unipolar depressive syndromes.

In the seventies, some authors advocated trying lithium with patients who had previously been unsuccessfully treated with tricyclic antidepressants, MAO inhibitors, or ECT. Neubauer and Bermingham (1976) described 20 depressive patients, mostly unipolar, with anergy, obsessional and hypochondriacal traits, and with a positive family history. These patients failed to respond to pharmacological and ECT treatments but rapidly responded to lithium. Kupfer, Pickar, Himmelhoch & Detre (1975) postulated that hypersomnia and hyperphagia were present in unipolar depressive patients who were responsive to lithium but not to tricyclic antidepressants. It is still not clear which specific features of unipolar depressive patients make them lithium-responsive during acute depressive episode. Presumably, unipolar and bipolar affective illness are not homogeneous conditions.

Of practical concern is the issue of recommending the use of lithium in the treatment of acute depression. In some American and British centers, it appears that lithium has been used routinely as a drug of first choice, especially with bipolar depressed patients who may be candidates for further lithium prophylaxis. Lithium may be also selected for treating unipolar depressions refractory to other antidepressant drugs. However this option was recently replaced by another therapeutic strategy, namely, adding lithium to antidepressants in order to potentiate their effect.

## LITHIUM POTENTIATION OF ANTIDEPRESSANT TREATMENT

Studies in recent years revealed a novel and interesting clinical feature of lithium. In a substantial proportion of patients with endogenous depression refractory to treatment with antidepressant drugs, the addition of lithium may turn antidepressant "nonresponders" into "responders."

The first controlled study of concomitant administration of lithium and antidepressants was performed collaboratively by Scandinavian investigators (Lingjaerde, Edlund, Gormsen, Gottfries, Haugstad, Herman, Hollnagel, Makimattila, Rasmusen, Remvig & Robak, 1974). This work comprised a total of 45 patients randomly assigned either to a tricyclic antidepressant alone or to an antidepressant combined with lithium. The authors determined that lithium did not interfere adversely with the therapeutic effect of antidepressants and might even synergize their action. However, the evidence of rapid potentiation by lithium of the therapeutic effect of antidepressants came from the observation of Canadian authors seven years later (De Montigny, Grunberg, Mayer & Dechenes, 1981). The terms "potentiation" or "augmentation" were coined to describe the beneficial effects of the addition of lithium to the antidepressant medication. It was also suggested that sequential administration of antidepressant drugs and then lithium may be necessary for this effect.

Between 1981–88, studies on lithium potentiation of antidepressants in about three hundred patients were reported. Many papers on this issue were small sample studies or case reports; the largest studies were presented by Price, Charney & Heninger (1986) (84 patients) and by De Montigny, Cournoyer, Morissette, Langlois and Caille (1983) (39 patients). The studies to date have not revealed any special choice to administer antidepressant drug prior to lithium in order to obtain lithium potentiation. The most frequent antidepressants used were tricyclics such as imipramine (e.g., De Montigny et al., 1983), clomipramine (e.g., Schrader & Levien, 1985), and amitriptyline (e.g., Rybakowski & Matkowski, 1987). The trials with MAO inhibitors included phenelzine (Nelson & Byck, 1982) and tranylcypromine (Price, Charney & Heninger, 1985). Furthermore, a variety of "atypical" antidepressants were given prior to lithium addition. A good potentiating effect was also described after lithium was added following previously unsuccessful treatment of depression with carbamazepine (Post & Kramlinger, 1988).

Although there is a relative predominance of unipolar depressive patients in the reports on lithium potentiation of antidepressants, this potentiation was found in patients with both unipolar and bipolar depression. The study of Price et al. (1986) suggests a tendency toward better efficacy in unipolar depression. In the second largest sample, that used by De Montigny et al. (1983), all the patients had unipolar illness. The study of Nelson & Mazure (1986), comprising depressive patients with psychotic features, demonstrated significantly better results in bipolar patients. In our recent study (Rybakowski & Matkowski, 1988), we found markedly better potentiating effects of lithium in patients with bipolar depression than with unipolar depression. Thus, any definite judgement on lithium augmenting efficacy in relation to the polarity of illness would be still premature. Furthermore, no relationship was demonstrated between lithium potentiation and the gender of depressed patients.

A remarkable proportion of patients with delusional depression appear in the reports of lithium augmentation. Delusional depression responds poorly to antidepressant drugs and usually requires adding neuroleptic or electroconvulsive treatment. In most cases, lithium was successfully added to an antidepressant-neuroleptic combination (Nelson & Mazure, 1986). However, there were also patients with delusional depression where the introduction of lithium to antidepressants was sufficient to obtain a substantial improvement or remission (Pai, White & Dean, 1986). There was also a significant representation of patients over 60 years of age. This might be due to the fact that endogenous depressive syndromes occurring in old age with concomitant organic or somatic conditions represent a subgroup refractory to antidepressant treatment. Good results were achieved by the addition of small doses of lithium in geriatric depressed patients, who were also medically ill (Kushmir, 1986; Dumlao, Perl, Bagne & Gurevich,

1988; Katona & Finch, 1988).

The report of De Montigny et al. (1981) indicated a very rapid onset of lithium potentiation (within 48 hours), but this was not unequivocally confirmed in the majority of subsequent studies. While some patients showed marked improvement within the first week of lithium administration, in others, a clinical alleviation was seen by the second to fourth weeks. The latter course may be similar to lithium therapeutic action when used as a sole drug in the treatment of acute depressive episodes. In the study of Price et al. (1986), only 3 patients, out of 26 with marked improvement, met the criteria for a rapid response within the first few days. In our own study, out of 24 patients having lithium added to tricyclic or atypical antidepressants, 8 of them showed significant amelioration within the first week. Rapid response was more prominent in patients with bipolar depression and usually preceded subsequent full remission (Rybakowski & Matkowski, 1988). According to De Montigny et al. (1983), rapid amelioration in most patients may continue even with lithium withdrawal. Nevertheless, it seems probable that the quick onset of action is more prevalent with lithium potentiation of antidepressants than when lithium is used as the sole antidepressant.

In most studies of lithium potentiation, serum lithium level was kept within the recommended therapeutic range, i.e., 0.6–1.2 mmol/l. However, it should be stressed that beneficial effects were also obtained with lower concentrations, such as 0.4 mmol/l (De Montigny et al., 1983) and, in geriatric depressive patients, even in the range 0.2–0.3 mmol/l (Kushmir, 1986). Recently, Stein & Bernadt (1988), compared the efficacy of the addition of 250 mg vs 750 mg of lithium carbonate in 26 patients with tricyclic-resistant depression in a double-blind trial. One-third of their depressive patients responded to a very low dose of lithium where the serum levels were 0.1–0.3 mmol/l. A further one-third improved on the increased dosage of lithium. This may suggest that in some circumstances even very low doses and low serum levels could effect potentiation.

The cumulative data concerning the efficacy of lithium potentiation may be misleading, because small sample studies and case reports described mostly patients with favorable response. In the largest sample, reported by Price et al. (1986), clinically significant response, within four weeks, was seen in 56% of their patients. De Montigny et al. (1983) showed greater than 50% improvement as measured by the Hamilton Rating Scale within 48 hours of lithium addition in 72% of unipolar patients. In the paper by Nelson & Mazure (1986) on lithium potentiation using an antidepressant-neuroleptic combination, the positive response rate amounted to 53%. In our own study the response rate was 69% (Rybakowski & Matkowski, 1988). The small sample studies demonstrated good results in 60–70% of cases. Probably, it would be safe to say that a beneficial effect of lithium may be anticipated in at least half of antidepressant-resistant patients within four weeks, and in about 1/4 of them within the first week.

From a theoretical point of view, the most interesting question is: what is the mechanism of lithium potentiation for antidepressant action? It is known that, despite administering the adequate dose of antidepressants, achieving optimal plasma levels, and continuing the treatment for a sufficient period of time, 20% of endogenously depressive patients may still remain unresponsive to such treatment. The reasons for such unresponsiveness are not fully understood. From the pharmacodynamic point, it may be due to the insufficient interaction of antidepressant drugs at the receptors sites in CNS. The most coherent hypothesis so far, put forward by De Montigny et al. (1983), postulates lithium-antidepressant interaction at central serontoninergic synapses. Experimental studies demonstrated that pretreatment with different kinds of antidepressant drugs (tricyclics, MAO inhibitors, atypical) causes an increased sensitivity of brain neurons to serotonin, probably due to heterogeneous mechanisms (De Montigny & Aghajanian, 1978). Acute lithium administration exerts mostly presynaptic serotoninergic effect by augmenting the tryptophan transport, but also exerts agonistic action on serotonin receptors (Sangdee & Franz, 1980). Thus, interaction of lithium and antidepressant drugs will markedly potentiate the serotoninergic mechanisms that may be related to the alleviation of depression.

In terms of practical recommendations, the introduction of lithium appears to be a therapeutic modality worth attempting in a broad range of antidepressant-resistant patients with both bipolar and unipolar endogenous depressive syndromes. Old age is not a critical factor disqualifying the patients from lithium addition, which may achieve good results in older patients. Adequate precautions connected with lithium dose and somatic effects must be taken. Adding lithium can also be considered in patients with psychotic depression which has been unsuccessfully treated with an antidepressant-neuroleptic combination. Such an option would be particularly helpful if the patient is reluctant to undergo ECT treatment or if such treatment proved ineffective in the past.

After adding lithium to antidepressant medication, it may be expected that a significant amelioration or complete remission of depressive symptoms will be achieved in at least half of the patients treated. Such a trial would be especially recommended for patients whose course of the disease makes them candidates for subsequent lithium prophylaxis.

## LITHIUM PROPHYLAXIS OF DEPRESSION

First observations of the possible prophylactic effects of lithium against recurrences of endogenous depressions were made in the early sixties by Hartigan (1963) in England and Baastrup (1964) in Denmark. Subsequent studies unequivocally confirmed the observed prophylactic effects (Baastrup & Schou, 1967; Angst, Weiss, Grof, Baastrup & Schou, 1970; Baastrup, Poulsen, Schou, Thomsen & Amdisen, 1970). This led to a new treatment approach in psychiatry. It has been gradually recognized that psychotropic drugs not only may be effective in treating the acute episode of the illness, but also, when administered longitudinally, may favorably influence the natural course of the illness. Periodic affective disorders are characterized by recurrences; the number and intensity of these recurrences may serve as a criterion for the severity of disease. Lithium was the first drug shown to exert preventive action against both depressive and manic recurrences and thus to attenuate their frequency and severity.

Prophylactic action of lithium was evidenced in a vast number of studies and for thousands of patients. The methods used compared the course of disease in equal time before and on lithium (mirror-image studies), compared lithium and placebo in a double-blind design, and followed the course of disease after lithium discontinuation.

There is extensive documentation on lithium prophylaxis in bipolar affective illness. Following lithium administration, in 40–50% of patients, the disease completely ceases, i.e., no more depressive or manic relapses occur. In 20–30%, the frequency and severity of episodes diminishes and in 10–20%, lithium fails to affect the course of disease. In our study (Rybakowski, Chlopocka-Wozniak & Kapelski, 1980), comparing equal time periods before taking lithium and while taking lithium in 61 patients with bipolar affective illness, we observed a reduction of affective episodes by 71% in patients on lithium, and that of hospitalizations by 72%. The complete prophylactic effect was seen in 44% of patients, a partial effect in 28%, and poor results in 28%. Therefore, there was some prophylactic effect for 72% of the patients.

In bipolar affective illness, the prophylaxis of depression is linked to the prophylaxis of mania. It has been postulated that lithium may prevent the occurrence of depressive episodes by preventing manias: in connection with this, some recent studies showed that the prophylactic effect of lithium was better in patients showing a sequence of mania-depression episodes, i.e., episodes of depression were preceded by the episodes of mania (Grof, Haag, Grof & Haag, 1987). In our own study (Rybakowski, Chlopocka-Wozniak, Kapelski & Strzyzewski, 1980), it was suggested that the relative prophylactic efficacy of lithium against depression and mania may also depend on gender, i.e., it was better against depression in male and against mania in female bipolar patients. No other drug for bipolar affective illness was more effective than lithium in terms of prophylactic efficacy against both depression and mania. In recent years, the anticonvulsant drug carbamazepine was shown to exert good prophylactic effects in rapidly cycling patients who responded poorly to lithium (Post & Uhde, 1987). Comparative studies of the prophylactic effect of lithium and carbamazepine are, for the most part, in favor of lithium (Watkins, Callender, Thomas, Tidmarsh & Shaw, 1987). The relative preventative action of the lithium-carbamazepine combination, which seems to be prophylactically superior than lithium alone, has not yet been determined (Svestka, Nahunek & Ceskova, 1987).

There are fewer studies of lithium prophylactic efficacy in unipolar depression than in bipolar affective illness. However, the investigations clearly show that the quality of the prophylactic effect of lithium in unipolar depression is similar to that in bipolar illness (Schou, 1979). Also, in many studies the prophylactic efficacy of lithium in unipolar depression was found to equal or to better that of antidepressant drugs (Coppen, Ghose, Rao, Bailey & Peet, 1978; Kane, Quitkin, Rifkin, Ramos-Lorenzi, Nayak & Howard, 1982). Thus, for long-term prophylaxis of depressive episodes, both in bipolar and unipolar illness, lithium still remains the drug of first choice.

The factors determining a good prophylactic response to lithium are somewhat difficult to asses due to the problems of unequivocally defining an individual patient as a prophylactic "responder" or "nonresponder." As Schou (1984) notes: "...one cannot ever decide with certainty whether the individual patient is a responder or a nonresponder. Even a patient who does not have a single episode during lithium need not necessarily be a responder, because conceivably he or she also might have been without relapse if lithium had not been given. And even a patient who has many relapses during lithium treatment could still be a responder, because he or she might had even more frequent relapses if lithium had not been given" (p. 413). Nevertheless, to some extent, determining factors appear to be different for bipolar affective illness and unipolar depression. Family history of bipolar illness and cyclothymic personality traits may be connected with a better response to lithium. In bipolar patients, a mania-depression sequence is a favorable prognostic, while rapid cycling is not (Dunner & Fieve, 1974). In unipolar patients with an endogenous symptom pattern (vital melancholia, marked retardation), the absence of neurotic anxiety traits, as well as psychogenic precipitating factors, may be predictive of a good response (Maj, Arena, Lovero, Pirozzi & Kemali, 1985). It was also suggested that good therapeutic effects of lithium in acute episodes and also for the initial two to three year period of lithium prophylaxis may be a harbinger of subsequent long-term favorable prophylactic response. There is still controversy whether some biological factors connected with membrane properties such as erythrocyte lithium or sodium transport activity or some HLA antigens can determine the quality of a lithium prophylactic effect (Rybakowski, 1982, 1987).

Whether the affective illness is bipolar or unipolar may also determine the psychotherapeutic approach to the patient on lithium prophylaxis. Part of the psychotherapeutic relation between the psychiatrist, the patient, and his family should be directed to the acceptance by the patient of such a long-term drug regimen. The gradual efficacy of lithium intake by itself exerts a psychological reinforcing effect on patients. During the early stages of therapy, as well as when there are relapses, the role of such an approach is especially crucial. Bipolar patients who have memories of their hypomanic state equate them with their "normal, good functioning." They sometimes blame lithium for dampening their mental functions and may, on this account, discontinue the drug. This frequently leads to a full-blown affective episode. This is not the case with unipolar depressed patients. They have recollections only of disastrous depressive episodes and are ready for compliance regarding medication to prevent these recurring episodes. This is further reinforced by their frequently perfectionistic personality traits.

Up to the end of the seventies, optimum lithium prophylactic blood plasma levels were thought to be between 0.8–1.2 mmol/l. Prien & Caffey (1976) described twice as many relapses in patients with serum levels below 0.7 mmol/l than in those above 0.8 mmol/l. On the other hand, in many studies, lower levels were repeatedly found to be prophylactic (Jerram & McDonald, 1978). Now there is a tendency to keep prophylactic lithium levels within a lower range, i.e., 0.5–0.8 mmol/l, which in most cases is sufficient for prophylactic action and also decreases the incidence of side effects (Schou, 1984).

A relevant question in lithium therapy is how long lithium maintenance should be continued. An early study of Baastrup et al. (1970) showed a similar incidence of relapse upon lithium discontinuation after a relatively short term (1–3 years) or for a long-term (4–6 years) lithium prophylaxis. Angst & Grof (1976), on the basis of the analysis of the natural course of affective disease, agree that prophylactic treatment should not be shorter than 10 years. Cases of acute confusional states following discontinuation of lithium intake after several years (the symptoms disappeared after lithium had been reinstituted) have been reported (Wilkinson, 1979). All this experience shows that lithium prophylaxis of affective illness may be compared to substitute therapy and that there is a substantial risk of relapse after lithium discontinuation, regardless of its previous duration of use. There are many successful experiences with over 20 years of continuous lithium prophylaxis. Thus, the recommendation would be to continue lithium indefinitely if the psychiatric results are satisfactory and somatic conditions do not preclude its use.

A vast amount of knowledge has also been accumulated on lithium-induced somatic side effects. For many years, the main concern has been suspected deterioration of kidney function as an effect of lithium. The latest studies show that these effects can be minimized by adopting lower prophylactic lithium levels, i.e., 0.5–0.8 mmol/l (Schou & Vestergaard, 1988). Also, many other somatic effects of lithium (e.g., hypothyroidism) can be successfully managed without discontinuating the drug.

The integrated approach has been recommended in the case of unsatisfactory response to lithium prophylaxis, taking into account both nonpharmacological and pharmacological factors (Schou, 1988). Nonpharmacological factors, such as proper selection of patients, their cooperation and compliance in taking medication, as well as a possibility of providing them with supplementary psychological support, may be linked to the outcome of lithium prophylaxis. However, in some cases, combining lithium with other drugs or switching to prophylactic alternatives such as carbamazepine may be a better option.

## CONCLUSIONS

The judicious use of lithium may be beneficial for a substantial proportion of patients with unipolar or bipolar depression. Lithium may be used at times in the treatment of acute depressive episodes and even more frequently for the potentiation of antidepressant treatment. So far, lithium still remains the drug of first choice for the prevention of depressive episodes in the course of both unipolar and bipolar affective illness. The most important lesson learned from nearly 30 years of experience with long-term lithium administration was that a pharmacological prophylaxis might be possible and effective in most patients with endogenous depression. Due to lithium prophylaxis, thousands of patients with affective illnesses have lived lives of far better quality. Recent studies also seem to show that prophylactic treatment may be connected with significant reduction of the risk of suicide, the main mortality factor of endogenously depressed patients (Schou & Weeke, 1988).

The scope of contemporary lithium use with affective patients may be illustrated by the fact that, on the average, 1 person in 1,000 in Britain or the United States is treated with lithium. The efficacy of lithium in reducing the number of disabling episodes and hospitalizations and its low cost as a drug make it a treatment modality with an extremely low cost/benefit ratio. If lithium is given to appropriate patients and the psychiatrists are knowledgeable enough about the therapy, the benefits of such treatment can be maximized.

## References

Angst, J., Weiss, P., Grof, P., Baastrup, P.C. & Schou, M. (1970). Lithium prophylaxis in recurrent affective disorders. *British Journal of Psychiatry*, 116, 604–614.

Angst, J. & Grof, P. (1976). The course of monopolar depressions and bipolar psychoses. In R. Villeneuve (ED.), *Lithium in Psychiatry: a synopsis*. Quebec, Les Presses de l'Universite Laval.

Baastrup, P.C. (1964). The use of lithium in manic-depressive psychoses. *Comprehensive Psychiatry*, 5, 396–408.

Baastrup, P.C. & Schou, M. (1967). Lithium as a prophylactic agent. It s effect against recurrent depressions and manic-depressive psychosis. *Archives of General Psychiatry*, 16, 162–172.

Baastrup, P.C., Poulsen, J.C., Schou, M., Thomsen, K. & Amdisen, A. (1970). Prophylactic lithium: Double blind discontinuation in manic-depressive and recurrent depressive disorders. *Lancet*, 2, 326–330.

Baron, M., Gershon, E.S., Rudy, W., Jonas, W.Z. & Buchsbaum, M. (1975). lithium carbonate response in depression: Prediction by unipolar/bipolar illness, average evoked response, catechol-0-methyltransferase and family history. Archives of General Psychiatry, 32, 1107–1111.

Beckmann, H., St-Laurent, J. & Goodwin, F.K. (1975). The effect of lithium on urinary MHPG in unipolar and bipolar depressed patients. *Psychopharmacology*, 42, 277–282.

Cade, J.FR.K. Lithium salts in the treatment of psychotic excitement. *Medical Journal of Australia*, 36, 349–352.

Coppen, A., Ghose, K., Rao, R., Bailey, J. & Peet, M. (1978). Mianserin and lithium in the prophylaxis of depression. *British Journal of Psychiatry*, 133, 206–210.

Corcoran, R.E., Taylor, R.D. & Page, I.H. (1949). Lithium poisoning from the use of salt substitutes. *Journal of American Medical Association*, 139, 685–688.

De Montigny, C. & Aghajanian, G.K. (1978). Tricyclic antidepressants: long-term treatment increases responsitivity of rat forebrain neurons to serotonin. *Science*, 202, 1303–1306.

De Montigny, C., Grunberg, F., Mayer, A. & Dechenes, J.P. Lithium induced rapid relief of depression in tricyclic antidepressant drug non-responders. *British Journal of Psychiatry*, 138, 252–256.

De Montigny, C., Cournoyer, G., Morissette, R., Langlois, R. & Caille, G. (1983). Lithium carbonate addition in tricyclic antidepressant-resistant unipolar depression. *Archives of General Psychiatry*, 40, 1327–1334.

Dumlao, M.S., Perl, E., Bagne, C.A. & Gurevich, D. (1988). Antidepressants and lithium in refractory depression in geriatric patients. Presented at the First International Conference on Refractory Depression, Philadelphia, 6–7 October.

Dunner, D.L. & Fieve, R.R. (1974). Clinical factors in lithium carbonate prophylaxis failure. *Archives of General Psychiatry*, 30, 229–233.

Egeland, J.A. (1988u). A genetic study of manic-depressive disorder among the Old Order Amish of Pennsylvania. *Pharmacopsychiatry*, 21, 74–75.

Friedel, R.O. (1976). Lithium and depression. *American Journal of Psychiatry*, 133, 976.

Goodwin, F.K., Post, R.M. & Dunner, D.L. (1973). Cerebrospinal fluid amines metabolites in affective illness. The probenecid technique. *American Journal of Psychiatry*, 130, 73–79.

Grof, E., Haag, M., Grof, P. & Haag, H. (1987). Lithium response and the sequence of episode polarities: Preliminary report on a Hamilton sample. *Progress in Neuro-Psy-*

*chopharmacology & Biological Psychiatry*, 11, 199–204.

Jerram, T.C. & McDonald, R. (1978). Plasma lithium control with particular reference to minimum effect levels. In F.N. Johnson & S. Johnson (Eds.), *Lithium in medical practice* (pp. 407–413). Baltimore, University Park Press.

Kane, J.M., Quitkin, F.M., Rifkin, A., Ramos-Lorenzi, J.R., Nayak, D.D. & Howard, A. (1982). Lithium carbonate and imipramine in the prophylaxis of unipolar and bipolar II illness. *Archives of General Psychiatry*, 39, 1065–1069.

Katona, C.L.E. & Finch, E.J.L. (1988). Lithium augmentation for refractory depression in old age. Presented at the First International Conference on Refractory Depression, Philadelphia, 6–7 October.

Khan, M.C., Wickham, E.A. & Reed, J.V. (1987). Lithium versus placebo in acute depression: a clinical trial. *International Clinical Pscyhopharmacology*, 2, 47–54.

Kupfer, D.J., Pickar, D., Himmelhoch, J.M. & Detre, T.P. (1975). Are there two types of unipolar depression? *Archives of General Psychiatry*, 32, 866–871.

Kushmir, S.L. (1986). Lithium-antidepressant combination in the treatment of depressed, medically ill geriatric patients. *American Journal of Psychiatry*, 143, 378–379.

Lange, C. (1896). *Periodische Depressionzustande und ihre Pathogenesis auf dem Boden der harnsauren Diathese.* Hamburg und Leipzig, Verlag von Leopold Voss.

Leonhard, K. (1957). *Aufteilung der endogenen Psychosen.* Berlin, Akademie Verlag.

Lingjaerde, O., Edlund, A.H., Gormsen, C.A., Gottfries, C.G., Haugstad, A., Herman, I.L., Hollnagel, P., Makimattila, A., Rasmusen, K.E., Remvig, J. & Robak, O.H. (1974). The effects of lithium carbonate in combination with tricyclic antidepressants in endogenous depression. *Acta Psychiatrica Scandinavica*, 50, 233–242.

Maj, M., Arena, F., Lovero, N., Pirozzi, R. & Kemali, D. (1985). Factors associated with response to lithium prophylaxis in DSM-III major depression and bipolar disorder. *pharmacopsychiatry*, 18, 309–313.

Mendels, J. & Frazer, A. (1973). Intracellular lithium concentration and clinical response: toward a membrane theory of depression. *Journal of Psychiatric Research*, 10, 9–18.

Mendels, J. (1976). Lithium in the treatment of depression. *American Journal of Psychiatry*, 133, 373–378.

Mendlewicz, J. & Fleiss, J.L. (1974). Linkage studies with x-chromosome markers in bipolar (manic-depressive) and unipolar (depressive) illnesses. *Biological Psychiatry*, 9, 261–294.

Nahunek, K., Svestka, J. & Rodova, A. (1970). Zur Stellung der Lithium in der Gruppe der Antidepressiva in der Behandlung von akuten endogenen und Involutionsdepressionen. *International Pharmacopsychiatry*, 5, 249–257.

Nelson, J.C. & Byck, R. (1982). Rapid response to lithium in phenelzine non-responders. *British Journal of Psychiatry*, 141, 85–86.

Nelson, J.C. & Mazure, C.M. (1986). Lithium augmentation in psychotic depression refractory to combined drug treatment. *American Journal of Psychiatry*, 143, 363–366.

Neubauer, H. & Bermingham, P. (1976). A depressive syndrome responsive to lithium. *Journal of Nervous and Mental Diseases*, 163, 276–281.

Noyes, R., Dempsey, G.M., Blum, A. & Cavanaugh, G.L. (1974). Lithium treatment of depression. *Comprehensive Psychiatry*, 15, 187–193.

Pai, M., White, A.C. & Deane, A.G. (1986). Lithium augmentation in the treatment of delusional depression. *British Journal of Psychiatry*, 148, 736–738.

Perris, C. (1966). A study of bipolar (manic-depressive) and unipolar recurrent depressive psychosis. *Acta Psychiatrica Scandinavica*, 42, suppl. 194.

Post, R.M. & Uhde, T.W. (1987). Carbamazepine as a treatment for refractory depressive illness and rapidly cycling manic-depressive illness. In J. Zohar & R.H.Belmaker (Eds.) *Treating resistant depression* (pp. 187–232). New York, PMA Publishing Corp., New York.

Post, R.M. & Kramlinger, K. (1988). Carbamazepine-lithium combination: clinical and laboratory effects. *Psychopharmacology*, 96 (suppl), S101.

Price, L.H., Charney, G.S. & Heninger, G.R. (1985). Efficacy of lithium-tranylcypromine treatment in refractory depression. *American Journal of Psychiatry*, 142, 619–623.

Price, L.H., Charney, D. & Heninger, G.R. (1986). Variability of response to lithium augmentation in refractory depression. *American Journal of Psychiatry*, 143, 1387–1392.

Prien, R.F. & Caffey, E./M. (1976). Relationship between dosage and response to lithium prophylaxis in recurrent depression. *American Journal of Psychiatry*, 133, 567–570.

Rybakowski, J. (1981). Lithium prophylaxis of depression. In T.A. Ban, R. Gonzalez, A.S. Jablensky, N. Sartorius & F.E. Vartanian (Eds.) *Prevention and treatment of depression* (pp. 173–182). Baltimore, University Park Press.

Rybakowski, J. (1987). Clinical and biochemical aspects of the prophylaxis of depression (in Polish). *Psychiatria Polska*, 21, 212–219.

Rybakowski, J., Chlopocka, M., Lisowska, J. & Czerwinski, A. (1974). Studies of the therapeutic efficacy of lithium carbonate in endogenous depressive syndromes (in Polish). *Psychiatria Polska*, 8, 129–134.

Rybakowski, J., Chlopocka-Wozniak, M., Kapelski, Z. & Strzyzewski, W. (1980). The relative prophylactic efficacy of lithium against manic and depressive recurrences in bipolar patients. *International Pharmacopsychiatry*, 15, 86–90.

Rybakowski, J., Chlopocka-Wozniak, M. & Kapelski, Z. (1980). Clinical evaluation of the prophylactic efficacy of long-term lithium carbonate administration to patients with endogenous depressive syndromes (in Polish). *Psychiatria Polska*, 14, 357–361.

Rybakowski, J. & Matkowski, K. (1987). Synergistic action of lithium and thymoleptics in endogenous depress (in Polish). *Psychiatria Polska*, 21, 115-120.

Rybakowski, J.K. & Matkowski, K. (1988). Lithium potentiation of various antidepressants. Presented at the First International Conference on Refractory Depression, Philadelphia, 6–7 October.

Sangdee, C. & Franz, D.N. (1980). Lithium enhancement of central 5-HT transmission induced by 5-HT precursors. *Biological Psychiatry*, 15, 59–75.

Schou, M. (1979). Lithium in unipolar affective illness. *Archives of General Psychiatry*, 36, 849–851.

Schou, M. (1984). Causes of and remedies for incomplete response to lithium. In E. Usdin (Ed.) *Frontiers in biochemical and pharmacological research in depression* (pp. 413–420), New York, Raven Press.

Schou, M. (1988). The integrated approach. On the significance of pharmacological and nonpharmacological factors when lithium prophylaxis fails. *Acta Psychiatrica Scandinavica*, 78, suppl. 345, 119–123.

Schou, M. & Vestergaard, P. (1988). Prospective studies on a lithium cohort. Renal function. Water and electrolyte metabolism. *Acta Psychiatrica Scandinavica*, 178j, 427–433.

Schou, M. & Weeke, A. (1988). Did manic-depressive patients who committed suicide receive prophylactic or continuation treatment at the time?. *British Journal of Psychiatry*, 153, 324–327.

Schrader, G.D. & Levien, H.E.M. (1985). Response to sequential administration to clomipramine and lithium carbonate in treatment-resistant depression. *British Journal of Psychiatry*, 147, 573–575.

Stein, G.S. & Bernadt, M. (1988). A double-blind trial of very low doses of lithium in tricyclic-resistant depression. In N.J. Birch (Ed.). *Lithium: inorganic pharmacology and psychiatric use* (pp. 35–36) Oxford-Washington, IRL Press.

Svestka, J., Nahunek, K. & Ceskova, E. (1987). Combined lithium and carbamazepine is more effective in the prophylaxis of affective psychoses than lithium alone. *Activitas Nervosa Superior (Praha)*, 29, 184–185.

Watkins, S.E., Callender, K., Thomas, D.R., Tidmarsh, S.F. & Shaw, D.M. (1987). The effect of carbamazepine and lithium on remission from affective illness. *British Journal of Psychiatry.*, 150, 180–182.

Wilkinson, D.G. (1979). Difficulty in stopping lithium prophylaxis? *British Medical Journal*, 1, 235–236.

Worall, E.P., Moody, J.P., Peet, M., Dick, P., Smith, A., Chambers, C., Adams, M. & Naylor, G.J. (1979). Controlled studies of the acute antidepressant effects of lithium. *British Journal of Psychiatry*, 135, 255–262.

# 14

# Lithium Salts: Implications of an Empirical Medical Treatment for Recurrent Affective Illness

Mitchell J. Cohen and J. Raymond DePaulo, Jr.
*Johns Hopkins University*

KEY WORDS: lithium salts, syndrome, disease, neurovegetative changes, motivated behaviors, biological markers, genetic heterogeneity, phenotypic marker, linkage, F.J. Cade, empathic, empirical, rational

## INTRODUCTION

In his book, *A Mind That Found Itself*, Clifford Beers, who founded the seed organization of the National Mental Health Association, describes his transition from profound depression of longer than one year's duration into mania in the summer of 1902:

> No man can be born again, but I believe I came as near it as ever a man did. To leave behind what was in reality a hell, and immediately have this good green earth revealed in more glory than most men ever see it, was one of the compensating privileges ...

> During the first few hours I seemed virtually normal. I had none of the delusions which had previously oppressed me; nor had I yet developed any of the expansive ideas, or delusions of grandeur, which soon began to crowd in upon me ... But the pendulum, as it were, had swung too far.

> My fellow-patients who for fourteen months had seen me walk in silence—a silence so profound and inexorable that I would seldom heed their friendly salutations—were naturally surprised to see me in my new mood of unrestrained loquacity and irrepressible good humor ...

> For several weeks ... I did not sleep more than two or three hours a night. Such was my state of elation, however, that all signs of fatigue were entirely absent ... [despite] abnormal mental and physical activity in which I then indulged (Beers, 1981, 72–75).

This alternation of melancholia and euphoria, which Beers vividly details from the perspective of the phenomenological experience, is so characteristic of manic-depressive illness that it is familiar not only to clinicians, but also to non-professional lay persons as a most recognizable aberration of mental life.

This chapter focusses on recurrent affective disorders, particularly manic-depressive illness in which episodes of significantly elevated and depressed mood occur, as well as mixed states in which manic and depressive features appear simultaneously. Lithium salts have greatest utility in this condition. We will use the terms manic-depressive illness and bipolar affective disorder interchangeably.

Recurrent unipolar depression is a significantly more common disorder in which exclusively depressive episodes repeatedly occur. Approximately twenty percent of patients with this disorder eventually develop a manic episode and are reclassified as bipolar. We will briefly consider the relevance of lithium treatment to recurrent depressive illness.

Patients suffering manic episodes without any depressions are relatively rare, and are considered by DSM-III-R nosology to be "bipolar"; clinically, these patients predictably develop depression at some point in their lives and respond to lithium like patients who have already suffered both mania and depression.

This chapter is about the significance of lithium treatment in the conception of recurrent affective disorders as diseases and the validative research establishing lithium as effective, empirical medical treatment. Also discussed are other aspects of our treatments, as well as their practical and conceptual implications for patients, clinicians, and research.

We see lithium as established treatment for recurrent affective illness, particularly manic-depressive illness, and as such strongly supportive of a disease formulation of these disorders. We start with a consideration of the concept of disease, particularly as applied to psychiatry.

## SYNDROMES AND DISEASES

In their book *The Perspectives of Psychiatry,* McHugh and Slavney (1983) emphasize that the concept of a disease ultimately seeks to understand clinical problems as the outgrowth of a demonstrable abnormality of a body part (or pathology) which is itself explained by a specific causal or etiologic agent. This concept guides medical diagnosis, treatment, and research into a variety of causal mechanisms, including genetic, infectious, degenerative, and post-traumatic processes (McHugh & Slavney, 1983, 33–37). (See Figure 14-1.) In psychiatry the concept of disease has been more challenging to apply because neuropathologies of most mental disorders have been elusive, and the clinical symptoms, when mild, merge imperceptibly with normal experiences. Despondency and elation are moods everyone experiences. Defining abnormal moods is, therefore, in large part a matter of degree and, at some level, arbitrary, if other kinds of information are not sought. Information about other signs and symptoms, such as neurovegetative changes, cyclicity, occurrence of opposite mood states, and family history, can be particularly helpful in distinguishing illness of mood from normal experience.

In the absence of neuropathology and etiology, we do best to construct the clinical evidence suggestive of a disease process by noting the commonalities in symptoms and course across various groups of patients. The more similarities in clinical features, the more likely we are defining a useful category if not ultimately a disease entity.

The first step is identifying a syndrome, a typical roster of complaints (symp-

## Figure 14–1

Diagramatic application of disease reasoning applied to dementia, a clinical psychiatric sign/symptom cluster (syndrome) with some established pathological findings and a known etiologic factor in the case of pernicious anemia. Subdural hematoma has the demonstrable pathology of a collection of blood on the brain (seen on radiologic study) and could have various provocative etiologies such as head trauma or surgery. Alzheimer's disease has some known neuropathological (brain) findings but etiology is not yet established. [Reprinted from McHugh and Slavney (2)]

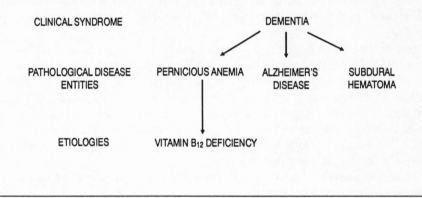

toms) and clinical observations (signs). McHugh and Slavney write:

> Patients complain not of diseases but of changes in their mental and physical states. To these symptoms physicians add signs (observations derived from examination) and data from laboratory tests. A collection of symptoms and signs occurring in a certain temporal pattern can then be used to categorize the patient's problem as a particular instance of a more general phenomenon (McHugh & Slavney, 1983, 33).

When pathological findings and etiologies are associated with such a category, a disease entity is established. At this point in the study of bipolar and episodic mood disorders, we have a solid clinical sign/symptom cluster or syndrome, but only suggestive evidence of pathology and etiology. We await conclusive neuropathology and causative factors that would make these disorders clearly diseases.

## BIPOLAR DISORDER AS A DISEASE ENTITY

The utility of Lithium in stabilizing the course of bipolar disorder is only one of various lines of evidence leading physicians for centuries to suspect a pathological basis for the disorder. It is actually one of the later observations. One of the most fundamental observations is the stereotypy of its clinical presentation. Greek and Roman physicians described clear melancholias, although the descriptions of mania were quite broad, encompassing various excited, agitated states. In the first century Aretaeus noted the occurrence of subdued and agitated episodes in the same patient (Georgotas & Gershon, 1981). In the nineteenth century more narrow formulations appeared which are the clear forbearers of current concepts of the disorder. Falret in the 1850s described *circular insanity* which he believed had a familial basis

(Sendler, 1983). In 1874 Karl Kahlbaum coined the term "cyclothymia", which is still in use to designate a mild form of the disorder. It was appreciated that a subgroup of asylum patients had similar mood symptoms and periodicities of illness, but Kraepelin (1921) organized prior observations and added clarity by distinguishing his *manic-depressive insanity* from dementia praecox (schizophrenia). He described an episodic illness with periods of relapse and remission, as well as alternating periods of euphoria and depression. He also delineated characteristic changes in appetites for food, sleep, and sex, changes in self-attitude, and typical content of delusions and hallucinations. He based his classification system on observations of thousands of patients and in so doing provided the foundation for modern nosology.

Stereotypy of course itself is suggestive of some biological foundation to mood disorders. Additionally, certain neurovegetative changes are indications of a bodily abnormality. Neurovegetative changes include alterations in *motivated behaviors*, namely sleep, eating, and sex, as well as changes in energy level and intellectual function. Patterns of change in these functions frequently but not always accompany mood illness. In manic episodes there may be a decreased need for sleep, increased libido, and increased hunger and eating. Severe depressions often involve anorexia, diminished libido, and sleep disturbance.

Motivated behaviors show patterns across the animal kingdom and lead us to believe they are internally regulated. For example, a subjective need to sleep or eat grows the longer rest and food are withheld and abates with satiation when interest in the activity quickly diminishes (McHugh & Slavney, 1983, 36). Derangements in these behaviors and their subjectively experienced drives or appetites is suggestive of internal pathological change. Changes in energy and intellectual function are seen in endocrine and neuropsychiatric conditions with known pathologies such as Alzheimer's disease; their occurrence in mood disorders suggests disease.

The familial pattern of the disorder is another old and powerfully persuasive observation supporting a disease process. This clustering of illness in families has been so clear that people historically have not spoken openly of mentally ill relatives, owing to misguided fear of bringing scrutiny upon themselves. There are frequent literary examples of families carrying the "curse" of madness, for example, Edgar Allen Poe's *Fall of the House of Usher,* in which various family members suffer psychosis and catatonic episodes. Mood disorders are the most likely basis for this lay awareness of familial clustering of psychiatric illness. Accumulated observations over the centuries have led to research into the genetics of bipolar illness.

Twin and adoption studies have provided substantial evidence of a genetic basis for affective disorders generally. Concordance rates in monozygotic twin pairs consistently exceed those for dizygotic pairs for unipolar and bipolar illness. One of the most well-done Danish studies, specifically on manic-depressive illness, compared 55 monozygotic and 52 dizygotic twin pairs, finding concordance rates of 0.67 and 0.20 respectively in these pairs (Bertelsen, Harvald & Hauge, 1977). Identical twins are over three times more likely to both show bipolar disorder if one does than are fraternal twins; all the studied twins of bipolars were much more likely to have bipolar disorder than the general population.

## Figure 14–2

Sites on Chromosomes 6, 11, and X associated with transmission of bipolar disorder in studied kindreds. (Reprinted from McKusick, V.A. *Mendelian inheritance in man.* 7th ed. Baltimore: Johns Hopkins University Press, 1986.)

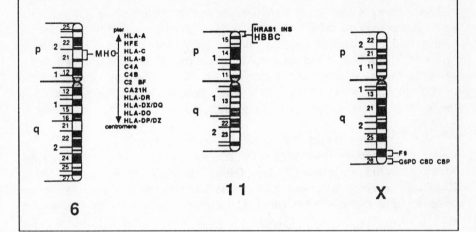

Adoption studies have shown that adopted out children of depressed parents have significantly increased rates of depression and suicide, suggesting genetic influences are more powerful than modeling of parents or other environmental issues. One study of manic-depressive adoptees by Mendlewicz and Rainer (1977) showed much higher prevalence of affective disorder in their biologic parents (31%) than in their adoptive parents (12%), the adoptive parents having a prevalence comparable to that in the general population (Mendlewicz & Rainer, 1977).

Kraepelin first suggested a genetic basis for manic-depressive illness. Since the late 1960s evidence for single-gene affective disorders has accumulated. It now appears that a number of different genes can individually give rise to bipolar affective disorder (DePaulo & Simpson, 1987). This situation is called genetic heterogeneity (see Figure 14-2).

There have been three basic approaches used in examining the genetic issue in bipolar disorder. *Segregation analysis* uses careful family pedigrees to make statistical estimates of the likelihood of a specific type of genetic transmission explaining the pattern of affected individuals in the kinship, for example, autosomal dominant or X-chromosome (called sex-linked) mechanisms. *Linkage* analysis takes advantage of genetic traits or *phenotypic markers* such as an enzyme deficiency occurring in individuals who also have mood disorder to demonstrate genetic basis for the mood disorder. This approach seeks to show that the marker and the mood disorder are linked when the marker and mood disorder always occur together in the studied families. This means there is statistically high probability that the genetic marker and the disease genes are located close together on the same chromosome.

Segregation analysis has produced useful but sometimes conflicting findings (Bucher, Elston, Green & Whybrow, 1981). Linkage studies depend on nature providing opportunities through phenotypic markers occurring in individuals suffering with mood disorders. Recent developments using *restriction endonucleases* to generate DNA fragments (RFLP technology) have allowed mapping of the human genome to progress and will guide further research. RFLP technology makes accessible to genetic study a much larger number of chromosomes and families with the illness.

Linkage studies have led to identifications of two markers at the same location on the X chromosome, which in certain pedigrees appear involved in the transmission of bipolar affective disorder (Baron, 1977; Mendlewicz, Linkowski & Wilmotte, 1980). One of the phenotypic markers carried on the X chromosome is color-blindness; the other is the enzyme glucose–6-phosphate dehydrogenase (G6PD). In other kinships transmission of the manic-depressive illness is linked to the human leukocyte antigen (HLA) region on chromosome 6 (Kruger, Turner & Kidd, 1982).

RFLP technology has led to the identification by Egeland et al. of a location at the top of chromosome 11 involved in the transmission of bipolar disorder in a large Amish family in Pennsylvania (Egeland, Gerhard, Pauls, Sussex, Kidd, et al., 1987). Hodgkinson et al. again demonstrated genetic heterogeneity in bipolar disorder by using the RFLP methods to show that bipolar disorder in an Icelandic kindred was *not* carried on this area of chromosome 11, but must be coded for elsewhere in the genome (Hodgkinson, Sherrington, Gurling, Marchbanks, Reeders, et al., 1987).

Thus the disorder is believed to have a variety of genetic abnormalities underlying it. This is a common situation in medicine. Probably the great majority of cases of manic-depressive disorder have genetic causes. Careful research utilizing RFLP methods is now underway to confirm and expand on present findings. Kindreds with the disorder in its various forms are being identified, and associations of mood disorder with markers located throughout the human genome are currently being sought in many centers.

Further suggestive of a bodily abnormality as the basis for these syndromes are the secondary manias and depressions (in DSM-III-R terms: organic affective syndromes). These are clinical manic episodes provoked most frequently by drugs, head trauma, or intracerebral processes such as stroke, especially right frontal strokes (Cohen & Niska, 1980; Jampala & Abrams, 1983). Depressions also can follow various somatic illnesses, drugs, and stroke, especially left frontal strokes (Robinson, Kubos, Starr, Rowe & Price, 1984). The antihypertensive drug Reserpine, known to deplete synaptic vesicles of neurotransmitters, caused profound depressions in treated patients and fell out of use as a result.

Conspicuously absent are pathological findings in most affective disorders. Having a chromosomal location does not give the pathology (bodily abnormality) even though etiology (genetic transmission) is established. Chromosomal location and genes (and study of the effects of gene products) should ultimately lead to identification of nervous system pathology.

While there remains an absence of clear pathology, a variety of somatic changes have been associated with mood disorders. These have been referred to as *biological markers* of mood disorder, and some are demonstrated more convincingly than others. These have included neurochemical findings in blood, urine, and cerebrospinal fluid (Schildkraut, 1965; Hollister, Davis & Berger, 1980), alterations in immune system function (Calabrese, Kling & Gold, 1987), and predictable electroencephalographic abnormalities in sleep architecture (Spiker, Cable, Cofsky, Foster & Kumpfer, 1978). The sleep findings and abnormalities of hypothalamic-pituitary-adrenal axis function (Carroll, Curtis & Mendels, 1976; Schlesser, Winokur & Sherman, 1983) in a subpopulation of depressives are examples of well-established markers. A role of serotonin in affective disorders is strongly suggested by various data, and other monoamine neurotransmitters are also clearly involved. However, no definitive pathological findings which always lead to or underlie the clinical disorders have at present been established.

Into this amalgam of clinical patterns, neurovegetative changes, familial clustering, secondary (organic) affective syndromes with known somatic origins, and biological markers is added lithium, a pharmacologic agent which appears to control acute manic episodes, decrease the recurrences of manias and depressions in a majority of patients, and to have some role as well in treating acute depressive episodes. The establishment of lithium's clinical utility in cycling affective illness is a significant additional line of evidence that these syndromes, as yet without fully delineated etiologies or pathologies, are disease entities.

The effects of lithium make the point that formulating these syndromes as diseases and then searching for bodily causes and medical treatments will lead to reduction of impairments and amelioration of suffering in our patients.

## THE ADVENT OF LITHIUM

Chemically, lithium is a monovalent cation. It has a long and, at points, notorious career in clinical medicine. It is one of the oldest agents in the modern psychopharmacologic repertoire, preceding the discovery of neuroleptics and the antidepressants, although its widespread use occurred later. Trace amounts of lithium occur in animal tissue (including man), aquatic and edible plants (including seaweed and sugarcane), and natural springs. Lithium was first isolated in 1817 by John A. Arfvedson. In the nineteenth century unsubstantiated claims were made of therapeutic uses in gout, rheumatoid arthritis, and renal calculi. Some of these ideas were based on lithium's ability to form a soluble salt of urate. Lithium's presence in European spa waters added to their popularity at this time. Garrod's report of treating rheumatic gout with lithium in 1859 is generally cited as the first medical use (Garrod, 1859). Lithium bromides were noted to be particularly sedating and were recommended as tonics and tranquilizers in the late 1800s (Georgotas & Gershon, 1981).

None of these early clinical claims were ultimately established as effective treatments. An unfortunate application of lithium occurred in the 1940s when lithium chloride was used liberally as a salt substitute in patients with heart disease. Several deaths occurred due to its toxicity at high serum levels and resulted in understandable timidity in the medical community to use the drug without reliable blood level monitoring.

Dr. John F. J. Cade's report in 1949 of the remarkable response of a small group of psychiatric patients to lithium marks the beginning of the delineation of its true medical utility. Cade, a gifted, experienced clinician, was also involved in independent research with self-described unsophisticated techniques. He was looking for an "endogenous" or "humoral" factor in his manic patients.

Believing this might be excreted in their urine, he injected manic patients' urine into the peritoneum of guinea pigs and observed that it seemed more toxic to the animals than "normal" human urine. He injected lithium salt into the animals along with patients' urine to dissolve uric acid crystals in his attempts to identify modifiers of the presumed "manic factor." He thought uric acid might be one of these modifiers and used lithium to solubilize it. When he injected the animals with lithium as well as manic patients' urine, he noted that lithium appeared to have a "protective" effect on the animals. He reasoned lithium was counteracting the "manic factor" in the patient urine. He also noted a calming effect on the animals.

This led Cade to try lithium in manic and other psychiatric patients. He was aware of the drug's use for centuries in man, although without significant benefit. He describes the first manic patient placed on lithium as follows:

> This was a little wizened man of fifty-one who had been in a state of manic excitement for five years. He was amiably restless, dirty, destructive, mischievous and interfering...in a back ward for all those years and bid fair to remain there for the rest of his life (Cade, 1970, 223).

He describes the response to lithium in dramatic terms:

> ... by the fifth day it was clear that he was in fact more settled, tidier, less disinhibited and less distractible. From then on there was steady improvement... (Cade, 1970, 224).

Cade goes on to report that the patient improved enough to be transferred to a less acute ward within three weeks. Two months later he was discharged from the hospital and resumed work, doing well until he stopped taking the medication some six months later. At that point he relapsed, was readmitted, improved when lithium was reinstituted, and was again back at his job within one month.

In his 1949 report Cade described this type of clear response in all ten of the manic patients he placed on lithium. He went on to describe improvement in the "excited" features of schizophrenic and "schizoaffective" patients to whom he administered the drug. He felt there was "no fundamental improvement" in psychotic depressives. He also discerned no noticeable effects himself when he took the drug. Thus he was led to postulate a specific antimanic effect for lithium.

Cade's report was followed by sporadic use of the drug in Europe in similar cases, generally with good results, but it was not until 1954 that a systematic study examining this effect appeared from Denmark by Schou et al. (Schou, Juel-Nielsen, Stromgren & Voldby, 1954). Gershon and Yuwiler (1960) published the first American clinical paper. In 1963 R. Maggs' paper in the *British Journal of Psychiatry* described a placebo-controlled trial of lithium in manic patients. Major clinical studies then accelerated, particularly in Scandinavia, England, and the U.S. The relative delay in the clinical research effort, particularly in the U.S., has been attributed to a number of factors, including the emergence, just after Cade's report, of neuroleptic drugs, as well as the major classes of antidepressants. Residual caution in the use of lithium owing to the deaths incurred during its use as a salt substitute, and Cade's small sample size and his relative obscurity also contributed.

As Schou has noted, by late 1967, over twenty-six positive reports had appeared in the literature, affirming the effectiveness of lithium in manic patients (Schou, 1967). Indeed only one small study in which the lithium dose was questionably low yielded less than positive results. Collapsing all the work to that point led to the conclusion that seventy to eighty percent of manics would begin to respond to lithium therapy within two weeks. Those conclusions essentially reflect current scientific data and clinical wisdom. However, new issues to confront were appearing at this point in the study of the drug. The episodic nature of manic-depressive illness raised conceptual problems. The possibility of spontaneous remissions of the disorder decreased confidence levels. Since episodes could vary in intensity, it was difficult to be sure a seeming improvement in course was not due in some cases to the natural occurrence of less severe episodes by chance after initiation of the drug. The question of efficacy in depressive episodes needed to be tackled as well. Fundamentally two problems existed: (1) an episodic illness cannot be adequately studied cross-sectionally; (2) since Cade's original doubts about efficacy in depression, no further clarity was obtained.

Following up claims by Hartigan (1963) and his own earlier work, Baastrup collaborated with Schou in an elaborate longitudinal nonblind study of eighty-eight bipolar patients treated intermittently with lithium over the course of nearly seven years (Baastrup & Schou, 1967). This extensive effort overcame the serious problem of studying this episodic illness at any particular point in time.

Summarizing over their full sample, comprised of all females, the authors noted that off lithium the patients suffered thirteen weeks with psychotic symptoms per year; on lithium this fell to two weeks per year of psychosis. The interval between episodes fell from an average of eight months off lithium to sixty to eighty-five months with lithium. Stabilization occurred in patients with any type of recurrent affective episodes, manic, depressed, or a combined course, irrespective of age of patient or duration of illness. The courses of illness in the studied patients were elegantly displayed in time-bar graphs which visually made clear lithium's effect (see Figure 14-3).

This study provided the most impressive evidence for a stabilizing or "prophylactic" effect of lithium in cycling, episodic mood disorders to date, but it was not without significant problems, and it launched an impassioned, productive controversy. Blackwell and Shepherd scrutinized reports up to and including the Baastrup and Shou study supporting a prophylactic effect and claimed evidence was less impressive on careful review than it appeared on first look, concluding "[A] controlled evaluation of lithium as a prophylactic agent is long overdue" (Blackwell & Shepherd, 1968, 968). A dialogue of letters ensued, and the problems with the accumulated research were identified. Blackwell and Shepherd wrote:

> ...[A] novel use for an old remedy has escaped the stringent demands for safety and efficacy ... This illustrates how treatments for which there is an appealing rationale and a widely felt need, or which are difficult to evaluate readily, become established and may continue to flourish. This is particulary true in psychiatry, where objective criteria are scanty, illnesses are chronic, and effective remedies are not always available for comparison (Blackwell & Shepherd, 1968, 971).

## Figure 14–3

Elegant time-bar depictions of the courses of patients studied longitudinally by Baastrup and Schou before and after initiation of treatment with lithium, showing decreases in frequency and length of severe manic, depressive, and mixed episodes in the majority of cases after starting lithium. Limitations of this study are discussed in text. [Reprinted from Baastrup and Shou (1967).]

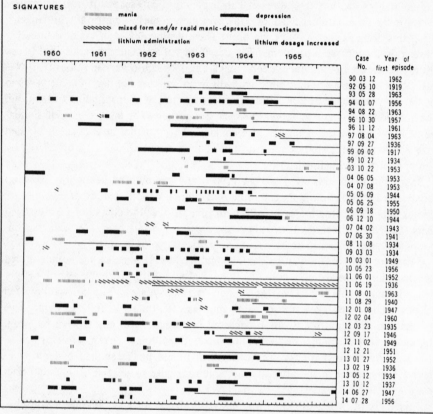

This largest study by Baastrup and Schou had been an open design. Selection bias, adequate documentation of cyclicity in some of the cases, and advantage of lithium over other treatments with some prophylactic effect were sound scientific concerns. Patients in the studies done to this point had received a variety of agents besides lithium including neuroleptics, ECT, and antidepressants. Periods on and off lithium varied in the studies, and placement on drug was not random.

At the same time, the drug struck many clinicians as so effective that placing some patients on placebo for research purposes raised ethical considerations. Finally, there is the issue of the prophylactic effect itself. It is an unusual effect in that it is neither cure nor full prevention. Antibiotics can cure infection by eradicating the pathogenic bacterium; banning leaded paint may be fully preventive of lead-related encephalopathy in children with pica. The prophylactic effect of lithium is a different but familiar type of effect in medicine. It is, however, more difficult to demonstrate this effect for an episodic psychiatric disorder than it is in diabetes mellitus, for example, where insulin clearly provides significant control of blood sugar and morbidity, but not cure.

These questions ultimately led to refined, blind studies which firmly established lithium as an agent which stabilizes the course of bipolar disorder in approximately eighty percent of cases. Lithium's role in depressive illness has been a focus of studies and controversy. At present lithium appears considerably more useful in acute manias than in acute depressive episodes, but it clearly has a utility in controlling at least a subgroup of recurrent unipolar depressive illnesses even in the absence of any manic periods (Coppen, Noguera, Bailey, Burns, Swani, et al., 1971; Mendels, Secunda & Dyson, 1972; Prien, Klett & Caffey, 1974; Mendels, 1976; Baastrup, Poulsen, Schou & Amdisen, 1970).

Other uses for lithium are less well established. Per Cade's original observations, it appears to have some utility in any syndrome that is episodic and has prominent affective features such as "schizoaffective" disorder and cyclothymic disorder. Further understanding of these disorders and clarity in their diagnosis will be required before the role of lithium in them can be fully determined. Lithium has also been used in alcoholism, behavioral dyscontrol syndromes, bulimia, personality disorders, and phobic and other anxiety disorders with varying or non-replicated effects (Schou, 1979; Sheard, Marini, Bridges & Wagner, 1976; Sheard & Marini, 1978; Judd & Huey, 1986; Merry, Reynolds, Bailey & Coppen, 1976; Lackroy & Van Praag, 1971).

Some of the difficulty in establishing lithium's utility in cyclic affective disorders came as well from a more fundamental issue than methodologic problems and the complexity of studying an episodic chronic psychiatric illness. Etiology and pathology of affective disorders remain elusive; moreover, the mechanism of action of lithium is undetermined. A persuasive case may have been easier to make if a cause or clear somatic pathology and a demonstration of some effect upon this by lithium were known.

There are a number of theories about lithium's mechanism of action. Its effects on neurotransmitter systems have been focusses of study and theory. Lithium cuts across various neurotransmitter systems with action on catecholamines, indolamines, and acetylcholine. This, in part, derives from important modulating effects on two second-messenger systems of known importance in the brain: the cyclic AMP and phosphatidyl inositol systems (Worley, Baraban & Snyder, 1987). These systems act as critical mediators in the effects of various neurotransmitters including serotonin, norepinephrine, and dopamine. Lithium inhibits the action of the enzyme adenylate cyclase in the cAMP system. The relationship of this inhibition to therapeutic effect is not yet clear; it is involved in lithium's effects on urination and the thyroid gland. It is also involved in the decreased prostaglandin synthesis and central levels of luteinizing hormone (LH) seen with lithium treatment. Thyroid and prostaglandin effects may be primarily or secondarily involved in therapeutic effect.

Distribution of the cAMP system is more localized in the central nervous system than is the inositol system. Lithium was actually important in the discovery of the inositol system and likely affects a variety of neurotransmitters through this system. Lithium's action as a calcium modulator and known effects on serotonin are likely mediated through this system. Lithium's calcium-channel blocking effects may well relate to therapeutic action. Another calcium-channel blocker, Verapamil, has growing evidence of clinical utility in bipolar disorder.

A variety of effects on the serotonin system have been postulated. Lithium may increase neuronal uptake of the serotonin amino acid precursor tryptophan. An increase in serotonin release from neurons and a decrease in activity of tryptophan hydroxylase, a rate-limiting enzyme involved in serotonin synthesis, occur at different points with lithium therapy (Belmaker, 1981; Treiser, Cascio, O'Donohue, Thoa, Jacobowitz, et al., 1981).

Lithium may also be involved as a cation in stabilizing cells and making them less excitable, intracellularly replacing or interacting with other cations such as sodium, potassium, or magnesium.

A broader question in terms of mechanism of action is whether lithium is an agent with specific effects on cyclic mood disorders or a broadly active agent particularly helpful in patients but with similar effects in "normals." Classically, the point of view has been that there is little activity in normals, based primarily on self-reports by lithium researchers such as Cade and Schou (Schou, 1968; Cade, 1970, 223). This turns out to be by no means clear as quite different self-reports and small studies have more recently appeared, albeit methodologically limited. Studies on normals are few, small in sample size, nonblind, and of inadequate duration to assess many lithium effects (Judd, Hubbard, Janowsky & Huey, 1977; Judd, Hubbard, Janowski, Huey & Attewell, 1977; Kropf & Muller-Oerlinghausen, 1977; White, Bhart, Whipple & Boyd, 1979). These suggest there may be a decrease in mood fluctuations in normals on the drug and raise the question of mild cognitive impairment, a side effect sometimes reported by patients. We are examining effects in normals at the present time in a placebo-controlled blind cross-over study.

As long as the etiologies of bipolar and other cyclic mood disorders remain unestablished, and the mechanism of action of lithium and its specificity are unclear, lithium will remain an *empirical* treatment, which implies that only its clinical efficacy is established.

## THE NATURE OF MEDICAL THERAPIES

In this section we will look at broad conceptions of treatment and how lithium best fits into these. Treatments in medicine can be stratified into the empathic, the empirical, and the rational (Folstein & McHugh, 1976, 284–286). In reality, each of these is a component of good patient care, but it is useful to separate them out for the purpose of understanding what we are doing in taking care of patients.

Empathic therapy involves "being in the world with the patient," "walking in his shoes," calling on resources of compassion and experience with similar patients to appreciate and acknowledge the symptomatic suffering of a *person*. This occurs at the "human" level of being understood as an individual in crisis and at the clinical level of an expert recognizing the distress that comes with certain illnesses. The patient feels some connection with the physician or therapist, perceives concern, realizes the clinician has seen patients like him before, and is often comforted and reassured. The sense that the clinician recognizes the presentation is particularly beneficial in patients who are least well informed or very depressed and believe they are alone in an unusual, grim illness; it also promotes confidence in the clinician's ability to help by virtue of his having treated others. Psychotherapy, which we elaborate upon below, can be seen as a systematically applied empathic treatment.

Empirical treatments address symptoms, but by unknown mechanisms. The applications of empirical interventions are validated by observation. The more systematic and controlled the observations, the more confidence clinicians can justifiably place in the intervention. The double-blind placebo-controlled randomized clinical trial is the most definitive method of studying treatment from the empirical perspective. This point is central here because the way the intervention works is not necessarily understood. An empirical treatment is established as working, but why it works is not yet known.

Rational treatments work by interrupting a disease process in a known way. These treatments work at the level of etiologic or pathological factors. We understand how they are effective; they interact with causal or disease maintenance mechanisms.

Empathic treatment should ideally be involved in every clinician-patient contact. It is most defined and developed in psychotherapeutic interventions. Empirical treatments are quite common in medicine. Chemotherapeutic agents are used for control or palliation in cancers with demonstrated efficacy in the absence of mechanistic or etiologic clarity. Many rational therapies are initially empirical. Salicylates were used for pain control empirically before their effects in prostaglandin pathways were clear.

Empirical and rational dimensions are involved in every medical treatment. Surgical removal of a localized malignant tumor could be both empirical and rational. Surgery may be known to decrease pain and prolong life through controlled study. It is also known that surgery for certain tumors decreases the possibility that malignant cytopathology will increase and be found in metastatic sites. Rational treatments also must be proven to have empirical efficacy. Coronary artery bypass grafting in patients with severe blockages of coronary vessels is a rational treatment which replaces occluded vessels with more patent ones; the empirical value of this treatment in terms of increasing longevity and decreasing symptoms has been the subject of study and controversy. Empathic methods such as psychotherapy also must be empirically tested through outcome research. The efficacy of lithium in attenuating the frequency and severity of exacerbations in patients with responsive episodic affective disorder is well established through a series of progressive, elaborate clinical trials. As we can tell approximately eighty percent of bipolar patients that lithium will offer some stabilization, but we cannot tell them why, it is an empirical medical therapy.

As empirically efficacious as lithium is, it must be accompanied by an empathic effort that recognizes the frustration and hopelessness which derive from a recurrent illness that profoundly affects emotional life. With the locus of symptoms being moods and associated views of self, the world, and the future, these patients will need to talk at varying levels of depth about the experience and management of their illness.

The treatment of lithium-responsive cyclic affective disorders thus requires the blending of pharmacologic and psychotherapeutic efforts. Fortunately, we have found these components can positively reinforce each other at the level of abstract therapeutic goals as well as at the level of practicality.

Frank has described psychotherapy as fundamentally combatting demoralization (Frank, 1974, 312–344). A person comes to believe his distress and circumstances will not change, feels hopeless, is enduring psychological symptoms, and most needs a sense of optimism that things will improve from the amalgam of relationship, setting, theoretical framework and technique that Frank suggests is universal to psychotherapy.

McHugh teaches that the goal of all therapeutic work is "setting patients free" from the burdens of difficult moods, thoughts, abnormal perceptions, patterns of behavior, or intense drive states that are dominating mental life at the time of presentation (McHugh, 1987, 582).

Psychotherapy's broadest goal can be seen as liberating the patient from the demoralization and enslavement that comes of persistent psychological symptoms. Psychotherapy empathetically addresses the suffering of a particular person in a dilemma. Frank (1974, 165–199) has further pointed out that the therapist-patient relationship is the central common agent of efficacy in psychotherapies and has been widely joined in this view. To this degree, this is a method that features empathic treatment. It is possible, however, to assess its effects empirically, and outcome studies are steadily being refined.

Lithium combats demoralization most powerfully by virtue of its clinical effects on the course of illness. When a patient can appreciate the stabilizing effect of the drug, a renewal of hope for the future often follows. Most psychiatrists are familiar with testimonials like that of one recent thirty-five-year-old woman who suffered recurrent mania and depression for ten years prior to being placed on lithium carbonate:

> "I thought this is the way I would always be and I just had to live with it, if I could, for the sake of my daughter. I hade no idea things could be so different."

This particular patient has a mother and sister who have similar affective symptoms and may benefit from lithium.

Lithium also gives the patient some liberation from the endogenous, autonomous cycling of illness. It thereby plays a significant role in restoring a sense of some mastery and control over the problem, neutralizing demoralization, and complementing our goals in psychotherapy.

At the same time the empathic, psychotherapeutic work supports the empirical chemotherapy. The symptoms of lithium-responsive illnesses are, after all, experienced in mental life. Unlike the signs of orthopedic injury, a laceration, or jaundice, the physician can only fully appreciate psychological changes occurring in the patient's private, internal world through a relationship with the patient. Perceived concern, compassion, and experience with such problems will lead patients to disclose troubling changes and events in mental life to their doctors, signalling times for serum level checks or dosage changes. Additionally, the psychotherapeutic work keeps treatment aimed at individual as well as illness; it also makes the important point for patients that treatment is more than a pill.

As Jamison has pointed out, patients with episodic affective disorders, especially bipolar disorder, have not historically been considered good psychotherapeutic candidates, particularly for psychoanalysis (Jamison, 1988). Their predictable unpredictability, intermittent compliance, provocative behaviors during periods of elevated mood, and impaired cognition in depression confound the psychotherapeutic process. Generally accepted clinical wisdom is that lithium treatment significantly reduces these psychotherapeutic problems.

Similarly, psychotherapy addresses some practical problems of lithium management. Noncompliance is probably the largest problem and grows out of a variety of patient concerns: loss of productive, pleasant hypomanias; side effects; difficulty accepting the need for long-term medication; a sense of inadequacy in not being able to master the problem "on one's own; " and others. Psychotherapy encompasses exploration of such feelings as well as work in helping the patient differentiate between "normal" and pathological mood shifts, a frequent issue that arises for us and others in clinical work with affectively ill patients and their families.

Family therapy and marital therapy may also lead to increased medication compliance if, for example, family members are fearful of psychotropic agents or believe the patient could fight off illness without medication if he just tried harder.

## IMPLICATIONS OF AN EMPIRICAL MEDICAL THERAPY

The advent of lithium has important implications for patients, clinicians, and research. We have already covered the reciprocally supportive interaction of lithium and psychotherapeutic efforts that clinicians observe, but the availability of a pharmaceutical treatment is not exclusively perceived by patients and families as positive or welcome. Normal moods swings, crises, and failures of coping pass; chronic diseases treated with medication do not. Lithium is symbolically a badge of medical patienthood. It threatens denial, making the problem difficult to attribute wholly to "stress" or transient decompensations of the individual or support systems.

At the same time, the clear effect of the drug removes blame from the family system and makes even less tenable metaphorical interpretations of psychiatric illness such as those proposed by Laing (1965) and Szaz (1974). This can provide considerable relief to family members who have borne unnecessary guilt and dispel misguided concepts that the patient is "sanely handling an insane situation" or expressing himself in an unconventional way. Family members then can become more effective in helping the ill relative. Of course the specter of heredity is less easily put out of mind by relatives as a result of lithium's "medicalization" of manic-depressive illness.

The appearance of effective chemotherapy also points out the need for the various accoutrements of responsible medical care, including blood tests, laboratories, provision for intensive management, including specialized hospitals or units, and standard teaching about medication that professionals provide to patients. Interpretive conceptualizations of hospitals as "ships of fools" designed to remove reformers and iconoclasts from threatened, conventional society (Szaz, 1971; Foucault, 1973) again become gratuitous in the face of what are overt realities of caring for suffering individuals.

The issues lithium brings to the "stigma" of mental illness are complicated, and our patients tell us neither a medication-controlled disease nor a psychological dysfunction is a particularly valuable social credential. Some patients and their families, however, do appear more comfortable dealing with a problem formulated as a disease.

A risk of medicalization of the illness is minimization of individual responsibility. This is one of many reasons why simply providing lithium with blood and side-effect monitoring will not be effective. Lithium is not a cure. The patient must be sensitive to the impact of alcohol and drug use, sleep deprivation, and other behaviors on his affective disorder. He must become ever more aware of the early symptoms of exacerbations. He also needs to enter a cooperative effort with his physician that includes maintaining a fairly stable sodium intake and complying with dosage schedules and blood and urine laboratory studies. Control of the disorder is still much more than a prescription. Jamison nicely points out the pitfalls of an exclusively medical or chemotherapeutic approach:

> Conceptualizing manic-depressive illness as a fundamentally medical disorder has many advantages to the patient—decreased stigma, effective and specific treatment, minimizing family and individual responsibility for its origins—but it can also discourage discussion of significant life issues, problems involved in adjusting to manic-depressive illness and its consequences, and psychological concerns about taking lithium, carbamazepine, or other medications (Jamison, 1988, 11).

Excepting some qualifications on issues of stigmatization and the continued importance of individual responsibility for behavior, this fully corresponds with our own view.

A new stigmatization may develop for manic-depressives who are not lithium-responders or are refractory to newer "second-line" agents like carbamazepine—the "sickest" bipolars, the "non-responders." In any event, the non-responders present a new psychotherapeutic challenge as their disappointment with agents quite helpful to other sufferers must be dealt with.

The concept of disease also appears to be one rallying point for self-help groups. Certainly Alcoholics Anonymous has used a less clearly evidenced disease model to build its treatment approach, which ironically then opposes most psychotropic medications. In this decade self-help groups have arisen for patients with episodic mood disorders. The availability of medication may have influenced a more useful attitude toward the medical community in these groups.

The National Depressive and Manic-Depressive Association (NDMDA) and the Depression and Related Affective Disorders Association (DRADA) are examples of groups started by patients and their families which seek consultation from physicians on issues of treatment, research, and education. We are closely affiliated with DRADA, which maintains an office in the Johns Hopkins Hospital and represents a combined effort of patients, families, and a variety of interested clinicians to support, educate, and conduct public outreach. We are persuaded that the notion of a disease that needs to be recognized, confronted, and studied serves as a crystallizing influence for this type of group.

## Implications for Research

Cade's serendipitous discovery of the antimanic properties of lithium make a powerful case for the importance of basic and animal research. As we have described, lithium had been used for centuries in humans without appreciation of its full utility in mood disorders. Cade's work with guinea pigs led him to conduct the first clinical trial. His work underscores the central role of the clinical trial and led to the described series of increasingly evolved, elaborate studies establishing lithium's efficacy. These must be seen as having advanced the state of the art of controlled drug studies. As Schou writes:

...the scientific scuffles focused attention on the treatment and led to further testing, and the result is that the prophylactic action of lithium treatment in manic-depressive illness is today one of the best-documented effects in psychiatric pharmacotherapy (Schou, 1988, 1834).

The advent of a treatment with clear efficacy allows subgrouping into responders, partial responders, and non-responders. Little clinical distinctions have emerged between bipolars with fairly typical courses who differ only in response to lithium; but, it is interesting to note that patients with depressions and hypomanias without full manic episodes (bipolar II) may have less benefit from lithium treatment (Dunner, Stallone & Fieve, 1976; Dunner, Stallone & Fieve, 1982). We are unaware of systematic studies of lithium response in seasonal affective disorders (SADS) in which depressions and/or manias predictably occur at certain times of year and may improve with therapeutic exposure to light (Rosenthal, Sack, Gillin, Goodwin, Davenport, Mueller, Newsome & Wehr, 1984). Clinical variants with less clear lithium response raise the question of whether they are etiologically, genetically, or pathologically distinct entities.

## SUMMARY

Lithium is a central piece in the conception of bipolar and other cyclic affective disorders diseases. It represents a well-established empirical medical treatment which joins other lines of evidence suggestive of a pathological disease entity in the absence of core pathological markers or full etiologic understanding. New technology is making genetic research the next wave of supportive evidence.

Lithium has revolutionized the treatment of episodic mood disorders, requiring medical expertise in combination with sensitivity to the symptoms and sequelae of a syndrome which affects work, interpersonal relationships, family life, and most fundamentally, mental life—its appetites and motivated behaviors, perceptions, cognitions, and of course, moods. Old issues of stigma may recede as new ones arise to challenge the clinician. Medicalization has favored the growth of novel self-help groups, some in collaboration with clinicians, to educate and support patients and families.

The advent of lithium marks a significant step in the appreciation of recurrent affective illnesses as diseases. Its systematically established stabilizing and prophylactic effects have pointed the direction for clinical trials of second- and third-line agents as well as emphasizing the relevance of further basic and animal research. Lithium has also made an important social point as it has been estimated by the National Institute of Mental Health to have prevented sixty-five billion dollars in medical expenditures over the past fifteen years (Harvard, 1988).

We can, however, be but temporarily satisfied with empirical treatment. Only a rational treatment, understood to interrupt a delineated pathological process, will rapidly lead to a spectrum of agents with fewer side effects and differential efficacy for subtypes of recurrent affective illness. Patients, their families, and society cannot wait for curiosity, clinical acumen, and serendipity to coincide as they did for Dr. Cade to reveal each new chemotherapy.

# References

Baastrup, P.C. & Schou, M. (1967). Lithium as a prophylactic agent. Its effect against recurrent depression and manic depressive psychosis. *Archives of General Psychiatry*, *16*, 162–172.

Baastrup, P.C., Poulsen, J.C., Schou, M., *et al* (1970). Prophylactic lithium: double-bind discontinuation in manic-depressive and recurrent-depressive disorders. *Lancet*, *2*, 326–330.

Baron, M. (1977). Linkage between an X-chromosome marker (deutan color-blindness) and bipolar affective illness. *Archives of General Psychiatry*, *24*, 721–727.

Beers, C.W. (1981). *A Mind that Found Itself.* Pittsburgh: Pittsburgh University Press.

Belmaker, R. (1981). Receptors, adenylate cyclase, depression, and lithium. *Biological Psychiatry*, *16*, 333–350.

Bertelsen, A., Harvald, B. & Hauge, M. (1977). A Danish twin study of manic-depressive disorders. *British Journal of Psychiatry*, *130*, 330–351.

Blackwell, B. & Shepherd, M. (1968). Prophylactic lithium: another therapeutic myth? An examination of the evidence to date. *Lancet*, *1*, 968–971.

Bucher, K.D., Elston, R.C., Green, R. & Whybrow, P., *et al* (1981). The transmission of manic depressive illness—II. Segregation analysis of three sets of family data. *Journal of Psychiatric Research*, *16*, 65–78.

Cade, J.F.J. (1949). Lithium in the treatment of psychotic excitement. *Medical Journal of Australia*, *36*, 349–352.

Cade, J.F.J. (1970). The story of lithium. In F.J. Ayd and B. Blackwell (Eds.), *Discoveries in Biological Psychiatry*. Philadelphia: J.P. Lippincott Company.

Calabrese, J., Kling, M.A. & Gold, P.W. (1987). Alterations in immunocompetence during stress, bereavement, and depression: focus on neuroendocrine regulation. *American Journal of Psychiatry*, *144*, 1123–1134.

Carroll, B.J., Curtis, G.C. & Mendels, J. (1976). Neuroendocrine regulation in depression: I. Limbic system-adrenocortical dysfunction. *Archives of General Psychiatry*, *33*, 1039–1044.

Cohen, M.J. & Niska, R.W. (1980). Localized right cerebral hemisphere dysfunction and recurrent mania. *American Journal of Psychiatry*, *137*, 847–848.

Coppen, A., Noguera, R., Bailey, J., Burns, B.H., Swani, M.S., Hare, E.H., Gardner, R. & Maggs, R. (1971). Prophylactic lithium in affective disorders. *Lancet*, *2*, 275–279.

DePaulo, J.R. & Simpson, S.G. (1987). Therapeutic and genetic prospects of an atypical affective disorder. *Journal of Clinical Psychopharmacology*, *7*, 52S–53S.

Dunner, D.L., Stallone, F. & Fieve, R.R. (1976). Lithium carbonate and affective disorders: V. A double-blind study of prophylaxis of depression in bipolar illness. *Archives of General Psychiatry*, *33*, 117–121.

Dunner, D.L., Stallone, F. & Fieve, R.R. (1982). [Letter to the editor] Prophylaxis with lithium carbonate: an update. *Archives of General Psychiatry*, *39*, 1344–1345.

Egeland, J.A., Gerhard, D.S., Pauls, D.L., Sussex, J.N., Kidd, K.K., Allen, C.R., Hosletter, A.M. & Housman, D.E. (1987). Bipolar affective disorder linked to DNA markers on chromosome 11. *Nature*, *325*, 783–787.

Folstein, M.F. & McHugh, P.R. (1976). Phenomenological approach to the treatment of "organic" psychiatric syndromes. In B.B. Wolman (Ed.), *The Therapist's Handbook: Treatment Methods of Mental Disorders*. New York: Van Nostrand Reinhold, 279–

286.

Foucault, M. (1973). *Madness and Civilization.* New York: Vintage Books.

Frank, J. (1974). *Persuasion and Healing.* Baltimore: Johns Hopkins University Press.

Garrod, A.B. (1859). *Gout and Rheumatic Gout.* London: Walton and Maberly.

Georgotas, A. & Gershon, S. Historical perspectives and current highlights on lithium treatment in manic-depressive illness. *Journal of Clinical Psychopharmacology, 1,* 27–31.

Gershon, S. & Yuwiler, A. (1960). Lithium A specific psychopharmacological approach to the treatment of mania. *Journal of Neuropsychiatry, 1,* 229–241.

Hartigan, G.P. (1963). The use of lithium salts in affective disorders. *British Journal of Psychiatry, 109,* 810–814.

Harvard Medical School Department of Continuing Education (1988). Treatment of Mood Disorders—Part I *The Harvard Medical School Mental Health Letter, 5, 2.*

Hodgkinson, S., Sherrington, R., Gurling, H., Marchbanks, R., Reeders, S., Mallet, J., McInnis, M., Petursson, H. & Brynjolfsson, J. (1987). Molecular genetic evidence for heterogeneity in manic depression. [Letter to *Nature*]. *Nature, 325,* 805–806.

Hollister, L.E., Davis, K.L. & Berger, P.A. (1980). Subtypes of depression based on excretion of MHPG and response to nortryptyline. *Archives of General Psychiatry, 37,* 1107–1110.

Jamison, K.R. (1988). Psychotherapy. [Draft] In F.K. Goodwin & K.R. Jamison, *Manic-Depressive Illness.* London: Oxford University Press.

Jampala, V.C. & Abrams, R. (1983). Mania secondary to left and right hemisphere damage. *American Journal of Psychiatry, 140,* 1197–1199.

Judd, L.L., Hubbard, B., Janowsky, D.S., Huey, L.Y. & Attewell, P.A. (1977). The effect of lithium carbonate on affect, mood and personality of normal subjects. *Archives of General Psychiatry, 34,* 346–351.

Judd, L.L., Hubbard, B., Janowsky, D.S. & Huey, L.Y. (1977). The effect of lithium carbonate on the cognitive functions of normal subjects. *Archives of General Psychiatry, 34,* 355–357.

Judd, L.L & Huey, L.Y. (1986). Lithium antagonizes ethanol intoxication in alcoholics. *American Journal of Psychiatry, 143,* 1166–1169.

Kraepelin, E. (1921). *Manic-depressive insanity and paranoia.* Edinburgh: E. & S. Livingstone.

Kropf, D., Muller-Oerlinghausen, B. (1977). Changes in learning, memory and mood during lithium treatment. *Acta Psychiatrica Scandinavia, 34,* 355–357.

Kruger, S.D., Turner, W.J. & Kidd, K.K. (1982). The effects of requisite assumptions on linkage analyses of manic depressive illness with HLA. *Biological Psychiatry, 34,* 1081–1099.

Lackroy, G.H. & Van Praag, H.M. (1971). Lithium salts as sedatives. An investigation into the possible effect of lithium for acute anxiety. *Acta Psychiatrica Scandinavia, 47,* 163–73.

Laing, R.D. (1965). *The Divided Self.* Baltimore: Penguin Books.

Maggs, R. (1963). Treatment of manic illness with lithium carbonate. *British Journal of Psychiatry, 109,* 56–65.

McHugh, P.R. (1987). [Editorial] Psychiatry and its scientific relatives: "A little more than kin and less than kind." *Journal of Nervous and Mental Diseases, 175,* 582.

McHugh, P.R. & Slavney, P.R. (1983). *The Perspectives of Psychiatry.* Baltimore: Johns Hopkins University Press.

Mendels, J., Secunda, S.K. & Dyson, W.L. (1972). A controlled study of the antidepressant effects of lithium. *Archives of General Psychiatry, 26,* 154–157.

Mendels, J. (1976). Lithium in the treatment of depression. *American Journal of Psychiatry, 113*, 372–377.

Mendlewicz, J. & Rainer, J.D. (1977). Adoption study supporting genetic transmission in manic-depressive illness. *Nature, 268*, 327–329.

Mendlewicz, J., Linkowski, P. & Wilmotte, J. (1980). Linkage between glucose 6-phosphate dehydrogenase deficiency and manic depressive psychosis. *British Journal of Psychiatry, 137*, 337–342.

Merry, J., Reynolds, C.M., Bailey, J. & Coppen, A. (1976). Prophylactic treatment of alcoholism by lithium carbonate. *Lancet, 2*, 481–482.

Prien, R.F., Klett, C.J. & Caffey, E.M. (1974). Lithium Prophylaxis in recurrent affective illness. *American Journal of Psychiatry, 131*, 198–203.

Robinson, R.G., Kubos, K.L., Starr, L.B., Rowe, K. & Price, T.R. (1984). Mood disorders in stroke patients: importance of location of lesion. *Brain, 107*, 81–93.

Rosenthal, N.E., Sack, D.A., Gillin, J.C., Lewy, A.J., Goodwin, F.K., Davenport, Y., Mueller, P.S., Newsome, D.A. & Wehr, T.A. (1984). Seasonal affective disorder: a description of the syndrome and preliminary findings with light therapy. *Archives of General Psychiatry, 41*, 71–80.

Schildkraut, J.J. (1965). The catecholamine hypothesis: a review of supportive evidence. *American Journal of Psychiatry, 122*, 509–522.

Schlesser, M.A., Winokur, G. & Sherman, B. (1980). Hypothalamic-pituitary-adrenal axis activity in depressive illness. *Archives of General Psychiatry, 37*, 737–743.

Schou, M. (1988). Lithium treatment of manic-depressive illness—past, present and perspectives. *Journal of the American Medical Association, 12*, 1834.

Schou, M. (1963). Lithium in psychiatry—a review. *Psychopharmacology—A Review of Progress 1957–1967, 109*, 701–718.

Schou, M. (1968). Lithium in psychiatric therapy and prophylaxis. *Journal of Psychiatric Research, 6*, 67–95.

Schou, M., Juel-Nielsen, N. & Stromgren, E. (1954). The treatment of manic psychoses by the administration of lithium salts. *Journal of Neurology Neurosurgery and Psychiatry, 17*, 250–260.

Schou, M. (1979). Lithium in the treatment of other psychiatric and non-psychiatric disorders. *Archives of General Psychiatry, 36*, 856–859.

Sendler, M.J. (1983). Falret's discovery: the origin of the concept of bipolar affective illness. *American Journal of Psychiatry, 140*, 1127–1133.

Sheard, M. & Marini, J.L. (1978). Treatment of human aggressive behavior: four case studies of the effect of lithium. *Comprehensive Psychiatry, 19*, 37–45.

Sheard, M.H., Marini, J.L., Bridges, C.I. & Wagner, E. (1976). The Effect of lithium on impulsive aggressive behavior in Man. *American Journal of Psychiatry, 133*, 1409–1412.

Spiker, D.G., Cable, P., Cofsky, J., Foster, F. & Kumpfer, D.J. (1978). EEG sleep and severity of depression. *Biological Psychiatry, 13*, 485–588.

Szaz, T.S. (1971). *The Manufacture of Madness*. London: Routledge and Kegan Paul.

Szaz, T.S. (1974). *The Myth of Mental Illness*. New York: Harper and Row.

Treiser, S.L., Cascio, C.S., O'Donohue, T.L., Thoa, N.B., Jacobowitz, D.M. & Keller, K.J. (1981). Lithium increases serotonin release and decreases serotonin receptors in the hippocampus. *Science, 213*, 1529–1531.

White, K., Bhart, R., Whipple, K. & Boyd, J. (1979). Lithium effects on normal subjects: relationships to plasma and RBC lithium levels. *International Pharmacopsychiatry, 14*, 176–213.

Worley, R.F., Baraban, J.M. & Snyder, S.H. (1987). Beyond receptors: multiple second-messenger systems in brain. *Annals of Neurology, 21*, 217–229.

# Sleep EEG Findings in Depression

John R. Debus and A. John Rush

*University of Texas Southwestern Medical Center*

KEY WORDS: sleep, depression, EEG, mood disorders,
polysomnography, REM latency

Biological psychiatrists, with their orientation toward mental illness as a physical or medical disease, are constantly searching for evidence of measurable biological abnormalities that can be used to improve diagnosis and treatment selection, and to better understand the pathophysiology involved in these disorders. The development of standardized laboratory methods for sleep assessment has provided researchers in the field of mood disorders with some of the most important biological findings as yet discovered in any psychiatric illness. This chapter reviews these methodologies, describes the characteristics of normal sleep, discusses the most consistent findings in depression and its subtypes and in other psychiatric disorders, and clarifies the relationship of these findings with other biological measures in depression. The theoretical and clinical implications of these findings are discussed.

To provide a basis for subsequent discussion of the abnormalities of the sleep electroencephalogram (EEG), we will first describe the typical findings in normal subjects and provide some definitions of the common terms used (see Table 15-1). In this chapter, the term "sleep EEG" is used in the generic sense, roughly equivalent to "sleep polysomnogram," which includes a number of possible measurements such as muscle activity (electromyogram), eye movement (electrooculogram) and others, in addition to the standard EEG.

An example of the normal progression of sleep stages in healthy adults is as follows: awake, Stage 1, Stage 2, delta (also known as Stage 3 and/or Stage 4), Stage 2, rapid eye movement (REM), Stage 2, delta, Stage 2, REM, etc. The first REM (formerly known as D or dream sleep) phase typically occurs 70–100 minutes following sleep onset and then alternates with nonREM sleep in a 70–120 minute cycle throughout the night (Gillin, Sitaram, Wehr, Duncan, Post, Murphy, Mendelson, Wyatt & Bunney, 1984). REM sleep is signified by desynchronization of the EEG with rapid, conjugate eye movements and muscular hypotonia. The other phases of sleep are sometimes collectively referred to as nonREM sleep. Stage 1 is a brief transitional phase marking the change from the awake state to sleep as indicated by EEG activity. Stage 2 is signified by K-complexes and sleep spindles on the EEG. Stages 3 and 4 (also called delta or slow-wave sleep) are characterized by the predominance of low frequency of delta waves (Rechtschaffen & Kales, 1968). Five to ten percent of total sleep time is spent in Stage 1, 45–55% in Stage 2, 20–25% in Stage REM and 10–20% in Stages 3 and 4 (Williams, Karacan &

Hursch, 1984). REM latency refers to the time from onset of sleep to the first REM period. REM density refers to REM activity divided by REM time. Sleep efficiency refers to the ratio of time spent asleep to the total time in bed. In normals, the usual tendency is for the REM periods to become longer as the night goes on, so that a greater percentage of REM sleep is spent during the second half of the night.

## METHODOLOGICAL COMMENTS

As far back as Hippocrates, clinical depression has been associated with sleep abnormalities. Early investigators substantiated these complaints, finding reductions in slow wave sleep and disruptions in sleep continuity, but were unable to discover consistent abnormalities in REM phases of sleep in depressed patients.

A number of significant advances in methodology have been necessary for sleep research to attain its current place in the clinical and research armamentarium (see Kupfer & Thase, 1983; Reynolds, Gillin & Kupfer, 1987 for reviews). Perhaps the most important of these was the establishment of rigorous, standardized diagnostic criteria such as the Research Diagnostic Criteria (RDC) (Spitzer, Endicott & Robins, 1978) and the Diagnostic and Statistical Manual of Mental Disorders (DSM-III and DSM-III-R) (American Psychiatric Association, 1980, 1987) which allowed for the study of more homogenous patient populations. The current awareness of complicating medical or neurological conditions and of medication effects also reduced intersubject variability. It is now a fairly standard practice to require a two-week medication-free period prior to sleep assessment, although the restrictions for various specific applications are still subject to debate. Another advance has been the acquisition of normative data in unaffected control subjects, thereby facilitating the use of the sleep EEG as an adjunctive diagnostic test.

Another methodological issue that has been dealt with is adaptation to the testing environment, or the so-called "first night effect." This adaptation may be of special importance in outpatients, since inpatients are often somewhat adapted to the testing environment. In outpatients, efforts have been made to reduce stress by previous exposure to the actual testing environment, such as by having the patient tour the laboratory prior to testing. Also, subjects are frequently asked to keep sleep diaries and to maintain a regular sleep-wake schedule for the five-day period prior to the sleep assessment. In general, concerns about this first night effect may have been overrated. Kupfer, Weiss, Detre, and Foster (1974) concluded that the first night effect is minimal in severely depressed patients, and more recent investigations indicate that this variation can be adequately controlled for, even in outpatients, by requiring at least two and sometimes three nights of sleep EEG recordings (Akiskal, Lemmi, Yerevanian, King & Belluomini, 1982; Reynolds et al., 1987). Other studies suggest that differences between the first and second nights may have diagnostic implications in themselves (Ansseau, Kupfer, Reynolds & Coble, 1985; Kupfer, Frank & Ehlers, 1989).

Of course, data obtained from sleep EEG recordings have to be scored, tabulated, and interpreted in a standard fashion in order to provide meaningful information. The establishment of standardized scoring criteria, procedural protocol, and sleep nomenclature by Rechtschaffen and Kales (1968) was another very important methodological advance in the development of sleep EEG techniques in psychiatry.

## SLEEP EEG FINDINGS IN DEPRESSION

As more and more investigations are published using the methodological advances described above, four distinct abnormalities have been relatively consistently reported in studies of depressed patients.

The first, and perhaps the most predictable of these abnormalities are disturbances in sleep continuity. These include prolonged sleep latency, mid-nocturnal awakenings, multiple stage changes, and terminal insomnia (see Gillin et al., 1984 for a review). Some of these sleep continuity disturbances may be related to a lower threshold for arousal to sound (Zung, 1969) and tend to be more severe in the older patient (Gillin, Duncan, Murphy, Post, Wehr, Goodwin, Wyatt & Bunney, 1981). An overall effect of these disturbances is that sleep in depressed patients is inefficient (i.e., a smaller portion of time spent in bed is actually spent sleeping). Sleep efficiency may be especially low in psychotically depressed patients who exhibit a marked reduction in total sleep time (Kupfer, Foster, Coble, McPartland & Ulrich, 1978).

A second area of rather consistent abnormality in depressed patients is a reduction or absence of the deeper stages (Stages 3 and 4) of sleep while more Stage 1 sleep may be found. Although delta sleep decreases with age in both depressives and normals, it is consistently lower at every age in depressed patients (reviewed by Gillin et al., 1984). This lack of deeper sleep may be one of the reasons that depressed patients complain of not feeling rested following a night's sleep, even in the absence of insomnia.

A third finding, and perhaps the most widely accepted and replicable, is the presence of a reduced first nonREM period, and subsequently the earlier appearance of the first REM period following sleep onset. This reduced time to the onset of the first REM period, or "reduced REM latency," while unique to depression, is consistently found in virtually all published studies of depressed patients. There may be a relationship between the severity of illness and REM latency in that the more severely depressed may evidence an even shorter REM latency than the less severely depressed (Kupfer & Foster, 1972).

Finally, the fourth consistent finding in the sleep EEG of depressed patients is an altered temporal distribution of REM sleep (reviewed by Gillin et al., 1984). REM sleep appears to be shifted so that more occurs toward the beginning of the night. This is accounted for both by reduced REM latency and by an increased length of the first REM period. Thus, a greater proportion of REM sleep occurs in the first third and less in the last third of the night, although a relatively normal REM-to-REM cycle length is maintained.

## SUBTYPES OF DEPRESSION

The sleep EEG with the above noted methodological advances has been employed in a variety of studies to subdivide the mood disorders. If the laboratory (sleep EEG) findings match best one or another clinically-defined subdivisions, while they fail to match another subtype, one might infer the relative validity of one or another subtype.

| TABLE 15-1: Brief Definitions of Human Sleep Stages[a] | |
|---|---|
| *Term* | *Definition* |
| Awake | EEG contains alpha waves and/or low voltage, mixed frequency activity. |
| Stage 1 | EEG shows low voltage, mixed frequency activity. Electrooculogram (EOG) shows no rapid eye movement (REM). |
| Stage 2 | EEG shows K-complexes and sleep spindles on a relatively low voltage, mixed frequency background activity. |
| Stage 3 | EEG shows moderate amounts of high amplitude, slow wave (delta wave) activity. |
| Stage 4 | EEG shows large amounts of delta activity. |
| Stage REM | EEG shows relatively low voltage, mixed frequency activity. EOG shows episodic REMs. Electromyogram (EMG) shows reduced amplitude. |
| Stage NREM | NonREM. Stages 1, 2, 3 and 4. |

[a] Adapted from Rechtschaffen and Kales (1968).

Within major depressive disorder, the primary/secondary dichotomy as defined by RDC (Spitzer et al., 1978) appeared to be a valid categorical distinction based on early sleep EEG studies. For example, Kupfer (1976) and Coble, Foster, and Kupfer (1976) discriminated primary from secondary major depressive disorder with a greater than 80% accuracy, based on REM latency and REM density. Gillin, Duncan, Pettigrew, Frankel, and Snyder (1979) reported that reduced REM latency was characteristic of 64% of patients with primary major depressive disorder. Akiskal (1981) was able to successfully distinguish between patients with primary and secondary depression and nondepressed healthy controls with 90% accuracy, using a REM latency threshold of $\leq 70.0$ minutes on two consecutive nights of sleep EEG recording. However, more recent reports (Feinberg, Gillin, Carroll, Greden & Zis, 1982; Rush, Giles, Roffwarg & Parker, 1982; Rush, Schlesser, Roffwarg, Giles, Orsulak & Fairchild, 1983; Giles, Schlesser, Rush, Orsulak, Fulton & Roffwarg, 1987a) have noted that a preponderance of RDC endogenous depressions were found within the primary group. These studies revealed that the endogenous/nonendogenous distinction rather than the primary/secondary dichotomy was validated by the sleep EEG. In fact, some patients with depressive syndromes "secondary" to other psychiatric disorders such as substance abuse, obsessive-compulsive disorder, generalized anxiety disorder, subaffective dysthymia, and schizophrenia also evidence reduced REM latency (see Gillin et al., 1984 for a review).

In our own laboratory, we have found that by utilizing a REM latency threshold of $\leq 60.0$ minutes, we are able to distinguish endogenous from nonendogenous depressed outpatients with a diagnostic confidence of 83% (sensitivity 71%; specificity 83%) (Rush et al., 1982).

The differentiation of bipolar from unipolar depression on the basis of sleep EEG measures has not been as successful as that for endogenous versus nonendogenous depression. Bipolar depression may have less efficient REM sleep with a longer REM duration than unipolar depression, but with more intrusions of wakefulness and nonREM sleep during REM (Duncan, Pettigrew & Gillin, 1979). Bipolar patients tended to have a shorter REM period duration at the beginning of the night and longer duration at the end of the night when compared to unipolar patients in this study. Overall, it appears that unipolar depressed patients tend to have poorer sleep efficiency than do bipolars, while bipolars experience more hypersomnia. No consistent differences have been found between unipolar and bipolar patients with regard to REM latency, REM density, distribution of REM sleep, or amount of slow wave sleep (reviewed in Reynolds & Shipley, 1985a). Confounding variables in making the distinction between unipolar and bipolar depressions are the phase of illness and the levels of psychomotor activity. An example of the former is that bipolar, mixed phase patients will have significant hyposomnia with sleep continuity disturbances, whereas both anergic unipolar depressives and bipolar, depressed phase patients will not infrequently evidence hypersomnia.

Overall, sleep EEG findings in bipolar disorder, depressed phase are very similar to those in unipolar disorder, especially in the unipolar endogenous group. Most studies to date have found reduced REM latency in groups of depressed patients with bipolar disorder, although as with unipolar depressives, not all patients in either group exhibit this abnormality. It is interesting to note that one study of nine manic patients found that they had reduced REM latency, increased REM activity and density, and a decreased time spent asleep compared to age- and sex-matched normal controls (Hudson, Lipinski, Frankenburg, Grochocinski & Kupfer, 1988), indicating a linkage to both unipolar and bipolar depression.

The distinction between bipolar I and bipolar II disorder has been largely ignored. Many studies of the sleep EEG in bipolar depression do not distinguish between the two groups. Chernik and Mendels (1976) reported reduced sleep efficiency in bipolar II compared to bipolar I, but were similar to unipolar depressions. Another study compared 10 bipolar I, 12 bipolar II and 22 unipolar endogenous depressives (Giles, Rush & Roffwarg, 1986). The bipolar II group had significantly higher REM latency and greater total sleep time than the matched unipolar group. Hypersomnia was found in both bipolar groups, although the incidence was not statistically different from the unipolars. Both severity and type of unipolar depression have been noted to contribute to sleep EEG differences (Rush et al., 1982) but were controlled for in this study. In addition, no sleep EEG measures discriminated bipolar I from bipolar II depressions (Giles et al., 1986).

Delusional depression is another category that has some relatively consistent sleep EEG findings. These patients tend to have impaired generation of REM activity, severely disrupted sleep continuity, and markedly reduced REM latency (often < 20.0 minutes), compared to nondelusional depressives, even after controlling for the effects of age, severity, and agitation (Kupfer et al., 1978; Kupfer, Broudy, Coble & Spiker, 1980; Thase, Kupfer & Ulrich, 1986).

Sleep EEG studies have recently been conducted with depressed children and adolescents. Puig-Antich, Goetz, Hanlon, Tabrizi, Davies, and Weitzman, (1983) found no distinct differences between the sleep of depressed children and healthy controls in a large study of prepubertal children with major depression. Interestingly, when depressed children were studied during remission, their REM latencies were significantly reduced compared to controls. Similarly, Young, Knowles, MacLean, Boag, and McConville (1982) did not find any sleep EEG parameters that discriminated between depressed patients and age-matched controls. Conversely, Lahmeyer, Poznanski, and Bellur (1983) found significantly increased REM density and reduced REM latency in 13 depressed adolescents when compared to age-matched controls. Goetz, Puig-Antich, Ryan, Rabinovich, Ambrosini, Nelson, and Krawiec (1987), while studying a group of predominately outpatient depressed adolescents, found evidence for sleep continuity disturbances, but no differences in REM sleep features. A preliminary study of 17 juveniles aged 9–14 with major depression, revealed reduced REM latency and increased early night REM density (Emslie, Roffwarg, Rush, Weinberg & Parkin-Feigenbaum, 1987) compared to normal childhood values reported by Coble, Kupfer, Taska, and Kane (1984). In an expanded study, 25 children (mean age = 11.5 years) with major depression were compared to 20 age-matched normal controls (Emslie, Rush, Weinberg, Rintelmann & Roffwarg, in press). REM latency was significantly reduced, with total REM time and REM percent of total sleep significantly higher in the depressed group. Non-REM sleep stages were not significantly different between groups. When a REM latency threshold of ≤ 70.0 minutes was used, 16 of 25 (68%) depressed subjects compared to only 4 of 20 (20%) normal controls had at least one night when REM latency was ≤ 70.0 minutes.

In summary, depressed children generally show fewer nonREM sleep and sleep continuity differences, when compared to controls, than has been reported in adults. As with adults however, children show evidence of increased REM pressure early in the night. These findings suggest that of the four major sleep EEG abnormalities found in depressed adults, REM sleep changes appear to be the most robust and are the earliest to manifest themselves.

## DIFFERENTIAL DIAGNOSIS

Perhaps the most exciting aspect of the sleep EEG is its potential utility in differentiating depression from other diagnoses. The search for a biological marker or clinically useful "laboratory test" for depression has driven much of the research in this field. Although there is still much controversy surrounding the clinical utility of the sleep EEG in day-to-day patient care, a brief review of the recent findings shows a great potential in this area.

A large concentration of sleep EEG studies have centered around differentiating the mood disorders from schizophrenia. There is still a great deal of controversy, but some of the major findings can be summarized. Many early studies found reduced REM latency in nondepressed schizophrenic patients. However, most of these studies have been criticized due to crucial methodological flaws (see review in Ganguli, Reynolds & Kupfer 1987). A more recent study by Zarcone, Benson, and Berger (1987) again found no differences in REM latency between depressives and schizophrenics. All met RDC criteria; however, a third of their patients received a diagnosis based on an unstructured interview only. Ganguli and colleagues (1987) pointed out another confounding variable which is often not controlled for, namely, the long-term and possibly even permanent effects of antipsychotic medication exposure. In their study of eight young, never medicated, nonschizoaffective schizophrenics, compared with eight delusional and 16 nondelusional major depressives and 16 healthy controls, the schizophrenics evidenced decreased sleep continuity compared to the other groups, with the exception of the delusional depressives. The percentage of slow wave sleep was similar to that of normals, as was the distribution of delta activity throughout the night. However, the delta count per minute of nonREM sleep was diminished as compared to normals. Slow wave sleep time was inversely correlated with the severity of negative symptoms in the schizophrenics, independent of the effects of age and presence/absence of depression. The schizophrenics evidenced normal REM latency and first REM period as compared to the depressives. Ganguli and coworkers (1987) suggested that decreased slow wave sleep should be further investigated as a possible marker for negative symptoms in schizophrenia. An earlier report of 42 never medicated schizophrenics who were studied by Jus and colleagues in Poland (reviewed in Ganguli et al., 1987) also commented on reduced delta wave activity and concluded that reduced Stage 4 sleep was characteristic of schizophrenics, but that REM abnormalities were not. Another study by Jus, Bouchard, Jus, Villeneuve & Lachance (1973) did not find this slow wave sleep deficit in elderly schizophrenics compared to age-matched controls. The use of larger patient samples with age-matched controls, automated scoring, and possibly multifactorial functional analyses may help to show the full value of the sleep EEG in discriminating schizophrenia from mood disorders. Also, valid ways of controlling for the potentially confounding effects of long-term antipsychotic medication exposure and psychosis itself as a separate variable need to be delineated.

There are indications that generalized anxiety disorder (GAD) can be differentiated from primary major depression by using REM latency and REM percentage in a discriminant function analysis (Reynolds, Shaw, Newton, Coble & Kupfer, 1983a). Papadimitriou, Linkowski, Kerkhofs, Kempenaers, and Mendlewicz (1988) compared a group of 10 inpatients with GAD and significant depression to another group of 10 age- and sex-matched GAD patients without significant depression and a group of primary major depressives. They found that the GAD patients with depression did not differ from the GAD patients with GAD alone, whereas the primary major depressives showed more stage shifts and a greater number of awakenings than either of the GAD groups. REM latency was significantly more reduced in the depressed patients than in the anxious group, which indicates that this feature is useful in differentiating some anxiety disorders from depressive disorders. However, this may not hold true for obsessive compulsive disorder (OCD).

Insel, Gillin, Moore, Mendelson, Loewenstein, and Murphy (1982) analyzed the sleep records of 14 patients with OCD and found significantly decreased total sleep time, more awakenings, less Stage 4 sleep, decreased REM efficiency, and reduced REM latency as compared to a group of age- and sex-matched normal controls. They commented on the similarities between these findings and sleep abnormalities seen in depressives and pointed to a possible biological link between OCD and affective illnesses. Rapoport, Elkins, Langer, Sceery, Buchsbaum, Gillin, Murphy, Zahn, Lake, Ludlow, and Mendelson, (1981) also found reduced REM latency and reduced total sleep time in a group of nine adolescents with OCD who were compared with 15 age- and sex-matched normal controls. However, in contrast to the Insel et al. (1982) findings, this group of patients showed a higher percentage of delta sleep as compared to normals.

Many patients in both studies evidenced depressive symptomatology. All patients in Rapoport et al. (1981) met criteria for major depression at some point in their history; four met criteria at the time of study. In the Insel et al. (1982) group, three patients met DSM-III criteria for major depression at some point in their history; all were secondary to OCD. Initial sleep EEG data in anxiety disorders appears to reflect considerable heterogeneity among these syndromes. Additional research must be conducted before generalizations about the utility of the sleep EEG in these disorders can be made.

Sleep EEG studies in eating disorders have yielded conflicting results. Of two uncontrolled studies, Weilburg, Stakes, Brotman, and Herzog (1985) reported increased REM latency, and Krahn, Shipley, and Canum (1987) reported decreased REM latency in bulimics. Two controlled studies (Walsh, Goetz, Roose, Fingeroth & Glassman, 1985; Levy, Dixon & Schmidt, 1988) showed no differences in REM latency between bulimic patients and normal controls. Hudson, Pope, Jonas, Stakes, Grochocinski, Lipinski, and Kupfer (1987) also found no differences between the sleep EEG in 11 normal weight women with bulimia and 20 normal controls, with the exception of a lower Stage 1 sleep. There was also no difference between bulimics with and without concurrent major depression. In a recent study of 12 bulimics compared to endogenous depressives and normals, Waller, Hardy, Pole, Giles, Gullion, Rush, and Roffwarg (1989) found that age-corrected mean REM latency for bulimics was reduced compared to normals and not significantly different from the endogenously depressed patients. The bulimics did not differ from normals in REM density or any other sleep variable.

Studies of anorexia nervosa also reveal inconsistencies. Katz, Kuperberg, Pollack, Walsh, Zumoff, and Weiner (1984) reported a reduced REM latency in patients with anorexia nervosa, particularly those with bulimic symptomatology. However, Walsh et al. (1985) found no significant differences in REM latency between eight anorectics and normal controls. Levy, Dixon, and Schmidt (1987) also found no differences between 6 nondepressed anorectics and 10 healthy control subjects, although low weight anorectics did exhibit less delta sleep. Many investigators in this field have attempted to use the various sleep laboratory findings to either strengthen or undermine the perceived linkage between eating and mood disorders. Interestingly, in Katz et al.'s (1984) sample of anorectics, most of whom also evidenced bulimic symptomatology, there was a significant negative correlation between Hamilton Rating Scale for Depression (HRS-D) (Hamilton, 1960, 1967) scores and REM latency. The confusing variation of sleep EEG findings in eating disorders may be largely due to methodological differences in assessing concurrent depressions and in the techniques of sleep recording, scoring, and controlling for such variables as binging patterns, weight, nutritional status, and even age. Further work needs to be done before major generalizations can be made about the sleep EEG and eating disorders.

The sleep EEG appears especially useful in the differentiating dementia from depressive illnesses. Reynolds, Kupfer, Taska, Hoch, Spiker, Sewitch, Zimmer, Marin, Nelson, Martin, and Morycz (1985b) conducted a study of the sleep EEG patterns in 25 subjects divided into three groups: elderly depressives, elderly demented, and elderly healthy controls. The sleep of depressives was characterized by reduced REM latency, increased REM percentage and REM density in the first REM period, altered distribution of REM sleep as well as diminished sleep maintenance (which correlated with HRS-D severity ratings). The demented patients evidenced reduced REM sleep percent, increased loss of spindles and K complexes (the later was correlated with severe cognitive impairment), and less severe sleep maintenance difficulties than did depressives. In a later expanded study of 235 elderly subjects, Reynolds, Kupfer, Houck, Hoch, Stack, Berman, and Zimmer (1988) were able to correctly classify demented and depressed patients 80% of the time using a discriminant function analysis. They found that four measures contributed to the separation of the two groups: REM latency (reduced in depressives); REM sleep percent (higher in depressives); indeterminant nonREM sleep percent (higher in dementia); and early morning awakening (more frequent in depressives). When applied to a group of 42 mixed symptom patients, these classification functions resulted in 27 of the patients (64%) with either depressive pseudodementia or with dementia and depressive features being correctly classified.

Buysse, Reynolds, Kupfer, Houck, Hoch, Stack, and Berman (1988) studied 26 elderly patients with mixed symptoms of depression and cognitive impairment following one night of sleep deprivation. Those with depressive pseudodementia showed a significant improvement in HRS-D and Profile of Mood States (POMS) (McNair, Lorr & Droppleman, 1971) tension scores following deprivation, while those patients with primary degenerative dementia with depression ($n = 18$) showed no change or a worsening in tension ratings. They also found that baseline REM percent and phasic REM activity/intensity were higher in the pseudodementia than in the dementia group. When considering REM sleep rebound alone (using a threshold of 25.0 minutes duration of the first REM period), Buysse et al. (1988) were able to correctly identify 88.5% of patients. Thus, the sleep EEG appears to be very useful clinically in discriminating depressed from demented patients, especially when some of the newer techniques such as discriminant function analysis and challenge techniques such as sleep deprivation and recovery are used.

The personality disorders have long been associated with sleep disturbances, including insomnia and hypersomnia. In many, these disturbances are thought to be associated with a chaotic lifestyle (Gillin et al., 1984), including an irregular sleep/wake schedule, poor nutrition and exercise habits, drug abuse, and a poor sleep environment. These patients are also prone to developing anxiety, depression, or other mood disorders with associated sleep disturbances. Akiskal (1981) reported that REM latency is reduced in outpatients with borderline personality disorders, comparable to that seen in primary depression. Reynolds, Soloff, Kupfer, Taska, Restifo, Coble, and McNamara (1985c) found that 75% of borderline patients and 85% of primary depressives had reduced REM latency compared to 35% of controls in a prospective study. These similarities in the sleep EEG are hypothesized to indicate some physiological similarity between borderline personality and affective spectrum disorders. Thus, the sleep EEG may be useful in identifying phenotypic variants of affective disorders.

Another area of application for the sleep EEG is in distinguishing between mood disorders and insomnia and hypersomnia which is related to organic factors such as sleep apnea and narcolepsy. It is a well-known fact that depression is frequently reported in narcolepsy and that patients with major depression frequently complain of the same sleep disturbances as do narcoleptics. Studies have shown that there are some similarities between the nocturnal REM sleep of narcoleptics and patients with endogenous depression (Reynolds, Christiansen, Taska, Coble & Kupfer, 1983b). REM latency, for example, is significantly reduced in both groups compared to age-matched healthy controls. However, compared to major depressives, narcoleptics evidence reduced sleep latency, more wakefulness following sleep onset (after age 40), reduced REM latency (before age 40), greater Stage 1 sleep percentage, and greater first REM period activity (after age 40). King, Akiskal, Lemmi, Wilson, Bulluomini, and Yerevanian (1981) found that low REM density helped to distinguish patients who had medical disorders and concurrent depressive symptoms from primary affective disordered patients.

Thus, the sleep EEG may prove to be very useful in clinical practice by assisting in diagnosis. Although not yet recommended as a general purpose test, it can be helpful in distinguishing patients with dementia, narcolepsy, and other sleep disorders, and possibly some of the anxiety disorders from pure depression. Other distinctions remain to be validated, such as for schizophrenia, OCD, personality disorders, and eating disorders.

## THE SLEEP EEG IN RELATION TO OTHER BIOLOGICAL MEASURES

As the evidence has mounted that the sleep EEG reportedly reveals certain abnormalities in the mood disorders, efforts have been made to compare these findings to other biological measures. Perhaps the most studied of these measures has been serum cortisol and the Dexamethasone Suppression Test (DST). This test provides information about the functional integrity of the hypothalamic-pituitary-adrenal (HPA) axis. A dose of the cortisol analogue dexamethasone is given at night, and the response is determined by measuring the cortisol level in the blood the following day. Normally, endogenous secretion of cortisol is suppressed by dexamethasone, indicating that the HPA axis regulatory feedback mechanisms are intact. Plasma cortisol nonsuppression after administration of dexamethasone (an abnormal DST) has been reported in about 50% of patients with mood disorders (Carroll, Feinberg, Greden, Tarika, Albala, Haskett, James, Kronfol, Lohr, Steiner, de Vigne & Young, 1981; Mendlewicz, Charles & Franckson, 1982), although the specificity (percent of those with a positive test that truly have the disorder) of the DST has been questioned. In a previously reported study (Rush et al., 1982), 70 adult patients with nonpsychotic, unipolar major depressive disorder by RDC were studied for comparison of sleep EEG and DST findings. In this largely outpatient sample, the DST proved to be a highly specific (95%), relatively accurate measure (confidence interval of 87%), although its sensitivity (percent of those with depression who evidenced a positive DST) was rather low (41%). A REM latency ≤ 62.0 minutes provided a more sensitive (66%), but less specific (79%) indicator of endogenous depression. DST nonsuppression was nearly always accompanied by a significant reduction in REM latency (only 1 DST nonsuppressor evidenced a mean REM latency <2.0 minutes). Conversely, over 40% of the patients showed neither abnormality, even though they were equivalent in symptom severity as measured by the HRS-D and Beck Depression Inventory (BDI) (Beck, Ward, Mendelson, Mock & Erbaugh, 1961).

In a later study by Mendelwicz, Kerkhofs, Hoffmann, and Linkowski (1984), the DST provided 100% specificity and 67% sensitivity, while REM latency showed a lower specificity of 78% and a higher sensitivity of 85% in 39 depressed patients as compared to 9 normal controls. Kerkhofs, Missa, and Mendlewicz (1986) compared 27 age-matched DST suppressors to 27 DST nonsuppressors. The DST nonsuppressors had significantly shorter REM latency, less slow wave sleep and more awake time than did DST suppressors. All had diagnoses of endogenous major depressive disorder by RDC, and the groups were similar with regard to depressive symptom severity as measured by the HRS-D. Neither Rush et al. (1982), Mendelwicz et al. (1984), nor Kerkhofs et al. (1986) reported a difference in REM density between DST suppressors and nonsuppressors.

In a subsequent larger study, Giles et al. (1987a) found the incidence of both DST nonsuppression and reduced REM latency was higher in a sample of 103 patients with endogenous depression, which replicated Rush et al. (1982). Findings in the other subtypes studied (probable endogenous, nonendogenous, primary, secondary, Winokur's family history) revealed no between-group differences. DST nonsuppression was slightly less specific (95% versus 85%) in this patient series, compared to the initial study (Rush et al., 1982). A REM latency threshold of 65.0 minutes provided a sensitivity of 68% and a specificity of 58%, with a confidence interval of 52%. A breakdown of the patient groups is shown in Table 15-2. Logistic regression analyses were used to estimate the effects of subtype of depression on reduced REM latency and DST nonsuppression (Table 15-3). Although severity contributed to the strength of the differences, coefficients associated with incidence of both reduced REM latency and DST nonsuppression were significant, even when severity was taken into consideration.

Kupfer, Jarrett, and Frank (1984a) suggest that extreme caution should be used by investigators who assume that biological measures may identify a homogenous group of severely depressed patients. They failed to find a significant association among several biological measures in 23 outpatients with recurrent, unipolar depression, including REM latency, DST status, and thyrotropin-stimulating hormone (TSH) response following stimulation with thyrotropin-releasing hormone (TRH).

Measurement of TSH following the TRH Stimulation Test (TRHST) is another putative biological marker in mood disorders, albeit one that is much more controversial than the sleep EEG and even the DST. Normally, the thyroid gland produces thyroid hormones in response to TSH secreted by the pituitary gland, which is in turn, regulated by TRH secreted by the hypothalamus. When TRH is given exogenously, as by intravenous infusion during the TRHST, the pituitary will increase its output of TSH, resulting in an increase in blood levels of TSH of at least 7.0 I$\mu$U/ml in normals. In a study at our center (Rush et al., 1983), 39.7% of a total sample of 68 depressed in- and outpatients evidenced TRHST blunting at the 7.0 I$\mu$U/ml threshold level and 26.5% at the 5.0 I$\mu$U/ml threshold value; 36.8% showed DST nonsuppression. Twenty-eight of these patients also had sleep EEG assessments performed. Twelve of 22 endogenous depressives had reduced REM latencies ($\leq$ 60.0 minutes). Seven of these patients also evidenced DST nonsuppression. Ten patients had a blunted TRHST at the 7.0 I$\mu$U/ml threshold and 7 evidenced this phenomenon at the 5.0 I$\mu$U/ml threshold. In a combination of all three tests, 15 of 22 (68.2%) at the 5.0 I$\mu$U/ml and 18 of 22 (81.8%) at the 7.0 I$\mu$U/ml threshold were identified by at least one abnormal test. None of the nonendogenous patients (n = 6) had two or more laboratory abnormalities. Conversely, Kupfer et al. (1984a) found no correlation among these three biological variables in their sample of depressed patients.

Overall, most studies comparing REM latency and neuroendocrine abnormalities reveal that most, but not all, patients with neuroendocrine dysfunction also evidence reduced REM latency. This finding is consistent with the notion that REM latency is more pervasive an abnormality, and that mechanisms involved in reduced REM latency may also facilitate the development of neuroendocrine dysfunctions.

## SLEEP EEG AND THE PREDICTION OF TREATMENT RESPONSE

As psychobiological measures such as the sleep EEG have gradually gained in their perceived validity with regard to clinical diagnosis, their utility is also being evaluated with regard to treatment selection and prediction of response. Kupfer, Spiker, Coble, Neil, Ulrich, and Shaw (1981), in a sample of 34 medication-free patients with primary endogenous depression, found that EEG-monitored sleep criteria proved more significant than clinical status alone in the prediction of response to amitriptyline. Difficulty in sleep onset and a prolongation of REM latency following a single 50 mg dose of amitriptyline were the main sleep variables that contributed to the prediction equation. Gillin, Wyatt, Fram, and Snyder (1978) reported similar results in 6 depressed patients. Hochli, Riemann, Zulley, and Berger (1986) also found that the degree of REM suppression predicted response to treatment with clomipramine. They did not find, however, that a shortening of sleep latency predicted treatment response as did Kupfer et al. (1981). Another study by Kupfer, Shaw, Ulrich, Coble, and Spiker (1982), using pretreatment automated REM analysis, found that average REM counts for the first three REM periods appeared to distinguish responders from nonresponders to amitriptyline.

Rush, Erman, Schlesser, Roffwarg, Vasavada, Khatami, Fairchild, and Giles (1985) studied the response to amitriptyline and alprazolam in a group of 49 patients (83.6% endogenous; 34.7% inpatient) with nonpsychotic major depression who evidenced pretreatment REM latency of $\leq$65.0 minutes. At the end of six weeks treatment, 79.2% of the amitriptyline-treated patients responded as compared to only 36% of the alprazolam-treated patients. Thus, amitriptyline appears to be more effective than alprazolam in patients with reduced pretreatment REM latency. In a preliminary study of placebo responders, Zammit, Rosenbaum, Stokes, Davis, Zorick, and Roth (1988) found that placebo nonresponders tended to have a greater number of abnormal DST results, less total sleep time, and a greater percentage of awake time than did placebo responders.

Jarrett, Giles, Roffwarg, and Rush (1988) studied a sample of 28 outpatients with unipolar major depressive disorder and found that one-half of the subjects who responded to treatment with cognitive therapy had reduced pretreatment REM latency and the remaining one-half showed nonreduced REM latency. Thus, contrary to the initial prediction, a positive response to cognitive therapy was associated equally with reduced and nonreduced REM latency.

With regard to electroconvulsive therapy (ECT), a case report by Grunhaus, Tiongco, Roehrich, Eiser, Feinberg, and Greden (1985) suggests that the sleep EEG predicts treatment response. In their patient, they were able to show normalization of two biological correlates (the sleep EEG and DST) prior to clinical response that appeared due to treatment with ECT. In fact, the sleep EEG improved several weeks prior to the DST.

In summary, although further work needs to be done in terms of replication and extension of these findings to other psychopharmacological treatments (e.g., in larger numbers of ECT-treated patients and in other treatments such as psychotherapy), the initial indications are that sleep EEG, either at pretreatment or within the first 7–10 days of treatment, may be a stronger predictor of response than traditional clinical signs and symptoms.

## PREDICTION OF COURSE OF ILLNESS

While the sleep EEG may be of value in predicting treatment response, relatively little is known of the relationship of the sleep EEG to the subsequent course of illness in depression. Estimates of recurrence range from 12–79% (Klerman, 1978), but clinical characteristics appear to have limited predictive value (Grof, Angst & Haines, 1974; Frank, Jarrett, Kupfer & Grochocinski, 1984; Angst, 1984).

Reduced REM latency appears to persist through an untreated period of depression (Coble, Kupfer, Spiker, Neil & McPartland, 1979) and through a period of remission following treatment (Hauri, Chernik, Hawkins & Mendels, 1974; Rush, Erman, Giles, Schlesser, Carpenter, Vasavada & Roffwarg, 1986). To investigate whether pretreatment REM latency during and episode of depression is a predictor of recurrence, Giles, Jarrett, Roffwarg, and Rush (1987b) performed sleep EEGs on 25 medication-free patients with RDC major depressive disorder (unipolar, n = 23; bipolar, n = 2), both prior to and following treatment with either tricyclic antidepressants or cognitive psychotherapy. At pretreatment, 15 of 25 (60%) evidenced reduced REM latency (≤65.0 minutes) and 10 of 25 (40%) evidenced nonreduced REM latency (>65.0 minutes). With various periods of longitudinal follow-up (from 6–26 months), 13 patients had relapsed. The REM latency threshold of ≤65.0 minutes identified 10 of these 13 who experienced a recurrence (76.9%). In the 19 patients diagnosed with recurrent depression at pretreatment, 12 (63.2%) had been predicted correctly to recur. In those diagnosed with a single episode at pretreat-

### TABLE 15–2: Estimates of Logistic Regression Parameters

| Independent Variables | Dependent Variables | | | |
|---|---|---|---|---|
| | Reduced REM Latency | | Dexamethasone Nonsuppression | |
| | *(1)* | *(2)* | *(1)* | *(2)* |
| Endogenous | 0.58[a] | 0.50[b] | 0.66[a] | 0.54[b] |
| | (0.21) | (0.22) | (0.25) | (0.26) |
| HRS-D | — | -0.03 | — | -0.06 |
| | | (0.04) | | (0.05) |

*Note*: Standard errors appear in parentheses.
[a] Estimated coefficient is significantly different from 0 at the 0.005 level.
[b] Estimated coefficient is significantly different from 0 at the 0.05 level.

(Reprinted with permission from Giles, D.E., Schlesser, M.A., Rush, A.J., Orsulak, P.J., Fulton, C.L. & Roffwarg, H.P. (1987a). Polysomnographic findings and dexamethasone nonsuppression in unipolar depression: A replication and extension. *Biological Psychiatry, 22*, 872–882.).

ment, 5 of 6 (83.3%) were predicted correctly. REM latency correctly predicted a recurrence and/or remission in 5 of 6 of the first episode patients. If replicated in a larger sample, these data suggest that the sleep EEG may usefully predict recurrence in major depressive disorder.

## THE STATE VERSUS TRAIT CONTROVERSY

Longitudinal studies allow us to track the sleep EEG over time and make correlations with clinical recovery, remission, and relapse. These types of studies may also allow us to determine whether the sleep EEG abnormalities found are state- or trait-markers. A trait marker is more likely a biological indication of vulnerability or predisposition for the development of an affective disorder, whereas a state marker is more indicative of current episode status. State markers have shown utility in differential diagnosis, treatment selection, response prediction and monitoring, and prediction and detection of relapse. Trait markers can be useful in the understanding of the pathophysiology of mood disorders, in the identification of those individuals at risk for development of a mood disorder (as an initial episode or relapse), and perhaps eventually in the prevention of such illnesses. Since no large-scale screening studies of the general population have been carried out, we do not know what type of sleep characteristics patients may evidence prior to the onset of the first episode of a mood disorder. We are, however, able to study patients during a symptomatic episode and then to follow them longitudinally to determine the evolution of the sleep EEG manifestations. Most such studies to date have shown that the majority of sleep abnormalities found during a depressive episode tend to remain

| | Suppressor | Nonsuppressor[a] | Total |
|---|---|---|---|
| **TABLE 15–3: REM Latency in Relation to Dexamethasone Suppression Test Response** | | | |
| Nonreduced REM Latency | | | |
| Endogenous | 7 | 5 | 12 |
| Nonendogenous | 30 | 4 | 34 |
| Reduced REM Latency[b] | | | |
| Endogenous | 15 | 10 | 25 |
| Nonendogenous | 19 | 5 | 24 |
| Total | | | |
| Endogenous | 22 | 15 | 37 |
| Nonendogenous | 49 | 9 | 58 |

[a] Nonsuppressor defined as ≥4.0 μg/dl.
[b] Reduced REM latency defined as ≤65.0 minutes.

(Reprinted with permission from Giles, D.E., Schlesser, M.A., Rush, A.J., Orsulak, P.J., Fulton, C.L. & Roffwarg, H.P. (1987a). Polysomnographic findings and dexamethasone nonsuppression in unipolar depression: A replication and extension. *Biological Psychiatry, 22,* 872–882.).

unchanged for a period of up to two years following remission (Rush et al., 1986; Hauri et al., 1974). At least one study has shown that sleep abnormalities follow a constant profile during two consecutive episodes of depression, although they may be more pronounced earlier in an episode (Kupfer, Frank, Grochocinski, Gregor & McEachran, 1988). Therefore, at least the initial indications are that sleep EEG findings, especially reduced REM latency, are probably more representative of a trait- rather than state-like marker. Thus, the combination of the DST and the sleep EEG may have additional utility due to this distinction, in that the DST tends to be more of a state-marker in mood disorders.

## FUTURE DIRECTIONS

Advances in methodology and technology have allowed the sleep EEG to assume its current important position in psychiatry, providing some of the strongest indications yet of biological abnormalities in mood disorders and related psychiatric syndromes. Further advances in new directions should enable the sleep EEG, with or without adjunctive measurements, to assume an ever more important role in research and clinical practice.

One of these future directions, automated analysis of sleep data by computer, has already been set into motion in some centers. Kupfer and colleagues at the University of Pittsburgh School of Medicine have found that automated measures of REM and delta sleep are highly reliable in normal subjects and that there was a good correspondence between manual and automated measures of REM in depressed patients. They also point out that besides this highly reliable scoring of sleep records, and thus division into the classic stages of sleep, this technology will also allow greater attention to the phasic components of the EEG with less reliance on the classic sleep stages. For example, Kupfer et al.'s report on spectral analysis of the sleep EEG and the electrooculogram mentions possible future investigations of changes in delta sleep produced by psychotropic medication, relationships between delta sleep and neuroendocrine and other biological rhythm variables such as activity and temperature (reviewed in Kupfer, Ulrich, Coble, Jarrett, Grochocinski, Doman, Matthews & Borbely, 1984b,c). In a later application of this technology, Kupfer, Reynolds, Ulrich, and Grochocinski (1986) looked at differences in sleep EEG measures between young and middle-aged groups of depressed inpatients. They found, in addition to expected differences in sleep continuity, increased Stage 1 percent, decreased Stage 2 percent, and decreased REM latency in the middle-aged depressives when compared to the younger group. The automated analysis also showed that the younger patients had an increased number of delta waves and that the middle-aged depressives evidenced a greater average REM count. They also found little statistical difference between manual measures of slow wave sleep and automated measures of sleep in their middle-aged patient population.

Another future direction that may allow greater application of the sleep EEG is the further development of ambulatory or portable EEG monitoring. In conjunction with computerized analysis of the data obtained, ambulatory monitoring may potentially provide increased convenience, patient compliance, and subject recruitment with reduced expense per study. A recent report by Sharpley, Solomon, and Cowen (1988), using ambulatory EEG for a total of three nights and automated sleep stage analysis, showed that this method produced qualitatively satisfactory at-home sleep EEG recordings with no significant first-night effect in normal subjects with no history of sleep difficulties.

Another future direction will be the addition of challenge tests to augment the utility of the sleep EEG. In biological systems, it is often more revealing to study responses to specific challenges to a system rather than simple baseline measurements. Such challenges can test the function of regulatory mechanisms involved, and thus reveal more subtle abnormalities that may be indicative of pathology at various levels within the system. Challenge techniques were first widely applied in biological psychiatry in the area of neuroendocrine systems, such as the HPA axis and the DST. With fairly specific challenges to relatively well-delineated regulatory systems and with easily measured consequences, specific hypotheses about the roles of various neurotransmitter systems in different behaviors and disorders can be tested.

One such hypothesis was proposed by Janowsky and colleagues in 1972. This hypothesis posits that affective states are determined by a balance between the cholinergic and adrenergic neurotransmitter systems. Depression is postulated to develop from a relative excess of cholinergic activity in the setting of relative adrenergic hypoactivity, with mania being described as the converse. In support of this theory, they cited the behavioral and subjective effects of medication that enhance cholinergic activity (Janowsky, Davis, El-Yousef & Sekerke, 1972). Since it was thought that the cholinergic neurotransmitter system is involved in the regulation of sleep as well as mood, the Cholinergic REM Induction Test (CRIT) was developed to test the hypothesized involvement of cholinergic hypersensitivity in depression (Sitaram, Nurnberger, Gershon & Gillin, 1980; Gillin, Sitaram, Nurnberger, Gershon, Cohen, Murphy, Kaye & Ebert, 1983). In this method, a subject is studied during sleep with a peripheral intravenous infusion line in place. An anticholinergic agent that does not cross the blood-brain barrier (such as glycopyrrolate or methscopolamine) is injected at the onset of the first REM period to block peripheral effects, and then a centrally active cholinergic agent (such as arecoline or physostigmine) is infused. Sitaram et al. (1980) found that infusion of arecoline during the second nonREM period caused an earlier onset of the second REM period in depressed patients compared to normal controls. A study by Berger, Lund, Bronisch, and Von Zerssen (1983) found that infusion of 0.5 mg physostigmine five minutes following sleep onset caused a significant shortening of REM latency, but did not differentiate endogenous, neurotic, and an unclassified sample of depressed patients from normal controls, and in fact, awakened the majority of patients from sleep. Another study by Sitaram, Nurnberger, Gershon, and Gillin (1982) with the CRIT showed that bipolar patients had an earlier onset of the second REM period than did normals following infusion with arecoline.

It is postulated that increased cholinergic sensitivity may be a biological marker for the depressive trait. Dube, Kumar, Ettedgui, Pohl, Jones, and Sitaram (1985) indicated that the CRIT may be helpful in distinguishing anxiety from depressive disorders. They found that REM latency was significantly reduced in patients with primary major depressive disorder (without anxiety), compared to patients with primary anxiety disorders with no concurrent major depressive disorder and to normal controls. They found that primary depressives (without anxiety or with secondary anxiety disorders) were more responsive to the CRIT than both the primary anxiety and normal groups. Spiegel (1984) found that RS 86, a direct acting cholinergic agonist, reduced REM latency in a dose-related fashion when administered orally.

McCarley (1982) summarized the data showing the relationship between REM sleep and depressive phenomenology, stating that: "(1) brain stem norepinephrine and serotonin systems suppress both REM sleep and depressive phenomena, (2) acetylcholine systems promote both REM and depressive phenomena, (3) in control of depressive phenomena, as in REM sleep control, opposite-signed monoamine acetylcholine neuronal systems interact and the balance of activity between these two systems, rather than absolute activity levels in either, is a critical factor."

Other potential future directions include the combination of the sleep EEG with additional measures of central nervous system function. Functional brain imaging is one such possible adjunctive technique, with the exciting potential for allowing the visualization of what takes place in the sleeping brain. Regional cerebral blood flow (rCBF) is closely linked to brain tissue metabolism, and thus is a way of examining the function of the brain. Townsend, Prinz, and Obrist (1973) used [133]Xenon inhalation and a multiple detector, nontomographic technique, to study rCBF in 11 healthy men. They found reductions in rCBF in all areas during slow wave sleep, especially in the precentral regions, and increases in all areas during REM sleep, especially in the temporal lobes. Sakai, Meyer, Karacan, Yamaguchi, and Yamamoto (1979), using a somewhat similar technique, found that mean hemispheric CBF in normal subjects during Stages 1 and 2 was about 10% less then when awake, whereas narcoleptic patients showed an average of a 20% increase (they did not compare rCBF during REM). Meyer, Ishikawa, Hata, and Karacan (1987), using a similar technology to Sakai et al. (1979), found that narcoleptics and sleep apneics had reduced rCBF in the brainstem and cerebellum in the awake state compared to normals, but during Stages 1 and 2 sleep the narcoleptics' rCBF paradoxically increased, while decreasing severely in apneics and mildly in normals. During REM, all subjects evidenced increased rCBF in all regions, especially in the right temporo-parietel areas.

Single photon emission computerized tomography (SPECT) is a more advanced version of the [133]Xenon method described above. SPECT can provide two- and three-dimensional images of rCBF, and thus cerebral function, in various stages of sleep or wakefulness. Blood flow can be quantified for any region of interest using SPECT, thus allowing statistical correlations with other measures.

Positron emission tomography (PET) can also provide high-quality images of regional brain metabolism and quantitative analyses, although at a greater expense than SPECT. Pilot PET investigations in normals show that this technique may prove valuable in revealing which brain regions are involved in sleep (Buchsbaum, Gillin, Wu, Hazlett, Sicotte, Herrera, Prager & Bunney 1988; Wu, Gillin, Buchsbaum, Hazlett, Sicotte & Bunney, 1988). To our knowledge, no studies have been published to date using SPECT to image the human brain in depressed patients during sleep. Improvements in imager technology and in radiopharmaceuticals are rapidly allowing us to image the functioning of the brain during sleep at lower expense and at greater convenience. The results may be far-reaching in terms of improving our understanding of the neurophysiology and anatomy of sleep, and in advancing the utility of sleep EEG assessment, with obvious applications in depression and other disorders in which sleep abnormalities have been discovered.

## CONCLUSIONS

Psychiatrists have sought various "windows on the brain" with which to decipher the underlying pathophysiology of various disorders. For depression, neuroendocrine measures and metabolites of various neurotransmitters measured in the urine, blood stream, or cerebral spinal fluid have been extensively studied.

In the last decade, the sleep EEG has been more widely used in these conditions. It has already shown utility in differentiating among different types of depression (endogenous versus nonendogenous). It also appears useful in discriminating depression from both dementia and anxiety disorders. Recently, its prognostic utility also appears promising. Further clarification of the underlying neurochemistry and neuroanatomy that account for these sleep EEG abnormalities in depression will likely lead to improved diagnosis and treatment selection for depressed patients.

**Authors' Note:** The authors wish to express their appreciation to David Savage for his secretarial assistance, to Tarak Vasavada for his comments and library investigations and to Kenneth Z. Altshuler, Stanton Sharp Professor and Chairman for his administrative support.
Preparation of this chapter was supported in part by a Mental Health Clinical Research Center Grant (MH–41115) from the National Institute of Mental Health to A. John Rush and by a grant from the National Alliance for Research on Schizophrenia and Depression (NARSAD) to John R. Debus.

# References

Akiskal, H. S. (1981). Subaffective disorders: Dysthymic, cyclothymic and bipolar II disorders in the "borderline" realm. *Psychiatric Clinics of North America*, 4, 25–46.

Akiskal, H. S., Lemmi, H., Yerevanian, B., King, D. & Belluomini, J. (1982). The utility of the REM latency test in psychiatric diagnosis: A study of 81 depressed outpatients. *Psychiatry Research*, 101–110.

American Psychiatric Association. (1980). *The diagnostic and statistical manual of mental disorders (DSM-III)*, (Ed. 3). Washington, DC: American Psychiatric Association.

American Psychiatric Association. (1987). *The diagnostic and statistical manual of mental disorders (DSM-III-R)*, (Ed. 3, Revised). Washington, DC: American Psychiatric Association.

Angst, J. (1984). *A prospective study on the course of affective disorders*. Consensus Development Conference on Mood Disorders: Pharmacologic Prevention of Recurrences, Bethesda, MD: National Institutes of Health.

Ansseau, M., Kupfer, D. J., Reynolds, C. F., III & Coble, P. A. (1985). "Paradoxical" shortening of REM latency on first recording night in major depressive disorder: Clinical and polysomnographic correlates. *Biological Psychiatry*, 20, 135–145.

Beck, A. T., Ward, C. H., Mendelson, M., Mock, J. E. & Erbaugh, J. K. (1961). An inventory for measuring depression. *Archives of General Psychiatry*, 4, 561–571.

Berger, M., Lund, R., Bronisch, T. & Von Zerssen, D. (1983). REM latency in neurotic and endogenous depression and the cholinergic REM induction test. *Psychiatry Research*, 10, 113–123.

Buchsbaum, M. S., Gillin, J. C., Wu, J. C., Hazlett, E., Sicotte, N., Herrera, D., Prager, E. & Bunney, W. E., Jr. (1988). PET study of REM and nonREM sleep in normal control. *Sleep Research*, 17, 23.

Buysse, D. J., Reynolds, C. F., III, Kupfer, D. J., Houck, P. R., Hoch, C. C., Stack, J. A. & Berman, S. R. (1988). Electroencephalographic sleep in depressive pseudodementia. *Archives of General Psychiatry*, 45, 568–575.

Carroll, B. J., Feinberg, M., Greden, J. F., Tarika, J., Albala, A. A., Haskett, R. F., James, N., Kronfol, Z., Lohr, N., Steiner, M., de Vigne, J. P. & Young, E. (1981). A specific laboratory test for the diagnosis of melancholia. Standardization, validation and clinical utility. *Archives of General Psychiatry*, 38, 15–22.

Chernik, D. A. & Mendels, J. (1976). Sleep in bipolar and unipolar depressed patients. *Sleep Research*, 3, 123.

Coble, P. A., Foster, F. G. & Kupfer, D. J. (1976). Electroencephalographic sleep diagnosis of primary depression. *Archives of General Psychiatry*, 33, 1124–1127.

Coble, P. A., Kupfer, D. J., Spiker, D. G., Neil, J. F. & McPartland, R. J. (1979). EEG sleep in primary depression. A longitudinal placebo study. *Journal of Affective Disor-*

*ders.* 1, 131–138.

Coble, P. A., Kupfer, D. J., Taska, L. S. & Kane, J. (1984). EEG sleep of normal healthy children. Part I: Findings using standard measurement methods. *Sleep*, 7, 289–303.

Dube, S., Kumar, N., Ettedgui, E., Pohl, R., Jones, D. & Sitaram, N. (1985). Cholinergic REM induction response: Separation of anxiety and depression. *Biological Psychiatry*, 20, 408–418.

Duncan, W. C., Jr., Pettigrew, K. D. & Gillin, C. (1979). REM architecture changes in bipolar and unipolar depression. *American Journal of Psychiatry*, 136, 1424–1427.

Emslie, G. J., Roffwarg, H. P., Rush, A. J., Weinberg, W. A. & Parkin-Feigenbaum, L. (1987). Sleep EEG findings in depressed children and adolescents. *American Journal of Psychiatry*, 144, 668–670.

Emslie, G. J., Rush, A. J., Weinberg, W. A., Rintelmann, J. W. & Roffwarg, H.P. (in press). Children with major depression evidence reduced rapid eye movement latencies. *Archives of General Psychiatry*.

Feinberg, M., Gillin, J. C., Carroll, B. J., Greden, J. F. & Zis, A. P. (1982). EEG studies of sleep in the diagnosis of depression. *Biological Psychiatry*, 17, 305–316.

Frank, E., Jarrett, D. B., Kupfer, D. J. & Grochocinski, V. J. (1984). Biological and clinical predictors of response in recurrent depression: A preliminary report. *Psychiatry Research*, 13, 315–324.

Ganguli, R., Reynolds, C. F., III & Kupfer, D. J. (1987). Electroencephalo-graphic sleep in young, never-medicated schizophrenics. A comparison with delusional and non-delusional depressives and with healthy controls. *Archives of General Psychiatry*, 44, 36–44.

Giles, D. E., Rush, A. J. & Roffwarg, H. P. (1986). Sleep parameters in bipolar I, bipolar II and unipolar depressions. *Biological Psychiatry*, 21, 1340–3143.

Giles, D. E., Jarrett, R. B., Roffwarg, H. P. & Rush, A. J. (1987b). Reduced rapid eye movement latency. A predictor of recurrence in depression. *Neuropsychopharmacology*, 1, 33–39.

Giles, D. E., Schlesser, M. A., Rush, A. J., Orsulak, P. J., Fulton, C. L. & Roffwarg, H. P. (1987a). Polysomnographic findings and dexamethasone nonsuppression in unipolar depression: A replication and extension. *Biological Psychiatry*, 22, 872–882.

Gillin, J. C., Duncan, W. C., Murphy, D. L., Post, R. M., Wehr, T. A., Goodwin, F. K., Wyatt, R. J. & Bunney, W. E., Jr. (1981). Age-related changes in sleep in depressed and normal subjects. *Psychiatry Research*, 4, 73–78.

Gillin, J. C., Duncan, W., Pettigrew, K. D., Frankel, B. L. & Snyder, F. (1979). Successful separation of depressed, normal, and insomniac subjects by EEG sleep data. *Archives of General Psychiatry*, 36, 85–90.

Gillin, J. C., Sitaram, N., Nurnberger, J. I., Gershon, E. S., Cohen, R. M., Murphy, D. L., Kaye, W. & Ebert, M. H. (1983). The cholinergic REM induction test. *Psychopharmacology Bulletin*, 19, 668–670.

Gillin, J. C., Sitaram, N., Wehr, T., Duncan, W., Post, R., Murphy, D. L., Mendelson, W. B., Wyatt, R. J. & Bunney, W. E., Jr. (1984). Sleep and affective illness. In R. M. Post & J. C. Ballenger (Eds.), *Neurobiology of mood disorders* (pp. 157–189). Baltimore, MD: Williams & Wilkins.

Gillin, J. C., Wyatt, R. J., Fram, D. & Snyder, F. (1978). The relationship between changes in REM sleep and clinical improvement in depressed patients treated with amitriptyline. *Psychopharmacology*, 59, 267–272.

Grof, P., Angst, J. & Haines, T. (1974). The clinical course of depression: Practical issues. In J. Angst (Chairman), *Classification and prediction of outcome of depression*. Symposium Schloß Reinhartshausen/Rhein (pp. 141–147). Stuttgart: F.K. Schattauer Verlag GmbH.

Grunhaus, D., Tiongco, D., Roehrich, H., Eiser, A., Feinberg, M. & Greden, J. F. (1985). Serial monitoring of antidepressant response to electroconvulsive therapy with sleep EEG recordings and dexamethasone suppression tests. *Biological Psychiatry*, 20, 805–808.

Goetz, R. R., Puig-Antich, J., Ryan, N., Rabinovich, H., Ambrosini, P. J., Nelson, B. & Krawiec, V. (1987). Electroencephalographic sleep of adolescents with major depression and normal controls. *Archives of General Psychiatry*, 44, 61–68.

Hamilton, M. (1960). A rating scale for depression. *Journal of Neurology, Neurosurgery and Psychiatry*, 12, 56–62.

Hamilton, M. (1967). Development of a rating scale for primary depressive illness. *British Journal of Social and Clinical Psychology*, 6, 278–296.

Hauri, P., Chernik, D., Hawkins, D. & Mendels, J. (1974). Sleep of depressed patients in remission. *Archives of General Psychiatry*, 31, 386–391.

Hochli, D., Riemann, D., Zulley, J. & Berger, M. (1986). Initial REM sleep suppression by clomipramine: A prognostic tool for treatment response in patients with a major depressive disorder. *Biological Psychiatry*, 21, 1217–1220.

Hudson, J. I., Lipinski, J. F., Frankenburg, F. R., Grochocinski, V. J. & Kupfer, D. J. (1988). Electroencephalographic sleep in mania. *Archives of General Psychiatry*, 45, 267–273.

Hudson, J. I., Pope, H. G., Jr., Jonas, J. M., Stakes, J. W., Grochocinski, V., Lipinski, J. F. & Kupfer, D. J. (1987). Sleep EEG in bulimia. *Biological Psychiatry*, 22, 820–828.

Insel, T. R., Gillin, J. C., Moore, A., Mendelson, W. B., Loewenstein, R. J. & Murphy, D. L. (1982). The sleep of patients with obsessive-compulsive disorder. *Archives of General Psychiatry*, 39, 1372–1377.

Janowsky, D. S., Davis, J. M., El-Yousef, M. K. & Sekerke, H. J. (1972). A cholinergic-adrenergic hypothesis of mania and depression. *Lancet*, ii, 632–635.

Jarrett, D. B., Giles, D. E., Roffwarg, H. P. & Rush, A. J. (1988). Predicting responses to cognitive therapy for depression from sleep EEG results: A preliminary report. In Perris C. & Eisemann, M. (eds.), *Cognitive psychotherapy: An update*. Proceedings of the 2nd International Conference on Cognitive Psychotherapy (pp. 67–69). Umea, Sweden: Umea University Printing Office.

Jus, K., Bouchard, M., Jus, A. K., Villeneuve, A. & Lachance, R. (1973). Sleep EEG studies in untreated, long-term schizophrenic patients. *Archives of General Psychiatry*, 29, 386–390.

Katz, J. L., Kuperberg, A., Pollack, C. P., Walsh, B. T., Zumoff, B. & Weiner, H. (1984). Is there a relationship between eating disorder and affective disorder? New evidence from sleep recordings. *American Journal of Psychiatry*, 141, 753–759.

Kerkhofs, M., Missa, J. & Mendlewicz, J. (1986). Sleep electroencephalographic measures in primary major depressive disorder: Distinction between DST suppressor and nonsuppressor patients. *Biological Psychiatry*, 21, 225–228.

King, D., Akiskal, H. S., Lemmi, H., Wilson, W., Belluomini, J. & Yerevanian, B. I. (1981). REM density in the differential diagnosis of psychiatric from medical-neurological disorders: A replication. *Psychiatry Research*, 5, 267–276.

Klerman, G. L. (1978). Long-term treatment of affective disorders. In M. A. Lipton, A. DiMascio & K. F. Killam (Eds.), *Psychopharmacology: A generation of progress* (pp. 1303–1311). New York: Raven Press.

Krahn, D., Shipley, J. & Canum, K. (1987). Sleep EEG abnormalities in eating disorders. Paper presented at the meeting of the Society of Biological Psychiatry, Chicago, IL.

Kupfer, D. J. (1976). REM latency: A psychobiological marker for primary depressive disease. *Biological Psychiatry*, 11, 159–174.

Kupfer, D. J., Broudy, D., Coble, P. A. & Spiker, D. G. (1980). EEG sleep and affective psychosis. *Journal of Affective Disorders*, 2, 17–25.

Kupfer, D. J. & Foster, F. G. (1972). Interval between onset of sleep and rapid-eye-movement sleep as an indicator of depression. *Lancet*, ii, 684–686.

Kupfer, D. J., Foster, F. G., Coble, P. A., McPartland, R. J. & Ulrich, R. F. (1978). The application of EEG sleep for the differential diagnosis of affective disorders. *American Journal of Psychiatry*, 135, 69–74.

Kupfer, D. J., Frank, E., Grochocinski, V. J., Gregor, M. & McEachran, A. B. (1988). Electroencephalographic sleep profiles in recurrent depression. A longitudinal investigation. *Archives of General Psychiatry*, 45, 678–681.

Kupfer, D. J., Frank, E. & Ehlers, C. L. (1989). EEG sleep in young depressives: First and second night effects. *Biological Psychiatry*, 25, 87–97.

Kupfer, D. J., Jarrett, D. B. & Frank, E. (1984a). Relationship among selected neuroendocrine and sleep measures in patients with recurrent depression. *Biological Psychiatry*, 19, 1525–1536.

Kupfer, D. J., Reynolds, C. F., III, Ulrich, R. F. & Grochocinski, V. J. (1986). Comparison of automated REM and slow-wave sleep analysis in young and middle-aged depressed subjects. *Biological Psychiatry*, 21, 189–200.

Kupfer, D. J., Shaw, D. H., Ulrich, R., Coble, P. A. & Spiker, D. G. (1982). Application of automated REM analysis in depression. *Archives of General Psychiatry*, 39, 569–573.

Kupfer, D. J., Spiker, D. G., Coble, P. A., Neil, J. F., Ulrich, R. & Shaw, D. H. (1981). Sleep and treatment prediction in endogenous depression. *American Journal of Psychiatry*, 138, 429–434.

Kupfer, D. J. & Thase, M. E. (1983). The use of the sleep laboratory in the diagnosis of affective disorders. In Akiskal, H. S. (ed.), *Psychiatric Clinics of North America*, 6, 3–25.

Kupfer, D. J., Ulrich, R. F., Coble, P. A., Jarrett, D. B., Grochocinski, V., Doman, J., Matthews, G. & Borbely, A. A. (1984b). Application of automated REM and slow wave sleep analysis: I. Normal and depressed subjects. *Psychiatry Research*, 13, 325–334.

Kupfer, D. J., Ulrich, R. F., Coble, P. A., Jarrett, D. B., Grochocinski, V., Doman, J., Matthews, G. & Borbely, A. A. (1984c). Application of automated REM and slow wave sleep analysis: II. Testing the assumptions of the two-process model of sleep regulation in normal and depressed subjects. *Psychiatry Research*, 13, 335–343.

Kupfer, D. J., Weiss, B. L., Detre, T. P. & Foster, F. G. (1974). First night effect revisited: A clinical note. *The Journal of Nervous and Mental Disease*, 159, 205–209.

Lahmeyer, H. W., Poznanski, E. O. & Bellur, S. N. (1983). EEG sleep in depressed adolescents. *American Journal of Psychiatry*, 140, 1150–1153.

Levy, A. B., Dixon, K. N. & Schmidt, H. (1987). REM and delta sleep in anorexia nervosa and bulimia. *Psychiatry Research*, 20, 189–197.

Levy, A. B., Dixon, K. N. & Schmidt, H. (1988). Sleep architecture in anorexia nervosa and bulimia. *Biological Psychiatry*, 23, 99–101.

McCarley, R. W. (1982). REM sleep and depression: Common neurobiological control mechanisms. *American Journal of Psychiatry*, 139, 565–570.

McNair, D. M., Lorr, M. & Droppleman, L. F. (1971). *Manual for the profile of mood states*. San Diego, Educational and Industrial Testing Service.

Mendlewicz, J., Charles, G. A. & Franckson, J. M. (1982). The dexamethasone suppression test in affective disorder: Relationship to clinical and genetic subgroups. *British Journal of Psychiatry*, 141, 464–470.

Mendlewicz, J., Kerkhofs, M., Hoffmann, G. & Linkowski, P. (1984). Dexamethasone suppression test and REM sleep in patients with major depressive disorder. *British Journal of Psychiatry*, 145, 383–388.

Meyer, J. S., Ishikawa, Y., Hata, T. & Karacan, I. (1987). Cerebral blood flow in normal and abnormal sleep and dreaming. *Brain and Cognition*, 6, 266–294.

Papadimitriou, G. N., Linkowski, P., Kerkhofs, M., Kempenaers, C. & Mendlewicz, J. (1988). Sleep EEG recordings in generalized anxiety disorder with significant depression. *Journal of Affective Disorders*, 15, 113–118.

Puig-Antich, J., Goetz, R., Hanlon, C., Tabrizi, M. A., Davies, M. & Weitzman, E. D. (1983). Sleep architecture and REM sleep measures in prepubertal major depressives. *Archives of General Psychiatry*, 40, 187–192.

Rapoport, J., Elkins, R., Langer, D. H., Sceery, W., Buchsbaum, M. S., Gillin, J. C., Murphy, D. L., Zahn, T. P., Lake, R., Ludlow, C. & Mendelson, W. (1981). Childhood obsessive-compulsive disorder. *American Journal of Psychiatry*, 138, 1545–1554.

Rechtschaffen, A. & Kales, A. (Eds.) (1968). *A manual of standardized terminology, techniques and scoring system for sleep stages of human subjects.* National Institute of Health Publication 204, U.S. Government Printing Office.

Reynolds, C. F., III, Christiansen, C. L., Taska, L. S., Coble, P. A. & Kupfer, D. J. (1983b). Sleep in narcolepsy and depression. Does it all look alike? *Journal of Nervous and Mental Disease*, 171, 290–295.

Reynolds, C. F., III, Gillin, J. C. & Kupfer, D. J. (1987). Sleep and affective disorders. In H. Y. Meltzer (Ed.), *Psychopharmacology: The third generation of progress* (pp. 647–654). New York: Raven Press.

Reynolds, C. F., III, Kupfer, D. J., Houck, P. R., Hoch, C. C., Stack, J. A., Berman, S. R. & Zimmer, B. (1988). Reliable discrimination of elderly depressed and demented patients by electroencephalographic sleep data. *Archives of General Psychiatry*, 45, 258–264.

Reynolds, C. F., III, Kupfer, D. J., Taska, L. S., Hoch, C. C., Spiker, D. G., Sewitch, D. E., Zimmer, B., Marin, R. S., Nelson, J. P., Martin, D. & Morycz, R. (1985b). EEG sleep in elderly depressed, demented, and healthy subjects. *Biological Psychiatry*, 20, 431–442.

Reynolds, C. F., III, Shaw, D. H., Newton, T. F., Coble, P. A. & Kupfer, D. J. (1983a). EEG sleep in outpatients with generalized anxiety: A preliminary comparison with depressed outpatients. *Psychiatry Research*, 8, 81–89.

Reynolds, C. F., III & Shipley, J. E. (1985a). Sleep in depressive disorders. In A. J. Francis & R. E. Hales (Eds.), *Psychiatry update. American psychiatric association annual review*, Vol. 4 (pp. 341–360). Washington, DC: American Psychiatric Press, Inc.

Reynolds, C. F., Soloff, P. H., Kupfer, D. J., Taska, L. S., Restifo, K., Coble, P. A. & McNamara, M. E. (1985c). Depression in borderline patients: A prospective EEG sleep study. *Psychiatry Research*, 14, 1–15.

Rush, A. J., Erman, M. K., Giles, D. E., Schlesser, M. A., Carpenter, G., Vasavada, N. & Roffwarg, H. P. (1986). Polysomnographic findings in recently drug-free and clinically remitted depressed patients. *Archives of General Psychiatry*, 43, 878–884.

Rush, A. J., Erman, M. K., Schlesser, M. A., Roffwarg, H. P., Vasavada, N., Khatami, M., Fairchild, C. J. & Giles, D. E. (1985). Alprazolam vs amitriptyline in depressions with reduced REM latencies. *Archives of General Psychiatry*, 42, 1154–1159.

Rush, A. J., Giles, D. E., Roffwarg, H. P. & Parker, C. R., Jr. (1982). Sleep EEG and dexamethasone suppression test findings in outpatients with unipolar major depressive disorders. *Biological Psychiatry*, 17, 327–341.

Rush, A. J., Schlesser, M. A., Roffwarg, H. P., Giles, D. E., Orsulak, P. J. & Fairchild, C. J. (1983). Relationships among the TRH, REM latency, and dexamethasone suppression tests: Preliminary findings. *Journal of Clinical Psychiatry*, 44, 23–29.

Sakai, F., Meyer, J. S., Karacan, I., Yamaguchi, F. & Yamamoto, M. (1979). Narcolepsy: Regional cerebral blood flow during sleep and wakefulness. *Neurology*, 29, 61–67.

Sharpley, A. L., Solomon, R. A. & Cowen, P. J. (1988). Evaluation of first night effect using ambulatory monitoring and automatic sleep stage analysis. *Sleep*, 11, 273–276.

Sitaram, N., Nurnberger, J. I., Jr., Gershon, E. S. & Gillin, J. C. (1980). Faster cholinergic REM sleep induction in euthymic patients with primary affective illness. *Science*, 208, 200–202.

Sitaram, N., Nurnberger, J. I., Jr., Gershon, E. S. & Gillin, J. C. (1982). Cholinergic regulation of mood and REM sleep: Potential model and marker of vulnerability to affective disorder. *American Journal of Psychiatry*, 139, 571–576.

Spiegel, R. (1984). Effects of RS 86, an orally active cholinergic agonist, on sleep in man. *Psychiatry Research*, 11, 1–13.

Spitzer, R. L., Endicott, J. & Robins, E. (1978). Research diagnostic criteria: Rational and reliability. *Archives of General Psychiatry*, 36, 773–782.

Thase, M. E., Kupfer, D. J. & Ulrich, R. F. (1986). Electroencephalographic sleep in psychotic depression. A valid subtype? *Archives of General Psychiatry*, 43, 886–893.

Townsend, R. E., Prinz, P. N. & Obrist, W. D. (1973). Human cerebral blood flow during sleep and waking. *Journal of Applied Physiology*, 35, 620–625.

Young, W., Knowles, J. B., MacLean, A. W., Boag, L. & McConville, B. J. (1982). The sleep of childhood depressives: Comparison with age-matched controls. *Biological Psychiatry*, 17, 1163–1168.

Waller, D. A., Hardy, B. W., Pole, R., Giles, D. E., Gullion, C. M., Rush, A. J. & Roffwarg, H. P. (1989). Sleep EEG in bulimic, depressed and normal subjects. *Biological Psychiatry*, 25, 661–664.

Walsh, B. T., Goetz, R., Roose, S. P., Fingeroth, S. & Glassman, A. H. (1985). EEG-monitored sleep in anorexia nervosa and bulimia. *Biological Psychiatry*, 20, 947–956.

Weilberg, J. B., Stakes, J. W., Brotman, A. & Herzog, D. (1985). Sleep architecture in bulimia: A pilot study. *Biological Psychiatry*, 20, 199–228.

Williams, R. L., Karacan, I. & Hursch, C. J. (1974). *Electroencephalography (EEG) of human sleep: Clinical applications*. New York: Wiley.

Wu, J., Gillin, J. C., Buchsbaum, M. S., Hazlett, E., Sicotte, N. & Bunney, W. E., Jr. (1988). Regional cortical metabolism after sleep deprivation. *Sleep Research*, 17, 32.

Zammit, G. K., Rosenbaum, A. H., Stokes, P., Davis, J., Zorick, F. & Roth, T. (1988). Biological differences in endogenous depressive placebo responders versus non-responders: Dexamethasone suppression test and sleep EEG data. *Biological Psychiatry*, 24, 97–101.

Zarcone, V. P., Benson, K. L. & Berger, P. A. (1987). Abnormal rapid eye movement latencies in schizophrenia. *Archives of General Psychiatry*, 44, 45–48.

Zung, W. W. K. (1969). Effect of antidepressant drugs on sleeping and dreaming. III. On the depressed patient. *Biological Psychiatry*, 1, 283–287.

# Depression in the Brain-Injured: Phenomenology and Treatment

Thomas W. McAllister and Trevor R. P. Price
*University of Pennsylvania*

## INTRODUCTION

Depressive syndromes occurring in the context of different types of neurological disorders are extremely common. In fact, depression is almost certainly the most common behavioral concomitant of disorders afflicting the central nervous system. It has been common to attribute this relationship to "reactive" or "psychological" mechanisms. However, evidence is accumulating from a variety of sources that the relationship may be much more complex than this. Rather than reflecting just the intrapsychic responses to chronic illness or physical disability, the expression of a mood disturbance may result from a complex interaction between the *type* of brain dysfunction, the *location* of the brain dysfunction or injury, the biological vulnerability of the individual to the expression of an affective illness, *and* the intra-psychic and psychological chaos brought about by the brain insult. Furthermore, the phenomenological expression, or clinical characteristics of a given depressive syndrome, may well be influenced by these same factors.

From a theoretical perspective, the ability to further define the contributions that pathophysiological mechanism and injury location make to the genesis of a depressive episode and its particular clinical characteristics ("phenotype") may hold particular importance for the understanding of primary or "idiopathic" mood disturbances. The advent of imaging techniques which facilitate more accurate, specific lesion localization, as well as techniques (such as positron emission tomographic (PET) imaging of specific receptor populations) which permit the integration of this information, with the gains made in neuropsychopharmacology over the last thirty years make this a potentially fruitful area of investigation.

From a clinical perspective, several factors are worth noting. For a number of reasons, including difficulties in language function (both propositional and prosodic functions), decreased cognitive function, atypical responses to psychotropic medications, as well as others, the presence of a brain injury alters the phenomenology and treatment of a depressive syndrome. Although one cannot lump all types of brain injury (cerebrovascular, epileptiform, traumatic, infectious, degenerative, neoplastic, etc.), together and assume that the pathophysiologic underpinnings and clinical phenomenology will be the same even when located in the same area, the presence of a brain injury does appear to have a predictable clinical impact in terms of difficulties in assessment, quantification, and treatment of an associated depressive syndrome regardless of the *type* of injury.

From a demographic standpoint, the number of individuals afflicted with important central nervous system (CNS) disorders is difficult to ascertain. Even more difficult is the percentage of those who also suffer from depressive illness. However, some reasonable guesswork suggests that the number is a large one. Using figures from Kurtzke (1982) on the incidence and prevalence of various neurologic disorders, and summing this data for 20 of the 61 categories listed[1] results in a summed average annual incidence rate of 1,194 per 100,000 population, and a point prevalence of 6,647 per 100,000 population (excludes mental retardation). This is a conservative number because for some of the disorders, the data assumes that only 10–20% of those with the illness need to be seen by a neurologist.

What percentage of these patients suffer from a depressive syndrome is not known although it is clearly quite high in *certain* of the illnesses. Cummings (1985) suggests that depression occurs in 47–71% of patients with Parkinson's Disease and approximately half of those with Huntington's Disease. Post-stroke depressive syndromes occur in up to 60% of those affected and 70% of patients with postconcussion syndromes (Merskey & Woodforde, 1972). Estimates vary, but probably at least 25–30% of patients with probable dementing disorders have clinically significant depressive syndromes (Reifler, Larson & Hanley, 1982). Depressive syndromes occur frequently as a complication of epilepsy, both as ictal events and interictal disturbances (Betts, 1981; Cummings, 1985; Himmelhoch, 1984; Robertson, Trimble & Townsend, 1987; Mendez, Cummings & Benson, 1984; Mulder & Daly, 1952). Although the exact frequency of significant mood disturbances varies according to seizure type, location, and study, it is clear that its effects are profound, with suicide 4 to 5 times more common in patients with epilepsy (and 25 times higher in temporal lobe epileptics) than in the general population (Robertson et al., 1987).

Thus, conservatively figuring that 25 to 50% of patients with the above mentioned neurological illnesses will suffer a depressive syndrome suggests that the number of brain-injured depressed patients is a large one.

This raises the question of whether depressive syndromes are a phenomenologically uniform, final common pathway for a wide variety of CNS insults, or a heterogeneous group of syndromes with phenotypic expressions determined by the location of the CNS insult, the pathophysiology of the insult, or a combination of these factors. It is assumed that an individual's psychological and environmental profile will further color the expression of a given depressive event.

We attempt in this Chapter to review the evidence that location and pathophysiology of the CNS insult influence the expression of depressive syndromes, as well as outline some of the important issues in the assessment and treatment of depressive syndromes associated with CNS dysfunction.

---

[1]  migraine, brain trauma, other headache, cerebro-vascular disease, transient postconcussive syndrome, epilepsy, dementia, Parkinsonism, persistent postconcussive syndrome, meningitides, encephalitides, sleep disorders, subarachnoid hemorrhages, metastatic brain tumors, benign brain tumors, mental retardation, mental retardation severe, multiple sclerosis and other demyelinating diseases, chronic progressive myelopathy.

## IMPACT OF LESION LOCATION ON RISK OF DEPRESSIVE SYNDROMES

Without fully addressing the largely unstudied questions of whether most "injuries" are the same (regardless of the exact pathophysiologic mechanism) with respect to associated risk of depression, one can begin by asking whether injury (of any type) to certain cerebral regions is associated with a greater risk of developing a depressive syndrome than injury to other regions. There are many different ways one could think about such regional differentiations, including simple "geographical" dimensions such as left versus right, anterior versus posterior, cortical versus sub-cortical, lobar (frontal lobe versus temporal lobe) and more complex schemes based on common neurotransmitter systems or shared circuitry and neuroanatomical connections (limbic system, language system, sensorimotor systems, etc.). Most studies to date have focused on simple geographic schemes, such as left hemisphere versus right hemisphere and, to lesser degrees, anterior-posterior gradients.

### Relationship Of Depression To Laterality Of Injury

An evolving body of literature suggests that the two cerebral hemispheres differ in terms of the roles they play in the experience, expression, and modulation of "normal" mood and affect, and the predictable manifestation of pathological mood and affect subsequent to injury.

A variety of work suggests that injury to the left hemisphere often results in dramatic paroxysmal displays of negative affect [described as a "catastrophic reaction" by Goldstein (1939)], whereas denial of impairment or relative indifference to the degree of impairment is more commonly seen in right-sided or non-dominant hemispheric injuries (Denny-Brown, Meyer & Horenstein, 1952; Hecaen, 1962). This has also been studied by unilateral barbiturate injections, and though the results are not unanimous (Gainotti, 1972; Sackeim, Greenbert, Weiman, Gur, Hungerbuhler & Geschwind, 1982), they have been interpreted as largely confirming of this schema. Gainotti (1972) further studied the verbal content of 160 stroke patients with primarily unilateral lesions (left or right) and concluded that expression and experience of catastrophic reaction-like symptoms and "anxious-depressive orientation of mood" were statistically more common in patients with left hemispheric injury. Of note, however, is that actual "depressive mood" symptoms were not unevenly distributed between the two groups, (discouragement, rationalizations, anticipation of incapacity, declaration of incapacity, etc.). Extending the above approaches, Hommes and Panhuysen (1971) studied the effect of carotid injections of amobarbital in eleven depressed patients and suggested that depression was associated with a decrease in left hemispheric dominance.

Sackeim et al. (1982) exhaustively reviewed the literature on pathological (exaggerated) displays of affect (laughing or crying), the effects of unilateral hemispherectomy on mood and affect, and cases of unilateral epileptic foci with associated ictal affect (in which the seizure itself is a crying or laughing spell). They interpreted the data as supportive of a pattern of cerebral organization wherein the left hemisphere largely subserves the more positive feeling states and laughing behavior, and the right hemisphere serves a more important role as substrate for negative feeling states and crying behaviors. Changes in mood and affect then result from relative deactivation of one hemisphere either by loss of function (i.e., through infarction) or over activation (i.e., epileptic focus) of the contralateral hemisphere. It is important to note in assessing this study that assignment of cases was based on *primary* hemispheric lesion location and that these were not all pure unilateral lesions. Further, although the paper discusses both *mood* and *affect*, most of the categorization was based on affective *display*, which may or may not be consonant with the internal feeling state (Green, McAllister & Bernat, 1987; Lieberman & Benson, 1977; Poeck, 1969).

Another line of studies bearing on this question comes from work on the risk of depression in patients with cerebrovascular accidents (CVA). Although the high prevalence of depressive disorders in this population has long been known, the factors contributing to this had not been studied, or had been assumed to be secondary to psychological mechanisms operating in response to such issues as physical disability, language deficits, cognitive losses, or other effects of the stroke (Fisher, 1961; Ullman & Gruen, 1960). The view that there was something unique about stroke as compared to other chronic, disabling injuries was advanced when 20 CVA patients were found to suffer more depression than 10 patients with orthopedic injuries and equivalent functional disability (Folstein, Maiberger & McHugh, 1977). Of interest, given subsequent work, is that the right hemispheric stroke group were particularly likely to be depressed, though the depression scores for all groups were in fact quite low. Subsequently, Robinson and Szetela (1981) studied a series of patients with left hemispheric injury, either due to stroke or traumatic brain injury (TBI). Although the CVA group had higher depression scores than the TBI group, this effect was negated when lesion location along an anterior-posterior gradient was controlled for. This confirmed the importance of lesion location in determining vulnerability to depressive symptoms and suggested that both laterality and anterior-posterior dimensions were potentially important factors.

Subsequent to these initial studies, this group has actively pursued a number of important questions relevant to lesion laterality and its relationship to depressive syndromes. The study population consisted of, for the most part, 103 consecutive patients admitted to The University of Maryland Hospital with thromboembolic stroke or intracerebral hemorrhage. Fifty-one other patients were not included due to depressed levels of consciousness initially or severe receptive aphasia and related comprehension deficits. Patients were primarily black males of lower socioeconomic status. They were evaluated for neurological deficits, cognitive deficits with the Mini Mental Status Exam (MMSE) (Folstein, M.F., Folstein, S.E. & McHugh, 1975), social functioning (Social Functioning Exam and The Social Ties Checklist [Starr, Robinson & Price, 1982]), and physical impairment (The Johns Hopkins Functional Inventory [Robinson & Benson, 1981; Robinson & Szetela, 1981]). Lesion location was assessed with computerized axial tomographic (CT) scanning, both in terms of laterality (left, right, or bilateral), and anterior-posterior gradient (described as the distance from the anterior tip of a lesion to the frontal pole). Mood was assessed and quantified by transposing scores on the 17-item Hamilton Depression Scale (Hamilton, 1960) and the Zung Depression Scale (Zung, 1965) to five point scales and summing them.

Using the above general paradigm, this group has reported up to 60% of stroke patients will have either a major or minor depressive syndrome in the first two years subsequent to the stroke (Lipsey, Spencer, Rabins & Robinson, 1986; Robinson & Forrester, 1987; Robinson, Starr & Price, 1984; Robinson & Szetela, 1981), that the risk of developing a depressive syndrome, as well as the severity of the symptoms experienced, is directly correlated with left hemispheric injury and proximity to the anterior frontal pole (Lipsey, Robinson, Pearlson, Rao & Price, 1984; Robinson & Forrester, 1987; Robinson, Lipsey, Rao & Price, 1986; Robinson, Starr, Lipsey, Rao & Price, 1985; Robinson & Szetela, 1981), and that this effect appears to be independent of handedness (Robinson, Lipsey, Bolla-Wilson, Bolduc, Pearlson, Rao & Price, 1985). Furthermore, the symptoms of depression increase over the first six months subsequent to a stroke, usually last at least six to twelve months, and acute and delayed onset depressive symptoms looked phenomenologically very much the same in this population (Robinson, Lipsey, Rao, Price, 1986; Robinson, Starr & Price, 1984; Robinson, Starr, Lipsey, et al., 1985). In addition, the presence of depressive symptoms apparently worsens stroke-induced cognitive impairment (Robinson, Bolla-Wilson, Kaplan, Lipsey & Price, 1986) and negatively affects recovery and rehabilitation (Robinson, Bolla-Wilson, et al., 1986; Robinson & Forrester, 1987; Robinson, Starr & Price, 1984).

From a theoretical perspective, Robinson and coworkers have suggested that disruption of asymmetrically distributed neurotransmitter systems may explain these provocative findings (Robinson & Forrester, 1987). Specifically, the effects of catecholaminergic disruption vary according to the laterality of the insult, and because of progressive breadth of distribution in an anterior to posterior gradient, anterior disruption of catecholaminergic pathways may result in more universal depletion "downstream" (Morrison, Molliver & Grzanna, 1979; Oke, Keller, Mefford & Adams, 1978; Robinson, 1979; Robinson & Forrester, 1987). More recently this group has reported a differential effect on certain serotonergic receptor populations as a function of laterality of CVA (Mayberg, Robinson, Wong, Parikh, Bolduc, Starkstein, Price, Dannals, Links, Wilson, Ravert & Wagner, 1988).

The above-described work has been well conceived, carefully carried out, and has produced some important and provocative findings. It is helpful to bear in mind, while synthesizing it, that most of the findings are from the same study population, that actual numbers of pure unilateral lesions in these groups are fairly small (10–17) and based on CT scan data (the actual numbers of bilateral lesions might be higher if now studied with magnetic resonance imaging (MRI) for example), and that the depression scores are actually quite low in most of the studies (for example, mean Hamilton Depression Rating Scale (HDRS) scores in the *depressed* patients of 11.7–16.6). Further, there is a fairly high percentage of alcohol abuse in the study population.

Surprisingly, there have been few other groups attempting to replicate these observations (Sinyor, Jacques, Kaloupek, Becker, Goldenberg & Coopersmith, 1986). The latter study supported the importance of location along an anterior-posterior gradient but did not confirm the strong laterality effects noted above. However, various case reports of the onset of depressive symptoms subsequent to left hemispheric injury, as well as manic syndromes subsequent to right hemispheric injury, continue to lend credence to the concept that the two hemispheres differ in terms of the role they play in the expression and experience of certain emotions (Cummings & Mendez, 1984; Freeman, Galaburda, Diaz Cabal, Geschwind, 1985; Stewart & Hemsath, 1988).

## Anterior-Posterior Gradient

Most of the information available on the effect of lesion localization with respect to an anterior-posterior gradient, comes from the body of work cited above by Robinson and coworkers (Robinson & Forrester, 1987). As suggested, both the risk of developing a clinically significant depressive syndrome and the severity of depressive symptoms have been found to be associated with proximity of the anterior tip of the lesion to the frontal pole. A potentially confounding factor is that left posterior stroke patients are more likely to have greater degrees of receptive language deficits and, as such, were eliminated from the original population. furthermore, one wonders about the validity of the mood scales in this sub-group of stroke patients.

## Cortical vs. Sub-Cortical Gradient

In addition to the laterality and anterior-posterior location of lesions, certain observations can be made with respect to cortical versus sub-cortical lesion location and its impact on risk of associated depressive syndromes.

Although small numbers of patients with sub-cortical infarcts (or both cortical and sub-cortical infarcts) were included in the body of literature cited above, the majority of these patients appear to have had primarily cortical damage. However, evidence from a variety of other clinical situations strongly suggests that several diseases with prominent sub-cortical components carry a very high risk of associated depressive syndromes. Several studies have suggested rates of associated depressive syndromes of 47–71% of patients with Parkinson's Disease (Cummings, 1985). Huntington's Disease can have a wide array of behavioral syndromes associated with the movement disorder and progressive dementia (Caine & Shoulson, 1983), but depressive syndromes are among the most common, reportedly occurring in approximately 50% of affected patients (Cummings, 1985). Affective displays, many of which can have features suggestive of a depressive syndrome, can occur in a variety of CNS disorders with sub-cortical damage, in particular pseudobulbar palsy (Green et al., 1987; Lieberman & Benson, 1977; Poeck, 1969; Wilson, 1924). In addition, several other small series and case reports suggest that basal ganglia calcification can be associated with important mood disturbances (Francis & Freeman, 1984; Munir, 1986; Sammet & Bucy, 1951; Trautner, Cummings, Read & Benson, 1988). Others have reported behavioral disturbances with affective features occurring in the context of brainstem lesions (Trimble & Cummings, 1981). The relatively recent applications of magnetic resonance imaging to the study of affectively disordered patients has led to the observation by some groups that a fairly high percentage of depressed patients referred for electroconvulsive therapy (ECT) (and, thus, perhaps a more severely depressed and/or refractory population) have MRI findings suggestive of sub-cortical ischemia, infarction, or demyelination

(Coffey, Figiel, Djang, Press, Saunders & Weiner, 1988; Krishnan, Goli, Ellinwood, France, Blazer & Nemeroff, 1988). Studies of patients with depression-induced dementia have suggested that the pattern of cognitive decline fits that seen in certain sub-cortical dementias, again suggesting a possible link to mood regulation (Caine, 1981).

Thus, it seems clear that there are important relationships between sub-cortical injury of a variety of types and locations, and disturbances in mood regulation. Given the distribution of neurotransmitter systems across several dimensions (left-right; anterior-posterior; cortical-sub-cortical), it is not surprising that a variety of disruptions occurring in a variety of locations could have clinical depressive syndromes as a final common pathway.

## IMPACT OF LESION LOCATION ON PHENOMENOLOGY

The proper assessment and treatment of an individual with a brain injury and concurrent depressive syndrome requires an appreciation for the effect that the nature and location of the injury can have on the expression of the depressive syndrome. This can be considered in terms of laterality effects and regional effects.

### Effects Of Laterality On Phenomenology

In considering the effects of laterality on expression of depressive symptoms, it is helpful to consider the various components which act (in the uninjured brain) in concert to produce what is then diagnosed as a clinically significant mood disturbance. Although a full discussion of this is beyond the scope of this chapter, the basic concepts can be mentioned. Ross and Rush (1981), in their discussions of depression in brain-damaged patients, suggest four basic components of depressive syndromes: the verbal-cognitive set (the propositional language used to describe the subjective experience); the mood, which is the actual internal feeling state experienced; affect, the non-propositional language components (facial expression, posture, gestures, melody, etc.) which supplement and augment the words and syntax used in communicating with propositional language; and vegetative behavior, which incorporates the usual "neurovegetative" or "biological" signs of depression (such as anorexia, anhedonia, sleep continuity disturbances, and loss of libido). Although the boundaries of these categories are arguable and not always clear, and it is not known that the concepts are clearly rooted in neuroanatomical or neurophysiological reality, the model is useful in considering some issues important in the evaluation and treatment of brain-injured patients.

### Dominant Hemispheric Injury

A common effect of injury to the dominant hemisphere, usually left, is impairment in propositional language function. This can lead to significant deficits in the patient's ability to convey the "verbal-cognitive set" of his or her depressive syndrome (Ross & Rush, 1981). Assessment of a mood disturbance must then focus on the other components of depression, including vegetative signs, pathological displays of affect, and more global hints, such as deterioration in neurological status and failure to progress with aggressive rehabilitative efforts (Ross & Rush, 1981).

## Non-Dominant Hemispheric Injury

Two common effects of non-dominant (usually right) hemispheric damage are germane to the experience and expression of depressive syndromes; denial syndromes, and aprosodias.

It has been noted for some time that certain patients with right hemispheric injuries can often demonstrate varying degrees of denial, which in its extreme form can manifest as a complete disregard of the left hemi-space (Denny-Brown et al., 1952; Gainotti, 1972; Sackeim et al., 1982). This can apply to denial of behavioral impairments and depressive symptoms as well as sensorimotor deficits (Ross & Rush, 1981).

Disorders of the prosodic components of language (emphasis, modulation of tone, "melodic contour"; Weintraub, Mesulam & Kramer, 1981) can be complications of right hemispheric injury and have been shown to have a significant impact on aspects of communication, both the expressive and receptive components (Monrad-Krohn, 1947; Ross, 1981; Ross, Harney, de Lacoste-Utamsing & Purdy, 1981; Ross & Mesulam, 1979; Weintraub et al., 1981). With respect to the assessment of the presence and severity of depressive symptoms in right hemispheric injured patients, the aprosodias result in a higher order level of complexity when the clinician attempts to match descriptions of the patient's mood, as described in the "verbal-cognitive set," with the affect expressed in association with that description (Ross & Rush, 1981).

## Frontal And Temporal Lobe Injury

Depression is a frequent concomitant of a variety of frontal lobe disorders, including: CVA's, tumors, and traumatic brain injuries (TBI's), among others. True depressive states must be differentiated from the so-called "pseudodepressed" syndrome with its characteristic apathy, psycho-motor slowing, and lack of motivation (McAllister & Price, 1987), which is typically associated with bilateral frontal convexity lesions. Frontal lobe lesions in other anatomical loci produce very different appearing clinical syndromes; those involving the orbitofrontal region are associated with the so-called "pseudopsychopathic" syndrome with its characteristic picture of disinhibited and impulsive behavior, while those involving the medial aspects of the frontal lobes are characterized by akinetic mutism (extreme verbal and motor inactivity) and unresponsiveness (Cummings, 1985).

As noted elsewhere in this chapter, depression is not uncommon with anterior frontal lobe strokes. They tend to occur with greater frequency the more anterior the lesion is, and with left-sided as compared to right-sided strokes (Cummings, 1985). Based on his review of available studies, Cummings suggests that frontal lobe tumors are associated with depression less frequently than they are with euphoria, and in any case only in a minority of patients. In his series of post-traumatic, brain-injured patients, Lishman (1968) found that depression was highly associated with frontal lobe injury, particularly when it involved the right as compared to the left frontal lobe. Others, however, have reported more frequent and more severe depressions with left frontal lobe involvement (Robinson & Szetela, 1981) as compared with the right.

Temporal lobe disorders are frequently associated with affective syndromes. The question of a predictable association of temporal lobe lesion laterality and the occurrence of affective syndromes, analogous to the association of schizophreniform psychoses with left temporal lobe disease, is complicated by conflicting research data. Flor-Henry (1969) first suggested a specific clinical association between right temporal lobe lesions and depressive symptoms. This finding was, however, based on a small sample of only 9 psychotic, temporal lobe epilepsy patients, 4 of whom had bilateral foci. Clinical data from several subsequent studies has cast considerable doubt on this putative association. Thus, Robertson et al. (1987), based on their sample of 66 depressed epileptics, 45 of whom had complex partial seizures, reported no specific association between right-sided foci and depression. In fact, among those patients in their study with localized electroencephalographic (EEG) abnormalities, left-sided foci were more common than right. Similarly, Keschner, Bender, and Strauss (1936) found that 20% of their 110 patients with temporal lobe tumors had depressive syndromes, and among patients with left, not right, temporal lobe lesions, Williams (1956) found that ictal depressive symptoms were more often associated with left (N=6), than right (N=4) temporal lobe lesions or foci, and that they tended to occur most frequently with lesions located in the mid-temporal regions. Mendez, Cummings, and Benson (1986), likewise found that 10 of 15 depressive epileptic patients with focal EEG abnormalities, most of whom had complex partial seizures, had left-sided foci. Perini and Mendius (1984) also found more depressive, dysphoric, and anxiety symptoms among patients with left as compared to right-sided temporal lobe foci.

## EFFECT OF TYPE OF INJURY ON PHENOMENOLOGY

Despite the known association of depressive syndromes with various types of brain injury, very little attention has been directed toward the phenomenology of these depressive symptoms, as a function either of location of injury (apart from that described above) or type of injury. This is surprising in light of what this might tell us about idiopathic or primary depressive illness.

### Cerebrovascular Accidents

Work from Robinson's group (Robinson & Forrester, 1987) has suggested that stroke-related depressive syndromes have similar natural histories, treatment responses, cognitive deficits, and abnormalities of the hypothalamic-pituitary-adrenal axis to depression in the non brain-injured population. Subsequent examination of the severity of Hamilton scores, as well as cluster scores from the Present State Exam (Wing, Cooper & Sartorius, 1974), of depressed stroke patients and depressed patients without brain damage showed that the two groups differed only with respect to past history of depressive illness, and two of seventeen Present State Exam (PSE) derived cluster scores.

## Dementing Disorders

The phenomenology of depressive syndromes in dementing disorders has not been directly studied. It has been suggested, however, that the natural history of associated mood disturbances varies with the type of dementia, worsening over time in sub-cortical dementias (Parkinson's Disease, Huntington's Disease), and becoming less severe in cortical dementias (Huber & Paulson, 1986; Pies, 1986). The profile of symptoms or symptom clusters has not been carefully looked at, although one group has reported that patients with depression and dementia were more impaired socially and with respect to work, and were noted to complain of and demonstrate more impairment in attention and concentration than a group of age-matched non-demented controls (Reding, Haycox & Blass, 1985). These differences would appear to be due more to the underlying dementing illness than the associated mood disturbance. Lazarus' group (Lazarus, Newton, Cohler, Lesser & Schweon, 1987) found that the depressive syndrome in demented patients tended to have higher scores in the psychological components of depression (as measured by such items on the Hamilton Depression Scale as depressed mood, helplessness, hopelessness, and worthlessness), rather than in the neurovegetative area (weight loss, diurnal variation). However, their control group consisted of healthy, age-matched volunteers, not non-demented, depressed subjects. We found that initial severity of depression and response to treatment were similar in a depressed group of patients with brain injury and a non brain-injured depressed population. However, the brain-injured group tended to have lower neurovegetative scores and lower anxiety scores (McAllister, Price & Ross, 1988).

## Traumatic Brain Injury

Although affective disturbances have long been recognized as a frequent complication of traumatic brain injury of varying severity (Leigh, 1979; Levin, 1987; Lishman, 1968; Lishman, 1973; Merskey & Woodforde, 1972; Miller, 1961; Strauss & Savitsky, 1934; Thompson, 1965), there is surprisingly little information available with respect to the phenomendology of these affective disturbances as a function of various injury parameters. Most observers have emphasized the "reactive" or "neurotic" nature of the affective symptoms while admitting that a certain percentage will also develop a more endogenomorphic picture as well (Fordyce, Roueche & Prigatano, 1983; Miller, 1961).

The overall degree of psychiatric disability appears related to a variety of injury parameters, including amount of brain tissue injured, the length of post-traumatic amnesia, the presence and time of onset of post-traumatic epilepsy, and location of injury (temporal and frontal lobes, left hemisphere greater than right; Lishman, 1968). Depression, in particular, appears related to some measures of extent of injury (*right* hemispheric injury, frontal lobe damage) and often is associated with a variety of somatic complaints, cognitive dysfunction, and other behavioral disturbances in a high percentage of cases (Lishman, 1968). The presence of agitation in the period following the injury has been shown to predict higher anxiety-depression cluster scores on the Brief Psychiatric Rating Scale later on (Levin & Grossman, 1978).

Depression has also been described as a common complication of minor head injury, occurring in 22 of 27 cases in one study (Merskey & Woodforde, 1972). Again, depressive syndromes often occurred in conjunction with a variety of other behavioral symptoms, including anxiety and somatic complaints. Further, it has been suggested that the latency between time of injury and onset of the depressive syndrome varies (to some degree) with the severity of the injury (Merskey & Woodforde, 1972).

Interestingly, the severity of the depressive symptoms may vary directly with the time elapsed from the injury, as well as the degree of cognitive improvement (Fordyce et al., 1983). This is, of course, somewhat the opposite of the pattern seen in the stroke population as previously described.

Others have also emphasized the clinical point that as in the stroke population, denial syndromes, deficits in propositional and prosodic (affective) language function, as well as the frequent mixture of symptoms seen can complicate the diagnosis and treatment of depression in the TBI population (Kwentus, Hart, Peck & Kornstein, 1985). From a treatment perspective, Saran (1985) suggested that clinically significant depressive syndromes occurring soon after minor head injury can have less vegetative features and be less responsive to amitriptyline and phenelzine than depressive syndromes of similar initial severity occurring in the absence of brain injury.

Thus, despite wide recognition of the prevalence, severity, and negative impact on rehabilitation that depressive syndromes can have, surprisingly little information is available with respect to diagnosis, phenomenology, and management of the depressed traumatic brain injury patient.

## Parkinson's Disease

Depression is the most common psychiatric concomitant of Parkinson's disease, with a reported prevalence ranging from 20%–90% (depending on the patient sample studied, and the criteria and methods used to diagnose depression), with 40%–50% being modal (Asnis, 1977; Harvey, 1986; Mayeux, Stern, Rosen & Levanthal, 1981; Mayeux, Stern, Williams, Cote, Frantz & Dyrenfurth, 1986; Schiffer, Kurlan, Rubin & Bock, 1988; Serby, 1980). While opinion has varied considerably over the years, the predominant view now, based on recent data, is that the depression associated with Parkinson's disease is largely an intrinsic part of the syndrome characterized most often by endogenomorphic clinical features. However, some patients may be reactively depressed in response to their neurological dysfunction and attendant physical incapacity, and both dysthymic disorders by DSM-III criteria (as many as 33% of depressed patients in one series of cases; Mayeux et al., 1986) and atypical depressions with concomitant generalized anxiety and/or panic disorder by rigorous diagnostic criteria (as many as 75% of cases Schiffer et al., 1988) have been reported.

The severity of the depressive disorders was characterized as "mild" in 65% of cases in one series of 55 patients (Mayeux, Stern, Rosen et al., 1981) and as "mild" to "moderate" in another series of 57 patients (Celesia & Wanamaker, 1972). There was a positive family history for depression in only 10% of cases in one carefully studied series of patients (Winokur, Dugan, Mendels & Huntig, 1978). A previous personal history of depressive illness was found in a like percentage of another series (Celesia & Wanamaker, 1972). Depression can occur at any stage of Parkinson's disease. It has been described even before the onset of clinically-apparent Parkinsonism in 34%–40% of cases (Harvey, 1986), and has been reported to be accompanied frequently by a relatively mild, though definite, impairment of cognitive function, which is different and distinct from the more severe dementia that often also occurs with Parkinson's disease (Mayeux, Stern, Rosen & Leventhal, 1981).

The neurological and affective symptoms associated with Parkinson's disease may vary (independently) in severity and both respond to treatment with antidepressants or ECT in as many as 70%–95% of cases (Harvey, 1986; Price & McAllister, 1989). Changes in these symptoms may also occur independently and over different time courses. The intrinsic endogenomorphic depressions associated with Parkinson's disease are believed to be related, at least in part, to decreased levels of dopamine and/or serotonin (Asnis, 1977; Mayeux, Stern, Williams et al., 1986).

## Multiple Sclerosis (MS)

It has been said that as many as 90% of cases of MS at one time or another have psychiatric and behavioral symptoms. These tend to be episodic, fluctuate widely, and are believed to be related in part to the brain dysfunction resulting from the process of demyelination, and in part to the stress of the disease and its associated disability (Brown & Davis, 1922). Estimates of the co-occurrence of depression with MS have varied from 20%–60% (Matthews, 1979; Schiffer et al., 1988), and it is considered by many to be one of the most common psychiatric complications of the primary illness (Goodstein & Ferrell, 1977). Depressive syndromes tend to occur more frequently in patients with a preponderance of cerebral as compared with brain stem or spinal chord demyelinating lesions (Schiffer, Caine, Bamford & Levy, 1983). Such affective syndromes frequently occur early in the course of the illness and may even be the presenting clinical problem. The occurrence of depression is not necessarily related to the degree of functional disability caused by the underlying neurological disorder but does seem to be related to the degree of severity of the neurological impairment associated with it (Dalos, Rabins, Brooks & O'Donnell, 1983; Rabins, Brooks, O'Donnell, Pearlson, Moberg, Jubett, Coyle, Dalos & Folstein, 1986), especially when it involves the temporal lobes (Honer, Hurwitz, Li, Palmer & Paty, 1987; Schiffer & Babigian, 1984; Whitlock & Siskind, 1980).

Earlier, it was believed that depressive syndromes, which can antedate the clinical presentation of typical MS signs and symptoms (Goodstein & Ferrell, 1977), usually occurred early in the course of the illness, only to be supplanted later on by inappropriate euphoric affective states co-occurring in conjunction with increasing organic cognitive impairment (Brown & Davis, 1922; Pratt, 1951; Surridge, 1969). More recently, euphoria has been less frequently described as an especially prominent clinical feature, either early or late, and increasingly, depression has been noted to become more severe as the underlying disease advances (Baretz & Stephenson, 1981).

The depressions associated with MS have frequently been noted to be virtually "classic," episodic and recurrent, endogenomorphic depressions, characterized by the full range of typical biological as well as psychological signs and symptoms (Goodstein & Ferrell, 1977; Schiffer et al., 1988), as well as a substantially increased risk of suicide (Kahana, Leibowitz & Alter, 1971). Many consider the depressive features to be due to a combination of biologically-based, endogenous factors as well as the painful external realities associated with the progressive state of physical and cognitive impairment.

A high frequency of "masked" depressions, especially early on, which become more overt as the disease progresses, has also been noted (Baretz & Stephenson, 1981), as has a pattern of increasing depressive symptoms at or around the time of disease "flares" (Schiffer & Babigian, 1984). A possible relationship between MS and bipolar affective disorders has been recently suggested (Joffe, Lippert, Gray, Sawa & Horvath, 1987; Kellner, Davenport, Post & Ross, 1984; Schiffer, Wineman & Weitkamp, 1986).

Despite their rather typical endogenous-like clinical presentation, however, the depressions associated with MS have been noted by some (Goodstein & Ferrell, 1977) to be poorly responsive to ordinarily effective antidepressant treatments, while others have reported more favorable clinical responses (Tucker & Price, 1987). Patients with combined major depressive disorders and MS are often intolerant of antidepressants, experiencing intolerable side effects or drug toxicity at relatively low doses that are likely to be homeopathic (Goodstein & Ferrell, 1977; Trimble & Grant, 1982). When antidepressant drugs are used to treat depression in MS, those with low side effect profiles should be used preferentially, and they should be given at the lowest dose levels consistent with favorable treatment responses. When indicated, electroconvulsive therapy can be given to MS patients safely and with a reasonable expectation of a favorable outcome (Abrams, 1988).

## Huntington's Disease

From 45% to 94% of patients with Huntington's Disease present with significant psychiatric disturbances (Brothers & Meadows, 1955; Heathfield, 1967; Oliver, 1970). Though some earlier studies had suggested that schizophreniform and personality disorders were the predominant types of associated psychopathology in Huntington's patients, more recent work has shown that affective disorders are very commonly seen. Thus, Whittier (1977) suggests that, after personality disorders, affective disorders, not schizophreniform disorders, are the most commonly seen in Huntington's patients. Caine and Shoulson (1983) found that 11 of their 24 Huntington's patients with behavioral disturbances (46%) met DSM-III criteria for major depressive (N=5) or dysthymic (N=6) disorders. McHugh and Folstein (1975) reported endogenomorphic depressions in 5 out of 8, or 63%, of the patients they studied. In Heathfield's survey of Huntington's patients, 8 of 29 patients, or 28%, had a clinical picture consistent with depression. Folstein, S.E., Abbott, Chase, Jensen, and Folstein, M.F. (1983) reported that 36 of their 88 Huntington's patients

(41%) had major depressive disorders. Of these, a significant majority (28 of 36 or 78%) had unipolar depression, while only 8 of 36, or 22%, had bipolar affective disorder. Heathfield (1967) and Brothers and Meadows (1955) found that 20% and 25% of patients respectively in their surveys who had presented with psychiatric symptoms had depression.

Depressive and other psychiatric symptoms can be present at a point in the natural history of Huntington's disease when neither the typical dementia nor characteristic chorea are present (McHugh & Folstein, 1975). In the 34 cases in the survey of Folstein et al. (1983), where the time course of the underlying disease could be clearly established, the depressive illness was present in 23 cases before the diagnosis of Huntington's had been established; it was coincident with the diagnosis in 6 cases and first appeared well after the diagnosis had been established in 5 cases. It has been shown that depressive episodes may antedate the appearance of clinically diagnosable Huntington's by anywhere from 5-10 years.

The depressive disorders seen with Huntington's tend to be relatively severe and not infrequently are of psychotic proportions with mood-congruent, nihilistic delusions (McHugh & Folstein, 1975) and are associated with a substantially increased risk of suicide. In a survey by Reed and Chadler (1958), suicide accounted for 7% of the deaths in one sample of Huntington's patients. The depressions associated with Huntington's are usually more reminiscent of endogenomorphic than reactive depression, with typical biological and psychological symptoms of major depressive disorders predominating. These depressions are usually recurrent, and when they alternate with manic episodes, as not infrequently may happen, they may meet the criteria for bipolar affective disorders (Caine & Shoulson, 1983; McHugh & Folstein, 1975). Overall, Folstein et al. (1983) suggest that secondary depressions associated with Huntington's disease are virtually indistinguishable from the primary depressions that are not. This is true in a number of respects: with regard to demography, in that they are more common in women than in men; in their rather classical clinical phenomenology; in their time and age of onset; in their natural history and progression, with recurrent exacerbations and remissions; and perhaps most importantly, in their response to standard antidepressant treatments. Thus, antidepressant medications and electroconvulsive therapy are both highly effective and relatively well-tolerated (Price & McAllister, 1989; Tucker & Price, 1987) in depressed Huntington's patients, and thus the clinician should not hold back on their use.

## Epilepsy

While little systematic clinical data and relatively few carefully-done, large studies of patients with epilepsy and affective disorders are currently available, depression is believed by some (Betts, 1981) to be the most frequent psychiatric concomitant of epilepsy. Betts (1974) and Gunn (1973) reported as many as a third of the epileptic patients in their respective series had depression or depressive symptomatology as their most prominent psychiatric clinical feature.

Depression and depressive symptomatology associated with epilepsy may be persistent or fleeting; pre-ictal, ictal, post-ictal, or not clearly temporally related to the ictus at all, i.e., inter-ictal. The symptomatology tends to be variable in severity but typically moderate in degree. Robertson et al. (1987) reported 21-item Hamilton Depression scores of 13–33 with a mean of 22 in their review of the depressed epileptic patients. The symptomatology is frequently accompanied by significant anxiety symptoms and is variable in phenomenology with both reactive (Mulder & Daly, 1952) and endogenous (Betts, 1974) presentation having been reported, though with the latter said to be more common (Betts, 1981). In the depressed epileptic sample reported by Robertson et al. (1987), 95% were classified by history as having unipolar depression, with only 5% bipolar depression. Twenty percent were described as being psychotic with mood-congruent hallucinations and/or delusions. Mendez, Cummings, and Benson (1986) also found a high prevalence of atypical, unipolar endogenomorphic, major depressive disorders in their sample of epileptics who frequently had episodes of agitation and psychotic symptomatology in association with their seizures. These patients also typically had a history of dysthymic features and usually had no family history of affective disorders.

Depressive disorders and affective symptoms associated with epilepsy are frequently atypical (Murray, 1985), episodic, often beginning and ending suddenly (Blumer, 1975), and lasting variable periods of time ranging from as little as only a few minutes (though according to Williams [1956], infrequently less than an hour) to as much as two weeks (Weil, 1956) or more. They are characterized by marked fluctuations in clinical features and have been hypothesized by some to be ictal or sub-ictal in nature, with the phenomenon of kindling playing a potentially significant role in their etiology (Himmelhoch, 1984).

Depressed epileptics have been reported by some workers not to respond especially well to standard antidepressants (Betts, 1981), which may also lower seizure threshold and potentially make the underlying epileptic disorder worse. Thus, not infrequently, such patients receive electroconvulsive therapy and often seem to respond well to it. Other authors have reported that depressive symptoms in epileptics do respond to antidepressants (Trimble, 1984). Still others report that such symptoms in epileptics frequently respond to anticonvulsants such as carbamazepine alone (Himmelhoch, 1984; Tucker, Price, Johnson & McAllister, 1986) or in combination with antidepressants (Murray, 1985).

Some have reported an inverse relationship between the severity of interictal depressive signs and symptoms and the occurrence and frequency of seizures (Betts, 1981; Landolt, 1960). In the past, it has been suggested that the occurrence of an occasional convulsion may have a salutary effect on affective symptomatology. This has also been advanced as a rationale to account for the otherwise seemingly counter-intuitive and even perhaps paradoxical efficacy of electroconvulsive therapy in such patients.

Consistent with the high frequency of depression in patients with epilepsy of unspecified type, it is not surprising that at least 33% of unselected epileptics in various studies have been shown to have attempted suicide one or more times (Barande, 1958; Delay, Deniker & Barande, 1957). Furthermore, suicide has been found to occur five times more frequently among epileptics than it does in the general population (Henricksen, Juul-Jensen & Lund, 1970; Prudhomme, 1941). Interestingly, temporal lobe epileptics commit suicide 25 times more often than do non-epileptics (Barraclough, 1981; Matthews & Barabas, 1981) and thus would be expected to have an increased incidence and/or prevalence of affective disturbances in comparison to patients with other kinds of epilepsy. The data reported by Mendez, Cummings, and Benson (1986) and Robertson et al. (1987) provides support for this relationship.

## Summary

As can be gleaned from the complexities described above in terms of the ways in which the type and location of a brain injury can influence the experience and expression of mood disturbances, the proper evaluation of depressive syndromes can be quite difficult and complex. Despite the differences described above, from a clinical standpoint it is our experience that the presence of a brain injury itself, almost irrespective of its underlying pathophysiology and to some extent its exact location, results in several general principles which need to be kept in mind when assessing this patient population.

### Reduced Cognitive "Reservoir"

A full examination of the relationship between lesion type and lesion location, associated cognitive deficits, and their relationship to the expression and experience of mood disturbance is beyond the scope of this chapter. However, most patients with a significant degree of brain damage will suffer from a mixed cognitive impairment syndrome. Most commonly there will be significant memory deficits, deficits in attention and concentration, as well as varying degrees of speech and language difficulties. As pointed out earlier, the superimposed presence of a depressive syndrome can, in and of itself, make these deficits worse. These factors conspire to make it difficult to get adequate historical information, as well as accurate descriptions of the chronology and sequencing of the symptoms being experienced.

### Fluctuating Symptom Picture

Although this has not been discussed in great detail, the presence of a brain injury, again, regardless of type and to some extent location, tends to increase the incidence not only of depressive syndromes, but also a variety of other disorders, including problems with impulse control, deficits in attention, and psychotic syndromes. The coexistence of mood disturbances with greater or lesser degrees of these other behavioral syndromes can frequently make the diagnosis and treatment of the mood disturbance much more difficult.

### Denial Syndromes

As mentioned previously, nondominant hemispheric injury and/or bilateral hemispheric injury often result in the patient being unable to fully comprehend the extent of his or her behavioral and functional deficits. This makes the establishment of a therapeutic alliance extremely difficult. Issues of compliance, especially around medications, become magnified when the individual has very little capacity to understand his or her need for treatment in the first place.

*Disruption of Language Function*

Both propositional and prosodic language function are commonly affected with any significant degree of brain injury. This can impair not only the factual description of the "verbal cognitive set" of the depressive syndrome, but in addition can make the matching of mood and affect a much more difficult task. One needs to bear in mind the potential presence of various degrees of aprosody, of both a receptive and expressive type. Greater attention must be paid to other clues relative to behavioral change, including changes in personality, irritability, level of function, degree of affective lability, and the presence or absence of neurovegetative signs that are commonly seen in depression. Complicating the injury-induced language deficits is the fact that these patients often have no prior history of significant psychiatric illness. They are thus unfamiliar with the common terms, language, and "jargon" that people who have a long prior exposure to mental health systems acquire and which thus facilitate the communication with psychiatrists and other mental health workers.

*Environmental Sensitivity*

The four factors described above combine to make patients with brain injury and behavioral disturbance, in particular depressive syndromes, exquisitely sensitive to changes in routine, environment, and psychosocial stress. This, combined with a common mixed symptom picture, results in prominent fluctuations of the prominent symptoms over time and requires prolongation of the evaluation and assessment period if one is to achieve an accurate evaluation and assessment. This is also true of the evaluation of treatment response. One must be careful not to attribute success or failure to any given intervention prematurely because of the extreme hypersensitivity to environmental or psychosocial stressors.

## TREATMENT ISSUES

There are surprisingly few studies which have looked at the treatment of depression in brain-injured populations (Cope, 1987; Gualtieri, 1988). Most of the literature focuses on the importance of diagnosis and the fact that depression is or should be a treatable behavioral syndrome regardless of the type of brain injury. Robinson's group (Lipsey, Robinson, Pearlson, Rao & Price, 1984) looked at the response of post-stroke depression to a trial of Nortriptyline and found that it did not differ significantly from non brain-injured patients. Reifler et al. (1989) studied the effects of Imipramine in patients with degenerative dementia and a depressive syndrome and found a significant improvement with resolution of symptoms. However, this was not different from that seen in the placebo group.

The consensus from the variety of case reports and other papers dealing indirectly with the topic is that the depressive syndromes do respond to traditional antidepressant regimens, including first and second generation antidepressants, MAO inhibitors, and even electroconvulsive therapy (see below). Despite this encouraging overview, it has been our experience in the last four years on the Brain Injury and Behavior Unit at the University of Pennsylvania that although depression does respond, it is not always an easy course of treatment. First, the assessment of depressive symptoms is much more difficult for the reasons already described earlier. Second, it is our clinical experience, as well as that of others (Cope, 1987), that the presence of a brain injury, again largely irrespective of type or location, carries implications for the use of antidepressant and other psychotropic agents. Thus, although the psychopharmacologic approach to depressive syndromes is much the same as that for the non brain-injured from the standpoint of specific available agents, there are certain principles which must be borne in mind in order to successfully treat depression in this group.

First, although the side effects of the various agents remain the same, their effect appears to be magnified in the presence of a brain injury. Thus, there appears to be increased sensitivity in this population to anticholinergic side effects, development of orthostatic hypotension, and sedation. Also, the potential lowering of the seizure threshold must be borne in mind, especially in the epileptic population. Related to this is that once side effects appear to have developed, resolution of the side effects and return to the "pre-morbid state" appear to take longer than in the non brain-injured population.

Second, there appears in some patients to be a worsening of affective modulation and control seen with a variety of psychotropics, including antidepressant regimens. Lithium in particular has been recorded to worsen agitation in "organic brain syndromes," although it can also be a very effective agent for the management of other dyscontrol type syndromes, such as affective lability, some intermittent explosive syndromes, and bipolar affective disorder occurring in the presence of various types of brain injury (Brown, 1973; Oyewumi & Lapierre, 1981; Rosenbaum & Barry, 1975; Shopsin & Gershon, 1976; Stewart & Hemsath, 1988; Kellner, Davenport, Post & Ross, 1984; Gualtieri, 1988). Perhaps, related to the enhanced traditional side effects and the propensity for worsening of affective modulation and control is the authors' and others' clinical impression that the anti-depressant agents all have a narrower therapeutic range in this population than in the non brain-injured population (Mysiw & Jackson, 1987; Trimble & Grant, 1982).

Given the factors mentioned above, it is wise to think of this population as analogous to the geriatric population, where one must essentially adopt a whole new set of dosing principles, such that one starts out at lower doses, increases the doses at longer intervals, and generally stops at smaller than expected doses for any given age level. It is as if the presence of a brain injury does carry specific implications for antidepressant dosing and management.

## Electroconvulsive Therapy (ECT)

Electroconvulsive therapy is a highly effective therapeutic modality which is generally well tolerated in the treatment of severe depressive disorders occurring in association with the primary degenerative dementias (Senile Dementia Alzheimer's type (SDAT) and multi-infarct dementia (MID)), Parkinson's disease, and Huntington's disease (Price & McAllister, 1989). As mentioned earlier in this chapter, the same tends to be true with major depressive disorders co-occurring with epilepsy or multiple sclerosis. The literature suggests that this is true as well for cerebrovascular accidents and traumatic brain injuries.

Among 31 depressed patients with cerebrovascular accidents, from eight different studies reported by Hsiao, Messenheimer, and Evans (1987), who had been treated with electroconvulsive therapy, 27 or nearly 90% improved. The only reported serious complications occurred when unmodified electroconvulsive therapy was used. Electroconvulsive therapy has been given to at least 6 patients who were as little as 4 days to 30 days after an acute stroke with no untoward effects (Abrams, 1988). Abrams (1988) suggests that electroconvulsive therapy given 3 months after a stroke carries with it little if any increased risk and that even when given as little as 30 days after a cerebrovascular accident, it may not represent a significantly increased risk.

A relatively large number of patients with traumatic brain injuries of a variety of types, ranging from lobotomies, to penetrating wounds, to blunt closed head injuries, who have received electroconvulsive therapy at variable intervals following the brain injury, have been reported over the years. As noted by Hsiao, Messenheimer and Evans (1987), 97 such patients, reported in 8 different studies, have been treated at intervals ranging from as little as 4 weeks to as much as 45 years post-injury (Moss-Herjanic, 1967). Among these patients only one experienced a major complication which was post-treatment status epilepticus. This patient had focal seizures resulting from a head injury 45 years earlier. Though the clinical and theoretical basis for the following clinical guideline has not been firmly established, it has been suggested that electroconvulsive therapy may well be safe by 6 months post-injury (Hsiao et al., 1987). Based on the favorable clinical outcome with electroconvulsive therapy in cases with various types of brain injury and associated psychopathology, such as those reported by Savitsky and Karliner (1953), Ruedrich, Chung-Chou, and Moore (1983), Silverman (1964), not only is ECT safe in the context of traumatic brain injuries, but it also has a high likelihood of resulting in a positive treatment response in such patients as well.

## CONCLUSIONS

The specific important points to be drawn from the preceding review of the literature on depression in the brain-injured are as follows:

- Depressive syndromes are an extremely common complication of a wide array of central nervous system disorders.
- The specific type of brain injury appears to be less of a predictor of risk of depression than the presence of some form of central nervous system insult.
- The weight of evidence to date would suggest that the location of a brain injury does impact on the risk of developing depressive illness. At least in patients with cerebrovascular disease, left hemispheric injury and anterior injuries appear to increase the risk and probably the severity of depressive syndromes.
- In many important ways, such as severity and natural history, the phenomenology of depressive syndromes in brain-injured patients appears very similar to major depressive syndromes seen in non brain-injured populations. How-

ever, given equal initial degrees of severity, brain-injured patients often appear to have more "reactive" or exogenous components, and score higher on the psychological dimensions vs. neurovegetative dimensions of the depressive syndromes than control groups of depressed patients without obvious brain injury.

- Response to treatment can be very gratifying and dramatic, yet tends to be complicated by difficulties in diagnosis and assessment. These difficulties are often a function of the reduced cognitive function, changes in language functions, denial syndromes, and the fluctuating symptom picture brought about by the brain injury.

- Appropriate psychotropic management of depressive syndromes in the brain-injured requires modification of dosages of the usual agents. Lower starting and maximum doses, and slower, smaller incremental increases are required. Electroconvulsive therapy can be quite effective and is not contraindicated.

As mentioned in the beginning of this chapter, depressive syndromes are clearly a major complication and potential block to progressive rehabilitation in a wide array of disorders afflicting the CNS. It seems clear from the evidence cited here that the association is greater than would be predicted on the basis of related disability, reaction to loss, or chronic illness patterns alone, though without question these are significant factors. Thus the implication is that the linkage between brain injury and depressive illness also involves factors related to the type of injury, amount of tissue injured, and the location (s) of the injury, which interact with the above factors to determine the risk, severity, and associated symptoms of depressive illness in the brain-injured patient. Further clarification of this linkage may lead to important insights into the pathophysiology of the primary affective disorders.

From a treatment perspective, depressive syndromes are very treatable but must be approached with a thorough understanding of the implications that the presence of a brain disorder has for the evaluation, psychopharmacologic approach, and assessment of treatment response.

## References

Abrams, R. (1988). Medical considerations: The high-risk patient. In R. Abrams (Ed.), *Electroconvulsive Therapy* (pp. 53–78). New York: Oxford University Press.

Asnis, G. (1977). Parkinson's disease, depression, and ECT: A review and case study. *American Journal of Psychiatry, 134,* 191–195.

Barande, R. (1958). Contribution a l'etude de l'etat dangereux chez les epileptiques. *Bulletin de la Societe Internationale de Criminologie,* 39–75.

Baretz, R.M. & Stephenson, G.R. (1981). Emotional responses to multiple sclerosis. *Psychosomatics, 22,* 117–127.

Barraclough, B. (1981). Suicide and epilepsy. In E.H. Reynolds & M.R. Trimble (Eds.), *Epilepsy and psychiatry* (pp. 72–76). Edinburgh: Churchill Livingstone.

Betts, T.A. (1974). A follow-up study of a cohort of patients with epilepsy admitted to psychiatric care in an English city. In P. Harris & C. Mawdsley (Eds.), *Epilepsy: Proceedings of the Hans Berger Centenary Symposium* (pp. 326–336). Edinburgh: Churchill Livingstone.

Betts, T.A. (1981). Depression, anxiety, and epilepsy. In E.H. Reynolds & M.R. Trimble (Eds.), *Epilepsy and psychiatry* (pp. 60–71). Edinburgh: Churchill Livingstone.

Blumer, D. (1975). Temporal lobe epilepsy and its psychiatric significance. In D.F. Benson & D. Blumer (Eds.), *Psychiatric aspects of neurologic disease* (pp. 171–198). New York: Grune and Stratton.

Brothers, C.R.D. & Meadows, A.W. (1955). An investigation of Huntington's chorea in Victoria. *Journal of Mental Science, 101*, 548–563.

Brown, S., II & Davis, T.K. (1922). The mental symptoms of multiple sclerosis. *Archives of Neurology and Psychiatry, 7*, 629–634.

Brown, W.T. (1973). The use of lithium carbonate in the treatment of mood disorders. *Canadian Medical Association Journal, 108*, 742–751.

Caine, E.D. (1981). Pseudodementia: Current concepts and future directions. *Archives of General Psychiatry, 38*, 1359–1364.

Caine, E.D. & Shoulson, I. (1983). Psychiatric syndromes in Huntington's disease. *American Journal of Psychiatry, 140*(6), 728–733.

Celesia, G.G. & Wanamaker, W.M. (1972). Psychiatric disturbances in Parkinson's disease. *Diseases of the Nervous System, 33*, 577–583.

Coffey, C.E., Figiel, G.S., Djang, W.T., Press, M., Saunders, W.B. & Weiner, R.D. (1988). Leukoencephalopathy in elderly depressed patients referred for ECT. *Biological Psychiatry, 24*, 143–161.

Cope, D.N. (1987). Psychopharmacologic considerations in the treatment of traumatic brain injury. *Journal of Head Trauma Rehabilitation, 2*(4), 1–5.

Cummings, J.L. (1985). *Clinical neuropsychiatry*. Orlando: Grune and Stratton.

Cummings, J.L. & Mendez, M.F. (1984). Secondary mania with focal cerebrovascular lesions. *American Journal of Psychiatry, 141*(9), 1084–1087.

Dalos, N.P., Rabins, P.V., Brooks, B.R. & O'Donnell, P. (1983). Disease activity and emotional state in multiple sclerosis. *Annals of Neurology, 13*, 575–577.

Delay, J., Deniker, P. & Barande, R. (1957). Le suicide des epileptiques. *Encephale, 46*, 401–436.

Denny-Brown, D., Meyer, J.S. & Horenstein, S. (1952). The significance of perceptual rivalry resulting from parietal lesions. *Brain, 75*, 433–471.

Fisher, S.H. (1961). Psychiatric considerations of cerebral vascular disease. *American Journal of Cardiology, 7*, 379–385.

Flor-Henry, P. (1969). Psychosis and temporal lobe epilepsy. *Epilepsia, 10*, 363–395.

Folstein, M.F., Folstein, S.E. & McHugh, P.R. (1975). Mini-Mental State: A practical method for grading the cognitive state of patients for the clinician. *Journal of Psychiatric Research, 12*, 189–198.

Folstein, M.F., Maiberger, R. & McHugh, P.R. (1977). Mood disorder as a specific complication of stroke. *Journal of Neurology, Neurosurgery, and Psychiatry, 40*, 1018–1020.

Folstein, S.E., Abbott, M.H., Chase, G.A., Jensen, B.A. & Folstein, M.F. (1983). The association of affective disorder with Huntington's disease in a case series and in families. *Psychological Medicine, 13*, 537–542.

Fordyce, D.J., Roueche, J.R. & Prigatano, G.P. (1983). Enhanced emotional reactions in chronic head trauma patients. *Journal of Neurology, Neurosurgery, and Psychiatry, 46*, 620–624.

Francis, A. & Freeman, H. (1984). Psychiatric abnormality and brain calcification over four generations. *Journal of Nervous and Mental Disease, 172*, 166–170.

Freeman, R.L., Galaburda, A.M., Diaz Cabal, R. & Geschwind, N. (1985). The neurology of depression: Cognitive and behavioral deficits with focal findings in depression and resolution after electroconvulsive therapy. *Archives of Neurology, 42*, 289–291.

Gainotti, G. (1972). Emotional behavior and hemispheric side of the lesion. *Cortex, 8*, 41–55.

Goldstein, K. (1939). *The organism: A holistic approach to biology derived from pathological data in man.* New York: American Book.

Goodstein, R.K. & Ferrell, R.B. (1977). Multiple sclerosis—presenting as depressive illness. *Diseases of the Nervous System, 38,* 127–131.

Green, R.L., McAllister, T.W. & Bernat, J.L. (1987). A study of crying in medically and surgically hospitalized patients. *American Journal of Psychiatry, 144*(4), 442–447.

Gualtieri, C.T. (1988). Pharmacotherapy and the neurobehavioural sequelae of traumatic brain injury. *Brain Injury, 2*(2), 101–129.

Gunn, J. (1973). Affective and suicidal symptoms in epileptic prisoners. *Psychological Medicine, 3,* 108–114.

Hamilton, M. (1960). A rating scale for depression. *Journal of Neurology, Neurosurgery, and Psychiatry, 23,* 56–62.

Harvey, N.S. (1986). Psychiatric disorders in parkinsonism: I. Functional illnesses and personality. *Psychosomatics, 27,* 91–103.

Heathfield, K.W.G. (1967). Huntington's chorea. *Brain, 90,* 203–233.

Hecaen, H. (1962). Clinical symptomatology in right and left hemisphere lesions. In V.B. Mountcastle (Ed.), *Interhemispheric relations and cerebral dominance.* Baltimore: Johns Hopkins Press.

Henricksen, B., Juul-Jensen, P. & Lund, M. (1970). The mortality of epileptics. In R.D.C. Brackenridge (Ed.), *Life assurance medicine: Proceedings of the 10th international congress of life assurance medicine* (pp. 139–148). London: Pitman.

Himmelhoch, J.M. (1984). Major mood disorders related to epileptic changes. In D. Blumer (Ed.), *Psychiatric aspects of epilepsy* (pp. 271–294). Washington, D.C.: American Psychiatric Press.

Hommes, O.R. & Panhuysen, L.H.H.M. (1971). Depression and cerebral dominance: A study of bilateral intracarotid amytal in eleven depressed patients. *Psychiatria, Neurologia, Neurochirurgia, 74,* 259–270.

Honer, W.G., Hurwitz, T., Li, D.K.B., Palmer, M. & Paty, D.W. (1987). Temporal lobe involvement in multiple sclerosis patients with psychiatric disorders. *Archives of Neurology, 44,* 187–190.

Hsiao, J.K., Messenheimer, J.A. & Evans, D.L. (1987). Review: ECT and Neurological Disorders. *Convulsive Therapy, 3,* 121–136.

Huber, S.J. & Paulson, G.W. (1986). Psychiatric presentations of the subcortical dementias [Reply to letter to the editor]. *American Journal of Psychiatry, 143*(6), 806–807.

Joffe, R.T., Lippert, G.P., Gray, T.A., Sawa, G. & Horvath, Z. (1987). Mood disorder and multiple sclerosis. *Archives of Neurology, 44,* 376–378.

Kahana, E., Leibowitz, U. & Alter, M. (1971). Cerebral multiple sclerosis. *Neurology, 21,* 1179–1185.

Kellner, C.H., Davenport, Y., Post, R.M. & Ross, R.J. (1984). Rapidly cycling bipolar disorder and multiple sclerosis. *American Journal of Psychiatry, 141*(1), 112–113.

Keschner, M., Bender, M.B. & Strauss, I. (1936). Mental symptoms in cases of tumor of the temporal lobe. *Archives of Neurology and Psychiatry, 35,* 572–596.

Krishnan, K.R.R., Goli, V., Ellinwood, E.H., France, R.D., Blazer, D.G. & Nemeroff, C.B. (1988). Leukoencephalopathy in patients diagnosed as major depressive. *Biological Psychiatry, 23,* 519–522.

Kurtzke, J.F. (1982). The current neurologic burden of illness and injury in the United States. *Neurology, 32,* 1207–1214.

Kwentus, J.A., Hart, R.P., Peck, E.T. & Kornstein, S. (1985). Psychiatric complications of closed head trauma. *Psychosomatics, 26*(1), 8–17.

Landolt, H. (1960). Die temporallappenepilepsie und ihre psychopathologie. *Bibliotheca Psychiatrica et Neurologica, 112* (Supplementa ad Psychiatrica et Neurologica), 1–96.

Lazarus, L.W., Newton, N., Cohler, B., Lesser, J. & Schweon, C. (1987). Frequency and presentation of depressive symptoms in patients with primary degenerative dementia. *American Journal of Psychiatry, 144*(1), 41–45.

Leigh, D. (1979). Psychiatric aspects of head injury. *J. C. E. Psychiatry, 40,* 21–33.

Levin, H.S. (1987). Neurobehavioral sequelae of head injury. In P.R. Cooper (Ed.), *Head Injury* (2nd ed.). (pp. 442–463). Baltimore: Williams & Wilkins.

Levin, H.S. & Grossman, R.G. (1978). Behavioral sequelae of closed head injury: A quantitative study. *Archives of Neurology, 35,* 720–727.

Lieberman, A. & Benson, D.F. (1977). Control of emotional expression in pseudobulbar palsy: A personal experience. *Archives of Neurology, 34,* 717–719.

Lipsey, J.R., Robinson, R.G., Pearlson, G.D., Rao, K. & Price, T.R. (1984). Nortriptyline treatment of post-stroke depression: A double-blind treatment trial. *Lancet, 1,* 297–300.

Lipsey, J.R., Spencer, W.C., Rabins, P.V. & Robinson, R.G. (1986). Phenomenological comparison of poststroke depression and functional depression. *American Journal of Psychiatry, 143*(4), 527–529.

Lishman, W.A. (1968). Brain damage in relation to psychiatric disability after head injury. *British Journal of Psychiatry, 114,* 373–410.

Lishman, W.A. (1973). The psychiatric sequelae of head injury: A review. *Psychological Medicine, 3,* 304–318.

Matthews, W.B. (1979). Multiple sclerosis presenting with acute remitting psychiatric symptoms. *Journal of Neurology, Neurosurgery, and Psychiatry, 42,* 859–863.

Matthews, W.S. & Barabas, G. (1981). Suicide and epilepsy: A review of the literature. *Psychosomatics, 22,* 277–378.

Mayberg, H.S., Robinson, R.G., Wong, D.F., Parikh, R., Bolduc, P., Starkstein, S.E., Price, T., Dannals, R.F., Links, J.M., Wilson, A.A., Ravert, H.T. & Wagner, H.N., Jr. (1988). Pet imaging of cortical S2 serotonin receptors after stroke: Lateralized changes and relationship to depression. *American Journal of Psychiatry, 145*(8), 937–943.

Mayeux, R., Stern, Y., Rosen, J. & Leventhal, J. (1981). Depression, intellectual impairment, and Parkinson's disease. *Neurology, 31,* 645–650.

Mayeux, R., Stern, Y., Williams, J.B.W., Cote, L., Frantz, A. & Dyrenfurth, I. (1986). Clinical and biochemical features of depression in Parkinson's disease. *American Journal of Psychiatry, 143,* 756–759.

McAllister, T.W. & Price, T.R.P. (1987). Aspects of behavior of psychiatric inpatients with frontal lobe damage: Some implications for diagnosis and treatment. *Comprehensive Psychiatry, 28,* 14–21.

McAllister, T.W., Price, T.R.P. & Ross, S. (1988). Depressive syndromes in patients with brain injury (organic affective disorder). Presented at Society of Biological Psychiatry, 43rd Annual Meeting, May 1988, Montreal, Quebec, Canada.

McHugh, P.R. & Folstein, M.F. (1975). Psychiatric syndromes of Huntington's chorea: A clinical and phenomenologic study. In D.F. Benson & D. Blumer (Eds.), *Psychiatric aspects of neurologic disease* (pp. 267–285). New York: Grune and Stratton.

Mendez, M.F., Cummings, J.L. & Benson, D.F. (1985). Epilepsy: Psychiatric aspects and use of psychotropics. *Psychosomatics, 25,* 883–894.

Mendez, M.F., Cummings, J.L. & Benson, D.F. (1986). Depression in epilepsy: Significance and phenomenology. *Archives of Neurology, 43,* 766–770.

Merskey, H. & Woodforde, J.M. (1972). Psychiatric sequelae of minor head injury. *Brain, 95,* 521–528.

Miller, H. (1961). Accident neurosis: Lecture I & Lecture II. *British Medical Journal, 1*, 919–925 and 992–998.

Monrad-Krohn, G.H. (1947). Dysprosody or altered "melody of language." *Brain, 70*, 405–415.

Morrison, J.H., Molliver, M.E. & Grzanna, R. (1979). Noradrenergic innervation of cerebral cortex: Widespread effects of local cortical lesions. *Science, 205*, 313–316.

Moss-Herjanic, B. (1967). Prolonged unconsciousness following electroconvulsive therapy. *American Journal of Psychiatry, 124*, 112–114.

Mulder, D.W. & Daly, D. (1952). Psychiatric symptoms associated with lesions of temporal lobe. *JAMA, 150*, 173–176.

Munir, K.M. (1986). The treatment of psychotic symptoms in Fahr's disease with lithium carbonate. *Journal of Clinical Psychopharmacology, 6*, 36–38.

Murray, G.B. (1985, April). Psychiatric disorders secondary to complex partial seizures. *Drug Therapy*, 145–155.

Mysiw, W.J. & Jackson, R.D. (1987). Tricyclic antidepressant therapy after traumatic brain injury. *Journal of Head Trauma Rehabilitation, 2*(4), 34–42.

Oke, A., Keller, R., Mefford, I. & Adams, R.N. (1978). Lateralization of norepinephrine in human thalamus. *Science, 200*, 1411–1413.

Oliver, J.E. (1970). Huntington's chorea in Northamptonshire. *British Journal of Psychiatry, 116*, 241–253.

Oyewumi, L.K. & Lapierre, Y.D. (1981). Efficacy of lithium in treating mood disorder occurring after brain stem injury. *American Journal of Psychiatry, 138*(1), 110–112.

Perini, G. & Mendius, R. (1984). Depression and anxiety in complex partial seizures. *Journal of Nervous and Mental Disease, 172*(5), 287–290.

Pies, R.W. (1986). Psychiatric presentations of the subcortical dementias [Letter to the editor]. *American Journal of Psychiatry, 143*(6), 806.

Poeck, K. (1969). Pathologic laughter and crying. In P.J. Vinken & G.W. Bruyn (Eds.), *Handbook of clinical neurology* (Vol. 3.). (pp. 356–367). Amsterdam: North-Holland Publishing.

Poeck, K. (1969). Pathophysiology of emotional disorders associated with brain damage. In P.J. Vinken & G.W. Bruyn (Eds.), *Handbook of clinical neurology* (Vol. 3.). (pp. 343–367). Amsterdam: North-Holland Publishing.

Pratt, R.T.C. (1951). An investigation of the psychiatric aspects of disseminated sclerosis. *Journal of Neurology, Neurosurgery, and Psychiatry, 14*, 326–335.

Price, T.R.P. & McAllister, T.W. (1989). Safety and efficacy of ECT in depressed patients with dementia: A review of clinical experience. *Convulsive Therapy, 5*, 61–74.

Prudhomme, C. (1941). Epilepsy and suicide. *Journal of Nervous and Mental Disease, 94*, 722–731.

Rabins, P.V., Brooks, B.R., O'Donnell, P., Pearlson, G.D., Moberg, P., Jubett, B., Coyle, P., Dalos, N.P. & Folstein, M.F. (1986). Structural brain correlates of emotional disorder in multiple sclerosis. *Brain, 109*, 585–597.

Reding, M., Haycox, J. & Blass, J. (1985). Depression in patients referred to a dementia clinic: A three-year prospective study. *Archives of Neurology, 42*, 894–896.

Reed, T.E. & Chadler, J.R. (1958). Huntington's chorea in Michigan. 1. Demography and genetics. *American Journal of Human Genetics, 10*, 201–225.

Reifler, B.V., Larson, E. & Hanley, R. (1982). Coexistence of cognitive impairment and depression in geriatric outpatients. *American Journal of Psychiatry, 139*, 623–626.

Reifler, B.V., Teri, L., Raskind, M., Veith, R., Barnes, R., White, E. & McLean, P. (1989). Double-blind trial of imipramine in alzheimer's disease patients with and without depression. *American Journal of Psychiatry, 146*(1), 45–49.

Robertson, M.M., Trimble, M.R. & Townsend, H.R.A. (1987). Phenomenology of depression in epilepsy. *Epilepsia, 28,* 364–372.

Robinson, R.G. (1979). Differential behavioral and biochemical effects of right and left hemispheric cerebral infarction in the rat. *Science, 205,* 707–710.

Robinson, R.G. & Benson, D.F. (1981). Depression in aphasic patients: Frequency, severity and clinical pathological correlations. *Brain and Language, 14*(2), 282–291.

Robinson, R.G., Bolla-Wilson, K., Kaplan, E., Lipsey, J.R. & Price, T.R. (1986). Depression influences intellectual impairment in stroke patients. *British Journal of Psychiatry, 148,* 541–547.

Robinson, R.G. & Forrester, A.W. (1987). Neuropsychiatric aspects of cerebrovascular disease. In R.E. Hales & S.C. Yudofsky (Eds.), *Textbook of neuropsychiatry* (pp. 191–208). Washington, D.C.: American Psychiatric Press.

Robinson, R.G., Lipsey, J.R., Bolla-Wilson, K., Bolduc, P.L., Pearlson, G.D., Rao, K. & Price, T.R. (1985). Mood disorders in left-handed stroke patients. *American Journal of Psychiatry, 142*(12), 1424–1429.

Robinson, R.G., Lipsey, J.R., Rao, K. & Price, T.R. (1986). Two-year longitudinal study of poststroke mood disorders: Comparison of acute-onset with delayed-onset depression. *American Journal of Psychiatry, 143*(10), 1238–1244.

Robinson, R.G., Starr, L.B., Lipsey, J.R., Rao, K. & Price, T.R. (1985). A two-year longitudinal study of poststroke mood disorders: In-hospital prognostic factors associated with six-month outcome. *Journal of Nervous and Mental Disease, 173,* 221–226.

Robinson, R.G., Starr, L.B. & Price, T.R. (1984). A two year longitudinal study of mood disorders following stroke: Prevalence and duration at six months follow-up. *British Journal of Psychiatry, 144,* 256–262.

Robinson, R.G. & Szetela, B. (1981). Mood change following left hemispheric brain injury. *Annals of Neurology, 9,* 447–453.

Rosenbaum, A.H. & Barry, M.J., Jr. (1975). Positive therapeutic response to lithium in hypomania secondary to organic brain syndrome. *American Journal of Psychiatry, 132*(10), 1072–1073.

Ross, E.D. (1981). The aprosodias: Functional-anatomic organization of the affective components of language in the right hemisphere. *Archives of Neurology, 38,* 561–569.

Ross, E.D., Harney, J.H., de Lacoste-Utamsing, C. & Purdy, P.D. (1981). How the brain integrates affective and propositional language into a unified behavioral function: Hypothesis based on clinicoanatomic evidence. *Archives of Neurology, 38,* 745–748.

Ross, E.D. & Mesulam, M.M. (1979). Dominant language functions of the right hemisphere? : Prosody and emotional gesturing. *Archives of Neurology, 36,* 144–148.

Ross, E.D. & Rush, A.J. (1981). Diagnosis and neuroanatomical correlates of depression in brain-damaged patients *Archives of General Psychiatry, 38,* 1344–1354.

Ruedrich, S.L., Chung-Chou, C. & Moore, S.L. (1983). ECT for major depression in a patient with acute brain trauma. *American Journal of Psychiatry, 140,* 928–929.

Sackeim, H.A., Greenbert, M.S., Weiman, A.L., Gur, R.C., Hungerbuhler, J.P. & Geschwind, N. (1982). Hemispheric asymmetry in the expression of positive and negative emotions: Neurologic evidence. *Archives of Neurology, 39,* 210–218.

Sammet, J.F. & Bucy, P.C. (1951). Symmetrical calcifications in the anterior limb of the internal capsules of the brain without demonstrable neurological or metabolic disturbances. *American Journal of Roentgenology, 66,* 880–883.

Saran, A.S. (1985). Depression after minor closed head injury: Role of dexamethasone suppression test and antidepressants. *Journal of Clinical Psychiatry, 46,* 335–338.

Savitsky, N. & Karliner, W. (1953). Electroshock in the presence of organic disease of the central nervous system. *Journal of the Hillside Hospital, 2,* 3–22.

Schiffer, R.B. & Babigian, H.M. (1984). Behavioral disorders in multiple sclerosis, temporal lobe epilepsy, and amyotrophic lateral sclerosis. *Archives of Neurology, 41,* 1067–1069.

Schiffer, R.B., Caine, E.D., Bamford, K.A. & Levy, S. (1983). Depressive episodes in patients with multiple sclerosis. *American Journal of Psychiatry, 140*(11), 1498–1500.

Schiffer, R.B., Kurlan, R., Rubin, A. & Bock, S. (1988). Evidence for atypical depression in Parkinson's disease. *American Journal of Psychiatry, 145,* 1020–1022.

Schiffer, R.B., Wineman, N.M. & Weitkamp, L.R. (1986). Association between bipolar affective disorder and multiple sclerosis. *American Journal of Psychiatry, 143,* 94–95.

Serby, M. (1980). Psychiatric issues in Parkinson's disease. *Comprehensive Psychiatry, 21,* 317–322.

Shopsin, B. & Gershon, S. (1976). Pharmacology-toxicology of the lithium ion. In S. Gershon & B. Shopsin (Eds.), *Lithium: Its role in psychiatric research and treatment* (2nd ed.). (pp. 107–146). New York: Plenum Press.

Silverman, M. (1964). Organic stupor subsequent to a severe head injury treated with ECT. *British Journal of Psychiatry, 110,* 648.

Sinyor, P., Jacques, P., Kaloupek, D.G., Becker, R., Goldenberg, M. & Coopersmith, H. (1986). Poststroke depression and lesion location: An attempted replication. *Brain, 109,* 537–546.

Starr, L.B., Robinson, R.G. & Price, T.R. (1982). The social functioning exam: An assessment for stroke patients. *Social Work Research and Abstracts, 18*(4), 28–33.

Stewart, J.T. & Hemsath, R.H. (1988). Bipolar illness following traumatic brain injury: Treatment with lithium and carbamazepine. *Journal of Clinical Psychiatry, 49*(2), 74–75.

Strauss, I. & Savitsky, N. (1934). Head injury: Neurologic and psychiatric aspects. *Archives of Neurology and Psychiatry, 31,* 893–955.

Surridge, D. (1969). An investigation into some psychiatric aspects of multiple sclerosis. *British Journal of Psychiatry, 155,* 749–764.

Thompson, G.N. (1965). Post-traumatic psychoneurosis—A statistical survey. *American Journal of Psychiatry, 121,* 1043–1048.

Trautner, R.J., Cummings, J.L., Read, S.L. & Benson, D.F. (1988). *American Journal of Psychiatry, 145*(3), 350–353.

Trimble, M.R. (1984). Epilepsy, antidepressants, and the role of nomifensine. *Journal of Clinical Psychiatry, 45,* 39–42.

Trimble, M.R. & Cummings, J.L. (1981). Neuropsychiatric disturbances following brainstem lesions. *British Journal of Psychiatry, 138,* 56–59.

Trimble, M.R. & Grant, I. (1982). Psychiatric aspects of multiple sclerosis. In D.F. Benson & D. Blumer (Eds.), *Psychiatric aspects of neurologic disease* (Vol. 2.). (pp. 279–299). New York: Grune and Stratton.

Tucker, G.J. & Price, T.R.P. (1987). Depression & neurologic disease. In O.G. Cameron (Ed.), *Presentations of depression* (pp. 237–250). New York: John Wiley & Sons.

Tucker, G.J., Price, T.R.P., Johnson, V.B. & McAllister, T. (1986). Phenomenology of temporal lobe dysfunction: A link to atypical psychosis. *Journal of Nervous and Mental Disease, 174,* 348–356.

Ullman, M. & Gruen, A. (1960). Behavioral changes in patients with strokes. *American Journal of Psychiatry, 117,* 1004–1009.

Weil, A.A. (1956, August). Ictal depression and anxiety in temporal lobe disorders. *American Journal of Psychiatry,* 147–149.

Weintraub, S., Mesulam, M.M. & Kramer, L. (1981). Disturbances in prosody: A right hemisphere contribution to language. *Archives of Neurology, 38,* 742–744.

Whitlock, F.A. & Siskind, M.M. (1980). Depression as a major symptom of multiple sclerosis. *Journal of Neurology, Neurosurgery, and Psychiatry, 43*(10), 861–865.

Whittier, J.R. (1977). Hereditary chorea (Huntington's chorea): A paradigm of brain dysfunction with psychopathology. In S. Gershon, C. Shagass & A.J. Friedoff (Eds.), *Psychopathology and Brain Dysfunction* (pp. 267–277). New York: Raven Press.

Williams, D. (1956). The structure of emotions reflected in epileptic experiences. *Brain, 79*, 29–67.

Wilson, S.A.K. (1924). Some problems in neurology: No. II.—Pathological laughing and crying. *Journal of Neurology and Psychopathology, 4*(16), 299–333.

Wing, J.K., Cooper, J.E. & Sartorius, N. (1974). *Measurement and classification of psychiatric symptoms: An instruction manual for the PSE and Catego program.* London: Cambridge University Press.

Winokur, A., Dugan, J., Mendels, J. & Huntig, H.I. (1978). Psychiatric illness in relatives of patients with Parkinson's disease: An expanded survey. *American Journal of Psychiatry, 135*, 854–856.

Zung, W.W.K. (1965). A self-rating depression scale. *Archives of General Psychiatry, 12*, 63–70.

# ABOUT THE EDITORS AND CONTRIBUTORS

## About the Editors

**C. Douglas McCann**, Ph.D., is Associate Professor of Psychology at York University. Dr. McCann received his graduate training at the University of Western Ontario and then completed a Post-Doctoral Fellowship at Ohio State University. His research interests include depression, social cognition, and communication. He has published empirical and theoretical papers in each of these areas. Dr. McCann has held research grants from the Natural Sciences and Engineering Research Council and the Social Sciences and Humanities Research Council of Canada.

**Norman S. Endler**, Ph.D., F.R.S.C., is Professor of Psychology at York University, Toronto, Canada, and Senior Research Associate at the Clarke Institute of Psychiatry. His areas of interest include anxiety and stress, depression, ECT, social interaction processes, and the interaction model of personality. Among his seven books is *Electroconvulsive Therapy: The Myths and the Realities* with E. Persad, 1988. He has written a description of ECT in *Holiday of Darkness: A Psychologist's Personal Journey Out of His Depression*, which has recently been revised and reissued (Toronto: Wall & Emerson, Inc., 1990). Dr. Endler was recently given the award of merit of the Ontario Psychological Association and is a fellow of the Royal Society of Canada. During 1987–89, Professor Endler was a Killam Research Fellow, Canada Council.

## About the Contributors

**Lyn Y. Abramson**, Ph.D., is Professor of Psychology at the University of Wisconsin in Madison. She studies vulnerability and invulnerability to depression from a cognitive perspective. Recently, Drs. Gerald I. Metalsky and Lauren B. Alloy presented Dr. Abramson's and their theory of "Hopelessness Depression" in the *Psychological Review*. Dr. Abramson has received a number of awards including the Distinguished Scientific Award for an Early Career Contribution to Psychology by the American Psychological Association.

**Lauren B. Alloy**, Ph.D., is Professor of Psychology at Northwestern University. She conducts research on cognitive processes in emotional disorders and has authored over 45 articles and chapters on the subject. She is best known for her work on "depressive realism" and hopelessness depression. Her recent book *Cognitive Processes in Depression* was published in 1988 by Guilford Press. In 1984, Dr. Alloy won the American Psychological Association's Young Psychologist award at the XXIII International Congress of Psychology.

**John A. Bargh**, Ph.D., is Associate Professor of Psychology at New York University. He received his Ph.D. in 1981 from the University of Michigan, and a B.S. from the University of Illinois, *summa cum laude*, in 1977. His research interests center on the role of unintended thought processes in social perception, judgment, behavior, and mental illness. Bargh received the Society for Experimental Social Psychology's annual Dissertation Award in 1982, and the 1989 American Psychological Association's Distinguished Early Career Contribution award.

**Mitchell J. Cohen**, M.D., is an Instructor in the Department of Psychiatry at the Johns Hopkins University School of Medicine. He has been involved in writing and research related to clinical effects of lithium salts as part of an abiding interest in affective disorders. He is very active in the educational efforts of DRADA (Depression and Related Affective Disorders Association), including outreach presentations in schools and the media. Dr. Cohen also directs satellite clinical programs for the Department.

**John R. Debus**, M.D., is Assistant Professor of Psychiatry at Southwestern Medical School and Assistant Director of Inpatient Services at University Medical Center, both of which are located at the University of Texas Southwestern Medical Center at Dallas, Texas. His major areas of interest are the neurobiology of mood spectrum disorders, their medical evaluation (including sleep assessment, neuroendocrine measures and brain imaging), and treatment (including medications and ECT). He is an investigator in multiple studies of new antidepressant compounds and in sleep EEG, regional brain perfusion and neuroendocrine measures in mood and related disorders, and has authored several publications on these topics.

**J. Raymond DePaulo**, Jr., M.D., is Associate Professor of Psychiatry and Director of the Affective Disorders Clinic, at the Johns Hopkins School of Medicine. Dr. DePaulo has been actively involved in patient care, research, and education during his 11 years on the John Hopkins Faculty. His major clinical and research efforts have focused on the genetic causes of and medical treatments for manic depressive illness. As an adjunct to his clinical work, Dr. DePaulo has also actively promoted the development of the Depression and Related Affective Disorders Association (DRADA), a group that has united the efforts of patients, family members, mental health professionals, and others to organize programs of education, mutual support groups, and research dissemination activities related to depressive disorders. As a member of the National Institute of Mental Health's "Depression: Awareness, Recognition, and Treatment" (D/ART) Campaign Consultants Group, Dr. DePaulo has participated in planning D/ART's national education program.

**Robert K. Elliott**, Ph.D., is Professor of Psychology at the University of Toledo. For the past thirteen years, he has been studying and publishing on clients' in-session experiences of significant therapy events, using a variety of methods including videotape-assisted recall and Comprehensive Process Analysis. He is currently conducting research on Experiential Therapy as a treatment for clinical depression.

**Norman S. Endler**, Ph.D., F.R.S.C. (See *About the Editors* above.)

**Lisa A. Feldman**, B.Sc., is a doctoral candidate in clinical psychology at the University of Waterloo. Her research interests include the role of self-structures and the role of self-consciousness in self-evaluation.

**Florence S. Foerster**, B.A., is a graduate student in the Graduate Programme in Psychology (Clinical/Counselling) at York University. She is interested in theory and practice of clinical and community psychology and is engaged in psychotherapy process research.

**Ian H. Gotlib**, Ph.D., C. Psych., is Professor of Psychology in the Joint Doctoral Training Program at San Diego State University and the University of California at San Diego. He serves as an Associate Editor of *Cognition and Emotion* and is on the Editorial Boards of the *Journal of Abnormal Psychology*, the *Journal of Social and Personal Relationships,* and *Cognitive Therapy and Research.* Actively involved in both research and clinical practice, Dr. Gotlib has published numerous scientific papers and chapters examining cognitive and interpersonal aspects of depression. He is co-author of *Treatment of Depression: An Interpersonal Systems Approach,* Pergamon, 1987.

**Leslie S. Greenberg**, Ph.D., is Professor of Psychology at York University. His areas of interest include psychotherapy process and outcome research with a special interest in studying how change occurs in psychotherapy, the role of emotion in psychotherapy, and marital and family therapy research. His books include *The Psychotherapeutic Process: A Research Handbook*, with W. Pinsof, and *Emotion in Psychotherapy*, with J. Safran. He is current president of the Society for Psychotherapy Research and an active contributor to the Society for the Exploration of Psychotherapy Integration.

**Donald P. Hay**, M.D., is an Associate Clinical Professor of Psychiatry at the University of Wisconsin Medical School and the Medical College of Wisconsin, Milwaukee, Wisconsin, and is the Medical Director of the Geriatric Psychiatry Program, Sinai Samaritan Medical Center. He is the president of the Wisconsin Psychiatric Association and the Executive Director of the Association for Convulsive Therapy, A.C.T. (formerly the International Psychiatric Association for the Advancement of Electrotherapy, I.P.A.A.E.). He is also the Midwest Regional Coordinator of the Regional Affairs Committee of the American Association for Geriatric Psychiatry. His publications in the areas of geriatric psychiatry and ECT include "Electroconvulsive Therapy in the Medically Ill Elderly" (*Convulsive Therapy*, 1989).

**Linda K. Hay**, R.N., Ph.D., is a registered nurse and a licensed psychologist. She is currently an Assistant Clinical Professor of Psychiatry and Coordinator of Research in the Department of Psychiatry at the University of Wisconsin Medical School. She has worked extensively in the area of ECT as an inpatient nurse and as a psychologist, providing patient and family education. She also delivers informational lectures for professional groups and the general public and has promoted mental health education through a local radio show. Her interest areas, in addition to ECT, include depression, psychopharmacology, and geriatric psychology.

**E. Tory Higgins**, Ph.D., is Professor of Psychology at Columbia University. He has previously held faculty positions at Princeton University, the University of Western Ontario, and New York University. He has held visiting positions at the University of Chicago, the University of Michigan, York University, the Clarke Institute of Psychiatry, and Macquarie University. In 1986–1987, he was a Fellow at the Center for Advanced Study in the Behavioral Sciences. His areas of interest include social cognition, self and affect, social development, and emotional vulnerabilities. He is Associate Editor of *Social Cognition* and was recently awarded an N.I.M.H. Research Merit Award.

**Nicholas A. Kuiper**, Ph.D., is Professor of Psychology at the University of Western Ontario and former Co-Director of the Clinical Psychology program. His research interests include personality variables relating to stress, coping, and adaptation. Dr. Kuiper has published numerous scientific papers on cognitive and social aspects of depression.

**Catherine M. Lee**, Ph.D., is Assistant Professor of Psychology at the Child Study Centre, School of Psychology, University of Ottawa. She is the author of papers and chapters concerning the relation between family factors and psychosocial adjustment. Dr. Lee is an investigator in two projects examining aspects of family adjustment funded by the Canadian National Health Research and Development Programme.

**Rod A. Martin**, Ph.D., is Associate Professor of Psychology at the University of Western Ontario and a current Co-Director of the graduate program in Clinical Psychology. Dr. Martin's research actively pursues the link between stress and personality, with a primary emphasis on the role of humour in coping.

**Thomas W. McAllister**, M.D., is Associate Professor of Psychiatry at the Hospital of the University of Pennsylvania, where he also serves as Director of Psychiatric Inpatient Services and Director of the Brain Injury Behavior Section of the Neuropsychiatry Division. His primary interest is in the phenomenology of depression and its relationship to regional brain function. He is currently directing the development of an integrated inpatient and outpatient program for patients with varying types of brain injury and associated behavioral disturbances.

**C. Douglas McCann**, Ph.D. (See *About the Editors* above.)

**Marlene M. Moretti**, Ph.D., C.Psych., is Assistant Professor of Psychology at Simon Fraser University. Her research interests include depression in children and adults, the development of the self and its relation to psychopathology, and the development of therapeutic techniques that promote changes in how individuals view themselves. She is currently investigating these issues with the support of research grants from the Social Sciences and Humanities Research Council of Canada and the Laidlaw foundation.

**L. Joan Olinger**, Ph.D., is a Clinical Psychologist at London Psychiatric Hospital, and also a Clinical Adjunct Faculty member of the Department of Psychology, University of Western Ontario. Dr. Olinger's primary research interests focus on cognitive factors relating to depression etiology, maintenance, treatment, and relapse.

**Emmanuel Persad**, M.B., B.S., is Associate Professor of Psychiatry at the University of Western Ontario and the Director of Education at the London Psychiatric Hospital. He has conducted research into mood disorders, transcultural psychiatry, and psychopharmacology. Prior to his appointment at the University of Western Ontario, Dr. Persad was at the Clarke Institute of Psychiatry, where he held various senior administrative research and clinical positions. His most recent book was on Electroconvulsive Therapy, which he co-authored with Dr. Norman S. Endler.

**Trevor R. P. Price**, M.D., is Professor of Psychiatry at the Medical College of Pennsylvania and Chairman of the Department of Psychiatry at the Allegheny Campus of the Medical College of Pennsylvania. He has written more than 50 papers and book chapters, is an editorial reviewer for 7 journals, and a member of the editorial board of *Convulsive Therapy*. His areas of interest include: neuropsychiatry, medical/psychiatric interfaces, ECT, and alcohol abuse.

**A. John Rush**, M.D., Professor of Psychiatry, holds the Betty Jo Hay Chair in Mental Health at the University of Texas Southwestern Medical Center in Dallas, Texas. In 1978 he established the Affective Disorders Unit (now called the Mood Disorders Program), a specialized program to provide diagnosis, consultation, and treatment for patients with various forms of depression and mania. In addition, the program provides a focus on clinical research into both the biology and psychology of depression and mania. Dr. Rush has authored over 80 articles, 45 chapters and 5 books on the recognition, assessment, and treatment of depression. He is co-author with Brian Shaw and Gary Emery of Aaron T. Beck's *Cognitive Therapy of Depression*, editor of *Short-term Psychotherapies for Depression*, author of *Beating Depression* (a guide for patients) and co-editor with Kenneth Z. Altshuler of *Depression: Basic Mechanisms, Diagnosis and Treatment*. Dr. Rush is a fellow of the American Psychiatric Association and a member of both the American College of Psychiatrists and the American College of Neuropsychopharmacology, and a past president of the Society for Psychotherapy Research. Dr. Rush's current interests and research span both the biological and psychosocial aspects of mood disorders.

**Janusz K. Rybakowski**, M.D., Ph.D., is currently Chairman, Department of Psychiatry, Medical Academy, in Bydgoszcz, Poland. He has been a Research Fellow and then Visiting Professor at the Department of Psychiatry, University of Pennsylvania, Philadelphia. Dr. Rybakowski has published more than 130 scientific papers and textbook chapters (e.g., in *Prevention and Treatment of Depression*, University Park Press, 1982). His main research interest is the psychopharmacology of the lithium ion. He was recently appointed to the Editorial Board of a new international journal, *Lithium*.

**Paul G. Salmon**, Ph.D., is Associate Professor of Clinical Psychology at the University of Louisville, and Associate in Psychiatry at the University Medical School. His areas of clinical and research interest concern cognitive aspects of anxiety and depression, especially as they affect musicians and public performers. He is co-author of a textbook on Abnormal Psychology, as well as author of a number of articles and chapters on various clinical disorders.

**Lisa A. Spielman** is a doctoral candidate in the social/personality psychology program at New York University. She earned her B.S. from Tufts University in 1988, graduating *magna cum laude*, and received her M.A. from New York University in 1989. Her research interests include social-cognitive factors in depression and anxiety; the effects of automaticity on affect and cognitive biases; and individual differences in social cognition. In addition to several publications, she has recently presented papers at the Eastern and Midwestern Psychological Association Conventions.

**Jesse H. Wright,** M.D., Ph.D., is Professor of Psychiatry at the University of Louisville School of Medicine, Director of the Center for Cognitive Therapy at the University of Louisville, and Medical Director of the Norton Psychiatric Clinic, Louisville, Kentucky. His research has spanned both biological and psychological approaches to the treatment of depression. Dr. Wright's recent publications have focused on cognitive functioning in depression and on interactions between cognitive therapy and pharmacotherapy. He is the author of "Cognitive Therapy of Depression" in Volume 7 of *The American Psychiatric Press Review of Psychiatry.*

# Name Index

# Subject Index